VOICES OF THE WORLD

Reinventing Social Emancipation: Toward New Manifestos

VOLUME 6

VOICES OF
THE WORLD

Edited by

Boaventura de Sousa Santos

V

VERSO

London • New York

First published by Verso 2010
© the collection Verso 2010
© individual contributions the contributors

1 3 5 7 9 10 8 6 4 2

Verso
UK: 6 Meard Street, London W1F 0EG
US: 20 Jay Street, Suite 1010, Brooklyn, NY 11201
www.versobooks.com

Verso is the imprint of New Left Books

ISBN-13: 978-1-84467-592-0

British Library Cataloguing in Publication Data
A catalogue record for this book is available from the British Library

Library of Congress Cataloging-in-Publication Data
A catalog record for this book is available from the Library of Congress

Typeset by Hewer Text UK Ltd, Edinburgh
Printed in the US by Worldcolor / Fairfield

Contents

COLOMBIA

INDIA

MOZAMBIQUE

PORTUGAL

SOUTH AFRICA

Preface

Boaventura de Sousa Santos

This book is the fourth in a series of five volumes that present the main results of an international research project that I have conducted under the title *Reinventing Social Emancipation: Toward New Manifestos*. The project's core idea is that the action and thought that sustained and gave credibility to the modern ideals of social emancipation are being profoundly questioned by a phenomenon that, although not new, has reached in the past decades such an intensity that it has effected a redefinition of the contexts, objectives, means, and subjectivities of social and political struggles. This phenomenon is commonly designated as globalization. As a matter of fact, what we usually call globalization is just one of the forms of globalization, namely neoliberal globalization, undoubtedly the dominant and hegemonic form of globalization. Neoliberal globalization corresponds to a new system of capital accumulation, a more intensely globalized system than previous systems. It aims, on the one hand, to desocialize capital, freeing it from the social and political bonds that in the past guaranteed some social distribution; on the other hand, it works to subject society as a whole to the market law of value, under the presupposition that all social activity is better organized when organized under the aegis of the market. The main consequence of this double change is the extremely unequal distribution of the costs and opportunities brought about by neoliberal globalization within the world system. Herein resides the reason for the exponential increase of the social inequalities between rich and poor countries, as well as between the rich and the poor inside the same country.

The project's assumption is that this form of globalization, though hegemonic, is not the only form and that, in fact, it has been increasingly confronted with another form of globalization. This other form—an alternative, counter-hegemonic form of globalization—is constituted by a series of initiatives, movements, and organizations that combat neoliberal globalization through local and global linkages, networks, and alliances. Their motivation is the aspiration to a better, fairer, and more peaceful world, which they deem possible, and to which they believe they are entitled. This form of globalization is as yet still emerging. Its most visible manifestation is the process of the World Social Forum, which has been unfolding since 2001 under different forms, from the seven global annual meetings so far to the hundreds of thematic, regional, and national social fora in an enormous variety of countries.

To my mind, this alternative globalization, in its confrontation with neoliberal globalization, is paving a new path toward social emancipation. Such a confrontation, which may be metaphorically characterized as a confrontation between the Global North and the Global South, tends to be particularly intense in countries of intermediate development, or, in other words, semi-peripheral countries. It is, therefore, in these countries that the potentialities and limits of the reinvention of social emancipation manifest themselves most clearly. This is the reason why four of the five countries in which the project was conducted are countries of intermediate development in different continents. The five countries in question are Brazil, Colombia, India, Mozambique, and South Africa.

The new conflicts between the Global North and the Global South occur in the most diverse domains of social, economic, political, and cultural activity. In some of these domains, however, the alternatives created by counter-hegemonic globalization are more visible and consistent, not only because the conflicts in them are more intense, but also because the initiatives, movements, and progressive organizations there have reached higher levels of consolidation and organizational density. I selected the following five domains or themes to be analyzed in each of the five countries included in the project: participatory democratic practices; alternative production systems; emancipatory interculturality and cultural and cognitive justice and citizenship; the protection of biodiversity and the recognition of rival knowledges against neoliberal intellectual property rights; and new labor internationalism. To learn about the choice of countries and themes, as well as the assumptions underlying the project and the challenges it aims to face, the reader should see the general introduction in the first volume of this collection.[1]

The series is constituted of five volumes.[2] The first three volumes deal with the above-mentioned five themes. This volume is different than the previous volumes. Rather than focusing on the scientific and social analysis of alternatives, it focuses on the discourse and practical knowledge of the protagonists of such alternatives. One of the core concerns of the

---

1 Boaventura de Sousa Santos, ed., *Democratizing Democracy: Beyond the Liberal Democratic Canon*, London: Verso, 2005.

2 Besides this English edition, this series is also being published in Brazil (by Civilização Brasileira), Mexico (by Fondo de Cultura Económica), Italy (by Città Aperta Edizioni), and Portugal (by Afrontamento).

project *Reinventing Social Emancipation* is to contribute to renovating the social sciences (see the general introduction to the first volume). One of the paths of renovation resides in confronting the knowledge the social sciences produce with other knowledges—practical, plebeian, popular, common, tacit knowledges—which, although being an integral part of the social practices analyzed by the social sciences, are always ignored by them. In this volume, voice is given to the leaders and activists of social movements, initiatives, and organizations, many of which were studied in the previous volumes. To this end, long interviews were conducted and transcribed.

Following some broad guidelines, the selection of interviewees was made by the social scientists who contributed chapters to the previous volumes. In order to gain a broader spectrum of the social and political contexts in which counter-hegemonic, emancipatory activism takes place, activists from two more countries were included: China and Portugal. It was thus possible to hear the voices of social and political activists from two countries in Africa (Mozambique and South Africa), two countries in Asia (China and India), two countries in Latin America (Brazil and Colombia), and one country in Europe (Portugal).

The selection did not follow any general criterion of representativeness, be it internal regional diversity, the type or theme of struggle, or gender balance. In this last case an effort was made, but unfortunately it was not successful. There are five female voices and nine male voices. The voices are representative only by their exemplarity—by the uniqueness of the struggles, life-stories, and narratives they lay before us with unsurpassable transparency. Millions of other voices might have been chosen, all of them equally representative according to the criterion of exemplarity. These unheard voices constitute the ungraspable planetary silence through which the voices in this book speak and whose heavy presence they acknowledge.

After a brief introduction by myself, fourteen interviews or life-stories are presented in alphabetical order of the countries from which the voices come. Each interview begins with an introduction in which the interviewer presents the interviewee, and ends with a commentary, also by the interviewer—often a self-reflexive commentary.

The first volume in this series, entitled *Democratizing Democracy: Beyond the Liberal Democratic Canon* (Verso, 2005), is concerned with high-intensity forms of participatory democracy emerging in the Global South. The main thesis of this book is that the hegemonic model of democracy (liberal, representative democracy), while prevailing on a global scale, guarantees no more than low-intensity democracy, based on the privatization of public welfare by more or less restricted elites, on the increasing distance between representatives and the represented, and on an abstract political inclusion founded on concrete social exclusion. Parallel to this hegemonic model of democracy, other models have always existed, however marginalized or discredited, such as participatory democracy and popular democracy. Recently, participatory democracy has attained a new dynamics. It has engaged primarily subaltern communities and social groups that, propelled by the aspiration to more inclusive social contracts and high-intensity democracy, struggle against social exclusion and the suppression or trivialization of citizenship. By this I mean local initiatives in urban or rural contexts that gradually develop bonds of inter-recognition and interaction with parallel initiatives, thus giving rise to the formation, as yet embryonic, of transnational networks of participatory democracy. To my mind, one of the major conflicts between the North and the South will increasingly result from the confrontation between representative and participatory democracy. Such a confrontation, often shown in representative democracy's systematic denial of the legitimacy of participatory democracy, will be resolved only to the extent that such a denial is replaced by the development of forms of complementarity between the two forms of democracy that may contribute to deepening both one and the other. Such complementarity serves to pave one of the ways to the reinvention of social emancipation.

Volume two, entitled *Another Production is Possible: Beyond the Capitalist Canon* (Verso, 2006), deals, on the one hand, with the non-capitalist production alternatives that for the past two decades have been gaining new life in their resistance to the social exclusion and wild exploitation brought about by neoliberal globalization, and, on the other hand, with the new struggles of workers against such exploitation, which signal the emergence of a new labor internationalism. Alternative models to capitalist development—generally known as solidary economy or social economy—are analyzed, and case studies are presented of popular economic organizations, cooperatives, communitarian or collective land management projects and associations of local development. Also analyzed are the new forms of the conflict between capital and labor, stemming on the one hand from the end of the Cold War, and on the other from the fact that in the last three decades labor has become a global resource, though without the emergence of any globally organized labor market. From this disjunction has resulted the weakening of the union movement as we know it. Meanwhile, it is clear today that labor solidarity is reconstituting itself under new forms, on both local and national levels, and on a global level as well. The book deals in detail with some of these new forms.

Volume three, entitled *Another Knowledge is Possible: Beyond Northern Epistemologies* (Verso, 2007), tackles the struggles and politics of the recognition of difference that in the past three decades have been confronting imperial identities, false universalisms, the coloniality of power, and imperial epistemologies, all of which are as germane to historical capitalism as the exploitation of wage labor. It analyzes the struggles and movements pursuing alternative conceptions of human, collective, and cultural rights, as well as the rights to local self-determination. New forms of racism and of reactionary multiculturalism are confronted with an emancipatory politics of cultural difference.

In light of both the global mercantilization of modern technical and scientific knowledge that is under way, and the more and more unequal access to information and knowledge it causes, the confrontation between rival knowledges acquires special relevance. Such a confrontation derives also from the latest advances in biology, biotechnology, and microelectronics, which have transformed the wealth of biodiversity into one of the most precious and sought-after "natural resources." Since most of this biodiversity is located in countries of the South and is sustained by popular, peasant, or indigenous knowledges, the issue (and the conflict) consists in deciding how to protect such biodiversity and such knowledges from the voracity with which scientific, technological, and industrial knowledge transforms them into patentable knowledge objects. The struggles and movements for the recognition of popular knowledges concerning biodiversity, medicine, environmental impact, and natural calamities are analyzed through a variety of case studies.

Finally, volume five, provisionally entitled *Reinventing Social Emancipation: Toward New Manifestos*, presents my theoretical, analytical, and epistemological reflections upon the major themes of this project and its main results. The objective will be to show some of the ways in which social emancipation—or, rather, social emancipations—might be reinvented.

Sixty-one researchers participated in this project; more than fifty-three initiatives were analyzed. A project of such proportions was possible only thanks to a demanding series of conditions. In the first place, adequate funding was available; I am grateful to the MacArthur Foundation for financial support. Secondly, the project was made possible by a number of coordinators, one in each country, who helped me to select the themes and researchers, and finally to bring the various strands of the research to conclusion. I was fortunate enough to have the collaboration of Sakhela Buhlungu in South Africa, Maria Célia Paoli in Brazil, Mauricio García-Villegas in Colombia, Shalini Randeria and Achyut Yagnik in India, and Teresa Cruz e Silva in Mozambique. My most heartfelt gratitude to all of them.

This project would not have been possible without the support of a dedicated and highly competent Secretariat. Sílvia Ferreira, Paula Meneses, and Ana Cristina Santos shared administrative, scientific, and editorial tasks, but they all did a little bit of everything. In the course of three years, they accomplished a remarkable amount of work, creating the best conditions to make my meetings with the country coordinators and the researchers productive, to meet all of the researchers' needs and requests, and to facilitate the production of all the texts. Theirs was a Herculean task, and I am only too happy to mention this here in order to keep it from lying buried in the many pages of this series of books. More recently, in the course of the publication of the different volumes, I have counted on the extremely dedicated and professional support of my research assistant, Margarida Gomes, for which I am most grateful.

This project was based at the Center for Social Studies of the School of Economics of the University of Coimbra, and greatly benefited from the support of the Executive Committee and its administrative staff. As usual, a very special word of thanks must go to Lassalete Simões, my closest collaborator and dear friend of more than ten years. She is the recipient of my most deeply felt gratitude.

The solidarity shown throughout by the governing bodies of the School of Economics of the University of Coimbra was always encouraging, as was the sympathy and support of my colleagues in the Department of Sociology—a gift all the more appreciated for being increasingly so rare in academic institutions. My sincere thanks to all of them.

I would like to thank Teresa Tavares for having coordinated the work of translation. Very special thanks to Mark Streeter, on whose generous time and competence I counted during the last phases of the preparation of the manuscript, and whose outstanding job as a copyeditor was invaluable.

Maria Irene Ramalho was ever an unobtrusive presence during the execution of this project. Thanking her, no matter how emphatically, would always be less than adequate. She alone knows why.

Boaventura de Sousa Santos

Introduction

Like the book itself as a whole, this introduction is different than those of the previous volumes. I write it reluctantly. I do not wish to use it, as in previous volumes, to contextualize or theorize what follows. That would be running the risk of imposing social-scientific knowledge upon the knowledge of the activists and leaders of emancipatory movements and organizations that constitute *Voices of the World*. Such an imposition would imply in this case a political-epistemological stance that contradicts the objectives of this volume. This is, therefore, a deliberately minimalist introduction.

ACTIVISTS' KNOWLEDGES

The inclusion of *Voices of the World* in the project *Reinventing Social Emancipation* stems from an epistemological stance that underlies the project and which will be fully developed in the final volume of the series. Stated briefly, such a stance is based on the recognition that there are many possible ways of knowing the world, scientific knowledge being only one of them; that scientific knowledge is incomplete and cannot be made complete by recourse to its own instruments alone; that the epistemological privilege granted to scientific knowledge for the last 200 years was motivated by the objective of transforming science into a productive force of capitalist development and social peace, and that the political forces that fought against capitalism saw in science, albeit often in an alternative science (the critique of political economy), an equally progressive force; that after 200 years it has become evident that the progressive promises of science have not been fulfilled, and that the suppression or marginalization of non-scientific ways of knowing has led to a waste of social experience and social agency that might have strengthened the paths of social emancipation; and that the recognition and valuation of non-scientific knowledges will allow for a broader conversation of humankind by means of which scientific and non-scientific knowledges will complement each other in reinventing social emancipation.

Non-scientific knowledges have been designated by scientific knowledge in many different ways: commonsensical, local, vernacular, tacit, practical, plebeian, empirical, traditional, native, and so on. All the previous volumes relied on social-scientific knowledge to analyze social struggles. Whenever the existence and value of non-scientific knowledge was acknowledged—in all volumes, but most specifically in volume three—it was up to scientific analysis to determine the terms of such acknowledgement. In a sense, non-scientific knowledge was an object of scientific research, rather than standing on its own as another way of interpreting social reality and social transformation.

The aim of *Voices of the World* is to present some concrete illustrations of non-scientific analyses and interpretations of social reality and social transformation emerging out of the social experience of activists in social struggles, and of leaders of social movements and organizations. Scientific knowledge is still present through the choice of the concrete manifestations of non-scientific, practical knowledge, through the selection of questions that structured the interview or the life-story and, above all, through the conversion or translation of an oral knowledge into a written knowledge. Still, the epistemological status of social-scientific knowledge is here different than in the previous volumes: rather than producing knowledge, scientific knowledge's role here is to facilitate the emergence and self-presentation of knowledges in another way—but not of any other knowledge. Rather, the knowledges presented are connected with the social practices that the social scientists involved in this project—another scientific "interference"—recognize as practices of social emancipation. In terms of the modernist epistemological canon, premised upon the distinction between science and common-sense, we could conceive of *Voices of the World* as a set of illustrations of "emancipatory common sense." In terms of the voices themselves, they are stories of chains of events caused or suffered by the storytellers and interpretations of the larger worlds that emerge from the storytellers' experiences in trying to transform the world into a better one. They are activists' knowledges as self-expressions of past, present, and future activism. They are both collective and extremely personal accounts. Because of their diversity, they are knowledges, in the plural, rather than diverse manifestations of a single form of knowledge.

It would not be possible—and if it were, it would not be adequate—to define the general characteristics of the knowledges presented in this volume. I can only list randomly a few ideas that come to mind, almost like a thought experiment. As I do so, I must say, I resort equally to my experience both as an activist and as a researcher.

1. These knowledges are knowledges that do not distinguish between theory and practice because they do not exist outside the social practices in which they occur. As a matter of fact, when we speak of these knowledges

we necessarily speak of the agents, individuals, and social groups that hold and produce them.

2. They are not written or recorded, but expressed through what they make happen in the world and their interpretations of it.

3. They do not distinguish between the true, the good, or the just, because they are obtained in the truthful processes of the struggle for a more just society and a better life. But they are not interested in abstract ideas of justice or good life, which in fact they do not even consider intelligible. Nor, for that matter, is the idea of social emancipation necessarily intelligible to them. They are concrete knowledges born of concrete struggles for survival, for a decent life, for dignity, for equality, for the right to difference—in a word, for the aspiration to a better life. What they have in common is conceiving of reality as a social task. They do not reduce reality to what exists, because what does not exist and ought to exist is truly their reason for being as knowledges.

4. They refuse to be defined by logical propositions. They prefer formulae, proverbs, stories, myths, gestures, silences. They become more precise by means of examples, illustrations, cases. They are capable of reasoning on the world, life, the future, God; but they do it always as if they were narrating concrete cases of worlds, lives, futures, gods.

5. They consider themselves neither traditional nor modern, neither secular nor religious, neither specialized nor non-specialized. They are pragmatic. They resort to everything, including modern science, that may be useful for the objectives of the practices in which they occur. They are nonetheless most unequivocal and clairvoyant in their definition of the enemies, forces, evils, and powers against which they fight.

6. They do not own the truth, but they do feel that they are at the service of practical truths in concrete contexts and situations. These truths are truths about knowing and doing; they are political in the sense that they only exist because they are adequate to the objectives to be reached; and they are ethical because they distinguish unambiguously between concrete goodness and concrete evilness.

7. They are not methodical knowledges, in the sense of establishing in abstract a single path to move from ignorance to knowledge. Their criteria of relevance and pertinence are vague, and for that reason they are willing to make connections between realities or conditions that are separated by science. Their gestation and emergence is always enigmatic for those facing them from the outside. They are collective, but assumed by individual spokespersons who are recognizable by the way in which they formulate these knowledges, above all before strangers.

8. They are probabilistic and anti-totalitarian knowledges, which do not assert themselves by way of demonstration but rather by practical

confirmation and persuasive argumentation. They are rhetorical knowledges that express themselves in common language, and whose arguments are validated inside the community, organization, or movement involved in specific social struggles.

WHO IS AN ACTIVIST?

The core idea underlying this volume is to allow for a confrontation between the social-scientific knowledge produced about the social struggles and movements analyzed in the previous volumes and the self-knowledge of the protagonists of those struggles and movements. The choice of interviewees was therefore, in principle, limited to the struggles and movements analyzed in the project. But, of course, this limit allowed enormous leeway. Moreover, it was agreed that the researchers in the project could make suggestions about interviewing activists or leaders of movements not specifically analyzed in the previous volumes, if they were particularly congenial to the specific analytical and epistemological objectives of *Voices of the World*.

In a first approach, one might say that the potential interviewees are the unknown Gandhis, Martin Luther King Jrs., Nelson Mandelas, Lech Wałęsas, Emiliano Zapatas, Rigoberta Menchús, Subcomandante Marcoses, Chico Mendeses, and so on. But how were we to identify them if our objective was to analyze ongoing struggles and movements, hence before the public reputation of their activists evolved? Let us bear in mind that some of the activists mentioned above were widely acknowledged only after death.

Alternatively, we could define the profile of the interviewees using the Gramscian concept of the "organic intellectual," or simply refer to common-sense philosophers and thinker-activists. This approach would not be correct either. Gramsci's "organic intellectual" implies a technical knowledge emerging within the working class, and geared to organizing it and preparing it to organize and run society as a whole. The designation would be correct regarding some (not all) of the activists involved in workers' struggles, but certainly not in many other contexts of social struggle. The other designations presuppose a distinction between thought and action, which is precisely denied by the knowledge to which we wish to give voice.

It is not surprising that there was some difficulty in defining the profile of the interviewees. Such difficulty resulted from the very global context that had led to the collapse, in the late 1990s, of the forms, languages, institutions, and agencies of progressive social transformation that had dominated in the previous hundred years, a (partial? total? reversible? irreversible?)

collapse out of which there emerged the need to *reinvent social emancipation*. It resulted, in other words, from the failure (for some) or the present lack of credibility (for others) of the great maps of social emancipation, such as national liberation, socialism, and communism. These maps having been set aside, whether definitively or temporarily, the great historical agents of social emancipation have now disappeared—the great leaders of national liberation, of communist parties and workers' or worker-peasants' movements. Some decades ago they might have been our potential interviewees. But then we would perhaps not be ready to think, as we are today, the reciprocal incompleteness of all knowledges, and perhaps the interview would be unthinkable, either because we would consider scientific knowledge the only valid one, in which case the interview would not be necessary, or because we would consider the knowledge of leaders and activists the only valid one, in which case they would not have to be asked questions, but only followed.

Ours is a time of small maps and guides. While augmenting considerably the stock of potential interviewees, at the same time this fact rendered the selection criteria far more ambiguous. Broadly speaking, we chose for our interviews activists or leaders of struggles, movements, initiatives, and progressive organizations engaged in resistance against oppression and fighting for a more just society and a better collective life; leaders or activists who had been successful in their struggles and had earned from them a practical experience and knowledge that they were willing to share with us. Their levels of formal education might have varied, some might even be illiterate. It mattered only that they held a practical knowledge and, having emerged from very concrete experiences and struggles, knew how to draw from the latter useful lessons for activists engaged in other struggles elsewhere. A subsidiary criterion we used concerned the exposure of leaders or activists to the media. With rare exceptions, it was better to select activists or leaders who had not been too exposed to the media. Such exposure often implies a kind of perverse training for a narcissist discourse, sprinkled with banalities, or even lies, whenever the latter serve the purpose of the interviewee's self-aggrandizement. As I mentioned in the Preface, I also tried to achieve a gender balance among the *Voices*. In retrospect, I think that the recommendation that the interviewer and the interviewee had to have known each other for some time and a relation of mutual trust had to have evolved between them was responsible for the unbalance: five female voices and nine male voices.

The interviews were conducted between 2001 and 2005. Each interview begins with an introduction by the interviewer in which she or he presents the interviewee and provides a brief summary of the social and historical context of the activist's struggles or movement. Footnotes were also added by the interviewer to clarify or contextualize what was being said. The interview ends with a commentary by the interviewer, conceived as an exercise of self-reflection on how she or he personally felt about the interviewee or the latter's knowledge as laid out in the interview.

There are different ways to give voice to the *Voices of the World*. Most of the researchers chose the most common one: the transcript of the interview. Some, however, making use of several interviews, composed the interviewee's life-story or a struggle story as a first-person account.

WHO ARE THE ACTIVISTS IN THIS BOOK?

It would be presumptuous on my part to introduce the activists whose voices the reader is about to hear. They themselves do the job much better on their own. In order to seduce the reader into listening to them, I present below a small excerpt of each interview.

Miguel Alves dos Santos

Rural worker, persecuted by the dictatorship, homeless, industrial worker, leader of the Rural Landless Workers Movement (MST).

You're on the street counting the days before you die. How can anyone think that people on the street have a good life? Because they don't. Today you're alive, tomorrow you may be dead. Because sometimes that same fellow you share your Marmitex with will kill you just to take your Marmitex, to take your shirt, to take your slippers.

I guess you have a road you just have to take. When you're a true person, a serious socialist, you know you're not going to have an easy time, you're going to meet with difficulties. And unfortunately in our country anyone involved in socialism is damned.

So I started the struggles; I got involved and put myself in God's hands. When you have already gone through suffering, you don't mind some more. What matters is that you reap a fruit that is meaningful, that everyone can benefit from, and that is lasting.

When I speak of struggle, I mean that all Brazilians have the right to fight for their rights. What does the struggle mean? It means a house, a roof for you to live under, the land for you to sow, to reap from, to live on your own means, without depending on anyone. It means to fight for education, with honesty, for healthcare, with dignity, to fight for serious socialist freedom, which is the respect we have for everyone. . .

To learn respect, to be young until you're one hundred years old—skin color, black or white, doesn't matter. We're all equal. That is important. The MST has that spark—it has that character of freedom. So this is why I have joined the MST, with a destiny—destined for something that was to come again, destined to go back to that old process, that struggle together, to commit to that common alliance; this is what I've always wanted: "to overcome, to overcome." Fighting to overcome. To see our children, our grandchildren, our comrades, laughing. To have a home, a home of plenty, of full bellies, in good health and with education. It is very important that you go around and see old people having fun, feeling joyful and satisfied.

It is a shame to say that this is a democracy. Because when you speak of democracy, it is a clean democracy, without filth. And what we see is filthy. A democracy that allows stealing, taking away the workers' bread, exploiting workers, plucking out their eyes? Is that democracy?

Read more in the interview . . .

Paula Lima

Housewife, organizer of the struggle against layoffs and for the right of women to participate in union activities.

I can still remember that I told them it had been the saddest Christmas of our lives, because it was. Because my husband had lost his job and that had been part of our life: him getting up at dawn, going to work every day, having a time for leaving the house and a time for coming back.

That was why I went there that day, so that I could have something, someone, to believe in. And at that moment, on that day, I left feeling confident that something would happen, if people did something. Because I don't think that people can just sit there waiting. You have to fight, get involved.

I didn't understand anything about the law, I never had. I'd heard people speaking about human rights, this and that, but I didn't know much about laws, you know? Still, I remember that I said this: "We have rights, and this is a right—it's a human right; what we have to do is fight for our jobs." I didn't understand anything, you know? It was unconscious, what I said.

Definitely, I've changed. I'm much more of a human being now, you know? If I was a supportive type of person before—because I always liked to help people—I got that from my family; well, now I do ten times more. If someone needs something, then I'll go and help that person first, and then they can help me later on, you know?

I'm much more of a human being nowadays. I'm much more of a woman—because I didn't know myself as a woman before.

When I saw women talking, getting up there and taking the microphone in their hands and speaking so clearly, without any fear of saying that they would go after things, that they would go to the Senate, that they'd go I don't know where, they'd get this and that, I was very proud to be born a woman, you know? Very proud.

Read more in the interview . . .

Pedro Inácio Pinheiro Ngematücü

Indigenous person belonging to the Tikunas of the Amazon, leader of the indigenous movement.

They killed the Indians, they killed all of them. Because they came out of the meeting house, came outside—they came out killing. Whoever went to the river, they killed them too—women, men, and children too.

So, after the massacre . . . no one stopped, because we knew that the massacre . . . everyone felt that blood had been spilt, we felt that in our bodies; but even so, we didn't stop fighting for the land, which is our land. Even today, there's still some land left to demarcate. . .

Because I had seen that the Constitution, the Indian Statute, said that it was the Indians that lived in this land—Brazil, as it is called today—which was not the land of Brazilians, as whites are called, right? So we based ourselves on that, and we understood that the land was ours because we hadn't come from other lands. We didn't come from another land, we didn't come from another planet—we came from right here. Our god was from right here. The god of the white man is different and maybe comes from a different place. Now our land is in the hands of our god, who is Yoi. So that's why when the bosses came here, the whites, like robbers, stole the land of the Tikuna. So, now we want it back.

Well, what happened after the demarcation? I mean, the demarcation of lands, the Tikuna needed to say that. . . Well, the Tikuna didn't understand what land is. Land for them is that there should be a contact with the whites, the timber merchants, the fishermen, who are interested in the lake and in the demarcated Tikuna area. And there are timber merchants interested in the demarcated Tikuna lands. So, we ask for the Tikuna's land, because the principle of demarcation is a security for the Tikuna, but then there were some leaders, some communities, saying that it's not Pedro that is providing for those folk. "Why does Pedro forbid cutting down trees and selling the wood since it's ours? So now the land is demarcated, we have the right to sell the wood!" There I said no, it's not like that, because the wood. . . there is good wood, there is softwood and there is wood that can be used to make canoes; so, if they're going to take out the wood to sell it to the sawmill, I mean, the land will be devastated. It will be destroyed. In conclusion, there won't be any more land, and the animals will go away and the animals will die. Time will go on and we'll grow up and we won't find anything.

Read more in the interview . . .

Han Dongfang

Railway worker, fighter in Tiananmen Square, organizer of independent union, prisoner, activist for human rights and democracy.

The first thing I remember is the bullets in the sky. Even though I served in the army for three years, I had never seen anything like this. The sky was dark and the bullets in the sky had a pink color. The color looked beautiful. There were bullets going in so many different directions—the bullets would whistle over your head.

My background is communism. Communism taught us to believe in heroes who save the people. We were taught to believe in saviors of the people—human saviors like Mao.

After I left the Square I was shocked at the terrible death and destruction. I believed that people would be serious and react to the violence.

I decided that the best thing for me would be to leave Beijing and work with the ordinary people to try and change things. I picked up my bicycle and started to travel around the country.

I reminded people that, under Chinese law, we were taking legal action: it was our legal right to act, to protest, and to organize a workers' organization. Second, I reminded everybody that, even though we were doing legal things, we were still taking a risk with our freedom and our lives.

When you are in a cell you are an animal, an absolute animal. What you need is food, more food, better food. You are only allowed to the toilet once a day and then only for one minute. Each person only has thirty seconds on the toilet. If you don't come back from the toilet after thirty seconds they will beat you and they won't give you water. So my first fight for human dignity in the prison was a fight over toilet time. I refused to leave the toilet, saying I haven't finished yet. I looked the policeman in his eyes and said, "Whatever you want to do, just do it."

Read more in the interview . . .

Gabriel Muyuy Jacanamejoy

Indigenous person belonging to the Inga people, leader of the indigenous movement, professor, senator.

My people resisted because they kept their Inga identity alive in their minds. They rebelled—and among them was my great-grandfather, who had libertarian ideas—because they refused to accept any rule which went against our culture. . .

I remember that, in this dispute, all the authorities were on the side of the settlers, who took concerted action to cause the disappearance of all the documents pertaining to the ownership of those lands. They burned down the registry office with the purpose of eliminating any evidence of our ownership of these properties. However, my stepfather and other Ingas proved to be astute, because all of them had copies of those documents that entitled us to keep our lands.

In the movement, we started to recollect our history—the deceit by the large landowners, the exploitation by the church, the government's violence—and we felt, all of a sudden, a historical rage, a retroactive rage, which had built up inside us.

Something deep inside made me feel that I had to prepare myself to fight for our cause. I understood the value of what it means to be indigenous. We were now awake, and we began to value our identity, and to understand what it is to be Inga.

We, the Inga, have specialized in the knowledge of our ancestral medicine, and this is our greatest cultural legacy from time immemorial to the present. We are experts in botanical medicine. The practice of this medicine is a cultural inheritance from our ancestors.

I came back to the Sibundoy Valley with a goal: to empower the Putumayo indigenous peoples—especially my own people, the Inga—so that they would no longer be subjected to the humiliations inflicted by the settlers and to the manipulation of the missionaries with their evangelization programs, which made them submissive, impoverished, and prey to discrimination. This became my major concern.

We did not stop the Inga people from attending church rituals or ceremonies, but we kept calling their attention to other things; we talked to them about the economy, about the workings of the state, and other issues that the priests failed to explain adequately because their sole concern was to catechize. So indigenous people began to get the whole picture, and started to think in a different way.

Today I believe we've achieved great constitutional and political victories. It was not a concession from the state or a "gift" from parties or governments: it was the outcome of an indigenous social process.

Read more in the interview . . .

Gerardo González

Peasant, guerrilla member, ex-guerrilla member, leader of the peasant movement.

We had to wait many years, and there were many deaths, before things got on the right course—and, I repeat, before we found a leader who refused to sell us out.

The gringos were obsessed with the Cold War, and saw agents from Moscow everywhere. I guess you could say that our main success in that war was figuring out how to organize defeat, and not scatter or turn into easy prey for the enemy.

The communists were extremely active, organizing groups of men, women, and children, and were establishing rural settlement councils, settlers' committees, and party cells. These were legal activities carried out along with others, like organizing peasant self-defense efforts. We knew the tide was turning, and in that we were not mistaken.

Out of that resistance movement came the name Independent Republics, simply due to the fact that we did not let them continue to govern as they pleased, were self-sufficient, and, above all, continued to grow stronger. That was the crime they accused us of. This accusation was conveniently used by the oligarchs to cover up their real crimes—and also by the military, to seal their alliance with the US government.

I began to travel around all the peasant regions, spreading the word about our experiences. I traveled by foot, talking to people. Agrarian reform began to become a goal once again. But this time there were also demands for education, healthcare, housing, and loans. People can learn how to fight back!

They refused to recognize the state—something that oligarchies find unforgivable, because the state was there to solve their problems, but not ours. There was some awareness of the fact that we were organizing another state.

The Cuban Revolution helped us a great deal. It gave us new ideas, and helped us see that it was possible to achieve what we had only dreamed about up to then. It was a great stimulus for the struggle, and showed the need for organization.

Our classmates were members of central committees from very important Communist parties, like those of Italy and Chile. On that trip we met Corvalan from Chile's Communist Party. We were sent to a fancy hotel, the Príncipe de Gales. Very luxurious, with a lot of velvet and feather mattresses. But as I was used to sleeping on the floor, and had been sleeping rough, out in the fields, I couldn't sleep on a soft bed, and so I slept on the floor. Jacobo laughed at me.

Read more in the interview . . .

Kaluram Dhodade

Activist of the struggle for the right to land, leader of one of the movements for the rights of the Adivasis.

My first focus was against the police, since everyone was afraid of confronting the police exploitation of Adivasis. People understood the police as being synonymous with the government. The Adivasi Sewa Mandal did not have the strength to oppose the atrocities against Adivasis. People also were scared to intervene if they saw someone being beaten up, because then they would be beaten up too.

We had used the technique of first harvesting the land that was within the law. Once we established that we were going according to the law, later, we would harvest all the land—whether it was within the law or not.

When all the Left activists—Mrinal Gore and others—were thrown in jail during the Emergency, we thought about doing a Satyagraha at that time. But all these city folks were so scared. But the Emergency was no new situation for us: we have been in an Emergency since we were born!

Complete authority should be given to people; only then can people begin to take democracy seriously. Funds should be given to the village, for distribution by the village. They will form a committee and decide who is needy, who should get what. Take the planning process in Kerala: that is what we are saying—planning should be from the bottom up. As long as the planning is from the top, people have no opportunity to reflect, to take part. If there is autonomy, then there can be planning in this manner.

These Left party people felt afraid, and were hesitant about sending their Adivasi workers. These parties had fought one or two struggles for Adivasis, but had no concept of the realities of Adivasi life or identity. We explained to them the need to articulate the Adivasi identity, the positive attributes of Adivasi culture. These are attributes that would benefit the human rights movement and society in general—attributes such as not begging, collective sharing, honoring oral commitments, respect for women.

The three foundation stones of any organization are its ideological base, its economic arrangements, and its programs. The economic base has to be independent—if you take outside funding, then you have to give false reports of your work.

The picture is so grim; an Adivasi is displaced not once, but several times. The situation has gone out of our hands; Adivasis alone will not be able to fight. All the oppressed classes, the 80 percent of society, have to unite so that all can live in human dignity. Today the situation of dependence in the country is so pathetic—we have mortgaged the Vidhan Bhavan and the Lok Sabha.

Read more in the interview . . .

Siddahraj Dhadda

Prominent Gandhian, writer, grassroots organizer.

I strongly feel that people have been cheated. Western culture and the adoption of English language are ruining the country. Western culture is a self-centered culture, and is unhealthy for a society. An extreme aberration is the Valentine's Day celebration in our country.

The only way out of this terrible crisis is for the society to free itself as far as possible from the clutches of money and the market, the bureaucracy and the government. This is possible through the building up of a self-reliant, cooperative, and decentralized social order with a rural orientation. The present situation poses a challenge to all revolutionaries who are distressed at the sufferings and tribulations of humankind. The people have also become fed up. They are on the lookout for an alternative. What is required is to go to the people and awaken their faith in themselves.

Some points are of great importance in regard to the economy of the villages. The first concerns agriculture. The first priority of agricultural operation in the village should be the fulfillment of the needs of the local community. The plan for the farming sector should be drawn up keeping in view the general principle that the food grains, vegetables, oil-seeds, and cotton for the cloth required by the community should be produced in the village. In regions that do not suffer from any deficiency in locally available resources, effort should be made to make the village communities self-reliant in the matter of food, clothing, housing, primary education, and health. Wherever the resource position is not favorable, the needs should be met through exchange, or cooperation with neighboring villages or regions.

The proper definition of Swadeshi is concern for and duty to one's neighbor. All the people of the world are our kin, but our first concern should naturally be for our immediate neighbors' well-being. The things we use provide employment to other people. Hence, in the matter of the things that we use, our first preference would be, after those we can produce at home, for those produced by people in our village or the neighboring area.

The lifestyle in consonance with Swadeshi is that in which people engage in productive labor themselves; there is interdependence and sharing among neighbors, wants are limited, and the life led is simple.

Read more in the interview . . .

Maciane F. Zimba

Traditional doctor, leader of the Association of Traditional Doctors.

But I managed to talk to Samora, and I said that I came to look for him because he used to say: "Even chained lions are free; and all my people are free." I said to him: "We are traditional doctors, sons of tradition, who look after traditional spirits. Who is going to liberate us if not you? Which president is going to liberate us, since we have heard that traditional medicine is not allowed?" [He answered:] Have you ever heard me say 'Down with the doctors'? Also, when we say down with something, it doesn't mean the end of it, only to diminish it. I want to tell you that traditional medicine is not going to end, but those who vaccinated the Portuguese so that they could come to Tanzania and murder Frelimo people without being seen, those are our enemies. As you have explained everything and came to see me, I am authorizing you—go and work!"

There is the problem that if you cure one person, another might die, even in the doctor's house. If it happens in hospital, no one is arrested. . .

A person can go to the hospital, but there are things that can never be cured there— there is no medicine for it. Modern doctors only bother to give medicines. There are illnesses that require ceremonies; if not there'll be no cure. There are illnesses only the traditional doctor can cure—it is not knowledge everyone has. You have to know what it is, how to treat it, know which medicine to get from the bush to give to the person—it's not easy.

That's right, because it's true Frelimo struggled until it won—but it wasn't only the warriors, it was also the dead, the ancestors. They were there to protect them. When [Frelimo] arrived, they should have conducted a ceremony—mhamba—so that all the dead would know they had returned, that the war had ended, shouldn't they?

Read more in the interview . . .

Carolina J. Tamele

Traditional doctor, leader of the Association of Traditional Doctors.

It is not only a question of tradition—it's that they don't do things right for us to live properly. A black is a black. There is always something difficult to resolve. He should find someone to look well into his life and its traditional base, to hear properly what the ancestors have to say to him . . . Our country will fail like this. But Chissano is worse—he is selling everything, even the land, to foreigners. He is selling our country— we know but we don't want to say it. This Chissano, it seems his head is not right.

Everything, everything you learn when you go looking for medicines in the bush and help cure people until the spirit comes out; and you are taught how to speak and to do the treatments.

It is the study course. First [I will] explain the nguni spirit, and then the ndau spirit. This is in the first year; in the second, you learn the medicinal plants. Then the master [(b'ava)] has to see that the person has properly learned to handle the spirits, both the strong and the weak. . .

It requires patience, because some spirits are really difficult to deal with. So there are people who take longer to train; it could take three or four years to finish the course.

You know, these Frelimo people forget that the bush, where people died, where the colonial soldiers burned houses, needs to be visited in the traditional way. The government should organize this, but it doesn't happen—they only go to visit the Heroes Monument. And those who don't rest there—who visits them?

Yes, there is a division of tasks. For this reason the majority of traditional doctors have these two spirits. The nguni is the one that throws the tinhlolo and looks for cures; the spirit has the job of bringing out the evil spirits, or those of the ancestors that show anger towards you for a variety of reasons.

When we go far away, the danger is greater. We get there, and there will be spirits that mean harm to us, which want to get what we have—they want to see if we are strong.

The person who taught me couldn't write. Would he have liked to see someone writing down what he said? He would have rejected this: even obliging the person to abandon his training. The might say that his house isn't a school, that it was not necessary to write all he knows. He would say that what he knows he has kept in his head, and until today he transmits everything he knows only through speech.

Read more in the interview . . .

Maincha Pitara

Women's rights activist, founder of a pioneering community court dedicated to disputes involving women.

To begin at the beginning for the person that is giving you information—we have to take that down, to listen, when it is a woman. Starting from there, we ask how and when they started to have the problem. First we ask the years of marriage—how many years of marriage. The person speaks. Then, in the early years, how did you live? Then the person starts telling everything. The conflicts related to the problem began in which year? Like that. The person also starts to explain. Then, they start explaining everything. . .

. . . then we give them some time to think: "Go away for so many days—thirty days, say, go away and think, stay together." When the day arrives, they come back to the office. Then, when they say "We're staying with our husbands," then we clap and it's all over, for the best, with the marriage and all that. There are cases when we do a reconciliation twice. But on the third day, if we see that the love doesn't stick, there's no way; so then we accept a divorce.

It's our shelter. It's here on the beach at Wimbe, near the village. It's a house where women can rest. Sometimes there are conflicts inside the home, so a person can't stay there.

People also started to ask, "Why don't you set up offices here? Because Pemba is far away. Here we are out of it, most of us—we still don't know about those rights that a woman has, that she can make a complaint in a place. So we want to have an office near us too." That's why we set up offices there in the districts, so that those who want to come to the office in Pemba, but can't, can have their problems solved there. That's why we have set up those offices, at the request of the majority.

I'm not talking about other matters, but about social problems, about widows, that sort of thing—not beating up, not killing people, social problems. . . I'm ready for that—I really am.

Read more in the interview . . .

Fátima Carvalho

Textile worker, grassroots trade unionist, leading activist in the struggle for the rights of working women.

April 25th was, for me and the others, the dream of freedom and hope—the end of oppression, and the right to think and express our opinions in freedom. It was about having standards of living that we had never had. It's enough to say that when they got a raise of 1,000 escudos, they were able to improve their living standards immensely. I was able to buy a fridge for my parents, a television, a cooker. In a few months, it was possible to afford all those things. It was a time when people made great investments, getting the main things they needed to live.

And so things started to change inside me, which I'm proud of today. I like being a woman! And I think that I've learned a lot about what men are like too. Often I had that idea about the boss, that the boss was someone who was frightening, who intimidated and repressed us. Those myths started to collapse as I gradually became aware of what I was capable of standing up to. I began to understand that men also have their weaknesses. And that let me realize where their weak points were, so that I could defend myself.

Things started to get complicated; no one knew how this was going to end, since positions were getting more and more extreme, in an area where there was no experience of struggle. Those women had never fought before! We had a group of unionists among them, but most of them were not members. I told them that we had to extend the movement—which was not difficult; and so the struggle took on a whole different tone, which was nice. The whole town of Poiares got behind those women. The nights were cold, but they didn't lose heart, and soon wood appeared, so that they could make a fire. The baker took them warm bread; other people took food and drinks. Those women felt almost like princesses with so much support, in spite of all the sacrifices they were making.

Sometimes feminists are very closed. That's the problem—women's rights seen through a single prism. I think that there are rights that we should defend for both women and men. I don't have the view that we have to work only for us, women. We all have to get involved, women and men. Maybe women should play a bigger role in educating men, or at least in trying to change their mentalities so that equality is not just an empty word.

I have always found it very difficult to fit into mid-ranking organizations, because the debate is generally quite far removed from daily union action.

Sometimes, I ask myself, "What is my role in all this? Is it worth being a unionist nowadays? Everything takes such a long time to change. And now we've even got a retrograde right-wing party in power. But what sort of political awareness do people have? What have I been thinking all these years? What is my role?" I wonder a lot about these things. I think that people's social conscience is still very fragile.

Read more in the interview . . .

Joaquim Gonçalves

Self-employed, leader of the ecological movement against co-incineration.

Let's say that the factory has been operating in its own universe, separate from ours, and that it pollutes because it has to pollute, because it can't make cement any other way, but it doesn't have the slightest awareness, or there hasn't been any awareness on the part of the people in charge of the factory, that on the other side there are human beings, plants, animals, and all the things that belong to these people, which at the very least ought to be discussed.

I had never been very involved in the political side; I was an independent at the time, but people were pressuring me, believing that I was strong enough to head the struggle—and also because of the fact that I was already self-employed at the time in Souselas, working as an insurance intermediary, which means working door-to-door, meeting people and talking to them. . .

And then [there are] some traumas that never leave you. Personally speaking, my father died of silicosis, my mother died of silicosis, and my grandfather died of silicosis—that is to say, there are some personal traumatic experiences that will always make us, at the very least, unable to trust. We are fighting to make our environment better so that the distrust lessens rather than increases, so that this lack of trust will gradually subside. So there are some things that we cannot give up on: we can't give up on spending our lives in Souselas, having our property in Souselas—we were born there, we live there, we can't just simply be thrown on the rubbish heap; we have the right to fight for the best possible quality of life.

No one cares about those who are against and say why: they might even be right, but if they're not aligned with those in power, it's extremely hard for them to get their message across.

But ordinary citizens—well, it's just not allowed. We present technical evidence, we present scientific evidence, and it's like beating your head against a brick wall, because they won't let us [speak].

And then, what's worse is that, as well as not allowing us a voice, the control they have over the media is so great that they manage to misrepresent the way the message is put across.

So, after all these questions, Souselas and I myself will never accept co-incineration. I can't accept it, because the failures in the whole process are so great that only the negative side stands out. My life is at issue here—I'm not even talking about the tangible side, money or material things, but my life itself; and nobody can tell me how much that is worth—they cannot, and I won't accept it.

Read more in the interview . . .

Manuel Graça

Footwear worker, member of the army that started the 25th of April Revolution, grassroots trade unionist, activist in the struggle for trade union democracy.

Well, the situation now is very different, totally different. At that time, there were a lot of workers who had the Eastern European countries as a reference, even socialists and independents that had nothing to do with the PCP—they saw in those countries a model for development. I didn't have that reference, but I was not systematically hostile to it either.

The militants from the PCP were reformists, and that was a caricature of socialism. But that did not prevent us from joining all together, united with the PCP crowd when there were struggles. But everyone thought that it was an obstacle to the development of politics and of the struggle for a socialist society—for a society based upon justice and solidarity.

And then they said to us, "Calm down, man. We've got the eastern countries, we'll get there one day!" But we knew what was happening to their political struggle through dissident groups—we knew all about the movements in Czechoslovakia and Solidarity in Poland. We knew what was going on from the start through political circuits and other autonomous organizations on the left. Of course, we knew very well what was going on—indeed, I was part of a committee supporting the struggle of the Solidarity workers in Poland—we held debates, showed films, news bulletins, and so on.

Now, how are we going to resist? This discussion is significant for those that took part in the post–April 25th period, when there was a great accumulation of new forces, a great popular participation, with important social achievements. This wounded the lion, but it didn't kill it, did it? Now, this crowd that was around at that time and had that experience has to resist, it has to try to resist all that, hasn't it? There is repression; people are fired; employers and those in power try to win people over to their side. These are times when we have to discuss new schemes to resist and reorganize.

When I speak of revolution, I mean with the participation of millions and millions of people, the extension of direct democracy, the participation of all the social and political movements, and not just the workers' and union movements, to help transform society. Obviously, in the countries of the east, for example, there was a complete fraud—that, for me, is not socialism. Now, I don't have the recipe for socialism. When I speak of emancipation on the level of women, on the level of rights to religious freedom, the secular state; when I defend ecology, employment, education. . .

There are people who say, "Listen, are you not tired of all this? Haven't you given up?" Because I never set rigid goals. Socialism is not made to measure. A more just society, a more fraternal society—that is something that will certainly not be built in my lifetime! I don't know—it's very difficult.

Read more in the interview . . .

Lydia Kompe-Ngwenya

Worker, community organizer against apartheid, campaigner for women's rights, trade unionist, member of parliament.

It was very difficult, you know, when I first came there, because I was the only woman among all these men, and there were a lot of things I was obliged to do like making tea, going to buy lunch—because we were eating in a group—and washing dishes afterwards, and then cleaning up. And in the meantime I was an organizer equal [to] them, so my job will delay and they will carry on.

If they allocate me a plant, I would have to organize that factory—and they would drop us at the gates of every factory to organize for thirty minutes only. At lunchtime. And within that thirty minutes you must have said something very, very special to encourage people to come to the office in Benoni. But you know, I survived. I had a lot of members, and without getting between sheets I managed! I had a lot of members. I survived, and I actually got a lot of respect from the very same men. They realized I can put my foot down and I mean what I say—that they will need to empower workers.

I first spoke to men themselves, and said, "I think this is wrong, what you are doing. You make decisions yourselves, and you don't convey this to women, and you don't plan with women, and they are the ones who are actually holding the knife at the sharp end. At the end of the day you are gone.

So I think that's why, when we launched COSATU, I just felt, "Oh my dreams came true. I am going to leave this union with the younger people, because now they don't have to run around. Stop orders are now legalized. Unions are registered. It's just a matter of strengthening the whole thing. The young ones can go around to the workshops—there's no more going to the gates pleading that people should join. People just come because they can see the benefits of trade unions."

I think I gained a lot of experience. I was really capacitated. I was really empowered. I could resist anything. I even said to myself, if I was empowered like this before my marriage I would not have divorced, because I would also empower my husband somehow or other.

And I learned to live with all races. Because I want to say, before I was very, very bitter with white people because of the laws that affected my life so much—particularly influx control. I never thought I would ever be friends with whites. When I saw white people, I just saw enemies.

Read more in the interview . . .

BRAZIL

1

Miguel Alves dos Santos

Rural worker, persecuted by the dictatorship, homeless, industrial worker, leader of the Rural Landless Workers Movement.

Interviewed by Marcelo Gomes Justo

"I guess you have a road you just have to take. When you're a true person, a serious socialist, you know you're not going to have an easy time, you're going to meet with difficulties. And, unfortunately, in our country anyone involved in socialism is damned . . ."

Miguel Alves dos Santos

MST is the acronym for what became known as the Rural Landless Workers Movement of Brazil. The struggle of the landless peasants is the result of the concentration of landed property and of a series of expropriations. Struggling to maintain their own or to gain new land, farmers have organized and have, in the recent history of the country, relied on the help of missionaries from the progressive wing of the Catholic Church, who created the Pastoral Land Commission (CPT—Comissão Pastoral da Terra) in 1975. At the end of the 1970s and the beginning of the 1980s, there were a few agrarian conflicts in the state of Rio Grande do Sul that were directly supported by the CPT. These conflicts were the embryo of the MST, which was officially founded in 1984 at a national meeting. According to data provided by the MST, there are in Brazil about 4 million families without land to live on or to work. Land occupation has been a common practice in the history of Brazil and, by engaging in this strategy, the MST managed to make the government expropriate a few landed estates and to settle thousands of families. However, in 2001, as is made clear in the interview, the federal government blocked this strategy of action.

The specificity of the Carlos Lamarca Settlement lies in the fact that it was the result of the joint organizational efforts of the MST and of the religious group Street Net (Rede Rua), which works with street dwellers in the city of São Paulo. The settlement is located in the municipality of Itapetininga, in the southwest of the state of São Paulo, about 190 km away from the capital.

In 1996, over sixty families from the cities of Campinas and São Paulo started occupying land in the municipalities of Itapetininga and Sarapui. About 20 percent of these families were living in the streets of São Paulo. They stayed in encampments for two years until, in 1998, they achieved the expropriation of the Monjolo estate, which came to be the Carlos Lamarca Settlement. Its area totals 883.3 hectares. The government settled forty-seven families in that area, and the remainder had to move to a different settlement.

I met Miguel Alves dos Santos on a visit to the encampment in 1998, shortly before the estate's expropriation. His personal trajectory and his capacity to relate his story to the history of the country attracted my attention. Two years later I started a doctorate concerned with the internal social conflicts in that settlement and with the *question of how the MST represents an alternative for street dwellers. My first step thereafter was to look for Miguel.*

Miguel was born in 1944, in Tabaiana Grande, in the state of Sergipe. He is presently married to Cida. Being the son of farmers, as a child he helped his parents work the land. His father introduced him to socialism. In 1962 he joined the army in the city of Santos, in the state of São Paulo, believing in a fairer country. At the time of the military coup, in 1964, he was an army sergeant, and was arrested on the accusation of being a communist. He was tortured and imprisoned with other soldiers. According to his account, they were released by a group of uniformed, hooded men, who led them into the thick of the jungle in the state of São Paulo. Miguel moved ahead on his own; he traveled to the state of Mato Grosso and later reached Paraguay, where he lived for two years. Back in Brazil, in 1966, he managed to obtain an army reservist's certificate. He worked for twenty-two years as a metalworker in the automobile industry, for companies such as Volkswagen, Ford, and Mercedes-Benz. During the 1970s he was active in an illegal Trotskyist socialist group. He participated in the labor movement, which would give rise in 1980 to the Workers' Party (PT—Partido dos Trabalhadores). He lost jobs for being considered a political agitator. He was also active in the homeless movement, participating in building-occupation actions. Unable to find any further jobs as a metalworker, he began working in construction, until he found himself unable to find any other sources of income. He lived on the streets of São Paulo for two years until he was found by members of Street Net (Rede Rua), through which he joined the MST and managed to be settled.

The interview took place in Miguel's home. We started the conversation in his yard, while he husked corn. As the sun started to burn, we went inside. We recorded for four hours, from 9.30 a.m. to 3.00 p.m., with a lunch break. We talked for most of the day. I present here a shortened version of the interview, containing its central moments. A few cuts were inevitable, given the prolixity of both the interviewer and the interviewee.

Marcelo Gomes Justo: *Miguel, last week, while we were talking, you told me your story. You have a past of political struggle, since the 1964 military coup.*[1] *You worked for twenty-two years as a metalworker, and you participated in the ABC strikes. When the PT was formed you were there in Vila Euclides.*[2] *You were working as a metalworker; and then, how did you end up on the street?*

---

1   On 31 January 1964, the Brazilian Army promoted a coup d'état and established an authoritarian regime that lasted until 1985, when a civilian won the presidency of the republic through indirect elections.

2   "ABC strikes" is the name by which the strike movement became known, especially the metalworkers' movement. The strikes took place in the late 1970s and early 1980s in the municipalities of Santo André, São Bernardo do Campo, and São Caetano, in the metropolitan area of São Paulo, where the country's largest automobile industry complex was located. The Workers Party (PT—Partido dos Trabalhadores) arose out of that strike movement. The meetings of the striking metalworkers took place in the soccer stadium of Vila Euclides, where hundreds of thousands of workers gathered.

Miguel Alves dos Santos: I guess you have a road you just have to take. When you're a true person, a serious socialist, you know you're not going to have an easy time, you're going to meet with difficulties. And unfortunately in our country anyone involved in socialism is damned. Because a socialist does not accept corruption. A socialist is someone who wants all to be equal, all to have the same rights. A socialist is not someone who wants to see some with a full belly while others starve, begging on the street. So my problem, my life, all my life, has been this struggle. Since 1964 I've been struggling to see these commitments that we have made fulfilled—to see if we can overcome this critical point, because this is what's been happening in this country. It's been all grief and suffering. And ever more we see the poor and the humble—not those with money, not the bourgeoisie. The bourgeoisie has privileges, but the poor man has poverty in his home. So the suffering that I've always endured, my struggle, since '64, has been against racism. It is against this racism that I'm in favor of democracy, a true democracy where we all have the rights stated in the Constitution. Because now and then they write it down, but they do not bring any of it into effect. I have always felt indignation and I have always felt suffering for being someone discriminated against, for being someone engaged in the struggle, the class struggle, and yet being discriminated against. This is what it has been like for a long time, and they say that if you speak the truth, you're the one who's corrupt. That's why I've been suffering: I've been through that hard path you mentioned as you started the interview, and that's why I've been suffering since '64. Because in '64, unfortunately—I wish I could forget it—I was in the military. I knew then what I've always wanted in life, which was freedom, which was a democracy without lies. What's the point of a democracy where you can speak up, but where you have nothing and people die of hunger? There's no point. The son of the bourgeois walks into a car dealer, an agency, and buys the car of the year. The son of the poor man watches TV and cannot even afford to buy a plastic toy car.

In '64 I went through hardship because they took me for something I wasn't. I was not and I am not a communist; I'm an honest person. I'm poor, but I've got my dignity; I don't put up with corruption and I don't put up with dishonesty. I had to get away from Brazil for two years, and I came back in '66. On my return to Brazil in '66 I felt discriminated against, being without papers, without anything. For two years I struggled to get papers to work as a civilian, because I have always wanted to fight for this—I have always wanted to fight for the working class, to be always among the working class, that's where I feel at home. I managed to get some papers. I started to work as a civilian, and I started getting involved in the struggle of my comrades, the homeless. I started getting involved in party struggles. I went ahead, but I always felt fear. Because once you've gone through suffering you know there's more of it ahead. I faced many threats after this, after I started to participate in popular movements.

Unfortunately, I don't have much learning—I have had little schooling. I'm like Rui Barbosa;[3] what I speak comes from my mind, and I have it recorded just like a computer. It is not the result of solid reading because I've never done that reading. I finished the fourth grade, and I'm proud of it, because that fourth grade does not ask me to do mischief, it only asks me to do good. Whereas there are people who are highly educated and they only plot mischief; they don't think of doing good.

I started with the alliance, the Socialist Convergence (Convergência Socialista),[4] in São Bernardo, in '75. That's where I started. I was already working in the metal industry then. I started in Volkswagen, and in '80 I had already been working at Volks for twelve years.

MGJ: *That was in 1980?*

MAS: Right. It all started for me at the Socialist Convergence in that struggle in '74. The struggle of '80 was the starting point for the emergence of a new party, the Workers Party. There was a call for a new party because there was no popular movement to fight for the working class. But how was it to be done, with our comrade Lula[5] in jail? He was being discriminated against. We signed the document for the foundation of the party. That's when the PT alliance was established. As we signed that document we committed ourselves to a party without lies, a class-conscious party, to fight for the working class, for the poor and the humble. Our party, the PT, is that kind of party. In the mid-'80s, as I was already seriously committed, and gaining strength, involved in politics together with my comrades, I said: "I'm going to go there and I'm going to get what I've always wanted, to help myself, to help my family and to help my comrades who are in need."

---

3   Rui Barbosa de Oliveira (1849–1923) was a Brazilian jurist, journalist, and politician. He stood for the abolition of slavery, which came into force in 1888. He was state deputy, senator, and chancellor of the exchequer.

4   The Socialist Convergence was a Trotskyist-leaning political group formed in the 1970s that contributed to the creation of the PT, and then merged into the party. At the turn of the 1990s, some members of that political group broke with the PT and founded the Socialist Party of Unified Workers (PSTU—Partido Socialista dos Trabalhadores Unificados).

5   Luís Inácio Lula da Silva was at the time the honorary president of the PT, which he helped to found. From 1975 he was president of the metalworkers' trade union for repeated periods. He led the ABC strikes in the late 1970s and the early 1980s, which were deemed illegal. He was arrested in 1980 under the now defunct National Security Law.

So I started the struggles; I got involved and put myself in God's hands. When you have already gone through suffering, you don't mind some more. What matters is that you reap a fruit that is meaningful, that everyone can benefit from, and that is lasting. While I was active in the PT, in the meantime, the rug was being pulled from under my feet. I started at Mercedes, and then I was laid off; I started at Ford[6] and then I was laid off.

MGJ: *Why were you laid off?*

MAS: They claimed that I was an agitator and that I wasn't fit to be among the class of people who were willing to work—that I was an agitator, not one who wanted to lead the life of a serious worker. They said that I was a communist, that I was of no use inside, and that they had to get rid of me. And why? Because I was the one who was pulling my comrades toward the truth, I was giving advice to them, saying that that was not our way, and that, going that way, we would end up being slaves in Brazil. I was saying all this, and people were following my ideas. And because of me there were other comrades who also started cooperating. They claimed that I was an agitator. So I gradually lost ground and my jobs were gone.

MGJ: *Is that why you were laid off?*

MAS: Yes, that's why. They kept turning me away, and I was pushed into a dead end. And I left, to work in construction. That was another trial for me. I started in the struggle again—I don't just turn my back, I started fighting. Soon the whole thing started all over again, they began pulling the rug from under my feet. I had no job, I had no place to live—I was struggling together with the homeless, but I was struggling in vain because there was no support. There was support from the families only; there was no serious support. So where did I end up? On the street, that's where I ended up, that's where I stayed for two years.

MGJ: *And you didn't manage to get any other job?*

MAS: I could get no job and I had no place to live, because I had always lived in rented places. That's something I've always fought for, but I've always fought for other people. For me and for other people.

MGJ: *And what was your last job?*

MAS: Basically I had my last job when I joined the homeless, when I found a job cleaning the streets, temporarily. I started working then, and I worked for three months, and I rented a room to get off the streets, because unfortunately if I hadn't got that room in Parque Dom Pedro[7] I

---

6   Mercedes-Benz, Ford, Volkswagen, and Scania were the most important automobile companies which, in the 1970s and the 1980s, were concentrated in the ABC region, and together employed hundreds of thousands of workers.

7   Parque Dom Pedro is a central area of São Paulo City where there are many street dwellers. There are services in the vicinity that provide assistance to this population.

would have had no job. Because they were already discriminating against anyone without lodgings: no address, no job.

MGJ: *Was that a shelter* (albergue)*?*[8]

MAS: Yes, I was in a shelter. But when I went to fill job applications, if I told them that I had no place of my own, that I was staying in a shelter, they would tell me straight to my face that it was no good, because jobs are for people with a fixed address. And I would leave with my head down, but I kept asking God for help, to hold me back from hurting anyone, to help me keep my way, because that is not my way. I moved on, and it was under the viaduct that I came across that temporary company. I was already a little involved with the Street People [Povo de Rua],[9] joining their groups to work with the homeless; and I was doing this, and I kept wandering. I got that tiny room, in Parque Dom Pedro; I stayed there for a while, in this boarding house, and that's where I got this temporary job sweeping the street and collecting garbage in trucks.

MGJ: *Working for the mayoralty?*

MAS: Yes, for the mayoralty. And that was my last job. It was then that I joined Father Naveen's community;[10] we started working together, and I joined the Landless Workers Movement. That was my last job. I earned a minimum wage[11] for sweeping the streets. Three months earning a minimum wage for sweeping the streets. What I made was barely enough to pay the rent. So how did I get food? I got food with meal tickets[12] given by the company and with the tips I got from people for doing the street-cleaning. This is what my life was like then. And then I joined the Landless Workers Movement, and my idea was just to get a piece of land to work on, to better my life and get off the streets, to get out of suffering. Because it is a sad suffering, to be lying on newspapers on the street, sleeping, when a homeless fellow just like yourself comes along and takes your slippers, your sneakers, your shirt, to trade for drugs, for liquor. . .

MGJ: *Is that what life is like on the street?*

MAS: That's it. It's a terrible life, a sad life. You're on the street counting the days before you die. How can anyone think that people on the street have a good life? Because they don't. Today you're alive, tomorrow you may be dead. Because sometimes that same fellow you share

---

8   A place that offers temporary and provisional shelter to the homeless.
9   The Street People Community, also known as Street Net, is an organization of Catholic missionaries, some of whom belong to the Divine Word Congregation (Congregação Verbo Divino), which conducts social work with the homeless in São Paulo city.
10 Father Naveen is a missionary of Street Net who contributed strongly to getting the homeless organized to join the struggle of the MST.
11 In the second half of the 1990s the minimum wage was 100 dollars.
12 Meal-tickets or meal-vouchers are wage supplements for the payment of meals.

your *Marmitex*[13] with will kill you just to take your *Marmitex*, to take your shirt, to take your slippers.

MGJ: *People actually kill for that?*

MAS: No doubt about it. Life is cruel there. It is each one for himself.

MGJ: *Right at the beginning, when you talked about corrupt people, you mentioned a "practical reality" politicians should build. What is that practical reality?*

MAS: That practical reality is a right—everybody has the right to have a job, to live on it; everybody has the right to have their own house. All Brazilians, rich and poor. All Brazilians have the right to have their own transportation. It is the duty of any decent Brazilian government to fulfill these obligations.

So, I believe this is a right we cannot take away from our comrades. We cannot take away your job, your house, leisure, schooling. Rich or poor, you are entitled to the most they can give you. There is a crisis in education, and it's even worse in healthcare. Only the bourgeoisie can get healthcare. Only the bourgeoisie can get education. The children of the poor, we are not far from seeing them become prostitutes to be able to move upward.

Fernando Henrique[14] is a great liar. But these lies come from way back. They come from all those endless crooked, lying governments. Those who are leaving are liars. And the new ones coming in are even greater liars, greater crooks. And that is why we're still in this situation, in this country. I mean, the working class, because the bourgeois has [everything]. It is the working class, the poor and the humble, who are suffering.

I have joined the MST and I have joined with a purpose. My purpose was to fight with the MST from the inside. I came to this conclusion: "I'm old already, I'm being discriminated against in getting jobs, so I'll join them just to get my piece of land, to stay there and rest. To stop. I have had no support from anyone, so if God helps me and I manage to get that support, to get at least that piece of land, I'm going to stop, I'm going to build by own house and stay put." But it didn't happen that way. I got there and just one month later I realized that the MST is not the sort of movement you join just to get your piece of land and stay put. The MST is a movement of struggle, a class movement, a movement of class struggle—it does not tie you to the land, to a piece of land.

---

13   Hot meal served in a tin container.
14   The sociologist Fernando Henrique Cardoso was at the time the President of Brazil, after having been re-elected in 1998. He was removed from his position as a university teacher in the late 1960s by the military government. In the 1970s he was elected senator of the opposition. He was one of the founders of the Brazilian Social Democracy Party (PSDB – Partido da Social Democracia Brasileira) in the 1980s. In 1994, as Chancellor of the Exchequer, he was responsible for the political and economic plan known as "Real," which controlled the high inflation rates with economic recession.

MGJ: *What is this struggle? Against whom? What is it for? What are its demands?*

MAS: When I speak of struggle, I mean that all Brazilians have the right to fight for their rights. What does the struggle mean? It means a house, a roof for you to live under, the land for you to sow, to reap from, to live on your own means, without depending on anyone. It means to fight for education, with honesty, for healthcare, with dignity, to fight for serious socialist freedom, which is the respect we have for everyone, to fight against Brazilian Constitutions[15]—we are against them. Some people are in favor, so be it, I'm against it. I know that in the MST most people are against the Brazilian Constitution. We are against it because it is a serious problem to fight against infiltrators and against drugs in our country; that's the one thing we struggle hardest against—it is important for a social movement like the MST, which is a movement of class struggle. [The struggle means] having that passion and fighting, because to fight against all this is a passion, and the roots of a better community in Brazil are already being created—a changed society, a society of respect, of classes. Because if we fight against those dirty, filthy practices I've just named and will keep on naming my whole life, what are we demanding for Brazil? We do not want rioting, we do not want anyone's power. What we want is the truth, a serious democracy. Because we are fighting against all this and also against discrimination.

MGJ: *What is that discrimination? You've been talking about it from the start.*

MAS: Discrimination on the basis of skin color and age. To learn respect, to be young until you're one hundred years old—skin color, black or white, doesn't matter. We're all equal. That is important. The MST has that spark—it has that character of freedom. So this is why I have joined the MST, with a destiny—destined for something that was to come again, destined to go back to that old process, that struggle together, to commit to that common alliance; this is what I've always wanted: "to overcome, to overcome." Fighting to overcome. To see our children, our grandchildren, our comrades, laughing. To have a home, a home of plenty, of full bellies, in good health and with education. It is very important that you go around and see old people having fun, feeling joyful and satisfied. You can't see any of that now. All you see is sadness. So we have to leave all this behind and overcome, to give that joy, to old and young people alike; to bring harmony, because harmony does not mean driving people into lies. Harmony means giving people what they need: fine schooling, education, health, leisure, respect. I believe that is something we all owe one another.

---

15   It is not clear whether MAS is referring to the Brazilian Constitution of 1988—which was fought for by the social movements—or to this type of legal document in general, suggesting that all constitutions are alike.

MGJ: *So you believe that this struggle for the land is also a struggle for all this? Then what is the place of agrarian reform in the struggle of the MST?*

MAS: Agrarian reform is part of that same struggle. Because, as I said before, the MST has a tradition. When the MST was formed—almost seventeen years ago now—it was declared to be a movement along certain political lines, a certain agrarian policy; it is not only about land policy. An agrarian policy is what we're talking about, along those political lines I've just named. It's not just the land. Agrarian policies involve the whole system—the system I've been telling you about. Everyone has the right to leisure, everyone has the right to fine schooling, everyone has the right to a good education, everyone has the right to own a house, everyone has the right to own a car. And also everyone has the same rights—black people and white people alike, old people and young people alike. The MST came to the conclusion that it is here to fight, that its mission is agrarian reform, to make agrarian reform. This is what it started fighting for. In '96–'97 we marched to Brasília, and then I learned more than I knew already. We marched for sixty days toward Brasília.[16] After sixty days of walking I stayed in Brasília for two weeks, in negotiations with the Congress.[17]

So I picked up some principles, even more than I was supposed to pick up from the MST. The MST is that sort of movement that cannot lie to society. It has to speak the truth. The MST is a movement with unique principles—it is a movement of struggle, a movement of agrarian reform. Before the MST there was the PT. The principles to the struggle the MST is leading today came from the PT. And I must apologize to my PT comrades, because I'm also PT, but the PT comrades became more interested in power, in getting more comfortable places for themselves—ties around their necks. We are allies of the PT. We love the party that is our own party. We have to respect the Workers Party, because we're workers. Now, those who aren't workers, they have no respect. This struggle was supposed to be the PT's job; but since the PT chose to remain in the background, the MST had to appear—the MST, the Landless Workers Movement, an agrarian movement. The PT handed the leading role in the struggle over to the MST, while it stays in the background, giving support.

MGJ: *Before 1964, when you were in the military, was agrarian reform already one of your causes?*

---

16   The national march of the MST to the city of Brasília, the federal capital, took place in April 1997. It was a long march of militants coming from various regions of the country with the purpose of attracting society's attention and of pressuring the federal government into negotiation.

17   The National Congress is composed of the Chamber of Federal Representatives and the Chamber of Senators.

MAS: Yes, it was. I remember, I was still a kid and Getúlio Vargas[18] was championing agrarian reform. His government was the only one to provide guidelines on how agrarian reform should be accomplished in Brazil. It cannot be done only by computers. Agrarian reform is not something for computers. Agrarian reform is a practice. It is not just statements and speeches. Sometimes I see 1964 in that light—class struggle for agrarian reform. And the struggle involves all the things I've been talking about, it involves all the complexities of our country. Back then we wanted change, to bring about that change and deliver it into the hands of all those comrades who had always suffered to get it. I got involved with the MST—I'm involved, and there's no stopping me, because I know that while I stay here, looking at this piece of land, there are thousands of comrades out there who need me to roll up my sleeves to bring them inside, to draw them to the struggle so they can get their own piece of land, a roof over their heads; maybe to form new militants for the MST and the PT. That's the most important thing. In the last five years—I have been with the MST for five years—I have brought in a few militants. With my little schooling, I have already brought in a few militants; I've brought a few militants to the truth.

MGJ: *Have you gone out working to form new militants?*

MAS: I went to build the base and I [ended up] forming new militants, drawing militants towards reality. I brought together many PT comrades who were sleeping their time away, and I brought them to the fight. I told them: "You see, comrades, this is our way, this is our class struggle and if you write down class struggle, then now is the time." A militant does not just organize in the MST, he does not just organize in the PT: inside your home you are a militant. You're going after your goal, as a sociologist, thinking of tomorrow and beyond. You never know, maybe tomorrow or after, you will want to be a Fernando Henrique in politics. So you're a militant. Because you don't want to see poverty in your home, you don't want to see your parents in poverty, your brothers and sisters, your children, your wife, your brother-in law, you want what's good for them. Then you're a militant. Now, when we say militant, what is a militant? Every breadwinner is a militant; now, the real militant is the militant of class struggle. Class struggle is an alliance employed in the process of agrarian reform. And when we speak of a process of agrarian reform, it's not that, once it's settled, it's not over and done with. It is no use joining a class-struggle movement such as the MST, just to say: "I go there; I grab my piece of land and hide. It's over." You join in if

---

18   Getúlio Vargas (1883–1954) was president of the republic twice, the first time from 1930 to 1945—he led a coup d'état in 1937 and remained in power until 1945—and the second time from 1950 to 1954, when he committed suicide due to political pressure.

you're an honest person, if you want something serious for your country; you don't just stay on the land, you commit yourself to class struggle; that's how you will start to press, to push, to change reality—and that's the MST.

MGJ: *Are you saying that a militant is the one who is also a militant inside his home?*

MAS: Obviously.

MGJ: *And how do you build the bridge between that struggle indoors and class struggle, as you name it?*

MAS: That bridge, how is it done? You're starting it right now, through what you're doing. Aren't you after a better life?

MGJ: *Yes, I am.*

MAS: You don't want to be a slave, do you? Do you want to be someone else's employee?

MGJ: *I don't want to be a Fernando Henrique, either.*

MAS: You don't want to be a Fernando Henrique, either; you want to be a man of truth, a man without lies; to live by your own means and honestly; to have what's yours—that is being a bit of an individualist, but it doesn't matter because everyone has to live a decent life. What is important is that you play your part well to drive away poverty from your country. Because there is the socialist and there is the individualist. The individualist lives his own life, has his own views, but it doesn't make much of a difference. You will always find him in the midst of a struggle to fulfill a role he has set for himself. I mean, this is part of the agrarian process. This is then the quiet militant. Now, there is this other militant who gets more involved. He is the sort of militant, like myself, who stays alert day after day. A militant like Gilmar Mauro, he is tough, he never stops, he keeps [working] day after day, and he is too busy to sleep at home. A militant like José Rainha, a strong comrade, a comrade of class struggle, an honest man. I really appreciate that fellow. I appreciate truthful people; I don't like people who lie. A militant like João Pedro Stedile[19]—here's another comrade I congratulate. Those are the real class militants, responsible militants, who really push the struggle, who don't push the struggle with lies. Because I'm a small part of these militants I'm talking about, because I don't have the ability of someone like João Pedro Stedile.

---

19   Gilmar Mauro, José Rainha Júnior, and João Pedro Stedile are national leaders of the MST. These three leaders are some of the best-known by public opinion. José Rainha Júnior gained prominence as a leader in the mid-1990s as a result of a series of land occupations in the region of Pontal do Paranapanema, in the western part of the state of São Paulo. He is now settled in that region. Stedile is one of the members of the MST National Board, composed of twenty-one members. He is the son of small farmers, and has a graduate degree in economics.

MGJ: *Why not?*

MAS: Because João Pedro Stedile is someone—he is practically a sociologist. He is well educated, he graduated and everything.

Gilmar Mauro is not much of a learned person, but he has got credibility, and Rainha as well, not to mention our other comrades and our other leaders in the northeast, in Mato Grosso do Sul, Mato Grosso, Belém do Pará,[20] where we have serious and honest militants.

MGJ: *Do you think it depends on having further schooling to be someone like Stedile?*

MAS: Not really. It depends on you being able to understand what class struggle is. Once you understand what class struggle is, you roll up your sleeves and you engage in true class struggle; to have a political awareness of agrarian issues. There is this saying Rui Barbosa kept repeating: "This is my land, this is my land." So what makes a man is his having the spirit, the ability—it is not schooling. You see, Rui Barbosa didn't have any schooling, he was illiterate, but he had this up here [*he touches his forehead*]. He had a computer in his head.

MGJ: *And he is a reference for you?*

MAS: He is. That's why I say this. Those of us who love class struggle, who want a liberal country, a free, well-formed country, with a political awareness of agrarian issues, will fight on this side. It doesn't matter. You may be white, you may be black, whatever, as long as you commit to an agrarian alliance; because that's what you want to do, something true, something beautiful, honest, and without lies. Now it is shameful to lie to Brazilian society. Because Brazilian society is full of the lies of politicians. But for us, as a class movement, of class struggle, to lie to society, that is shameful. The day I come here to lie, to skip over what I've always said, you can charge me. But to charge me you have to know how to do it, because you'll never see that lie. You'll never see such selfishness in me, of only wanting things for myself. You'll never see me on the dirty side; you will only see me on the clean side. Because I eat beans with plain flour, but I don't want anything that is not my own.

MGJ: *You talk about class struggle, you talk about the bourgeoisie and corrupt politicians. Don't you think that those corrupt politicians are looking after their own interests?*

MAS: Of course. Of course they are looking after their own interests, because they are not concerned about the interests of Brazil. They have to look after their own interests because they have never had any interest in Brazilian society; they have never had any interest in the poor, humble

---

20   The northeast is a region composed of nine states: Mato Grosso do Sul and Mato Grosso are states in the central-western region of the country; Belém do Pará is the capital of the state of Pará, in the north.

working class. Do you expect the bourgeoisie to have any interest side by side with the working class, side by side with any begging, starving, poor man's son, side by side with a fellow who is lying on the street, starving to death, begging for bread? Someone living on a plate of soup, delivered in the night, by the community itself? Because the community itself is doing something right, and at the same time it is doing something wrong. I'm in favor of providing soup, because there are comrades who are unable to get their own piece of food and they may starve to death. A plate of soup may keep [a comrade's] life for another day. But it does not keep his life for the class struggle, because he is being manipulated. So, those crooks, that bourgeoisie, that's what they do.

Corruption is terrible, more so than pride; discrimination, double-crossing. When I speak of social integration, you may ask me the question: "What is social integration?" Social integration is what I've just mentioned: a socialism, where you have your rights, your benefits, for you and for your child, where the poor man's child has the same thing.

MGJ: *You're saying that power is a problem, but don't you think that in this case, for example, the MST needs power to be able to transform the country?*

MAS: Not power! Because anyone living inside the MST with that power business, to make revolt, to create a serious problem in this country, to revolutionize the country, in order to make things better in the country—he is not in the movement, he is into power. The MST is a movement of class struggle, so the MST comrades, the militants, they are not after power. The honest MST members are not after power. They are after a rightful democracy, a class democracy, of hand in hand, of hearts together. This is what we're going to fight for, not for power. If there is anyone inside the MST who is fighting for that sort of thing—and I know there is—someone in disguise saying that he is MST, he is anti-movement, he is an infiltrator in the movement. I speak with absolute honesty: I may die with a knife in my throat, but I won't lie to anyone. Today movements need to be careful; all movements, the MST, popular movements, they all need to be very careful. Everyone in the church needs to be very careful, because if you're going to weigh a goal, to choose a correct goal—if there was a scale to weigh the faithful, they would be only a few.

MGJ: *Do you go to all the meetings of the MST?*

MAS: Yes, I go to all the meetings. I've been working more on the outside, organizing national and state marches. Doing grassroots work, with the Mass Front (Frente de Massas),[21] to strengthen the struggle. I've never stayed put here, not even for six months. Just a while ago I was talking to

---

21   The Mass Front is a division of the MST organization, considered to be the gateway to the movement.

my wife and I told her: "If I had thought that, after being settled, there was going to be too many luxuries, I would have never settled here." I was going to stay, even if I had to wait another ten years, I was going to become settled. But I'm not chained to this stuff, because this is not mine, this [the lot where he is settled] belongs to the people, to the community. Those who want to claim the land as their own, it's ok by me, but I say that the land belongs to the community. I'm aware of what I've always fought for. Right now I'm feeling chained. I'm ill and it was illness that chained me, unfortunately. All these illnesses of mine come from earlier sufferings. Because work doesn't make anyone ill. When I'm not away, I'm here, working the land. What you see here is no one's work but mine—I did it myself, with my wife. When I go away, to be with the communities, with society, our people on the street, I feel good. Because I know I'm among my own people.

MGJ: *How did you find them? Or did they find you? Father Naveen? Was it the Street Net group?*

MAS: Yes, it was the Street Net group. Our meeting was a delicate matter, which I wasn't expecting. I had an argument with Sister Berta. She got there at midnight, with Father Naveen [and two others]. They got there at midnight and called me to give me a plate of soup and some bread. When she called me, I got up. I said: "Instead of giving me that plate of soup, why don't you find me a job so I can work? A house for me to live in? Because if you did that for me, you would be doing something for my life, and for all these brothers lying here." [She answered:] "But son, are you suggesting that I'm manipulating you?" So I said: "Not suggesting, I'm saying it! Because I can't take this. Let me starve to death, so you can feel shame and start looking for the truth." Then Naveen came by. She said: "Naveen, listen to what he's saying, that we are manipulating." Naveen let his head down and this is what he said: "He's right, he's right. Miguel, the problem is, we're a group of people and we're doing this work on the streets, only with the people on the street, and we do not want to manipulate. It is true that we're giving that plate of soup, but we call people to the struggle, to class struggle. And through class struggle you get what you were talking about." I said: "I don't believe you. I'm not saying you're a liar, Father, but I want to see something true. If you say you're going to do this and that, and then the following day I go there to see if you did it. . . you're like those politicians today, who only tell lies. Look around, Father." At that time, you know, there at Mesbla, in São Paulo,[22] do

---

22   Mesbla is a large department store in the central area of São Paulo whose porches provided shelter to a huge number of street dwellers.

you know how many were sleeping there? Between two and three thousand every day.[23]

There were between two and three thousand people. I showed this to Father Naveen and I said: "Look at what the politician does to the people. See these people here? They are not bums, they're all working people." But who will come here and try to take you to the truth? Who will give you work, give you land to sow, so you can live on your own means, so you will not live being manipulated for a plate of soup and an old shirt? No one will. He said to me: "That's what I'm doing and that's what she's doing. Do you want to see the truth? Come with me, this is the address."

MGJ: *Do you remember what year that was?*

MAS: That was '96. I took that address and said: "OK." Then I felt rage. Not rage—more like distress. I don't want your soup. Then on Sunday, I dropped by, to see. Because I was on the street. I walked on the street, I slept on the street, but you couldn't tell I was a beggar, because I was always clean. Do you know how I did it? Early in the morning I picked up my stuff and hid it somewhere. When I went out I took any dirty clothes I got, and if I couldn't find any job to do, I would take off to wash my clothes away from there. So my clothes were very clean. On Sunday I dropped by. When I got there the place was full.

MGJ: *What were they talking about?*

MAS: They were saying that people had to get organized, they had to be aware, be socialists—they had to care for one another on the streets, have friends, so that no one would be left out. That you have to socialize, have unity; that no one was going to offend others, and that way we would get organized—we would engage in the struggle to get a piece of land to live on, to plant on, to live on our own means. They didn't say they were MST.

Right then I started attending. Three months later an MST militant came by. He started talking to us, with Father Naveen and Sister Berta, and they laid the cards on the table. They said: "People, this is the Landless Workers Movement, the MST; it is a movement of class struggle. You join this movement to struggle with the rest of us, and you will get those lands. They are not going to give you the land, you are going to fight for it. There's no point in saying that we're going to give you land: you are going to fight, we are going to support you, and you will succeed." Their words reminded me of '64—the movement was supposed to have been working since 1964, but it died away and now it was back.

---

23 In 1994, São Paulo's Municipal Office of the Family and of Social Well-Being carried out the second official census of the population living on the street, counting 4,549 individuals.

MGJ: *Had you heard of the MST before?*

MAS: I had, yes. I knew about it since the setting up of the [Socialist] Convergence. I kept hearing the name of that popular movement, which was not openly the MST. Some popular movements were campaigning for agrarian reform, and they gained ground. In '84 the occupations in Rio Grande do Sul had already started.

MGJ: *Did you follow that episode?*

MAS: I was following it, yes. But I wondered. I followed that episode, but I wondered: What is really happening there? Is it going to be another '64, or is it going to be a military coup again? Because sometimes the military join the struggle just to destroy the principles that are hidden behind the curtain, which are us. I thought about all this in '84, when the movement declared itself to be the Landless Workers Movement. It was only in '96 that I found out that the MST is a movement of class struggle, the movement we had always longed for to struggle in Brazil, to have the right decisions made about agrarian reform. Fortunately, this talk about agrarian reform has already been going on since 1952.

The MST embraced the struggle, a just cause. This is a just cause that the MST has embraced and has been accomplishing. It does not lie to anyone. If the MST hadn't embraced the cause, who would? The PT. But the PT does not want to embrace such a cause. Because, for the PT to embrace such a cause, it would have to leave politics aside. Their land policy, they [would] have to drop it and embrace agrarian policy. So the MST embraced this cause, and that's why I'm saying that our militants suffer great pressure.

MGJ: *You've already mentioned that the MST is doing what the PT should do. How do you see the connection between the struggle of a popular movement and political struggle? Because then you attacked power. What is your understanding of this?*

MAS: How can you trust them, if they are involved in filth? That's why I said that we have to be very careful, because those people that say those things, they are. . . But you have to be very careful. If we had freedom, true freedom, true democracy, you wouldn't be watching them playing those ridiculous parts.

MGJ: *So, do you think that we're not living in a democracy?*

MAS: We aren't. It is democracy between quotation marks. You have the right to speak, but if you speak, you die. So you have to be very careful. Because when you say democracy—that is the real democracy, without quotation marks, a democracy where you can speak, where you have rights and they are respected; it is delivered in the hands of society for it to act, the way it is done in other democratic countries. It is a shame to say that this is a democracy. Because when you speak of democracy, it is a clean democracy, without filth. And what we see is filthy. A democracy that allows stealing, taking away the workers' bread, exploiting workers, plucking out their eyes? Is that democracy?

MGJ: *But that was already happening before, under the military dictatorship.*

MAS: So this is the reality I'm talking about. Because that is what it was like during the dictatorship. "You be quiet, don't say a thing, otherwise you're dead"; and you die anyway, of hunger. Then in came this thing between quotation marks, so you can speak, so you can die speaking, not quietly. Let that clown speak, he will be dead soon. He is going to die of hunger, he is not going to resist, he is going to steal and he will be caught in the act, he'll be shot and die on the street. He is going to deal drugs, he's going to be a drug dealer, he'll be a drug casualty. He is going to become a thief; he is going to be tortured to death, because if he survives the hands of the police, he is going to fall into a prison; he is going to be raped, and if he resists raping, he will die, because he will be hanged inside. And none of this will happen if we make a true democracy in Brazil, because we can prevent all this. Jobs, land to harvest from, houses to live in, education, health, respect, honesty towards everyone: we are not going to enjoy any of this. Because most of those miserable liars make their living from this, from this dictatorship. Which is a democracy between quotation marks. This is a process we have to work on very carefully. When you've got a fair and honest democracy, you can work freely. You come out and do whatever you want to help your comrades and get help, which is very important, because today it is very important that you help. I feel good helping you to get your project going, to search for your truth, the way you wish to, because you're a student. Unfortunately, much of the support we're getting in Brazil these days comes from students; male and female professors from the greatest universities are with us, seeing as they do that we do not lie, that we speak the truth, and that's why they are with us. I feel happy because I'm showing something that is the truth. I'm not telling lies; I'm not after power. I'm bringing the truth to society. An illiterate person, addressing society, with a truth that must be fulfilled, which is true democracy. We are not following lies.

MGJ: *I understand from what you're saying that your struggle, the MST struggle, is well organized and at the same time also depends on the government implementing agrarian reform. So I think this raises a question: What role can politics play, institutional politics, side by side with the MST? You said that the PT should be leading the struggle the MST has undertaken, but the MST depends on a parallel struggle. While agrarian reform is being accomplished through the occupation of land—and that has so far been the only feasible agrarian reform, as you yourself said—there have been politicians in the history of Brazil who were willing to bring* *about agrarian reform and were prevented. So it also depends on having a higher power to implement agrarian reform. How do you see this? Doesn't it also depend on the struggle of both the MST and the PT, which happens to be one of the very few parties that identify with the struggle of the MST, which are fighting, within institutional politics, for agrarian reform?*

MAS: Yes, that is important. Because the PT. . .

MGJ: *Sorry, but before you go on, I understand when you speak of this democracy between quotation marks, because right now the government of Fernando Henrique is making propaganda on TV, saying that they are going to make agrarian reform, that they are settling a given number of families, and that they will no longer allot land to people who have been identified as property-invaders. The estates that have been occupied will not be expropriated, and the families that did the occupation will not be settled. This is clearly one measure more to repress the MST. So this is a democracy between quotation marks because his policy is to hold back this social movement.*

MAS: I'll tell you what the problem is. Of course it is between quotation marks, because the PT and the MST, if we look closer, are a single star.[24] As I was telling you, these struggles go back to '84. If there hadn't been a movement of class struggle like the one in '84, like the MST, which the PT appeared to make. . . The PT and the MST have taken the form of a movement of class struggle. Now, the PT has drawn away from its principles, because it hasn't gone after the truth, it hasn't truly engaged in this class struggle. It has gone after its own policy, a policy of information. It has gone after a bit of power and it has left agrarian policies behind. That's where the MST took over, and it has been leading [the struggle]. This agrarian policy of ours, it was thought through, it was seriously debated by the MST. We won't let it suffer political manipulation. And there have been, as there always are, opportunists who try to do that. That can't happen. Fernando Henrique is making comments on this agrarian reform because he is registering people with straight lies, because he is not looking after the families; they are being fooled, as they always will be, because all their lives they've been fooled. The government's part has been to allow INCRA[25] to register people, to let twenty or thirty years go by without calling anyone [to be settled]. And his repression of the MST. . . He knows that if he represses with lies, the MST will pass over all those dirty, filthy projects he has, because it is the only movement of class struggle. He is using that dirty, filthy strategy, as

---

24   A reference to the star in the PT's flag.
25   INCRA: Instituto Nacional de Colonização e Reforma Agrária (National Institute of Settlement and Agrarian Reform). It is an agency of the executive, controlled by the Ministry of Agrarian Development, and one of its functions is to coordinate the whole process of settling rural workers.

you said, fooling the workers with lies. Only cowardly workers will fall for that, those who don't have the courage to come up and ask for their rights. Because that worker who has the courage to come up and ask for his rights, honestly, he does not believe that Fernando Henrique is carrying out agrarian reform. Because, as I said, the occupations our comrades are carrying out are all taking place in lands bought from the large estate owners. And that money belongs to the union. And who makes up that union? Workers themselves. So that is not agrarian reform. It is struggle, it is shedding the blood of the worker, of the working class, of the MST, which wants this cause to be just. The government is not carrying out agrarian reform in the settlements they are making. Actually, it is not the government that's making anything, it is the MST; these are class struggles, hard struggles. That minister of agrarian reform, Raul Jungman,[26] he is a liar, he's not doing anything. He is another Fernando Henrique. He's going to resort to all sorts of lies and wickedness to knock down the MST; because the MST should have been wide awake for some time, since that last march, our second national march; we should have taken that decision then, because we had society's general support. We let the occasion go by, because we had everything in our hands and we just had to mobilize society to join us and we would have accomplished agrarian reform without lies. We would have accomplished a fair agrarian reform, without lies, without abuse of power, because our militants are not after power. If he says that MST militants are after power, he's lying. The MST does not want power, it wants the truth, and class struggle.

MGJ: *Do you really think that even the leaders that emerge inside the MST don't want power?*

MAS: They don't want power. They want the truth that the government is not accomplishing. I'm absolutely sure about that.

MGJ: *And how could that democracy without quotation marks be achieved?*

MAS: It's obvious. You just have to be honest, go after the truth. Do it the way we are doing it, calling upon people, society. This government does not want to have anything to do with society; it does not want to have anything to do with society playing a decent role; it does not want foreign countries to see that. . . He is being manipulated.

MGJ: *Who's being manipulated?*

MAS: Fernando Henrique. He doesn't want to show what Brazil is like, who Brazilian people are—people who want Brazil to be part of that first world he talks about. For Brazil to be part of that first world, it has to go through changes first, starting from below, getting the people out of poverty, out of drugs and out of crime, because crime is the result of

---

26   Raul Jungman was then the minister of agrarian development in Fernando Henrique Cardoso's government. This office used to be called the Ministry of Agrarian Reform.

hunger and poverty. Because when there is no true agrarian reform in a country, one without lies, there are no jobs, there is no proper education, no healthcare, no respect, no justice. If the country is willing, if it engages in class struggle—like we do—if it makes an honest agrarian reform, it can show the world that Brazilian society is honest, who Brazilians are and what they want. Because it is a lie what they say abroad, that Brazilians only want to steal. But it is the ones in the Senate, in the Chamber [of Representatives] who want to steal, who are the outlaws. Not the working class. This is a class of poor, humble, and honest people, who want sincerity and respect. The working class does not behave like that; if it did, the MST would fight it. The government claims that the MST does not want agrarian reform anymore, that the MST wants power, that it wants to overthrow the government and take over. People in society who have no political understanding believe that the MST wants power. But those people in society who understand reality, who honestly want a fair agrarian reform, they support the MST, because they know that it is not after power. Still, inside every social movement or party there are always wicked people.

MGJ: *You keep saying that the MST has to be honest and truthful, and at the same time you identify dishonest and corrupt politicians as being this country's biggest problem, as we all can see. Inside the MST there is this need for everyone to be truthful, without lies. But then you meet this situation where it is inevitable that you should find people inside the movement whom you do not recognize as being honest and true. Doesn't this take you back to the question of conflicting interests, between groups who are self-seeking, who are individualists, and groups who have other interests?*

MAS: We have an ethic to deal with that. We know that happens. But we work mostly within our settlement and our encampments. If we, as a movement of class struggle, were to repress people who want to be individualists, who go hand in hand with power, we would be using a strategy of enslavement, which is unfortunately used in dirty politics—that of repressing people, saying: "You can only do this." In the MST we do not accept this sort of taboo. Because our statutes say freedom, social-ist freedom. Socialist freedom is the most important one, because we do not accept dictators. Let's suppose, inside there may be someone who is fighting for power, who is getting into politics to promote themselves in politics.

MGJ: *When you say power, what sort of power?*

MAS: Political power—what else? I mean, if we repress people, saying, "No, this is what you have to do," aren't we using the language of dicta-torship? That's what we call a dictator. The MST does not want that role; the role of the MST is to move [people to action]. When people play that role [of the dictator], the MST gives up on them. Time destroys them. The MST does not destroy them, because the MST is here to move [people], not to divide [them]. This is why today you can find in most settlements individualists and others, people of both kinds. Because the role of the MST is to move people, not to police them, because we are not dictators. If inside the MST we apply the rule of dictatorship, then we'll be playing the role of the bourgeoisie and of the dictatorial government, and that's not what we are. Why don't popular movements banish them? Because they don't want to act like the government. Why doesn't the Church banish them? Because it does not want to act like the government—because the Church's role is the same as the MST's, which is to bring in believers, not to banish them.

The MST is showing the truth. So if there is no unity, if society does not pay enough attention, people will say that the MST is encouraging riot. So you have to look at reality, see what's really happening. Take our case. What have they [the government] done to us? They planned the whole thing, they set us up, they sent the bastards to strangle the settlement. Corrupt officials come up here and all they do is lie. You know, for these uninformed people, money is everything. So these guys attracted a few people, bought those few, and these began putting those lies into the heads of other suckers, other poor souls. They were destroying the settlement with downright lies. Look at this road, what it's turned into. If you don't want underbrush creeping into your house, you have to do like I do, grab the hoe and clean the way in. Where is the [electric] power? It's downright shamelessness. It destroyed. . . This is what those crooks' agrarian reform is like. And yet they keep saying that the MST is fighting for power. "The struggle of the MST is no longer for agrarian reform, the struggle of the MST is for power. What they want is to have power over here." They are liars. The struggle of the MST is a serious struggle, it is class struggle. For true and fair agrarian reform. The statutes of the MST do not mention this business of power. When we say class struggle. . . class struggle is very different from power.

MGJ: *But don't you consider getting power necessary, in order to transform society?*

MAS: No, I don't. Those who turn to a struggle for power are no longer part of the movement. You see a few MST militants who have turned to the PT to run for elections. Why? Because when they get on the wrong track, the MST immediately tells them: "Your place is over there, because over here we're into class struggle, not power struggle."

MGJ: *But, for instance, the Mass Front, as the movement names it, in which you were involved, forming militants, what is it for?*

MAS: The Mass Front is groundwork. Unprepared people don't know what to say when they go out there. Unprepared people go out into society and they won't say much of any good, they won't speak properly, they won't speak with competence. Let's suppose you take one of these settled here and send him into society to call people to the struggle. That comrade you chose has no political experience in social struggles, to be able to deal with politicians. Because in class struggle the party he belongs to is not important. As long as he's a socialist, he may belong to the PT, the PDT,[27] it doesn't matter. If he is committed to class struggle, he may even belong to the side of Fernando Henrique. If he is committed to class struggle, if he is a militant who has always fought for a better country, there's only one thing that matters: that he is going to play his part in class struggle. That's the purpose of the MST. So it's not fair to take somebody who is unprepared and send him out there. This is what the Mass Front is for. To train our comrades. We train children, grownups; we train everybody.

MGJ: *How did you come to be that way? Right then, when you joined the movement in '96, right then you started organizing and participating in basic training. Were you chosen by someone from the movement because you were good at giving that training?*

MAS: The problem is, this training was given on the way, during the march, on the road.

MGJ: *In 1996?*

MAS: Exactly. Because here, unfortunately, when I first joined, at the time of the encampment, I was food coordinator, I was the one who delivered the food. From being food coordinator. . . I didn't want to stay at it, because when you're the one who gives food to people, what you give to the one you have to give to the other, but there's always someone who thinks you are favoring somebody else. So I said to myself that wasn't working for me, because what I do to one, I do to all. So I became work coordinator, of the work group. They soon moved me from this and placed me as general coordinator of ethics.

MGJ: *Who did this?*

MAS: The settlement's council. I've never wanted to harm anyone. Because we're here to bring people in, not to throw them out. They kept saying at the meetings that they had to throw out certain people, and I kept saying that they should think it over because the MST is here to bring people in, not to throw them out. You see, I've come a long way; I don't come from the MST. And if our movement is one of class struggle, we have to consider what class struggle means. Class struggle is here to bring people in, not to throw them out. That is where my rush started. People in the movement started saying that I was a guide and that I should be

27   PDT: Partido Democrático Trabalhista (Democratic Labor Party), organized in 1979, which has at times formed coalitions with the PT.

given the place I deserved. When the idea of the march to Brasília came up, my name was the first to be called.

I started learning on the road. After two weeks of learning I started coordinating the march I was doing the general coordination of the march, with another comrade. I was general coordinator, and he was the one who made the speeches. I coordinated the march, the march work, I coordinated the kitchen, food. It was all on my back, on our way to Brasília. When we got to Brasília, they wouldn't let go of me, interviewing me, filming me, everything. That's how far I had gone. And I didn't ask for anything, it was the people.

MGJ: *What is interesting about your story is that you were in a position where you needed an opportunity to be able to survive, because you were in a difficult situation, being on the street. You wanted to settle your personal life and you moved from your personal situation to a larger struggle and you started fighting for this, because you had been politically active in the past. Then your struggle was directed to other people, to make them understand this, that there's a need for individual struggle as well as collective struggle.*

MAS: You see, if you're a fighter, there's a point when. . . Jesus was one of our greatest revolutionaries—you know that well, you read about it in the Bible. That's why he was tortured, stabbed, nailed to the cross, beaten and called a liar. Because he was only preaching the truth, he didn't preach lies. As a man of character, my struggle has always been the same; I consider myself honest, but I ended up being poor. Because it is shameful to have no character, to be a dirty thief, but there is nothing shameful about being poor, but honest and true. What I've been saying, since I joined the MST, is that I came to fight for my share of land and be someone, to have a place to live, to have a roof to live under, to have peace and be at peace with everybody. But because of all the pain I went through when I was on the street, some years ago, being hurt, fooled, lied to, paying for what I didn't owe—that happened because I was a simple person. And when you're simple you're mistaken for a dangerous person. Unfortunately, in Brazil our governments mistake simple people for dangerous people and dangerous people for simple people. I came to get my share of land. But when I got to my share of land, I looked back on my past struggles and I realized that I wasn't meant for that. That was not the life I had always fought for. I didn't feel it was right for me to join the struggle, get my share of land and stay at home. Because that is not my role, the role I bound myself to before society, the role I committed to as I took part in class struggles. My role was to take part in class struggle— the struggle for everyone to have a decent life. I didn't feel it was right for me to struggle for a decent life for myself alone, while my comrades were without it. The working class, it doesn't matter if they are from the country or from the city, the people on the street, we're all Brazilians. So I couldn't play that role. It was a ridiculous, individualistic role. Because I would be wanting to settle down in life, to get peace for myself, and leave others in poverty. So that wasn't the right role for me. The right role for me was to struggle for myself and for my comrades. And I swear that I will struggle until the end of my life, to see my comrades settled in life just like I am.

Today we've got the MST and other popular movements that have their roots in '64. And in '84 the MST took up the struggle that was the PT's. And the PT thanked God for that. Because if the PT had kept the political guidelines the MST has got today, the PT wouldn't have moved ahead. Because agrarian policy is one thing, and land policy is another.

MGJ: *What is the difference?*

MAS: There is a huge difference. Land policy is about getting power. Agrarian policy does not involve power—power belongs to everyone. We are going to build a new Brazil. When we talk about a new Brazil, we mean a country that belongs to everyone. So if the PT had kept these principles, the PT couldn't have senators of their own inside, federal representatives, people running for president of the republic, governors, mayors. They just couldn't. The PT had to train these politicians, make an alliance with the PC do B[28] and stick to the principles of agrarian policy. It was the role of the PT to do this.

MGJ: *According to you, then, the PT and the PC do B should be acting together?*

MAS: They should, obviously. They set that goal of acting together. They weren't supposed to wander from it. And then the PT would be making the decisions on agrarian policies that the MST is making today. If there was any issue involving politics, the PC do B would take over and lead the way. And if the PT and the working class, in our struggle together, were getting involved in politics, we would hand it over to the PC do B. These were the political lines of agrarian policy. In '84 these guidelines of agrarian policy came from Rio Grande do Sul, where it had all started. Those who started it were the comrades from the time of Getúlio Vargas. They stood up and started thinking up agrarian policy. The PT joined in with open arms. The PT started getting into politics and the MST was right beside it. But the thing is, the MST is committed to a clean agrarian policy. Opportunistic militants set on getting into politics, they walk away and join the PT, they don't stay here. This is the role of the MST,

---

28   The PC do B (Partido Comunista do Brasil) is the Communist Party of Brazil, which appeared in 1962 after a split in the old 1922 Communist Party. Militants of the PC do B turned to guerilla tactics against the military government at the turn of the 1970s.

to get an agrarian policy.

MGJ: *And when did you start working on basic training? Was it before or after you came to the encampment here? At first you came here to carry on with what you're doing today?*

MAS: Right. I came to the encampment at the time of our first occupation.

MGJ: *Was that in 1996?*

MAS: Right. In the Cercadinho estate.[29] That was our first occupation. That was my first occupation with the MST, because I had already been involved in other occupations for the Homeless [Movement].

MGJ: *Were you active in the Homeless Movement?*

MAS: I was. I participated in many occupations. At the time I was working at Ford and Mercedes, but that was not all I was doing. I was participating in occupations, I was working with the unions. So my struggles come from way back. And we carried on this occupation here with the MST in '96.

All this time I was giving basic training, working in management. So this is my life, this is my struggle. It's not a struggle for power.

MGJ: *You mean you don't see this as power?*

MAS: I don't, no. If I come to my comrades and say, "This is what you have to do," I know that's power. But when you're in a struggle as a socialist you say: "Listen, could you help us out on this?" and that's comradeship. It's not power. Now, if you command people, that's power. The dictator is the one who comes to you and keeps saying "I" all the time.

MGJ: *But when you have a social movement like this one, that is a sort of power. It is the power of the whole.*

MAS: It is the power of the whole. It is power, but it is the power of the whole. Because as a whole you need directives and those directives need someone with a good head on his shoulders to lead the way. But it is not the power of the mighty. It just means that he's got better understanding, and he is staying to teach something. It's like a school. Schools have teachers, teachers have headmasters, right? That's it, then. But he is not into power, he's someone with a better understanding, someone who's ahead of you. He is not all-powerful, he is just ahead of you, so he will pass on to you the political directives, he's going to show you. . . so you won't slip. Power is when someone, a dictator, a politician. . . "Such and such is a mayor," "Deputy such and such," that's power. A mighty person. Someone like Saddam Hussein, someone like Fernando Henrique. All those guys. That's what power is like. But inside popular movements, just because you become known, and speak in the name of the people—that's not power. Because the people need public speakers. Because when Jesus

---

29   An estate in the neighborhood of the Carlos Lamarca settlement.

was in this world he spoke in the people's name. Now if someone takes advantage of it, if he uses the people to become a dictator, then it is power. But if he is honest, goes out there and speaks in the people's name; if he's a socialist, it is not power. He's our brother. It is a good thing to be able to find your way inside popular movements. Suppose there wasn't someone like Gilmar Mauro, someone with an education, someone committed, who can set the path for society, who knows how to reach the media, how to deal with the media. What if there wasn't someone like José Rainha, who knows how to argue in the media?

MGJ: *What do you think about that?*

MAS: What if there wasn't someone like João Pedro who knows how to act before the media?

MGJ: *Do you think they are essential?*

MAS: They are. These people are essential. Because they are the ones who carry society's name outside. This is not to say that they are the power. Outside they are thought to be powerful, but they aren't. Because every popular movement needs someone to carry its name outside. The church needs bishops to carry the church's name outside, to carry the name of their flock outside. It needs priests, the pope. Look at us, we don't have a pope. The pope is not the one who carries the name of all nations. But if we think of it, priests are not dictators, they are sheep as well. They are not dictators—they can't command anyone. They are like us, in the MST. We have got these educated people I've just mentioned, who had better schooling, who carry our name outside, and who can debate in the media. Then we've got people who are not so strong, who gather around them. But we're all equal. All of us together, more and less educated, we're a popular front.

MGJ: *And those people who are better educated, do you consider them leaders?*

MAS: No, they don't act like leaders. No one is a leader. As I said, we're all equal. No one is a leader. When you say leader—a leader is a dictator. So no one is a leader here. We're all equal. For me it is a matter of political trust.

MGJ: *If you're all equal, how come only those turn up in the media?*

MAS: It's obvious: because they are chosen by the community. Because we can't all turn up. Can you imagine all of us on show in the media? That's what they wanted, so tomorrow or later, if there was a revolution, they could go after them, one by one. And popular movements would then be over. It's the same in the church. Can you imagine, if the media filmed the priests who support popular movements, the bishops who support popular movements? One year later, if there was a revolution, they would go after these priests and bishops. That's why they stay in the background. It's the same with us. Suppose—I pray to God this will never happen—someone brings down Gilmar Mauro, or José Rainha, or João Pedro; other militants will come forth. If another militant is brought down. . . there are countless militants in the making, so the MST will never fall down. This is what unity is all about. It's the same in the PT. You should never get rid of a single militant.

MGJ: *What is the stage you think the MST is at, right now? Do you think it is at its height. Will it keep growing? Will it decline?*

MAS: No. Let me tell you this: the MST is not at its height. The MST is level. It is not large. It will grow, yes. The MST will grow, but now it is level. It is calling society to break with the lies of the government.

MGJ: *Does "level" mean being at a standstill?*

MAS: Yes, a standstill. It's quiet. It doesn't feel choked by the lies of the government. Because the role of the government is to lie to society and the role of the MST is to show society that it is digging up freedom for the people. To show that what the government is saying is all lies. That it is not true that the MTS is after power. [The government] is the dictator, [the government] and its scum.

MGJ: *And inside the settlement, how do you get organized? Is there anyone here you consider a leader?*

MAS: No way! The families are the leaders here. Everyone is the leader of their homes. Everyone has the free, equal right to get organized.

MGJ: *But you've got settlement coordinators, haven't you?*

MAS: These coordinators you see, who have work to do outside, they all have a political conscience—they are the ones who support the MST; they know what has to be done. Some of those who fight for power also know what has to be done. We're not going to hang anyone for not doing what the MST wants. Everyone is free. We just ask everyone to get organized. That's what's important here. Everyone getting organized.

MGJ: *But some decisions are made collectively?*

MAS: Yes, they are.

MGJ: *How are you organized?*

MAS: We've got two collectives in here.

MGJ: *This collective you're talking about—is it collective farming?*

MAS: It's collective farming—it's raising cattle together.

MGJ: *But each one farms his own plot?*

MAS: Yes. I farm here, the next one farms over there, and so on.

MGJ: *So what belongs to the collective? Is it collective when you sell?*

MAS: We manage the vegetable garden together; the cattle belongs to all. Because there is the collective area and there are individual shares, these crops, which supply each household.

MGJ: *Is that a different area? A common sector belonging to all?*

MAS: Exactly. Just like I have this part here, which has been divided and which is where I'm going to build my house. We are going to plant beans in the collective area. In Edna's[30] plot we are going to grow vegetables, and the cattle are there. And all have their individual plots besides. You may raise chickens, a pig, or even a calf for food, for whenever you want to have a private barbecue. I'm trying to get these comrades together, to have them organize a collective. And we're starting to get things going. But we need to be aware, politically—take it easy, not overreact, not challenge our comrades. We struggle democratically for everyone to have their rights, without slavery. If we make demands on these people, that's dictatorship. Comrades have the right to choose what's best for them. Because there's the saying, "If you want the people, show them what you're made of, do it yourself, don't send anyone to do it for you." That's what we're doing inside. These people understand reality. They know where the truth is. Because there's no point in telling you to do something when I'm not doing it myself. That's wrong. And you'll never be persuaded.

MGJ: *Do you think that setting an example is more effective than talk?*

MAS: Obviously. I must set an example.

MGJ: *Do you go out there and talk as well?*

MAS: I go out and talk to people and, besides, I set an example, so they can see what it's like. There's no point in telling people to do something and not do it myself. If I do that, I'll be behaving like a dictator. We have to share the bread among our children, share the chores with our wives, because they should not just be in the kitchen. They can also participate in class struggle. Because class struggle is not just a man thing—it is for women as well. We have to take our share of the chores. If they are involved in class struggle, we have to cook the food, do the laundry. This is what socialism is all about, what class struggle is all about. To be able to demand something from my comrade, I must do it myself first, to show him. There's no point in telling him to farm in the collective while I stay in my share. This would mean I behaved as a socialist only for my family.

MGJ: *Are there others in the settlement who share your view of socialism?*

MAS: Well, yes. But it is complicated. Because true socialism is all this. You may be a socialist, but the true socialist is the one I've been talking about. It is difficult to practice this socialism. I don't know what's wrong with some people, that they're not doing their part. Because they were brought up in a bourgeois system. They are here, inside the MST, but they live by a bourgeois system. They talk about the MST and at the same time they refer to the bourgeoisie. Because it's like I've just said. This here, it is not mine, it belongs to society. And when I say

---

30   Edna is a resident in the settlement who participates in its organization.

society I mean the people. If I say this is mine, I'm representing the bourgeoisie. The landowner, what does he say when he goes to your place? "I have this many estates." It's the system. He is in the bourgeois system. And this makes it hard work to build a new Brazil within that system. Because many comrades are inside that capitalist system, which is a terrible system for this country. If we had a socialist system in Brazil. . . because this is what we've been fighting for, for years. But fortunately we have got other supporters. Not just João Pedro Stedile, Gilmar Mauro, José Rainha. We have other comrades outside, who are socialists. This system is being brought from the outside by them—by our comrades in class struggle. You go out and join the class struggle for society, and you see these comrades in the popular movements.

MGJ: *Is there a place here in the settlement where you discuss these issues? With everyone?*

MAS: There isn't, no. Because if we discussed the question of socialism with everyone. . .

MGJ: *But you hold assemblies, don't you?*

MAS: We do, yes. But if we discussed the question of socialism with everyone, that would scare society—the same way it scares many people in the encampments and in the settlements, because they don't know what socialism is. The same happens outside. Society doesn't know what socialism is. Most popular movements outside talk about socialism. Some know what it is, but others don't. If you talk to them about socialism, honestly, they are going to be afraid, because they will think it is communism. Communism, for those who don't know—true communism is the same as socialism. But there is radical communism, which is not socialism. So those who don't understand what socialism is, they will say it is communism, the bugbear that kills you for food. Those who are not ready to accept socialism, they will take it the wrong way. True socialism is something good. To have your rights. If the son of the bourgeois has a right, you have it, too. That's socialism. If I have the right to build a house of my own, my comrade has the same. How come I'm entitled to so many spare bags of cement and my comrade gets none? He has the same right. That's socialism. But unfortunately, if you try to discuss it inside the settlement, inside the encampment, unless people are aware [they'll think:] "He just wants to take from me all I've got." Even the ones in the settlement will say that. They've come from that dirty politics of the capitalist system, so they won't accept you as a socialist. They're not going to listen to you. It's the capitalist system: each one tries to get things for himself alone and forgets his brother.

MGJ: *You were saying that the INCRA was. . .*

MAS: The government used INCRA, which is a governmental agency, as a strategy. They came up with INCRA, brought it inside, and engaged most of the families in the capitalist system. And through that system they destroyed most of the settlement.

MGJ: *What do you mean, they brought in the capitalist system?*

MAS: That's what the capitalist system is like. You know that the government doesn't want to see results from the struggles of the MST. Because all they want is to bring damage. They talk about agrarian reform, but it's worthless talk. Then they see what the MST is saying and doing. Because they can't stop the MST, what do they turn to? They turn to government agencies, the INCRA and the ITESP,[31] to cause damage. They infiltrate their people inside and they look for the families who are unfortunately still under the hold of the capitalist system, which is the system of money. They get involved with these people, so they infiltrate into and ruin most families. They can sometimes destroy a whole settlement. That's the problem with these families. [Those infiltrators], they know their business well. They turn the families one against the other, to bring disagreement, to bring misery, the sort of thing the MST has never put up with inside the settlement. Unfortunately, here in this settlement, we need to be very careful, because we've had those cases and we need to be very careful. Because inside we have comrades who say they're with the MST but who are government infiltrators. They have allied with the government to destroy the MST.

MGJ: *But do you depend on INCRA to demarcate the lots, to divide the land? Because that was the problem you had, of not being able to give a share to everyone, wasn't it?*

MAS: The problem is, all settlements, at pre-settlement stage, need the damned INCRA, because they're the ones who are doing the demarcation. When they are fixing the damned lots, along come the ITESP with their lying rotten technicians to complete the infiltrating and to stain our comrades. Because for every one hundred there may be ten or thirty who aren't aware yet, who are still set on getting things for themselves alone. When that is the case, the INCRA takes advantage of it to pull down the MST. We've had this here in the Carlos Lamarca settlement; we still have it. Even the poor fellows who came from the streets, who came for the struggle, who came after a piece of land to be able to survive and stand before society with dignity—even these got involved with those people. And now these poor fellows are living on the edge. They're being treated like slaves. They have to be very careful if they don't want to lose their

---

31   ITESP: Instituto de Terras do Estado de São Paulo (Institute of Land of the State of São Paulo). This agency is under the control of the state secretary of justice, responsible for assisting the land policy of the state government. In the 1990s it began to mediate agrarian conflicts in the state of São Paulo.

piece of land. There's a lot of complicated stuff going on in here which I don't like and don't give my support to. I'm in favor of all that we've been stating at the meetings, to the public and to society: a decent life for everyone, not just for a few.

MGJ: *So you believe there are people inside who are set on destroying the movement?*

MAS: Yes, I do. Definitely. They're infiltrated inside. Since the time of the encampment. These people are inside, and they're giving us a hard time. The thing is, politically, they are tough. They can argue. To be up to them, you need to play serious politics. You have to be able to give them a reply, to destroy them politically. Because they are deeply infiltrated and well organized.

MGJ: *And what means have you got to deal with these people?*

MAS: The means to deal with these people. . .

MGJ: *How do you deal with that political dispute?*

MAS: The political dispute with these people has to be run with caution. The political dispute with these people demands strategy. The first strategy is to leave them be, for a while—but always watching their moves closely. When they are well into their business, it's time to talk things over with them and get them off the line. Because if we don't do things this way, if we stand up to them at once, face to face, we'll be doing what the government wants us to—to cause trouble, deaths, murders. That's what you're going to get.

MGJ: *So you have to debate with these people publicly, or is it done behind the scenes?*

MAS: No, we debate publicly. We can't take it too easy with them. It is done publicly. We treat them like friends. Because there's the saying: if you can't beat the bandit, and you see that he's going to win, then join him. You join him to cut his throat later on. It's the only way. Imagine what can happen if you stand up, face to face, to such bandits. They are trained to destroy. Since the time of the encampment.

MGJ: *And how did you settle that matter of the division? Because INCRA was fixing the lots for the families and everyone had to be settled, but there was not enough land for everyone.*

MAS: The first thing was a process we had been working on since the time of the encampment—the collective, cooperatives.[32] We were well into the process. We planned having an agro-village,[33] and everybody settled.

---

32   The MST has a policy of implementing production cooperatives among residents. In the case of the Carlos Lamarca settlement, the residents who support collective production have not yet managed to form a cooperative. In recent years, many academic studies have been done on MST cooperatives.

33   Agro-villages are a type of housing devised for agricultural settlements where the houses are built close to one another. In the Carlos Lamarca settlement, the majority decided against the agro-villages and, as a result, families live in lots that are far from each other.

We even began building the agro-village down there.

We were well into the process, but when INCRA came in to start dividing the lots we had our first setback. It was the beginning of the settlement's ruin. Because we had already debated all this in meetings and assemblies and we had decided that none of those forty-six families would be left unsettled. All the families were going to be settled, because there was enough land. Even if we had to reduce the size of lots. But it was enough for everybody.

Everyone in the assembly had agreed on this. But the INCRA turned up to destroy. They came with a mean and false intent: "We are here today to decide about the settlement. For this we have to make a decision today. We're here with a list of forty-one families."

MGJ: *Who decided there would be only forty-one families?*

MAS: INCRA did. The guy [INCRA's technician] spoke these words and threw money up front.[34] We insisted: "Sixty-three, and end of discussion." And right then, from among those forty-one families: "But we have to get that money. We need that money for this and that." We managed to destroy what he set on. Not right then, he let us decide. We rose against it and we were left with a group of twenty-two families who were in favor of settling those sixty-three families. There were even death threats.

MGJ: *Among yourselves?*

MAS: Yes. I was threatened with my life. They came back with the same ideas, and there was trouble, because no one accepted them. It could only be settled if everyone. . . one vote against, and it could not be settled. We had that to our advantage. In the meantime, the people caught in the capitalist system started arguing because of the money. We told them that the money was part of the government's craftiness. That was the government's strategy to destroy. "Listen, people, we've been struggling together all this time and now we're going to let our comrades down because of 1,425 reais. Not for all the money in the world. Let's have courage, decency, pride." I showed them the truth; I shouted before the assembly, but they turned away. So what did we do?

MGJ: *But those people you're talking about, do they see you and the others as leaders?*

MAS: Obviously. They thought that we were the ones who were upsetting their process, because they wanted the money and we were not giving in, because of the others who were not being settled, who happened to

---

34   Under federal regulations, settled families can obtain financing from federal banks to support the costs of agricultural production. This program is called Pronaf (Programa de Apoio à Agricultura Familiar—Family Agriculture Support Program) and each family is entitled to 1425 reais per year.

be the first comrades to come to the encampment, the first in the struggle. We sat down and debated until we decided what we were going to do. We decided to take those forty-something-thousand reais and divide the money among those sixty-three families. We did that. I went ahead in good conscience.

MGJ: You *did, not everyone.*

MAS: We debated for some time. Then we called people to the assembly: "People, we have reached a decision. It's almost Christmas and New Year's; there's no basic basket, nothing. So this is what we're going to do. We're going to take the money and divide it among the sixty-three families. Everyone is entitled to it, no one will be in need." Everyone agreed. See what the capitalist system is like? Everyone agreed.

MGJ: *And that was your decision, not everyone's.*

MAS: No, it was our decision.

MGJ: *Of half a dozen of you?*

MAS: Yes. But they all agreed. Then we went up to INCRA's people to tell them that everyone had agreed. They handed out the checks. When we least expected it, INCRA came again. We started negotiating with them. We told them that those comrades who were being left out had suffered together with us—that they had been in the struggle longer, that they had been in hard struggles. We were all a bit embarrassed.

MGJ: *Did everyone agree that the sixty-three families had to be settled?*

MAS: Everyone agreed. Then in comes another guy from INCRA. He got here and said: "Listen, the number of families to be settled has increased to forty-seven."

MGJ: *So INCRA decided to settle forty-seven families instead of forty-one?*

MAS: Right.

MGJ: *And you were looking at sixty-three.*

MAS: Right. The other families had to stay on a waiting list. You can guess who they were looking after. They were looking after. . . Those six guys who were included were all from the capitalist system. Six guys from the capitalist system who had fallen on the street. You can guess their kind!

MGJ: *So they settled only forty-seven families?*

MAS: Only forty-seven, yes. Forty-six, as it turned out, because someone from the first list died. The government agency managed to destroy things. The damned money did it—the greatest capitalist scheme of all. That's why the MST needs to be very careful dealing with this filthy government, and to have strategies to crush those shameless crooks. Because they use a few families inside the settlement—families without a political conscience; they use them to destroy the others.

MGJ: *Maybe this is all their conscience comes down to. They are not concerned with building socialism. But they'll get something for themselves, and that's it. That's* *enough.*

MAS: They are not concerned because all they worry about is whether they have something, whether their families have something. They don't care if your family has nothing, if you're starving to death. They don't care. "My children have food, my wife has food, I have food." They are the sort of crooks who, as long as their houses are provided for, they couldn't care less. Anything you have, they will come over to take it away from you. They want to have you under their feet. This is the sort of people we have here. I regret having been settled here, because mine is a different system. My system is the socialist system. I have a conscience.

MGJ: *And all the while you talk about democracy. This means that we have to coexist democratically with those who think differently.*

MAS: Like those capitalists. Because, you see—suppose you have half a dozen socialists in the middle of forty-seven capitalists. I mean, half a dozen socialists. . . So you have forty-one capitalists. What are you going to do in the middle of those forty-one capitalist families? You have to be good at crushing, politically speaking. Crushing them, good and proper. Because the problem is this: I am politically aware. I'm a socialist, I have very sensitive class struggles before me. I've had many and I'll have more. I fight for a given socialism, true socialism. Piecemeal socialism is no use. I'm going to face those capitalists.

MGJ: *Is socialism what you expect for the future?*

MAS: Socialism, yes. Socialism is a bright future. You'll see your son. . . even if you don't enjoy it yourself. Everything I say today, I do it and will keep on doing it, but it's not for myself. Unless I die, unless God takes me. But as long as I'm alive, I'll keep on doing it. For my comrades' children, for my comrades' grandchildren, for my nephews. Well, for all of them. For the whole of the Brazilian working class, the poor and the humble. I'll keep on doing this for them, because I'm almost fifty-eight, so I can't say that I'm doing this for myself. Everything I do from now on, I'll be doing it for society. This is what I can do. I'm not doing this to be on the media, to appear in the media. That's not what I want. What I want is the truth. I'm not doing this for my wife, for myself. Because I and my wife, I'm glad we're of one mind.

MGJ: *But you and a few others—half a dozen, as you said—have that awareness of what socialism is, and at the same time you have those people whom you call capitalists who don't have that awareness. How can you achieve a democratic space—because you also talk about democracy—to deal with those differences, with those people who think differently, people who I believe aren't really capitalists—though they aren't socialists either—who just happen to have a different conscience, not that of socialist struggle, but which doesn't necessarily mean they think in a capitalist way? How will you live democratically, side by side with these* *different interests, when you expect the future to be one of socialism?*

MAS: I see what you're getting at. You mean. . .

MGJ: *This is what I'm getting at: we're all concerned with individual interests, and we have collective interests as well. How can we bring them together?*

MAS: It's like you said. We're over here, a bunch of nobodies, socialists. But you know, a few socialists together, being socially aware, they're worth more than one hundred opportunists. Because if one hundred socialists sit together, discuss reality and set the example, you can be sure they will destroy those individualists, those capitalists. Because everything they do, they do it for socialism. Besides demanding society's attention, they demand the attention of those comrades who are lost among those individualists. Because there are many comrades among those individualists who are lost, who play the part of capitalists, who are at a loss. They are at a loss, floating around, not knowing what the capitalist system means, not knowing what socialism is. And when they see socialism working, being true, those who are floating around, lost in time, they will come over here. They will say: "Look, things are working over there." Because those people who are inside the capitalist system and the others, who are floating around that same capitalist system, and who don't understand a thing, they'll be kicked all over. The capitalist system is an exploiting system. Because all capitalists want is to get ahead. So they will only help others like them. Do they help each other? Of course not: they will compete with each other. Because it is a competition. Not so with socialism. Those who are out there floating around, they will come over here. It's true they come here moved by opportunism. There's that too. They are floating around—they are not getting anything from capitalism; they look at socialism and say: "I'm going there, and as soon as I'm in control, I'll come back." That's what the system is like. But their coming over ends up being good for us. Because when they come here, they bring comrades with them. When they get here, they're under that system of. . . then the others come in and change them, make them stay. There's a proverb saying that you should never work thinking of getting very far; you have to work and expect to grow step by step—you pull forward step by step. Because if you pull forward step by step, you will not be pushing anyone. You'll be pulling forward all those people who know what they want. I fought for so many years. Then, at the time of the unionists, when all I did was fight, from inside popular movements, I was fighting without support.

MGJ: *And democracy, what is democracy?*

MAS: It's socialism! Serious, honest democracy—that's socialism!

There is in Miguel's discourse a guiding line, an internal logic: the truth. The idea of truth is repeatedly present in his words: it is the truth of the MST against government lies, or the truth of class struggle versus corrupt politicians. He presents himself as someone who is poorly educated, but whose words are true. His belief in God, in what is right, fair and honest, allows him to claim that the MST is true. For him the truth is class struggle; or rather, class struggle is the truth. The class struggle of the MST is a struggle for the truth, not for power; the MST does not want power, it wants the truth—because politics, power and the Constitution are false. When the PT seeks power, it stops seeking the truth. But the contradiction apparent here—how, for example, can one speak of class struggle and reject the struggle for power?—uncovers an ambiguity. If, according to Miguel, the search for power is a false path, the possibility of a "true" politics without a power established through the state is still open.

At times, throughout the interview, I wanted to interrupt Miguel's apparently "ready-made discourse" on class struggle—to me it seemed merely a distant concept. But I came to understand that this is the heart of his thinking. And, at that moment, he was precisely structuring his political view of the world. That was the "awareness of the other" I was searching for. Class struggle gives it its meaning.

In the end, after hours of interview, I realized how strongly I was interested in the issue of conciliating different interests in a democratic way—to deal with the "individualists," as Miguel claimed—and of thinking about the construction of socialism. Miguel's major contribution, as I see it, is the idea that, although there is a minority of socialists facing a majority of individualists, the collective form can become attractive, because many of the latter feel lost—"at a loss, floating around."

We can find in an MST settlement something that appears in a diffuse form in the metropolis of São Paulo: the building of a public space of open debate between socialists and "individualists." In turn, when you see a farmer claiming democratic conviviality among people with different views, you realize that the "rural world" has become distant from a homogeneous way of living that may have existed in the past.

2

Paula Lima

Housewife, organizer of the struggle against layoffs and for the right of women to participate in union activities.

Interviewed by Roberto Véras[1] and Maria Célia Paoli

"When I saw women talking, getting up there and taking the microphone in their hands and speaking so clearly, without any fear of saying that they would go after things, that they would go to the Senate, that they'd go I don't know where, they'd get this and that, I was very proud to be born a woman, you know? Very proud . . ."

---

1 The interview with Paula Lima took place on two separate occasions. The first session was conducted by me at the headquarters of the ABC Metalworkers Union. The second session was conducted by Maria Célia Paoli and myself about five-and-a-half months later, at the same place. The texts were written by me, although they have benefited from the helpful suggestions made by Maria Célia.

Paula Lima

Paula Lima was born in the interior of the state of São Paulo, in Timbó, near the city of Presidente Prudente. In 1988 she moved to São Bernardo do Campo, which is part of the Greater ABC region.[2] She has been married twice and has two children. She has had several jobs, the majority of which were very precarious. In order to survive, she has almost always combined working with being a housewife. Her second marriage was to a worker at the Ford factory in São Bernardo. This is how she became involved in the movement of the 2,800 workers dismissed by Ford in December 1998.[3]

At Christmas, the ABC Metalworkers Union and 2,800 Ford workers received redundancy notices. The factory had closed for its end-of-year recess and the return to work was scheduled for January 4th. The workers agreed that no one would sign the termination of contract, and that they would hold a meeting at the factory gates on that day to demand a full return to work. Large demonstrations followed, with full coverage in the national media and significant displays of solidarity. Throughout the month of January, the company refused to negotiate the return of the dismissed workers, but was unable to conquer the rising tide of public opposition. The result was that, in an unprecedented manner, Ford retracted, suspended the dismissals, and entered into negotiations with the union about the future of the company in the region. From then onwards, successive agreements were made that involved, in most cases, the adoption of programs of voluntary redundancy, the almost full payment of the salaries of the workers whose contracts had been suspended, the maintenance of a healthcare plan, and the reinstatement of a certain number of workers. By the end of June 2001, around 700 workers, who had been receiving gradually diminishing salaries over the previous six months, were still on suspended contracts. The last

---

2   Santo André, São Bernardo, and São Caetano are the three main cities in the area that, together with four more municipalities, makes up the metropolitan region of São Paulo. It is a highly industrialized area and the main center for the automobile industry in the country, although in recent years it has been experiencing some profound changes. It was here that the so-called new unionism emerged at the end of the 1970s, leading to the creation of the Workers Party (Partido dos Trabalhadores—PT) in 1980, and of the Single Federation of Workers (Central Única dos Trabalhadores—CUT) in 1983.

3   This represented 40 percent of the total workforce in the factory.

agreement led to the return of 100 more workers, making the total around 900, and the rest accepted a new voluntary redundancy package.[4]

The participation of Paula and various other families of the dismissed workers contributed moving symbolic images to the movement, and gave it a special vigor and a distinctive aura. A great performance was mounted, depicting the social drama of unemployment and the struggle of certain individuals to remain on the stage: it was politics as spectacle.[5] Although in the beginning the world of the union and of politics was completely alien to them, Paula and her companions soon found themselves promoted to the center of events, facing the TV cameras and increasingly taking on new responsibilities within the movement. They thus became part of this environment, making contacts, establishing connections, arousing interest, in ways they had never imagined before. New horizons were opened to them. Let us accompany them for a while. . .

In the latter part of the interview, Elenir, who also played an important part in the events, appears as a respondent as well.

Roberto Véras: *When Ford announced the redundancies, in December 1998, the newspapers printed a phrase of your husband's explaining the reaction you both had when you received the redundancy letter. According to one article, he said, "At that moment we just sat down and cried." What was it like for you?*

Paula Lima: It was just before Christmas, on 23 December. We'd been to my niece's wedding in Presidente Prudente. She was getting married and we were the godparents. She's like my adopted daughter. I brought her up until she was eleven years old. We got back from that on the 22nd. On the 23rd I was having a shower before going out to the market to do some shopping, to get something for supper. Well, it wasn't exactly a supper, because of all the money we'd spent paying off a plot of land at the end of the year, and also traveling. Anyway, I was just getting changed to go out to the market to get a few things for supper when the postman knocked and I had to go downstairs to sign [the form]—he said I had to sign it—and there he was looking at me, and I could see it was something from Ford. I even thought it might

4   See R. Véras, "Perspectivas do Sindicalismo CUT: Rupturas ou Continuidades? O Caso do Setor Metalúrgico na CUT," São Paulo, mimeo, 2000 (paper presented at the 24th Annual Conference of the Associação Nacional de Pós-Graduação e Pesquisa em Ciências Sociais [National Association for Postgraduate Studies and Research in the Social Sciences], held 23–27 October 2000, in Petrópolis, Rio de Janeiro).

5   In the sense described by Rancière, who sees an essential nexus between politics and theatre. According to him, popular insurrection, "far from being the actions of an enraged or hungry mob flooding into the streets," is, rather, "a means of occupying the street and disturbing a space normally dedicated to the circulation of individuals and commodities by staging a scene and redistributing roles" (*Folha de São Paulo*, September 29, 1996).

be a Christmas card, because Ford usually sent us something every year wishing us a Merry Christmas. Then he looked at me and said, "Dona Paula, Ford is reducing the workforce." But I didn't pay any attention. I thought he was just joking. Then he said, "I've delivered a lot of these today." And I ran off upstairs, still thinking it was just a joke. I handed it to my husband, who was putting on his shirt. I said to him, "You know what the postman said? 'Ford is reducing the workforce!'" But then I saw that it was a telegram, not a letter. He opened it—he went off into the bedroom and opened it. He looked at it and read it, and it started like this: "We hereby inform you that the company no longer needs your services. . ." or something like that. My God! He couldn't believe it. He started again, and I said, "Read it again, because it might be a memo saying that it's going to dismiss people, right?" Then he saw the line "termination of contract." Oh my God! Then he said, "Read this line here."[6] I looked at him and he looked at me and then we just clung on to each other, you know? We were paralyzed right then and there. We just held on to each other and sort of leaned against the wall, trying not to cry, you know? And then we did cry, sitting on the floor, kneeling down on the floor. At first we just knelt there, crying, holding on to each other; and then, I don't know, I just felt something inside me and I said to him, "Come on—we're not going to take this lying down, let's go and find the union. You always pay your dues—let's go and speak to the union." So he called them and he spoke to someone from the union. They asked him not to go and do the medical exam they were asking them to have. So he said, "OK, I won't go." He put down the phone, and I said to him, "For God's sake, we can't let this happen." I said, "This can't happen, I'm going to call the union, I'm going to speak to someone." And I rang them.

RV: *Had you already been in contact with the union before?*

PL: I hadn't.

---

6   The letter read, in part: "São Bernardo, 18 December 1998. Subject: Notice of termination of contract. As is generally known, factors of an economic and financial nature are profoundly affecting our economy, with serious consequences for the automobile sector. Strictly unavoidable measures to rationalize expenses and restructure operations have therefore made it necessary for us to eliminate one complete working shift, namely the night shift [. . .] Several alternative measures have been attempted throughout 1998 in order to maintain the workforce as it is at present, including the banking of hours, collective and individual holidays and paid leaves, but there was no recovery in the automobile market. We therefore regret to inform you that the company has no alternative but to terminate your contract of employment on 04/01/99, the date of the beginning of the notice now given, for which you will receive severance. We request your presence at the date and hour indicated below, for a final medical examination [. . .] We would like to thank you for your hard work and dedication throughout the time you have been employed at Ford Brazil, and hope that we may be in contact with you again in the future, if circumstances permit. Yours sincerely, Ford Brazil."

RV: *Had he?*

PL: My husband had, yes. But it was very difficult for him to go to union meetings.

RV: *Was he a member?*

PL: He was a member, he always had been. So, at that point I said, "I'm going to ring the union, I'm going to talk to someone, because this is really upsetting me." So I rang and I said, "Look, I'm nearly going out of my mind because of what's happening. Talk to some of the families—let's do something."

RV: *So you already had this instinct to search out the other people who were in the same situation and get together with them?*

PL: At that time, yes. I said, "Let's go and find someone." At the union, they said, "At this moment we are talking to a family that is also coming here." And I said, "I'm going to get in touch with some of the families, because I can't sit here doing nothing." So I started calling my husband's friends to see if they had received the same letter. Some said yes, others said no. So I invited people round to my house. They didn't come because they were afraid to do anything. I invited them to come to the factory gates on January 4th.[7]

RV: *What were they afraid of exactly?*

PL: Afraid of. . . well, they wouldn't say, would they? But they said they were afraid of going to the factory gates in case the shock troops[8] were there and there was some kind of repression, or something like that, and people would get hurt. I told my husband that I was going there on the 4th because I couldn't accept that, and I wanted to know what they could tell us about the situation. And my husband said, "Very well, then you go." On Sunday we went to Mass and we met some people there who were saying, "I'm not taking my wife," and others saying, "I'm not taking mine either—you're crazy to let your wife go." On the way home, my husband said to me, "Look, you're not going, because if you do—no one's taking their wife, you'll be the only one." And I said, "Well, I am going, whether you like it or not, whether you take me with you or not; because I'm not going to stay at home suffering on my own, waiting for something to happen; I have to go there and see." So he went with me. We were expecting that group, you know? But no one showed up.

RV: *Were you the only wife that went?*

---

7   The date set for the return to work, after the end-of-year recess at Ford. The union called on the dismissed and non-dismissed workers to hold a meeting on that day at the factory gates, to begin protests against the redundancies.

8   The Riot Police—a regiment of the Military Police responsible for suppressing mass demonstrations.

PL: No, there was one other family that stayed right at the back, near the exit gate so that if anything happened they could get out quickly. But I didn't—I was up at the front, because I wanted to see what was going on. I remember that I was at the front, hugging my son; my thirteen-year-old son, he gave me a lot of strength, he went with us; he said, "No, Mum, let's go, nothing's going to happen; let's go, Dad, we'll all go together." And my husband said, "OK then." We got the morning bus, we went to the factory gates—all that noise, that crowd of people. I had never seen a factory; I'd never worked in a place where there were so many people as that, you know? I got there and everyone was talking about things.

RV: *You'd never been to the factory before?*

PL: Never.

RV: *Even though your husband worked at Ford? How long had he been there?*

PL: For. . . it was six years in March.

RV: *Had he worked in a factory before that?*

PL: He's always worked in a factory.

RV: *And you'd never been to a factory?*

PL: Well, I knew what a factory was like, because I worked in textiles once. But not a factory with such a great number of workers. Anyway, when we got there, me, my husband and my son, arm-in-arm, everyone was staring at us because, you know, a woman, there. . . Still we got there, at dawn, and the gates were locked because they weren't going to hold the meeting inside. Even the sound truck was outside, and all. I remember that—I think at about six in the morning someone said that they had the right to go into the yard where they'd always held the meetings. I can still remember. . .

RV: *Was it inside, in the inner yard?*

PL: Inside, yes. I can still remember Barba[9] breaking the chains on the gate.

RV: *And this was on January 4th, when they were due to go back to work, right?*

PL: Yes, on January 4th. I remember him breaking the chains so that all the employees could get in, the ones that had been fired and the ones that hadn't, so that they could go to the meeting in the yard. So we got in; I went right up to the front. There were Isawa,[10] Vicentinho,[11] and everyone up on the truck. I can remember it as if it was yesterday. God! It almost, like, hurts to remember. So, everyone was there, talking and talking—and I remember when Vicentinho looked over and said, "Here you have an image of an unemployed family, husband, wife and son, there they are." At that moment I wasn't expecting anyone to be looking

---

9   A member of the Ford Factory Committee at the time.

10   Vice-president of the union at the time.

11   Ex-president of the union and president of the CUT at the time.

at me. I remember he and Marinho[12] saying that it would be a very diffi
cult struggle, very tough, very hard, but that we had to fight, that we
could achieve something, and so on. When he'd said that, the meeting
was over; and then the journalists were all crowding round me and my
husband and my son.

RV: *Was that because you were the only family present?*

PL: The only family, at that point, yes. And they all asked me what
Christmas had been like, what it had been like getting the letter. I can
still remember that I told them it had been the saddest Christmas of our
lives, because it was. Because my husband had lost his job and that had
been part of our life: him getting up at dawn, going to work every day,
having a time for leaving the house and a time for coming back.

RV: *Were you expecting him to be made redundant?*

PL: I wasn't expecting it, because my husband has always been a very good
worker, and very honest; he never took time off work for anything. He
even avoided going to the doctor—he always did, he only went if it was
something really serious. He was always very hardworking, you know?
And he, like, sweated away in the factory to provide for us, to give us
a life. So it was very hard. And I was very disappointed, because he was
such a good worker.

RV: *Disappointed with the company?*

PL: With everything, with the government, with everything, because
these machines are taking over the job market and there isn't any more
work for human beings to do. If you look for a job, it's all computerized
nowadays. Metalwork, nowadays, is really difficult. If a metalworker who
works in a car factory and earns not bad pay—because that's where they
pay a bit better—ends up out of work, he won't get another job, because
they can't reduce the wages, they can't do this, they can't do that. If you
haven't had any education, you won't get in, and that's that. There aren't
any jobs for you anymore.

RV: *Your eldest son was made redundant too, wasn't he?*

PL: Yes. He was dismissed at the same time as my husband, so that made
me even more desperate, you know?

RV: *Did you hear about any other dismissals in your neighborhood?*

PL: There were lots of people in my neighborhood.

RV: *From other companies as well?*

PL: Oh yes. Near us there were other people who'd been dismissed from
other companies. So, I think the last year was the saddest of all, with all
this unemployment situation. Critical even. It even happened to me, at
the beginning of the year. I used do some washing for a football club,

---

12   President of the union.

and in early January I also lost my job. But when all this happened, this unemployment problem, and I saw that my husband was going to be unemployed as well as my son, I sprang into action. I phoned the company where my son worked and I said, "Look, he's seventeen, he needs to work, I don't know what I'm going to do now." I was desperate, you know? I spoke to the people at the company. And then they asked my son to carry on working, out of consideration for everything that had happened. My son had already received notice in December.

RV: *Going back to January 4th, when you were listening to the union leaders talking, did you feel hopeful that the situation could be reversed?*

PL: I felt it when Marinho said that it would be a very difficult struggle, but that if we put up a fight, we would win. I believed it then, at that moment, I believed in what they were saying, because I didn't have anything else left to believe in. That was why I went there that day, so that I could have something, someone, to believe in. And at that moment, on that day, I left feeling confident that something would happen, if people did something. Because I don't think that people can just sit there waiting. You have to fight, get involved. And then that was when everyone saw me on the television, in the papers, everywhere. Women started phoning up, from some union, I think, but I don't know where, asking who I was. They all started calling me—even the people I had rung at the end of the year to invite them to come over, they started asking for my husband's number and contacting me. We began talking about starting a campaign. People started to appear. On the 8th, I think, there was a meeting here, at the union, at six in the evening, and I went. And that was when I asked to speak for the first time. Before that, after the meeting on the 4th, we had been in a Rede Globo[13] report. They came to my house and did a report. After that we came running over here from my house, because there was going to be a meeting here; but when we arrived it had nearly ended. From then on, I didn't want to miss anything else. I wanted to grab everything, everything. Then, on the 8th, we came here to the union. They opened the doors for the people who had come to the meeting. And I remember. . . I don't know how I had the courage then to ask—I only remember that I said, "People. . ."—the union was packed—I said, "People, there aren't many of us, but we're going to do it; there aren't many of us to face what has happened, to face all this, the 2,800 who have been fired, but we can fight and we can win." I didn't understand anything about the law, I never had. I'd heard people speaking about human rights, this and that, but I didn't know much about laws, you know? Still, I remember that I said this: "We have

---

13 TV network.

rights, and this is a right—it's a human right; what we have to do is fight for our jobs." I didn't understand anything, you know? It was unconscious, what I said.

RV: *And this was at the meeting on the 8th?*

PL: Yes, at that meeting.

RV: *Were there any other women there?*

PL: A few that I had invited came. We arranged a meeting at my house for the Sunday afternoon.

RV: *What were you thinking of doing at that meeting?*

PL: It was because they had arranged a meeting at the factory gates.

RV: *For the Monday?*

PL: For the Monday. So we invited those people to come to my house so that we could talk about the movement, the Christmas dinner we'd spoken of, a symbolic Christmas dinner that we were going to have at the factory gates.[14] After this dinner, we were going to march to Rudge Ramos.[15] We wanted to make banners and placards and talk about things, make friends with people so that we would have a movement—start doing something good, you know? Not with that feeling that the factory gate is where the mob is, where there is conflict, where people fight and thump each other.

RV: *Was that what you had heard them say?*

PL: It was.

RV: *Pickets, fights. . . ?*

PL: It was the police, it was the shock troops. But I just saw a lot of human beings there. I didn't see any thugs, nothing like that—you know? I saw human beings; I looked at the faces of each one of them and I thought: "Has this one been fired? Has this one?" I kept trying to imagine what each person was thinking at that moment. I saw there was a gentleman, like this, with a walking stick, a dark-haired gentleman, whatever. Everyone was there—some were sweating, from nerves I think—the sweat was dripping off them. I looked from one face to another, someone else was in tears. And it made something inside me grow stronger. That was why I invited those families. At the time, at two in the afternoon, thirteen families turned up. Some brought two children, others brought four. Someone brought six. Dear Lord! I was like this—because my house is small. And I never thought that so many people would turn up. And I had to have people sitting in the corridor, on the stairs. My house is small, you know? When I talked to them I had to stand at the

---

14   On January 13 the union organized a Christmas dinner as an ecumenical act, aiming to exploit its strong symbolic appeal in order to publicize the movement and win support from society.

15   The cathedral square in São Bernardo do Campo.

foot of the stairs. That's how it was, but it was really nice. People started to suggest things, make up slogans—nowadays I know what a slogan is, but before I didn't know any of that stuff. Because I wasn't educated—not at all, you know? So, anyway, we did all these things, not knowing what was going to happen. I remember that at the Christmas dinner at the factory gates, some people came up to congratulate me, because they had seen me on the television, and because I'd had the courage to go to the factory gates, because I'd managed to get other women together. The women themselves came up to congratulate me; and I looked at all of it, all those children, and I felt desperate, because I didn't want to see anyone, you know, kicked out. We made banners, placards—I knocked together some phrases for the placards.

RV: *Can you remember them?*

PL: Some of them. I remember that one man came up to me and said, "What am I going to be without my work?" So I made up a phrase like this: "A man's dignity lies in his work; give us back our jobs." That was in one of the banners. My son and two other kids carried another banner that had this phrase: "In the Children's and Adolescents' Charter, it should say that every child has the right to have a working father." That banner got a lot of attention, you know? Because I really do think that—I do think that every child has the right to have a working father, because if he isn't working, if there isn't any money coming into the house to pay the rent, to pay the bills, the milk, the water, the electricity, what's going to happen to them?

RV: *Paula, a right is something that we demand of somebody. From whom were you demanding this right? The company, the government, society?*

PL: At that point we didn't know from whom we were demanding it. We made banners criticizing the government, because it was doing nothing to help those who had been fired.

RV: *The government did nothing, in your opinion?*

PL: In my opinion, it did nothing. It only did one thing: when it saw that the movement was at the factory gates, it called the union people to tell them to go there; but I think that, even so. . . Look, I've still got doubts about the government, OK? I voted for Fernando Henrique. . . I voted for Lula, once. Then I voted for Fernando Henrique, which was a mistake. One day I hugged Lula, in tears, and I said, "Lula, I'm really sorry about what I did." I don't know if he remembers that, but I was really sorry, you know? Because this government we've got now doesn't give the poor any hope. There are factories closing every day that goes by, leaving, closing their doors. The small businesses, which could be employing people, are going away too because they can't survive. It's too much. . .

RV: *So the government didn't do its job properly, in your opinion?*

PL: It didn't. Our only hope was the union. Our biggest hope was that the union could do something. So people believed in it—they were behind it. There were people here every day at the union. I think the people here were even getting tired of seeing the same faces every day.

RV: *Did you feel you were getting any support from other people?*

PL: Yes. Lots of people came to help—sometimes a lot of people called to support us. Even the television, the Bank Workers' Union, the Chemical Workers' Union, the Metro Workers' Union, lots of places, you know?

RV: *Workers from other factories?*

PL: Yes, workers from other factories, too. Especially when we began collecting food and money, to keep the movement going. The factories got together and began to help people with provisions, with money, with anything they could. One day I remember really well was when we went to. . . We closed Sandre-Car,[16] we went there to demonstrate, to get the attention of the president of Ford. I invited thirty families—I think only one of them didn't turn up. But, thank God, we were well received by the manager there. And he even collaborated with us and sent a fax to the Ford president's office. Yes, he treated us quite well. We stayed there very quietly, all the families. Because when you've got the whole family there, you don't want any violence, do you? And they didn't even call the police or anything. In our movement there wasn't any bad behavior, any violence—nothing like that. We had hope, because we were fighting for hope.

RV: *Out of everything that happened in the movement, what was most important for you?*

PL: The thing that was most important for me was that I would speak to people, to the women, especially the women. I don't know what they saw in me, but I would say something and they'd do it, you know? There was one day at the factory that I spoke, I was there at the meeting, and I said, "If something doesn't happen. . ." It was before the day of the victory, it was on the Monday. I got there and I spoke to them like this: "Let's do something because if we don't, I don't know what's going to happen." I remember that I called on all the women. I sat down first, on the curb, and I said, "Dear God, help me to do something to get someone's attention, to show them how much these families are suffering." Then, I got up, caught my son by the arm, and called on all the women to link arms, and we went out to the factory gates, where the barriers were. And we stayed there, you know, with our arms linked.

RV: *Was that the day when you made that cordon around the factory?*

---

16   A Ford concession in the city of Santo André.

PL: Yes. It was, I don't know, a moment of faith, a moment of unity. It was the same day that we brought saucepans to the factory gates, laid a tablecloth on the ground, and the pans were all empty and they had "hunger" written on them, because we no longer had enough rice, beans, milk, no more bread. There was a little child sitting there, a little girl called Aléxia, sitting on the tablecloth, and her bottle was all empty, and it had "hunger" written on it as well. It was one of those days when, I don't know, I cried a lot. And that other day, when we had the symbolic Christmas dinner and I saw a woman who had brought her paralyzed son in his wheelchair and pushed him the whole way—I can't remember if it's 7 or 8 kilometers to Rudge Ramos. And that child there in his wheelchair. And a man with a walking stick, with his son by his side. . . I remember I saw a child who looked at Lula[17] and yelled, "Lula, don't let my Dad lose his job, please!" But he couldn't hear him properly, so he said, "What did you say?" And the child repeated, "Don't let my Dad lose his job, please! We need him to work." My God! At that moment I just cracked, I cried, you know? I knelt down on the ground and prayed to God—I've always been very religious. And I remember that all through the movement I prayed, I held my rosary, I asked for help, I had faith. It was very sad, what we went through. We had days when we didn't have any bread to eat. But we ate in each other's houses, we bought odds and ends, we left the factory gates and went to someone's house to make lunch. So we ate, and we had faith.

RV: *Out of everything the leaders and the union said, what made the most impression on you?*

PL: It was all a lesson in life for us, a very big lesson. The struggle of the union, people's struggle to get everyone back in, that motivated us a lot, you know? It motivated us to have the strength to do something for our own, didn't it? What moved me most were the other industries—Volks, all of them, making a chain of solidarity.

RV: *The workers?*

PL: Yes, the workers, all of them, making that chain of solidarity, to help. The Citizens' Committee of Rio de Janeiro[18] brought us two truckloads of food. That day when they came, bringing the food trucks—dear God! Our Christmas had been so miserable, and then suddenly, when we were in so much need, two trucks of food arrived, you know? That motivated people to fight even more.

---

17   The rise of Luís Ignácio Lula da Silva, political leader of the Workers Party (PT), was one of the main expressions of the "new unionism" that emerged in the ABC during the late 1970s and early 1980s.

18   A movement led by the late sociologist Herbert de Souza, a.k.a. Betinho, which began in the early 1990s with the aim of organizing the participation of the population in campaigns for ethics in politics and in food collections for those living below the poverty line.

RV: *Do you think you have changed because of this movement?*

PL: Definitely, I've changed. I'm much more of a human being now, you know? If I was a supportive type of person before—because I always liked to help people—I got that from my family; well, now I do ten times more. If someone needs something, then I'll go and help that person first, and then they can help me later on, you know? I'm much more of a human being nowadays. I'm much more of a woman—because I didn't know myself as a woman before.

RV: *What do you mean by that?*

PL: I didn't know the strength I had, to be able to do something for someone, to help—I didn't lose the fighting spirit, you know? Now I always try to be involved in something; now I belong to the Feminina de Santo André (the Santo André Women's Group)—it's a feminist movement. So, now I'm part of that movement. And I'm also in the Frente Regional de Combate à Violência Contra a Mulher (Regional Front to Combat Violence Against Women). The Frente Regional is in São Bernardo. Yes, I got involved. I wouldn't just stand there watching. I take part in discussions. I got very fond of the people in the union. I didn't know the CUT.[19] I only got to know them after the struggle.

RV: *You didn't know anything about the CUT?*

PL: Nothing at all.

RV: *But you'd heard about them—you'd seen them on television?*

PL: I'd only heard about a women's movement, a few years back, where the women went out in the streets banging saucepans with wooden spoons.

RV: *The Movement against Inflation?*

PL: Yes, that's it.

RV: *What was the impression you had of them before? When, for example, you saw the CUT on television, and Vicentinho, the union, the Movement against Inflation, what was your impression of them? What did you think of them?*

PL: I didn't have any opinion, you know? I didn't pay attention; I wasn't interested. I only remember that people used to say that the PT. . . the union were a bunch of thugs—they were this, they were that. So I was scared to death of them. Only that. But when I got to know them, I had a different idea. I saw that they were nothing of the sort. I met Feijó,[20] I met Vicentinho, I met Grana,[21] I met Rafael, I met Bagaço[22]—everyone. And they all said what I wanted to hear—I learned to value them all.

19   CUT [Central Única dos Trabalhadores] is—according to its official publications—a mass Brazilian national union organization, autonomous and democratic, with class character, whose commitment is to protect the traditional and immediate interests of the working class.

20   President of the São Paulo CUT at the time.

21   Secretary-general of the Metalworkers Union at the time.

22   The latter two were members of the Factory Committee.

The way they love their work. Because if it isn't for these men, what will become of us? What will become of our husbands, who really need workers' rights? If they don't have someone to fight for them, to look after them. . . ?

RV: *Do you think that society, the Brazilian government, could do more about the unemployment problem?*

PL: Definitely. I think that if they have computerized everything, if they have machines taking people's places, they should open two or three positions in other kinds of jobs so that things wouldn't be so bad. These are people who are turning to crime, because they don't have jobs. Girls and women who can't get their first job become prostitutes. Even the lads today are working as prostitutes, because they can't get a job any more. So, this is violence by the government against the people, right? Yes, the president should do something, should give some support. Because if we have these industries, these automakers that come from abroad, they have to do something, because these are foreign companies coming here—they get free access, they get lower taxes to set up in our country, and they take the money back home with them. Why can't he do something about that? Surely he could do something.

RV: *When the workers, the union, demanded a solution, Ford said, "But we have to dismiss people, we have no alternative; the other companies are doing the same." Do you think you managed to reverse this situation?*

PL: The union was the one who managed to reverse the situation, and it asked everyone to believe in it. And everyone believed and hoped. They fought for this. They fought hard and did everything they could. So if the situation was reversed it's due to the work of the union people, the people up there who fought for this. And they were so successful that Ford was just recently asking people to go back, weren't they?

RV: *How many have already gone back?*

PL: Altogether, I don't know. I only know that my husband was one of the first. And a few more went back this week.

RV: *What's your general opinion of the movement?*

PL: Ah, I've only got one thing to say and that is: if you don't fight, you don't get anywhere, do you? And struggle is life—it's hope. It's what I said, hope; we had hope, we believed in our leaders, and we've achieved something because of that.

RV: *So you think that the movement was victorious?*

PL: Sure, definitely. A lot have already gone back. And those who don't want to wait until July are taking their pay and leaving. Because there's been a lot of people wanting to leave, because they're starting to see that

São Paulo, São Bernardo, these big cities don't have anything for them any more. I'd leave as well, if I could.

RV: *Did you get to talk to the people who accepted redundancy when the movement was at its peak?*

PL: Dear God! We talked to them, begged them to do something, begged them not to sign the papers. Some of them, I think, had already signed but hadn't received their dues. Then they came back—they believed in the movement.

RV: *And those who accepted redundancy, despite all your efforts, what did they say?*

PL: "Oh, no, it's over. Ford won't take on anyone else. So let's get out, let's pick up our pay and leave" OK then, there were some who did that. So now we've got the situation of people in need. They took the redundancy pay, spent the money, and now they need help.

RV: *And what arguments did you use with them?*

PL: "Oh, let's believe in it, let's have some faith." This was what people said: "Let's believe in the union, let's have some faith." And that's what we did, we believed and we had faith.

RV: *What has happened to you is something that is happening all over the world: mass redundancies. If you had to say something to these other people in the world, what would you say, on the basis of your experience?*

PL: I would say that people have to believe, fight, and have faith. Because people who don't have faith won't move mountains. You have to have a lot of faith. And we had a lot of faith. I think it's because of this that we are where we are today, because we had a lot of faith and hope. We were fighting for our hopes, weren't we? For people to have more confidence in themselves, to be able to do something for themselves, not just stand there waiting for something to come to them. Go on, get involved, do something for yourself, for the ones you care about. People have to feel useful. I like to feel useful, now. Before, I didn't know myself as a woman, that I had the strength to do things. Now, I know I can.

Maria Célia Paoli: *What struck me most in your previous interview was what you discovered about action, especially in terms of women's participation. So I'd be interested to know if you already knew about the women's movement, if you'd heard of it, if you'd had any connections with it?*

PL: I didn't understand a thing about the feminist movement, or about women taking part in movements. I'd seen something on the television, someone talking—but I'd never taken part myself. I know that it was, like, unexpected for me to be accepted as a leader at the time, in 1999, when it all happened. At the end of 1998, 2,800 workers were dismissed. And on January 4th I said to my husband, "Whatever happens, I'm going to the factory gates with you, because I can't just stay here in the house, like this, suffering, worrying about whether you'll go back to work or not." But I believed what Paulão[23] said to me: "We'll go to the factory gates and when we get there you'll hear what the union people have got to say to you." I went—I couldn't stand staying in the house; and I said to my husband, "I'm going, whatever happens." His friends had warned him not to let me go because they said it would be dangerous.

MCP: *The union was seen as something dangerous?*

PL: It was. People used to say that, didn't they? My husband went to the meetings sometimes, but he wasn't really closely involved. And I was even afraid for him to go because sometimes you would hear that it was dangerous because "those people are thugs," as they say—they just want a brawl, and all that. But suddenly, when I saw the situation we were in, I couldn't just sit there doing nothing and watch my husband being sent packing, so I said, "I'm going to the factory gates," and I started ringing up loads of women, and no one would go. There was only one other family, who stayed by the back gate, and I said, "I'm not going to stay at the back there by the exit, afraid of a riot. I want to go up to the front to hear what the people on the truck are saying."

MCP: *Were there women in the union at that time?*

PL: There were already some women taking part.

MCP: *But they weren't the ones you were talking about?*

PL: No—they were the wives of the workers. I didn't even know that women were in the union at all. I went directly to the wives, to the husbands, I rang people up to get them to go to the factory gates. It was like. . . I don't know how this suddenly happened, but it was like something inside me burst. And my son said, "No Mom, we'll go too, to defend my dad's job"—he was twelve at the time—"Yes, let's go, I'll get up at dawn with you and I'll go." So I dug my heels in and I told my husband I was going. And on the 4th we went there. We even went dressed in black because we were in mourning, in protest against unemployment. I said to my husband, "We're going in black, to protest against unemployment."

MCP: *And you all went in black?*

PL: Yes, me, my husband, and my son. When we got there, we were listening and that, and then suddenly Vicentinho saw us there in the middle and he said, "Look, here is an image of an unemployed family." And suddenly all the cameras were turned on us—everyone started taking pictures of us and asking questions. And then I begged people, for the love of God, to do something, not to leave their husbands alone but go with them, accompany them, because we couldn't just stay at home and let this happen, you know?

---

23   A member of the workers' Factory Committee at Ford, at the time.

MCP: *And then afterwards didn't the female unionists get in touch with you?*

PL: Yes, they did. After they'd seen me on the news, in various papers, the Santo André Women's Advisory Office[24] called me the next day to find out who I was, to give me some encouragement and to talk to me. They invited me to go there, and I went to find out what they wanted of me. Suddenly, the telephone started ringing non-stop in my house. It never used to ring, and then it was going non-stop. It was the wives of the Ford workers, women from the movement, from São Bernardo, from Santo André, from all over, from São Paulo, from the CUT, everywhere, suddenly, all giving their support: "Come on, my friend, don't let this movement die—let's turn it into something really big." That's when Elenir[25] appeared with her daughter to give us strength. Her daughter was a symbol of the struggle for us. And suddenly, a force had been created—every time I went to the factory gates I saw women, children, husbands. . .

MCP: *And did you meet the unionists?*

PL: I did, several of them.

MCP: *And what was that like? What was your impression of them?*

PL: They gave me a lot of strength, especially Luci, the head of the union at the time. Luci gave me a lot of support. She would say, "Come on, comrade, you're doing the right thing, if you want to win a struggle, you have to fight, go after what you want." The Santo André Women's Advisory Office, as well—they made me get up on top of a truck to ask for people's support.

MCP: *What was it like, speaking from on top of a truck?*

PL: My God! I don't know, we were there on the day of the Christmas dinner and suddenly everyone knew me from the telephone, the television, the newspapers, and I looked at all those people and it was a sea of faces—you could only see their heads. Then Arlete and Matilde, from the Women's Advisory Office, arrived and said, "No, comrade, you have to get up there and tell all these people not to give up on the movement, to keep going." I didn't even know how to begin, because I'd never spoken into a microphone before. They asked me to get up there and speak, and I climbed up onto the sound truck, and suddenly there I was with a microphone in my hand, looking at this crowd of people, not knowing what to do, what to say. I only know that some words came out, but I don't remember them.

RV: *You don't remember what you said?*

PL: I don't remember what I said. I just remember one thing: I felt hot; it felt as if there was a volcano ready to explode inside me. I only remember

---

24   A local feminist organization.

25   Like Paula, Elenir was the wife of one of the dismissed workers.

that I asked the families who were there not to let the movement die, because everyone had to take part and keep bringing their families to the factory gates. And when I looked down, I saw a child in a wheelchair, a mother with a child, holding on to him ready to go on the march to Rudge Ramos, a man with a walking stick, women, the mothers of the sons who worked there, and that gave me strength. And suddenly Elenir came up to us, with Aléxia, and I saw that tiny little girl there in her mother's arms.

RV: *How old was Aléxia then?*

Elenir: She was nine months.

PL: She was so tiny and she didn't cry; it seemed like she understood. From that day on, she took part in all the demonstrations—she was down at the factory gates every day. That child gave people more strength to keep the movement going.

MCP: *Were there women working in the factory?*

PL: There were some. Today there are a few more because of the Ipiranga truck factory coming to São Bernardo.[26] But not many.

Elenir: There were four women among the 2,800 who were dismissed.

MCP: *Did you see any difference between calling on the women to help their families, as the wives of the dismissed workers, and calling on the women who worked in the factory?*

PL: I think that. . . I don't know; now I can see the difference, you know? Women who work have a different attitude compared to the wives of workers; they've got another attitude, they believe more in their jobs. Women are more confident if they are working than if they are at home. If you stay at home, you feel lost, because you're just thinking all the time about the job that's gone. I don't know, there is a difference that I just can't explain to you at the moment, but there is a very big difference between a woman who works and the wife of a worker.

RV: *Did the four female workers who were dismissed take part in the movement?*

Elenir: Only one took part right up to the end. The three who didn't take part went back. That was revolting.

PL: And the one who stayed to the end didn't get to go back to work.

MCP: *Did the unionists keep in touch with you out after this?*

PL: After the movement ended, I always did. But I realized that I was a bit of an outsider. I kept seeking the union people, so that I could go to the CUT, see the work of the women at the CUT. I did go a few times. Because I was active, I followed the Santo André Women's Advisory Office, the Santo André feminist movement, all that, but when you're

---

26 Ford maintained an old factory in the city of São Paulo, in the Ipiranga area, which manufactured trucks. This unit had been transferred to the São Bernardo plant a short time before the interview took place.

not working, when you're unemployed, you don't have a job, you're a bit sidelined, aren't you? I began to see that—that I was always on the sidelines, and I was very sad about it. I was very upset.

MCP: *Why do you think this happens, if you've got so much to offer?*

PL: I think that if I was a worker, if I was a metalworker, they'd find a way in for me. But since I don't work, it's my husband that does. I get left out.

MCP: *Do you think the unions don't know what to do with people like you?*

PL: Look, if there's someone who's strong, who wants to fight, who's always available and ready to do something to help, I think they should pay attention to them and say, "Yes, this person could be useful to us, let's find you something." But now I'm unemployed, and I can't get a job.

MCP: *What work did you do?*

PL: I used to work in textiles, and I've worked as a receptionist, in radiology.

MCP: *Until you got married?*

PL: I've been married twice [*laughter*].

MCP: *Did you work until you got married?*

PL: I worked until I got married, and then I separated. I got married again, worked again, and I'm still working now. Just that I'm not registered, so that means I'm unemployed, as of last week.

MCP: *Were you working when the movement started?*

PL: No, I was just a housewife.

MCP: *Do you think that the unionists only call on the people who are directly affected, those in the workplace? Do you think they should involve more people?*

PL: I do. I think that someone who has the will, who has the strength of will to do something, who finds they've got dedication. Because I was like that, totally dedicated to taking part in all this. And suddenly I saw that I was a leader, everyone sought me; if something happened it was me that they sought out. And suddenly. . .

MCP: *Why do you think they didn't keep you on?*

PL: I don't know. Male discrimination [*laughter*]. But the women in the movements who are union leaders should say, "Hell, we've got a comrade here who's as strong as an ox and she wants to do something. Let's try her out on something, shall we?"

MCP: *Did you ever get to see what the CUT unionists do?*

PL: We don't get much involved, we know that the women are always fighting, always doing something—like Luci, who's always away, traveling, even outside the country.

RV: *Did you ever get to take part in any of the work at the CUT?*

PL: No. I only went to some meetings in São Paulo. I asked to take part in things, when they happened. I went, I think, about two or three times, I can't quite remember, to see what work the women did in the union, in the CUT, and so on. And I saw that women are really strong. When I saw women talking, getting up there and taking the microphone in their hands and speaking so clearly, without any fear of saying that they would go after things, that they would go to the Senate, that they'd go I don't know where, they'd get this and that, I was very proud to be born a woman, you know? Very proud.

Elenir: Only a few women participate. If a majority of women were in charge of the union. . . because the union is big. Imagine if we were in charge, just like Marta [Suplicy] in São Paulo[27]—then I'm sure we could change this a bit.

RV: *And what about the episode with Ford Ipiranga?[28] You were invited to go there, weren't you?*

PL: We were. We went, and we even got up on the truck and I got ready to speak. Marta asked us to go, just to give a bit of encouragement to people there, who were also having problems with Ford Ipiranga. We got there and I said, "My God, I don't want to just stay down here looking at all the people, all these women inside the factory." Then I spoke to someone from the union there, and I said, "For the love of God, speak to these people and tell them not to give up on the movement." And they said, "Well, you get up there and speak." So I got up there and I spoke to them: "Come on, people, let's fight for our jobs, let's go for it, let's take part, bring your families"—because the family is very important in a worker's life. My son would say to me, "Mom, I'm coming with you on the march tomorrow against the blackouts[29] and against corruption." And I would say, "Yes, of course we'll go together." He started at twelve and one day, who knows, someone else will follow him, someone will go along with Elenir's daughter too.

RV: *It would be interesting if you could talk a bit more about this Ford Ipiranga episode, because some of the workers there were women.*

Elenir: That day when Paula got up on the truck there, it was great, because after that two women invited us there—they asked Marta to call us, for us to go inside the gates and give them some ideas. They asked for information about how they could start, about what we were doing; they asked for our help. And that broadened their ideas. Because there they were, a bit shy and not doing anything, only the men were speaking. And after Paula went there, it all changed.

PL: They made a huge circle of women, like this. . . Lots of women. They all asked us what we had done, what it was like, if it was dangerous.

---

27   The mayor of São Paulo at the time, connected to the PT.

28   In mid-1999 Ford announced its intention to close down the Ipiranga unit, which produced a strong reaction from the workers.

29   Brazil was then in the midst of a severe energy crisis, and there was the constant risk of blackouts lasting for hours.

"Look, there's no danger at all, it's an honest fight, we're doing something for our future, for our children's future." And Marta was there with us. Afterwards we went out and went on a march, all together. Some of them are still working, even though the factory has been transferred to São Bernardo. I recently went to visit the factory, because we were invited. . .

RV: *Ford has been inviting families to visit the factory in São Bernardo, hasn't it?*

PL: It has. Some of them saw me go past in Ford Caminhões, and they waved, like this, you know? I think they recognized me. The men saw me passing by and called out "Hey comrade! Hey comrade!"—and all that. And everyone was looking, and I said, "Hello, good afternoon, are you all fine?"

RV: *Had you ever been in the factory before?*

PL: I'd never been inside before, but I really enjoyed it. I really wanted to go, to see what kind of place my husband worked in, because it's important for us—he brings the money back from there to feed the family, you know? So we'd always wanted to see it. And that day we went. Me, my youngest son, and him. It was great!

MCP: *Did he start to take part in the union?*

PL: No, he doesn't. Well—he goes to the meetings, he goes on the marches when he can, because he's studying. He hasn't got the time at the moment, has he? He's trying to get us a better future. I'm more willing to go. On Saturday there's going to be a lunch at the São Judas restaurant with Lula,[30] and I told my husband I wanted to go no matter what, and he told me that if that meant I was going alone, I wouldn't be going, I could only go with him. So I said, "Well, then, let's go, let's both of us go because if you don't, I will." He's a bit like that.

MCP: *You have to push him, do you?*

PL: I do. And tomorrow I'm going on a march and he's coming too.

MCP: *Why is it that the union isn't able to involve people like you, except when this type of campaign is going on?*

PL: I used to go almost every day to the union, because I felt that I was part of it. I could no longer do without the union, without seeing the women, without seeing the work people were doing there, without finding out about other movements. So, when I started to get involved, I began reading the *Tribuna Metalúrgica*[31] almost every day. And I keep asking my husband, "Bring the *Tribuna*, so that I know what's happening in the factories, on the shop floor, because I want to know everything—because if something suddenly comes up I'll know what to say, what to

---

30   An attempt by PT unionists and militants in the ABC region to persuade Lula to run for president in the 2002 elections.
31   The daily union newspaper.

do, where to go." But he is always forgetting the *Tribuna Metalúrgica*. Whenever I pass by here, I get one. Because I'm stuck now, I'm out of action—but that volcano's still here inside of me. And suddenly. . .

MCP: *Have you ever thought of getting involved in something, for instance, in the local PT?*

PL: The women's movement in the São Bernardo PT is very weak. I went to some PT meetings, but you can see that it is very weak—people are rather down. No one is bothered. And you only feel like doing something when you see that there's a movement, that people are after something, that they want to grow—don't you? Like the Santo André women. There it's different; there you can see that they've got the strength, they're always doing something, fighting, having meetings. The work the Santo André women do is really worthwhile. I took part in a lot there. But since I didn't have money for the bus, it got a bit difficult, because I needed the money to get there and back. So I stopped going, because of the money and because I was feeling a bit sad, because I was always a bit left out. But they were the only people who didn't forget me, the Women's Advisory Office in Santo André. And I'm also involved with the women's group, which has a meeting every month.

MCP: *If the Women's Committee in São Bernardo wasn't so weak, it would be a lot nearer for you, wouldn't it?*

PL: It would be a lot nearer. I could walk it.

MCP: *Have you ever thought of joining and, I don't know, giving them some ideas?*

PL: No, because it's only for people who are members.

MCP: *Is it closed?*

PL: I think those places are cliques, like you get everywhere. To get in, you'd have to. . .

Elenir: If you do go there you don't get the same welcome you get at Santo André. You get there and. . . I don't know. The girls in Santo André, when we get there, they already know who we are and invite us for something: "Oh yes, you're invited for such-and-such." And it makes you feel better. The welcome is very important.

MCP: *Do you also think that in São Bernardo the discussions are weak, apart from the reception you get? That's to say, what they talk about—the contents?*

PL: Yes, in São Bernardo—that's to say, not in the union but in the PT, I think the meetings I went to were very weak. It wasn't, like, solid, consistent. I didn't like it very much. I voted for Vicentinho,[32] I helped get some votes for him, and all that—but in terms of women being involved, it left a lot to be desired. At that time, the women's movement itself in politics left a lot to be desired.

---

32   The defeated PT candidate for mayor of São Bernardo in 2000.

RV: *And nowadays, do you campaign in any particular area? Or do you take part in one thing here, another thing there?*

PL: No, I only, like, go on marches. If they say there's a march in aid of this cause or that one, I go. If they say it's somewhere else, I go. I'm always like that—but I'm on my own.

RV: *How did you hear about the march against the blackouts?*

PL: Through the *Tribuna Metalúrgica*. And I decided to go. I read the *Tribuna Metalúrgica* every day.

RV: *How do you feel about having voted for Fernando Henrique[33] in the last elections? How do you feel about marching against Fernando Henrique? [laughter]*

PL: If I could, I'd run him off the face of this earth. I'd get rid of him, exclude him from politics altogether. I feel terrible about it. I don't even know why I voted for him.

RV: *You can't imagine why you voted for him?*

PL: Well, I can. It was because people said, "You're not going to vote for Lula? Lula hasn't had any education. You're going to vote for a person with no education, who doesn't understand anything?" Come again? If he didn't understand anything, he wouldn't be where he is today. He's done so much for our country, for our workers. It's an honor for us to know that someone has come from nowhere, and achieved something in a city as big as ours. It's an honor that a person without an education has grown into the person he is.

MCP: *And do you try to keep up with the policies of Fernando Henrique?*

PL: We talk about it, especially within the family. At home, you know? We talk a lot about things at home—because we need to prepare the youngster now, so that he knows what's best for him and for the country.

MCP: *Have you ever thought of forming a discussion group to continue the work you did?*

Elenir: Well, before, the people in the movement were very united. But now most of the women have lost interest.

PL: It was because they were jealous, wasn't it? Because the union, the magazines, the papers were all asking for me and they thought they should have been asking for them. But they weren't there every day working for the struggle like us, were they, Elenir?

Elenir: The fact is, whether they like it or not, the one who started it all was Paula. Because if Paula hadn't had the idea of going to the factory, to the factory gates, I'd never have had that idea.

PL: Many of them lost interest because their husbands managed to get their jobs back, and then they were afraid to fight in case their husbands lost their jobs again. But, damn it, nobody's doing anything wrong. It is the

---

33   The then president of the country.

husband who's working, and we're not going around insulting anyone. How many times did we talk about getting together and having a meeting, but suddenly there wasn't any interest?

Elenir: Now Paula's had this idea that she's passed on to me, that we should get in contact with the union people to try and get some women together to pay a visit to Marta Suplicy, as a way of thanking her. Because she helped us a lot.

RV: *How did she help you?*

PL: She helped us with her presence, she gave us strength, she advised us.

Elenir: She passed on information, gave us ideas, as well. Marta was the one who was by our side when we came out of Ford and went to the Ministry of Finance. Often, when I was with my daughter, she would help me to carry her—she and her husband, Eduardo. I mean, for us it was very important. The fact that she was there by our side was very important. She made our movement bigger, her presence made it bigger. It was a way for us to grow. So Paula had this idea and I took the liberty of speaking to Paulão about it. He said he'd look into it, but it might take a bit of time because Marta had a full schedule. But I said, "Paula will talk to you about it later."

PL: Yes, I did, because Marta, as a woman, is very important to us; knowing that she is a woman gives you encouragement. A city like São Paulo, which I think is the biggest city in Latin America, with her elected mayor, it encourages you.

MCP: *Are you thinking of doing anything to support Marta's work?*

Elenir: Before she was elected mayor, Paula and I, we said to her, "Marta, if you need anything. . ."

PL: "Or anybody. . ."

Elenir: "You can count on us, we'll help you."

PL: If she needs our help, my God, I'll get help for her—I'll get people, I'll go after things, because we're always going after something. Here in São Bernardo, I know a lot of people, in my neighborhood I walk down the street and everybody knows me, because I do volunteer work for a football club, which has 613 needy children, you know? So, we do things in the neighborhood, we help people, we work in the slums—and so you end up knowing a lot of people. But the councilors and the mayor don't seem to know that we exist; we are excluded.

MCP: *It's amazing that, with all this potential, you almost seem to be on your own. Do you think that there are too many obstacles against you joining an institution, such as the union or the Mayor's Office?*

PL: Two years ago, more or less, I came here to the union and I spoke to some people. I said, "Hell, my husband is a worker and he always pays his dues, so don't I have rights too? Why can't I, as a woman, take his place?"

They said, "But you aren't a worker, he's the one that's working. If you were a worker, you could." And I was very sad about this, because I really wanted to be involved, to do something, to be with the women. Because I think it's great, you know, that women can participate by doing something or other. But it wasn't very well accepted, this idea of mine.

Elenir: I've been thinking—I've got the strength, the will to work, to participate, to help organize the movement, but at the same time. . . Nowadays the market requires qualifications, and I haven't got any. I'm trying to do something about it now, and, God willing, I'll do it because I'm still young, you know? I'm studying to achieve my big dream, which is to work, to have my rights as a woman, just like all the other working women. Because nowadays most people in the jobs market have got qualifications, and I haven't. I can't even speak well. That's what they tell me—and I think they are right, because I haven't had a proper education, you know?

MCP: *Do you think that people who use this justification are right?*

Elenir: No, they aren't, no.

PL: No, because there are other people here who haven't had a proper education either.

RV: *Like what we were saying about Lula, right?*

PL: Yes, exactly.

Elenir: No, they're not right about that, because lots of people haven't had a proper education. I've got a lot of will to work, to organize movements, to join in with the poor, get people together, to see if we can't change Brazil a bit, you know? At least, if I could get in, then I definitely could, a bit, and I'd give all I've got to achieve. . .

PL: We've achieved a lot of things.

Elenir: We did, we did. And I'm sure we could achieve a lot more.

PL: A lot more. My son was talking to me about those days. He saw the movement of the wives of the Military Police[34] on the television and he said to me, "Mum, did you see that? We've been a lesson to those people. Why do you think those women are out there in the streets, fighting for their husbands' salaries? It's because we did it here and lots of people saw it in the papers and magazines and on the television, and saw the women taking part in movements, and so we've been a lesson to them." And I said, "We have, son, we really have been a lesson to them." And I am proud that, after us, many other people have organized movements in other cities and other states. Because at the time people from other states began ringing us up, congratulating us and the movement, encouraging us, people from other unions, other states, and even foreigners.

---

34   In the state of Tocantins.

MCP: *What I see is that you only have room for action when there's a crisis* [*laughter*].

PL: That's true, we can only show up when there's some kind of crisis. And, God, what I really want is to be able to do something.

MCP: *You'll have to find yourself a niche some day, won't you?*

Elenir: Well, I've already tried. At the time of the elections in Santo André, I gave everything I could to help a friend, a councilor, who was elected there.

RV: *Did you take part in the campaign?*

Elenir: The whole campaign. I went out in the drizzle, at six in the morning; I left the house to join them in the streets, to organize. I'm well known in my neighborhood because I do a lot of agitating [*laughter*]. Whatever I can, I get going, I do a lot of agitating. And we took advantage of the elections, because we need a lot of things there. In that period I got to be well known for helping my region, and I helped a lot—I gave everything I could, went everywhere, got home late at night after leaving the kids on their own. I've tried to find a place for myself, but it hasn't worked out.

MCP: *And things like asking for health centers, schools, that type of thing—did you do that?*

Elenir: There we've got Participatory Budgeting.[35] We organize people to vote for the things we need most. I participate directly, directly. . . We needed a really big retaining wall there. My house is down below and there's a hill, like this, all of it is municipal land, and we built a retaining wall, all together. This was long before politics came into it. So I organized a nice deal for our candidate, didn't I? I was the one that organized it, for her. I put myself out for this. We have health centers that need improvements, and there are so many other things. And we're also campaigning for a station for our community, but it's difficult. Because it used to be a nice, quiet neighborhood, but now it's. . .

RV: *Is it a police station?*

Elenir: Yes, it's part of the Military Police. I believe that people have to fight to get things, but this isn't within the jurisdiction of the town council, so it can't be included in the Participatory Budget because it is a state matter, and the town council has to have a partnership with the police, so they have to talk it over. But I haven't stopped, you know—I'm still agitating. And there are people who still criticize me, you know?

PL: If one person doesn't start something, no one will follow. So you start, you participate, you start to do something, and suddenly someone's there trying to mess you about. That's how it is in my neighborhood, too.

---

35   A model for planning the municipal budget that allows for citizens' participation by region within the city. It was introduced by PT administrations, in particular the first PT administration in Porto Alegre, but has come to be adopted by other parties.

MCP: *You were saying that you were able to build the wall "before the politics started." Do you separate politics from these kinds of actions?*

Elenir: Politics actually helped, didn't it? Because this was the time of the "fat cows," as people say.

MCP: *But before politics, is there a space where you have more freedom, where people can. . . ?*

Elenir: Yes, you don't have party divisions at all, you know?

MCP: *Paula, have you also had the experience of working for an electoral campaign?*

PL: I voted PT, but I had to do work as a volunteer for a councilor from another party, because he had helped my neighborhood. We were asking for a hall, and he went there and helped and did a lot of things for us. So, I had to go over to him, to help; but my area isn't really for Maurício,[36] it's for Vicentinho. Even so, on the day of the elections, I went there and worked for him, because of all the work he'd done for us. He didn't get anything out of it—he didn't even ask for our votes; he just did it with such good will that I think it would have been unfair not to have supported him.

MCP: *What you're saying is that to gain some room for action, so that you can use all your experience, you have to take advantage of any opportunity, is that it?*

Elenir: Yes, you have to be flexible.

PL: You have to dance to the music. So, if this side offers you something, you get behind them. And then if the other side offers you something, you go over to them. But I'm loyal to one person only, you know? After that day when I regretted my vote. . . I'll never do it again. From now on I'm going to study things very carefully. It's no use people talking to me and putting things in my head. It has to be my ideas, my judgment.

RV: *It seems that you're much more aware now, aren't you? Do you feel that there is a difference, before and after the movement, in the way you look at life, at society, at politics?*

Elenir: You wouldn't believe it, but before all this the most difficult thing for me to do was to watch the news. Now I watch it all.

PL: I watch it all day long now.

Elenir: Now we're more aware of what's happening—we're always interested in things. Before, I wasn't at all.

PL: The newspapers, magazines, television—they're much more important nowadays for me. Knowing what's going on, in the country as well as in the city, in general, in the state—it's much more important to me nowadays. If I could, I'd be in every single one of those places.

MCP: *If I understand you correctly, the most important thing for you is actually to make people more aware—is that it? In other words, to make people understand*

---

36 The candidate for mayor representing President Fernando Henrique's party, the PSDB (Partido da Social Democracia Brasileira—Brazilian Social Democratic Party).

that they have something to do with the decisions of the president, with politics, with the union—to make them engage more with the world and not just with a political party?

PL: That's right. It's like with the children at school—I'm always in touch with my son's school; I'm often there talking about politics, about whom to choose, about what they think. So, it's making them aware of what's right and what's wrong, which path they should take. I'm always trying to make my son aware of what's right and what's wrong, so that he can explain in his classroom what's right and what's wrong. Because teenagers are the future of our country. And I'm always trying to make them aware; I would like to make the whole world aware, of everything, of what is good, what to do, how to fight, how to get involved. Not just by listening; if you just listen, you'll get nowhere. Staying at home doesn't get you anywhere, you have to get out into the streets. If you don't get out into the streets, if you just sit there waiting, then we'll just wait around for one another and there'll be nobody out on the day of the march. You have to keep on getting people involved: "Come on, let's do this." If I stay at home, that's just one more person at home. If I go out into the streets, it's one more person in the streets.

MCP: *Why do you think people don't go in for this? This blackout package, for example, is going to mess everyone up, isn't it? But people still don't take advantage of these opportunities. Why do you think this is?*

PL: People are quite resigned to the money they earn—it's a kind of conformity. Because I don't agree with a minimum salary of 180 and something reais.[37] A family of four, what are they going to do on a salary of 182 reais? Well, what are they going to do about it? I don't resign myself to it, no. We have to fight for better salaries, for everything—for no blackouts, for no corruption. People have to fight, have to go for it, protest.

Elenir: People are paying no attention to the things that have been happening—they're paying no attention and leaving. I think that something has to happen, like, well. . . I think that once there's really a blackout, they'll go out into the streets. Because it's like this: you're there; oh, ok, it's over, it's finished, "Let others go, I'll go next time," and this next time never comes. It isn't happening to you, because when it does happen to you, then you'll go out there. We were in our nice home, enjoying it, and then things happened to us and we had to go out and fight for our interests. People need motivation—they need someone to give them ideas, to clear their minds.

MCP: *And how can we do this? What needs to be done?*

---

37 In 2001, US$1 was equivalent to slightly more than 2.3 reais.

PL: You need to back the people who have the will to do something.

Elenir: You have to open people's minds, to get them out demanding their rights, because, I'm not educated, but I think that Fernando Henrique is only going to be there until people get out on the streets. Because when people get out on the streets, that's when he'll be out. He's only there because we put him there, right? If we want to change this country, we will. It's just that people are sitting about waiting for someone else to do it.

RV: *Were you on the March of the 100,000?*[38]

Elenir: We were.

PL: And we would go more often if there were more opportunities.

Elenir: The last time, we were planning to go, but with Ford working again, it wasn't possible. My husband couldn't go. But he does participate. Before the movement, he used to come to the union. Once we were having a barbecue at my neighbor's, and he said, "I'm going down to the union." They had a meeting with Lula. And I said, "You're not going to leave the barbeque to go to a union meeting?" And he said, "Of course I am!" He was always like that—he always took part. He's even got three holes in his leg, you know? They threw a bomb at him, in Minas.[39] That was frightening! He called me from there—it was on the TV—and he said, "Have you seen the news, love?" I said, "No." And he said, "Just as well, because you'd get a fright." He was in a wheelchair, at the hospital, covered in blood. It was nasty, what happened in Minas. But when he got better, he said that if they had to go again, they could count on him.

PL: I didn't go only because my husband wouldn't let me, but I wanted to go with Elenir.

Elenir: Yes, and I phoned Paulão—do you remember? I phoned Paulão and I said, "Paulão, what do you think about us going to Minas?" And he said, "If you want to go, fine, we won't stop you, but it's not going to be nice there." I still wanted to insist, but my husband said, "Oh no, not if he said it's going to be like that, because we can run for it, but I don't know about you." So I shut up about it, like Paula, but it made me want to go—it really did.

---

38   A demonstration against the policies of the government that took place in August 1999.

39   In the second half of 1999 the metalworker unions linked to the CUT and Força Sindical (Union Strength) federations organized a "Festival of Strikes," involving the six states where automobile and auto parts plants were located, under the banner of a national collective contract. In Betim, Minas Gerais, the stoppage was marked by conflicts with the police and the Fiat security forces. See Véras, "O Sindicalismo Metalúrgico, o 'Festival de Greves' e as Possibilidades do Contrato Coletivo Nacional," São Paulo, mimeo, 2001.

RV: *Did you start studying again because of your experiences, Elenir? Did that have an influence on you?*

Elenir: My God—it certainly did! It did! Because I hadn't cared about school at all. I used to say, "I was born to be a cleaner, really." I left school, I think, when I was fifteen. I did a bit of studying in Ceará, where I come from, and then I left for here. And I did work as a cleaner—I stuck to that, then got married, stayed at home and had children. And when I thought about studying, I thought, "A housewife, with children—no, it's impossible." But after all this, my little girl stays with my husband now. When he gets in, it's "I'm off now, bye!" And I only get back at eleven.

MCP: *Was it through him that you started to learn about the union?*

Elenir: Yes. I used to say, "Hell, what's the union got to do with your job?" I didn't even know what the union had to do with Ford, you know? "Don't you work for Ford?" "I do, but. . ."; "So why are you going to the union?"; "I'm a member and I have to participate"; "And if you don't, what happens?" I didn't understand it properly—I really didn't. I didn't know anything; I didn't even know what a union was for [*laughter*]. I soon found out.

PL: I even used to feel jealous when my husband went to some of the union meetings straight after work. I'd say, "Meeting, what meeting? You're up to something else!" I was jealous. Then afterwards, when I was part of the movement, I understood. So today, when I tell him, "Go on, dear, you can take a day off school, can't you?" he says, "No, I can't miss." Now it's I who want to go [*laughter*].

MCP: *So, for you this union became the headquarters for the fight, did it?*

PL: A symbol of the fight, even, for us. When I go past here on the bus and I see the name of the union up there, it makes me want to get off and go in and do something, or, I don't know, go in at least.

RV: *Do you ever try to find a pretext to come here?*

Elenir: Many times I spent long periods without coming here, because I'd be trying to think up a reason for coming. I tried to find a pretext to come in, just to come in.

PL: You know that you're in a really powerful place, don't you? Because so many decisions come out of here; it is the union and the union leaders that make the decisions that are so important for the factories—it's this, it's that. And all this business about having separate unions—I don't know how many thousand separate unions there are in Brazil. I think there should only be one union, one single union.

RV: *Are you following the debate about the creation of a CUT National Metalworkers Union?*[40]

---

40   A process that is still continuing.

PL: This proposal to have a national union is very important—it's going to be much better for metalworkers throughout the whole country.

Elenir: I think it would favor the big cities more, wouldn't it? Because the big companies leave here and go to other states in the interior, and so if there's a single union, they won't be able to do what they're doing now. Because it's one thing here and another thing there.

PL: In other states they offer less.

Elenir: And people there are desperate to earn a pittance. They take advantage of people who are really in need.

MCP: *You've had a long working life, haven't you?*

PL: God, yes! I've been working since I was a child, and we were hungry—we didn't have enough to eat; there were eight brothers and sisters. We were really desperate. I always talk about this from the bottom of my heart, about not having anything to eat in the house. I used to go to the butcher's to beg some bones, for stock, for the marrow, so that we could make a meal, so that we could eat.

Elenir: I remember, there's one thing I'll never forget, during the movement, for those who lived in rented houses, those who depended on the salaries to pay the rent, the food, everything—it was really hard. For us it wasn't so difficult; we don't rent, we've got our own house. But we asked everywhere for help, for basic food; we got it from the churches sometimes, wherever we could. It was a really hard time, and I couldn't explain to people what I was going through. Out in the country we were needy, but there you could fish, you could grow things, you could eat, there we always had some food, you see? And here it's so difficult, there's nowhere to get it from, and you can't ask for things. If you knock on someone's door to ask them for something, they'd shut it in your face. I remember that TV report that was live. The reporter asked me something and I. . .

PL: She didn't say anything.

Elenir: I was struck dumb for a few seconds. I didn't know what to say.

PL: Her husband managed to say something. The reporter asked her and she couldn't speak. I cried a lot at that time.

Elenir: He asked me what I thought about the situation, because it was a very important day for us, because we'd been out for days and days at the factory gates—and the factory kept saying, "No, no, no. . . " That was the day Ford retracted. Dear God, there was Marinho up there—it was a huge celebration. And it was so different for me; it seemed as if it hadn't been me that had taken part in all that, you know? Then, after the interview, after they turned off the lights, I just burst into tears! [*laughter*]

PL: She was crying in her house and I was crying in mine.

Elenir: It was a really difficult time. Every day Paula organized something, someone had one idea, someone else had another; we were doing all kinds of things.

PL: And that day when we linked arms—remember, Elenir?

Elenir: At that moment some of the staff were already trying to get into the factory.

PL: The staff wanted to get in, and I said, "No, we're not going to let them—let's link arms," and we did. Everyone got hold of someone else's arms, like this, like a human chain, made of women and children—we made this chain all round the factory gates, and everyone turned back, didn't they? And then the TV helicopter came down very low to find out what the commotion was, what was going on. They thought we were having a brawl. But we were just making a human chain to stop people from entering.

Elenir: Lula was there that day as well, and we started to cry.

PL: I even said to him, "Lula, I'm really sorry I didn't vote for you." I hugged him, in tears, and talked to him. I'd like to go on Saturday, but I don't know if I'll be able to get near to him because a lot of people are going to be there. But I would like to go up to him and ask him, "Lula, do you remember the Ford movement, when I gave you a hug and I was crying and asking you to forgive me, and saying I was sorry for not voting for you? Well, it was the only year I didn't vote for you—the only time. I was really stupid and I bitterly regret it." My God, I think he lost the election because of us.

Elenir: But I think our turn's coming. In 2002, we're going to get back all those lost votes.

PL: You bet—and this time I'm going all the way, I'm really going to fight. I'd like to be doing things, to be part of it, because I don't see myself as a housewife any more, not just a housewife.

Elenir: Would you believe that sometimes I'm just waiting for the phone to ring, for someone to ask me to join in something?

RV: *What was the March of the 100,000 like for you? What did you feel when you were there, at that moment?*

Elenir: What I thought was, "What if, instead of us, all the students in Brazil were here?" Because students have a different kind of mind.

PL: My God—just looking at each person that was there, that was in the movement, demanding something—people with little shacks. . .

RV: *What do you think they were calling for most? Why did 100,000 people suddenly gather there?*

Elenir: Look, this country's in chaos, total chaos. So the people that were there were the conscience of Brazil. It was a sign that not everything was lost. I think the biggest thing was salaries—so many things are wrong that you can't even explain them all; it's too much. Each one of them was looking for a little bit of. . .

PL: Yes, each one was looking for something.

Elenir: There are so many things—the country's healthcare system, which is really. . .

PL: Housing, healthcare, corruption—there's corruption in everything you see. I think that if people fought for things, if everyone got out there, if each person got ready to do their bit—damn it, we'd never have. . . We'd start by replacing the president, and getting rid of his mob, the lot of them. Why can't anyone see what they really are? Everyone knows, but people just go on doing stupid things like I did and vote him in again. I just know that if we could, each one of us, housewives or workers, manage to make our next-door neighbors more aware, then that would be two more people from each of us. I know I went there to demand the end of the IMF, an end to unemployment; I was there, God knows, to demand anything I could. That day it was so good to see everyone calling for something, there were even people there with shacks on their backs. They'd made these little wooden shacks and they were carrying them on their backs, asking for proper housing. And nowadays people have no houses, no healthcare, nothing, in this country. If they don't get rid of all this robbery, all this corruption that's going on. . . I don't think just getting rid of the president will do it. We have to get rid of the whole group that's in there, in command. I'd say that if Lula gets in, he can't do anything on his own—he can't do very much. We have to get rid of the whole mob, right?

Paula's trajectory, as the interview suggests, is striking for what it reveals of both the potentialities and the limitations that exist within unionism and the political environment of the ABC Metalworkers Union, the CUT, the PT, popular movements, and feminist organizations, particularly in the region where she lives.

Her trajectory in the movement of the 2,800 dismissed workers developed rapidly. Paula and some of her companions were abruptly lifted out of the anonymity of a strictly private life, totally alien to the world of politics, into instant media exposure, gaining a place in the public arena and becoming deeply involved in politics. They were thus introduced to a tradition and an area of experience that is a central point of reference and engagement for the ABC Metalworkers Union, but which extends much further than this into other sectors of society and into party politics. The movement was influenced by this political field, and established itself in the social and political scene of the country in opposition to the paths adopted by the hegemonic forces, disputing their directions (the movement claimed unemployment as a public issue) and questioning their rationality (the movement claimed that politics was the decision-making arena par excellence). Paula shared in this experience, both affecting it and being affected by it.

Different conditions took shape in the period that followed. At the end of the month-and-a-half in which the movement had been active, the situation returned, to a certain extent, to normal. The workers who had not been included in the redundancy lists, as well as those reinstated, returned to work and to their daily concerns. The workers on suspended contracts (some remained on these for around 15 months) lived under special circumstances, receiving almost their entire salary, but without working. Those who had accepted one of the innumerable voluntary redundancy programs began a new phase in their lives, usually condemned to further insecurity and instability. The activists and union leaders returned to their daily routines, according to the positions and the responsibilities they held. And what became of women such as Paula and Elenir who, as the wives of workers threatened with redundancy, had become fully involved in the movement? As the interview shows, they were left with a feeling of restlessness. They could find no spaces where they could use their energies and fulfill their desire to campaign, to participate, to remain involved. The obstacles proved formidable. It seems that the institutional consolidation of entities such as the unions, the political parties, and other popular organizations led (as in the 1970s and '80s) to the shutting off of channels for direct participation, other than in exceptional circumstances such as the movement described here. The persistence of Paula and Elenir, however, is impressive. Against the avalanche of the neoliberal technocratic argument, and in clear contrast to the institutional crystallization of the social movements, their attitude is simple, determined and unflinching: "We want to participate."

3

Pedro Inácio Pinheiro Ngematücü

Indigenous person belonging to the Tikunas of the Amazon, leader of the indigenous movement.

Interviewed by Fábio Vaz Ribeiro and Lino João Neves

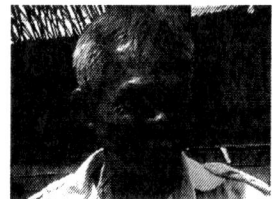

"We didn't come from another land, we didn't come from another planet, we came from right here. Our god was from right here. The god of the white man is different, and maybe comes from a different place. Now our land is in the hands of our god, who is Yoi."

Pedro Inácio Pinheiro Ngematücü

The Tikuna Indians, the original inhabitants of the Upper Solimões River, have a long history of contact with different agents who, at various historical moments, imposed their presence in the frontier region that Brazil shares with Peru and Colombia.[1]

Having suffered the repercussions of the contact initially established by religious missionaries, the groups that occupied the great river's shore were profoundly touched by the violence of the extractive system, whose power of life and death over the native populations was scarcely affected by the protectionist actions of the Brazilian state, which, from the beginning of the 1940s, installed bases in the Upper Solimões. At the end of the 1970s and the beginning of the 1980s, the establishment of seven indigenous outposts in Tikuna villages limited the power of the regional commercial interests, interrupting the cultural massacre and progressive abandonment of customs to which all of the ethnic groups had been subjected. In the 1980s, the need to form a representative body with base support in order to negotiate the regulation of the land with the State resulted in the organization of the group, through its most representative leaders, and intensified the struggle for the recognition of a territory that might correspond to the communities' needs for subsistence as well as protecting their sacred sites.

This struggle led to new forms of organization, giving rise to the General Council of the Tikuna Tribe (CGTT—Conselho Geral da Tribo Tikuna) and causing the emergence of new roles determined especially by the need for articulation between the villages and for the coordination of common action for the defense of ethnic interests. The creation of the CGTT, which was constituted as an authority above the clan divisions that mark Tikuna society, was the result of meetings that succeeded in overcoming political and religious factionalism.

Pedro Inácio Pinheiro, fifty-six years old and known among his people as Ngematücü (a name that in the Tikuna language indicates his affiliation with the Onça [jaguar] clan), was born in a village along the São Jerônimo tributary, near

---

1   These introductory paragraphs are taken in part from Fábio Vaz Ribeiro de Almeida and Regina Maria Carvalho Erthal, "Breve Nota sobre a História do Movimento Indígena no alto Solimões," Manaus, Rio de Janeiro, 2001.

the border between Brazil and Colombia, in the heart of Évare, a mythic area where Yoi, the hero-creator of the world, fished for the Magüta ("the people fished from the river"), the self-denomination of the ethnic group designated by Brazilian indigenous ethnology as the Tikuna.

With the death of his mother, Pedro Inácio, while still a small boy, was taken by a regional businessman to live away from his community. With the passage of time, Pedro Inácio was able to discern the dishonest and harmful manner in which the rubber plantation owners, the owners of both the lives and the labor of the Indians, exploited his people. At the same time that he became acquainted with "non-Indian things," just as he already knew "the nature of the Ticuna people," Pedro Inácio was becoming conscious of the suffering experienced by his relatives. Refusing to allow the ease and comforts of that time in his life with the regional population to influence his manner of viewing the world, Pedro Inácio took up again the Magüta way of life, later entering into the struggle for the defense of indigenous rights.

At the forefront of the CGTT, Pedro Inácio Pinheiro (Ngematücü) played a fundamental role in the transformation of the scene of subordination and dependence to which the Tikuna people had been subjected in the recent past. For leading a long struggle against constant territorial invasions, and principally for the demarcation of the Tikuna lands, Pedro Inácio is, without a doubt, one of the most significant and steadfast leaders in the recent history of the indigenous movement in Brazil.

The interview was recorded at Filadélfia Village and the Magüta Center, Benjamin Constant Municipality, State of Amazonas, Brazil.

Fábio Vaz Ribeiro de Almeida: *Pedro, what is your name and your age, and where were you born?*

Pedro Inácio Pinheiro: Well, I am Pedro Inácio Pinheiro, known among our people as Ngematücü, because I'm from the jaguar clan. Today, in the year of 2001, I am fifty-six years old. I was born in 1944 at the *igarapé*[2] São Jerônimo, in the Évare I area.[3] Now I'm here to do. . . to finish some things that still have to be done in our documentation.

FVRA: *Pedro, I know that many of the Tikuna call you "Pocu," which is the Tikuna word for the* pirapitinga fish.[4] *Why do they call you that?*

PIP: Back in the *igarapé* São Jerônimo, when my mother was still alive, my father had gone fishing. When I was a child I would always cry to go with my father, until he took me in his canoe. But I don't remember any

---

2 *Igarapé*: brook, creek.
3 According to their mythical stories, the Tikuna originated from the *igarapé* Évare, located near the source of the *igarapé* São Jerônimo, which is in turn a left-bank tributary of the Upper Solimões River, in the area presently recognized by the Brazilian state as Indigenous Territory Évare I. Indigenous Territory: area of land occupied by an indigenous population in accordance with current Brazilian legislation.
4 *Piaractus brachypomus Cuvier*: an Amazonian fish, light gray in color, very similar to the *tambaqui*.

of this—it was my aunt that told me. So my father took me fishing in the *igarapé*. When the sun was beating down hot, I cried and cried until I fell asleep on the bottom of the canoe, I lay down there. So he gave me a black shirt. He took off his shirt and covered me with it and put some leaves over the top, and then came back after 12 hours. He came back, arrived at the harbor. Then my aunt said, "Ah! my brother's back! My brother's back—he's at the harbor! He's caught a *pirapitinga*. It's there on the bottom of the canoe!" But he had already taken out what he'd managed to catch. So, my aunt came down and took away the leaves, and it was me there, lying down. When she got home, she said, "Ah! I thought it was a *pirapitinga*, but when I got there, I saw it was him lying on the bottom of the canoe, it was him." Since then, they've called me *pirapintinga*, because of that.

FVRA: *Before you tell me about how the CGTT[5] emerged and about the Tikuna struggle, we'd like you to talk a bit about how you learned about the white man's stuff.[6]*

PIP: Well, at the time, this was in 1950, I was alone, at the *igarapé* São Jerônimo—you see, my mother had died. In the boss'[7] day, a long time ago, at that time, the boss took me from the *igarapé* and took me to his house. It was for a long time, right—a long time I lived there. I wasn't used to it; so I'd run away home and they'd come after me again, until I got used to it. For a year, two years, I got used to living in my boss's house. So then, for two years, three years, I learned the white man's customs. So, when I was two, three, four, until five years of age. . . no, not of age, I mean, I was ten there. For five years I lived there like the white people lived, and I got used to it. So, during those five, six years of living with the whites, I knew white men's stuff as well as I knew the stuff, the nature, of the Tikuna people. Well, during the time I was there, in the boss's house, I saw a lot of Tikuna from my family—not only from my family, different Tikuna families—that the boss was exploiting, he was exploiting the Tikuna at that time. He took the Tikuna products, things they had brought for the boss to sell, things like rubber, sorb, animal skins, meat;[8] and the boss got rich on those products. He would also tell the Tikuna to pay what they owed him and so he became richer.

---

5 CGTT (General Council of the Tikuna Tribe): a political organization set up in the 1980s to represent the interests of the Tikuna people.

6 White man or white ("branco" in Portuguese) a term used in the region to refer to anyone who is not Indian.

7 Boss ("patraõ" in Portuguese): a regional merch who, even today, controls the trade products extracted from nature.

8 Products: the result of the work of extraction. Rubber: natural coagulated latex; sorb: elastic gum extracted from the rowan tree; skins from wild animals; meat from wild animals, usually salted, which is still today one of the staple foods of the region.

So, at that time, I saw how my people suffered. Then some time later. . .
after the '70s . . . in '69, I had to get away from the boss. By that time I
was with my wife. My father and my family came and got me from the
boss's house and took me back to my father's house. Between '69 and
'70 I left the Évare I area. From Évare, I went to Colombia, to Letícia.[9]

FVRA: *How long did you live in Letícia?*

PIP: I lived in Letícia for two years. During those two years. . . it was
in '72, when the Religion of the Cross[10] arrived. It was in '72 when
Brother José passed by there in Vendaval.[11] At that time, my wife's
uncle came there to Colombia, where we lived, and said that the
messiah had come, the father, Yoi,[12] and told stories, many things.
We thought: "Who could this be? What has happened?" And we
went along to see what was happening. So we went to Vendaval.
When we got to the Vendaval community, when we got there—
today, it is being built—only bits were marked out, because it was
one of the boss's cattle pastures at that time. The boss had got the
cross and planted it, right? And he stayed with the people, to soften
them up, make them work for him. So when we arrived, that was in
'72, almost at the end of the year, we stayed almost the whole year
of '72 and '73. "So what's happening? Is it really religion?" Then we
went down there, to talk to Brother José, to find out what it's all
about. So we took off from there in our canoes, paddling—no one
had an engine in those days[13] like they have today, so we paddled
along. And we went to find Brother José, in New Italy, in the Tikuna
community, by the Amaturá *igarapé*.[14] We found him; we talked to
him, and more or less took to Brother José's reality. And then we
went back. When we got back, we made a house there in Vendaval
because our folk were in Colombia, and no one had a house. We
lived nearby, near Gracila's father.[15] So, the time went on. From
'75 onwards, I saw how the Tikuna continued to be exploited. So,
I [thought], What is happening to the Tikuna people? It was already

---

9 Colombian city on the banks of the Solimões River, on the border with Brazil.
10 The Santa Cruz (Holy Cross) religious movement established itself in the region
from the end of the 1970s. Led by a white man, Brother José, the movement used
Christian biblical figures to instill strict norms of conduct, including the use of clothing, weddings, worship, food, and so on. The Santa Cruz brotherhood spread rapidly,
creating various communities of indigenous followers from different ethnic groups along
the Solimões. After the death of its founder, the "Religion of the Cross" gradually lost
strength, although there are still communities today that continue its religious practices.
11 Tikuna village located in the municipality of São Paulo de Olivença.
12 Mythical hero, creator of the Tikuna people.
13 A small engine used to propel canoes.
14 Tikuna community, located on the *igarapé* Amaturá, in the Upper Solimões.
15 Gracila Pinheiro, wife of Pedro Inácio.

a community at that time. So we set off with ten people, paddling, until we got to the Umariaçu community.[16]

FVRA: *Who was leading the Tikuna at that time?*

PIP: At that time the captain[17] here in Umariaçu was Paulo Cruz.[18] We went to him. He told us the story, why he was captain of the community, what the community was like, what was its reality. He told us the story of the Tikuna people. And I told him everything that was happening. So, at that time, when I was there, he said, "Listen, do this, this, and this. . ." The law that was in force then in the Constitution, the "indigenous people's law," was called "Indian Statute Legislation" at the time.[19] So I based myself on that. So when I got back to Vendaval, then I said no. Today, if there is a community. . . . So, at that time, the people chose me, put me at the front of them. So at that time I was made captain of the community. I explained to the boss, saying: "Listen, now that time has passed when you told us what to do, sent us to work; now we go to work only if we want to. We don't have a boss any more. We are free now. We work if we want to. We're going to sell our stuff, but to other people as well, not just to you. Because the land is going to be the Tikuna's." He got really mad. He wanted to hit me, send me to the army.[20] He wanted to ask the army to arrest me, you know? Get me and send me to jail—because he used to do that. So I said that I wasn't afraid, no. Because I hadn't killed anyone, so I wasn't a criminal. Now, they are the criminals, aren't they? I kept on talking to them like that. Then he said, "But you were brought up here in my house—you are like a son to us, I don't know how. . ." So I said, "You said that I'm a son to you.

---

16 Tikuna community located in the municipality of Tabatinga, on the Brazil-Colombia border.

17 Pedro Inácio refers to the "Indian Statute" (Law no. 6001, of December 19, 1973), which regulates the indigenous rights defined in the old Federal Constitution of 1967, drawn up by the government of the military dictatorship that ruled Brazil from 1964 to 1981. This was replaced by the new Constitution of 1988, but the "Indian Statute" is still the legal mechanism that regulates the state's relations with the indigenous peoples of Brazil.

18 Former Tikuna leader, also known as Paulo Canhão, who moved away from the indigenous movement and today works for the National Indian Foundation (FUNAI), the organ for indigenous action that succeeded the SPI.

19 Captain: chief, leader. Term adopted in the wake of the military influence of the Indian Protection Service (SPI), a protective body set up by the Brazilian state with a strongly military character, which was established in the Upper Solimões in 1942. Tikuna society, which was traditionally very divided, has never had a centralized leadership; the authority of political leaders is generally restricted to villages formed on the basis of close kinship.

20 Throughout the region of Brazil's three-way border with Peru and Colombia, the Army historically played a strong role in policing and social control, often allied to local political and economic interests. In this instance, Pedro Inácio is referring to the military mase at Tabatinga.

But talking like this about having me arrested, I don't think you are my father, and I am not your son. I'm independent of you. If I was arrested, you would arrest all my people too, because the Tikuna are with me." Then he got furious. He went to Tabatinga. But he didn't get anything in Tabatinga, so he went to Manaus,[21] to get the law. Then he came back. He hadn't managed to get the law at all. Until today, we don't know what happened to him. He decided to sell his boat—he sold everything he had left. And that was it! So, at that time, when he was away traveling, the Tikuna broke into his warehouse[22] and we threw everything out. Then he couldn't find his house anymore. So he got even more furious. He went off again to find out about his rights. But he never did. While he was doing this, the people, the rest of the Tikuna, when they saw that I was doing them a favor and getting rid of the boss, they made me their chief—I mean, their captain. So I stayed like that. Then, someone from Campo Alegre[23] came to ask me how I was doing things. I told the whole story: "Because Solimões, all this that we have is ours. Because the white man came from outside. Today . . . the land, he stole it from us. Now we have to get our land back and get it back for ourselves. Send the whites away!" The people from Campo Alegre and Belém do Solimões[24] had a boss at that time. So we decided to have a meeting. We had the meeting in Vendaval itself.

FVRA: *Why did you hold that meeting?*

PIP: We had it to choose the new captain of our Tikuna people. That was the first step for this experiment in a small area. It was Pedro Severiano,[25] at that time. We did the same in Vendaval. So it happened like that. That was my struggle in '78 and '79. At that time the meeting was held with the whole people to sort out the question of the land. I had remembered that there were people in other places too, like in the South. I told the Tikuna about other people. Because the Tikuna didn't know that other people existed. They thought there were only the Karajá,[26] that Indian people. I said that they were fighting too. And so, in '80, there was an

---

21   State capital of Amazonas, the political center of the Brazilian Western Amazon.
22   Warehouses are generally located at the headquarters of the rubber plantations, from where the tools and merchandise used for the extraction of rubber were distributed and the products of extraction collected.
23   Tikuna community in the municipality of São Paulo de Olivença, founded by American Baptist preachers.
24   Tikuna community located in the municipality of Tabatinga. This is the most populous Tikuna community, with around 4,000 inhabitants, where there is a Catholic parish and a large number of followers of the Santa Cruz faith.
25   Tikuna leader connected to the Santa Cruz movement, who was very important at the beginning of the struggle.
26   Karajá: an indigenous people whose lands are located on the Island of Bananal, in Central Brazil.

invitation, that there was going to be the first—or the second, I can't remember which—National Meeting of the Indigenous Peoples, in São Paulo do Sul.[27] At that time, as I said, Paulo Mendes[28]—he is from here, a relative of Paulo Cruz—he saw that I was fighting with my people, there in Vendaval; he heard the news that had got around everywhere. So he found out who took part in the general assembly of the indigenous peoples, in São Paulo, and he came to me to ask me if I would go to that assembly that was taking place there. At that time, I didn't know anything about it, but I accepted, and I went. I went there.

FVRA: *And what happened at that meeting in São Paulo?*

PIP: So there I got more experience about what the folk had been talking about, about peoples from all over Brazil. I got more experience. I also told my story to various leaders that were there at that time. The strongest leader I met was Domingo Veríssimo, of the Terena[29] people. I met some others who are dead now. There, they told the story, how it is. So I got more experience down there from those people. So, when I got back from that assembly, I told my people everything. So we saw how we could do it, more or less. At that assembly I met João Pacheco.[30] He was young at the time. He was working and writing. There he met with me and such. He gave us his address and told us that he could help us in any way, whenever we needed anything. He wanted to help in something, in a project, in anything that he could do, in an assembly or something. So, some time later, we thought about it, when we were back here. I told the folk. We had a meeting ourselves. No one knew what a project was. No one even knew what the word meant. So the folk got together. We brought family, all kinds of food. We got together just like that. We used our own resources to hold our first assembly[31] in Vendaval—that was in '83, '84. There I told the whole story, the other peoples' struggles, and how we had to struggle. Then I spoke to the people: "How can we

---

27   Pedro Inácio is referring to the First Assembly of Indigenous Peoples, held in the city of São Paulo, in the southeast of Brazil. The reference to "São Paulo do Sul" distinguishes it from São Paulo de Olivença, a municipality in the Upper Solimões, frequently mentioned in the region as simply São Paulo.

28   One of the most important Tikuna leaders. Today he works for FUNAI as head of the Indigenous Center at Vendaval.

29   Terena: indigenous inhabitants of the lowlands of Mato Grosso. Domingos Veríssimo, a former Terena leader, was one of the creators of the Union of Indigenous Nations (UNI), the first indigenous organization in Brazil.

30   João Pacheco de Oliveira Filho, an anthropologist from the National Museum/Federal University of Rio de Janeiro, who has studied the Tikuna since the 1970s, making them the theme of his masters and doctorate. Since that time he has accompanied the struggle of this people as their main consultant in the areas of anthropology and indigenous policy.

31   Pedro Inácio made a mistake here. The First Assembly of the Tikuna People was held in 1980 in the community of Campo Alegre.

get our land back that the boss took control of and that the boss is saying now is his? That land that he says is his, he has nothing to do with. The land is ours! He stole our land. He says he has a rubber plantation on that land—he says he has goodness knows what, on that land of his. But he didn't plant anything. It is not his land! We have rights because the Brazil nut plantation that he has there, the rubber trees, everything else that's there, they belong to nature herself.[32] And the boss came and took charge of it all, he killed all our people, our leaders, our old folk and grandparents died, and he took charge, and we were afraid, so he took over. But now we are coming back, to see if we can get our land back." I told them that story. Everyone was listening, all enthusiastic and such. "Come on, how are we going to do it?" At that time, this small assembly had only ten leaders. At that time, there were only a few people that understood. There, we managed to get more people involved, supporting us. Because at that time we'd only got the folk of the CIMI[33] with us. The person who was working with us was Silvio Cavuscens.[34] So he gave us a better idea of what it was like. So we did it with small projects. He sent us all over the place. They got the project approved for us to hold another assembly, with more people. And so it was like that that we got on with the struggle, slowly. We managed, little by little, to get the whole of the people to meet up. So that was what happened at that time.

FVRA: *So you set up the CGTT at that time?*

PIP: No—not then, no! That was in '72, '73. The CGTT was set up in '78, or around then. I don't know how to explain this to you. In our heads, we created it, but on paper it still didn't exist. For the people of the communities it existed. But that stuff, getting it down on paper, making a document—that, no. It was not the CGTT at that time.[35] It was all

---

32   Rubber and Brazil nuts are the main products of the extraction industry, which were always the object of disputes between bosses and Indians. The idea that the nut and rubber plantations and everything else are "of nature herself" may be opposed to the cultivated rubber plantations, which were state-financed from the mid 1970s, as a way for the federal authorities and regional traders to bolster the sagging rubber production system.

33   CIMI: Indigenous Missionary Council, a body of the Catholic Church that provides community support, counseling, consultancy, and other services for the indigenous peoples of Brazil.

34   A volunteer for Operation Anchieta (OPAN), an indigenous body that worked with the Tikuna from the late 1970s to the early 1990s.

35   In 1986 the Tikuna, together with researchers from the National Museum, set up the Magüta Documentation and Research Center of the Upper Solimões, to provide support for the indigenous movement. Despite their lack of independent legal status until 1997, the CGTT oversaw the Center and defined its policies, establishing partnerships and generating projects in the areas of education, healthcare and development. Within a project for the gradual implantation of an entirely indigenous directorate, in 1990 a new directorate was elected, mostly indigenous, also headed by Pedro Inácio Pinheiro.

down on paper back at home. So then, we had to do a mini-project to buy petrol, food, to invite the rest of the people, to hold that assembly. That was when we contacted João Pacheco. He joined in. He picked up that project and sent it to. . . I don't know the name of the place where he sent it. But they approved the money and we could hold our assembly.[36] We got together twenty more captains. That was in Campo Alegre. There in Campo Alegre, we discussed the problem of the land with all the other captains, to see how we could do the drawing.[37] "Each chief has to make a drawing of how the area should be." And after that meeting where the people discussed the land, it was then that they chose the captain-general for the whole people.[38] At that time, the people always chose me, so it always had to be me. So I kept moving up for that work.

FVRA: *Why did they choose you?*

PIP: I believe that they think that I am interested in winning rights for my people. So, they thought that there was no point in someone else having a turn. Well, they'd get a turn to talk about other things. But to get back our rights, to take the news further—for that they thought I was one of those people who's got more; for them, they think that I know people from farther away, I've got better contacts. So they made me their representative. So when there were those projects, meetings to hold, I invited all the other folk. I held the meetings like that. That's why they chose me to be their captain-general. So, after I was chosen, we discussed what was going to happen. I had already made the map that looked like this.[39] I had already done that. So, some of the other leaders also made maps, and in our meeting they presented them in order to decide which would be the definitive one. So we voted, and it was decided to have it like this, like it is on the map.[40] And so that's how it was. So, we had that assembly,[41] and in the third assembly we went back again to Vendaval.[42] Another assembly—this was in '82—we held it in Vendaval to invite other Tikuna from Colombia and Peru. That was to get more experience about how they are there and how they are here. To see if we could get more support, we invited João Pacheco again, and people that we knew. And so the struggle went on, and goes on today, until now. If we told

---

36   Second Assembly of the Tikuna People, held in 1982, in the community of Vendaval. Pedro Inácio once again made a mistake as to the location of this assembly.

37   A sketch map marking the area claimed as Tikuna territory, to be sent to FUNAI.

38   The CGTT, which was constituted in order to be above the clan divisions that characterize Tikuna society, resulted from meetings that succeeded in overcoming political and religious factionalism.

39   Those Tikuna areas currently recognized by the state as "indigenous territories."

40   The map represented the Tikuna areas recognized by the state as "indigenous territories."

41   The Second Assembly, held at Campo Alegre.

42   Third Assembly of the Tikuna people, held in 1983, in the community of Vendaval.

the story from the beginning of my struggle, we wouldn't get through it in an hour, two hours, not in two weeks, not in two months, not two years. That's why I've told you just a bit of each, so that you know and remember that this is not a joke. Because there were lots of other leaders at that time when we were fighting—some of them are dead now, others have given up, they couldn't keep going on that path. So the only person that kept it up was me; I've been going since the beginning of the struggle, when we set up the CGTT with the folk from Peru and Colombia, and gave it the name it has now.

FVRA: *At that time, you had a problem with the bosses. So you went to get help from FUNAI,[43] from the church, from OPAN and CIMI. That was the first step. But then, what other problems did you have? After you'd got rid of the boss, was it easy to get your land back?*

PIP: No, it wasn't easy getting the land. I mean, there was no violence, but it wasn't easy. The problem was that we had a lot of obstacles in the middle, and lots of people tried to trick us: the boss, the mayor—other authorities from the community and from the municipality. So people started to say that I was crazy, that I was doing it because I was crazy: "Only folk that don't have a good memory do things out of the blue, without any right"; "Pedro's going to die on the road and he's tricked you, you shouldn't go after him because he's half crazy, he doesn't know what he's doing . . ." So my suffering was always that. So, while all that was happening, we continued to struggle, explaining that with time . . . But in the middle of all that, the Tikuna themselves got together and threw the whites out of the area, the boss, who was the owner of the property in Ribeiro, and the boss of Cajari.[44] Then those two communities got together with a hundred people on the boat and went in and knocked down all the houses and sent everyone away. Then, the worst was that some that spoke of the boss, even the chief, even the same folk from the communities, said that I was crazy, that I could die at any moment—be arrested, I don't know what, because I was doing things I shouldn't be doing, because I was going against the law; and the ones that talked the most were the religious folk.[45] I always said, "No! I know religion, I'm religious too, but when it's the hour of need, of struggling for rights, I don't want to hear any more about religion! What I want is for my people to live—for the boss to stop ordering us about! It's the people themselves that are going to be in command of our land, not the

---

43   See note 18.
44   Ribeiro and Cajari are two Tikuna communities near Vendaval. The former is part of the Indigenous Territory Évare II, the municipality of São Paulo de Olivença, the latter of the Indgenous Territory Évare I, in Tabatinga.
45   The Tikuna connected to the Santa Cruz movement.

boss." I always spoke like that. So there was suffering; we had to get over obstacles in our struggle.

FVRA: *Then, you wanted to regularize that land at FUNAI. How did that happen?*

PIP: Exactly. We went to FUNAI. The problem is that FUNAI always makes out that it doesn't have any money—that it can't do anything on the spot, that it has to get funds. It always happens, even today, I think. FUNAI began to say it had no money. Even so, we kept on struggling. We had to struggle more and more with our own community, until we managed to get some time, and traveled to Brasília;[46] and after that we set up our own organization, the CGTT. The people said that at least five chiefs should go to Brasília to talk to the president of FUNAI, because FUNAI here had not sorted out anything. Anyway, we took the map we had made to the president. And so we went. That was in '80-something. It was when Paulo Moreira Leal was the president of FUNAI.

FVRA: *Where did you get the money for the trip?*

PIP: The money for this trip was given by the church, by OPAN and CIMI, which made a contribution for the journey. So, we began the struggle like that. We went to FUNAI in Brasília, and had a meeting with them to discuss the matter—and of course, at that time, we didn't know much, did we? How should we do it? Who should we talk to? We talked to João Pacheco on the telephone about what we should do. Based on what he said, we did something. Until we found we weren't getting anywhere, so he phoned the president of FUNAI, who said he'd sort it out. He'd send his team over to see the area, see how it was, see if it would stay like that, like it was, and do a survey of the area[47]—to do that map in the way it should be, to be properly legal,[48] like we explained. After a while they came, but they didn't say that they were arriving at that moment, and they came as if they were just passing through. They went into the municipality, with the boss, but they didn't talk to anyone; they passed through São Paulo, Benjamin, but didn't speak to anyone. It was only after they came back[49] that we saw other documents saying that FUNAI, the people from the region themselves, the whites saying, "Oh!

---

46   The federal capital of Brazil, situated in the central region of the country, where the main office of FUNAI is located.

47   The first phase of the process of regularization of the indigenous territories involves a series of ethnographic and agrarian surveys, undertaken by a technical team generally consisting of anthropologists, specialists in indigenous cultures, agricultural technicians, and surveyors.

48   If it satisfies the demands of the indigenous population, and is in accordance with the rights of the whites that have vested interests in those lands.

49   As a result of Tikuna mobilization, a team from FUNAI was sent to the area during January and February 1982 to select areas for future demarcation.

because Pedro Inácio, who's famous, is running in Brasília, I don't know what. Today, he wants to get the land back off the whites, now they want to give all the lands to the Tikuna." So they [the Tikuna] began turning against me, at that time. Then I said, "No, I'm against those who are taking the land from us. I'm on the side of our people. If you say I'm wrong, come and see later, in ten, twenty years' time—you'll see that it'll work out well for you." I don't know if everyone understood, at that time, when I was in the struggle. And so I stayed to get in touch with the others, with João Pacheco, other people that gave me support. That was how we struggled.

FVRA: *When you asked FUNAI for land, why did you think that they would have to "give" the land to the Tikuna? Was it because the Tikuna had the right under the "white man's law," or was it because the Tikuna had always lived there and had their own customs? Why did you say that you had to have the land, that the land belonged to the Tikuna, and had to be regularized?*

PIP: Because I had seen that the Constitution, the Indian Statute, said that it was the Indians that lived in this land—Brazil, as it is called today—which was not the land of Brazilians, as whites are called, right? So we based ourselves on that, and we understood that the land was ours because we hadn't come from other lands. We didn't come from another land, we didn't come from another planet—we came from right here. Our god was from right here. The god of the white man is different and maybe comes from a different place. Now our land is in the hands of our god, who is Yoi. So that's why when the bosses came here, the whites, like robbers, stole the land of the Tikuna. So, now we want it back. But the boss says that we don't have rights over the land: it is he who has the rights. So, based on the law that told that story. . . "Look here, we are going to fight to see if we can do it today!" As it says that we do have a right, because the land is ours. Since they'd taken our land, at least we have the right to some little portions of it. That's how we found out the land was ours. For we're not on other people's lands; we're on our own. That was how we saw it. That was why we asked FUNAI that our land be recognized by the proper authorities—on the other side too, we talked to the authorities, saying that the Tikuna people was the Tikuna people, when they were saying that the people didn't exist any more. "The Tikuna don't exist, they have died out, all gone. . ." They said we weren't Indian any more—we wore clothes and watches, spoke Portuguese, cut our hair. So we said, "But we have our own language, our clan—we have our own god." So it was like that. We sorted it out, that we had rights like any other citizen.

Lino João de Oliveira Neves: *So, what happened when you*[50] *got there, to see the president of FUNAI?*

PIP: The president of FUNAI was Paulo.[51] We told him that we had had that Tikuna land for a very long time, that we are natives, that we didn't come from outside. We started to tell the story to the president of FUNAI. We said that there was our so-called boss in the region, who said he owned the land. So, at that time we also told him that we were asking for land, for the Tikuna, and that it wasn't for just a few Tikuna—there were 18,000 of us at the time. He said that what would happen was that he had to send his people to do a survey of the area and study the area, get to know it, and do some research first. So he promised that—I mean, he agreed that it was good to do that. Meanwhile, the other areas of other peoples[52] had the same problems, didn't they? So he was going to send these persons from the study group to the Tikuna area. So, at the same time that we received this message from the president of FUNAI, he told us to go back, to have a meeting with the Tikuna people and tell them that they would come and study the area. So, we left Brasília. And when we got back, we held a meeting. We always have meetings to explain everything to the folk, and to let them know what we've managed, what we've done. So we stayed waiting for the date they'd booked. Some people, instead of looking for us, went to the whites from the town—they didn't look for us, they went to FUNAI itself, people from the town council. And it was like that: they came and did the study without consulting us. But they did it the same, based on the map that we had left with him,[53] and they did their study. After the study, they came back. And again, later, at another time, they did the study and sent us a letter saying that it was all right, all legal, saying when the president of FUNAI was going to call the representatives of the Tikuna and people from Manaus,[54] to let them know about the demarcation[55] of the lands, how it would be. As for this, he sent a message here a long time after. When the invitation came, I was doing other work, and when people heard about it, someone from Tabatinga went to

---

50   The Tikuna representatives who went to Brasilia to request recognition of their lands.

51   Paulo Moreira Leal, who was president of FUNAI between 1981 and 1983.

52   Pedro Inácio refers to the situation of the other indigenous peoples of Brazil, who generally face problems similar to those experienced by the Tikuna.

53   The map that the Tikuna representatives took to Brasília to present to the president of FUNAI.

54   Staff of the regional administration of FUNAI-Manaus.

55   The recognition of the indigenous territories by the Brazilian state is a long process involving five distinct phases: identification; delimitation; demarcation; legal ratification; agrarian regularization. The process of official recognition of the indigenous territories is commonly called simply "demarcation."

Vendaval, where I live, to tell me that the president of FUNAI had sent for me for the meeting.

Meanwhile, the president of FUNAI was in Manaus having a meeting with the people of Rio Negro, with the Sateré-Maué[56] and the others from Amazonas. He was asked what would happen to the Tikuna lands. All of a sudden, without knowing what was happening. . . So he sent someone to my home, [saying] that I was to get ready to go to Manaus, to talk to the president of FUNAI about the land. But there was no one there, in the morning, at ten o'clock—everyone was working except me; only my wife and me were at home. I needed two people. "And now?" There was no one else, there was no more time, only half an hour to get ready, the motorboat had to get back. So, as there was nothing to be done, I took Gracila, just the two of us, to meet with the president of FUNAI, to see what he would say to us. And that was how it was in Manaus. He brought the result of what we'd talked to him about before, in Brasília, but he tried to trick us, saying that the demar-cation of lands was almost ready—that we shouldn't be worried, that it was almost ready. But he tricked us! He made the paper[57] of all the areas and gave us a copy. When we got back, we tried to find out, consulted people about if this was real, if he had done the study correctly, if this was really the demarcation of the Tikuna lands or if it was just a trick. Then, the people of OPAN who worked here showed us that it was not quite like that, that this was only a study. The president of FUNAI tricked us just to shut us up. Because he knew that we would make a fuss. So he did this to trick us. Just so that he could say, "Look, here it is. . ." We waited and waited, but it didn't happen. So the time went by. After that, we had to do everything all over again. Then, after that, the president changed again; then another president. Then we had to do another work in order to get it done. And so the time was passing, on and on. . . Everything was stopped, always. It was like that at the beginning when we requested the demarcation of the lands. At the beginning it was like that.

FVRA: *So, when the study was done, the military called you. What was that story?*

PIP: That was at the time when the study was already quite legal, between '84 and '86. So we met with two more of the leaders; one of them was Armando Guedes, from Santa Clara.[58] We met with the colonel,[59] who

---

56 'Sateré-Maué': an indigenous people inhabiting the mid-Amazon River area.

57 Maps and descriptive records.

58 Tikuna community located in the Indigenous Territory Évare I, in the municipality of São Paulo de Olivença.

59 Colonel Antônio Carlos Carneiro da Silva, representative of the National Security Council (CSN) for the evaluation and processing of the demarcation of indigenous territories.

was in charge of security on the border strip,[60] at the Ministry.[61] So we went to talk to him, and he told us what type of land demarcation we had to accept, in his opinion. In his opinion, we had to accept it. He wouldn't accept our opinion because he was the one who knew. "The Tikuna don't know, I don't know what. . ." So he started to explain it to us. He said that the land would be forest and goodness knows what else. He gave two names to the land. He said that where there was indigenous land, the demarcation would be done as "forest land" and the demarcation of the indigenous land as "indigenous colony."[62] We said no to that: "We don't want the land as a colony. We want it to be 'indigenous land' not 'indigenous colony.'" So he said, "If you won't accept my opinion—and you're giving your own opinion—I won't accept your opinion, because you don't accept my opinion. So, the land you ask for, this indigenous land, well, you can go back, you can die on that land, because you're never going to get that land." Yes, he spoke like that. So, at that moment when the colonel spoke—at that moment, Armando Guedes got up from his chair and said, "Colonel, since you won't give the land to the Tikuna, then we'll fight." He hit the table, right in front of the colonel. And the colonel backed off, as if scared of Armando! Someone from his security came to calm things down, because Armando was really furious. He wanted to hit the colonel there in his office, where we had our meeting with him. So he finished with these words, that he wouldn't accept the demarcation of the "indigenous land," which in his opinion was "forest land" or "indigenous colony." So that was his opinion—that was what he would accept on this border strip. Our opinion he wouldn't accept. He said, "You'll never get that land!"

FVRA: *What is the difference between "national forest" and "colony"?*

PIP: It means that the white man who lives on the border next to those areas can use it just like the Indians. So his intention was to demarcate the

---

60   A 150km-wide strip of land, extending along the whole frontier of Brazil with the other countries of South America. The military are against the demarcation of indigenous territories in this area on the grounds that they "put national sovereignty at risk."

61   Generic reference to the "Esplanada dos Ministérios," the place where the different ministries and main federal bodies are located in Brasília.

62   Even after the end of the dictatorship, the military continued to exercise great influence over questions relating to the Amazon. Pedro Inácio refers here to the Brazilian government's intention to limit the territories recognized as belonging to the indigenous peoples to a small portion around the villages (then called "indigenous colonies"), which would be surrounded by "national forests" (which Pedro Inácio calls "forest land") destined for private economic exploitation, and from which the indigenous peoples would be excluded. Associated with the project of militarization of the Amazon, this proposal also functioned as a mechanism for restricting the concept of "indigenous territory," by means of which some sectors of society tried to exert influence in order to deprive traditional lands of indigenous rights in the new Constitution of August 1988.

land, but it didn't mean it wasn't ours. It's as much his as the Tikuna's. So there could be problems later. That was the idea he gave. So no one accepted it. So, it all got stopped for some time after that because no one accepted the colonel's opinion about "indigenous colony" and "tropical forest." So we carried on fighting; we said that, even if we don't get the land, we'd still carry on fighting. "We will start killing whoever is there. Those that are inside, anyone coming in will die; a lot of blood is going to run." We told him we'd do that. "And we won't leave our land in somebody else's hands. If our people die inside, our bodies will be buried in this land, so if the white man takes this land, our bodies will be buried in the land!" And we continued fighting like that.

FVRA: *Did anything violent happen? Tell us about that.*

PIP: No, there wasn't much violence during the great struggle. We fought for other lands, like that of the Uati-Paraná, Macarrão,[63] Santo Antônio do Içá, São Paulo de Olivença. There were folks living there and saying they owned the property, and when the land was demarcated, they didn't want to get off the area demarcated for the Tikuna. So, it only happened near here, in the Benjamin Constant municipality, with Oscar Castelo Branco,[64] in the São Leopoldo area. Then there was the massacre of 8 March '88. What happened was that, after the demarcation, there was the matter of the compensation for those people who lived in the Tikuna area, to be compensated.[65] It went to anyone who had made improvements. Most didn't have improvements, just the plantation that they themselves had planted. The only one that stayed in the area was Oscar Castelo Branco, who didn't believe it, saying that he'd only leave after a lot of Tikuna blood had run. He spoke like that to a lot of Tikuna. Meanwhile, we were setting up meetings with the people to explain the matter and everything. The best thing was to leave it in the hands of FUNAI—the federal folk. But, when the massacre of 8 March happened. . . One of the Tikuna who was involved in that religion business, a Baptist, I don't know if he was Baptist or Adventist,[66] I think it was Baptist; so he had religious contacts, both with Tikuna and non-Tikuna. So he was giving a party to inaugurate a Baptist church, I think—there in the area where the massacre happened. So he invited some people

63   Tikuna lands located in the municipality of Tonantins and Foz do Jutaí, in the mid-Solimões region.

64   Local tradesman, who claimed to be the owner of the lands occupied by the Tikuna community of São Leopoldo, in the municipality of Benjamin Constant.

65   With the official recognition of the indigenous territories, the state promoted the payment of compensation to the white occupants, with the purpose of contributing to their resettlement in some other area.

66   In addition to the Catholic Church and the Brotherhood of the Cross, the baptist and adventist churches are also present amon the Tikuna.

from communities like Espiritual[67] to celebrate. So at that moment, as they[68] all knew about it, they also met at that moment. The Tikuna were inside the white man's area—they should be meeting in their own area, eh? So they met, the white people, more than fifty of them, to carry out the massacre of the Tikuna. So, the whites met in a house, came out and killed the Tikuna. There were explosions and shooting. They killed the Indians, they killed all of them. Because they came out of the meeting house, came outside—they came out killing. Whoever went to the river, they killed them too—women, men, and children too. I mean, it was a really serious problem, what was happening; a problem like that had never happened before, that was the first problem that happened. It caused great suffering.

FVRA: *How many people died?*

PIP: Fourteen Tikuna were killed. Some of the bodies were found and some of the bodies were taken by the water down the Solimões River, and they didn't find the bodies.[69]

FVRA: *Were the murderers ever charged?*

PIP: Well, time passed. We made a trip to see if we could get those people charged, arrested. We denounced them all over the place, in Brasília and in other places, so that the authorities would know about the problem, and even then nothing happened quickly to resolve the problem. Because of the massacre, those murderers have been out there all this time. More than twenty or so years of struggle have passed,[70] and we are still suffering from the massacre. It think that's the way it is: one year, two years, three years, five years, and they never managed to catch that person and arrest him and put him in jail; nothing ever happened. But I think that now, recently, there's been some work done. We have never stopped, to get that person caught and arrested and put in jail.[71]

FVRA: *That was in '88. Some of the Tikuna lands had been demarcated at that time. After that, did you manage to demarcate other lands? How did those cases happen?*

---

67   Porto Espiritual, a Tikuna community located in the municipality of Benjamin Constant.

68   Oscar Castelo Branco and his men.

69   The "Massacre of Igarapé Capacete," as it has come to be known, was perpetrated by the trader Oscar Castelo Branco and his employees. Fourteen Tikuna lost their lives, and some of the bodies that fell into the waters of the Solimões River were never retrieved.

70   When the interview took place, thirteen years had passed since the massacre.

71   Only in May 2001, and as the result of the untiring mobilization of the Tikuna, were seven of the fourteen assassins convicted, while the instigator, due to his advanced age, was sentenced to house arrest in Benjamin Constant. One man was absolved for lack of evidence, and six are still at large today. The vague and evasive way in which Pedro Inácio responds to this question is evidence of the severity of the trauma that this massacre caused to the Tikuna people.

PIP: The demarcation—after that, what happened? It went on. Even so, we did other kinds of work to see some profit from the Tikuna blood that was spilt, to see if the authorities would pay for that Tikuna blood that was spilt. And so we ran to Brasília and other cities to get our rights to the rest of the lands. And so we managed to get the lands demarcated as the area of Betânia,[72] and at the same time we got the areas of Évare I and Évare II. Then, after that came all the others. The demarcation happened after the massacre. But, even so, there are some areas that haven't been demarcated yet, that still have to be finished. So, after the massacre, I mean, after what happened at the massacre, no one stopped, because we knew that the massacre. . . everyone felt that blood had been spilt, we felt that in our bodies; but even so, we didn't stop fighting for the land, which is our land. Even today, there's still some land left to demarcate, like for example Matitin, Maraitá, Nova Esperança and São Francisco do Canimari,[73] and other areas that have not been demarcated yet.

FVRA: *Tell us what it was like at the time of demarcation. What did FUNAI say so as not to carry out the demarcations? And how did you manage to get it done?*

PIP: Well, we went to Brasília and we made a committee to go to Brasília. After we got there, to the Ministry in Brasília with Colonel Carneiro[74]of the border strip, and him saying that. . . he replied to us, and when we were asking for land, FUNAI was saying no, that they had no money to demarcate the land. So, as we heard straight afterwards that FUNAI had no money, so we had to go back, like that. So, right after Eco 92 in Rio,[75] we were invited, and we met up with a chap who came from Austria.[76] João Pacheco gave us that contact so that we could have a discussion about our land. So he was interested in the type of support that they could give, from Austria. They said that the people's organization would have to get alternative support from outside the country—the Indians themselves from the organization—because a great many countries were managing it like that. So, as we couldn't manage to get any more here in Brazil, not from the responsible authorities, nor from FUNAI, as no one could, so we had this in our heads. We talked, we met, and we said that we had to go and get what we heard at Eco 92. So, at that same time, we

---

72   Area occupied by the Tikuna, demarcated as indigenous territory in 1993.

73   Matitin: a community located in the municipalities of Santo Antônio do Içá and Tonantins; Maraitá: a community located in the municipalities of Amaturá and Santo Antônio do Içá; Nova Esperança: a community located in the municipality of São Paulo de Olivença; São Francisco do Canimari: a community located in the municipality of Amaturá.

74   See notes 59 and 60.

75   United Nations Conference on the Environment and Development (CNUMAD), also known as the Rio Conference, held in the city of Rio de Janeiro in June 1992.

76   A representative of the Austrian government, who showed an interest in supporting the demarcation of Tikuna lands.

said to João Pacheco, we wrote him a letter explaining our problems. So, after that, there was a world indigenous conference in Austria, and at that moment we were on a trip outside the country, so we used the occasion to go see the government of Austria. At that time, I was a participant in that World Indigenous Conference. So, at that time, I was in Austria and the agreement with the President of Austria could be drawn up and signed, so that money could be given to the Tikuna people, for the demarcation. And that's what happened. So, as I was in Austria, I signed it, because at that time I was president of the CGTT—I had the right to sign the agreement.[77] And it was like that that we managed to get the land that was demarcated with the money that we got ourselves. After we had that money, a company here in Brazil[78] appeared, and they took control of that money, so that the CGTT could contract the company to do the demarcation of the land, do the clearing, the money for the topography and for the rest—all the work they did came out of that money from Austria. So we managed to get the demarcation done, and so the land got demarcated.[79]

FVRA: *How did the Tikuna oversee this demarcation?*

PIP: The Tikuna kept up with it all. Before the demarcation we had a meeting with the people to find out how the land would be demarcated.[80] Because the company demarcated many other lands, because they had contacts with the government, which was concerned with the people living in the land, with interests in the land. If the Indians want the land like that, they are going to take out[81] a small part. So we held that meeting so that one person from the community of each area would oversee the company. How? We had already got a map, and we left one person there to see how the demarcation would be done. But even so, some of them didn't oversee it properly. In some areas there are problems, the demarcation wasn't completed. So we held a meeting so the Indians themselves could keep an eye on the land demarcation. Some of them

---

77   On the basis of a convention previously signed between the CGTT and FUNAI, in which the Brazilian state recognized the CGTT as the body promoting the demarcation of Tikuna lands, and of negotiations held during Eco 92, the Magüta Center received funds from the government of Austria for the demarcation of the main indigenous lands.

78   With the resources provided by the Austrian government, the Magüta Center contracted an engineering firm, through a process of public bids, to carry out the physical demarcation of the Tikuna lands.

79   Thus, in 1993, six of the most important Tikuna areas were physically demarcated: Évare I and Évare II, Beruri Lake, Porto Espiritual, Betânia, and Vui-Uata-In.

80   Physical demarcation is the process of opening up trails in the forest and setting up markers and plaques indicating the limits of the indigenous territory, based upon maps produced from the surveys carried out in the Identification and Delimitation phase.

81   Take out ("tirar" in Portuguese): demarcate.

had problems—I don't know if they caught some disease in the middle
of the journey. And some didn't stick it until the end. And that's why
things stopped in some lands, some bits are not finished yet, and that's
what happened. I mean, the Tikuna kept an eye on it, yes, but those who
were overseeing it didn't really know how to do it, because at that time I
had other work to do, I had to make another trip. And so I was traveling
and couldn't keep an eye on it at that moment, and so another chief did
it instead.[82]

FVRA: *Do you know how much it cost to demarcate those six Tikuna areas?*

PIP: I think that more or less. . . the information I have about money is that
it cost around US$600,000 or so to demarcate the lands.[83]

FVRA: *Those are the most important Tikuna lands. After the demarcation, how
did the Tikuna movement continue?*

PIP: After the demarcation of the lands, when the land was already in our
hands, there was no more problem—I mean, no more danger of making
clearings, of working the lands; I mean, that stopped, there was no more
of that. The land demarcation was in the hands of the Tikuna. Well, what
happened after the demarcation? I mean, the demarcation of lands, the
Tikuna needed to say that. . . Well, the Tikuna didn't understand what
land is. Land for them is that there should be a contact with the whites,
the timber merchants, the fishermen, who are interested in the lake and
in the demarcated Tikuna area. And there are timber merchants interested
in the demarcated Tikuna lands. So, we ask for the Tikuna's land, because
the principle of demarcation is a security for the Tikuna, but then there
were some leaders, some communities, saying that it's not Pedro that is
providing for those folk. "Why does Pedro forbid cutting down trees and
selling the wood since it's ours? So now the land is demarcated, we have
the right to sell the wood!" There I said no, it's not like that, because the
wood. . . there is good wood, there is softwood and there is wood that
can be used to make canoes; so, if they're going to take out the wood
to sell it to the sawmill, I mean, the land will be devastated. It will be
destroyed. In conclusion, there won't be any more land, and the animals[84]
will go away and the animals will die. Time will go on and we'll grow
up and we won't find anything. Even if they don't come in, the Tikuna
themselves will work in fishing and make products and sell fish, right? So

---

82 Demarcation was followed step by step by the communities involved, with the full
participation of the CGTT in the negotiations to remove trespassers, define limits, open
up trails, and so on.

83 The demarcation of six indigenous territories, encompassing an area of approximately 1 million hectares, cost around US$496,000, an amount covered in full by the
funds from the agreement signed between the CGTT and the government of Austria.

84 Wild animals, which are still today a staple element of the diet of the indigenous
populations of Amazonia.

I kept saying that we shouldn't let that happen to this area. So folks started to say, "Oh, Pedro interdicts those areas that are demarcated. Aren't they ours? Are they only Pedro's?" That's when we started to fight, because of this. Because I was trying to get laws against cutting down trees, except to make canoes, clearings; fishing in the lake only for consumption. If anyone needs it, they can fish a *pirarucu*.[85] They can fish one, two, three and sell them to buy something they need: kerosene, matches, soap, sugar or clothes, things like that—not to always keep selling the product. So we started to argue because of that. "If the land is the Tikuna's now, why does Pedro still forbid us from selling what is from the land?" That's how the quarrel started. And then, after that quarrel, they started to say: "Now Pedro is not making things work for us." One group had a meeting, and they set up another organization;[86] they put another name on the organization so that they could choose the president, to see if they could make contacts to get money or whatever. Something like that—to be able to cut down the cabbage palm, the *buruti*; economic interests again, right?

FVRA: *Why didn't they go to the CGTT and try to get you out and elect another president? How was that?*

PIP: That's because they were in the minority, those people interested in doing that. First, the people saying they had studied, saying that they knew how to study, like at the university—those people are a minority, aren't they? So the majority, like me, haven't studied at all, that can't read or write, that never studied, that only have got studies from their own heads, knowing things, reality. So, because of that, they didn't let them take charge of the CGTT, because their great fear was that they would mess it up in the CGTT, and so they weren't able to take charge of the CGTT. So they set up another organization. That's when the split started, because they had another group and the CGTT was on the other side. When they did that, they spread it about, among all the Tikuna, that I was stealing money. Now, they were going to give money to all the chiefs, who were going to have a salary, going to have money, goodness knows what else. So, after a while, people started to leave the CGTT. So there were few people left in the CGTT. Some of them

---

85   The biggest fish in the Amazon region, which has been so intensively fished for commercial purposes, particularly in the extractivist period, that the species is at risk of extinction.

86   From 1995, and particularly between 1996 and 1998, as a result of the competition for resources that were becoming scarcer, the indigenous movement of the Upper Solimões suffered a great crisis, due to the exacerbation of internal factionalism and the creation of the Association of the General Council of the Tikuna Tribe (ACGTT), which later changed its name to the Federation of Organizations and Chiefs of the Indigenous Communities of the Tikuna Tribe (FOCCITT), a rival organization to the CGTT.

didn't understand; those who didn't understand wanted to go over to the other group,[87] which was against the CGTT. That's how the split started, for that reason.

FVRA: *Who is entitled to vote in the CGTT? What are the positions in the CGTT?*

PIP: The CGTT is like this: it holds meetings; the chief, captain of the community, holds a meeting to see how the CGTT is going to work. He has a position within the CGTT, and so does whoever has responsibilities. So the CGTT invites the chiefs of all the communities. So the CGTT means all the chiefs of the communities. So if there are a hundred villages, there are a hundred chiefs. So the CGTT is those hundred chiefs, with their peoples. Now, of those hundred chiefs, there are some that are more important: the one that is responsible for the CGTT, the captain-general, and a second person;[88] after that you have the members—it goes on like that. So the directors have to invite those chiefs to a meeting, to discuss things.

FVRA: *Who else takes part in the meetings alongside the captains?*

PIP: The CGTT also invites health workers and a bilingual monitor, who is the teacher of the community.[89] If the teacher is not present, he can send another person to represent him. The same thing for the health worker and the captain.

FVRA: *Those people who are invited, the health workers, the teachers—do they vote too?*

PIP: No. Only if the CGTT allows them to vote. Now, the ones who vote are the chiefs of the community or anyone that is chosen to be a member of the CGTT.

FVRA: *Who is the captain-general of the CGTT today, and what is his role there?*

PIP: Well, in the CGTT the one who has taken on the role of director—before, I was the captain-general, I was in charge, and not long after several other organizations appeared, of teachers, health workers. So I was very tired, of all the work, of all the things I'd done, and someone else had to take over, another person had to be chosen as councilor of the

---

87 The fact that Pedro Inácio does not mention the name of the "other organization" may be taken as an indication of the severity of the problems and the intensity of the rifts and ruptures that emerged in the indigenous movement of the Upper Solimões.

88 The second person that Pedro Inácio mentions is the vice-coordinator of the CGTT. The Tikuna usually refer to the second captain of each village as the "second person."

89 In the Upper Solimões region, bilingual education, with an indigenous teacher, is implanted in almost all the Tikuna communities. As for healthcare, according to the guidelines adopted by the Brazilian state concerning partnerships, it is provided by the Special Indigenous Sanitary District of the Upper Solimões, using indigenous health workers from the communities themselves, and peripatetic teams that develop special programs and supervise the health workers.

CGTT. So it was Nino Fernandes that took over[90]—he's in charge now, here inside the office of the museum;[91] it's him that is general councilor of the Tikuna Tribe.

FVRA: *Who else is involved in the Directorate?*

PIP: The other members are Paulino, Manduca,[92] and other people that are under him. So he took over looking after everything. Now they've made me honorary president of the CGTT. That's what I do today.

FVRA: *Do you still take part in the CGTT's courses and activities?*

PIP: I still take part in CGTT activities, I still take part in teachers' and health workers' courses, etc. I give support to the leaders.

FVRA: *What is the CGTT working on today, now that it has managed to demarcate the lands?*

PIP: I think the land is all demarcated now, thanks to the work that the CGTT did to get hold of the land. Now, recently, the Tikuna, the CGTT are thinking of doing other things. A lot of people here in the region, the whites, are saying that we asked for so much land and nothing is being done with it, but we are thinking of doing something now. The CGTT wants to do some plantations, like, for example, of *urucum*, *tucum*,[93] and some other things for the good of the Tikuna people.[94] Where there is no fish, where there is no lake, we will build a dike, things like that. For the future, we are thinking of other things like breeding animals—I don't know, like pigs or chickens. That's what the CGTT is thinking of for the future.

FVRA: *In those works that you want to do, how do you decide how you're going to do it and when you're going to do it? How do you discuss matters like the land or questions of development, improvement of quality of life, healthcare, education, and so on?*

PIP: The CGTT has a plan for what it does. The CGTT makes a plan and then takes it to the council, discusses it, and then takes it to all the

---

90   Because of his position as captain-general of the CGTT and director of the Magüta Museum, Nino Fernandes (Metacü) now divides his time between the seat of the municipality of Benjamin Constant and his community, Filadélfia, located a few minutes from the city.

91   Headquarters of the CGTT, operating from the Magüta Museum.

92   In 2001, the Directorate of the CGTT consisted of five people: Nino Fernandes, coordinator; Paulino Manoelzinho Nunes, vice-coordinator; and Silvio Mariano Lopes, Sildomar Estolando and Orlando Luciano Geraldo. Manduca Manoel Jonas was vice-coordinator of the CGTT in Pedro Inácio's administration.

93   *Urucum*: a substance extracted from vegetable seeds, used as food coloring; *tucum*: a palm tree with a fiber that is used in the production of crafts.

94   At the time of the interview, Pedro Inácio's presence in the Filadélfia community was connected to the activities of the Project for the Ethnodevelopment and Training of Tikuna Managers. The activities of this project involve the creation of nurseries for the production of seedlings of plant species for the sustainable occupation of lands, and are associated with the surveillance of the Tikuna territories.

communities to discuss what we are going to do on such and such a day, at such and such a time. So there is a plan to be discussed.

FVRA: *Do you discuss that in the General Assembly?*

PIP: Yes, it's discussed in the General Assembly.

FVRA: *What sort of matters do you discuss in the General Assembly?*

PIP: In the assembly we discuss the problem of the land—what land we should have in our hands, who's going to organize it, not to abandon it after the demarcation, take care of the clearing so that others don't come and take it. Because if no one knows where the land is demarcated. . . You have to choose some people, set a date and choose who will clean and keep watch on the demarcation line of the lands, or what type of work. So, all this is discussed in the assembly.

FVRA: *In what way do you think the Tikuna's life has improved since that time of struggle?*

PIP: I think that at first it was very hard. It was like the time when the people got independence from their boss, wasn't it? Because, at that time, we were imprisoned like animals in a corral. We were imprisoned, and the boss was in charge of that body, and now that we are free, the Tikuna today. . . What has the CGTT done to improve the life of the people? What improved for the Tikuna was the demarcation of the lands, which is done now; healthcare is taken care of; education is taken care of; and then there's this house[95] that we have, which we didn't have at the start of the CGTT's work. What this work has shown is that the museum is the main thing for the Tikuna, to make the whites of the city, both those nearby and others farther away, respect the Tikuna people. The CGTT thought that it could improve the Tikuna's life in this way. So, I mean, the CGTT did that and improved the life of the Tikuna a lot, because of the museum, because of the office. And it's not just that—the CGTT has also managed, in the course of time, to improve the life of the Tikuna. Each community has a radio for communication,[96] and in the office there's a telephone, fax—those things for the office to have contact with other people far away, like newspapers, to be able to communicate by fax or telephone when there's some problem in the community, when a Tikuna has had an accident or has a health problem, and we can't solve it here. That has improved the life of the Tikuna, with the work of the CGTT.

FVRA: *You said people around here know and respect the Tikuna. What is the relationship of the Tikuna with the other people here in the municipalities of the*

---

95   Pedro is referring to the Magüta Museum, where this part of the interview took place.

96   Radio equipment that establishes daily communications between the different communities and the Magüta Museum.

Upper Solimões? How are the Tikuna seen by the population of the region? Have the Tikuna participated in politics?

PIP: Well, as I'm not really into politics, I'm right out of politics, I don't understand it much. I more or less understand some comments—what the politicians have done with the chiefs of the communities. The people who have some authority, like the CGTT, those people, they talk to those people and deal with each community as if they controlled it like in the boss's time, to be able to elect whom they want from the community for the municipality. So, that kind of political work, for me, for the CGTT, for the minority, is not good. It is not very correct to do that, because they're doing the same thing as the boss. Because the boss already did that to us, and the moment we go inside as a councilor or mayor,[97] it's like we are the employees of a boss, as if we were back in the boss's time.[98] That for us isn't very good, because that person who is inside the white man's community, in the municipality, near the mayor, he deceives his own relatives in the Tikuna community. He's in the Tikuna community. He [the white man] wants to catch that person so that he no longer has a voice in the community and for his people, because that person is imprisoned in the municipality and doesn't go to his community any more to explain to his people what's happening, the white men's problems.[99] So that isn't very good, because the politicians of this region, of Benjamin, São Paulo de Olivença, Amaturá, Tonantins, São Antônio do Içá[100] and various others... That's what's happening.

FVRA: *Do you know how many Tikuna are elected, today?*

PIP: No, I'm out of all that, I don't know how many there are; there must be more than fifteen, something like that.

FVRA: *Besides that problem you spoke about, what other problems do you come up against?*

PIP: The problem that we are seing is that... Before the CGTT's work began, what happened was like I said before: we were imprisoned like animals; and as they couldn't manage to do that to us, now they use many other ways. What I'm seeing with my eyes is that they are picking out those important people, those who can do things, that can speak Portuguese, understand the white man's things, they are picking out

---

97   In the Brazilian political model, municipalities consist of an executive power, exercised by the mayor, and a legislative power, exercised by a chamber of councilors.

98   Pedro Inácio criticizes local politics, which reproduce the kind of domination characteristic of the times of the rubber plantations.

99   Pedro Inácio is also criticizing the ethnic distancing that has characterized the political practice of the Tikuna elected for local government, and the co-optation of indigenous representatives by local politicians, who harness them to the whites' interests.

100   Benjamin Constant, São Paulo de Olivença, Amaturá, Tonantins, and São Antônio do Içá are all municipalities of the Solimões River.

those people to put them in there so that we cannot say, "Look, the white man out there, the government out there is doing this and that against our land, against the Indians, against the Indians' law." That's it. So, they pick out those people, throw money at the councilor, give them money to shut those people up. This is what we are seeing and what we fear most, because they pick out those people, and they are the clever ones—the ones that have studied and have a weak heart,[101] they go in there and have their mouths gagged and don't have a voice any more. That is what I see happening here in the region.[102]

FVRA: *What about the invasion of timber merchants and fishermen? Is that still a problem?*

PIP: In some parts, yes; not so much in others. Someone is in charge of this in each municipality. They are taking the wood from the indigenous areas, and it's the Tikuna councilor[103] who should deal with that—he's on the inside. So this is what's happening. The same thing with fishing, too. The councilor is responsible inside there, because he is an authority alongside the mayor, isn't he? He should do something with the people of the municipality, because when they come to the community without permission, they don't respect anything—they invade [the area], and when the folk from the community want to take over, they don't respect them. So that's what's happening.

FVRA: *You mentioned the problem that is happening to those people that get an education and then are "bought" by the mayors and shut up. But what is the CGTT doing so that those people will join the movement?*

PIP: The CGTT is thinking especially about the students, that they could do some kind of course every three months, for those people who have the ability to study. To explain how the Tikuna struggle was at the beginning, the suffering of the Tikuna at the beginning—explain to them what happened in the past and what it is today and what it will be in the future, to get it into their heads. Because if they just study the white man's things, they won't remember anything else, especially the people that live near the city. They won't know about what's happening where I live,[104] farther away, out there in the jungle, outside the city, where you don't

---

101   Pedro Inácio means "a weak will."
102   Pedro Inácio is referring here to those Tikuna who, after completing their education and/or professional training, are attracted to work in public institutions, and distance themselves from the indigenous movement.
103   In the local elections of 2000, thirteen Tikuna councilors were elected in the Upper Solimões region.
104   Using the metaphor of the "jungle" in opposition to the "city," Pedro Inácio observes the degree to which the young students are involved in the knowledge and "all the things" of the city, in the "white man's world," and thus are increasingly at risk of forgetting what happens inside the "Tikuna world."

see the white man's things, where there is no television, modern things the whites have. So I think that, for those people to remember... because we are going to stop at some point, and the ones who are going to take over are those that are studying, so that, when we stop or die, as the case may be, they are prepared in their hearts and minds to carry on the struggle just like we struggled before. I think that this could improve life in the future—because those young people are literate; because we fought with our heads, but they can also fight with the tip of a pen, today, to fight for the rights of the Tikuna people.

FVRA: *What do you think was wrong about the Tikuna struggle, and what could have been done better to solve your problems?*

PIP: I don't think the CGTT made many mistakes. I think that everything that the CGTT did was the right thing to do. Now, what isn't quite right is the people that work in the CGTT.[105] Because we know that the CGTT is the Tikuna people, and that there are 30,000 or so of us[106]—that is the CGTT. But out of those 30,000 or so, there is a good-sized group that doesn't think. If I think alone, the rest don't have to think. That's what's happening. So, there weren't so many mistakes in the CGTT. What I have seen wrong in the CGTT, today, is perhaps because there are other communities that have the ability to study, and I don't know how they can put it in their heads and fight for Tikuna rights. But I think that it is because of lack of funds too, because for this you need money.[107] There is not enough money for those people to do something. Because if we said, "Right, today we want those people that have finished primary school or secondary school, we want to make them into lawyers for the Tikuna, for the CGTT!" But how?! Those people will not clear the ground, or work in fishing. They will sit down, working with their pens. They will make trips, get themselves invited to meetings—and for that you need money, for the journey, for food, and for daily expenses. So, that's what's needed. That is not a mistake of the CGTT, it's because we don't have anywhere to get money from. So, that's what's missing.

FVRA: *How has the Tikuna struggle affected your personal life? Were there good things? Bad things?*

PIP: During the struggle, which lasted more than twenty years, that struggle for me was a personal one, what I dreamed of—this is perfect. Because

---

105   Pedro Inácio criticizes salaried work, instituted by the CGTT some time before the interview.

106   According to data provided by the CGTT itself, and also by the Special Indigenous Sanitary District of the Upper Solimões, the Tikuna population is today estimated to be around 54,000 people, with 32,000 in Brazil, 12,000 in Colombia, and 10,000 in Peru.

107   Pedro Inácio is referring to the personal financial needs of some people, particularly those who have had an education, that make them turn to salaried work outside of the indigenous movement.

I have dreamed of it since I was a child. When I was a young man, I became free, I became independent from the boss; I achieved everything that I dreamed of, at that time. So, I did this as much for me, it is a good life for me, as for my family. Now, I don't know if it is very good for the other Tikuna. I'm just saying that for my family it's good. Because I'm free, I do everything that I can do—I don't owe anyone anything; I don't have to worry about any debt. I don't have to worry about paying for where I'm going to make my clearing, where I'm going to get my bread each day, my fish. I don't pay for water, I don't pay for electricity, I don't pay any rent. So that's really good. This struggle of my life has been very important for me, because I got my freedom. So, I think that my work of struggle, for me, for my family, is very important because I got freedom—I stayed with nature, and I will die close to nature. I will be free in nature. I will always have my soul in nature, because nature owes nothing to anyone, nature is free. So, that's good. My struggle has meant a lot of good things in my life, as much for my family as for my people.

FVRA: *How did your family and your community see it when you were not at home? Did they understand, or did they complain about it?*

PIP: I know the family understood. Now, the families that are not nearby, that are far away, didn't understand, or they understood some things; some of them remembered the time of the boss, and they said that we had gone off because we had a contract, like an employment contract, and were going to get a lot of money. Many people think that. A minority thinks differently, that it's not like that. Now, my own family doesn't think that.

FVRA: *When you went off on those trips spending a month or so away, struggling for the rights of the Tikuna, what did you feel? Was it worth it?*

PIP: Well, I think that when I got involved in this struggle, during the struggle, at the beginning of the struggle. . . thinking of the memory of the man who struggles, he has to leave his home for a long time. So, during the trip, I didn't remember that I was traveling, or that I was at home, or in the forest. Because I have dreamt about what nature says: "Them, the people, a nature person lives just like the rain. The rain is everywhere, wherever you see it!" That's what I think when I'm traveling. I don't think about the family, I don't think of my son, I don't think of my daughter, I don't think of my wife. If I thought about my family, of course I'd never leave my home—I wouldn't go anywhere, I wouldn't achieve anything that I was fighting for. I would never have achieved it. Because the history of the Tikuna says this: "Anyone who thinks evil will find evil; and he who thinks good, thinks he will achieve something, and he will get it." He who thinks of bad things, who thinks of his family when he's far away, who thinks, "Ah! maybe my son is ill, maybe he's hungry, maybe he's not living in good conditions"—that holds you back, the person at home and you yourself. . . It's like now that I'm here. Now I'm not thinking if I'm at home, or if I'm here doing this work, talking, explaining important things. . . So it's the same thing when I'm traveling. I don't care if I have a family or if I'm alone, I just care about what I will get to bring back in my basket for my family to eat, for my family to enjoy. That's what I think.

FVRA: *In the struggle that you've had, the things you've done, is there any figure that inspired you, who gave you the idea? Or has it all come out of your own head?*

PIP: Well, it's like this. Around 1920, before I was born, around then[108] there were some important leaders that died, like. . . I can't remember their names, but I've got it written down. The old people then used to give a lot of parties and told stories of what happened, how it used to be. While I was growing up and when I was with the whites, I remembered then, in there with the whites, what happened when I saw people being beaten and suffering. And I remembered that it was exactly what the old folk had told us and what happened to those people, and some of them that were still alive told us what happened. So I felt it in my flesh, because it happened to me too. When they wanted to do something, they put pressure on us. So, when I grew up, I remembered it even more, because it wasn't someone who'd told it. The final element was that the late Calixto, father of Jeremias,[109] became captain of the people at that time and taught us the history of what happened, the past. So some of his words I knew were right. So I base myself on that. At that time, I was a big boy already. I got hold of the Indian Statute that was at FUNAI—we saw that it was like that, just as Pedro[110] said. That's why we remembered. So that's how I did that work. Because, in fact, the old folk were telling it as it was, so that was why. It wasn't because someone said, "Look, you've got to do this, do that. . ." So when I did this it worked out, and other communities, other captains gave me support, strength; that's why it worked out.

FVRA: *In other countries, and even in other parts of Brazil, did you get to meet people who were also doing things in this way, or did you meet people that were doing things differently?*

---

108   Pedro Inácio is probably referring to the 1940s, when the German ethnologist Curt Nimuendaju was in the Upper Solimões. This is confirmed by the following reference to Calixto, who was Nimuendaju's main informant. The confusion over dates probably arose from the fact that Nimuendaju was with the Tikuna for the first time in 1929, for a short period.

109   Jeremias Calixto, son-in-law of Pedro Inácio, married to his daughter Carmelita Pinheiro.

110   Pedro Severiano, an important Tikuna leader. See note 16.

PIP: Yes, because many other leaders of other peoples talked to us: "Look, what is your people like?" And they started to talk to those persons:[111] "Look, it happened like this, in such and such a way. . ." We explained it to them; they also explained to us how it happened in their country and in other countries, and even here in Brazil. So I got the idea. That was how it happened. That's why I have done that.

FVRA: *Do you think it's difficult organizing a movement with the Tikuna? What sort of advice would you give to a young person just joining the movement?*

PIP: What's important? I think that if. . . Because, as I said before, the young people of today are not like in my time. In my time, it was not like today, with these young people, girls, who have had an education,[112] who study, speak Portuguese, understand the white man's things. In my time, there was no education, there was nothing, we were like animals.[113] We grew up without an economic movement[114]—that didn't exist at that time. So what is difficult is for us to organize ourselves, and meet with those people that have got the ability to study, to speak Portuguese and understand the white man's things, to let them get skills in order to help their people, in order to do even better what I was doing before, for the future—so that when I die they can take my place, or even at the moment when I stop, they can take over and deal with everything I'm dealing with today. I think that this would be hard for me, because what could I do to keep on working to improve the future? But what we are seeing today, I think it's like I said: they were born within the economy, for money. They only want to work for money, no one wants to work for free, no one wants to work voluntarily. So when they go out, they go in search of something, they need to earn every day a good wage, like the whites get. "When the arm goes to work, it needs to get something back!" So the young man, the boy that is here, we could meet with him, explain how we were doing things before, and in that way we could win him over, [but] it's very difficult to keep him here with that kind of idea in his head. I think that we will never win him over to do what I was doing before. So we can do it today with money, through projects, through the economy. That we can manage, but it will be temporary, not definitive, because the money runs out, the project finishes, and of course those people will not want to continue working—it will stop there. So that's why I find it hard, unless there's some other way of doing it.

111　Pedro Inácio is referring to the exchange of ideas between the leaders of the Tikuna and the leaders of other indigenous people.

112　School education.

113　Here Pedro Inácio reproduces the stereotype common in the region, which sees the Indian as a "wild animal" that lives far away from civilization.

114　Without being inserted into the market economy, at least on the level that the Tikuna are today.

FVRA: *What do you think is the most important thing in the education of the Tikuna, of the child, irrespective of what he will go on to do?*

PIP: Well, I'm not a teacher; but we often discuss that problem of the education of the Tikuna in the assembly. We discuss whether the indigenous teachers themselves should teach first our mother tongue, in the first year and even in the second. Since we know the Tikuna story of the creation of the indigenous Tikuna people, where they were born, where they came from, know the history, the reality of the Tikuna people, they should learn about Évare[115]—why it is Évare, why Yoi exists, why Ngutapa, Aicuna, Mowatcha,[116] all those people that are important, the eternal father, who is the owner of the world, of the group, who was the creator of man, the creator of the indigenous Tikuna people. So the teachers should insist on teaching this first to the children, to get it into their heads, and after they've understood it and have all that knowledge in their heads, then they can study the Portuguese language, because they already know what is Tikuna history and what is the white man's history. That would be very important, very good; but we've tried hard, the teachers have tried, and many don't want it. They don't want to be considered Tikuna—they don't want to be considered indigenous, because they do not—maybe they don't have a grandfather, a father that would explain it to them, tell them what is the white man's way and what is the Tikuna way.

FVRA: *So, do you think that it is the parents and grandparents that have to pass on those teachings to the young people, or is it the school?*

PIP: It's both. It has to be passed on by the father, mother, grandfather, and then afterwards by the school. Because the teachers have to teach Tikuna history first. So it would be good like that. Both sides. He should study Portuguese to be able to talk to the white man's authorities, because he is required to do it. But he must learn first the Tikuna's own cultural history.

FVRA: *You said that there is a Tikuna way of thinking, a Tikuna knowledge that it is important to learn. What about the white man's? What is the difference between those two ways of thinking? What is the difference between being Tikuna and being white?*

PIP: For me there is no difference. Me being Indian. . . When someone comes from somewhere and asks me, and I am all dressed up, with a watch and all, just like the white man, so I'm fine, I don't want to be Tikuna, I don't want to be indigenous, I don't want anything—I just want to speak Portuguese, in that language, everything fine. And if

---

115   The myth of Tikuna origins, arising from the Évare River, which in turn gives its name to the land.
116   Yoi, Ngutapa, Aicuna, Mowatcha: the most important figures in the Tikuna myth of the creation of the world.

someone who can't speak Portuguese would come up to me, I would be ashamed of not knowing my own language. So, I would have denied my nation, my people. So, that would not be good. So I want it to happen that when there is a crowd of other men that can't speak my language, a relative comes up to me and asks me a question in my own language, I have to speak in my language, if they offer me a drink I have to take it in front of everyone. So I think that it has to be like that, in order to achieve that. But I see the young people of today, the girls, the boys that are there, they have lost their culture and they're attaching themselves to the white man's culture. Instead of defending their culture, their mother tongue, history—no, they are losing it and running after something they don't know. I think that is perdition. That worries me a lot, because for me it is very difficult to manage it. There must be some way. . . If they forget their mother tongue, their history, the people will end.

FVRA: *You were saying that it is important to have pride in your culture, to show that you can speak the language, know how to drink the traditional drink. Why is it good to be Tikuna and not Brazilian? Why do you think it is better being Indian than Brazilian?*

PIP: For me, for my people, it is very important not to stop being Indian. Because, on the one hand, it is good to be Indian, even if you are educated and have studied at a high level, got a degree, become a deputy—I don't know, an authority. But you have to know your own language, your history, your culture and your god, that's the main thing. So, that's why, in the law of the Brazilians, who wrote the legislation, the chapter about the Indians says that the moment when the Indians can no longer speak their language, can no longer tell their history, when they have no more name, no clan of their people, they no longer recognize their brother, relative, cousin, then that people is lost. So this is a way of calling them Brazilian, white. So we are lost because of our land. We can lose our land just as we can lose our culture. Then we will have to buy the land, buy water, buy various things, just as they do in the cities. That is my fear. That's why we have to have pride in our language, in our culture. That's why it is good to be Indian; even if you are a high-level authority, you die an Indian, because of that.

FVRA: *Do the Tikuna Indians that live here in Brazil consider themselves Brazilians?*

PIP: We consider ourselves Brazilian because we are on Brazilian soil, as they say, no? The moment we leave to go to Peru or Colombia, then we become Colombian because we are on Colombian soil. But in reality, our blood is of the Tikuna Indian; Brazilian because we were born in Brazil.

FVRA: *What is the difference between the Indian that lives in Brazil and the Indian that lives in Peru or Colombia?*

PIP: The only difference is the language, because the history is the same. The Tikuna language is a little different, and non-indigenous language is different too. Only that difference. The clans are the same, the history is the same. Because all the Tikuna that live in Colombia or Peru came from Brazil—they were born in Évare.[117] So it was only at the time of the conquest, the war,[118] that they left Brazil and went to Peru and Colombia.

FVRA: *Do the people from the CGTT have any contact with the Tikuna of Colombia, or with the indigenous movement of Colombia and Peru?*

PIP: We have more contact with the people and the indigenous movement of Colombia than Peru. They are always writing, their leaders come here—they invite us to their meetings, and we always keep in touch.

FVRA: *Are you in touch with other indigenous groups in Brazil? With the Brazilian indigenous movement?*

PIP: Here in Brazil itself, we are in contact with various ethnic groups, organizations. Whenever we have an assembly, we get in contact through COIAB.[119] That's why we have contacts with various indigenous organizations in Brazil.

FVRA: *Besides COIAB, are you in touch with other indigenous organizations?*

PIP: Besides COIAB we are in touch with other organizations like, for example, UNI in São Paulo, which is another indigenous organization; UNI-Acre—like that, there are various organizations that we are in touch with.[120] They write, send letters, send recordings. That's how we keep in touch with various organizations.[121]

FVRA: *Do you think that this type of indigenous organization will continue to be important in the future, or that after the land demarcations they will no longer be necessary?*

---

117 Here Pedro Inácio is emphasizing the mythic origins of the Tikuna people, identified with the area covered at present by the Indigenous Territories Évare I and Évare II.

118 The dispute between the Portuguese and the Spanish over the definition of the borders of their respective colonies.

119 Coordination of the Indigenous Organization of the Brazilian Amazon, the body that brings together the different organizations of indigenous peoples located in the Amazon region.

120 UNI: Union of Indigenous Nations, the first nationwide indigenous umbrella organization, with headquarters in the city of São Paulo. From the 1990s, UNI gradually lost its role as connector of indigenous struggles, and was replaced by local organizations such as UNI-Acre (Union of Indigenous Nations of Acre and Southern Amazonas), which represents the populations located in the so-called Western Amazon.

121 The vague references to the indigenous organizations with which the Tikuna have relations should be understood in light of the fact that Pedro Inácio's no longer holds the post of general councilor of the CGTT, being more involved with internal aspects of the Tikuna movement.

PIP: For me they are always important. Because we are going to let our father die just because we are organized and have achieved certain things—we can't let him die, because then we will be orphans. We can't do that. Our organization should always go on, because it comes from the root of our culture, so it can't die. We should put it down on paper that when our people dies, the Magüta dies, the lands will also finish, the water will finish, the light will finish. The only one who can create another indigenous Tikuna people is Ngutapa; it is Yoi who can put an end to the whole movement of the people on the earth and can create another, but we cannot put an end to our way of life. We stay just like this, even if we have a house that was built, that is safe, but we keep our culture and the organization that we have today.

FVRA: *You have spoken several times of Évare, Yoi, Ngutapa. What is Évare? What is that story?*

PIP: It is the story of the Tikuna people, who were born in the Évare. But the words that explain what is Évare are difficult. So there are simpler words that I can use to explain what Évare means. It is because the Tikuna people that is not known today, the Magüta,[122] from the beginning of creation, today is called Tikuna. So the Magüta was fished, which means Magüta, not Évare. "*É* because it is!" *É* is the fruit of the *genipap* tree.[123] So, the creator is Ngutapa, who is the eternal father of the Tikuna and the father of Yoi. So, when they had a son, they grated some of the *genipap* to paint the body of the children, and they tossed the rest of the *genipap* into the Évare River. So, the rest of the *genipap* changed into a fish, and over time the fish came up the Évare River. So, that's why it's called Évare; it is because the leftovers of the *genipap* mean Évare. That's why we call it Évare I and Évare II. Because at that time it was all one continuous area.[124] Only afterwards did they leave the area where the eternal father of the Magüta people, the Tikuna, lived, and went to Peru. So at that time they split up the Évare, where the people was fished. That's why it's called Évare I and Évare II, because the Magüta people was created in that place that we call the sacred land of the Tikuna people, in the field of Évare, inside the Évare area, where our eternal father—that is, Ngutapa—fished Yoi, his son, who is the creator of the Tikuna people.

FVRA: *How did he fish?*

PIP: In the beginning, they fished in various different ways.[125] They fished with cassava, and they didn't change into people. They thought of fish-

---

122 Magüta: self-denomination of the Tikuna people, which means "people fished from the river."

123 *É*: name of the fruit of the *genipap* tree in the Tikuna language.

124 Évare I and Évare II, the main Tikuna lands, formed a single area in the mythic historical era before European colonization.

125 Another reference to mythic history: Yoi and his brother, Ipi, founding heroes of the Tikuna world.

ing with bait of *tucuma*,[126] and they changed into animals, pigs, tapirs, jaguars—those things. And he tried and tried until he managed to find a tree: the *macaxeira*.[127] So he fished with the *macaxeira* and tried and changed into people. Before, he tried fishing with corn, cassava, those things—but they changed into foreigners, the other nations. They said that his brother spoke funny.[128] His words were half-stuttered. "Brother, brother, let me fish my people too!" He fished with corn and cassava, and everything came out foreign. Everything that exists that is foreign is his people.[129] That's why, it happened like that. He got it all and was happy. Then Yoi said, "You have done your homework, brother, now I'm going to fish my people, cultivate our land!" And Yoi fished with corn and other things, but they didn't change into other animals; whenever he fished, it was people—male, female, male, female. And after he'd gathered together the people and the Magüta was already in a corner, the males and females separated;[130] then, at that moment, on the same piece of land, someone was sent to find a *jacarerana*.[131] He killed it, right at that moment, and Yoi ordered a big clay pot to be made, to see if he could manage to create that people. A long time passed, and the people did not respect one another any more, and it always happened as if they were animals. An animal does not respect its mother, brother, sister. So Yoi, Ngutapa were sorry. "Let's do something!" So he did. He cut the *jacarerana* up and cooked it. Then he invited everybody to try the *jacarerana* soup. He would ask each person that tried it, "What taste does it have?" They said, "It tastes of *sauba* ant!" So, that person was received into the clan of the *sauba* ant. They were all done like that, each person that exists today, both male and female, and the *curassow* clan, the jaguar clan, the *maguari* clan, the different kinds of clans were made from the *jacarerana* soup. That's how it was created. Then he put them into pairs, male and female, and today that's known as boy cousin, girl cousin, uncle, aunt, of feather, of tree, of branch, various. . . That was how Yoi made the separation in the creation of the Magüta people, within the Évare area.[132]

LGON: *What else would you like to say?*

---

126 Species of palm tree that produces a small edible coconut.
127 Species of cassava, whose root may be eaten without being ground into flour.
128 In the myth, Ipi is always referred to as being more impulsive and childlike than Yoi, who is always wiser, more prudent, and often cunning.
129 Ipi, who stuttered, created the "Peruvians," the generic name for all foreigners, or non-Indians.
130 Yoi was the creator of the Magüta or Tikuna.
131 Jacarerana: a small type of alligator, with a red head.
132 Tikuna social organization, described here by Pedro Inácio in terms of mythic origins, consists of exogamic halves (here classified as uncles and cousins) of patrilineal descent. The two halves are divided into the "feather clans," related to birds, and the "featherless nations," related to certain animals and plants. Marriage within each half would be considered incestuous.

PIP: The Tikuna people thinks that only the Tikuna exist—they don't know that there exist Xavante, Karajá, Bororo,[133] other peoples out there, that there are three hundred or so ethnic groups in the country.[134] So I think it would be worse. There are peoples that are suffering, too. The Magüta, the Tikuna, are suffering like the other Indian brothers in Brazil and outside Brazil too—they experience the same suffering, and they have to know our suffering too. We also have to know their suffering to be able to make demands in the country, so that the owner of the country, the president of the republic, the authority of the country, will have respect for the indigenous people. I think that is very important.

FVRA: *Briefly, what is the CGTT?*

PIP: The CGTT, for the Tikuna people. . . It is because for a long, long time there wasn't this organization that is called the General Council of the Tikuna Tribe. So, that is what CGTT means. So, today, it is known as the Magüta, which is a council that was organized, that has achieved a lot—things we never dreamed of, like living in freedom today.[135]

PIP—"Ngematücü", or "Pedrinho", as all of us who live the struggle of the indigenous peoples respectfully call him—is, without a doubt, one of the most important indigenous leaders in Brazil.

At the height of his political activity and effectiveness, and of his renown as a great leader, Pedro Inácio withdrew from the frontlines of the indigenous movement, retiring to his family's group in the interior of his people's traditional lands and to the innermost core of Magüta culture so that, with his unique experience as a "man of the struggle," he might renew the "Tikuna Indian blood" of his people. Withdrawn from the frontlines of the indigenous movement, though without ever withdrawing from

---

133 Xavante, Karajá and Bororo: indigenous peoples from the central region of Brazil.
134 Recent data indicate that there are around 240 different ethnic groups in Brazil—a number that is growing due to the reappearance of peoples considered to be extinct, and which are now demanding recognition of their indigenous identity.
135 The CGTT directorate, which formally represents the CGTT, consists of the president of the Council—a position held by the captain-general—and the vice-coordinator. As Pedro Inácio has already explained, the CGTT is a group of chiefs who meet to present to the directorate the plans and programs proposed by their respective communities. After these have been examined by the General Assembly, which counts on the participation of the directorate, the captains and other guests, the projects are returned to the community to be programmed and implemented. In December 1996, in General Assemblies of the CGTT and the Magüta Center, it was decided that the latter association would be dismantled; non-Indian employees and consultants were dismissed, and its patrimony was transferred to the CGTT. From then on, the CGTT, consisting only of indigenous people, with the occasional participation of non-Indian consultants, became the representative body of most traditional Tikuna leaders, continuing the struggle for land, and for their traditions and development. This proposal of the Tikuna captains to centralize in the CGTT all decisions about struggles in general, and projects in particular, had the effect of reinforcing their autonomy and self-management, and became a key for the constant strengthening of the important role that the CGTT continues to play.

the Tikuna struggle, Pedro Inácio seems to want to express by means of his personal example that the lands for which the Tikuna are fighting belong to the Tikuna because they "didn't come from another land, didn't come from another planet," but came from that very place—from Évare—and that they therefore have the right to live there with their gods, with their sacred beings, with their lives being constantly reinvented each day in complicity with the forest.

Coherent in the objectives and firm in the principles that he marks out in the steady rhythm of his peaceful voice, the trajectory of Pedro Inácio's struggle reaffirms the certainty that the success of an initiative, of a movement, can be guided and nourished through actions taken from within that initiative or movement itself, through simple actions that can nourish and strengthen our motivation and reinvigorate the struggle more than grand projects can; that the consolidation of victories often occurs away from the grand stage, distant from the focus of the public lights, with the quiet action of coherent, ethnic force.

Conducting this interview with Pedro Inácio allowed us to rediscover, yet again, the teachings that so many other Indian elders have already given us: that utopia is possible, and that, more than that, the possibilities for constructing it are always there.

CHINA

4

Han Dongfang

Railway worker, fighter in Tiananmen Square, organizer of independent union, prisoner, activist for human rights and democracy.

Interviewed by Robert Lambert

"I reminded people that, under Chinese law, we were taking legal action. It was our legal right to act, to protest, and to organize a workers' organization. Second, I reminded everybody that even though we were doing legal things, we were still taking a risk with our freedom and our lives . . ."

Han Dongfang

Freedom is born and bred in the depths of my soul. I long for democracy, I long for freedom. We have been deprived of our rights and our human dignity. There has been a prolonged silence. We have tolerated the injustices and the monopolization of power and wealth.[1]

Han, a tall, dignified, quiet-spoken man, was born in Beijing in 1963 and lived his early years in the poverty-stricken town of Licen, in Shanxi province. As a young boy he experienced the turmoil of the Cultural Revolution, and later entered the army. He became a railway worker in Beijing in 1984.

His life story was transformed by the dramatic events that occurred at Tiananmen Square during April, May, and June of 1989. His life reveals how individuals are transformed by history's freedom struggle. However, Han's story shows that this transformation does not simply occur automatically, mechanically. The individual's psychology, his or her deepest self, the soul is touched only by the stirrings for emancipation if they are open to the times, if they are willing to embrace history, to feel, with Dostoyevsky, that "Each of us is responsible for everything and to every human being"; or to identify with Goethe's Faust: "Whatever is the lot of mankind, I want to taste within my deepest self."

What was it that touched the soul of Han and stirred him out of the ordinary, routine patterns of work and family? It was the passing of Tiananmen Square in early April that changed his life forever. The Beijing square is one of the largest public spaces of any modern city. Mao planned it for the Communist State's mass rallies. Symbolism abounds as significant buildings surround the huge stone-based square. Tiananmen faces the Forbidden City, symbol of the old China; on the left is the Great Hall of the People; on the right, the Museum of Chinese Revolutionary History; and facing the Forbidden City is Mao's mausoleum. There is an obelisk in the center—the Monument of the People's Heroes. Then, as if to usher in a new

---

1 Extracts from a profile of Han Dongfang, "Revolutionary worker Han Dongfang," in Asia Monitor Resource Center, *A Moment of Truth: Workers' Participation in China's 1989 Democracy Movement*, published by the Hong Kong Trade Union Education Centre, Hong Kong, 1990, pp. 122–7.

heroic age, fast-food restaurants have proliferated on the right-hand corner of the square. McDonald's is prominent.

In November 1998, I visited the square at dusk. In ever-busy Beijing, crowds of people moved and walked and talked, as people do at Trafalgar Square in the heart of London, or Times Square in New York. But this had a different feel. There was something to be remembered. What is the spirit of the place? I walked alone in the growing darkness and tried to envisage those days between April and early June 1989. From mid-April 1989, Beijing University students gathered at the square demanding the restoration of the honor of Hu Yaobang, the Party general secretary who had recently died. They called for an end to profiteering and the elimination of corruption. As the student protest grew, workers began to take an interest. A worker leader at Tiananmen commented, "Workers should not stand on the sidelines; we should stand up and protect the students and give support to this great democratic movement." Over the next four weeks, workers became more actively involved in the protest, encouraging other workers to leave their workplaces and participate in events at the square. This led to the establishment of the Autonomous Workers' Federation (WAF) on April 21st.

On the day of its formation, the WAF advanced several slogans: "Down with official profiteering, eliminate corruption!"; "Stabilize prices and raise the wages of the workers!"; "Publicly reveal the wealth and the assets of Deng Pufang and the sons and daughters of leading cadres!"[2] On April 26th, the Public Security Bureau declared WAF an illegal organization. The leadership of WAF responded, "We workers have no fear of such threats and firmly believe that the questions that we and the students raised are correct. The people are the ones to judge what is right and wrong."[3] On the same day, April 26th, two large battalions of soldiers were sent to Beijing. Students and the WAF organized massive protest marches. On May 13th, students began a hunger strike in protest against the regime. On May 20th, martial law was declared. In the tense situation that developed, WAF advanced the slogan, "We won't fight back when hit; our petition is peaceful." The WAF declared that they were against the ruling class of all dictatorial regimes:

We need clean officials and not bureaucrats who sit on the heads of the people. We don't want a government who lives in beautiful villas, who wear fine clothes and who ride in luxury cars. Sell your crowns and the people can dress; sell your villas and the people can live; sell your Mercedes Benz and the people can eat.

On May 26th, WAF led a march, chanting: "The Beijing workers' spirits are high. They don't fear the tanks and planes in the sky." On the morning of May 30th

---

2   Deng Pufang, the son of Deng Xiaoping, was reported to have overseas business interests, and was rumored to have hidden assets (ibid.).
3   Liang Hong, "Beijing Workers Autonomous Union: Origin and Activities," in *ibid.*, p. 3. Liang was a leader of WAF.

several WAF leaders were detained. Han Dongfang and other leaders led a protest at the Public Security Bureau, where the leaders were detained. Meanwhile, substantial numbers of troops made their way to Tiananmen. At three in the afternoon on June 3rd, a large number of soldiers appeared on the western side of the square. There were continuous clashes between the soldiers and the students and workers. At ten in the evening more PLA[4] troops arrived from the underground railway station on the south side of Mao's mausoleum. They lined up in two formations. Then tanks appeared in the southwest corner of the square. Gunshots were heard from all sides. WAF leader Liang Hong commented, "I sensed a massacre was beginning." Troops fired red tracer bullets into the air. At 2 a.m. that morning, more troops advanced onto the square firing randomly from near another symbol of the new China—the Kentucky Fried Chicken restaurant. Bodies lay everywhere.

Han emerged as one of the key leaders of the protesting workers. In the following interview, he describes this historical moment and the way its tragic events shaped his soul. His lifelong commitment to social emancipation was forged in the fiery furnace of Tiananmen.

Robert Lambert: *What influenced you to become so dedicated to the struggle for social emancipation in China?*

Han Dongfang: In a way it was a coincidence. Eleven years ago, I was a railway worker—an electrician trained in Beijing. My wife and I were on a bus. I saw the people gathering as the bus passed by the square. My wife was really curious. She said, "Let's go and have a look—let's get off at the next stop." I said, "No, let's go back home." I told her that I did not like getting together with people I did not know. What is the point of getting together with people in the street that you don't even know? You don't even know what they are there for and what they are talking about. I didn't want to get off the bus and have a look. I reacted to my wife's suggestion strongly.

She wouldn't give in—she insisted that we go and have a look. I said, "OK, if it's only for ten minutes I will go, because I want to get home." We went there. I started talking to people. I couldn't pull myself away. After a while, my wife tried to pull me out. I refused to leave. Yes, my commitment to struggle was due to this coincidence. This is how I discovered the democracy movement. I joined the democracy movement because of the students, but I soon realized I had to get workers involved.

The student movement talked about democracy and human rights and the corruption of the political leadership. I spoke to them as a worker. I did not know much about the system of democracy and human rights. I had never heard people talking like this before. Because I was a worker I

---

4   People's Liberation Army (PLA). Established in 1927, the PLA is the unified military organization of air, sea and land forces of the People's Republic of China.

started talking about the factory situation. I said, "Well, you see, we don't have democracy in our factory." The ideas started coming to me as I spoke. I said that I believe that if we are going to fight for democracy, we should also fight for democracy in the factory, not just political democracy. Workers should have the right to have a say in how things are run in the factory. They should be able to express workers' interests. I told them about my experience as a worker. I explained that we didn't have democracy in the factory that I worked in. But even though I touched on the workers' issue I didn't really understand what the labor movement was supposed to be. I also discovered that the students wanted a pure students' movement. But I met other workers at the square who wanted to form a workers' organization. So I joined the workers' organization.

The students did not really create the opportunity for workers to get involved. They made a circle around the square, but you had to be a student to join in. That is why we formed a workers' organization. We organized elections for the workers' organization so that we could determine our direction. We did not just want to be a support group for the students. Five people were elected to a preparatory committee. I was one of them. I was also appointed spokesperson for the committee. This was the starting point of my involvement in the struggle for democracy and worker rights.

RL: *When you think back to that time at Tiananmen, when you remember that experience, what memories come to mind? What was the atmosphere and how did this affect you?*

HD: Well, there were several things. Of course, it was an experience that could never be forgotten—never in one's entire lifetime. The first thing I remember is the bullets in the sky. Even though I served in the army for three years, I had never seen anything like this. The sky was dark and the bullets in the sky had a pink color. The color looked beautiful. There were bullets going in so many different directions—the bullets would whistle over your head.

I was shocked. I served in the army, and the main education we received was that the army was there to serve the people. Just one hour before I saw the bullets in the sky some colleagues in the worker organization warned me: tonight they are going to shoot! The army will do whatever it has to do to take over the square. They will sacrifice lives if they have to. They don't care. I told them I don't believe this. I told them I served in the army for three years; I believe that there is not a single soldier who will shoot people in the street: trust me. When I was forced to flee an hour after the bullets began to be fired, there is one thing that broke into my mind—this terrible event ended all trust in the communist government in China.

While I was witnessing these events everything seemed to go in my mind. My brain seemed empty. I didn't know how to react. In the chaos, people were looking for leadership. Many were asking me what we should do. I just said, "I don't know." They looked on me as their leader, but I just didn't know what we should do. This is something I will never forget.

Another thing that I could never forget was when ten people came to the workers' tent that I was in. They told me that I had to leave the square. They said I had to come with them. I asked, who are you? They said, "Don't ask questions. You have to go." I said, "Sorry, I can't go; I am responsible—I am the spokesperson for the workers' organization." They said, "We know your life is in danger; you have to leave." I said, "Everybody's life is in danger." They said, "No, your life is more valuable. You know the history of what has happened here. You have a duty." I went with them. I must be honest and say that I had mixed feelings.

My background is communism. Communism taught us to believe in heroes who save the people. We were taught to believe in saviors of the people—human saviors like Mao. Sadly, I was also confused. I worked together with these people for two weeks. Suddenly someone says my life is more valuable than their own life. But weren't we struggling for equality, democracy? Statements like they were making were not right.

At this point, I remembered one thing—I am embarrassed to say this—I remembered Stalin at a critical period of the war when he refused to leave Moscow. It was a very dangerous time. I thought, you say I am a leader; if I am, I should not leave the square at this critical time. I told them, I will not leave. I am responsible here. I will wait until the soldiers come, even if we cannot do anything. They went out of the tent and left me. They had a discussion and then came back in and said, "We are sorry but we have decided that you don't have a choice; you have to leave." They said, "We need people like you in the future. You cannot die. It is not your choice; it is our choice." So they took me like a hostage out of the tent. When we were out of the tent, the leader of the group said, "Let's walk in a circle with Han in the middle to prevent the bullets from hurting him."

That is how they took me out of the square.

Even today, I don't know who they are, or where they are. I would really like to meet them and share my experiences and my thoughts with them. I will never forget them. This is a heavy burden I still carry. It is a burden that keeps me working hard to build a worker movement and fight for freedom. It is not as though I want to be a big-name leader as they wished it, but I feel a duty because I don't know what happened to these people, because after they took me out of the square they went in

again. They said they had to because they had other people to take out.
I don't know—are they still alive today or not? And until the day I meet
them to make sure they are okay, I don't think I can stop working in this
way. I feel this as a great pressure on me.

RL: *When you left the square, did you get arrested?*

HD: After I left the square I was shocked at the terrible death and destruction. I believed that people would be serious and react to the violence.

I decided that the best thing for me would be to leave Beijing and
work with the ordinary people to try and change things. I picked up my
bicycle and started to travel around the country. I planned to travel for a
year or two trying to collect real information from people in touch with
real life. I felt that if I traveled by rail, I would not really touch people's
lives, so I decided to travel on a bicycle.

I left Beijing on June 14th. After I had traveled for ten days, I took
a rest in a small TV store. The TV program listed twenty-one students
from Tiananmen. I was curious to see if there was anyone I knew. I just
stood there and watched.

Yes! I knew some of them. I recognized some of them. Suddenly, the
state TV put out another list—this was a list of wanted workers. I was
at the top of the list. When I saw the screen, I was so shocked. I was
shocked that things had come to this. I suddenly felt that everybody's eyes
were on mine—looking at the screen but really looking at me. I suddenly
felt that way. So I just sort of turned away. Then I saw the front pages of
the newspapers. They had pictures on the front page—my picture was
there on the front page. I realized that I was one of the most wanted men
in the whole country. I went somewhere very quiet to think about my
situation. I went to this small river bed and I lay down there on the bank.
I had to try and think what I should do.

As I lay there, my mind went back to the events on the square. There
was a time when elections were organized. Ten people were invited up
on stage in front of TVs. They had to say why they were running for this
election, and what they would do if they were elected. I reminded people
that, under Chinese law, we were taking legal action: it was our legal
right to act, to protest, and to organize a workers' organization. Second,
I reminded everybody that, even though we were doing legal things, we
were still taking a risk with our freedom and our lives. I reminded everyone there that we were running not for power, not for position—we
were running because we accepted the risk. I asked, "Who is prepared to
accept the dangerous risk?" I said, "I am ready for this." I warned, one
day we could face jail. We must be prepared for this. I told the crowd, if
that day came, I would accept prison. The government would not need
to send ayone running after me. They wouldn't need to send someone

to catch me—I would go to prison because I believe in what I am doing and saying today.

As I lay alone on the river bank, that speech came back to me—I thought, Oh my God, what should I do? I knew I couldn't run and hide anymore, even though I wasn't really running because, before seeing my details broadcast, I didn't really realize the dangers. Now I told myself, any second I could be taken by the police in the street. This situation made me think of my promise to the people at Tiananmen. I promised I would walk to jail rather than run away. If I decided to run away, how could I face these people in the future? What would I say to them if they asked me why I ran away, if they reminded me of what I had said in the square? Was I really prepared to run away and leave others in jail? I knew that there were already lots of people from Tiananmen in jail.

Finally, I decided to accept my responsibility, to accept what I had promised at the square. Even if I suffered, even if I was filled with regret, even though I knew I was not ready for what they could do to me in prison, even though I knew this was a big risk in my life, I knew I had to do it. I had to encourage people, even if this was a bitter experience for me personally.

So I took my bicycle and rode back to the Beijing police headquarters. There I saw pictures of myself and others on posters on the walls. I spoke to the soldier at the gate and told him my name. I told him that the Public Security Bureau had asked that I be here—now I was here. The soldier told me to go to the reception. Suddenly, I thought, what a stupid decision! You think everybody knows you because of the stupid posters. I don't think that is the situation, because even the soldiers don't know you. I said to myself, oh, should I go away?

At that moment, a person walked out of the main building. He stood in front of me. He looked at me and he asked, "Are you Mr. HD?" I said, "Yes I am." He then asked a very strange question: "What are you doing here? You are the one negotiating with us the other day?" I said "Yes. I saw my picture on a wall in the street and on TV. This is why I am here." Suddenly, he realized what was happening. Suddenly, the person he wanted to arrest was in front of him. He changed his voice. He ordered me to come in. He said, "You did terrible things, evil things, now you feel bad and you want to give up—right? You want to save your life, right?"

I said, "No, wait a minute! I come here not because I want to say I was wrong. I come here because I want to accept responsibility for what I did. What I did was not wrong. I am not giving up."

By now people had begun gathering at the gate, and he became nervous. He said, "I know you are not violent. Just come inside so that we can talk more." I walked in with him.

When I was detained they just kept questioning me: "Why did you give yourself up?" Every day they took me for two or three hours, either at midnight or early morning, three or four times each night, always the same question: "Why did you give yourself up?" I kept explaining why. Finally, they picked me up very early one morning and they said, "You are giving yourself up, aren't you? This is the only way you will save your life. This is your last chance. Tell us why you are giving yourself up? Accept that you did wrong."

I told them, "I am sure you don't want to be cheated. Of course I want to survive. I want to save my life. If you want to be cheated, I can say what you want me to say to save my life, but this is not true." He became angry and said, "You really are a brave man and I respect you a lot. There is one thing I don't respect you for. One day when you face the gun, don't blame me—I tried my best." After one month I realized that I would spend my life in prison. They would not kill me.

RL: *During that first month in prison, how did you cope with the experience? You have mentioned that the feeling of change in the movement carried you forward and you said things during those days in the square. When you were imprisoned and on your own, what difficulties did you experience, and how did you cope with these difficulties at a personal level?*

HD: This was an experience. You learn what real fear is. You see other sides of human beings. You see what can be done to human beings by their "masters."

When you are in a cell you are an animal, an absolute animal. What you need is food, more food, better food. You are only allowed to the toilet once a day and then only for one minute. Each person only has thirty seconds on the toilet. If you don't come back from the toilet after thirty seconds they will beat you and they won't give you water. So my first fight for human dignity in the prison was a fight over toilet time. I refused to leave the toilet, saying I haven't finished yet. I looked the policeman in his eyes and said, "Whatever you want to do, just do it." I don't know why he didn't do anything. I was there for about ten minutes after all the prisoners had left. I found that he came to respect me.

I saw police beating people for no reason. Each day they would come to the cells and select a prisoner and beat them. You could hear the cries from your cell. I couldn't keep quiet about this. It was the same thing every morning. I decided to speak out. I told the police, "You know we are animals. We are not human beings—we can't say anything. We can't escape. We can't charge you for assault in court. You can just do it. But I do feel sad for you because you must be a person who is suffering deeply. It must be very hard for you. There must be a huge pressure in your life. You are not a happy person; that is why every morning you need to be here and do this to be released." He was shocked at first. He said, "What do you mean?" I said, "I feel sad for you and I hope you will get better." He was embarrassed, and he said "You are probably right." After several weeks he stopped the daily violence. He probably felt some sort of shame because I said we are animals.

During the two years of prison, I went on hunger strike a number of times, demanding medical treatment. They refused. That is why I now have a heart problem.

They never touched me physically, perhaps because I was known internationally. They used another method to harm me physically. They put me in a small fourteen-meter cell with another twenty prisoners. The police officer who took me to the cell commented, "You are a brave person. We respect you. We have decided to put you into this cell so that you will learn to change your ways." I entered, and I was shocked when I saw all these peoples' faces. It was horrible. I asked them what was special about this cell. They answered, "You don't know why you have been sent here? Do you have TB? This is a cell for TB sufferers." It was a terrible place. Everybody had TB. Some had liver problems, some had skin problems. Any person with a serious sickness was sent to this cell. This nearly killed me. They had discovered my weakness. I had said to several police officers that I would live longer than my ten years in prison. Every day I did exercises in my cell so that I kept fit and healthy. They knew my desire to be healthy and fit—they had finally found my weakness. They believed that they had found a way to make me give up my commitment. I spent nine months in that cell. I started to cough and develop a fever. Eventually, I could not even speak.

Eventually they released me because I was dying of TB. I was about 19 lbs. in weight. I couldn't walk anymore. They put me into hospital for three weeks and gave me injections. They checked, but said they couldn't really find anything wrong with me. The doctor says it was strange. He said my right lung was so badly damaged that it didn't function anymore. It was like a piece of old rotting paper. The doctor said that he believed I had AIDS. I didn't know what AIDS was.

I was suddenly crushed. After two years in prison, after all of the terrible things that happened to me, I was crushed. I was crushed because I was led to believe that I had AIDS and that I would die of AIDS. But I kept asking how could I have AIDS? He took tests and told me to wait for three days for the results. Those three days were really like days from hell. I felt that I was dying. On the third day the doctor came in. I really felt that this was God giving the Judgment. He said, "Good news. It is not AIDS." I entered a state of joy—it was like I was flying across the sky. He said that they did not know what was wrong with me, and so they would do a blood transfusion. I believed I was dying, and so I asked the police to bring in my family. I wanted to see my wife and my sister. I told them that this was my final request. There were tears in the eyes of the nurse and the doctor. He said he would do his best. The chief of the Beijing police's political section soon visited me. He said, "Don't worry, you will be OK. We are working on your request. On the next morning, I heard my wife's voice and my sister's voice outside my room. They came in and they were crying. They said that they had permission to take me home.

After I went home, a doctor working for the organization called Physicians for Human Rights assisted me. They sent a doctor to Beijing. They X-rayed me and discovered that I had serious TB. He immediately put me on a course of TB drugs and I got better and better, and the fever reduced. And he said that it is TB, there is no question: just start to take the TB drugs. So I started to take the TB drugs and started getting better and better. I was sent to the United States to recover. I received lung surgery. One of my lungs was removed.

Six months after I was released I was ordered to come to the police headquarters in Beijing. The prosecutor gave me a notice ordering me to go to the police headquarters. I went, together with leaders from my workplace—the railway factory—and my wife. I had to face ten to fifteen people. I was forced to stand in front of them. The prosecutor read a statement that said that I was a serious criminal who was to be charged and sentenced. They went on to argue that, because I gave myself up and was cooperative, the crime of revolutionary action would be dropped.

I responded by informing them that I intended to sue for the physical harm that they had done to me in prison. I also demanded a formal apology and compensation. The prosecutor was shocked. He warned that the case and the charges against me would not be closed if I acted in this way. He asked me to go back home and think carefully. He told me that there was no procedure whereby an ex-prisoner could sue the authorities. I told him that I had never acted illegally, I was never armed, and that I believed that my actions were correct. He again said that he was not prepared for this, and that I should go home and think about this for seven days so that the case could be closed.

I insisted that I wanted to sue the authorities. He went away for about three hours, and then came back and said, "OK, give me your complaint," which I did. I then demanded a receipt. He went away for another half an hour and then came back with a receipt.

I then left, and to this day I have had no answer to my case.

RL: *How did this whole experience change your outlook on life? In a real sense, this was an attempt to destroy you as a person. The terrible personal repression challenged your right to exist.*

HD: Through this experience, I kept thinking of the future of labor. I knew very little about labor movements or labor law, or how workers could address labor issues that arise in the factory. I thought about this a lot in prison, and during the months that I was waiting for lung surgery in the United States.

When I joined the movement in 1989, it was more a democracy movement than a labor movement. At that time, the official Chinese "unions" were really just in the service of the state and the Party. We had no idea of unions that were independent of a party. I started to think about these issues seriously and took opportunities to discuss them with different union movements outside of China. I spoke to labor leaders in Europe who told me how hard unions had to fight to win conditions for workers. I was naïve at that time. I was surprised that union organizers got victimized in a democratic system. This helped me develop my ideas on the democracy movement. I realized that workers everywhere have to stand up and fight for their rights. That's why I remain focused on labor. I have to remind Chinese workers about this.

I have to get this message of struggle across to the Chinese workers. For the last three years I have been broadcasting from Hong Kong.[5] Workers respond and ask me about the concrete issues in their factories. For example, they tell me, we have 1,200 workers here and we get no salary for nine months. We can't survive anymore, we have spent all of our savings already, so how can we survive?

In these cases workers rise up and take action. I tell them, having a general election and just winning a democratic government in China is not the complete answer. Workers have to struggle—they have to study the labor law, and they have to learn from the trade union experience in other countries. I tell them that they have the right to a decent wage, paid monthly. I tell them that if they are not paid, it is illegal. I tell them about democratic unionism. If a factory worker is not happy with a union leader, he or she can elect a new leader. Every union member has these rights.

Some say they are scared. They say if you raise an issue you will be fired. Nobody will follow. I told them that this is an example of workers feeling powerless. This has to be changed: we have to be responsible for

---

5   After he had recuperated from his lung operation, Han attempted to return to mainland China, determined to begin his lifelong work of organizing Chinese workers. He was arrested at the border and sent to Hong Kong, where he set up an organization to support independent worker struggle in China.

fighting for our interests. Your wage belongs to you—you have to fight for it when it is not paid.

Workers also raise many technical questions about how to organize that we try to answer on our radio station. Workers are very fearful of the economic and political situation in China today, with all the market changes. I tell them that, if we can organize union elections inside the factories and workplaces, that this will be a big step forward for democracy itself. Workers will learn to have a say in their own lives—they will learn that they can create power and begin to influence events. Workers will learn to elect leaders and control leaders in their democratic unions.

RL: *How often does the radio station broadcast?*

HD: The radio station runs every day for twelve hours.

RL: *That is quite an achievement!*

HD: There are different programs on this station. My program is called "Labour Bulletin." I have two slots each week that run for about ten minutes. It's a short-wave radio, and sometimes it gets jammed and it is really hard to hear.

People call me regularly from public phones. They tell me, for example, that there are a hundred people from a factory gathering in front of government offices and stopping the traffic. They want their issues addressed. Demonstrators call me on a public phone to tell me what is happening. So I call up government officials and ask, "Why are things happening this way? Why don't you pay back the workers and explain to them?"

The state-run union is useless in these situations. I discuss these crises with them, but they are powerless. They are just like a transmission belt between workers and the government. They don't negotiate for the workers. This failure shows workers the real face of the state union. Workers tell me that the union is useless because it is Party-controlled, Party-organized and Party-paid. These organizations are corrupt, so they do not serve workers. That is the nature of the organization.

RL: *Finally, how would you summarize the situation of Chinese workers in the new market-oriented China—the China of privatizing state enterprises, the China that is reliant on attracting foreign companies? What is your assessment?*

HD: Between October 1999 and November 2000, there were approximately 10,000 demonstrations throughout the country. These were mostly worker demonstrations.

Workers responding to my radio program tell me demonstrations are happening in their county and their city. It is interesting when I asked them, "Is there any demonstration in your city?" They tell me that there are usually two to three a week, involving more than 500 workers. It is a real demonstration, because they stop traffic—really stop traffic, and so make trouble. Even if they are ignored, they keep going back and demanding action from the government. The big issue is workers are not being paid their wages.

Layoffs from the privatizations are a big issue. There is no social security cover. They have absolutely lost their trust and confidence in government. The government responds by putting their organizers into detention centers. Despite this, they demonstrate again and again because they are suffering hunger—their families are suffering. At the moment the demonstrations are peaceful. My fear is that, if the government doesn't respond, there might be violence. Some may make bombs, and innocent people will be killed. The arrests of the leaders of the demonstrations will do this. The arrests will lead to secret underground action. This will be a nightmare for the future of the country, for the future of the labor movement—that is why my radio program and my conversations with the workers always tells them to organize. Don't accept the price of violence—it will create a violent society.

The sad thing is, worker leaders who try to organize get arrested. Recently, a lawyer put up a banner in his office: "I serve the workers." He was arrested and imprisoned for a year. He was accused of trying to overthrow socialism. He is paying a price.

RL: *What about China's entry into the WTO?*

HD: This will bring more big MNCs into China. The MNCs are every-where. At the moment we are in a very weak position: we don't have the money that they have; we don't have the political power and influence that they have. The only power we have is our traditional one: solidar-ity. We have to keep talking to Chinese workers to organize themselves. We have to build solidarity that is global. This is where our real power lies—the only power that workers have.

The alternative is despair, hopelessness, a feeling that we are going nowhere.

I had met Han briefly during a visit to China in 1993. He made a lasting impres-sion. A committed person—a person who has suffered deeply, personally, in the cause of social emancipation—attracts like a magnet. There is a spirit there, far from the mundane, the routine cycles of living and working. Commitment, and the spirit that calls forth that commitment, enliven a new depth of communication, of sharing, of hopes and dreams of a different world, a liberated world.

I was again in downtown Hong Kong—the busy, bustling, noisy, polluted, money-making heart of the East. The high-tech city of fast money, business deals, and quick personal fortunes for the elites. I waited in the busy street on a mild winter morning to be taken to the offices of the China Labour Bulletin, *the organization Han had set up to stimulate, encourage, and support worker struggles in China. Ushered into a small lift, I soon clasped the hand of Han. He is a tall, well-built, handsome man. There are few outward signs of what he has endured. We spoke for two hours.*

I was struck by the fact that Han's story could easily be lost to all but a few specialists on Chinese labor. What would be lost if the story remained untold? We would lose the sense that the rhythms and movements of history are also shaped by the powerless and the marginalized, and that there exists within the exploited a deep desire for freedom, a desire that drives some to extraordinary sacrifice in its cause.

On that fateful day when he stopped at the square, Han became driven by an awakening spirit of freedom—in the events around him, but also within him. As he noted, "Freedom is born and bred in the depths of my soul." He discovers a power to speak, to encourage, to enthuse, and to lead. Han and the movement for change become one; the movement's fate becomes his fate.

The interview had a deep impact on me. I shared Han's choices, his courage, his sufferings, his dignity, and clear sense of direction. There were times when I felt as though I were in the prison with him as he relived his experiences. There was the sense of the powerful, brutal repression. Get caught in its grip, and you may well be crushed—gone, forgotten, just another nameless number, lost to the world. Han is disciplined, outspoken, assertive, determined to survive. Freedom comes at a price. Who will pay the price?

If the spirit cannot be broken, then the body can. Let's erode, corrode, destroy the body, the temple of the spirit that will not be broken. A broken body is mended. The irrepressible spirit is again at work. China's crisis—workers on the streets protesting—is the focus. History has not ended; courage, daring, and political commitment have not vanished from the earth, as Fukuyama would have us believe, driven away by the powerful money-driven ethos of liberated markets— "Let individualism reign supreme."

Han's story breaks the ice age of individualism that we are now living through—the age in which the only interest is self-interest; the only worthwhile activity, profit-making; the only worthwhile value, market value. The age in which anything goes, provided these interests, activities, and values are promoted.

The spirit of freedom rises to contradict the "End of History"; there are other interests, activities, values: community, dignity, security, justice. Han's story, like all the other unsung stories, all the other Voices of the World cutting freedom's pathway, is attractive because he lays his life on the line for those values.

Self-sacrifice inspires others and demonstrates that deep commitment to the other is possible in a world cluttered by an array of incentives for self-indulgence and self-ishness: get rich quick; seek power, status, and recognition. Han's story is a story of personal choice, of commitment to those injured by exploitation, of moving in the world of the powerless.

Han's life is a sign of hope that the drive for freedom and solidarity has not waned before globalization's glittering prizes for the few. The struggle for an alternative social order has not died—it lives on in the spirit, commitment and drive of the unsung heroes of our age.

COLOMBIA

5

Gabriel Muyuy Jacanamejoy

Indigenous person belonging to the Inga people, leader of the indigenous movement, professor, senator.

Interviewed by Alfredo Molano
and Maria Constanza Ramirez Silva[1]

"Something deep inside made me feel that I had to prepare myself to fight for our cause. I understood the value of what it means to be indigenous. We were now awake, and we began to value our identity, and to understand what it is to be Inga . . ."

---

1   In order to maintain the flow of the text, the interviewers have eliminated the questions and transformed the interview into a first-person narrative.

Gabriel Muyuy Jacanamejoy

Gabriel Muyuy Jacanamejoy: Leader of the Inga people; son of María Jacanamejoy and Luis Muyuy; husband of Antonia Agreda, herself an Inga, and the father of Tupac Amaru and Waina Capac; philosopher, anthropologist, and theologian; prominent indigenous leader at national as well as international levels; senator of the republic for two mandates; full professor; present deputy ombudsman for indigenous peoples and ethnic minorities at the Office of the Ombudsman (Defensoría del Pueblo) of Colombia.[2]

I am an Inga, a descendant of the Mitimak group of the Inca people. At the time of the conquest, we, the Incas, already had a history. Our language is the Inga language, belonging to the Quechua family. In the old Incario, and by delegation of the Incan sovereign, the Mitimak were in charge of the Tawaintisuyo borders, which the conquerors named the Inca empire. History tells us that, when the Spanish conqueror arrived, the shock was extremely violent. At that time, the Incario faced many internal problems: two Inca brothers, Waskar and Atahualpa, the sons of Waina Capac, were both claiming their father's power. During this dispute, the conquerors arrived and took advantage of this circumstance to subdue them. The Mitimak group was forced to disperse; some headed south, down to the Napo River; others stayed north of the Tawaintisuyo, hiding and scattering to protect themselves. We, the Inga, descend from the group that settled on the banks of the Napo River, but, in the course of time, we moved to the Sibundoy Valley. We are thus the descendants of the Incas, of the Mitimak group, and we speak the Inga language.

Around 1535, the conquerors arrived at the Sibundoy Valley (Putumayo, in southern Colombia), accompanied by missionaries. According to the chronicles, they found an organized, working, peaceful people. However, we know that there were intense battles with the Ingas that had settled in the area of Mocoa. Terrible massacres were perpetrated by the conquerors

---

2   Alfredo Molano and María Constanza Ramírez Silva's comments on the life stories of both Gabriel Muyuy Jacanamejoy and Gerardo González are presented at the end of the following chapter, on Gerardo González.

at that time. We don't know if the same happened in Sibundoy. Next
came the period of evangelization. To the Sibundoy Valley came the
"Mercedarios," the missionaries of the Vírgen de la Merced. They stayed
for a long time, but beyond that little is known of their presence. After
them came the Capuchins, and with them a period of forced evangelization. In the memories of the Inga, especially of those who are from the
Sibundoy Valley, these were times of harshness. The missions had great
influence over our people's political and cultural decisions. Whatever they
said was the law, and only if it was spoken and understood in Castilian.
They forbade the use of the Inga language in schools and colleges; they
seized our best lands and manipulated our authorities. There are records—
dating as late as the beginning of the twentieth century—attesting to the
fact that the missionaries forced our grandparents to sign documents
stating that they would yield our lands to them in exchange for evangelization. As a result, our parents and grandparents ended up working as
serfs on our best and most beautiful lands. Even so, in spite of the power
of the missionaries and the threats of governments, our people resisted and
fought for their rights in various ways.

About 1700, Carlos Tamabioy, one of the great Inga leaders, rebelled and
recovered some of the lands in what is now the Sibundoy Valley. Carlos
Tamabioy left a will where he vowed "to recover our lands, our authorities and our own culture." This will is preserved in the Cabildo Inga[3] del
Resguardo Aponte[4]. We guard it as a treasure because it reminds us of
the struggle of our ancestors. Around 1850, the struggle was resumed to
defend our territory, our autonomy, and our cultural identity. The priests
excommunicated all those who rebelled against injustice. Among them
was my great-grandfather, whose name was José Muyuy. It was a difficult
and dangerous struggle, because the missionaries had great power over the
government and over the indigenous people, and used our own authorities
to secure obedience from the community. This situation led many Inga
families to change the names and surnames of their children, who came
to have white people's names: López, Hurtado, Rosero, Cruz. My people
resisted because they kept their Inga identity alive in their minds. They

---

3 The "Cabildo" is the political institution recognized by the Ingas. The "Gobernador"
is the leader who represents the community, connects with other institutions, manages
community projects, and tries to find solutions to the conflicts, holding the power of
punishment and forgiveness.

4 According to the Article 21, Decree 2164 of constitutional reform of 1995
"Resguardo Indigena" is defined as "a legal and socio-political institution with a special
character, composed of one or more indigenous communities that with a collective land
title enjoy the guarantees of private property, possess territory and control its management and the internal life of the community through an autonomous organization
governed by the indigenous community's own normative system."

rebelled—and among them was my great-grandfather, who had libertarian ideas—because they refused to accept any rule that went against our culture.

At the beginning of the last century, after the One Thousand Days War (1899–1902), settlers from Nariño and Cauca arrived to take possession of the scarce territory still in the hands of the Inga. With lies and fraud, with alcohol and food, they took our lands from us. The agrarian colonization of the Sibundoy Valley cost us much of the land, including that of my grandparents. Imposed evangelization and strong colonizing pressure led many Ingas, mostly those from the Sibundoy Valley—among them my paternal grandparents and my father—to move to various Colombian cities and also abroad, where they dedicated themselves to promoting, teaching, and commercializing our traditional medicine. It was a strategy for the defense of Inga dignity. We, the Inga, were the first to be displaced from our ancestral territory in Colombia, which forced us to face the unknown and to struggle daily for subsistence.

I was born in 1957, during that difficult period of colonization and forced displacement, in a place called Chunga Kaspi ("the place of ten trees"), in the village of Waira Sacha ("the place of trees and winds"), which is today part of the San Francisco municipality, Putumayo. It used to be a very wild region, with bears, rabbits, armadillos, and tapirs. My father died when I was eight months old. He was killed at the time of the Inga migration, by thieves who wanted to take the scarce savings he had made from promoting and selling Inga medicine.

An important event that molded the first stage of my thought and consciousness was the settlers' invasion of the lands that belonged to my family and to other Ingas. My mother remarried and my stepfather played an important role in the fight to stop the seizing of our lands. I remember that, in this dispute, all the authorities were on the side of the settlers, who took concerted action to cause the disappearance of all the documents pertaining to the ownership of those lands. They burned down the registry office with the purpose of eliminating any evidence of our ownership of these properties. However, my stepfather and other Ingas proved to be astute, because all of them had copies of those documents that entitled us to keep our lands.

I went to school in 1965, at the age of eight. At the time I didn't speak Spanish; I could only speak my mother tongue. The first rule I was required to obey was not to speak Inga, which made learning to read and write quite difficult, because I didn't speak Castilian. The teacher who taught us to read and write was extremely harsh.

Until the age of ten I wore Inga clothes: the *cusma,* which is a homemade tunic, and the *kapizayu,* a cloak woven in a manual loom by Inga women.

I walked barefoot. To eat, I took in my satchel a little *mute*,[5] *arepa*,[6] and *chicha*,[7] while non-indigenous children ate at the school cafeteria. As a child, it seemed to me that they were better nourished because they ate sweets. At school, everything was strange: the words, the food, the clothing. In the first year there were twenty-five children, five of us being Indians. The non-Indian children looked down on us because of our clothes and the sort of food we ate. It was in this difficult environment that I went through primary school.

Under the Concordat, the Colombian state, among other issues, granted the Vatican the right to develop evangelical work. In this way, the state hired the church to provide educational services, but without establishing clear terms, and my view is that the church used education to make converts. Later, adjustments were made and the contract became a specific means of regulating the education of indigenous peoples: under the ploy of evangelization, the church established very strict rules, which implied the denial of our cultural specificity. In the first place, to speak our mother tongue was considered to be a sin, in religious terms, and backward, in terms of education, so you had to stop speaking your own language and speak Castilian, because your own language supposedly limited the learning of the truth. Second, the whole Christian moral ethic was the correct ethic, while elements of the indigenous ethic and morality, based on indigenous spirituality, were bad, and sometimes even said to be diabolical. The ritual elements of Catholic Christian practice were good, whereas the ritual elements of the indigenous practices were the opposite. For example, the *yagé* ritual[8] was evil and had to be eradicated, because the proper behavior was to go to mass and practice the sacraments. All of this tended to lead to the denial of identity, which developed in indigenous people a set of complexes in their relations with others.

When I concluded my fourth year, a problem arose: there was no further schooling available in the village, and to get it meant a three-hour walk to the seat of the municipality. Since we lacked economic resources, I interrupted my studies and started working in the fields, tilling the *chagra*[9] for three years.

Three years later, our village school started to offer a fifth year and, encouraged by my mother, I gathered the resolve to go back to school,

---

5   Boiled corn.
6   Cornbread baked in the oven with eggs and butter.
7   A fermented drink made from corn.
8   The *yagé* is a hallucinogenic plant. In the literature the plant is described as the amplifier of the experience, a substance causing a modified state of consciousness. People who have taken it report that it aids introspection into emotional states and past and present experiences.
9   A plot of land where a wide variety of products is cultivated.

although I was quite grown by then—I was already fourteen. According to my mother, after primary school I could take a practical course, allowing me to face life better equipped. My mother is a humble Inga woman who can't read or write and who knows very little Spanish. The reason why she sent me to school was to spare me from suffering the humiliation she had to endure for not knowing how to read and write.

My mother didn't want me to be deceived like other Ingas had been, when the settlers, with the help of the Corregidor de Indígenas,[10] forced them to sign documents relating to their lands. The settlers asked someone who could read and write to sign at the request of the Indian, who was unable to do so and thus couldn't know what he was signing. This was the strategy used by the settlers to deceive us, and in this way many of our lands were taken from us. But the way the lands were recovered, which is recorded in our collective memory, was also fundamental to the lives of the Ingas, and it never involved violence. The Ingas that had gone to the cities came back to the Sibundoy Valley in waves. With the earnings from the sale of traditional medicine, they bought back from the settlers the same lands that had been taken from them. It was a political and peaceful way of resisting and of recovering the lands. Today, some of these lands belong to Inga families, each of which owns one to four hectares of private property. Many of the settlers lost the lands they had stolen. Before dying, my father managed to buy a little less than two hectares, and that is what we still own today. It was this land that I worked, growing corn, beans, and vegetables, and raising chickens, pigs, ducks, and rabbits. The Inga diet is mostly based on corn: corn soup, *chicha, arepa,* and also vegetables and some meat—mainly domestic animals raised by the families.

I grew up in this environment of work and study. After school I helped at home, preparing the feed for the chickens and pigs. With the sale of these animals, we bought essential goods and clothes to wear to school. I used to get up at 4:30 a.m. and go to bed at 10 p.m. During certain periods of the year I did community work, group work. A few families would get together to clean the fields and improve the roads. This traditional system is called *minga* or *divichido,* and it consists of working for a day in a family's *chagra* and then doing the same for a different family. This system of communitarian work is still in use, although with decreased vitality, surviving as a cultural practice among the Inga people. During school vacations, I worked as a day laborer for the settlers, cleaning the stables on their properties. I needed to earn money to buy clothes and school items, and to help with our household needs.

---

10 Official with administrative and judicial powers in charge of local Indian affairs.

After that I started my secondary studies at the Champagnat School, run by Marist monks. During the first four years everything went fine, but the last two were difficult because of my family's financial problems, in addition to my mother's health problems, which almost made me decide to give up studying altogether. There were three indigenous boys in the school—two Ingas and one Kamentsa[11] and we experienced strong discrimination. We were marginalized by our teachers and by our non-indigenous peers. There were exceptions, of course. Some of our classmates treated us well, without any sort of racial discrimination, but the majority made a point of stressing the difference. I felt discriminated against, marginalized.

Around that time, I and my two indigenous classmates joined a youth movement organized by the Social Pastoral[12] of our region, Putumayo. The main reason for my involvement in this movement was to claim our indigenous identity. In the movement, we started to recollect our history—the deceit by the large landowners, the exploitation by the church, the government's violence—and we felt, all of a sudden, a historical rage, a retroactive rage, which had built up inside us. We understood the value of the past, of everything I had been told by my father [i.e., stepfather] and my mother—the heavy physical work the settlers submitted them to. So I started to recall the struggle with the settlers who wanted to seize the lands of the Ingas in abusive ways, the authorities who connived with them and took advantage of the fact that indigenous people could not read or write. Something deep inside made me feel that I had to prepare myself to fight for our cause. I understood the value of what it means to be indigenous. We were now awake, and we began to value our identity, and to understand what it is to be Inga. The youth movement of the Social Pastoral was led by Brother José Cruz, from the Congregation of St. Afonso María de Ligório. It was here that many young Indians first felt the urge to resist injustice, discrimination, and marginalization. Physical abuse, humiliation, and deceit persisted. This made us aware of the need to do something for the cause. I actively participated in different social, cultural, sporting, and even political actions, which were socially formative for me.

When I finished secondary school I had the opportunity of going to Medellín and attending the university supported by the Marist brothers—a religious institution of French origin dedicated to education. When I completed secondary school, two circumstances coincided: the Marists invited me to study with them, and my paternal grandfather, an ancestral medicine doctor who lived in Medellín, offered

---

11 Another indigenous people from Sibundoy Valley.
12 The "Social Pastoral" is a Catholic social justice organization.

to support my studies. This encouraged me to study philosophy and theology in Medellín at the Bolivariana University. In the second semester, however, I applied to study anthropology at the University of Antioquia, and was accepted, and so I did both courses almost simultaneously. My future career was influenced by the social experience I had during secondary school.

It is obvious for me that the principles of Christianity and the gospel are compatible with, useful for, and important to the development of humanism in society. For example, the respect for human dignity: Christianity and the gospel state that this respect is essential. Another example of this compatibility is the principle of the relationship between humans and nature, which is one of the most important principles that Christianity embodies and preaches. The principle of the value of history, of historical legacy, for example, present in both Old and New Testaments, is also important for Christianity. These and other aspects are important and compatible principles. In this respect, the spirituality of Christianity is compatible with indigenous spirituality—in principle, that is. But not all of the expressions of this principle allow compatibility between Christian and indigenous spirituality. The relationship within a community and among people is spontaneous and open in indigenous spirituality, whereas Christian spirituality poses ethical limits that go against the natural dynamics of people and the community—we cannot agree on this. No one can deny any community the right to speak their own language—this is written nowhere in the gospel; nowhere does Christianity purport to deny any group of people, indigenous people in this case, the possibility to further their education unhindered, or the right to practice their own rites, or the right to speak their mind and express their feelings. None of this is in the gospel. The religious agents acted, let's say, in opposition to what should have been—today things have changed slightly. So, one of the reasons why I wanted to study theology was because there was much submission, much incoherence. While the Ingas and Kamsas were being preached to about issues of faith, the hereafter, and austerity, and were encouraged to "have patience and to work," the religious agents were well-off, had the best lands (which they had taken possession of), and had all the conditions to live comfortably, including indigenous people to serve them. They preached austerity for others, but they themselves did not live by it. So, in order to understand all this, I started to study theology. It is not a case of my being against Christian principles; I am, rather, against the structures of the institution and the way that institution shapes its agents.

I left my territory, my community, and my family at the age of twenty-two. It was the first time I was moving away to an unknown place, to a city. My paternal grandparents lived there, and I felt safe. My grandfather was a *sinchi*,[13] a *taita*. He worked in the promotion and commercialization of our ancestral medicine.

We, the Inga, have specialized in the knowledge of our ancestral medicine, and this is our greatest cultural legacy from time immemorial to the present. We are experts in botanical medicine. The practice of this medicine is a cultural inheritance from our ancestors. Both the Ingas who left and those who stayed in the Sibundoy Valley have knowledge of and use medicinal plants, but not all of them can be *taitas*. *Taitas* are the sages (*sinchi*), the experts, our spiritual guides; they are the pillars of our history, our identity, and our autonomy as a people. They are born to be *taitas*, but someone has to teach them, and the basis of the learning and wisdom of the *taitas* is *yagé*. *Yagé* is our spirit, our soul. When the *sinchi* treat someone, they immerse themselves in *yagé*. With *yagé*, people have revelations; they contemplate the depths of both the inner self and the outer world.

There are different types of *yagé*, and the *taitas* know that you cannot take just any kind of *yagé* without their help, because some are very strong. For example, the "aya waska," which is called snake *yagé*, is extremely strong; in contrast, the "tocto waska," or flower *yagé*, causes a very pleasant reaction: you hear chanting, see gardens, and contemplate wonders. The *taita* knows which *yagé* the patient needs according to his or her illness and personality. *Yagé* opens the mind of the *sinchi* and makes him see more deeply than what he can see with his eyes. *Yagé* may even touch the soul. So, after taking *yagé*, you become clean and at peace, your mind becomes clear, you become as new, like a newborn child. All evil energies are driven away, and this enables you to see things. The *taitas* live their lives fulfilling their mission; this is what they focus on, and they are able to examine thoroughly what is the matter with the patient. *Yagé* is not produced in the Sibundoy Valley, but in the Amazonian area of Putumayo. The masters are Ingas and Kofanes from the wild region of the lower Putumayo. Our medicine is known and respected because it is effective; the *taitas* heal, and the people trust and respect them deeply. My grandfather was a *sinchi*; forced to move by the violence of colonization, he was greatly attached to his territory and to its teachings, although his life ended in the city of Medellín.

Nowadays our ancestral wisdom is in decline, because colonization led to the destruction of many medicinal plants. And, what is worse, the Sibundoy Valley has been turned into cattle-raising territory. The traditional *chagras* are disappearing because the settlers grow beans as a single crop, and use chemicals that poison the vegetal mantle. Because of this, all plants have become vulnerable, and you need to go to the lower Putumayo to get them. Still, the *taitas* are able to find the plants to produce purgatives, ointments,

---

13   A sage of Inga medicine.

and *contras*.[14] It is a tradition that is being kept alive. My paternal grandfather taught me, and so I know a lot about plants. I know what they are good for, and sometimes I use them to treat myself when I have health problems.

At the University of Medellín I met other indigenous students: Rojas Birry, who took part in the Constituent Assembly of 1991, studied at night and worked during the day; Abadio Green studied philosophy, and was later the president of the National Indigenous Organization of Colombia (ONIC); and many others, leaders of their own communities. We used to meet on weekends to talk about our concerns, and as we discovered what bound us together we thought about asserting the cause of the indigenous peoples. In 1979 and 1980 we organized the first urban indigenous meeting, known in Colombia as Chibkariwak—an organization that brings together indigenous students and workers from both formal and informal sectors, as well as indigenous people visiting the city. Because of this, I discovered a new world in Medellín, and it came as a big surprise to actually meet other indigenous people who shared the same feelings and the same resentment for having been deceived and abused.

I learned about what was being done in Cauca[15] against indigenous peoples, and this too fed my commitment to the struggle; the same was happening to the indigenous peoples of Vaupés, Tolima, Chocó, Antioquia, throughout the country—and also in other countries of our continent. I took a solemn vow to fight for our cause.

Around that time, the first National Indigenous Congress took place in the country, and some of us belonging to the indigenous university group actively participated in the creation of the National Indigenous Organization of Colombia (ONIC). We were very active, especially in publicizing our conclusions: we organized conferences and debates; we did everything that could be done to make the Congress' conclusions known throughout the country—what the actual situation of the indigenous peoples was, their relation with the state, and with society in general.

As we finished college, we scattered throughout the country, and each of us went back to his community. For ten years I dedicated myself to teaching in Nariño, in Ipiales, and in the city of Pasto, and after that I lived in Brazil, in Rio de Janeiro, for almost a year. I came into contact with the network of Latin American philosophy of Enrique Dussell, a Mexican anthropologist who is the leading exponent of Latin American philosophy, and I participated in their reflections on the theology of liberation. I continued to teach, combining classical philosophy with indigenous philosophy. I strongly encouraged the reading of Quintín Lame, and also Carlos Tamabioy, who is one of our leaders. But I also got involved in social work among indigenous

14   Protective or preventive substances.
15   Another region in southern Colombia.

peoples. While I was living in Nariño, I traveled almost every weekend to Putumayo to support the process of indigenous organization and to develop practices of reflection and empowerment with the purpose of creating a new organizational dynamic.

I came back to the Sibundoy Valley with a goal: to empower the Putumayo indigenous peoples—especially my own people, the Inga—so that they would no longer be subjected to the humiliations inflicted by the settlers and to the manipulation of the missionaries with their evangelization programs, which made them submissive, impoverished, and prey to discrimination. This became my major concern. In the Sibundoy Valley, the Inga continued to have a conforming attitude, and were obedient to the priests out of habit. The phrase "May God's will be done" was very much in use. With this kind of submissiveness, it was easy to abuse people. Injustices were being committed by the institutional authorities, by the missionaries, and by the settlers. My first action was to let the indigenous peoples of Putumayo know of the existence of other indigenous peoples throughout Colombia, of the outcomes of our first Congress, and that we had rights written down in the law, such as Law 89 of 1890—a century-old law that is still in force, and which guarantees our rights to the territory and to autonomy. They had to know it to be able to use it. Together with other Inga leaders, I started to talk to them about economic injustice, about how we were excluded from the political and economic life of the country, and about how our culture was being disregarded. My awareness-raising activities among the community were condemned by some of the priests and settlers.

In a meeting of the clergy, the bishop urged the priests from all over Putumayo to stop me from going on with my activities, because I was bringing "disorder into the indigenous communities." It was actually the case, because I traveled throughout Putumayo telling people what had been said and denounced at the National Indigenous Congress. Our response was to organize a group of young Ingas to implement a comprehensive empowerment program between 1983 and 1985.

During that same period I organized a strong movement, called Musurunakuna (new men), which involved mobilization and action directed towards the strengthening and recovery of our culture, making people aware of the value of our dignity as indigenous peoples.

Pressure arose when some of the indigenous people who were not familiar with our organization objected to the process we were leading. It was not an easy task to get rid of the shame associated to being an Indian. On weekends, for example, the Ingas went to the village to get drunk with rum and beer, and the settlers took advantage of this to make deals with them. With the Musurunakuna organization, we proposed to start producing *chicha*, our traditional drink, and by doing this we managed to prevent the traders from depriving indigenous people of the little money they earned with their daily work. The taverns felt the effects of this, and rum vendors became infuriated because we had ruined their business. Today, as a result of this process, the indigenous authorities are more aware of things, and we've achieved more autonomy.

Another important action involved reflecting with indigenous people about the issue of Catholic rituals from a critical perspective. The evangelization of indigenous people, as well as the talk about the economic, social, and political issues of the period, emphasized the idea of people's suffering in this world. Reward was to come after death. The result was compassion and conformism. I explained biblical issues in a broad sense, in historical terms. I called attention to Jesus Christ as a man and a fighter; we spoke of Jesus Christ as a historical being, the person who fought for the poor, against oppression, against injustice, and for the truth. At that time, the ideas of the theology of liberation were latent, and I studied the writings of liberation theologians like Leonardo Boff and others. We did not stop the Inga people from attending church rituals or ceremonies, but we kept calling their attention to other things; we talked to them about the economy, about the workings of the state, and other issues that the priests failed to explain adequately because their sole concern was to catechize. So indigenous people began to get the whole picture, and started to think in a different way.

We also revived our traditional festival, the Atún Puncha—the great day—which is the end and the beginning of the year, and which takes place in February. It is related to the celebration of the "Inti raimi," the Inca festival of the Sun, held in June in Peru and Ecuador. In Colombia, the church had forbidden this festival, and the priests organized religious pilgrimages to the Lajas Sanctuary, near Ipiales[16] designed to coincide with the "Inti raimi," in order to prevent people from participating in their own festivities. We syncretized the festival by holding it the week before Ash Wednesday, so that it wouldn't die out. The celebration lasts for a week, and it includes food, drink, and games. We always make reference to our place of origin, because Ingas, no matter where they are, always have the Atún Puncha in their minds: it is the time for homecoming, the most important time of family reunion. On the day of forgiveness we greet people with these words: *kausankamalla suma kausasunchi, sug watacama*, which mean "as long as we live, let us live well, until the new year." For this greeting we usually place a few petals on the head of the person who is being greeted, as a sign of peace, tranquility, and understanding. That is why Ingas, no matter

---

16 A city in the province (*departamento*) of Nariño, in Southern Colombia.

how far away they are, are always thinking of their place of origin, in the Sibundoy Valley; and that is why this is a time when most Ingas return to their place of origin.

In 1986 we held a very important forum. We called on the church, the traders, the politicians, the teachers, to examine the way in which each of them had contributed to the progress or to the neglect of the indigenous people. We prepared a document with an overview of our historical, political, cultural, social, and economic context, and we stated our case at the forum. We managed to make people see that the problem was not restricted to the assertion of indigenous rights, and that the situation of all parties involved mattered as well, and therefore it involved the commitment of them all. This was a very important event and, three or four years later, it resulted in a process of reflection, empowerment, and even organization, because for the first time we were heard as equals, and strategies were sought jointly to achieve the improvement of socioeconomic and cultural conditions in the region. Among the group of young people and leaders with whom we organized the Musurunakuna was the Inga Francisco Tandioy, professor at the University of Nariño, and other men and women who have become prominent since then.

In the same period, in 1986, I participated actively, with other Inga leaders, in the Second National Indigenous Congress called by ONIC. I met many indigenous leaders there; I continued with my training as a leader, participating in national and international meetings; and I left the country to contact other indigenous peoples, in Ecuador and Mexico. I was in Chile, and afterwards in Brazil, visiting different places and peoples, always talking about the situation in our country and the indigenous struggle in Colombia, and sometimes acting as a delegate of ONIC. I was involved in social and educational work in Putumayo, combined with teaching at the Champagnat School.

The Third National Congress of the Indigenous Peoples of Colombia took place in 1990. A very significant delegation of Colombian Indians, among them the Inga, put my name forward for the presidency of ONIC. I agreed to be a candidate for the presidency, and was elected vice president of ONIC. During that period of my life, as vice president, with other indigenous people elected at the Third Congress, I lived the experience of setting up the participation of Colombian indigenous peoples in the National Constituent Assembly. For the first time, we—Colombian Indians—were in a place where the future of the country could be decided.

I had never thought about participating in politics. I was part of the academy, and also supported the social process from the educational angle, and we made our own program of education with a very good team of teachers. It was this work that led to my election as vice president in 1990, and it was in that capacity that I was part of the negotiating committee for the Constituent Assembly, together with José Caldono, who is from Cauca, and Alfonso Palma, the president of ONIC, who is from Tolima. The three of us attended all the preparatory meetings for the Constituent Assembly, and we met with the representatives of all the parties and social movements. My first experience was a political speech in Caldono, Cauca, to present our list of candidates, and I was shaking all over.

Today I believe we've achieved great constitutional and political victories. It was not a concession from the state or a "gift" from parties or governments: it was the outcome of an indigenous social process. Neither the Liberal Party nor the Conservative Party, nor even the M-19, which had been negotiating with the government, were willing to support indigenous people, to allow our participation to start out with minimum guarantees: the lists of candidates they proposed offered no guarantee of there being any indigenous deputy to the Constituent Assembly. So we decided to participate directly with our own list, which was headed by Francisco Rojas Birry, and I was number three. I accompanied the indigenous deputy as one of his advisors. It was a valuable experience. I remember Horacio Serpa, who represented the Liberal Party, Alvaro Gómez, for the Conservative Party, Otto Patiño for the M-19, and many other political leaders. It was hard work, but it all went well, and when the Constituent Assembly came to its close we had obtained the recognition of our rights, including two seats in the Senate of the Republic.

After the Constituent Assembly, it was necessary to elect the indigenous representatives who would fill up those two seats in the Senate. I was chosen as a candidate by ONIC. There was some internal tension, because there were other indigenous people with political aspirations, but the majority chose my name and I was elected to the Senate for the period between 1991 and 1994. My parliamentary experience was very hard in the beginning, because I did not understand the workings of politics in this country. When I arrived in Congress I was pleasantly surprised, because they all seemed nice people and everyone patted you on the back, saying "We will help you." But three months later I had my first disappointment. Anatolio Quirá, who held the other seat assigned to indigenous people, Floro Tunubalá, an indigenous senator elected by Cauca, and I wanted to join a few committees that were of particular interest to us. I wanted to participate in the First Senate Committee and Anatolio in the Fifth. Our interest derived from the issues to be discussed in these committees, but we needed votes to become members. We organized the lists with other senators, but when all seemed settled we realized that the rules had suddenly changed, and support was withdrawn. We felt betrayed. It was at that moment that we suffered our first shock, and we began to realize that not everyone was quite what they seemed.

It worried me, and surprised me, to see that everyone talked about ethics—everyone was loud in speaking of a front against corruption—but when we were well into debating important issues and laws in favor of Colombians, they voted against. On one occasion, in the Ethics Committee, I asked what ethics it was we were talking about, whether Christian or other, and demanded that this point be clarified, because, if this was about trying people, we already had courts for that and there was no need for an ethics committee—problems of corruption should be tried in courts, in the Supreme Court or any other appropriate court of law, but not by us, because I too had an ethics which was different from theirs. It was an interesting debate.

My first mandate was very hard. I managed to get to know people— know who was who in the legislative field—to define strategies to draft bills and see them through. It was a good experience. Thanks to my work and my commitment, I carried out a second mandate: I was re-elected for the 1994–98 period. During this second mandate, I was able to produce more because of my prior experience. We made significant progress in lawmaking. I believe that during this second mandate a great volume of legislation was produced in support of the indigenous peoples and of the Colombian people. The indigenous forum was instituted, but it remained on paper—it was never brought into practical existence. We achieved the opening of important political-legal spaces where indigenous people can have a voice and a vote—they participate in decision-making, for example, on the boards of the INCORA (the Institute for Agrarian Reform), of the Regional Autonomous Corporations instituted by the environmental legislation, and so on. This was one of our political lines of action. Another one consisted in securing economic resources through guidelines for the development of social programs for the indigenous peoples and other marginalized groups. One of my achievements was the allocation of the resources relating to the transfer of oil royalties to the *resguardos*,[17] even though many distinguished senators, who are still in office, did not approve of regulating Law 60.[18] We fought a great legislative battle on this. Because of this, the indigenous reservations obtain resources from the Colombian state that are entrusted to the indigenous authorities, who have had to learn how to manage them as their "own." I think that we, the indigenous people, are still learning. In this period, during President Samper's administration (1994–98), we managed to get 2 percent of the

---

17   Reservations.
18   To "regulate" means to determine the mechanisms for the implementation of the law once promulgated. Law 60 of 1993, also known as the Transfer Law, was implemented in 1994, when the indigenous *resguardos* started to receive funds from the national budget, to be administered by the indigenous communities.

national budget earmarked for investment in the needs of indigenous peoples, and this was included in the social section of the National Plan for the Development of Colombia. The government did not carry it out exactly as prescribed by law, but still those resources were very important. A third important area I worked on was the strengthening of the autonomy of the indigenous groups. This work was the basis of several articles in different laws. This is why I say that, in my second mandate, my greater knowledge of lawmaking allowed me to act more effectively.

I am at present the deputy ombudsman for indigenous peoples and ethnic minorities of Colombia, at the Office of the Ombudsman. This is something I'm doing because I want to keep fighting for the indigenous peoples and for the poor people of my country, so they may win back their self-confidence and so that their rights stop being abused. My wife, Antonia, is Inga, and we have two children—ten-year-old Tupac Amaru and one-year-old Waina Capac.

As I take stock of the whole process of organizing and asserting the indigenous cause in Colombia and my role in it, I think that, until 1990, when we still didn't have any constitutional rights—as everyone in this country knows—we had no options other than concrete actions, such as marches and demonstrations. This helped to further the political and social process of indigenous peoples: social programs in health and education had broad support and were swiftly set up, and many people showed their solidarity and gave us quite a bit of help as advisors; many good people supported us until 1990. Unfortunately, after that year, at the time of the Constituent Assembly, there was a kind of regression in the effort to legitimize the rights obtained in social and legal terms, because many indigenous leaders dedicated themselves to electoral politics and neglected the social and educational work. We began to show signs of internal problems, among the indigenous people themselves, because not all had the same aspirations. We have to be self-critical in this respect; we have to be capable of evaluating our own processes. We achieved many rights, but they are still only on paper. They still have to be brought into practice. For instance, in the matter of the revenue from oil royalties, people should have had training on handling money, because they were not prepared to do so; they were on a different level, culturally and historically speaking. And because of this many problems arose, aggravated by the fact that the money does not come directly to the indigenous people—which means a further loss, because we end up with almost nothing at all.

Traditional politicians were largely responsible for this situation, by putting many obstacles in our way, because they thought it unacceptable that the Indians should have power and autonomy. In the end, we fought in the Senate but we lost, in the sense that the administration of the transfers was put in the hands of the *alcaldes*,[19] who sometimes resort to manipulation, bribing the leaders and using the money for petty politics, thus creating a series of problems of corruption and misuse of public monies. The fact is that indigenous people have been educated by whites, and have learned from them all the vices of their dealings with the world.

But we have been learning. Before 1990 we fought for the land. Between 1990 and 2000 came a period of political build-up. Now is the time for cultural change among the indigenous peoples, who are searching for new institutional relations with the state. New administrative mechanisms and structures of representation are being created; and in this struggle I will continue to support—as I'm now doing at the Office of the Ombudsman— the defense of pluralism and equality for the indigenous peoples.

Gabriel Muyuy Jacanamejoy's life story illustrates very well the importance of the struggle against the official forgetting of both social oppression and the resistance to it. History plays a fundamental role in the development of a people, allowing them to preserve and reproduce their identity, and to prevent the disintegration of the customs that give strength to it. Still, there are two histories: one is the history that is taught in school—that of heroes, great men, generals, presidents, literati, grand engineers, and events that power wishes to transmit from generation to generation, so that they acquire materiality; the other history, which has been forgotten or silenced by the victors, is that of great yet failed movements.

---

19   The *alcalde* is the head of the municipal administration.

6

Gerardo González

Peasant, guerrilla, leader of the peasant movement.

Interviewed by Alfredo Molano and
Maria Constanza Ramirez Silva

"The Cuban Revolution helped us a great deal. It gave us new ideas, and helped us see that it was possible to achieve what we had only dreamed about up to then. It was a great stimulus for the struggle, and showed the need for organization . . ."

Gerardo González[1]

In Gerardo González's account of his life one learns of the peasant movement's resistance and its struggle for land and the right to a dignified life throughout the course of the twentieth century. His testimonial reveals the causes of the conflict that has had the greatest social repercussions for the country's daily life. From his youth, Gerardo was a protagonist in the agrarian struggles taken up in defense of peasant property. He took part in one of the first instances of resistance to the violence that, in the 1950s, gave rise to armed conflict and the formation of guerrilla bands. After some years in hiding, he came to the forefront of the civil opposition in such movements as the National Association of Peasants and FENSOAGRO, always at the risk of his life.

BACKGROUND

My maternal grandfather moved to Pasca after the Thousand Days War.[2] He was a Liberal, a native of Chipaque, to the east of Cundinamarca, who told us of the daring deeds of the Liberal armies. He was old and lame, and would sit with us when we were children and tell us what he knew about those times. He liked to remember them. Back then, he was a second lieutenant under Uribe Uribe, and was a very strong man. Whenever he could, he would give impassioned speeches to the people, encouraging them not to give up the battle that they, the Liberals, had started and never finished. He felt they had to keep on going, because if they got organized, all was not lost.

The old man kept saying that the Conservatives had not won, but that the Liberals had surrendered to the government in a cowardly fashion. He always harbored hope that there would be a new Liberal uprising, and insisted that when the Liberals went back to battle they should not make

---

1   In order to maintain the flow of the text, the interviewers have eliminated the questions and transformed the interview into a first-person narrative.

2   The Thousand Days War (1899–1902) was won by the Conservative government with the help of the United States, which got the Panama Canal in return.

the same mistakes that Uribe Uribe and his people had made. According to him, before accepting defeat they had had time to retreat, regroup the army, and continue fighting.

He was involved in the uprising of the peons and day laborers at the Hacienda el Retiro; he was one of the people who helped people stand up for themselves and challenge the owners—or rather, the alleged owners—of those lands. That is how my mother came to be a leader at La Colonia; and now, after all these years, I realize that we all have fighting in our blood, inherited from my maternal grandfather, and later from my mother. I never knew my paternal grandparents. My father was born between Boyacá and Cundinamarca, in a village called Villapinzón, but moved to Sumapaz after a fight about some land in the upper part of his village—a skirmish that left several people dead. By the time I was old enough to understand a little, he had already taken another name. His real name was Salustiano González, but he had identification that said he was Eliseo Castillo. Years later, when I was older, he went back to using his real name. To explain to us why he was now called Salustiano and not Eliseo, as everyone had always called him, he told us he had had some problems with some land having to do with the coal mines. There were some galleries near the mines, and some people claimed the land for the coal and wanted the others to move down to the lower areas, because they were settled in the mining area. The fight was between those who wanted the land to mine the coal and those who wanted it to be left alone—like my father, who wanted the land for the peasants. My father was certainly Conservative, and when La Colonia was founded in Pasca, Sumapaz, there were several Conservative and Liberal families, people of both persuasions. Besides my father, there were other Conservative sympathizers who gradually left their Conservative affiliations behind, because Erasmo Valencia and the La Colonia people believed that, regardless of political beliefs, everyone should fight for their plot of land and throw off the yoke of the landlords. That was their banner.

CHILDHOOD AND ADOLESCENCE

I was born in 1936 in the house of Ifigenia (my mother) and my father. We were born on a plot of land that the owners of the hacienda had assigned to my parents, a place of abject poverty. My family, with a total of ten siblings—eight boys and two girls—all lived in a two-room hut with an outside kitchen. Life was hard, and we grew up in that miserably poor place. It was very rough. The house and bedroom had dirt floors, and stones were still used for grinding the corn. Life was miserably harsh, but within that poverty-stricken environment of the settlers there was still the will to fight. The Hacienda El Retiro belonged to the Cubillos or Adolfo León Gómez.[3] The climate was one of the coldest on the savannah, suitable for potatoes, corn, *arracacha*,[4] broad beans, cold-weather crops, but they used it mainly for dairy cows that they took to Fusagasugá. My parents began as sharecroppers, but instead of turning over a percentage of the crops they raised, they had to work for the landlord. They were given a small plot of land to work, a very small plot, in exchange for going so many days per week to help till the crops at the hacienda, mend the fences, herd the cattle, and clean the stalls—tasks divided up during the week. They were not paid, and of course there was a certain freedom for the settlers, or share-croppers, to work their own land. From what I've heard, there were about 230 families. Each got whatever they were allotted, probably on the basis of their relationship with the boss. There were some small plots, but they were generally 10 or 15 hectares. Since it was a big hacienda, and was being opened up for farming by clearing out the low mountain areas, the families who cleared more land were given more to clear. They would plant crops for a while, and then it would be used for cattle. So the plots were not all the same size, and there were people who had up to 30 hectares because they were very good at clearing land. Starting in 1912, near Cabrera, in the *vereda*[5] of Pueblo Viejo, a family named Molina and a woman called Eufrosina Moya began to fight for their land, to get organized, and to have meetings. That was the atmosphere we grew up in.

In a neighboring hamlet, called La Esperanza, we worked together to set up a school, with the help of the government of the Department. That is where we studied. My mother worked hardest of all on it, so her children could learn to read and write. I owe my love of reading and learning to her. And we were fortunate to have a teacher, Leonor Cuevas, who was very knowledgeable. When my uncles were in their third and fourth years of high school, I helped them with geography, although I was only in the third grade. I particularly recall that one year there were 106 students, all in one very big room. We sat wherever we could, and she taught us all, from first to fourth grade. Just one woman. She worked from eight to eleven-thirty or twelve, if I remember correctly, and then from two to four in the afternoon. And Saturdays too, from eight o'clock to noon, without a break. There were a great many opportunities to learn. The teacher organized a library for the older students, and we had to pay one or two cents for book loans. We would read it, and the next Monday, we would all talk about the part we were reading. My mother, who didn't know how to read or write, paid the library rental fee, and had us read aloud so she could listen. This led us

---

3   Owners of the Hacienda el Retiro.
4   A garden root vegetable.
5   Hamlet.

to read several novels, by Vargas Vila and other authors. She truly enjoyed it, and when she was working in the kitchen, getting our breakfast ready for the following day at six in the morning, our job was to read to her. And so went our childhood, in the midst of the ups and downs of all the La Colonia settlers' fight for the land.

My siblings and I began to attend the meetings with my mother. At first, they seemed very long to me, and I didn't really understand what was being said, although I liked seeing so many people together, all pulling in the same direction. They were large meetings, of 300 to 400 people. Then there were special meetings, with an open character held the first Monday of each month, and people who did not attend were fined. I remember quite well a very heated discussion, as we would say today. My uncle was the controller on the La Colonia council, and he said it made no sense to start so many lawsuits about the land; it was better just to move in and squat on it, and not leave it up to the judges who were appointed by the landlords—just move in from all sides and then the government would be helpless. My uncle's initiative was cut short when Act 200[6] was passed. It worked to our favor, but they ended up replacing it with Act 100.[7] I always say that that reversal sowed the seeds of all the violence that still goes on today. There was one very well-known case that I personally was very familiar with, because my own father was involved. One wealthy landlord family, the Cubillos, was buying up land from peasants at low prices. If they were willing to sell, it was a friendly purchase; but if they weren't, other methods were used. Whatever the method, the Cubillos always got the land they wanted. The Cubillos had their eye on some land owned by the Indians in the hamlet of Púchica. But the Indians refused to sell or leave the land. They said they had deeds for the land granted by the king of Spain. My father and other people went to take a look at those old land grants, and they were authentic. So, the Colonia people bought the land from the Indians and registered it again to defend the Indians from the tricky lawyers and corrupt judges. It was a very touchy business, because the Indians were afraid to take that step, which was really a great leap forward. It was harder to get at the peasants, because they were organized and also had political representation. Gaitán[8] was the spokesman for a multitude of cries of rebellion, and he made himself heard. That's why they had to kill him—to shut him up and put a stop to that.

---

6 The Act 200 [Lei 200] of 1936 was an attempt to accomplish the Agrarian Reform beyond the simple model of parcelling lands.

7 The Act 100 [Lei 100] was an accomplishment of the landowners retarding the application of Act 200 until 1956 where it concerns the benefits and guarantees to the partners and tenants and declaring as a public utility the partnership contracts.

8 Jorge Eliécer Gaitán was a leader of the populist movement in Colombia and one of the most charismatic leaders of the Colombian Liberal Party. He was assassinated in 1948 during his second electoral campaign for president.

After that battle, things got better for us. At least now we had land of our own to work. People started building houses, and my father had us laying bricks every Sunday, until we had our own brick house to live in. We were still poor, but at least we had a decent, sturdy place to sleep that didn't rattle in the wind.

So we—and particularly I, from boyhood—began to take part in things. I started going to the meetings of the *Junta*, as it was called, every Monday. I went because my mother took me. I would sit there and listen. The meetings started at eight o'clock in the morning and went on until three or four o'clock in the afternoon, with long discussions of all the ongoing problems, because there was a lawsuit that had been filed by the former renters and the settlers. I remember it as part of the training we had, and the forms of rebellion we learned, as children. But then, after having lived through the effects of Act 200, Act 100 went into force. My father and mother sent their children to cut wood in a certain part of the hacienda, telling us to avoid being seen by anyone. We loaded it on some donkeys that we had and then took it either to Fusagasugá or to Pasca, to exchange the wood that was used for baking bread or for making *chicha*,[9] for salt, sorghum, soap, and other household staples. One time, when I was seven years old, I was with my brother César cutting firewood, when we were arrested and taken to Fusagasugá, where they held us for about eight hours or more. They finally released us, gave us our freedom, but we were naturally very angry, and everybody protested because they had thrown little children in jail. So this feeling of rebellion, together with the stance we have always maintained, was added on to other life experiences.

We continued with our studies, with our work, and our reading, and one day Erasmo Valencia's newspaper, *Claridad*, began arriving at La Colonia. My mother had us read that newspaper aloud to her every night, and the next day she would gather her fellow workers and talk to them and share the advice and points of view Erasmo Valencia expressed in his newspaper, along with the news about what was happening in other parts of the country concerning the organization and struggle of the settlers.

I later earned my first wage working with my Uncle Luis, my mother's brother, helping guide the team of oxen. Since the oxen were not very well broken in, they would always hire a young boy, a *chino* as they called them, who would go along helping with the team and the plow wherever they went. Later, when I was older, I began to work with my father. He gave us a lot of advice and guidance, and said we would have to work hard for the things we wanted in life. The main thing then was for us to be able to buy our own clothing, since he fed us, and of course we lived in the house [he

---

9   A traditional fermented corn drink.

had built]. He let us keep the money we got for the crops we sold on our own, and allowed us to buy whatever we wanted.

My father assigned each of us a small plot, telling us what would grow there, and giving each of us tasks and obligations according to our ability and the quality of the soil. You had to know the land in order to know what to sow, because not all crops did equally well in the different types of soil. He also inspected our work. We learned a lot from him. He did not use fertilizers or pesticides for plagues or weeds, and that is why I am still so strong and in such good health today. The newspaper *Claridad* published articles with information on farming methods, health advice for peasants, and also on laws and norms that could help us, along with news from different regions of the country. That is how we found out that the government used violence not only against us, but also against other peasants in other regions. This information put us on our guard and helped us decide what to do. It warned us about all the dangers that beset the peasants and their leaders. In those days there was a very cruel punishment called *extrañamiento*,[10] which consisted in expelling people from the village they lived and worked in. This could be applied to one or several people, who could not return for a specified period of time or, in some cases, never at all, depending on what the authorities decided. I have vivid memories of the exile of Facundo Díaz, who was my godfather and also had fought the Thousand Days War. He was a Liberal leader and also one of the peasant leaders, so the right-wingers had him in their sights. They declared his expulsion, but the mayor took longer to write out the order of expulsion than it took Don Facundo to come back through the foothills in the middle of the night. Of course we all took him in and protected him, because he was valuable to all of us. The settlers did what they could to keep him out of harm's way. They hid him in their homes, or made sure he was hidden out of sight in the foothills, away from the roads. This made it hard for the police to catch him by surprise. The older people taught us all the tricks they used to stay alive: never give any information to a stranger, and if you do, give him the wrong information. We would send them west instead of south, say yellow instead of white, all to make time for our people to flee or set up a defense. If they were caught again, they would be put on road gangs, to build roads with picks and shovels, or locked up and forgotten in the Panóptico, a prison built in Bogotá for the Liberal prisoners taken in the last civil wars, and for the people who protested against Conservative governments. During General Reyes's dictatorship, they filled that prison up with "reds."

---

10   Banishment, exile.

ERASMO VALENCIA

Erasmo Valencia was from the province of Caldas—the village of Manizales, I think. He started the newspaper *Claridad*. It was only published occasionally, whenever they were able—meaning when the money collected from the peasants was enough to pay the printer, and when Erasmo had time to write it. As I understand it, Erasmo did everything, from writing to proofreading. He had been an officer in the cavalry. According to the older Sumapaz Colonia directors, one day, riding down from Monserrate, he fell off his horse—the horse took off, bucking. He hurt his leg and requested a discharge from the cavalry.

He had studied law, and although he wasn't a lawyer, he used to hire lawyers for trials. Valencia and Jorge Eliécer Gaitán opened an office here to deal with social problems. He and Gaitán were great friends. The settlers said they had heard about a person who defended peasants, and that person was Erasmo Valencia. He later defended some people from north Boyacá, and many people then found out that the land did not really belong to those who said they owned it. According to the old settlers—there are still a few left—in 1928 or 1930, after some trouble that happened with a peasant who lived in the hamlet of Hollerías, who was whipped for not meeting his commitments as a sharecropper, some settlers got together and went to look for the man they had heard of, who knew that those lands did not belong to the *hacendatarios*.[11] And that is the story of how people learned about Erasmo Valencia. A complaint was filed in the Cundinamarca regional assembly; later it went to Congress, to the parliament, and several commissions were formed. Erasmo Valencia was on those commissions that traveled around with the government making reports, and he was already very well known throughout the region. He visited different areas of Sumapaz and the east of Tolima, around Iconozo and part of Villarrica, and this kindled his passion for legal battles. He was a pacifist, and wanted no part of any battles except legal battles. That is why he had many differences with the communists—because they said that the landlord system had to be done away with completely, by whatever means, and Erasmo Valencia did not agree. He said that only the landlords who were not legitimate should be eliminated, and those who held legal deeds to the land should be left alone.

He fought very hard for the upper region of Sumapaz, because he was sure it was not legally held. Eduardo Rocha had no deed for his property. People from Púchica, and later from Degolladero, got organized for the fight. It was after the Pueblo Viejo incident in 1912 that they were brutally repressed, in 1914, in a massacre higher up in the moorland in Púchica. Since

---

11   Landlords.

each department had its own armed forces, the Cundinamarca Guard went up there to a meeting being held by the settlers; the settlers fought back, and several people were killed. Erasmo Valencia had an idea about forming an organization to be consolidated throughout the region of Sumapaz, in Púchica. Púchica was part of the concession of the highlands, near Huila, on the way to Meta. There, things were rougher, and there was a battle, with the police wielding rifles, and the peasants too. Although Erasmo Valencia was a pacifist, many settlers had arms, since they knew that eventually they would have to fight. I should also add that the Sumapaz area had a lot of game that the locals hunted. There were deer, and everyone had their shotguns and muskets, and some also managed to get rifles called "grasses." Some of these arms were from the Thousand Days War, and changed hands among people who knew where to get clandestine ammunition, because anyone who had one of those was very well armed. They were *Pardo Roche*, which is the name of one of the weapons they used.

ACT 200 AND ACT 100

The Land Act was passed the year I was born; but the difference was that I grew up and Act 200 was killed, in 1944, and replaced with Act 100. I was still a boy. What Act 200 did was recognize our right to the improvements we made on the land. It guaranteed that sixty days after an improvement was made, nobody could fail to recognize it, or throw the peasant off that land. There could be a hearing before a land judge, but the landlord could no longer send the police with a long bullwhip to throw people off the land. The peasants who lived in Viotá, who were no fools, came up with the idea of planting coffee up in the foothills, and when they reached a certain height, about 20 centimeters, they would clear out the land around them and keep the crops. It would all happen very quickly; all of a sudden the crops were there and had grown to a good size. When the inspector came around, there was nothing he could do, because the plants had grown tall, and the law recognized them, because they had been there more than sixty days. After that, there would always be a legal complaint and a hearing, but no one could do anything about it, because the crops were two months old. The landlord, who usually didn't hold the deed to the land—or if he did, it was false—had no legal recourse really, because he had already lost possession of the land, due to the right acquired through growing crops. After that, Erasmo taught us how to enhance these improvements, in order to make it harder to lose possession of the land they had taken. The peasants built fences, stables, brought in cattle, and built houses. This meant that, even if they lost in court, their work to improve the property had to be recognized; and if they weren't awarded the land, they at least had the right to be paid for the work done. In many cases, the improvements made were worth more than the land itself, so the peasant won the lawsuit, because the owner, or the alleged owner, was not willing to pay more than the land was supposedly worth. That is how they started to win over the land, due to the peasant's skill at conserving his land by working it.

That is how my father got his own land. His work was recognized as an improvement, and the improvement as title to the land. My old man had built fences, improved the roads, cultivated the fields, and every time the judge came to serve the papers to evict us, there was some new improvement—even if it was just a plot of carnations or roses. The idea was for a high value to be placed on the improvement, so that it wouldn't be worth it for the landlord to pay the price. The price could be high or low, but the important thing was to fetch a price that recognized the settler's work.

The Agrarian Councils (Juntas Agrarias) were there to back up the peasants. After Erasmo Valencia's efforts got the high region of Sumapaz for the peasants, things got moving. In Púchica, in the hamlets of Hollerías and la Playa, where the incident with the hacienda supervisor took place, everyone began to get organized and attend meetings. Erasmo Valencia placed only one condition on fighting back at the landlords, and that was to do it in an organized fashion. That's why everybody in that region ended up being members of an organization where attendance was taken before each meeting, dues were paid, group work was done, and people obeyed the leaders: the president, the controller, and the treasurer. It was a peasants' union. The people got themselves organized, and that was the instrument, the tool they used to fight for their land. Whenever they heard the horn being blown— or *cacho*, as we called it—they had to drop everything they were doing and go see what was going on. The horn was the signal that something was either happening or might happen, and everyone responded to that signal. Blowing the horn was like firing a shotgun. I learned later, as I got older, that there were different types of horn blasts to warn that the rural guards were coming, or that a head of cattle had been lost, or to call people to a meeting. When the judge came to serve papers, there was a horn signal, so that when he got there to evict people he would find all the peasants waiting for him. The women in charge of the midday meal would usually build big fires. I remember one day when my mother and Alicia Solórzano, a huge woman, started boiling water in big pots like they did to make coffee; but when the guards arrived they knew it was not for coffee: the women were boiling water to throw pots of it on the guards, and scald them like chickens. Once they arrested two women and took them to jail for that, but the next day people rose up in protest, and they let the women go free. Some of the women played a very important role; they were even more daring than the men. Today, looking back, one can see that the essential thing was the organization and the discipline. The horn signaling was a very valuable tactic, because all the people, gathered together and on guard, would begin to shout at whoever had come, sometimes in unison, chorusing out their protests. At times, the visitors were shouted down and forced to leave without having said a word. And that is how many official visits to serve eviction papers were thwarted. Anyway, it was the strength of the organization that managed to uphold that law, the one that was favorable to us. We developed a great sense of solidarity and were very much aware of our rights.

There were few evictions, but some people did get thrown off their land. Looking back, there was no political rationale behind this, because the landlords controlled the mayors, and the mayors controlled the judges. There were some judges, the so-called land judges, who did do their job honestly and independently, and respected the law. In particular they enforced Act 200, which was not a bad law. Those judges specialized in land disputes. They paid no attention to the mayors and did not obey the landlords. Also, I should point out that the peasants had good lawyers, who were on top of the game. I remember the case of one man, Julio Rodríguez, who was elected president of the Pasca settlement's peasant union, and shortly after, it came to light that he had bought another plot of land and a team of mules, when everybody knew he didn't have a penny. They looked into it, and found out he was making deals on the side with the landlord Germán Cubillos. The people reacted immediately to this and threw him out, not only of the union, but also out of the settlement. And so, traitors were successively discovered and punished. People were no longer so easy to fool, and in the end the people won that legal dispute with the hacienda.

I remember many important leaders who did not sell out: Alberto Clavijo, Neftalí Prieto, Julio Ramos, Salvador Castellanos, Pedro Díaz, my uncle, Florian González, and my mother. They were a highly respected group, because they had been elected by the community and because of the positions they defended in the interests of all, including the children. Although they didn't understand everything, they heard things, and listened, and little by little came to understand. The bosses exploited the children even more, because they were weaker and afraid of adults. I was paid to guide the oxen. My job was to walk along with them, using a long switch to keep them moving. Crops like potatoes and wheat were sown at the hacienda, and at home we grew beans, *arracacha*, and green onions for food. Sometimes, when I got home, I would have to weed the bean patch after working with the oxen. There was no rest, even on Sundays, because we had to haul water and then go to market. It took up the whole day.

It was a long, hard fight, because even though Act 200 recognized land improvements, it did not recognize the peasant's right to the land. In other words, this act became a way to make the landlord pay for land improvements, but it didn't take the land away from him. The Land Act never gave us the land. What it did was try to reduce the pressure about land rights, and force the owners to pay for improvements. Even so, the landlords didn't accept it, and killed it off in 1944 with Act 100, which basically gave them the right to evict, by increasing the time they had to prove legal title. This affected the peasants and the settlers, because it made it harder to obtain proof of improvements and so gain a legal right to the land. Act 100 worked against Act 200. Using it, landlords began to reconquer their land, like they did in northern Boyacá and Córdoba.

There were some very large estates in Soatá province, and Erasmo Valencia also came into the picture there. The whole Cocuy region was full of these huge estates, and he organized people there too. That was one of the places where the fight began, and it was where the *chulavitas* appeared. *Chulavitas* is what we called the Conservative peasants, who were duped by the "Christ the King" tale and organized to kill Liberal peasants. The same thing happened in el Valle, near Cartago. There Erasmo reared up his head once again, and organized people, and the Conservative government of Ospina also gave arms to the Conservatives (who we called *pájaros*) to kill Liberals.

The struggles of the 1920s came to bear fruit in the 1930s, became a problem in the 1940s, and have been a source of bloodshed from the 1950s on. In February 1934, Gaitán was arrested in Fusagasugá after a huge peasant demonstration organized by Erasmo Valencia to protest the death of several peasants and at the same time demand land. Gaitán had founded his party, UNIR,[12] and Valencia had founded PAN, the National Agrarian Party. They exchanged ideas and reached agreements. Gaitán was a national political leader and Valencia was a regional peasant leader. They were two strong influences. Valencia started his party in Sumapaz and then extended it to include other areas—not many, but a little along the Córdoba coast, and a little on the Atlantic side, somewhat into the Cauca Valley and also to the east of Tolima, around Chaparral. This is where Isauro Yosa, a Liberal socialist, had a stronghold. Yosa and Manuel Marulanda were the founders of FARC.[13] Gaitán had a big movement, but so did Erasmo Valencia, and that's where their friendship stemmed from. Erasmo Valencia controlled everything from Pasca up, but Gaitán ran Silvania. The Communist Party, headed by Dussán, ran everything from Alto to here on the Tequendama side, toward Viotá. Much of the work was shared in Viotá and Aguadita. People from Viotá came to Aguadita to help clear the foothills, filling the

---

12   Unión Nacional de Izquierda Revolucionaria—National Left-wing Revolutionary Union.
13   Fuerzas Armadas Revolucionarias de Colombia—Revolutionary Armed Forces of Colombia.

region with peasant camps. The same thing was done in La Colonia. That's why the Fusagasugá demonstration was so important. People cleared the foothills to take possession of the land, but the political struggle was needed to ensure that the possession became legal title. Whenever they found out that a landlord did not hold legal deeds, people started to make improvements, clearing foothills to cultivate banana and coffee, and then made that fact known. It was the battle between the alleged owners and the settlers. The peasants were organized in agrarian leagues, and Gaitán was in charge of the settlement. From Alto to here, they were known as Peasant Leagues—in Tibacuy and also throughout Quipile, in San Juan de Río Seco.

THE STRUGGLE FOR LAND

The struggle for land came out of the need for peasants to get their own land, and stop being at the mercy of the large landowners. For example, the Viotá landowners were very important, even though they were a very small group of people. In Tibacuy—at a village called San José—the fight against the Caballero family had a major political effect, because they had enormous power—they had their own currency and their own jail, and made their own laws. I got firsthand knowledge of the Caballero family's jail during my time as one of the ANUC[14] leaders. In other areas, the landlords did not have jails because they used the police. In some regions they started charging tolls, forcing people to pay to travel along their roads. The people using the road had to cross the hacienda land, because there was no shorter, less steep route, and to cross it they had to pay a toll as they went in and came out. They paid to enter when they took that route from Soacha, and to exit when they came in from Fusagasugá. If they were leading a calf, or even a dog, they had to pay a toll for themselves and the animal. There were two famous toll roads: one at Alto de Rosas, in the area of Chocho, and another at the exit of Silvania, because the hacienda, whose main house is now a golf club, was located there. But Gaitán turned all that system upside down and fought against it. The repercussions were enormous, and of course he ended up being murdered.

What made Gaitán different from other politicians was that he was on the side of the people. For example, when Lleras Restrepo was Secretary of Agriculture for Cundinamarca, he bought land from the El Soche landlords using public funds from the Agrarian Bank, so that they would not be lost to the peasants who had made use of the Land Law. Lleras was not on the peasants' side—he was rather on the other side. Later, when INCORA[15] was

---

14   Asociación Nacional de Usuarios Campesinos—National Association of Peasants.
15   Instituto Colombiano de La Reforma Agraria—Colombian Institute for Agrarian Reform.

established, he tried to do the same thing—buy the worthless land from the landlords to sell it to the peasants at high prices. He failed because neither the peasants nor the landlords were happy about it. So, between both sides, they stopped that practice.

But Gaitán was a lot like Erasmo Valencia, even though he had his differences with Valencia about what areas should be left alone and what areas should be invaded. Valencia respected the legally owned lands that were being tilled, but Gaitán wanted a land reform that included even those lands. That was the main difference. That is why, when in the 1940s President López Pumarejo organized a group of horsemen to go meet the settlers in Sumapaz, Valencia went out to meet him, and that caused a great rift between him and the Communist Party. The interesting thing was that, despite all the differences between Gaitán and Valencia, and those that later arose between Gaitán and the Communist Party, the solidarity among the peasants never broke down, because they were not losing anything as a result of those differences.

For years, Eufrosina Molina had been saving some petticoats she had made out of Samacá cloth. It was a thick and coarse, but very sturdy fabric that was highly valued. She had kept them tucked away, with no particular purpose in mind, until the problem of Pueblo Viejo came up. Pueblo Viejo was a hard three-day walk through the foothills. In those days there was still dense foliage in the Sumapaz foothills and mountains; there was a great deal of water, and also deer, which we called *soches*, a lot of armadillos, and even bears. Her husband had to go testify before the Pueblo Viejo authorities that the land was not owned by anybody, so she sold her petticoats. Nobody had dared to challenge the word of the bosses about who owned the land, until Eufrosina sold her petticoats to pay for her husband's trip, and so help peasants defend their right to keep the fruits of their labors. Defending that right led to the 1912 deaths, which, like Eufrosina's petticoats, were a carefully kept secret—until 1928, when it all came out and was denounced in the newspaper *Claridad*.

Viotá was the original site of the organizational movement. It was where the struggle had begun in the 1920s—the struggle of the *tabloneros*[16] and *aparceros*[17] of the large coffee plantations of Tequendama against their landlords. It was because the labor contracts they were forced to sign were literally robbery, sanctioned by the law, or at least backed up by the authorities. That struggle was undertaken by the newly founded Communist Party,

---

16   Rural workers from Cundinamarca and southern Tolima who got paid by the *tablón* (a measuring unit)—that is, by the amount of coffee they picked for the plantation owners.
17   Workers who, in exchange for living on a plot of land that they could cultivate, had to work for free for half of each week for the landowner.

as a kind of proof of its existence. If I'm not mistaken, it was Gilberto Vieira who started organizing people, educating them about their rights. He made friends with a certain Leopoldo Niño, who was a highly respected peasant, and the two of them were key to opening up the doors to the rebellion. They began with something very simple: tilling land at three o'clock in the morning and planting good-sized plants, so that by 8 a.m. the judge could see that they were there.

The big disagreement between the communists and the pro-agrarians had to do with the methods used. The communists were out to eradicate the landlord system and the large estate holdings, whether or not their owners held legal title. The pro-agrarians wanted the fight to be only against illegally held land. That is why the communists became so strong and received so much support from the peasants, particularly after 1934, when a resolution was passed condemning the landlord system unconditionally and with no exceptions. That was very well received by the peasants, and particularly by indigenous people. Those were the struggles that reached Pasca and Sumapaz in the early 1940s, when Act 200, defending land rights, was already in place. That resolution helped the communists gain strength. One of the best things that I truly value is the fact that, despite all the discussion between the pro-agrarians and the communists, the solidarity remained, even as each group argued to uphold their ideals. Neither side lost sight of what was most important, and there were no fights. With Juan de la Cruz Varela, who was a radical pro-agrarian, there were major arguments and shouting matches, but never, ever did they let those differences get in the way of maintaining a united front.

JUAN DE LA CRUZ VARELA

Juan de la Cruz Varela came to Cabrera, Sumapaz, with his father, Don Dionisio, in the 1920s. They had left their home, Ráquira, not to escape violence, but due to a lack of land. It was a migration born of poverty, and people came to Sumapaz to seek a better life, to find work. In Boyacá, the lands at Sáchica, Ráquira, and Sutamarchán had been appropriated since colonial times. It was dry, poor soil, and there was no water. The father, Don Dionisio, had also been a bugler in the Thousand Days War. The Varela family ended up in the hamlet of Pueblo Viejo, where the Molina family owned many tracts of land and controlled people's lives. The Varelas managed to survive by day-jobbing, which is all you can do if you have no land and don't have a special, friendly relationship with the landowner.

Juan de la Cruz was a very intelligent boy. He had learned to read and write by the time he was eight years old, and was put in charge of the mail between Púchica and Cabrera. That is how he gained experience, and also knowledge about life in other villages. They say that after an argument with old Don Dionisio, Juan de la Cruz took off for Tolima, near Villarrica, and settled down in a hamlet called Mundo Nuevo, because, as he was passing by, the peasants asked him to help them write a document defending their livelihood. Juan de la Cruz, who was well informed, and also felt in his blood the need to fight for the land, not only stayed on at Mundo Nuevo, but also helped the peasants fight for their rights. He put together a very well drafted document, and people became very fond of him. They gave him work and a plot of land. But he was a rolling stone, and took off for the east, further inland, to a hamlet that was in the process of being founded, called La Colonia, which belonged to the village of Icononzo. He stayed there for a while, and cleared another plot of land, but got wanderlust again and went to look for land around Cunday. He settled there in a place called Alto Palmar, started anew, began organizing people, and also used it as a base to fight battles in other areas. Juan de la Cruz Varela and Alto Palmar were soon seen as one and the same. There, he became a peasant leader and a political leader as well, because he was elected councilman for Pandi and Icononzo. He was elected by both the Pandi and Icononzo settlers, and served on the councils of both. He was a man who read a great deal, and continued to learn and evolve. He organized the peasants, taught them to fight back, and that is why the violence in those regions was so terrible in the 1940s and '50s. The natural bridge at Icononzo became a place to dump the dead. And the municipal dump trucks hauled all the bodies of the Liberals killed by the public works gangs. Piles of dead bodies were dumped over the side, from where they fell into a bottomless pit so dark that even the local birds, the *guácharos*, have no eyes.

He was a very studious man. I remember that during the violence of the 1950s they burned up his library, and he never forgave them for that. He always denounced the tactics used to deny education to the people, and always encouraged their desire to learn. After the period of violence passed, in 1954 or '55 he was elected deputy to the Tolima Assembly, and also served as its president. He then filed a lawsuit against the state for burning down his library, and won—and so the provincial government ended up paying him for the damages. Later, I saw him again in Duda, in a meeting with Jacobo Arenas. He asked me to take him a list of books because he had nothing to read, and always felt desperate when he had no way to learn something new. Juan de la Cruz settled down there, and as a leader, became very good friends with Valencia. It was a personal and political friendship that lasted until the death of both. Juan de la Cruz held Erasmo's ideas in great esteem, and both were left-wing Liberals who opposed all privilege.

THE DEATH OF GAITÁN

The day Gaitán was killed we were up working on a beet patch we had. At around two o'clock we heard the horn. It was a Friday. We thought it was strange, but we gathered up our tools and went to the settlement head-quarters, and it was there that we found out that they had killed Gaitán. Nobody knew what to do. We all knew it was serious, very serious, and that all hell would break loose. Some of the settlers got out the shotguns they had kept hidden since the war, but everybody was waiting for orders from Bogotá. Everyone was ready, but since it would mean going back to war, we all needed a general, or at least a leader of some kind. Echandía came forward to lead us, but he sold out. Ospina bought him out. The people would have given up their lives to avenge Gaitán, but Echandía betrayed us and turned over the entire movement, bound hand and foot. It's true that people managed to gradually free themselves from those ties; but we had no leader, and so all those individuals became their own leaders, and that is why the people got organized, without waiting for any orders, and took to the hills. It was a long time before we had another leader who wouldn't sell out. There was some hope when the people in los Llanos rose up, but they managed to buy out their leader and lead him to the slaughter.

Here, things got started with Pablo Bello and Pedro Acosta, who were leaders from Cunday, but had come from Chaparral after hearing speeches by the Indian leader Quintín Lame. They took off for the hills alone, to gain support from the coffee pickers first, and then, little by little, from the peas-ants. When Juan de la Cruz joined the movement, things began to change and to gain new significance. He was a very serious individual. There was no declaration of war, or *pronunciamiento*, as there had been in the wars of the nineteenth century, because there was no general. That was a mistake, because the civil war—and that is exactly what it was—was never recog-nized as such. It ended up as a bloody confrontation between armed groups, not a social and political struggle. We had to wait many years, and there were many deaths, before things got on the right course—and, I repeat, before we found a leader who refused to sell us out.

In truth, the peasant organization of the 1930s was a training ground for guerrilla commanders. Many of the commanders from Marquetalia, Riochiquito, Pato, and Guayabero came out of those early conflicts. The school of hard knocks, frustration, and deception teach a lot more than books and speeches ever could. The repression they were subjected to led people to learn to defend themselves, and the crimes committed by the *chulavita* police forced them to arm themselves. Besides, I should also point out that many peasants—or, rather, many sons of peasants—who were fighting for their rights, did military service and learned to use weapons.

I did my military service in 1950. You had to have your papers certifying compliance with the draft, or you could not find work. Before that, things were different: on market days, the army would close off the roads leading in and out of the villages, and any young man who got caught inside and who was physically fit to serve would end up in the army. That is why most young men never left their homes on Sundays—and if they did, they were always on guard, checking out all corners of the marketplace, so they could get away, fast, at the first sign of a uniform. But by 1950 the army had figured out another way to get recruits: deny the right to work. If you didn't have military service papers, you were stuck. You couldn't sign legal documents or contracts, couldn't go to school, and were almost confined to the farm, because there were soldiers strategically staked out on all the roads. The violence that year was something to behold. There were dead bodies all over; public order ceased to exist. I was sent to a region of La Colorada, near San Vicente de Chucurí, where a Liberal follower of Gaitán, whose name was Rangel, had led the uprising in Barranca on April 9th. He was the local mayor and had led the army on a merry chase for weeks, until eventually he found himself surrounded and betrayed, and fled to the hills. We had heard of him in Sumapaz, but had never seen him. Since I was an officer in the army, I tried to make contact with him, and I even managed to send him some rifle cartridges through some women who offered to take them, but another officer reported me. I was arrested and they investigated the case, but couldn't prove anything against me.

When I finally got my discharge papers, I returned to Pasca. Things had gotten much worse there. Erasmo Valencia had died a few days after they killed Gaitán, and the settlers had appointed Juan de la Cruz to replace him. Juan had his people around La Concepción, and he stayed there, and from there ran the movement which, after April 9th, was not only fighting for the land, but also for survival. It was at La Concepción, the entrance to Sumapaz, that the army attacked us one day. Thank God we managed to defend ourselves, because we had gotten good information. The soldiers came out much worse than we did. I heard the shots. We left La Concepción with Juan de la Cruz, to go to Duda. The idea was to fight, push back the Conservatives, and so take power. That was our response to the violence started against us on April 9th, and we got organized for the fight. It was Alvaro Vásquez del Real who was responsible, to a great extent, for this turn towards the goal of taking power, rather than simply fighting to get the land. He was a general trial court judge in Icononzo, just out of law school. A bit later we reached a peace agreement with Rojas Pinilla, in Cabrera. That agreement gave us valuable time to regroup and regain our strength, because, despite the peace agreement, the problems had not been resolved.

We worked on that for a time, but it was not very long until Rojas decided to attack us in Villarrica to keep the gringos happy. The gringos were obsessed with the Cold War, and saw agents from Moscow everywhere. I guess you could say that our main success in that war was figuring out how to organize defeat, and not scatter or turn into easy prey for the enemy. Several marches were organized, inspired by Mao Zedong's great march in China. After the bombing and military invasion of Villarrica and Cunday, we conducted an organized retreat towards the Duda Canyon, towards El Pato and Guayabero, while the people who had fought in the south of Tolima organized self-defense for the Marquetalia and Riochiquito regions. The communists were extremely active, organizing groups of men, women, and children, and were establishing rural settlement councils, settlers' committees, and party cells. These were legal activities carried out along with others, like organizing peasant self-defense efforts. We knew the tide was turning, and in that we were not mistaken.

We went out and got to work organizing regions from Meta, Huila, Tolima, and Cundinamarca, founding several self-defense groups, because self-defense meant the protection of the people themselves and their communities. The self-defense groups were part of the organizations, but were kept anonymous. We took advantage of the country's situation and used the experience gained from the agrarian struggle, dating back to the 1920s. Both the army and the state intelligence agency would frequently send their spies disguised as doctors, clergymen, beggars, and day laborers. The self-defense groups were in charge of keeping track of them all, and also of calming tempers in the face of provocations, whose purpose was to incite new violence, a new war against the regions with peasant settlements—because it was above all the peasants who fought for the land, who worked it, settled down, farmed, and improved whatever land they held.

THE INDEPENDENT REPUBLICS

Out of that resistance movement came the name Independent Republics, simply due to the fact that we did not let them continue to govern as they pleased, were self-sufficient, and, above all, continued to grow stronger. That was the crime they accused us of. This accusation was conveniently used by the oligarchs to cover up their real crimes—and also by the military, to seal their alliance with the US government.

The peasants' self-defense groups were a thorn in the government's side, because they simply never gave up. They might be beaten, but they would never surrender. Another reason was that we were seeking self-government, because the national government persecuted and repressed us, and was always against us. We weren't after independence from the nation, because first and foremost we are Colombians; but we did want to share some of the decision making with the government. Our elected authorities were respected because they defended us, and helped solve people's problems— all those small-scale conflicts between neighbors, communities, families, and even between husbands and wives. Natural conflicts. If there was a government-appointed police agent nearby, people would not go to that authority, but would call on the self-defense groups, who knew the people and who solved problems without taking sides. The government always took sides, and it was always the side of the rich and never ours. Problems were solved calmly, with tranquility, and without resentment. They started calling our movement Independent Republics, because we stopped obeying those who worked against us. In addition, they were interested in taking the land that we had farmed.

That was the case of the Gómez family. A brother of Alvaro Gómez— son of Laureano, the most bloodthirsty leader we have ever had—had lands up above Villarrica, on the limits of Dolores. But beneath Gómez Hurtado's patriotism were hidden economic interests. At that time, Marulanda was the Southern Tolima Highway inspector. He always was a big one for highways and roads, but he did not neglect his people, because he knew what was good for him. He worked inside and gave guidance, as he was well informed of everything that was happening in Marquetalia and Riochiquito, where the self-defense groups were in charge. There were other leaders, like Ciro Trujillo, in Riochiquito, and Isauro Yose, in Marquetalila, but the ones people really respected and trusted were Manuel Marulanda and Charronegro. Charro was Indian, and when they killed him in Santiago Pérez, Marulanda went back up into the hills, and has never come out. Marulanda gave up his job as a highway inspector without notice, and began to lead the movement—also because Charronegro had been a beloved friend of his, and they had grown very close during their military and political battles. So, Marulanda made this decision, and became more radical. When the government found out he had gone back to arms, they came up with the Independent Republic business, suggested by Alvaro Gómez Hurtado, and attacked.

The important thing about the self-defense groups was that they proved to be an organization capable of helping the communities prosper; they helped them recover economically, provided education and healthcare for the people, and opened up new paths. These were peaceful populations who stuck to their own business, and worked on their concerns, their crops and markets. They grew and improved their cattle, increased coffee production, and also potato crops, in the colder areas they farmed. That helped a lot, because those struggles, which were organized by committees, also had a political side. They discussed things and presented arguments to the government, and the government did not like that at all. With each passing day, the needs of those communities increased, and they and their leaders kept looking for ways to meet those needs. This was frowned upon by some sectors of the oligarchy. Here were groups that, to a certain extent, were isolated from the rest of the country, but hadn't allowed themselves to be forgotten, isolated, or confined. Just the contrary: they expanded their scope of interest, made contacts with the cities and also, in the case of Sumapaz, participated in elections and won. In many areas, electoral alliances were formed with López Michelsen and his party, the MRL.[18] They were politically active in the cities, spread the word about the movement, and above all demanded people's rights. When the MRL split and López returned to the Liberal Party and to the right, we started up the MRL's so-called hardline policy. Our strategy was to win over the masses and convince them to support armed struggle, armed resistance throughout the country, because the same things were happening all over the country. The movement reached the Cauca Valley, Nariño, and the Santanderes, and worked with the universities and unions. The Communist Party made sure of that.

THE STRUGGLE IN THE CITIES

We did not limit ourselves to the countryside, but fanned out into the cities. I went to Nariño to work with a peasant movement that was just getting organized. In Nariño people were easy to organize, because they have always worked in what we call *mingas*—collectives they form to build things and help one another out. Besides that, there were people at the university, in teachers' unions and public institutions, and there was certainly indigenous and peasant organization. The understanding was that we had to organize the whole population.

In the Cauca Valley we ran into one problem we didn't know how to solve. We felt that, since there was only a very weak peasantry, we should work with laborers from the city, with sugarcane workers, and with intellectuals. This led to divisions between the MRL and the Communist Party. We believed that there was actually a peasantry, and that we needed their support.

The same thing came up in the Santanderes. But, of course, agriculture was dominant in that department, and industry was less influential. It is interesting that, while the agrarian movement was crushed in 1946 and in 1950, the agrarian problem was not solved, and rose up again, alive and kicking, in the 1960s. There were new peasant mobilizations, agitation in the communities, the occupation of properties. When Act 200 was overturned by Act

---

18   Movimiento Revolucionario Liberal—Liberal Revolutionary Movement.

100, the issue didn't stop there. It was reborn, and became an insurrectional objective. By violently repressing the demand for land, they turned it into the main cause of the guerrillas. The movement was concentrated in the so-called Independent Republics, which is where it really began: Sumapaz, southern Tolima, and northern Cauca. But, at any rate, those agrarian groups had the support of the whole country—well, not the entire country, that's true; but in Colombia the peasants were and are a major force motivated by discontent. I began to travel around all the peasant regions, spreading the word about our experiences. I traveled by foot, talking to people. Agrarian reform began to become a goal once again. But this time there were also demands for education, healthcare, housing, and loans. People can learn how to fight back! We did everything we could to help people solve their own problems without going to the authorities, encouraged them to take things into their own hands, both problems and solutions. That was explosive! They refused to recognize the state—something that oligarchies find unforgivable, because the state was there to solve their problems, but not ours. There was some awareness of the fact that we were organizing another state. That period was extremely valuable, because we began to realize that the problems in the countryside could not be solved without also solving the problems in the cities—in other words, without solving the country's problems. We looked at everything with clearer heads—a broader vision. We began to see the whole picture. That moment was marked by the death of Charronegro and by Marulanda's return to armed resistance. It is also when the US embassy and the Colombian armed forces decided to attack the Independent Republics: the generals running the operations had been under US command during the Korean War. There was a very famous debate in Congress with Alvaro Gómez, who defended the idea of war, and forced President Valencia to declare it. It was known as Operation LASO.[19]

There had been recent events in those zones. In Tequendama, the struggle had been for land, but also for higher pay for the coffee harvest, for wages. They were two sides of the same coin, and people were fighting for both. The Viotá leaders were skillfully pressing for the hacienda lands to be divided up into plots, while demanding better pay. The biggest achievement was raising awareness about the agrarian problem. In Pato and Marquetalia, the settlers fought to be able to organize their own work and property without the authorization of the government. There the land did not belong to landlords, and the issue was not about deeds or wages, but about the right to organize our lives as we saw fit. Land was cleared and settled, and there was armed defense of the settlements, going against the rule that whatever land peasants opened up and cleared always fell back into the hands of the

19   Latin American Security Operation.

landlord. The truth was that the idea of peasant self-defense came into being in Sumapaz. It was born of experience, of seeing how, over and over, the government was on the large landholders' side. They always ruled against us. In Marquetalia, Ríochiquito, Sumapaz, and Pato, we defended the region, denounced provocateurs, and punished the traitors. And the government did not sit still. They stuck us with commission after commission, always hiding their real purposes. I remember one commission in Sumapaz, made up of a priest and a civilian who turned out to be army officers, provocateurs. That whole set-up was gradually uncovered because Juan de la Cruz was then a deputy in the provincial assembly, and used all the information he gathered to publicly denounce those methods. That helped the nation recognize our struggle. The decision was made to refuse to recognize the authorities, because what we couldn't fail to recognize was the underlying problem: land. In Ríochiquito, it was different because it was already a centuries-old fight: the Indians' fight to regain their land, stolen by the rich landowners and the priests from Cauca. There were different types of struggles, but all were due to the same problem: land.

THE INFLUENCE OF THE CUBAN REVOLUTION

The Cuban Revolution helped us a great deal. It gave us new ideas, and helped us see that it was possible to achieve what we had only dreamed about up to then. It was a great stimulus for the struggle, and showed the need for organization. This was particularly true along the Atlantic coast, where the peasants were landless, but would drink rum with the boss. Radio Havana broadcast in their coastal dialect, *costeño*, and when Radio Havana explained what the [Cuban] Revolution was doing about agrarian reform, it opened up their eyes. Another thing that the Cuban Revolution taught us was the usefulness of armed resistance, because here in Colombia we had seen time and again how the rich people defended their interests with bullets. On the other hand, it showed that you had to open the door to democracy, make room for democratic struggles, although that door was gradually closed. Charro's murder was a turning point. After that and the Cuban Revolution, for a major sector headed by Marulanda, Isauro Yosa, Jacobo Arenas, and many others, it became much clearer that it would be impossible to resolve the conflict in a peaceful manner. So, while the Cuban Revolution, on the one hand, stimulated a democratic struggle, on the other hand it showed us that, with weapons, we could achieve our ideals.

I lived through the Sumapaz battles, alongside Juan de la Cruz, and became part of a commando unit when the time came. That was during the Rojas Pinilla dictatorship. We needed to form a group of military chiefs of staff, and, even though I was very young, I was asked to serve, because of my mother's integrity and contribution to the struggle. I got married around the time Rojas fell from power, which was also when we decided that part of our group would stay and guard the weapons we had buried—because we never turned them over to the enemy—and another part would get into politics. I left with that group. I married a woman from Pasca, a neighbor. Her father was an agrarian leader and we got along very well, since we were both working towards the same goals. So there was no problem there. Just the opposite—she encouraged me to fight, and continue to fight.

It was when we were still living in Sumapaz, in Cabrera, almost still on our honeymoon, that the case of that doctor happened—the one that lived among us and then betrayed us. They killed him on a bus between Venecia and Pandi. Then I was accused of killing him, but I was with other people who had been forced to flee. And I decided, "I'm not leaving—I'm not leaving the region." And so I ended up staying there for a long time. The internal debate between Juan de la Cruz and our political leaders continued. It eventually spilled over into the government, and they came after us, and there were deaths. There were still some *chulavitas* and government *pájaros* out there. There were deaths in Icononzo, Pasca, and Venecia, and they blamed us, the recognized leaders [of the movement], and some of us had to go into hiding. I was the first to say I refused to leave the region, and a lot of other people stayed too.

LIVING UNDERCOVER

I lived undercover for six years, but really only had to hide from the army and the police, because I worked night and day out with the people, and if we had ever had to confront the army or the police, everyone would have looked after us. There was great solidarity. I believe that solidarity was because we understood and interpreted people's interests, defended their rights and their reasons, and helped them make themselves heard. So we really didn't have many problems, and I was fortunate because I was able to travel everywhere on foot or on horseback. Where you really had to go underground and hide was in the cities, because there nobody knew you, and there were more police and more snitches. We would pass straight through the cities, not go to *cantinas*, and avoid gatherings of people as much as possible. We would cross the cities taking peripheral routes, and head straight for the rural settlements. That involved a lot of walking, because most of the journeys were done on foot, from foothill to foothill, settlement to settlement.

We would travel from Sumapaz to Meta, using the old Duda River road, wind through Esperanza to go down to Ucrania, and then down further to Uribe, and from there to San Martín. It was a three-month journey. Mesetas had not even been founded yet (it was founded later by the brothers of Juan de la Cruz), but Uribe had been there before the start of the Thousand Days War. In 1955, the first time I went there, Aljure had burned down the village. One of the hardest things about those trips was the hunger, because the Duda Canyon was totally unpopulated—it was nothing but foothills, almost cliffs, that dropped sharply off into the river. It was poor, dry land. So, as we used to say, when you can't eat *cat* (food we got from people along the way), you have to start eating *dog*. That was when we would eat a kind of meatless meatball, made of toasted corn, beans, and sorghum. You put them in your pocket and walked for one day, two days, sometimes for a week. Then all you needed was water, but there was water all over. The "meatballs" could also be made with dried peas. But the most important ingredient was the sorghum, because it kills hunger, quenches thirst, and cures wounds—plus it keeps your mouth busy. It is blessed among all plants. We couldn't have survived or fought without it. Coffee was a true luxury. If you had that in your rucksack, you felt almost festive; you were doing great. We didn't travel alone, but stayed in small groups to avoid ambush. We were all young, between twenty-five and twenty-eight years old. My wife supported my attendance of those meetings, which sometimes lasted for months. Of course, the women also had their women's organization and did very important jobs. Without their help, it would all have been much harder to bear, more difficult. Meanwhile, the children began arriving. The first was born in 1959. We named him Byron. Later we had three girls, and after that, no more. My son is now carrying on the fight.

JACOBO ARENAS

On one of those trips I met Jacobo Arenas. It was in Santodomingo, and he was coming from Chaguaní, where he had been out organizing people. I also met Richard, who was from southern Tolima. That was our first meeting. Later we ran into each other again in Villarrica, Dolores, Prado, Usme—we ran into each other all the time. There was a great deal of activity, and it all led to the First Conference, where the Political Directorate was established. We gradually came to know and understand one another. He was not an easy man to get to know, but once you bridged that gap, you had a friend for life. Whenever he was passing through Pasca he would always come see us, the González family. We were a large family, with ten siblings, all good workers and all committed to the struggle. Everyone respected us, and so they could sit down with our family and have a drink. All the kids followed us around. We were called to mediate all kinds of conflicts. We earned the authority we held, and there were never any fights when we were around. So, I say that it was the training we had, especially from my mother, in good behavior. She taught us about solidarity with our people. As a result, we were well loved and respected within the municipality. When they attacked Marquetalia, Jacobo came to Pasca for a few days while reorganizing the forces that were dispersed, but not defeated. He continued his visits to Sumapaz to give speeches. We saw a lot of each other then. He was an unpretentious man who treated you as an equal, a real human being. He was a noble man who was considerate of people, but as a leader was very hard on the enemy.

He had his faults, one of which was that he would run over anybody to keep a united front. Jacobo thought on a higher plane—he focused on the future of the struggle. He was quite a drinker, liked to drink, but you hardly ever saw him drunk. He preferred to talk, converse, and share stories, and make you laugh while making his point. Above all, he was a studious man. He could read a book in two days, and then get you to give him one you had, saying: "Show me that book"—he would say—"it's no good." And then he read it himself. He was a very studious, cultivated man. He was always reading something, and knew a little bit about everything, and a lot about life. He knew things about philosophy and shoemaking, economy and carpentry. He could talk to you about historical materialism while he was curing an animal of some illness or injury; he knew about weapons, about how to build a house or a bridge, and could recite whole poems by Mayakovsky and Neruda. We became very good friends. He met my mother, and they got along very well. He was my best man at my wedding. I was about to leave for Buenos Aires, for a course in politics, when Jacobo came up to me one afternoon and said, "Comrade, marry her before you leave, so you will have a good reason to come back." He knew that Anita and I were engaged. Anita was a schoolteacher. She was eighteen years old. And so I said, "You know what? I will, comrade." And so, on July 16th we got married, and I left on the 17th for Buenos Aires with Jacobo. He was a good influence on me.

ARGENTINA

In Argentina we were at an international school for cadres. We had a very good German teacher who taught us about the history of the Internationals. Very well read. She and I hit it off, and she praised me, a peasant, for having been sent to that school for proletarian leaders. Our classmates were members of central committees from very important Communist parties, like those of Italy and Chile. On that trip we met Corvalan from Chile's Communist Party. We were sent to a fancy hotel, the Príncipe de Gales. Very luxurious, with a lot of velvet and feather mattresses. But as I was used to sleeping on the floor, and had been sleeping rough, out in the fields, I couldn't sleep on a soft bed, and so I slept on the floor. Jacobo laughed at me. The school helped me a lot, and I began to understand what we had lived through. We read Marxist philosophy, political economy, the history of the revolution-ary movement. There, I saw people from sixteen countries with my own eyes, and heard them talk about the struggle all over the world. I became convinced, despite the theory, that in Colombia the peasants were the most revolutionary force, and that our struggle represented the vanguard of the movement in Latin America. In Argentina they had organized the pampas, and Bolivia had its indigenous movement—but none of those could compare with ours, either in awareness or organization. I became aware of that fact—of how our commitment was seen through the eyes of the worldwide revolu-tionary movement. Perón had already fallen from power, and communism was outlawed in Argentina. The school itself was clandestine.

But we, the two Colombians, were used to that life. Even so, we were arrested because the intelligence agencies were looking for a Panamanian, and instead they found us. We learned that much later, in Moscow. Halfway through the course, the police showed up and arrested us. They took us all to jail, and released us after five or six days. The lawyers got us out, but the legal process against the foreigners continued until the government expelled us. We were thrown out of Argentina! Jacobo didn't finish the course in Buenos Aires, and left for Moscow. He was much more radical when he came back to Colombia, convinced that the only solution was armed combat. He started a huge discussion. I had my differences with him. We had had different life experiences and training, but the differences were never ideological; rather, they had more to do with temperament. At any rate, I had more in common with Jacobo than with Juan de la Cruz.

AGRARIANISM VS. COMMUNISM

Juan de la Cruz began having run-ins with Julio Merchán, a leader from Viotá. They got drunk one day and, even though they had always said a war between the peasants would not be permitted, shots were fired due to the differences between the agrarian stance of Juan de la Cruz and our commu-nist position. That damaged the relationship, but it went no further. Later, the brothers of Juan de la Cruz were killed in the Mesetas area.

There was great consternation. The Cabrera police commander, a colo-nel who was in charge of the entire Sumapaz region, told Juan de la Cruz that I had killed his brother. But Juan de la Cruz was a noble man who knew who his enemies were, and said that wasn't true, because "Anzola was in such and such a place on that day." And that was true. I had been in Paquiló trying to solve a problem about some stables that had been burned down, and this was being discussed in a meeting. Despite our differences,

Juan de la Cruz refuted the colonel's accusation. He refused to swallow the version of the police. That taught me a lot about how to handle differences among the leftists.

Jacobo and Juan de la Cruz had their political differences, but they never broke off relations. They would argue, and even shout, but they never got really mad at each other. Jacobo was after power; Juan de la Cruz wanted the land. But in that sense, from a political standpoint, the Cuban Revolution ended up proving that Jacobo was right: it was possible to take power, but no true agrarian reform was possible without a political revolution. For me, those differences were hard to take, because I had begun to fight on Juan de la Cruz´s side, but felt more political affinity with Jacobo, whom I felt was my comrade and teacher.

I felt closer to Jacobo because of the way he saw the country—based on facts—the way he treated people and listened to them, and the way he lived. He ended up convincing me that only by using weapons could we solve the class conflict we were in. I was more inclined to think like that. After returning from Argentina, I spent all my time teaching the masses. I wasn't part of the self-defense movement, but supported its struggle. I'm not good at writing, but I debated, spoke, gave speeches, and studied. Despite my limitations, with Raúl Valbuena—a comrade who was highly respected by Manuel Marulanda—I did write several documents for the struggle, about the actions and future of the self-defense groups. I helped by giving opinions, and then helped correct the drafts. By then, I was on the official most-wanted lists, and had to be very careful about my movements. But one night, at the Lagunitas settlement in Sumapaz, I had a few drinks at a party, began to feel sick, and went home to bed. At around four o'clock in the morning, I heard them banging on the door. It was the army. We let them make all the noise they wanted until they knocked the door down. My son Byron was about six years old. He started yelling and yelling until he woke up the whole settlement, and people realized I was being arrested. That saved my life, because we found out later that the idea was to accuse me of trying to escape and shoot me: in other words, to murder me. I did end up in a military garrison, but at least not in a common grave like most people they had under watch. From there they took me to the former Colombian Intelligence Service, the military police prison. I spent something like eight days in there, but they had to let me go because they had no charges to bring against me. A lawyer got me out. Ironically, he was a Conservative, but he was the son of an agrarian leader from Pasca, a neighbor. And to round it out, it turned out the judge was from Fusagasugá, and had a farm in Pasca. The judge was independent, and overruled the prosecutor to get me out on parole. So I went back to organizing.

They sent me to Europe, and so I went. While I was there a woman from

Bogotá came to me and said, "They are sending you word not to re-enter the country through El Dorado." Here we go again. Fortunately I was staying at a hotel the Communist Party had in Moscow. It was a very famous hotel where everybody went. There were people from Brazil, Argentina, and Chile. So, when that woman told me I shouldn't go back through El Dorado, I told my comrades and they organized my return trip through Italy, Spain, Brazil, Argentina, and Chile. In Milan I was fortunate to meet an Italian who had been a soldier with the resistance and had taken part in the firing squad that killed Mussolini. He was very old, and had been a partisan. The Communist Party military command gave the order to shoot Mussolini before the Americans found out, because they would have saved him for sure. I was very pleased to be in the home of a man like that. I went to Madrid to catch my plane, but when I got there, it had taken off two hours earlier. I had to wait a week for another flight, without a penny in my pocket. I sold some gifts I had bought, paid to sleep in a fleabag hotel, and started walking the streets. I believe I saw everything there was in Madrid—I walked until the soles of my shoes fell off. When I could see my toes peeking out, I went to the airport to wait for my flight—thirty-four hours ahead of time. I arrived in Chile when Allende was coming into power. The Party gave me some new shoes and put me up in a good hotel, and I spent a whole week talking to revolutionary leaders.

We didn't trust the political project of Allende and the Chilean CP. We told them that the army would end up crushing and destroying the democratic alternative, and that they should get prepared for war. But they didn't believe us—they didn't believe us. From Santiago I flew to Quito, and entered Colombia through the Rumichaca border, guided by the CP cells from Ecuador, who put me in touch with the Communist Youth movement at Tulcán, and so I returned through there.

ANUC

I was gone for fifty-eight days and nobody at home had known where I was, because that was the order. And so, when I went back to Pasca to see my family, people said, "The lost sheep has come back." Those were the days of ANUC.[20] I dedicated myself body and soul to organizing the peasants. It was a race against the clock. Either we got organized, or they would take away everything we'd achieved over twenty-five years of struggle. During that period Tirofijo showed up again, after all the business in Marquetalia, being run off, everything that had happened in Inzá. Then Manuel Marulanda appeared, disproving all the propaganda they had made

---

20   Asociación Nacional de Usuarios Campesinos—National Association of Peasants.

up about having done away with all the armed groups. The takeover of Inzá
was not a very important military action, but it announced to the country
that the guerrilla movement was alive and still fighting. Then, in the heat
of the Cuban Revolution, the movement grew even stronger, and people
started believing in it again. Peasants became united in Córdoba, Sucre, and
Norte de Santander. Thanks to the effects of the Cuban Revolution propaganda, people began to organize; the ANUC grew stronger and started to
move away from the government, although it was the government itself that
had created it. I felt like a fish in water, helping to strengthen peasant unity.
I was elected to represent Cundinamarca on the National Directorate. The
ANUC had a lot of authority by then. The agrarian policy of Lleras was
still new when he appointed a group of young leftist professionals to defend
his creation, because old man Lleras had plans for re-election. That was
when the Mandato Campesino[21] came on the scene. It was truly a hand-
book of discontent. We helped write that document, and it was approved
in a congress held in Cúcuta. After it was published, we began to break off
relations with the government, and the division came with Pastrana. That
was exactly when the land occupations started. First they started in Sucre,
but little by little continued all along the coast, and throughout the country: the Santanderes, Valle, Tolima, Caquetá. A march was organized to
Bogotá. We planned to send 100,000 peasants to the capital to demonstrate.
The idea was to take Bogotá by storm and demand land, loans, seeds, and
roads. We could see the Chicoral thing coming—the agreement between
the Conservatives and the Liberals to reverse the agrarian reform, what little
had been done anyway, and above all [to stand in the way of] what still
could be achieved. At that time, something really interesting was going
on: the so-called *parcelaciones*.[22] There were already concentrations of these
in Soacha, Silvania, and Jamundí. And so, under the guidance of ANUC,
people started occupying properties almost everywhere in the country.

   And, once again, you began to hear the slogans and cries of "The land
belongs to those who work it!" "Land without landlords!" "Tear down the
fences!" It was a very fruitful period, and I traveled all over the country. But
the party was soon over, and then came the repression: deaths, disappear-
ances, prison, evictions, and beatings. The landlords are very sly. In Córdoba
and Sucre, many landlords buddied up to their workers; they drank with
them and managed to create divisions within the movement. It was a bit
of a farce, and there was a lot of that going on. It was at that time that the
President appointed Dr. Jaramillo Ocampo as minister of agriculture. He
was from Caldas, and was skillful and intelligent, but a reactionary. They put
him there to fight against us. That is why, during the opening of ANUC's

21   Peasant Mandate.
22   Divisions of large estates into plots for peasants.

first Congress, I made it my business to tell him a few things. First, that the oligarchy was never going to allow an agrarian reform; second, that stopping it would only fill up the cities with poor and unemployed people; third, that if we didn't manage to divide the land up in a peaceful and orderly way, the armed struggle within Colombia would reach unprecedented levels; and fourth, that if there was no peace, Colombia would end up being invaded by the US. I finished by telling the minister that he was a member of the oligarchy, that we expected nothing from the government, and that we, the peasants, would end up taking by force what we were denied access to by peaceful means. But we were far from achieving the advances we announced. Just the opposite: they were the ones who were poised and prepared to defeat us. They managed to create divisions into two groups. One, headed by Velázquez, a leader from San Bernardo, followed our position and wanted the land; the other they managed to convince by buying them out and making promises. They accused us of being communists, the press launched a furious campaign against us, and the armed forces followed us constantly. Then dead bodies began showing up, and the leaders began to disappear. They met in Armenia, under the protection of politicians, and we met in Sincelejo, as a way of honoring those fallen in battle, and to show respect for the fight of those who invaded the landlords' lands. I continued my work as an organizer, without losing touch with the armed movement. I had always worked in legal organizations, such as ANUC and others.

The armed movement supported the land occupations and organized many themselves. But I have to say that the INCORA staff also joined the fight—particularly the lawyers, who were well aware of how the lawsuits went, how things were going, and they passed on a great deal of information to us. All of this led to the division of the peasant movement.

We kept up the fight from there, but ANUC fell into anarchy when all the internal factions started trying to take over. It became a big mess, and everyone wanted to control their own patch. Those differences were not dealt with well, mainly due to the arrival of party professionals from political groups that wanted to throw out the opposing groups. In Cundinamarca they screwed us because the advisors tried to take over as spokespersons. I was on the board, and was scheduled to preside over the meeting. I had to fight back, and so when opening the session, the first thing I did was bring up the question of whether these "gentlemen," who were not peasants but advisors, had the right to speak and to vote, as they had in the past. And it worked, because the majority supported us and denied the "advisors" the right to vote, but did let them speak up in the meeting. I was re-elected to the board. Jaime Vásquez, who was leading a group of his own, delivered a highly reactionary speech against me, but the decision had already been approved.

And so ANUC continued its course. The government was trying to isolate us, using every means available, and wanted to push the radical Sincelejo peasant group into a corner, using the Armenia group. That crisis coincided with one of our meetings within the Communist Party, in which we discussed the possibility of leaving ANUC and forming our own peasant organization. We had the support of the CSTC, the trade union federation with Communist Party influence. Víctor J. Merchán, a longstanding, experienced leader, gave us his support. A proposal had been made to the central trade union committee to form an agrarian organization, what with all the rural and land-based struggles underway. Since the meetings we were holding, along with the committee's meeting there, were all part of this federation, and given the anarchy within ANUC, with so many fractured small groups all pulling in different directions, we decided, then and there, to leave ANUC and found our own organization. In 1976 we scheduled a Congress to officially found the new organization. But before that came a two-year preparation period, when we worked nationwide, organizing ourselves into union federations in the departments, and into chapters in the municipalities. And so it was that in 1976, in homage to the struggle of the Santa Marta banana workers, we founded our federation, FENSA (Federación Nacional Sindical Agropecuaria—National Union Federation of Farmworkers).

THE ARMED STRUGGLE

This opened up new horizons for me, and I began to understand the need to join forces with the unions of workers and government employees, and all the grassroots organizations in general. But that same unity that we sought, and managed to achieve little by little, brought a violent reaction from the bosses and the government, which, if you stop to consider it, is really no more than an association of businessmen. Many people died for the peasant demands—there was a great deal of persecution, and the armed movement became stronger as a result. This was no coincidence. Our position had a lot in common with the ideas defended by FARC. The repression unleashed against the peasants and the union movement fortified the guerrilla movement. People did not know what to do and, given the repression, they ended up going to the hills or supporting the guerrillas directly. That is one of the main reasons for FARC's growth, because the people could see that the political system was not going to solve their problems.

I want to make it clear that this is why the armed struggle became stronger. The armed struggle is also the people's struggle, which is closely linked to the concentration of land ownership. It began, and continues, due to this problem. There is something very interesting in all this, at least as I see it: the oligarchy is not willing to give up anything at all. During all these years of fighting I've been recounting, the oligarchy has only given up crumbs, and then comes back and takes even those away, like it did with the Lleras Act. The Lleras Act was initially a victory for the peasants, but the government later twisted it around and stripped it of all meaning, and the trading and loan programs ended up being the ruin of many people. For many people, it's not that they don't want the land, but that they don't have the means to work it, so they prefer to leave their plot and go somewhere else. The state is only interested in making money off the banks, and that is why it defends them instead of us, the peasants. The high interest rates bankrupt the peasants. So, the agrarian reform they trumpet about simply never happened. That is why I say that, in the course of this long struggle, the oligarchy has never been willing to give so much as an inch.

The bourgeoisie took advantage of the divisions within the peasant movement that had led to the formation of two diverging factions: the government-backed Armenia faction, and the peasants' Sincelejo faction. You have to remember that the philosophy behind ANUC was that of defending the "users," since this was the term for people who received plots of land, so there were no landless people or wage-earning workers involved. For us, the organization should include all peasants, whether they owned land or not. The Chicoral maneuver, which we called the "Chicoralazo," was a plan by the Liberals and Conservatives to reverse what little progress the Lleras Act had helped us make in our fight. In Chicoral, the agreement between the peasants and the government was violated, and the result was a resurgence of repression of the peasants. It was very severe repression, because they went after the peasants who tried to take back the land or worked it, and more than a few were thrown in jail or murdered. This made the armed movement grow in an unprecedented manner, as many peasants turned to the guerrillas. And to complete the picture, we had the example of the Cuban Revolution, right there. Many people went over to FARC, to the ELN,[23] the EPL,[24] and to the Movimiento Armado Quintín Lame,[25] which was just getting started. Those movements grew due to the stance taken by the government, and to the delay in providing any solution to social problems. In Colombia, armed struggle has these social roots. The Chicoral Pact had a lot to do with the armed movement that exists today. In 1970, '75, and '80, the armed movement flourished. It was because people realized there was no other solution. And you have to remember that, in those days, there was a revolution underway in Chile that helped create a climate of rebellion in Colombia. The Chicoral Pact was the ideological

---

23   Ejército de Liberación Nacional—National Liberation Army.
24   Ejército Popular de Liberación—Popular Liberation Army.
25   Quintín Lame Armed Movement.

agent responsible for the growth of the armed movement in the 1970s and 1980s.

This period is important for two reasons: one is that the Chicoral balloon burst, and repression of the peasant movement and democratic sectors ensued. The violence increased in line with the resistance. But besides that, the people who didn't head for the hills and the guerrillas became active in the struggle, and we organized different land occupations and advised them, particularly in Sucre, Córdoba, on the Atlantic coast, and in some parts of central Colombia. Some smaller-scale actions were organized towards the south of Tolima, in Valle, and Nariño. We encouraged people to continue to demand their rights; and above all, we never gave up on the fight for agrarian reform. This part is very important. Later, after the Misael Pastrana government, first came Turbay Ayala and then Dr. López, who used the DRI[26] to revive the parceling out of lands. Nevertheless, we said that the peasant movement should get inside those organizations and try and find out what good things there were about the organization of renters and sharecroppers that was backing the new López Act. We got involved in the legal aspect to continue to fight from inside the law, without denying the battle outside the law. Although in our documents and speeches we showed that it was a step backwards, we found ways to use it to our advantage and keep the movement alive. That we did, and it helped us quite a bit. While the movement did lose ground, it did not disappear. We learned how to combine our claims with political efforts to strengthen the movement as a whole. At that time the agrarian movement enjoyed very good relations with urban movements, since peasants were migrating to the city, and the cities were full of revolutionary, left-thinking peasants who continued to participate in national organizations such as Provivienda.[27] Many people got organized around the fight for housing. They began squatting on large land-holdings and built up whole neighborhoods on them. They also built their houses on vacant lots; many went to jail, and many died, but [those who remained] got their houses in the end. That was a very positive experience, because the people who had been activists and leaders in the agrarian fight for land were now using their experience in a different context. But the underlying problem had not changed. We often combined urban and rural efforts. During that period we had excellent relations with workers, with the CSTC.[28] We joined this confederation and received a great deal of help and a lot of solidarity from affiliated unions. It was during that time that we formed FENSA, today known as FENSOAGRO. There were also unions

26 Integrated Rural Development program.
27 An organization promoting housing rights.
28 The Confederación Sindical de Trabajadores de Colombia—Union Confederation of Colombian Workers.

that helped us out, like the one in Avianca, SINTRAVA, which gave us a car and the means to travel throughout the country. The metalworkers, public employees, and teachers also helped us. In short, we were not lacking for help. Many unions gave us a small monthly contribution—very small, but they gave it to us. And so we managed to consolidate our work of organizing the peasants at the national level. The time came when we had covered nearly the entire country with agrarian union organizations.

THE 1977 STRIKE

Taxes, inflation, and very low wages all led to increased social discontent under the López government. Poverty grew, and with the participation of the UTC, CTC, and CSTC, the 1977 strike was organized. In those days, the union movement was strong and respected all over the country, and we had done a very good job in the banana-growing area of Urabá and Magdalena, and in major regions such as the Cauca Valley, Cundinamarca, Boyacá, Tolima, Nariño, and Norte de Santander. The peasant movement played an active role in the 1977 strike against López, and this mobilization against López was extremely positive. The strike was a challenge to the government, a challenge to public forces, and people stopped being afraid to stand up and fight, face to face. During his term in office, López had done some progressive things that people liked. He built schools and health centers, made loans to rich peasants, and tried to govern without imposing a state of siege. He had been our ally when he opposed bipartisan politics, and especially the alternation of the two parties in power. That is why many people did not understand why we attacked him and called a strike. It took a lot of work to unmask him, in his game of using the left to gain power, only to later govern with the right. But we managed to do it.

During that time—or during that strike, I should say—I was working in Bogotá. We had just founded the National Agrarian Federation and, much to my dismay, I needed to stay in the city. But I did get away once in a while. I went to Tolima and Huila to hold meetings with the different union chapters, promote the strike, and organize people, and also to get an idea of what the different regions were doing in the movement against the government. Although our actions then were not as forceful as they are today, we did organize some big protests, like closing main roads and mobilizing large groups of peasants to march on the cities. I particularly remember the march on Neiva. We brought people in from Pitalito, La Plata, Campoalegre, and from several different municipalities to join the workers in the strike. We brought people in from the west to Bogotá, and people from Sumapaz and Tequendama to demonstrate in Fusagasugá. Each leader, each activist, had a specific task. Some were to block off the bridges, others to put obstacles in the roads, such as rocks, felled trees, whatever they could. The success of the strike depended on the freedom the activists were given to use their own ideas and do whatever they felt necessary, while complying with the general instructions issued. We managed to cut off the entrance to Bogotá. People can be very resourceful and efficient, and come up with totally unexpected ideas. There were twenty-seven deaths in the whole of the country, fourteen of them in Bogotá. And we gained very little—a few claims for higher wages, and other adjustments. The biggest success was that it taught people to fight back in an organized way.

THE REPRESSION

But the bourgeoisie also learned from it, and when Turbay took office after López, the first thing he did was declare a state of siege, called the National Security Statute—one of the most arbitrary and repressive measures ever used by governments. President Turbay had many more ties to transnational companies than López, and was much more submissive to big capital. He was also a very good friend of the military, hand-picked by the highest ranks. He was much more right-wing than López. That statute was a carbon copy of the measures the dictatorships used in Argentina, Chile, and Uruguay. It gave the army and the judges the power to break and enter during the night and to make secret arrests; it also got rid of habeas corpus, thus clearing the way for the disappearance, torture, and assassination of thousands of activists, along with innocent citizens. During that period, although the government went after the democratic left, people also became more radical, and so the armed insurgency grew stronger. The bourgeoisie began to realize that it was a counterproductive policy, and that it would be better to negotiate, so that opened up a slight hope of peace negotiations. But, since Turbay thought "negotiating" meant our unconditional surrender and surrender of arms, that initiative failed. They slowly came to the realization that taking a hard-line attitude simply did not work. When Betancur took office, he proposed negotiations based on other foundations. Looking back at the course of history after 1950, there is clearly a sector of Colombians who did not lose hope or perspective about the possibility of building a new Colombia. So, after those periods of violence, in the 1950s, the days of Ospina Pérez, Laureano Gómez, and later Rojas Pinilla and Alterto Lleras, the ruling class has had to include at least a few democratic nuances in their governments, and has not dared to implement only repressive policies.

Even so, out in the different regions, and particularly those regions with strong and defiant peasant groups, the government has always used armed violence as a tool of repression. What's more, I would even say that the violence organized by the landlords and politicians in rural areas triggered and fuelled the war. The paramilitary groups, lately called self-defense groups, have always been backed by the state. Since the 1950s, the *chulavitas* and *pájaros* have always had close ties to regional politicians, certain factions of the police force and the army, and also to the landlords and wealthy businessmen. In northern Boyacá, the *chulavitas* were paid by the church in Soatá and the Conservative Directorate of Tunja; in southern Tolima, by Liberal politicians; while in the northern parts of Valle and in Santander, they were funded by the Conservative Party. There have always been groups of murdering thugs protected by the authorities and paid by the wealthy. The National Security Statute was one step further along the path of organizing and arming a right-wing irregular army. But, on the other hand, you had the drug-trade mafia, which was already getting organized. MAS,[29] for instance, was as much a creation of Turbay's National Security Statute, which watched over its birth, as it was of the drug lords who financed it. They are the putative fathers of the paramilitaries.

THE SOURCE OF DRUG TRAFFICKING

You have to take a good look at history. We do not have a history of drug trafficking. Here in Colombia, ever since the Spanish colonization, we have always had smugglers, but never drug traffickers. Before there could be drug trafficking, there first had to be marijuana, coca, and poppy farming, and we did not invent those drugs. Marijuana was first sown by the Peace Corps workers in Sierra Nevada de Santa Marta. There was the coca plant, and the Indians chewed its leaves, but we did not invent cocaine. Neither did we invent heroin—for us poppies were flowers, not drugs. In the early 1970s, when the Chicoralazo happened, I was in the banana plantation zone trying to reorganize the union movement in Cénaga, and I saw the hippies, who were with the Peace Corps, bring in marijuana seeds and sow them around the mountains. They had contacts with the peasants, with people in the poor neighborhoods, and were their guests in the everglades. The hippies gave the peasants and Indians the seeds, and then bought the leaves from them, which were valued for the effect they caused. They did it for their own consumption, but little by little they discovered there was money to be made, and with the help of ex-Vietnam pilots organized the first shipments—and that is how drug trafficking got started. And it was soon taken over by the ruthless dominant class, the rich and idle landlords and smugglers who set up companies with the gringos to export it to the US. And so they made incredible fortunes. Turbay permitted that alliance, and soon the

---

29   Muerte a Secuestradores—Death to Kidnappers.

police were in on it, ready to get rich. The peasants only grew the crops, but they had eyes and ears, and everyone knew who those groups were.

I found out about coca in a different way. It was in Uribe, Meta, when the FARC burned a shipment while journalists watched, and the news was published, hailing the work of the guerrillas. I was out organizing an agrarian union in Mesetas when that happened. Drug trafficking has nothing to do with the political ideas of the guerrillas. But how I really came to learn about coca is a funny story. I was working as an advisor for a union of African palm plant workers located in San Martín on the La Nohra plantation. The union began to disintegrate, because the workers just disappeared and didn't come back to work. I thought it was strange, but, as sometimes happens, I let it go, forgot about it. Much to my surprise, I was then invited to a peasant assembly at Calamar, Guaviare. From the small plane we were traveling in, I saw some pretty but unfamiliar crops. I was a peasant, and couldn't tell what they were. When we landed, I was greeted by some comrades who had disappeared from La Nohra, and I asked them what had happened. They told me they had come to farm that plant I was so curious about: it was called coca. So I asked them why, and they told me because they could earn five times as much by harvesting coca leaves as they did working on the African palm plantation for making palm oil. I learned a lot from that meeting. People gave a lot of money for the association, and it all came from the coca plant. How could we stop it? How could we tell people who had gone hungry for years to keep on going hungry? I had to keep my mouth shut and accept the fact that it was not a problem of just a few people, but rather a general social problem. It was an economic and political problem, because there were many persecuted union leaders among them.

I also learned that, long before the FARC showed up, there was terrible disorder and anarchy. They killed people. For example, a coca crop day laborer would collect his day's wages and along the road would be killed by the same people who had paid him. A lot of people died. And when the FARC came into the picture, things changed. They imposed order, but they were also responsible for the really serious problems with the drug traffickers and mafias, the planters and buyers, that followed. That fight began then, and got more serious as the drug traffickers started buying up land and getting together large tracts of land and throwing off the peasants and their cattle, just like in Sumapaz fifty years earlier.

FARC had imposed only one condition: the peasants also had to plant banana, yucca, and corn. This was because so much money could be earned from coca that the peasants would have preferred to buy it and bring it in from Villavicencia, rather than raise it themselves. But the FARC saw that this was not a good idea, because what the people earned from coca, they would end up turning over to the merchants. It was clear that raising their own food would eliminate that problem, and would also keep the peasants from becoming drug farmers, and from forgetting about their traditional fight for land and a better life. Coca was a huge threat to the peasant movement—it was a time bomb against their interests and the beliefs they had always defended. That is why peasant associations have never agreed to raise coca to finance themselves. It was different if the settlers decided to use their earnings and savings [from coca] to help the associations. That money was at least the result of their farm work. It was a moral issue, but also a very wise political condition. Many settlers spent part of their earnings on works that should have been built by the state, such as roads, schools, and health centers. In many areas, teachers and police inspectors made a living from harvesting coca to compensate for the starvation wages they supposedly earned, but never actually received. And so it went—from the teachers to the police, the mayor, the lieutenant and captain, the priest, the minister up to the president. It was a long, heavy chain.

CONCLUSION

Then came Belisario Betancur's government. They tried ceasefires, agreements to grant local political power for the popular election of mayors; they also tried to found a legal political party, as a political arm of the insurrection movement, which was supposed to slowly help create conditions for a new, nonviolent political system. But just the opposite occurred: as people dared to come out of hiding and get into politics and public life, they were murdered. As soon as the new party gained strength, they killed us. They wiped out 3,000 of our activists at gunpoint! Only two people are in prison for such monstrous acts of genocide! No political organization can resist such criminal assault. They destroyed us. Two of our presidential candidates were assassinated before the eyes of the entire country. How could the guerrillas possibly trust them enough to go back to peace talks? And what kind of guarantees would there be from any agreement reached with the state, which had been an accomplice to all the killing? It was this great political frustration that led the peasant movement and the armed movement to take the same route, and the agrarian claims were transformed into programs that go beyond agrarian reform, and that call for substantial changes in the economic and political structures. It's not just a matter of land, but also of the financial and tariff systems, and of international treaties. Democracy today means a new concept of security, public influence, citizen participation, regional participation. Things have changed over fifty years of struggle, and they have changed for all Colombians.

Like that of Gabriel Muyuy Jacanamejoy, Gerardo González's life story reads as struggle against the official, hegemonic history in the name of an emancipatory history—that is, history as a form of the social production of knowledge, a knowledge that is constructed by means of social memory, and that permits a particular reading of the past; one linked to the manner in which both the present and the future are perceived. Social memory is everything that individuals remember of their local and regional experiences. History is the music of a people, their food, their rites, and their myths; it is the ancestral ties of their communities, which are transmitted orally and which give them the strength necessary to resist the forgetting and the disintegration imposed by globalization. It is the memory of their constitution as a people, and often the sad testimony of their destruction.

It is for the sake of this history that one undertakes the recuperation—or, better, restoration—of oral history and life stories as an instrument that contributes to emancipation. The right to memory is increasingly necessary as a defense of the other rights of a people—a right that is inscribed in the Principles for the Protection and Promotion of Human Rights of the UN. A people's knowledge of the history of their oppression is a part of their patrimony and, because of this, ought to be conserved actively by the state. It is out of forgetfulness and oblivion that revisionist or deceitful theses emerge.

INDIA

7

Kaluram Dhodade

Activist in the struggle for the right to land, leader of one of the movements for the rights of the Adivasis.

Interviewed by Achyut Yagnik

"These Left party people felt afraid and were hesitant about sending their Adivasi workers. These parties had fought one or two struggles for Adivasis, but had no concept of the realities of Adivasi life or identity. We explained to them the need to articulate the Adivasi identity, the positive attributes of Adivasi culture. These are attributes that would benefit the human rights movement and society in general. Attributes such as not begging, collective sharing, honoring oral commitments, respect for women . . ."

Kaluram Dhodade

Kaluram Dhodade, one of the most powerful voices among Adivasi[1] leaders of India, leads a simple, spartan life in a small Adivasi village, Damkhind, surrounded by the hills in the vicinity of Bombay. Widely recognized as a pioneer of the Adivasi movement in western India, Kaluram, now in his sixties, is popularly called "Kaka" or "Uncle" by Adivasis and non-Adivasis alike. If you move with him in the remotest villages, in the industrial areas, or on the national highway stopover or suburban railway station north to Bombay, you will find that everywhere he is greeted with a raised fist by Adivasi men and women, whether farm laborers, industrial workers, rickshaw drivers, or vegetable and fruit vendors.

In the world of social movements in India, Kaluram's name is associated with Bhoomisena (Land Army), the organization that he initiated in 1970. As the name suggests, the issue of land—ownership, occupancy, and entitlement of land for

---

1 "Adivasis" is the collective name used for the many indigenous and tribal peoples of India. The term derives from the Hindi word adi, which means "of the earliest times," and vasi, meaning "inhabitant" or "resident." Officially they are termed "Scheduled Tribes." According to the 1991 census, there are about 84 million Adivasis, constituting 8 percent of the Indian population. About 30 percent of Adivasis are literate, though literacy among Adivasi women is a mere 18 percent.

Special provisions have been made in India's Constitution for the protection and development of Adivasis, ranging from the reservation of seats in the national parliament, state assemblies, and in the local self-government structures at the district and village levels, as well as positive discrimination in institutions of higher learning and government jobs.

States with Adivasi populations have enacted various laws for Scheduled Areas to prevent the appropriation of Adivasi land to non-Adivasis, as well as to restore alienated lands to Adivasis. Under the Fifth Schedule of the Constitution, the governor of a state having Scheduled Areas has been vested with special powers of making regulations, *inter alia*, for the protection of Adivasi interests in land. In the Sixth Schedule, the District Autonomous Council has also been given powers for protection of Adivasis' land interests.

Simultaneously, and apparently paradoxically, Adivasis are also the victims of development. Social science researchers estimate that 40 percent of the people displaced by development projects are Adivasis, and that this amounts to about 10 million persons. It is projected that another 10 million will be displaced in the next couple of decades. This means that, at the dawn of the twenty-first century, almost a third of the entire Adivasi population of the country will be development-displaced persons.

Adivasi—was at the core of the organization in the early years. The period from the late 1940s through the 1950s, which coincided with Kaluram's youth, witnessed a series of agrarian reform measures by the Bombay state government. The declared objective was that of "land to tillers," but poor and illiterate Adivasis were caught in the web fabricated jointly by the landlords, moneylenders, bureaucrats, and law enforcement agencies. After twenty years of intense experiences of legal advocacy in one form or the other, Kaluram realized the futility of legal intervention and moved to the path of struggle.

With some initial success in getting land for Adivasis, he engaged himself with activities related to agricultural development using credit from nationalized banks, and found himself and Adivasi farmers lost in the labyrinth of the financial world. Dissociating himself and his organization from the labyrinth, Kaluram embarked upon greater awareness-building among Adivasi youth by mobilizing and organizing Tarun Mandals (youth groups) in more than 200 villages. In turn, these groups continue their struggle against exploitation and injustice either in the field or in the factory.

Active in the Socialist Party since 1961, Kaluram fought in many elections, for the provincial assembly as well as for parliament, and lost all of them. By the time he was in a position to win the parliamentary elections in the late 1970s, he was thoroughly disenchanted. As a result, he put forward a friend, who won, and thereby kept himself free for his social emancipation work through Bhoomisena.

After about five decades of work, and having passed through many vicissitudes, in the early 1990s Kaluram was convinced that non-Adivasis who belonged to the world of social action or to political parties never gave Adivasi people their due, and hardly accepted their leadership. In 1993, with other Adivasi social activists from western India, Kaluram formed an autonomous network of Adivasis alone, called Adivasi Ekta Parishad. In the following seven years, AEP has reached far and wide, covering four western states of India with a message of Adivasi renaissance at the national and global levels.[2]

I don't know the exact date of my birth. The schoolteacher estimated my year of birth as 1936. In that period, there was no one in my village, Manor, who was literate. I got an education because an ashram[3] school had opened in the village. My father was afraid that if I went to the school I would be

---

2   This interview was conducted with the assistance of Ashok Chaudhary, a senior Adivasi leader from Gujarat and one of the founders of the AEP, and of Bina Fernandes, a social activist who works with Adivasi women. In order to maintain the flow of the text, the interviewer has eliminated the questions and transformed the interview into a first-person narrative. The interview was originally conducted in Marathi, the language of the state of Maharashtra, and later translated into English by Bina Fernandes.

3   Residential school, run according to the Gandhian vision of education. These schools focus on children from marginalized communities, and have a strong emphasis on working with both mind and hand.

recruited into the military. I ran away from home and went to the ashram school.

At that time there was a tremendous famine. When the Congress Party[4] started a school in the village, none of the children would go at first. Only when they started giving *pej*[5] did the children attend for one or two hours in the beginning. Previously, there were not really any schools in this area. After independence, a few schools were established. We would not go to the schools in urban areas. I went to high school in Wada, where I studied until the 11th standard. There was no college in this area—one had to go to Pune or Mumbai.

BEGINNINGS OF SOCIAL ACTION: ADIVASI SEWA MANDAL

In 1947, I was eleven years old and in the 4th standard. I started volunteer work with the Adivasi Sewa Mandal.[6] In school they did not teach you about *sat bara*,[7] but I used to fill out *sat bara* forms and police complaint forms as part of my work as a volunteer. The law stated that debt should be repaid in cash, at a limited interest rate. People had no knowledge of the law, and therefore the *saokars*[8] would take repayment at exorbitantly inflated interest rates—without giving receipts. Then they would send another notice asking for repayment of the debt! Then, after two or three notices, they would make a claim for the land by putting their name on the *sat bara* revenue record at the village.

After independence, the oppression experienced by Adivasis was greater than it had been under British rule. Earlier, Adivasis lived off the roots and fruits of the forest, and got by. After independence, the whole process of corruption, the oppression of Adivasis, and the appropriation of Adivasi land began, in which the *saokars* took over mortgaged lands. After the Maharashtra government passed the Tenancy and Agricultural Lands Act in 1948, the ancestral ownership of land could not be changed. Earlier, that had not been the case—if one could not pay the *khand*[9] then land was forfeited. This was the period of the Telengana revolt,[10] and the revolt led by the veteran Communist leader Godutai.[11] This was a movement against the *saokars*, and those who had earlier been afraid were instilled with new courage.

---

4 Established in 1885, the Congress Party led the freedom struggle in India and, after independence in 1947, became one of the main political parties.
5 Rice gruel.
6 Gandhian social organization working for Adivasi welfare.
7 Section of the Revenue Code pertaining to land entitlement.
8 Moneylenders.
9 Moneylender's rent.
10 Land movement started after independence by the Communist Party.
11 Godavari Parulekar.

In 1945, it was declared that land would be given to the tiller. Yet, until 1952/53, the Congress government gave the *saokars* assurances that they could divide the land with the Adivasis. As a result, the Adivasis did not think they had any rights to the land. Then, on April 1, 1957, the law of "land to the tiller" was passed. In 1956, all over Maharashtra, when the poor tillers refused to leave the land, the *saokars* sent *goondas*[12] to force them to give up their claims to the land. The other way land was alienated was through the collusion of the police with the *saokars*: the police scared people into giving up their lands, even though we had rights to the land under the law. So, after the *Kul Kayda*,[13] the land that had once been 100 percent Adivasi went out of their hands; 80 percent of the land was now controlled by 20 percent of the *saokars*, and 80 percent of people were left with 20 percent of the land. Even for this 20 percent of land, the *saokars*, in collusion with the *talati*,[14] would manipulate the records and prevent the registration of the harvested crop in the Adivasis' names. A lot of this land too was mortgaged.

Then there was the system of *palomodi*.[15] If I needed 5 rupees to go to the hospital, even for such a small amount of credit, I would become a bonded laborer. And even after one year's labor, the *saokar* would not give freedom to the bonded laborer. The *saokar* would pay the bonded laborer 20 *paili*[16] of rice as wages. If the laborer fell ill for a few days, 5 *paili* would be cut from the wages. Then, if the police caught the Adivasi, the *saokar* would arrange for his release, setting up a whole nexus of extortion.

The exploitation was so high, post-independence, that the rate of interest on loans was between 800 and 1,200 percent. So, even if the law was on the side of people, they were forced to mortgage their lands. The land and the crop became the *saokar*'s—nothing was left for the Adivasi. Almost all the Adivasi land was alienated in this way. I would work in the complaints resolution center of the Adivasi Sewa Mandal and, as a result, some Adivasis managed to hold on to their lands.

From 1945 to 1947, the movement against *saokars* was quite strong. After that its strength decreased because, in the 1952 elections, the leftists decided to enter the political struggle for power. Since the environment had been corrupted, I got fed up and went to Wada.

The environment at the Adivasi Sewa Mandal was such that even if Adivasis were being tortured, beaten up, their homes burnt and possessions destroyed, they were not ready to organize the Adivasis to protest. They

---

12   Persons employed to threaten or attack people.
13   Maharashtra Tenancy and Agricultural Lands Act, 1948.
14   Village revenue officer.
15   System of bonded labor.
16   Approximately 0.75 kg.

would limit their work to relief—helping the Adivasis rebuild their homes. After independence, even police repression increased, but these Gandhians do not confront police violence. Adivasis used to be afraid of the police, who would beat them up and throw them in jail. At that time, though the people in the Adivasi Sewa Mandal may have been good, they had no thought of helping Adivasis oppose the atrocities they were suffering. Their role was strictly charity-based—there was no struggle against exploitation.

Since the oppression by police and *saokars* was so heavy, I had decided to do something for Adivasis to oppose this oppression. People also felt they wanted to protest, but didn't know how. First, they would have to get rid of their fear of the police. Without that, nothing was possible. The next time the police raided people (confiscating property or chickens) we wrote down what they took and sent a report to the SP[17] the next day. We started this daily campaign against the police, and sustained it for a year. After a year, people saw that, of all the social workers in the area, no one else was confronting the police, and they began to trust me.

When I started this work, my family felt that I should take up a job instead of roaming about dangerously like this. In those days, people used to have the old silver coins as savings. They would make small contributions so that I could go to Jowar, Mokhada, and other block headquarters. For two to three years it went on like this.

Then the Jungle Kamgar Sanghatana[18] asked me to help them. There was a charcoal depot at Palghar where there was a lot of exploitation, because the management was in the hands of the upper classes. They would claim losses that would never be recovered. When I was in the Adivasi Sewa Mandal, I saw this exploitation of Adivasis in the charcoal pits. The first society of the Jungle Kamgar Sanghatan was in my village in Kondan. They ensured that if the saokar was getting 100,000 rupees profit, they would get at least 20,000 rupees—in the form of bonuses, provident funds, and so on.

At that time, the chairman of the cooperative was a nominal figure and would not be available when we needed his signature on checks, which was a problem. Also, he would travel all over the country on the union's money. When we decided to rent a space for an office, he started staying there.

I was not affiliated with any party, but the Congress people did not have a good opinion about me because they said I used to mislead the Jungle Kamgar Sanghatana. They prohibited me from coming to their meetings because I used to organize Adivasi meetings. I used to keep a diary, a record of the financial transactions—how much the laborers were paid, how much was pocketed. The cooperative leaders realized that this was dangerous, so one day they checked my bag. I had hidden away the records, so they did

17 Superintendent of police.
18 Jungle Workers Cooperative, supported by the Congress Party.

not find them. On May 10th, 1962, I publicly exposed how the leaders were looting the Kamgar Sanghatana.

Between 1962 and 1966, two Adivasi acquaintances were working in a sweatshop in Manor, and I was trying to get their wages increased. The sweatshop owner retaliated by accusing them of theft, and getting them arrested. The police beat them to death. This incident deeply affected me. I demanded a postmortem, in accordance with the rules. To protect the police, this was not done. I thought that this was not right, that this was how Adivasis were denied justice. The police asked me, "How are you related to these people?" I replied, "I am not related."

I witnessed so many incidents like this while I was in school, where, for one rupee, people were beaten up. There was this man from my village, hardworking and poor. They beat him up until he defecated, and then forced him to eat his feces. We had no justice. People were afraid—of the police, of the *saokars*, of the *goondas*—and people were not ready to organize. In that environment, I started working.

I decided that the first task was to get rid of this fear. One experience was in Ghot village, where the *seth*[19] was trying to capture the land of a widow, and the village united to prevent it from happening. In those days, women would go to work just five days after giving birth. When the *seth* came, threatening to throw them in jail, they protested, saying she had young children. The village collected 500 rupees to give to the *saokar* and free the woman. Since the *sat bara* was clearly in the name of the Adivasi, even the Supreme Court would not give a judgment in favor of the *seth*. I went to the regional office, and got a stay order. I also made a complaint to the SP that the *seth* had taken the 500 rupees. The PSIs[20] came to the village and got fifty people to testify that the money had been given. At the end of it, the *seth* was forced to repay the 500 rupees.

In general, though, the land that was recorded in Adivasis' names was not under their control for cultivation. We went in protest to the collector,[21] who sent the applications to the regional office, and enforced Section 144, *manai hukum*, which prevents the assembly of more than four persons. This is applicable to both parties, but the *saokars* paid off the police and brought seven ploughs and 300 men to till and sow the land. It was clear that the government was not on our side. People were afraid—if we stepped out of our houses to go to our jobs we were arrested. People said, if you help us, then we can do something; otherwise how can we fight 300 men? The

---

19 Landlord.
20 Police sub-inspectors.
21 Head of the district bureaucracy.

Wada sarpanch,[22] Dinkar—who everyone knew was a big *goonda*—had brought a gun.

So the *seth* started planting. We decided that, to stop them, we would first have to catch those who had guns. There were ten or twelve of us. We went to the land and beat up Dinkar. It became a case against Parsuram and other activists. What could we do in court? We had made a complaint against them. The person who was going to make the identification was Dattu Patkar. At that time, in the CID[23] there was Patankar, who came to investigate after forty-eight hours. The 300 men had fled by then. The police kept changing the names of the accused and arresting different people.

The DySP,[24] who was Saldanha at that time, said the wrong persons had been arrested. The whole group of us went to Bhivandi Court, where the case was being tried. I argued that the real culprits were the police, because they had not enforced the Section 144 order. When Dattu Patkar stood up to make the identification, I protested against the impartiality of his testimony, saying that he was guilty of raping an Adivasi girl and that the case was on record. When Dattu Patkar was questioned as to whether this was true, he started trembling, and had nothing to say. The case was closed. Some four or five men were put in jail with a ten-year sentence. But we appealed and eventually got them released also. This was in 1969.

This way, I began to work independently, to unite Adivasi society. My first focus was against the police, since everyone was afraid of confronting the police exploitation of Adivasis. People understood the police as being synonymous with the government. The Adivasi Sewa Mandal did not have the strength to oppose the atrocities against Adivasis. People also were scared to intervene if they saw someone being beaten up, because then they would be beaten up too.

When people realized that I was prepared to take on the police, they started coming to me in large numbers for help. The Adivasi Sewa Mandal would not take up Adivasi land-appropriation cases, so I took up the issue. I followed up the cases with the *mamlatdar*,[25] but nothing came of it. After fifteen years, some people got their land back.

FAMILY BACKGROUND

We had an extended family in the old days, and I had four brothers. I was in a boarding school, and all my schoolmates used to come home. There

---

22 Head of village council.
23 Criminal Investigation Department.
24 District superintendent of police.
25 Most senior official of the Revenue Department at the block level.

was always plenty of *harbara*[26] and other things to eat. In those days there were very few things we bought with money; we did not even buy salt. We used to exchange with others in the community. Because it was a joint family, a few people extra would not make a big difference. There was a lot of loving hospitality shown to visitors, which is not there in today's culture. People never thought of it as a burden or loss. My parents were illiterate, but they were always happy to greet guests. There is not a single friend of mine who has not visited us. This stood me in good stead when I roamed about holding meetings. I would always have food and shelter. There were no buses in those days. But I roamed around a lot more then than I do now, even though there are buses—from one village to the next. There was no expense of bus tickets.

My family did oppose my roaming around somewhat, saying that I got into problems. They thought I should get a good job and settle down. They did not understand what the meetings were about, why I was going. Their biggest fear was that either the police would arrest me or that the *saokars* would kill me. If I got a job I would be safe, they thought. But I would never go when job calls came.

I got married in 1968. My parents decided the match—they said, since you are not going to do the agricultural work, we need to find someone who will. They said that I was getting into too much trouble, I should be married off. I said that I was not going to stop my roaming about—so if someone was prepared to accept that, then I would marry her. Twice my wife returned to her parents' home, saying, this fellow is never at home. I said, I told you from the beginning, this is the kind of person I am. I did not go to bring her back, but my father felt very bad. So he went and brought her back. After my children were born, she stayed. I have two sons and a daughter.

INFLUENCES

I read novels in school. But the novels one read were of one type, and social reality was another type. What was in books was not in society. So I realized that books are also the monopoly of the oppressive, upper castes. Even as a youngster I had understood this. They would take our grain, our land. The police used to support them—they were all together in this exploitation.

The Socialists also fought in the land struggle from 1966 to 1968. The Socialist leader, Ram Manohar Lohia, had first talked about a land army. I never met Lohiaji, but I read two or three of his books—not then, but later, between 1972 and 1975. After our struggle had taken off, the Socialists

---

26   Green chickpeas.

joined us. The Socialist leader S. M. Joshi came here a few times to see the land army that people had formed in a jungle area.

I was not much influenced by the Bhoodan Andolan.[27] In Bhoodan, mostly waste and non-arable land was given. The movement could have been a success, but people's understanding of it was very limited—75 percent of the people were on the opposite side, because the *saokars* had frightened them off, saying that they would have no land left. So it never took the shape of a movement here.

It was because of the Telengana movement that the Congress government was forced to enact land reforms. The Telengana revolt was primarily by Adivasis. After this revolt, there was a movement here in Thane district too. The *saokars* would burn the grass of people, break down their huts. The Tenancy Act was made after Telengana. After that, in West Bengal, the same thing happened—college students were also involved.

But apart from the Adivasi struggles in the rest of India, we had our own history of struggles. In 1894, there were Adivasi movements here led by Bagoji Bagda and Bagoji Naik. The military used to take Adivasi young men from the jails. Three or four people from this area were in the military. At that time, nothing could be bought without the permission of the Nawab.[28] In the whole stretch from here to Nashik, whoever looted the maximum was rewarded. So Bagoji and these four military men in this movement taught all the poor Adivasis to shoot. They organized people against the oppression of the Nawab.

There is nothing written about him in Marathi, but the people from Mokhada (in Nashik) came from village to village and told us, through *thala* and *pat*.[29] The Adivasis always resisted the British. I learned these old stories as I moved around in this region. I did not learn this from books—there was no connection between this and what I studied in school.

PARTICIPATION IN ELECTORAL POLITICS

In 1962, M. G. Kadu was representing the Congress in the Bhopoli region. People wanted me to campaign for him but I refused to campaign for the Congress. Instead I helped the Communist Party in Kasa and got their candidate, Sutar, elected. In Palghar ward I campaigned for Navneetbhai Shah. I

---

27 Literally meaning "land donation," Bhoodan was a movement started by the eminent Gandhian Vinoba Bhave, who tried to persuade landowners to donate land to the landless.
28 Muslim king.
29 An oral tradition in which a metal plate is hung on a rope and drummed on with sticks, while a story of ancient times is told. This tradition used to be common—there would be a storyteller for each village. Today, however, it is a disappearing tradition.

asked people to vote for his symbol *jhopdi* [30] Navneetbhai lost, though he got a good number of votes. I had opposed him all these years because he was a Gujarati and a businessman, and belonged to a community that had oppressed us. But when I needed a certificate to join a sanitary inspector's course (on the insistence of my family) I went to him, and he treated me with respect. He was a member of the Socialist Party. Since 1940, there had been a socialist movement in this area. When they went on foot to Thane to protest, I began to think that these were people of integrity and that I should join them. So I started the Socialist Party's Manor office in 1961.

Earlier, all the *panchayats*[31] were controlled by the Congress. But between 1962 and 1967, except for a few seats, all the elections were won by the Socialist Party because of my efforts. But I did not find any difference between the Socialist *sarpanch* and the Congress *sarpanch*.

In 1967 I was nominated by the Socialists to contest the Legislative Assembly provincial elections. I got defeated in the mixed electoral ward of Dahanu and Palghar, while Navneetbhai got elected from Palghar. In 1967–68, I gave him records of all the lands lost by Adivasis, and he raised the issue in the Assembly. As a result, the government appointed the Pande Commission, which gave a false report declaring that this was all just a political stunt and that no Adivasi land had been taken over by non-Adivasis. After that, I was convinced that laws and commissions of inquiry would never be able to secure justice for Adivasis. When I saw that after ten years of efforts I was not able to release even one plot of Adivasi land, I felt we had to do something else.

Meanwhile, in 1971, I bowed to pressure from the high command of the Socialist Party and ran in the Lok Sabha parliament election in 1971. India

---

30   Hut.

31   The traditional *panchayats*—community councils and village councils—are very ancient features of the Indian subcontinent. For more than 2,000 years, these councils have been resolving conflicts within and between communities. During the colonial (British) period, traditional *panchayats* lost their importance, as they were replaced by British legal and administrative institutions. Mahatma Gandhi strongly advocated village councils with greater autonomy. After independence, and particularly after the constitutional amendment of 1960, *panchayats* were gradually developed and accorded more power. A three-tier system with village-, block-, and district-level representatives, and development activities at the local level such as education, health, road building, and so on, are managed by the *panchayat* system. It is noteworthy that the introduction and development of the *panchayat* system has eroded the traditional village council among Adivasis. In 1996, the Constitution was again amended (Panchayat Extension to Scheduled Areas Act, 1996) to give greater power to *panchayats* in Scheduled Areas where Adivasis form the majority of the population. Significantly, this amendment made it mandatory that land acquisition in Scheduled Areas could take place only after the informed, written consent of the *panchayat* of the area. It is using this power that Adivasis are resisting the entrance of multinational projects into their areas following the advent of India's new economic policies.

had just won the war against Pakistan, and there was a wave of admiration for Indira Gandhi,[32] and all opposition candidates lost. In this election, between 5,000 and 6,000 paid workers of the Jungle Workers Union campaigned for the Congress. In 1972 I fought in elections for the provincial assembly of Kasa.

After the Emergency,[33] in 1977, the Socialists started insisting that I contest elections once again. I was sure I would get elected from all the Bhoomisena villages with 80 percent of the vote. I refused, because it would have affected the basic work of the Bhoomisena youth groups. I suggested the name of Arjun Shingade, and it was accepted. Due to ill health, he campaigned only during the last eight to ten days, but we got him elected by a large vote. And I remained free to build the youth groups.

THE BEGINNINGS OF BHOOMISENA

In 1970 I had started a movement against the Anjuman Trust, which controlled 2,000 acres of Adivasi land. During this agitation, we were put in jail for ten to fifteen days. Datta Samant's[34] men also came. All those who were in jail had also fought for independence. In jail, we discussed what we would do after we left. Some said that clothes should be available in the public distribution system; some said that sugar should be available for the common person.

They asked me, "Why haven't you said anything? What will you work for when you leave jail?" I said "What can I say? The issues you have raised are not our issues. An Adivasi does not drink tea, not even by mistake. And where do they have the money for clothes? Clothes and sugar will be bought by others—these are not our questions. The struggle I intend to start is to gain control over Adivasi land that has been alienated. We will harvest the crops on such land." This was the birth of Bhoomisena.

When I left the jail and organized the first meeting in my village, Kondan, 1,500 people attended. We labored in the fields, we harvested the crop. People asked, "Will we get the land?" I replied that if we were united, we would. Men, women, and children should participate in the struggle. From today, we should stop doing salaam[35] to the sahebs[36] and court-kacheri.[37]

---

32 Daughter of India's first prime minister, Jawaharlal Nehru, Indira Gandhi rose to power in the late 1960s, and was Congress prime minister in the 1970s and 1980s.
33 State of internal emergency declared between 1975 and 1977 by Prime Minister Indira Gandhi. Fundamental rights were suspended, and the period was marked by widespread human rights abuse and gave rise to the civil liberties movement in India.
34 A prominent union leader from Bombay.
35 Salute.
36 Officials.
37 Courts and government offices.

At that time, my brother and father were bonded to the *saokar*. They asked me, "What are you up to? What is this *vanar sena*[38] you have formed? We are not going to let you do this in our village." The landlord had a meeting that nine people attended and they decided to beat me up. Word got around and people warned me against holding any meetings. I said, "If 1,500 attend our meeting and nine attend their meeting, who is in the right? If they pick up sticks, we will pick up stones!" We decided to harvest the crop, but it was not yet ripe. Meanwhile, the *saokar* ran to the police for help. The police and the *saokar*'s *goondas* were threatening to beat up the village. We decided that we should stay united—we should keep watch and, if the police came, no one should face them alone. One of us kept a lookout on the road and he would quickly inform us if the police were approaching.

I was about twenty-five or twenty-six years old then. People were afraid of the *saokar*'s repression. So I told them, "The law is on our side. How can the police be on their side?" When four policemen came, we told them that we are a thousand, we are not coming unless you can show us a written order. So we chased them off.

Meanwhile, since the rice had not ripened, we could not move ahead with the harvesting, and people were getting uneasy; they needed to take action. So we harvested the unripened grain, because otherwise the momentum would disintegrate. Again the police came, and again we chased them off, saying that since our title was on the land revenue records, we had the law on our side. The police stated that the debt of the Adivasi had to be repaid to the *saokar*. We said, then you can confiscate the *jhopdi*, but you have no legal license to the land.

Some people backed out of this struggle and wanted their names to be taken off the Bhoomisena list. We decided to prevent more people from leaving the struggle, and formed units of thirty, fifty, a hundred people for crop harvesting. We selected those plots of land that were in the interior and not easily accessible, so that by the time the *saokar* or the police arrived we would have finished the harvesting. When the police confronted us, we said we were bound to return the original debt incurred, but we also had the right to reclaim the value of the harvest these past ten to fifteen years. We agreed to go to the police station, and the next day 2,000 people went. There we told the DSP that the 1957 law was on our side. The SP asked for time to study the law.

We had used the technique of first harvesting the land that was within the law. Once we established that we were going according to the law, later, we would harvest all the land—whether it was within the law or not.

---

38 Literally, "army of monkeys"—a term used since Gandhian times to refer to youth groups.

When people heard that we were harvesting the land, many approached us. But we could not go everywhere. So all over Thane district, people started harvesting the land on their own, in the name of the Bhoomisena. Particularly during the Emergency, if they tried to stop us harvesting, we scared them off by threatening to have them thrown into jail.

BHOOMISENA STRUGGLES

Since we started with the struggle for the liberation of land, we decided on the name "Bhoomisena," which literally means "land army." The inspiration for the Bhoomisena was the Bhoomi Mukti Andolan,[39] though we used the word *sena* in the sense of *sanghatan* or collective—that is, a militant, struggle-based organization.

One of our first struggles was in 1972, when we had undertaken the crop-harvesting in one village called Hatna, where the *saokar* had captured two acres of land by giving the tenants 10 kg[40] of flour. I told the Bhoomisena activist to show us the *sat bara*. Since it was in the Adivasi's name, we assembled fifty to a hundred people and forcibly harvested the crop. The *saokar* came to the *godown*[41] with his pistol; but the public was large in number, so he went to the police and made a complaint.

This was during Diwali, when the youth were on holiday from college and had come to watch and learn about this harvesting program. When the police came from Vikramgad, they started talking to these fresh youth recruits. The police took all of us to jail in Jowhar—those of us who had done the harvesting and these youth too. Although the *sat bara* was in the Adivasi's name, the *talati* manipulated the records, and so we became the criminals. The youth with us were worried that a jail record would reflect badly on their character, and they would not get jobs. So we organized discussion and song sessions in the morning and evening and, after fifteen days, their fear of jail had disappeared. Meanwhile the socialist activists put up the bail, and we were released. The day we were released, we decided to stage a rally protesting against the tyranny of the *saokars*. Everyone was taken aback that the time in jail had only strengthened us further.

Then came the fight for payment of minimum wages in Maharashtra. All the Left parties, trade unions, and Right parties organized a rally in Mumbai where between 200,000 and 300,000 people participated. We went as part of Bhoomisena. People from Wada and Palghar *tehsil*[42] walked to Virar, and from there took the local train. There was a great unity on this issue. Finally,

---

39 Land Liberation Movement.
40 Worth 10 rupees.
41 Warehouse.
42 Block (unit of a district).

in 1973/74, the Minimum Wage Act was implemented in Maharashtra. At that time, people would not even get the 3 rupees that was the minimum wage.

From 1972 to 1976, after we released the Adivasi lands, we decided to start a constructive program. So we went to the Gandhian people and asked them what help they could give. Nothing came out of that. Then, in 1972, Aba Karmakar and Mrinal Gore of the Socialist Party came to do some constructive work. But agriculture requires a lot of investment, so we did not get support.

This newly released land had no clear title, because it was on forest lands. So no banks were willing to issue loans. Due to a lack of trust, when Karmakar came, only twenty people in Kondan joined the program for cultivation. When people questioned where the money was going to come from, he told them that this was not their worry, and that they should form a Kshetkari Mandal.[43] That first year, somehow or other funds were collected for payments. As a result, in 1973, forty villages in the area joined the program. People thought some *seth* had come, who was distributing loans. Karmakar had convinced the manager of the Bank of Maharashtra to give productive loans to these twenty Adivasis, even without the *sat bara*, arguing that it made more sense than giving poverty-alleviation handouts.

This was "modern" agriculture; you had to use this much fertilizer. The fertilizer was brought to Palghar direct from Pune. People got scared, because usually one requires 500 to 1000 rupees for cultivation. Some people had loans of up to 60,000 rupees. Karmakar would go personally to see the fields. But these people were *chapter*.[44] They would show somebody else's cultivated fields as their own, and Karmakar did not know any better. We told Karmakar not to distribute the loans without consulting us, but he went ahead anyway. When the people on whose names the loans had been taken started expressing concern, he assured them that the money would be repaid. That year the harvest was very good.

In 1974 there was a drought, and we decided to urge people not to trade in the black market. Before we started this movement, the *saokars* were buying up the land. They kept watchmen for the land—from among us— by giving them food and drink. Two of these, Sukriya and Jipriya, helped us out against the *saokar*, even though we were not sure that they would. The movement picked up momentum at this time. We would go walking from village to village. When the collector came and saw that the Bhoomisena was doing social work, preventing people from selling grass on the black market, he cancelled all the cases pending against us.

43   Farmer's Cooperative
44   Overly smart.

The hold of the *saokars* in this region was so strong that people were forced to sell their grass to them—or face being beaten up, and their bullock cart confiscated. Everyone who has ever gone to sell grass has been beaten up at some point or other; no one has escaped. We raised an outcry, saying that we would not let the grass be sold off in this exploitative way. The CPM and Congress people would not oppose the *saokars*. The *saokars* had Pathani[45] guards against whom no one could make a police complaint, even if they beat up and murdered fifteen or twenty people.

We decided to organize the sale of the grass in Bombay. We thought it would help us to repay our outstanding loans too. A lot of college students, professors, and reporters used to come here at that time—like a *jatra*[46]—to help us in this revolution. These people did not know the difference between grain and grass. For them it was all sensational—"People survive by eating *imli* leaves, and we have helped them get grain."

The rate for grass was 50 rupees for 500kg. We decided on 60 rupees, but the *saokars* raised their rate to 150 rupees. So a lot of people did not sell to us. Those in the movement sold to us. We took the grass to Andheri and kept it in a *godown* there waiting for the price to rise. But the *saokars* used their connections in Mumbai to ensure that we were not able to sell the grass at a good rate. We suffered a loss of between 10,000 and 20,000 rupees.

So the loans remained outstanding in the Adivasis' names. The bank sent notices to these people. Some consultants came for digging wells, and so on. They bought cement for constructing the wells from the black market—which I opposed, saying that we should stick to our principles of not trading on the black market. From that point on, I used to hold separate meetings with the college youth, who had also questioned Karmakar on this.

We still had to figure out what to do about the bank loans outstanding against Adivasis. Karmakar had not only been unable to create a resource for Adivasis; he ended up getting them hugely indebted. This debt was a critical issue; it became an Assembly question, and inquiries were instigated against me. People were ready to give statements against me. We held a meeting of all those who had taken loans, and got them to give promissory notes. Even so, not all the loans were repaid. In this way the Kshetkari Mandal became a failure. It was not that Karmakar was corrupt, but he had mismanaged affairs and created a bigger problem. By 1975, we had chased him off from this area.

Meanwhile, the movement had also received a setback, because we had put our energies into this. Meanwhile the atrocities had increased, so I

---

45   Men from the northwestern frontier of present-day Pakistan, known for their physical strength.

46   Cultural or religious procession.

decided to reactivate the struggle-oriented work. The *saokar's* hold would not be broken just by constructive work.

EMERGENCY

In 1975 and '76, during the Emergency, Navneetbhai and others suggested that we organize another loan-recovery meeting with the bank officer, Joshi. The *saokars* had spread the propaganda that I was against Indira Gandhi, and that I was giving speeches against her. We were continuing the crop-harvesting program in our area. I fixed a village meeting program with Joshi; he would come to talk about the loan recovery. I would go ahead to that village and mobilize people against bonded labor and to harvest the crops. When the police wised up to what was happening, they came to one village; but Joshi said, "We are doing a loan-recovery meeting." Joshi didn't know what I was doing.

The well-known journalist, Premila Lewis, had done an exposé that Indira Gandhi had bonded laborers from Bihar in her farmhouse. I started telling people about it in my speeches. Kumar Saptarish and other activists from Palghar and Thane were all arrested, but I was not. When Indira Gandhi's Twenty Point Program[47] was announced on the radio, I thought people should understand what is useful for them and what is not. Meetings were banned, and the city folks were scared. I roamed about and mobilized the youth to come to a *shibir*.[48] Some thirty youth attended. We had to keep it very secret; we told the youth to look out for the red-ribbon guide who would guide them to the green-ribbon guide, and then to the yellow-and black-ribbon guides, ultimately to reach the spot of the *shibir*. The issues from the Twenty Point Program that we selected at the *shibir* were bonded labor, minimum wages, freedom from indebtedness, and mortgages. I got some pamphlets and forms printed in Mumbai about bonded labor and minimum wages. We decided to give copies of the completed forms to the *tehsildar*[49] and collector. The Emergency was in force, so it was decided that the youth should go, not I. Our program was good, but we had no support from outside. Because we had filled out the forms, those who opposed us from the Congress got demoralized. The Tarun Mandals that had attended the *shibir* were strengthened.

Then we decided to release all the mortgaged gold, ornaments, and vessels. Some fifty or sixty people came to recover the mortgaged goods. We scared off the *saokars* saying this was the law of the Emergency, and recovered

47   Populist development program mooted by Mrs. Gandhi during the Emergency years.
48   Camp or meeting.
49   Revenue officer at the block level—also referred to as *mamlatdar*.

between 75,000 and 80,000 rupees' worth of goods. It was not possible for us to go to all the *godowns*. We started writing letters to all the *saokars*, demanding the return of mortgaged goods, or else they would be thrown in jail. They got scared and handed over the goods—emptied out the *godowns*.

When all the Left activists—Mrinal Gore and others—were thrown in jail during the Emergency, we thought about doing a Satyagraha[50] at that time. But all these city folks were so scared. But the Emergency was no new situation for us: we have been in an emergency since we were born! During the Emergency, people were scared to speak. We called a meeting at night in the jungle with the youth. We knew the Manor police would come. So we told the police *patil*[51] of the village that if he saw the police coming, he should approach with a candle and we would disperse. It was the monsoon season and we were in the jungle, running from the police. We hid out in one house in the jungle.

BHOOMISENA'S TARUN MANDALS (YOUTH GROUPS)

> *Four months we sow the rice in monsoon mud*
> *Drenched by the rain*
> *When the grain is ripe*
> *The* saokar *comes with his car*
> *Why has it become his father's goods?*
>
> *Don't do* palomodi
> *Form a Tarun Mandal in the village.*
>
> Bhoomisena songs

In each Tarun Mandal there would be one person responsible for songs, and he would teach the others, pass it on. This was in the 1970s, when the environment was such that people came together in song. There were some songs comparing Adivasi religion to Hindu religion. The Hindus begged from the gods; Adivasis did not. Begging was not a practice among Adivasis. Some songs were about marriage and how women had the maximum rights. Adivasi marriages were democratic, which was not the case in Christian or Muslim marriages. Among Adivasis, marriages are decided in the community. Women made the songs about marriage. Now, because of modernization, many of these songs have disappeared. When the 1996 panchayat legislation came, we put the information into songs of this style. We even made a cassette of the songs—for use all over Maharashtra. Even before this legislation, we had a campaign for "Our rule in our village" in Maharashtra.

---

50 Nonviolent protest movement evolved by Gandhi.
51 Person in charge of maintaining law and order in the village.

The Tarun Mandals were formed mainly after the Emergency. There was one group here in Nagjhari that held a night-long meeting and decided to free bonded labor. The question that arose then was, "How would people get married then? How would people meet the wedding expenses?" According to custom, we have to give the police patil liquor, feed the village, and incur a lot of unnecessary expenditure. Could we think of something different? The first low-cost wedding was organized during the Emergency. The older folks protested, saying that tradition should be followed. But the youth objected, saying they did not want to live as debt slaves for the next twenty or thirty years like the previous generations had.

The Tarun Mandals were organized in such a way that their weekly meetings were on different days, so that the message quickly spread from one group to the next. At that time there were about a hundred active Tarun Mandals that took part in the struggles.

In 1976 and '77, during the Devkhop struggle to get alienated Adivasi land back, the Tarun Mandals played an important role. Due to intense repression, rape, and beatings, people were very demoralized in that village. Earlier, I had not been able to do anything alone, but now we had the support of the youth groups. I told Banibai of Devkhop village to organize a meeting in the jungle, and told them to bring their land records.

We could organize a meeting in that village because of Banibai's courage. We went to harvest the lands for which we had *sat bara* records. Overnight the *saokar* bribed the *talati* to make the records in his name. This was during the Emergency, so the news did not get published in the papers. We wanted the *saokars* who had beaten people up to be arrested. We told Banibai that there were 200 Tarun Mandals to support our actions. The law and the records were on our side. These police and revenue officers have to follow the law, as we are the ones who are paying for them. We are poor, but what is the point of living like dogs? Better to consume poison and die than live like this. Even with all this persuasion, no one in that village was ready. Banibai then expressed her disgust, saying that the youth of the Tarun Mandals were real men, and her villagers were not. Finally, after "If he will, I will," some twenty-five people were ready to harvest the crop of one Maya Tandel. This was not enough, so we told them that they all had to take part. We devised a strategy in which the most fearful would be put in front and the fearless at the back, so that when the former turned tail and ran, the latter would break their heads first!

When the Bhaiyya[52] realized that the crop had been harvested, he sent three trucks of *pehlwans*[53] who came with swords and sticks to the village,

---

52 Term used for migrants from the northern state of Uttar Pradesh; in Kaluram's area, some of them had become landlords.
53 Muscle-men.

who told the people "Seth bulawa."[54] The people refused to go, saying they had not taken any property from the *seth*, so why should they go? They were hiding on the mountain, and were surrounded on all sides. We started throwing stones at the *pehlwans*. They dispersed in a shambles. They were too ashamed even to go to the police station and make a complaint that Adivasis had beaten them up! I asked them, "How many trucks does the *seth* have? Three? I have thirty-four trucks with Adivasi drivers that I will fill and bring!" Of course, I had no trucks, but we fooled them properly. We did not let the Bhaiyyas take the grass; we burnt it. When they came to confront us, we beat them up again.

Now the people were confident that, even if a thousand Bhaiyyas came, they would be able to deal with them. In Devkhop, from then to now, there is a tremendous unity—all due to Banibai's tremendous courage and initiative. She was unafraid of confronting even the police. The village has now become "modernized," so many people have fallen into bad habits, but you will still find some people who hold on to the old ideals.

Some men from Uttar Pradesh who were going to Wada got lost along the way, and were looted of their money. The people of Devkhop were wrongly accused of being responsible for it, and a false case was made against them in Palghar police station. When we protested, they were released. Then the police went with two jeeps to Umbargaon, which is a small village of twenty-five houses. They opened fire and Mangal Raghu Mandal was hit. The police caught some men and put them in the jeep. The first attack happened at nine o'clock, and the second shooting happened at ten o'clock at night.

My colleague Neelam and I went there. When we arrived, no one had any idea how many had been killed in the shooting. We did not know for sure if shooting had occurred. The village was deserted; everyone had fled to the jungles. We could see the blood stains and the empty cartridges. Neelam and I decided that lodging a complaint with the guilty would be of no use—we would have to go to Mumbai and meet the police commissioner. People made a contribution for our tickets, and we went and met the commissioner.

We took out a *morcha*, demanding to know where Mangal Raghu Mandal was. It had no effect. We then made a habeas corpus writ petition to produce Mandal in court. A CID inquiry was initiated in all the police stations from Vikramgad to here. I roamed around for a month with Deshpande, the inquiry officer. He supported the police, so nothing came out of it.

---

54   The *seth* was calling them.

AFTER THE EMERGENCY

After the Emergency, when the Janata Party came to power, we decided that we would not collaborate with any party that was part of the capitalist system. The Congress is a devil with teeth, and the Janata is a devil with no teeth: they will help us until their teeth grow.

In 1978 we organized our first meeting on the environment. This was after a visit to the Chipko Jungle Bachao movement.[55] We had a good meeting on this issue, and people came from as far away as Pune. We printed a booklet that we sold for small contributions of 25p[56] and 50p. This enabled us to buy some vessels for the Bhoomisena office.

We had completely left constructive programs, and went into struggle-based actions. The implementation of the Minimum Wages Act was our next struggle. People were still not getting minimum wage. The Rashtriya Swayamsevak Sangh[57] and Congress leaders threatened to beat up the Adivasis in the same way in which Dalits[58] were beaten up during the Marathwada riots.[59] They said they were not going to put up with the Bhoomisena's *dadagiri*.[60] They started a "Save Justice" movement. But justice had been done: Who were they going to save?

The upper castes thought they could suppress the Adivasis in the same way in which they had tried to suppress the Dalits. The central government at Delhi was in their control. We sent a memorandum to the government saying that we were being labeled unjust for trying to implement the minimum wages law. Releasing bonded labor is an injustice, according to them. They wanted us to continue to slave for them. When an inquiry was instituted, they got scared and became quiet. In fact, some of the *saokars* started fighting among themselves, because they were not willing to come into conflict with the Bhoomisena and risk damage to their property.

At this point both Adivasi and non-Adivasi poor people were ready to work together to enforce the minimum wage, and wanted the Bhoomisena to organize meetings in interior villages. At Vangaon, one of our activists had been beaten up and was missing. So we decided to hold a protest march. I reached the meeting late, and the speeches had already started and other supporters of the Bhoomisena, including lawyers, were present,

---

55 Movement to save the forests, initiated in the northern state of Uttar Pradesh under the leadership of Suderlal Bahuguna. The movement became famous for its modus operandi of hugging trees to prevent them from being cut down.
56 Paise (singular paisa) it's a subdivision of the rupee.
57 Extreme right-wing Hindu political party.
58 Castes at the bottom of the Hindu social hierarchy, formerly considered untouchable.
59 These riots took place in 1980 over the proposal to rename Marathwada University after the eminent Dalit leader, Dr. Ambedkar.
60 Bullying and domination.

because it was a Sunday. The *saokars* were all ready to beat me up, but they did not know what I looked like. I went when the meeting was almost over. They thought that one big strong fellow at the meeting was Kaluram Dhodade, and caught him. When the beatings started, people fled, and the main people and I went and hid inside a house. These people told me I should do something—but what could I do?

After this incident, the Bhoomisena once again stood strong. I held a meeting with the Tarun Mandals. We decided that anyone who came into our area should not be able to come in directly. The Shiv Sena[61] fellows got scared. They couldn't come to Thakurpada, but in Thanepada a landlord had captured all the land. He would not offer minimum wage. I went to a meeting in Thanepada. The landlord brought *goondas* with swords and sticks, and there was a confrontation in which eight or ten women were injured. People realized that the *goondas* were going to escape on the milk train to Mumbai. They stopped the trains and checked the whole train, including the toilets. By this time between 200 and 400 people had amassed at the station, and they were ready to beat up whoever they caught, regardless of the police. The Shiv Sena protested that the Bhoomisena's *goondas* had beaten them up. They tried to call a meeting, but no one from here would go. And how could they call a meeting with outside people? They were scared off. The Shiv Sena was strong in Mumbai at that point, but they could not gain entry into this area.

In 1982, in Manor, we started work on *palomodi*. We had the records of the repayment, and we started the work of releasing pawned goods. We had the records of all the 80,000 rupees' worth of goods released. So when the cases were filed against us, we had proof. We had a good lawyer too. In court, the *saokar* got scared.

In 1984 the Maharashtra Industrial Development Corporation (MIDC) zone was being constructed, and the site laborers were not getting minimum wage, and women were being harassed. So we decided to organize a meeting there. There was much resistance from the *goondas* there, but we overcame it and sat down by the bridge to have our meeting. Meanwhile, the DySP drove up in his jeep to the bridge and summoned me. I said I would go when the meeting was over. People thought we would all be arrested. But the DySP and I were old acquaintances, and I told him that this *saokar* contractor was not paying minimum wage. So he told the police station not to take the *saokar*'s complaint, even though it was true that we had beaten them up. As a result, the 300 workers on the site stopped working and construction came to a halt. The *saokar* was on his way to meet the collector to resolve the dispute, and offered me a ride there. I refused, saying

---

61   Extreme right-wing Hindu political party.

I had a State Transport bus worth 13,000 rupees to travel in. Finally, he had to pay the backlog of wage difference and pay minimum wage before the work could recommence.

The government officials got quite tired of us. Every day we had a new issue—bonded labor, land appropriation, the minimum wage. As far as they were concerned, we might be doing "good work," but we were a pain. People were motivated, though. If minimum wages were not given, they would go on a protest march. When they were confronted by guns, the women grabbed hold of the gun and marched to the police station and deposited the gun there. In all the struggles of the Bhoomisena, women were at the forefront; about 70 percent of the participation was from women.

We established a trade union in 1974, and a second in 1978. We registered the trade union to fight legal struggles. The truck drivers and mine workers were part of the union. We struggled for a minimum wage for them, and made the collector and *mamlatdar* conduct inquiries. Some were released from bonded labor through the movement; others were released through legal struggle. In some orchards, people were made to work 12 or 15 hours with no wages; Adivasi women worked on a contract basis in cleaning freshly caught fish. All these were exploited. So our union covered the whole region and forced the signing of contracts.

This union was active until 1992, after which we did not renew it because there was no one to run it. Now, if there are any labor struggles, we take them on through the Bhoomisena. Two years ago we got the MIDC drivers' salary raised from 1,000 to 3,500 rupees; the truckers' rate was raised to a minimum of 150 rupees per day. We struggled for bonded laborers, fishermen, hotel workers, grass laborers, jungle workers, and contract construction workers. Now, if we need to do official or legal work, there is no registered body because we have never registered the Bhoomisena, and do not intend to. If you register an organization, then you are bound within a legal framework. To implement the law we had the trade union, and to break the law or struggle for a new law we have the Bhoomisena.

THE 1970S AND 1980S IN RETROSPECT

In the 1970s there was a lot of hope and expectations—that things could change. One of the reasons was that the officials at that time were good; they would support us. For example, although we harvested the crop, we were not able to get control over the land. We did not have money to go to court. We are people who sell our chickens to go on a *morcha*[62] where would we get money? In fifteen years, we were not able to get one favo-

---

62 Protest march.

rable judgment. Then came Collector Chaudhary, who said that he would clear our cases in five minutes. He actually cleared five people in three minutes. Now, this same Chaudhary came just last year when the Enron pipeline business had started, and told people how he was an old friend of mine and that the Bhoomisena had given permission for the Enron project! He came here, had tea, and said that he would ensure that we got adequate compensation. We said we did not want the money, and we did not want the gas pipeline going through our area.

In the 1970s, if we had any complaint, it used to be considered by the top-level officers. The lower levels were loose, but our work would get done. Bureaucrats had more integrity in those days. They would tell the truth. Now people will say or do anything for personal gain. Then, the lawyers of that period were from the movement, so they had a greater sensitivity to Adivasi life, language, and culture. They would support us in front of the magistrates. Today, few lawyers have that understanding—even among the human rights lawyers. The leaders today have no idea about Adivasi life.

Activists of that time had a lot of integrity too—if they gave their word, they would do it. They were very loyal. The reason why Godutai[63] was able to work in the area was because she inspired their loyalty by living like them. People from outside will taste *pej* or *kadu kanda*[64] once out of politeness, but will not have them otherwise. Those that come from upper-class society and could live like us, they immediately get greater acceptance.

PANCHAYATI RAJ AND ADIVASI AUTONOMY

In the 1970s, when we formed the Bhoomisena, we had realized that the state is corrupt, and against Adivasis. The nature of the state had not changed since independence. It is worse than the British. When Panchayati Raj came, things got worse.

Earlier, our people would never beg. But this government machinery is such that it has made beggars of people. Today's democracy means there is nothing in the hands of people, but those that control affairs from above have the power to distribute resources. And they distribute assistance in such a way that those that have a surplus benefit further. Those who have nothing do not get anything. In that situation, how can democracy exist? Today's government results in the destruction rather than the development of people.

Until today, all the laws have been made by the oppressor society, and have been against Adivasis. During British times, Adivasi law was different;

63   Godavari Parulekar.
64   Adivasi food items.

they had no relation with the *court-kacheri*. Decisions would be taken in the village—about land, adjudication of marital disputes, and any other offences. The total concept of the law of the oppressors has been forced on us. As a result, more displacement, more repression. We don't have any knowledge of this law. The lawyers in the courts don't understand our language. In these courts, a criminal can go free. But in the village court, a criminal is punished.

At the time of independence, there should have been the equivalent of the Indian Penal Code for Adivasi society. That did not happen. We should be able to decide what law we should have, not have someone else's forced on us. The second thing is, whatever good laws the state has made have been because there was an Adivasi movement. Even though there were constitutional provisions, they were not implemented. So there were resistance movements. The state would never have made the law if it had not been for these movements. And it was passed only because the Speaker was an Adivasi.

If you look at the amendments in the Tenancy Act, some sections were included because of the struggle of the Bhoomisena. These sections are about lawful and unlawful transfer of lands. Earlier, land transfer could take place with the collector's permission and the Adivasi could not get back the land. This section, which ensures that the government itself cannot take Adivasi lands, was a result of the Bhoomisena movement. It was not there before. Now, even if a big organization holds the land with the permission of the collector, it has to be returned to the Adivasi.

Since the Gram Panchayat has come, it has become clear that the government is the *mukhia*.[65] As a result, people's concept of development, which used to be collective, has now become individual. Earlier, if someone was ill, the village would help out in the cultivation, and there was no question of wages. Now, the urban concept of development has entered people's minds. The collective attitude has disappeared.

After Panchayat Raj, the question "Whose development?" is now not in the hands of the village. The control is from outside the village. Under Panchayat Raj, if 1 billion rupees are spent on "development of Adivasis," 900 million rupees of that budget is spent on vehicles, buildings, air travel, and so on. I don't accept that this is "development." Even the 100 million rupees that reaches Adivasis—suppose it is for 10,000 people, and is distributed among five, then the remaining 9,995 are left with nothing—inevitably causes conflict. From Bihar to Nagaland, everywhere I see the same process—not just in the government, but also among NGOs. There is no difference from what the government is doing. There is money for work with Adivasis, so you work among Adivasis.

---

65 Headman.

The 1996 legislation should have happened earlier. Now everything has been destroyed—the land, the jungle. If that had been enacted earlier, then something could have been saved. Then, all the Adivasi land has been sold already. In Maharashtra, the Adivasi's *sag* trees were sold off in 1973 for 50 paisa per tree to the contractors. The *saokars* stole the trees, and now we are given the rights! If we had been given the rights then, we would have had property worth tens of millions of rupees, money that Adivasis cannot even visualize having in their whole lives. Even if not in the form of money, it would have been a supportive resource for us.

The Panchayat Raj legislation has left nothing in the hands of people. All the decisions are taken from a distance. Today, what the Gram Sabha[66] decides does not happen. If someone's house is destroyed in the floods, does he get any assistance? It is the people who are not affected who benefit most. Whose names are in the "Below Poverty Line" lists? Those who have good land—not the Adivasis. Even for the simple *gharkul yojana*,[67] those who already have get homes; those that don't have don't get. The whole affair is in the hands of the upper class. It is true that, with the Panchayat Raj, a new Adivasi leadership has emerged—in the *panchayat*, the *tehsil* and the *zilla*.[68] But inequality has not been removed. Those who are in need continue to be deprived. I don't accept that the development of four people can constitute the development of the village. If all people are to enjoy equality, then inequality has to be destroyed first. For this Panchayat Raj or democracy to work, people have to be given the power to make laws.

After independence, the traditional council among Adivasis gradually disappeared. As a result we suffered a great loss. Our traditions of people's justice have been destroyed. If they had survived, our situation would not have deteriorated so badly. Now, they are telling us that we have the 1996 legislation. But it has become very difficult. People's mind-set has changed; they now see themselves as separate from government. If there is a movement, then people can learn. Otherwise there is nothing.

Now they tell us that the Gram Sabha has been given rights. But what are the upper classes doing? Bringing pressure by saying this is wrong, that is wrong. If the Gram Sabha has been given rights, it should be the ultimate authority. It has not been given that sort of right. Decisions should be made in the village. Now everything still comes from the top. Decisions should go from the village to Delhi; the village should be able to formulate schemes. Only then can they be successful. They can never be successful if they are forced from above. That is our experience to date. The village should have the right to decide. The decision may be wrong—everyone can

---

66 General assembly of a village.
67 Housing scheme.
68 District.

make mistakes. But it should be accepted. So, the *panchayat* should be given independence to develop the village.

In this context, for Panchayat Raj to be effective, it cannot be just in one village, but must be in the community of a whole region. The region will have a different lifestyle; people will learn from each other; the decisions of one village will be communicated to other villages. Through experience and exchange, the development of the village can happen. Today, even if villages have the right to take decisions in the Gram Sabha, how much influence do they have at the state level? Only if that influence increases can anything happen. The leaders and the people—the distance between the two should decrease. The leaders should have the trust of people, and should implement the decisions of the Gram Sabha.

With Panchayat Raj, on the one hand there is supposedly the right of the village; on the other hand, in real terms, those rights do not exist. What good things should be preserved cannot survive when *Dunkel*[69] is forced on us. The government does not consider the good things. Only the horrific things are considered, like the gas pipeline, the Enron projects, mega-projects—all of which result in more exploitation of rural people.

After independence, corruption and the desire to "get rich quick" have increased among people. And among these people, there is no movement to offer resistance. They do not consider their lives to be dependent on the Gram Sabha. In many areas the land has been sold off without the Gram Sabha's permission. The distribution of land has not gone to the needy, landless people. Today the land that has been sold off has gone to those with black money—to thieves, smugglers, and *goondas*. It is just a means for them to store their black money. False records are made showing that this is their ancestral property. It is not even that they use the land to harvest crops. All the land along the highway to Mumbai has been bought by black money.

WHICH DEMOCRACY?

The government says there should be democracy. But there is a difference between the democracy of the village and urban democracy. In a village there is no distinction between big and small. A democratic meeting is for all people, and all are viewed equally. In today's democracy, there are many different agents who interfere. This is where the difficulty starts. Since 1996 the Gram Sabha law has come, but in my opinion the government Gram Sabha is different from the village Gram Sabha. Even today, people accept

---

69   Reference to the Dukel Draft, a proposal for major changes in India's patent, science, and investment laws.

the decisions of the village Gram Sabha. In the government Gram Sabha, the Gram Sevak[70] will say this or that and create difficulties.

People are united when there is a religious festival or holiday—the organizing is fixed by custom: where and how to hold the *puja*,[71] how much collection will be made, and so on. On that day, the village law is also implemented and cases are adjudicated. This is the village Gram Sabha, the democracy of the people.

The only solution is that those areas that are in the Fifth Schedule[72] should be given Sixth Schedule[73] status. Complete authority should be given to people; only then can people begin to take democracy seriously. Funds should be given to the village, for distribution by the village. They will form a committee and decide who is needy, who should get what. Take the planning process in Kerala: that is what we are saying—planning should be from the bottom up. As long as the planning is from the top, people have no opportunity to reflect, to take part. If there is autonomy, then there can be planning in this manner.

In a place like Thane district, which is highly industrialized, with big factories, there is nothing for the development of Adivasis. They are afraid to declare it an autonomous Adivasi district, because then they would not be able to benefit from the process of industrialization. Today there are no Adivasis in these factories; the workers have all come from outside Thane district. At that time, there were no educated Adivasis, and now, when there are, there are no jobs.

In my opinion, if we went according to the 1996 legislation then a court should be created there where people would have decision-making power. As long as an autonomous Adivasi district council is not created, the Scheduled Areas cannot implement democracy. Until the autonomous district council is constituted, the village will not be able to exercise full power. We do not have such power in the current Thane Zilla parishad.[74] The question is, how big should the district be? Even a *taluka* can be a district, like in Dangs where non-Adivasis cannot enter without permission. This demand should have been made at the time of framing the Constitution—autonomous districts could have been formed in Surat and Dhule.

They did not do it; as a result, today we are dependent. The Zilla parishad is not autonomous. This dependence has to be broken; we should be able to

---

70   The Gram Sevak is appointed to work as secretary to the Gram Panchayat. He prepares the budget, maintains the records of the Gram Panchayat, and also advises the village in matters of health, farming, village development, and education.
71   Religious ritual.
72   Section of the Indian Constitution protecting Adivasi rights to land.
73   Section of the Indian Constitution granting autonomy to Adivasis in selected areas.
74   District Council that looks after the administration of the rural area of the district. Thane is the name of the village.

implement our own decisions. People can accept this, but the government is not ready to accept it. We can implement all the programs democratically. For example, people would be able to cultivate this land collectively. We would be able to revive the lost ethic of people helping each other out. From this, people's trust would grow. There would be no necessity for money. People would unite together and work.

Now, such a village cannot fit into the government structure. The government erodes people's trust. As a result the *panchayat* and democracy cannot survive. It has become something the government does.

MODERN AGRICULTURE AND BIODIVERSITY

If you look at the harvest, it has gone down. The people at the top say, "You should use this fertilizer, use that pesticide." One year the harvest may be good. But after two years, the land becomes infertile. Earlier, people would use cow dung and leaves. What crops I saw in those times! In the name of "modern agriculture," all the land has been destroyed. If we could develop organic fertilizers, we could increase our harvest. Even the seeds we get now from the government are good only for two years; after that they have to be thrown away. The old seeds used to last for many years. The effect is also on people's health—as long as there was nature and the jungle, people's health was good. Even if they did not eat much, what they did eat was nutritious. Now, there is no nutrition. People just manage to survive.

Day by day, agricultural land is being taken over by factories, by dams. The process of displacement is huge. If they cannot enter this village, they will go to the next village. This is increasing in Adivasi areas. The jungle also is taken over in this manner, until nothing is left. We used to survive eating the roots and fruits of the jungle. Even that is gone. Before, the big enterprise was the jungle. People used to get work in the jungle, so people did not have to go elsewhere for work. Now the jungle is finished. The big benefit of independence was that the jungle was finished.

URBANIZATION—DISPLACEMENT

As urbanization increases, the oppressed classes will increasingly get displaced. The process of urbanization is against them. We need to think about how people can have sustainable livelihoods in their villages so that they don't have to migrate to cities.

In a globalizing world, the wars of the future will be over natural resources, between countries. This is why they want to establish relationships with Third World countries. Their situation is such that they are forced to, because resources are limited. We are useful to the capitalists as long as we have resources they can exploit. This question of resources is crucial not only to the Adivasis, but to all marginalized people in the Third World.

ADIVASI SOCIETY AND ADIVASI IDENTITY

There were some good attributes of illiterate Adivasi society, which the educated, urbanized people have destroyed. For example, if a woman died in childbirth or if she was unable to produce milk after childbirth, it was the responsibility of the entire village. She would be provided with milk by the village. If a husband and wife had conflict and they were unable to live together, they could separate and could remarry. There was no question of going to court. Also, the village *panchayats* were mostly on the side of women. Rape did not exist in Adivasi society anywhere—even by mistake.

Earlier, when the jungle was there, outsiders used to fear tigers and would not come to our villages at night. Now, with the jungle gone, and with motorcars, they can come at any time.

Take our *dongar dev*[75]—there is a custom determining which vegetables should be taken at which season. As a result, the forest was preserved, because people observed the rules of allowing the plant to grow, even when it was plentifully available. Today these plants are sold; they are no longer for consumption or to meet the needs of the community. Money has become the basis of relationships. Unless people reflect on these traditional values, village social life cannot survive. It is the imposition of external values that has destroyed democracy.

Among urbanites, the perception of Adivasis is that we are like grubby insects, ignorant and illiterate. Adivasis never had any form of idol-worship, but now they have started bringing these idols into their homes. The RSS[76] and other groups like it are trying to misdirect Adivasis. They have started saying that Raja Pantha and Ganda Thakur[77] are the same. The "Hindu-ization" of Adivasi gods and goddesses is going on. They are equating them with Hindu mythological gods and characters. Then, they have introduced their customs of fasting for this and that. Adivasis would never fast beyond the fast imposed by nature. They have realized that unless they change the mind-set of the Adivasis, they will not be able to influence us, so that is the direction in which they are working. Only when the Adivasi culture is destroyed can your ideology be propagated among them.

Now I find that superstition is increasing. The rituals and customs of the upper castes around the Kohlapur area are increasingly being followed. In these past fifteen to twenty years, many temples have been built to Adivasi

---

75 A mountain god.
76 Rashtriya Swayamsevak Sangh is a is a Hindu volunteer organization.
77 Raja Pantha and Ganda Thakur are mythological warrior deities.

gods, which would not be the case earlier. On the Maohik side, there is a lot of *bua baji*.[78] These men gain the trust of the Adivasis and then become informers to the *saokars*.

The government has never tried to preserve Adivasi identity. For them, we are a people without history. They sent us to be hung as criminals in the Andaman and Nicobar islands. Even among the Naxalites,[79] it is the Adivasis who fill the Ranchi jail.[80] We are used in the movement, but with no benefit to us. This is a trend I perceive in all movements.

ADIVASI SOCIETY IN TRANSITION

The new generation of Adivasi youth has become very urbanized and Westernized. So now, even if an autonomous district was constituted, would this process of Westernization be reduced? The other thing is that the culture of consumption has permeated society. People don't think they have any responsibility to society beyond my house, my wife, my children. I may think that the new life that has come in the last fifty years is not right, that the new generation has become consumerist. My son is more consumerist than I am—he tells me, "You are middle class, and I am upper middle class." He is a human rights lawyer and does his work well, but he wants to live a particular lifestyle.

All this will continue to increase. In Adivasi society, too, a middle class is being created. Your son or daughter will like the life of Mumbai. They do not understand or accept the language and ideas of the Bhoomisena. How can we say they should not have these clothes, these lifestyle aspirations? Take education. The Hindu Rajas[81] of Satara, Dhule and Khapar—in the pre-British times—would never let the Adivasis have access to education. In Jowhar, Surbana, and Chandrapur, where there were Adivasi Rajas, and even under the Nizam,[82] where there were Muslim Rajas, there is a tradition of education among Adivasis. Nowhere in India has there been education for Adivasis under a Hindu Raja. In Bihar and Nagaland, because of the missionaries, there is a tradition of education. The Nizam had even made efforts to ensure that education should be in Gondi language and schools and the Gondi script, and books were promoted. After independence, these Gondi schools were shut down, and they were forced to learn Telegu.

---

78 Manipulation by godmen.
79 Group of far-left radical communists, supportive of Maoist political ideology.
80 A prison in the village of Ranchi.
81 Kings.
82 Title of the native sovereigns of Hyderabad State, India, since 1719. They were considered to be among the wealthiest people in the world and they were great patrons of literature, art, architecture, culture, jewelry collection and rich food.

If educated people learn the values of the oppressor society, then that is what they will become. Where autonomous councils have been created, why don't they change the syllabus? Why have these autonomous councils been formed? They have demanded it for the same reasons as the mainstream development framework. The syllabus is ready, but who will decide? The autonomous council can do it only if it *is* autonomous. In Maharashtra—and even in Gujarat—the textbooks are the same. Whether you are in Nagpur, Chandrapur, or here. But what is the lesson? In what way do they learn? It is a question of the method.

The demand is that education should be in English. The majority of urban Adivasis will want to have their children learn English—not even Marathi. In an urban area, that would be the result of the environment surrounding them. The critical question is not about the language so much as the *content* of education. Whether the *Ramayan* is in Dangi or Bhili—there is no difference. It is still the *Ramayan*[83] of Ram,[84] not of Ravan.[85] As long as the content does not change, the struggle over language is meaningless. Until the values change, nothing can change.

The loss of integrity, the readiness to say or do anything for personal gain, has come from the education process. In this area, it is difficult to find any person who has *not* been exploitative. The Adivasis would not understand the process. Thus, at the root, this is an ideological struggle—whether it is among Adivasis or among non-Adivasis. The difference is that among the former it is 90 percent, and among the latter 99 percent. To preserve and strengthen that 9 percent is the work of Adivasi Ekta Parishad. Otherwise they will also disappear.

ADIVASI EKTA PARISHAD (AEP)

In 1991/92, Vaharu[86] and I thought, "We keep struggling, but who supports us?" In none of the Leftist parties was there any attempt to create space for Adivasi leadership. Adivasis were never participants in the top-level decision-making process. When we examined the NGOs too, we found the same thing. As a result, our dependence increases. We cannot stand on our own feet. So we thought there was a need for discussion with all these groups—political parties, NGOs, and individual Adivasi activists and intellectuals.

If we decided to hold such a meeting, then some NGO would donate funds. But we did not want to do it with their funds. We wanted it to be

---

83 Epic Indian poem which narrates the journey of virtue to annihilate vice.
84 Hero of the Ramayan, Ram is the seventh incarnation of Vishnu.
85 There are some versions of the Ramayan that portray Ravan as the hero.
86 Eminent Adivasi writer and thinker of western India.

organized with individual contributions. Our Mumbai supporters agreed to collect these contributions. With this money, we were able to travel all over Maharashtra for one year. We started meeting all these people, and initiating discussions. This was how AEP was formed.

In Dhule, Bhima Shankar, and other places, we found that Adivasis did not have any Adivasi customs left. The Hindus prohibited Adivasi puja rites. The RSS had taken over, and insisted that the rites be performed by Brahmins; there was no place for Adivasis. In Ratnagiri, too, Adivasis had started worshipping Hindu gods. Adivasi animism was being replaced by Hindu idol-worship.

We decided to have a meeting in some central place. The Adivasis we met observed that they were also excluded from policy making and leadership. When we discussed the meeting with the CPM leaders in Mumbai, we told them that they should not attend this first meeting, because then Adivasis would not speak up.

These Left party people felt afraid, and were hesitant about sending their Adivasi workers. These parties had fought one or two struggles for Adivasis, but had no concept of the realities of Adivasi life or identity. We explained to them the need to articulate the Adivasi identity, the positive attributes of Adivasi culture. These are attributes that would benefit the human rights movement and society in general—attributes such as not begging, collective sharing, honoring oral commitments, respect for women. Women work in Adivasi society, so they are considered equal to men, and not their slaves. Women have the right to divorce. Even if widowed, a woman is never destitute or forced to beg. Rape does not exist in Adivasi society, nor dowry deaths or *devdasis*.[87] The concept of Lok Nyayalaya[88] is also from Adivasis, but people are ashamed to acknowledge this source.

In 1993, after the Nashik meeting of Adivasis, we called another meeting in Pune to which we invited everyone—parties, NGOs, and all. Although the non-Adivasis agreed that there was much to learn from Adivasis, only a few people attended. It was as if they had boycotted the meeting. Those that did come did not speak much or discuss our ideas. All these years that these different parties have worked among Adivasis, none of them have really learned what Adivasi culture or customs are about. They have never acknowledged that the values of Adivasi culture could be useful for them. That is why we needed to found the AEP.

We decided to continue our process, and had the next meeting of Adivasis in Dhule. This was attended by some doctors and lawyers, as well as the activists. There was general agreement that Adivasis are treated as second-class citizens; there is no space for our leadership, therefore there is a need

---

87   Prostitutes.
88   People's courts.

for us to unite. We held the first AEP Convention in Shahada in 1994. The second was in MP, the third in Rajasthan, the fourth in Aundhiya, Gujarat, the fifth in Maharashtra, the sixth again in MP, the seventh in Rajasthan, and the most recent in Gujarat.

The strength of the AEP is increasing—people can understand the ideological and political perspectives. We now want to organize the next convention in Maharashtra—somewhere in the center, like in Nagpur. The state that takes responsibility for the convention has to gather the funds for it.

In sum, the attitude to the AEP has been: How dare they set this up without our permission? Our challenge to the NGOs who are working in Adivasi areas is that they should stop being so territorial. We are working as a movement, so no one gets a salary. So it is difficult to increase our activities and impact. Change cannot happen unless poor people have the opportunity to travel and learn from struggles in different regions. When we organize a program, people travel on *jhindabad* ticket.[89] We have been stopped many times, but we say, "The railway is ours—we have broken the stones to build it. Who are you to ask for tickets?" There are some among us who have traveled to Delhi with 15 rupees in our pockets. Only then can they get an idea of how big our country is and how big our struggle needs to be. We cannot limit our struggle to Thane district.

In Bihar too now they are thinking of setting up a platform like Adivasi Ekta Parishad. People don't think they will get justice from the political parties, because the exploiters, local and international, also belong to these parties.

Between 1992 and 1996, we met Adivasis in all the political parties—the CPM, Congress, the BJP—as well as social activists. They all agreed that wherever there were Adivasis, and no matter how well they worked, they were never part of the decision-making process. In our first meeting, the three of us—Vaharu, Devaji Tofa, and I—told the CPM people that they should not be in the meeting, because then Adivasis would not speak freely. They agreed that we should have a separate meeting, and be free to speak openly. But some people felt we were destroying the movement, and said, "Vaharu and Kaka's legs should be broken." We went ahead and had our meeting in Nashik. The first few years were difficult, but recently we have been getting a very good response—not only from urban areas, but mainly from the rural areas. There is a feeling that we should stand up and create a place for ourselves in society. This time, when we went to Gujarat, the police and the political leaders could also see how we practice democratic principles. We have hope that people will see, and change. The members

---

89   Ticketless travel.

of the AEP board have no special names. This is the banner under which we work, whether it is in Delhi or anywhere in the world. I have learned more working in this movement than I have working for any political party.

We have to think about renewing the traditional council, and for that we will need to think about what its character should be and what the role of Adivasi Ekta Parishad in this can be. In the current context, different societies are coming together. People are reconstituting social rules and customs. The bad is being discarded. For example, the custom of bride-price is being reduced. Although it was not that the father took the money—it was made into ornaments for the woman. A ceiling of 8,000 rupees has been put on even this practice.

The second thing is that committees are being formed in the villages. It is difficult to bring together all the people in a village to a Gram Sabha, but at least a few thinking, concerned individuals in the village can come together. These are Adivasi committees. It is difficult in places where the population is mixed and there are the merchant classes. The local Adivasi "leaders" are often the puppets of the local industrialists or landlords. This is what happened in Umbergaon—there were too many internal conflicting interests, and so the struggle was broken. We are trying to rebuild it from the bottom.

The other challenge is that of biodiversity. First, our traditional knowledge of the jungle, plants, medicines, and so on is threatened by foreign patents—like with *haldi*.[90] Second, there is the issue of seeds: today the seeds that are available can be used only for one year, so we have to buy seeds every year—we cannot store and use. This challenge is bigger than that of the forest.

In Kashele, Adivasis have started an endeavor where they collect the old varieties of seeds. People had switched to hybrid seeds because, in the first years, the crop was good. The old seeds got destroyed. So now, at Kashele, they collect the seeds, the herbs and plants, and disseminate them to people. Some *vaidyas*[91] also come every week to learn from each other. There is a lot of research into herbal medicines there. They are now the protectors of seeds that are not available anywhere else.

Today, the soil has been destroyed by inorganic fertilizers. It is a big issue for farmers everywhere. There is no jungle, no vegetation to create organic compost. Only if there is reforestation taken up in villages can this compost be created. We can improve the soil quality with compost; but people's mentality has to change. They are too dependent on chemical fertilizers, even though they recognize the damage done to soil. We have to propagate this in the Gram Sabhas. We have to also retrieve the indigenous knowledge

---

90   Turmeric.
91   Practitioners of traditional Indian medicine.

from the older generation about which leaves are especially good to create compost, and so on.

We have to also recover our old seeds. Today, we sell our grain for 100 rupees, and then are forced to buy seeds for sowing at 500 rupees. In the interior area of Dangs, there are a few varieties of rice that are used especially during drought years. Our old seeds would last for twenty to thirty years. People would not perish during droughts, as we had varieties that could give us crops with less water. AEP is also working on retrieving this knowledge, these preservation techniques. Ultimately, people's awareness is the biggest protection. This is why AEP is forming village committees. We have reached 1,500 villages in four states. Our target is 10,000 villages in three years. We are trying to get the village committees recognized as the traditional *panchayats*, since, in many places, these *panchayats* have been weakened. They will take forward the concerns of customary laws. Where there are local organizations working—like Tarun Mandals or Mahila Mandals[92]—we have not duplicated AEP structures. In the beginning we were also not sure if these small groups would join AEP. Gradually, they also realized a need to go beyond the limitations of a small group. AEP helps them formulate their vision.

Recently, on August 9th, 2000, we organized a mass demonstration in fifty blocks of twenty-five districts in protest against the proposed Land Acquisition Bill. Thousands of people turned out. After this we felt confident that we have the strength to mobilize, to stop them. People can feel our strength, and the feeling of helplessness is decreasing.

To mitigate the influence of market forces we have to create institutions for consumers in Adivasi areas. Our goods will be exchanged "house-to-house." We will directly exchange rice for *jowar*, *tuar*, and so on. The use of money and cash trading will be reduced. We will link this system to the women's self-help groups. This is the system we want to create. The Mahila Mandals would reflect on their problems, and what kind of laws they would want implemented.

If you look at the Dhan Kosh,[93] they are in a position of surplus now, where they can exchange. Until now it was subsistence level—meeting the needs of the village. We did not have cash purchasing power until now. Now some of our groups buy *jowar* from another group, and distribute it in the village. So we have started on a small scale—we intend to do it on a large scale, but that will require larger funds. There is no scheme that promotes such natural cooperation between groups.

---

92   The Mahila Mandals are voluntary organizations of rural women working for the promotion of Nutrition education, family welfare, food storage, immunization of children, small saving accounts of women, provision of bathrooms, etc.
93   Grain banks.

We wouldn't say no to bank loans. Our ultimate goal is to use our own resources. The experience of the marketing federations—of sugar or agricultural products—is that it is not in the hands of the producers, like the forest cooperatives are. People cut the trees and sold the forest to contractors. The farmers sell sugarcane to the factories, and have to buy sugar. The 1 billion rupee annual turnover of the sugar factory does not benefit the farmer. In Calcutta, rice from Malaysia is now cheaper than local rice. The buyer will always go for the lower price. Therefore we will also have to make alliances with the farmer's organizations to counter the globalization process. Last week we had a meeting with the farmer's cooperatives—they are also open now—in the struggle against the multinationals. It has become difficult to survive alone.

Among the new generation, there is a capacity to reflect, to support. Another signal of hope is that, though Adivasi languages are different, the customs are the same everywhere you go. After eight years of AEP, I do have hope in the new generation. In the beginning, there were not many youth in the movement. Earlier, educated Adivasis would not listen to someone like me. Now they do.

Fifty years ago, Adivasis did not go to the cities, they stayed within the community and at the most had contact with the police, the *saokars*. Now there are changes—they go to cities for education, for jobs. They come into contact with other communities who look down on them, disrespect them. As a result, the question of identity has become very important to them. That is the reason why they feel drawn to the AEP.

GLOBALIZATION AND ADIVASI SOCIETY

Due to globalization, the situation has become extremely desperate for Adivasis. Decisions are taken internationally and forced on us. In the name of "development," Adivasis are displaced. The constitutional rights of Adivasis are on paper only. The political leaders totally ignored these rights when they pursued different projects that have displaced us. Internationally there is recognition that the environment is endangered, but here the contractors continue to destroy the jungle. This destruction is called our "development," and we are supposed to accept it. There is some awareness today, but it is in pockets, and there is no link between the different struggles.

Adivasi society is scared; even the urban-educated are concerned that privatization will negatively affect them as well. The next generation will have to live like insects. We will be destroyed in this process, but even those just above us, the OBCs,[94] will also be destroyed. The OBCs and Dalits

---

94   Other Backward Class.

have understood that, with globalization, 80 percent of the resources will flow out of the country, and we will all drown in the process. For a movement to happen, we have to realize that we can combine against the *saokars'* exploitation, but we cannot fight exploitation among ourselves. Our leaders are taking international loans, and we have to repay them, including the interest debt.

The picture is so grim; an Adivasi is displaced not once, but several times. The situation has gone out of our hands; Adivasis alone will not be able to fight. All the oppressed classes, the 80 percent of society, have to unite so that all can live in human dignity. Today the situation of dependence in the country is so pathetic—we have mortgaged the Vidhan Bhavan[95] and the Lok Sabha.[96] At the time of independence, the country had assets worth 50 million rupees, because even if the British exploited, they built the railways. Today you do not have a paisa—instead you are a debtor! In India, 75 percent of people depend on agriculture for survival. This livelihood is destroyed today.

The struggle against the American multinational, Enron, took place four or five years ago. Their people came here, but we organized Gram Sabhas and did not let them enter. They were proposing a private highway from Dahisar to Talasari. This highway would have walls, and would be only for vehicles traveling at speeds of 120 km/h. Gates are supposed to be at 7km intervals, so if the highway went through your land, you would have to walk that distance with your plough to get to the other side!

Vasai passed the highway because they have no jungle, so it is to their benefit. But it has got stuck at Palghar and Dahanu. This is all Adivasi land, so when the collector sent notices, we sent back the Gram Sabha resolution against the proposal. The Gram Sabha is posing a problem for them. This is all Fifth Schedule land. After that the mamlatdar and other officers came to try and make us understand, but we refused. The highway was going to pass through my village, just behind that mountain.

But before dealing with the highway, we would have to attack the Enron project in Umbergaon, too. They set up the project by misleading people, saying that we will get jobs and benefits. All the gas will go to Malaysia and other countries. We had opposed the project when it was first proposed here in Dahanu in Wadwan. We chased them off, so they went to Umbergaon, in Gujarat.

The Gram Sabha will have to develop greater strength to resist these challenges. People will have to join in the Satyagraha. We have to organize meetings in the villages and resist. We have to explain the serious significance of the issue to the whole village or area, and the possible impact of

---

95 Provincial assembly building.
96 Parliament building.

the proposal. We have to form a committee for the whole region, so that, no matter from which side they approached whichever village, we would be prepared. All the parties—the Congress and the Left—should also be included in the committee.

MODERN NGOS

After the AEP was formed, the support of the non-Adivasi activists was reduced. We had expected that we would be able to identify issues for joint action—that had been the discussion in Pune. Now a lot of these people take funding from outside to do their work, so there are limitations on what we can do together. They are all earning an income in different ways. They want the Bhoomisena, but have a problem with the Adivasi Ekta Parishad. The relationship got broken then. We had a difference with their process.

The problem with all these mass organizations is that Adivasi leadership is not being created. And then they also changed their focus from mass organizations to small groups—voluntary agencies or NGOs. The resulting limitation was that leadership from the masses could not emerge in these structures, even if they wanted it. These organizations also became more of the corporate type, which the Adivasi people cannot understand. Adivasi workers in these organizations do a lot of work, but cannot write the reports.

Even among the political parties, there was no attempt to create Adivasi leadership—they would say it, but it never happened, again because of the structure. If you have to allow others' leadership, you have to go into the background.

The three foundation stones of any organization are its ideological base, its economic arrangements, and its programs. The economic base has to be independent—if you take outside funding, then you have to give false reports of your work. For our kind of work, no one gives funding. The NGOs running on foreign funding cannot be independent. Initially they took money, saying they would ultimately get independent. Twenty years down the line they are still dependent; but, more importantly, a global connection has occurred that influences their agendas.

We were against foreign funding from the beginning, since it would mean giving false reports, and toeing the funders' line. We decided at first that we would take the contributions from friends in Mumbai, for a fixed period. We realized though that our membership would not increase like this, and that the distance between people and the leadership would increase. We could not claim to have formed a *sanghatana*.[97] Now our effort for the past

---

97 Organization.

eight years has been to take membership fees and strengthen the AEP and Bhoomisena.

THE IMPORTANCE OF MOVEMENTS

In 1981/82, when Indira Gandhi was back in power, the labor movement here was very strong. Her plan was to bring the Forest Bill in secret, to make the forest out of bounds to all. Entering the forest for water, let alone fuel and fodder, would be a criminal offence. No one knew anything about this bill. They were getting ready to pass the bill. Many senior activists got a copy of the bill from some positive government officials. The copy was circulated among all of us. A national seminar was organized in Dehradun, to discuss what kinds of bill we wanted, one that was beneficial to Adivasis. We went to visit the Chipko movement. At another meeting in Delhi, some forest officials were invited, and they made speeches saying that Adivasis and forest officials have a good relationship—which we countered.

Many reports and papers were given to the government, and there were discussions on the international level also. Finally, social forestry and forest protection started. But the problem was that they started plantation-style forestry of trees that had no uses in herbal medicine, or as food, fodder, or fuel. Adivasi participation was limited to digging the ditches. There was no attention paid to increasing the forest cover and species. There was World Bank funding, so it was undertaken. Where there was no movement, it was difficult to verify whether the forestation work was actually done.

Now the population in the villages has dropped since people had to migrate for work. Before, the forest would be their source of livelihood. Even if a drought is declared, there is no work—unless there is a movement.

LOOKING BACK, LOOKING FORWARD

During the Emergency I was in bad shape. But, seeing that people were living in such desperate situations, I felt forced to take up the role of struggle. There are people who are much poorer than I am, living like insects, and they continue to survive. Without a movement, none of us will be able to move from mere survival to living.

To get out of the cycle of poverty, we had to break dependence. From 1978 we started to collect rice as contributions. Now our economic strength has increased. We get contributions from city people, from youth members who have salaried jobs. Earlier we would not collect from them—we had written them off as lost causes. But now we feel that we should involve them too. They give contributions, so we don't have to beg before anyone, and our needs can be fulfilled within our *samaj*.[98] Also, in this process, the urban Adivasi's consciousness gets created.

Fifty years ago, I did not think that we would be where we are today. Earlier I thought that people's awareness would bring strength. Now it seems more difficult. Even in Adivasi society, some are associated with the oppressor class. But there are also some people of integrity in some places, who maintain the values and traditions of old. Only if these customs survive can Adivasi society survive. The role of AEP is to spread awareness about this.

If we are not able to urgently take action now, there will be nothing left after fifty years. The entire country will be completely mortgaged. Just as we are reflecting as a village, as a nation, the non-Adivasi society will have to also start this process of reflection. Or else we will not have a village or a nation left.

Unless the non-Adivasis also join the struggle, there is no way out—whether one owns land or factories. Today, even the Tata-Birla[99] factories are being forced to shut down. In some years, the factories of the world will come here and the few Adivasi Scheduled Areas that remain will get finished. The situation of the non-Adivasis will become like [that of] the Adivasis. Shouldn't city folks also think about the environment? If they don't, it means that they do not see the need for self-examination. It is a lacuna in your leadership that you do not see.

Therefore, at the state and national levels, we should have exchanges of information and ideas so that we can strengthen our struggles. Adivasi Ekta Parishad has been able to create awareness among the Adivasis quickly because, for Adivasis, the question of identity is closely linked to the struggle for survival. The identity of other societies, especially among the upper classes, has eroded. Among them, the feeling of superiority has increased. So they have not joined the struggle.

We are displaced within this country as a result of privatization. In America, the Adivasis have been destroyed. In India too, we are in that situation. No part of the country is going to be spared from globalization, so we need to all unite for strength to stop this process. But this will take time—only when non-Adivasis reach our desperate situation will they start to consider uniting. The people of cities are immersed in a consumerist culture—dependent on money, on jobs. They are far from the concept of sharing with each other.

Once people join a movement, and are confronted with different situations and opportunities, then they learn. The situations may be good or bad—but one can learn from both, and use it in the next Emergency.

---

98 Community.
99 Large Indian corporations.

When we were at the Bhoomisena Center in Damkhind, ten Adivasi youth from the neighboring country, Nepal, had come to learn from Kaluram. He was telling them about the struggle around land and the forest. It became obvious that Kaluram's influence had already crossed the country's frontiers.

On the second day of our visit, some Dalit youth were organizing a struggle against the American multinational, Enron, and had come to invite Kaluram for the meeting. He went through the document about the meeting very closely, suggested some alterations, and assured them of his attendance as the chief guest. His life of struggle is not over, and the injustice of globalization has been added to the many causes that he continues to fight for.

He offered us impeccably gracious hospitality. Thinking that we would not like the simple Adivasi food cooked by the Nepali youngster, he himself went and bought biscuits and milk from the nearby town. We later realized that he had no money, and that these items had been bought for us on credit.

Kaluram came to see us off at the railway station 50 kilometers away. He told us that, the next time we came, all we had to do was to show a raised fist as a sign to any of the Adivasi women selling vegetables and fruit outside the station, and they would escort us to him.

8

Siddharaj Dhadda

Prominent Gandhian, writer, grassroots organizer.

Interviewed by Achyut Yagnik

"I strongly feel that people have been cheated. Western culture and the adoption of the English language are ruining the country. Western culture is a self-centered culture and is unhealthy for a society. An extreme aberration is the Valentine's Day celebration in our country . . .

The only way out of this terrible crisis is for the society to free itself as far as possible from the clutches of money and market, the bureaucracy and the government. This is possible through the building up of a self-reliant, cooperative, and decentralized social order with a rural orientation . . ."

Siddharaj Dhadda[1]

Siddharaj Dhadda, now in his nineties, is an eminent Gandhian of India, respected in his peer group as the "salt of the earth." A firm believer in the unity of thought and action, words and deeds, he represents the Gandhian tradition, evolved and expounded after India's independence by Vinoba Bhave[2] and Jaiprakash Narayan.[3]

Siddharaj was attracted to Gandhi from his school days. He joined the freedom struggle when Gandhi issued a call to "Do or Die" in the Quit India movement of 1942, leaving behind a lucrative job as the secretary of the Indian Chamber of Commerce and Industry at Calcutta. Between 1943 and 1945, he was imprisoned by the British rulers. Later, between 1975 and 1977, he was imprisoned by the government of free India during the Emergency, when fundamental rights were suspended by the prime minister, Mrs. Gandhi, and Siddharaj was in the forefront of the pro-democracy movement.

Currently, he is chairman of Kumarappa Institute of Gram Swaraj, and a trustee of the Gandhi Memorial Fund. Leading a simple life in his ancestral house in Jaipur, he edits a weekly periodical, Gram Raj, *and a monthly,* Satyagraha Mimansa. *Both are in Hindi, and focus mainly on Gandhian praxis. Through these journals, as well as his lectures throughout the length and breadth of India, he underlines the Gandhian alternative based on people's power and village self-reliance. He strongly feels that, within the next ten to fifteen years, the forces of globalization will*

---

1   In order to maintain the flow of the text, the interviewer has eliminated the questions and transformed the interview into a first-person narrative.

2   Vinoba Bhave was an associate of Gandhi, and during his lifetime Gandhi declared him his "spiritual heir." After independence, Vinoba started the "Bhoodan movement" to resolve land problems in India. He walked the length and breadth of India, trying to persuade landowners to donate their land (*bhoodan*) to the landless. The movement was later expanded to include the donation of land by entire villages (*gramdan*). Bhoodan and Gramdan formed the foundation for his Sarvodaya ("development of all") Movement.

3   Jaiprakash Narayan (or JP, as he was known) was a great Indian freedom fighter and a pioneer of the Socialist Party. In the early 1950s he renounced active politics and joined Vinoba's Sarvodaya movement. In the early 1970s JP gave the call for Sampoorna Kranti ("Total Revolution"). In the mid-1970s, when Prime Minister Indira Gandhi declared a state of emergency, JP and his associates were arrested, including Siddharaj Dhadda. During this time, JP spearheaded a nationwide pro-democracy movement.

crumble under their own weight, and that the next century will be one of alternative social orders. Of course, he cautions against any kind of complacency, and points out that the onslaught of globalization is very powerful. Even today, he participates in people's movements—whether it is the Narmada movement against big dams, or the grassroots water-harvesting movement in Rajasthan.

EARLY LIFE

I was born on February 12th in Jaipur, and was adopted at birth by my grand-uncle Gulabchand, who did not have any sons. Gulabchand and Mahatma Gandhi were the two people who influenced me in my life. Gulabchand was a postgraduate who did his MA in 1889, the second person to get a degree in Rajasthan, and the first in his Oswal Jain community. Father was the president of the Shwetambar Jain Conference. Thus, the Gujarati influence has been substantial, as the majority of Shwetamber Jains are in the neighboring state, Gujarat. I am not a practicing Jain, but the influence is very much there.

My father worked as a civil servant and was involved extensively in social and community service. I accompanied him to all such gatherings and meetings, and observed him conduct the meetings and take decisions, and so on, which had a lasting influence on me. Besides learning, he was also inspired to do social service and community work. I recall two inci-dents when he taught me valuable lessons in life. Once I did not polish my shoes; my father noticed it as he was going out. He did not scold me or tell me to go and polish them, but simply said, "If you will maintain the honor of others, they will maintain yours." Another value that my father inculcated in me was "waste not, want not." My father taught me my values in life. Though I am a non-practicing Jain, this religion had an influence on me.

From 1920 onwards I was influenced by Gandhiji. I was in high school, in VII or VIII standard. Then, in my college days, I wanted to join the freedom struggle but was unable to do so due to loans that the family had to repay. My father and I regularly exchanged correspondence and, through letters, discussed this and other issues. In 1942 I finally resigned from the Chamber of Commerce to join Gandhi's Quit India struggle. When I gave my resignation, the industrialist K. K. Birla had joined. He told me not to worry about earning a living, but to join the struggle. He said he would take care of that aspect. To this day, the Birlas have kept their promise. I have never had to work for a salary. I did not even claim my freedom fighter's pension. Recently, I had to ask for it because I required a travel pass, since I could not afford to pay the train tickets. George Fernandes was then the railway minister, and he advised me to get a permanent pass to save myself the trouble of having to renew the pass every year. But permanent passes were given only to those getting pensions!

Two people have influenced me most in my life—my father and Mahatma Gandhi. Though I had heard Gandhiji many times at meeting and gatherings, I met him twice, face to face. The first instance was in 1941, when I asked my friend Mahadevbhai to fix an appointment for me. All through my journey to Gandhiji's center at Wardha, I kept thinking about the possible questions I would ask Gandhiji. When I met Bapu,[4] I forgot everything and was struck dumb. Bapu asked me several times why I had come, but I could not answer. Finally I said that I had come for his *darshan*, and went back.

In 1947 I started Rajasthan's first daily paper, *Lokvani*.[5] I wrote about Hindu-Muslim unity and took the cuttings to show Gandhiji, who was staying in Delhi at the Bhangi colony. I had fixed an appointment. I showed Gandhiji my cuttings. He smiled and wrote something on a sheet of paper. It was then that I realized that, being Monday, it was Gandhiji's day of silence.

Thus, I met Gandhiji twice. Once I was *maun*,[6] and the second time Gandhiji was *maun*!

IN THE FREEDOM MOVEMENT

During the Quit India Movement, I was arrested in January 1943 at Banaras and imprisoned in Banaras Central Jail. After my release in 1945, I went to Jaipur and became active in Jaipur State Prajamandal.[7] At the national level there was an organization called All India Princely States Conference, in which I was working as the secretary of the Rajasthan branch. These organizations were very active in the freedom struggle in the territories under the princely states—other than British territory. Later, this Rajasthan branch was transformed into the State Congress Committee, and I was its general secretary.

A MINISTER IN RAJASTHAN

After independence, the process of integration of the princely states with the Indian Union started, and when a ministry was formed in the newly created state of Rajasthan, I was asked to join the ministry as industry and commerce minister. For two and a half years I was in that post. As a minister

---

4   The Indian people also called Gandhi "Bapu"—the father.
5   Voice of the people.
6   Silent.
7   People's organization.

I took two or three important decisions to protect rural cottage industries and the rural market. It was the beginning of the manufacture of Vanaspati *ghee*,[8] and I banned it in Rajasthan, since it was destroying the local *ghee*[9] market. I also decided that, in an area with less than 2,000 residents, no factory run on electricity should be allowed. The central government at Delhi was not happy about this decision. I resigned from the government, and also the Congress Party.

At that time, Mr. Balwantrai Mehta, who later on became chief minister of Gujarat state, was secretary of the All India Congress Committee. He asked me if I was going to join another political party. I replied that I had realized that change would not take place through the state and through the Congress Party, or any other political party. But change would come through the people themselves, and I wanted to work with the people.

IN THE BHOODAN MOVEMENT

Vinoba Bhave had started a movement in 1951, and I joined him. Vinoba had advocated that, in order to be truly free, one had to be free of the lure of gold.[10] Later, he initiated the Bhoodan and Gramdan Movement, and started his historical *padayatra*[11] throughout India.

Bhoodan failed because everyone was against it. Our power or energy was also inadequate. The original concept was lost after Vinoba died. But the revolution was not a failure. An idea does not fail the society; it is the people who fail. For example, independence was not a failure, people failed. Ideas or concepts do not fail; people who run on those ideas fail.

PERSONAL LIFE AND VALUES

I have two children, a son and a daughter. I sent my son to the *buniyaadishala*,[12] and later to Wardha. It is unfortunate that children from such schools find it difficult to get jobs. Even my son sometimes complained that he was not given a proper education. My grandchildren studied in an English-speaking school. My grandson is in the jewelry business.

I strongly feel that people have been cheated. Western culture and the adoption of English language are ruining the country. Western culture is a self-centered culture, and is unhealthy for a society. An extreme aberration is the Valentine's Day celebration in our country. We have the festival of

---

8   Vegetable oil.
9   Clarified butter.
10 Money.
11 Journey on foot.
12 Gandhian school.

Holi, where you have fun as well as express your affection. This "I love you" culture is devoid of modesty.

Earlier, parents chose marriage partners for their children; they saw the family and the girl. The family background and the values of the family were the guiding factors. I had an arranged marriage, though she had visited my home before marriage and I did speak to her. I had just turned seventeen when we married, and she was my constant companion and supporter. She died just last year. We had a happy family life together. Now boys just choose by themselves after seeing the girl, and hence the increase in the number of separations. This selfishness breaks society too. The way to counter this is through self-reliance and a de-emphasis on economic prosperity through money.

The Jaipur of my childhood had its own character. It was the first planned city of India. Inside the walled city was the township, which was planned according to the various vocations. Of course, there have been changes in Jaipur too; but compared to Delhi and Bombay, it is better. None of the cities have been able to retain their character. Cities are aberrations. They did not develop naturally. After independence, most of the villages have been uprooted and people have left their villages to come to cities, and slums have formed.

THE PRESENT CRISIS

A handful of people in the world, organized in giant multinational corporations and financial institutions, have acquired control over all natural resources and means of production—in the name of growth, increasing production, and promoting development and welfare. People have been reduced to virtual slavery by the excessive centralization of economic and political power. Corruption, nepotism, irresponsibility, and cheating at work have become socially accepted because of their inevitability in a centralized system. Self-reliance and autonomy of the people and their capacity to resist injustice have been systematically destroyed. People have been enticed into the vices of drink, drugs, gambling, and promiscuity and hooked on to spectator sports, and thus made spineless so that they may not be able to raise their head. In the pursuit of lust and ever greater profits, advertisements in the electronic media and the newspapers and other media are being used to tempt the people to consume more and more, knowing fully well that the craving for material goods can never be satisfied, since there is no end to greed and the resources on our earth are limited.

Production of and trade in armaments has become a means of making money on a large scale, and nations are competing to produce newer and more destructive weapons. The unceasing exploitation of natural resources, their misuse, and the pollution caused by it, to satisfy the profit motive and the lust for an affluent lifestyle of a few is sure to leave a legacy of destitution and misery for the masses, and also for the coming generations. Governments, which are supposed to safeguard the rights of the people and work for their welfare, have become handmaidens of these processes. The survival of life and humankind on the earth has been endangered by acute pollution and the threat of war.

The self-centered and consumerist culture that has its origin in the West is rapidly eroding the individual's awareness of his or her obligations to the larger society. This is happening everywhere in the world. The very basis of social existence is community life, mutual cooperation, and tolerance. But the growing egotism is destroying these foundations of social existence.

At the moment this process of social disintegration is nearing its climax. On the one hand, the inner strength of society to sustain itself has been almost destroyed, while on the other, the impersonal power of the state and its laws is growing day by day, and society is unable to face the aggression of this inimical force. In spite of the paeans of praise for democracy that are being sung day in and day out, the people have lost all control or influence on the government. Consequently the government has lost its original purpose of promoting the welfare of the people, and has become a tool in the hands of authoritarian or dictatorial forces. The institutions and forces that were created for the protection of the social order have begun to feed on it. Barriers have been erected in every direction in which society may attempt to move ahead. The man in the street has been reduced to impotency, and is being forced to live a life scarred by humiliations. It is obvious that such a system cannot last for long.

The only way out of this terrible crisis is for the society to free itself as far as possible from the clutches of money and the market, the bureaucracy and the government. This is possible through the building up of a self-reliant, cooperative, and decentralized social order with a rural orientation. The present situation poses a challenge to all revolutionaries who are distressed at the sufferings and tribulations of humankind. The people have also become fed up. They are on the lookout for an alternative. What is required is to go to the people and awaken their faith in themselves.

THE ALTERNATIVE

I think social life should be organized so that the interests of individual and society are not antagonistic, but are mutually supporting. Also, social life and nature are interrelated and interdependent. Human beings are not entities set apart from nature; they are inseparable parts of it. The attitude that looks upon nature as subordinate to human beings, and on human beings as her masters who may treat her in any way they like to enjoy her gifts, is erroneous. Nature works according to regular laws. There is no place in it for willful behavior. Nature punishes us when we transgress her laws, and problems are created for human society as a whole. Creating is meant to be a source of joy for all creatures living in it, not a source of sorrow and suffering. Nature provides enough for the sustenance and growth of all living beings, provided people understand the laws of nature and follow them.

A meaningful and satisfying life based on these principles can be achieved only if we are guided by the conviction that cooperation is the law of life, not competition or struggle for survival. Self-control should replace self-indulgence, leading to a simple and uncomplicated style of living. Productive physical labor is the foundation on which our lives are built, and self-reliance has to be the goal: decentralization instead of centralization, and social responsibility.

Both individuals and the society as a whole can be happy and contented if the above principles and guidelines are followed in our social life. What form should such a society take, and how can it be brought into being and run?

PEOPLE'S POWER

One common characteristic of both the socialist and the capitalist democratic systems is that both repose faith in the centralization of economic and political power. The centralized state had evolved as a powerful instrument in feudal times, and those who brought about revolutions to establish political and economic equality through parliamentary democracy and socialism retained the centralized state in the belief that it would serve their purpose. The state has come to be looked upon as the only agency for managing and reforming society. As a natural corollary of this, the relatively small number of people in charge of government—either the elected representatives or the bureaucrats—have gone on acquiring more and more power by ever greater centralization. Fantastic progress in the technologies of transportation, communication, and in the means of subjugating the people has facilitated this centralization. As a result, the people have little say in the management of their or their country's affairs, except for the nominal right of casting votes in democracies. They have been doomed to suffer the trials, the tribulations and hardships heaped upon them by the centralization of power. In a just social order, the people should not be thus reduced to the role of mute spectators. In every sphere of life—whether political, economic, social, or any other—control over power and systems will have to be acquired by the people and exercised by them directly. Self-reliant and self-regulating village communities would be the natural base of such a social order.

Today, man has become a slave of the administrative structure. The latter becomes the dominant factor in a centralized system. The administrative machinery, or the state, is not the same thing as society, as we are prone to think. There is a great difference between a society and the state, or its administrative machinery. The latter is a wooden and insensitive structure, while a society is a living organism of sensitive and live individuals, interacting and leading their lives in cooperation with each other.

PANCHAYATI RAJ AND GRAM SABHA

Whatever is being passed off as Panchayati Raj[13] is merely meant to hoodwink the people. This is just a burglar throwing some scraps to the victim after having robbed him of everything. The sovereign authority of the village assembly or the Gram Sabha finds no place or recognition in the officially established Panchayati Raj system. The Gram Panchayats are meant to be merely agents or tools of the central and state governments.

It is necessary to properly grasp the import of the concept of "people's own government in each village," or Gram Swarajya. It means that the Gram Sabha[14] of each village, composed of all adult men and women, will be the symbol and the vehicle of the sovereign power of the people, and the highest authority in the village. The Gram Sabha will have the right to take decisions about all affairs of the village. Decisions pertaining to the smooth running of the affairs of the village, its development plans, and so on, will be made by the Gram Sabha. The Sabha will settle disputes that may arise in the village. At present, the weaker sections of a village have no security; but it needs to be realized that no outside agency can provide them with permanent protection. Ultimately, only the Gram Sabha can do so. This was ensured in our indigenous Panchayat system through the practice of decisions by consensus rather than by majority. This is necessary to promote the feelings of solidarity and cooperation in the villages. The Gram Sabha should aspire to strive for the welfare of each and every member of the village without fear or favor, like the mother of a family. Only this can ensure the welfare and security of all villagers.

---

13 The traditional Panchayats—community councils and village councils—are very ancient features of the Indian subcontinent. For more than 2,000 years, these councils have been resolving intra- and inter-communal conflicts. During the colonial (British) period, traditional Panchayats lost their importance as they were replaced by British legal and administrative institutions. Mahatma Gandhi strongly advocated village councils with greater autonomy. After independence, and particularly after the constitutional amendment of 1960, Panchayats were gradually developed and accorded more power. A three-tier system with village-, block-, and district-level elected representatives and development activities such as education, health, road building, and so on, at the local level are managed by the Panchayat system.

14 General village body.

VILLAGE ECONOMY AND AGRICULTURE

Some points are of great importance in regard to the economy of the villages. The first concerns agriculture. The first priority of agricultural operation in the village should be the fulfillment of the needs of the local community. The plan for the farming sector should be drawn up keeping in view the general principle that the food grains, vegetables, oil-seeds, and cotton for the cloth required by the community should be produced in the village. In regions that do not suffer from any deficiency in locally available resources, effort should be made to make the village communities self-reliant in the matter of food, clothing, housing, primary education, and health. Wherever the resource position is not favorable, the needs should be met through exchange, or cooperation with neighboring villages or regions.

Today agricultural plans are not drawn up with the needs of the local community in view. Every farmer grows crops in his own interest, and the tendency for most of them is to grow such marketable crops as would be most profitable in monetary terms. Policies adopted under international pressure by the government are also encouraging market crops. This seems to serve the narrow self-interest of the individual farmer, but in fact it is a bad deal for him. The farmer does not get a proper price for his produce because he has no control over the market. The market for money crops has become global, and the control of the same has now become centralized in the hands of powerful international agencies. These agencies always seek to buy agricultural products and other raw materials cheap and sell the products manufactured out of them at the highest possible price. The farmer is forced to sell his produce at unremunerative prices and buy his daily necessities like clothing, foodstuffs, and so on at exorbitantly high prices. Thus the farmers are being subjected to a double plunder. The farmer is not conscious of this, and feels that he is getting a fair deal because he is able to get loans for raising crops, occasional subsidies, waivers of loans, an so on. He is kept in the dark about the real situation and is misled in various ways, and his greed makes him walk into the trap. If the farmers are to be saved from this exploitation and plunder, the village plan for the agricultural sector will have to give the first priority to making the villages self-reliant in the matter of their primary needs. Other things will have to come later. Formerly there used to be land set apart for grazing in every village, but politics has enabled and encouraged powerful families to usurp these lands. This has done great harm to animal husbandry, which is an essential part of agriculture. Hence, efforts should be made wherever possible to free grazing land from illegal encroachment and put it under the management of the Gram Sabha.

FARMING SHOULD BE SELF-RELIANT

The second important thing about farming concerns the inputs needed for it. Three other essentials for farming, apart from land and labor, are seeds, manure, and water. All these three inputs can be easily sourced locally. Traditionally, our farmers have been self-reliant in the matter of these three things. They carefully selected and preserved their own seeds from season to season. They used cow dung and other animal wastes to make organic manure, and devised their own pesticides out of neem leaves and other such locally available materials. They depended for irrigation on rain-fed wells, tanks, and so on. There were reservoirs in every village to store rainwater. The water stored in these reservoirs also raised the level of groundwater, so that the wells were perennial. Normally there was no need for irrigation from external sources. It should also be noted here that heavy irrigation is required mostly for cash crops.

Now, the farmers have allowed all these inputs to go out of their hands due to their imprudence and their hankering after quick profits. Multinational corporations have acquired control over all the farm inputs: seeds, fertilizers, pesticides, and water. Our state and central governments have become agents of these multinationals. The farmers have been enslaved by this unholy combination, either directly or indirectly. The farmers have to free themselves from this slavery—otherwise, one day they will find that their land has been taken away from them. This is what is happening. Land is passing from the hands of small farmers into those of the big landowners or capitalists. Therefore the farmers and the village community will have to strive to be self-sufficient in the matter of seeds, fertilizers, and water if they are to be saved from this disastrous development.

CHEMICAL FERTILIZERS AND PESTICIDES

Apart from this aspect of self-reliance, chemical fertilizers and pesticides pose another serious problem. One of the false and misleading "facts" propagated by the capitalist—i.e., profit-seeking—system, relates to chemical fertilizers. In recent times the argument that there is a serious shortage of food in the world and that this can only be met by increased production through the use of chemical fertilizers has been used to boost the use of the latter. Both these assertions are baseless and false. The food shortage that the world is experiencing is not so much due to shortfalls in production as to the affluent countries like the US and those of the European Community destroying large quantities of foodstuffs like wheat, milk, butter, and so on in order to create artificial shortages in the market to earn larger profits.

It is also not true—or at best it is a half-truth—that artificial fertilizers help to increase production. Just as an addict experiences a transient surge of energy after consuming alcohol or some other stimulating drug and is able to exert himself vigorously for a short while, soil fed with chemical fertilizers produces more for a few years, but afterwards its fertility gets exhausted and production drops. The quantity of fertilizer has then to be increased from year to year only to maintain productivity at the earlier level. The farmer is thus caught in a trap. It is also a well-established fact that many useful insects and other organisms found in the soil that help to control pests are destroyed by the toxicity of the chemicals. Every farmer knows from experience that the use of chemical fertilizers is followed by an increase in the incidence of pests and plant diseases. Increasingly stronger and more toxic pesticides have to be used to save the crops. This vicious circle does not merely cast an increasingly heavy financial burden on the farmer, but also makes the soil unproductive in a short time. The use of chemical fertilizer also requires larger doses of irrigation, and this makes farming a very expensive business. Excessive irrigation also leads to waterlogging of the soil, and a lowering of the groundwater level caused by excessive pumping out of groundwater. Thus a vicious circle inimical to farming is set up, and land gradually becomes unproductive and barren. On the other hand, organic manure produced by composting cow dung, urine, droppings of other farm animals, organic farm wastes, and so on, helps maintain the fertility and improves the texture of the soil.

It is also now well known that the consumption of food produced by the use of chemical fertilizers and pesticides lowers the resistance of the body and makes it more vulnerable to diseases. On the other hand, the consumption of food produced by the use of organic manure actually helps to increase immunity and improve health. Hence, nowadays there is an increasing demand in the Western countries for foodstuffs produced by organic farming, and people are willing to pay higher prices for such products.

The farmers have become easy victims of exploitation by big business and multinational corporations as a result of their dependence on chemical fertilizers and pesticides. The latter fleece them mercilessly, making farming a losing practice, while land sold by farmers who are unable to continue farming is being taken over by rich businessmen and companies. The erstwhile farmers become day-laborers working for these new owners on the same land that was once their own. The use of organic manure and indigenous methods of pest control will save both the farmer and his land from certain ruin.

CONTROL OVER SEEDS

As mentioned earlier, the farmer used to preserve his own seeds, and this had been going on for centuries. Now half a dozen or more multinational companies are striving to capture the seed markets of the whole world. All the seed that the world needs has to be bought from them. They are pushing high-yielding seeds in the market, and government departments are helping them. These genetically engineered seeds are so structured that seed from their crops would not bear fruit, or only very little. The farmer will thus have to buy seeds from the corporations every year. The multinationals have patented their seeds, and are forcing the government of India to amend our patent laws so that they are favorable to them. Under this law farmers will be barred from choosing and keeping seeds from their own crops grown from seeds bought from the company. They may not use, sell, or even give away such seeds. They will be liable for fines and imprisonment if they do so. The multinationals have already adopted many tricks to make the farmers give up their own seeds, so that they may not have any alternative to seeds purchased from the corporations. They are already selling their seeds at amazingly high prices. Once they have a monopoly of the market, they will increase the prices still further. So the farmers have to be very careful not to let their own seeds, handed down to them for thousands of years, be lost.

DEVELOPMENT AND ECOLOGY

Natural resources of this earth like forests, water sources, mineral deposits are being rapidly exhausted or polluted by consumerism, the luxury-loving lifestyle, and the faulty policies of development that are being pursued nowadays. The greatest damage has been caused to forests. Most of the hills and mountains of our country have become denuded of green cover, and forests that had been there for millennia are disappearing fast. Some clearing of forests was inevitable with the growth of population, but the most damage to them is being done to supply raw material to paper and plywood factories and other industries, and by unregulated quarrying. These harmful activities are being indulged in to satisfy the needs of a consumerist culture in both our country and the other affluent countries. Forests in Third World countries are being denuded to satisfy the ever-growing hunger for timber and its products. Acid rains, caused by the accumulation in the atmosphere of large quantities of carbon dioxide from the exhaust gases of motor vehicles and factories, are destroying thousands of acres of forests in the US and Europe. This is also going to happen here at no very distant date. Corruption among the officials entrusted with the responsibility of protecting and developing the forests is also resulting in their depletion by greedy businessmen. Thus deforestation has become a matter of immediate and grave concern. Soil erosion has become a serious problem, and the underground water table is also going down because of the disappearance of forests. Floods have become more frequent and devastating. The cycle of seasons has been disturbed, and rains have become irregular and insufficient. Famines due to droughts, and dislocation and misery caused by floods have now become regular features of life. Moreover, the lives of people who depend for their livelihood on forests are becoming intolerable, and they are becoming rootless destitutes.

Thus, the highest priority should be given to the regeneration of forests. Their wanton exploitation for commercial purposes should be ended. The people will also have to be awakened to a consciousness of their responsibility in this matter. Laws relating to forests will have to be suitably amended so that the rights of the people dependent for their livelihood on forests are re-established, and they are enabled to participate in the work of conserving the forests.

Unsound irrigation projects and faulty methods of water utilization, use of chemical fertilizers and insecticides, heedless despoliation of mineral deposits and other such activities have caused serious damage to the land surface of our country. Immediate attention will have to be given to measures like soil conservation, checking erosion, and introducing proper methods of farming that do not injure the environment.

Similarly, the decay of the traditional system of collecting and conserving water (which was in vogue in all villages), due to the abolition of the right and control that the villagers had over these and their handing over to state irrigation departments, as well as the blind and senseless competition to build huge dams, have caused great damage to the country's water sources. Most of these have become polluted or are drying up. Priority must be given to the revival of the traditional system of water conservation in the villages.

Toxic effluents from factories, whether solid, liquid, or gaseous in nature, are causing serious injury to the atmosphere, rivers, lakes, reservoirs, the seas, and the land. This has become a very serious problem. The affluent economies are adopting all kinds of tricks to dump their toxic wastes in the poor Third World countries. Disposal of highly toxic and dangerous wastes from nuclear power plants is posing an insoluble problem, and poor villagers are being exposed to dangerous radiation from such disposal sites, the ill effects of which will continue to affect generations of their offspring. Adequate steps must be taken to stop such mischief, and to adopt systems and processes of production that do not injure the environment and people.

SWADESHI

Swadeshi has a very important place in Sarvodaya economy,[15] and is its cornerstone. Ordinarily, Swadeshi is taken to mean products manufactured in the country. But when looked at from the philosophical point of view, this differentiation between indigenous and foreign goods does not seem very meaningful. The proper definition of Swadeshi is concern for and duty to one's neighbor. All the people of the world are our kin, but our first concern should naturally be for our immediate neighbors' well-being. The things we use provide employment to other people. Hence, in the matter of the things that we use, our first preference would be, after those we can produce at home, for those produced by people in our village or the neighboring area.

Many articles of daily use are now manufactured by multinational corporations within our country. Apart from these, many firms that were indigenous until recently have been taken over by, or have entered into collaboration with, multinationals. The brand names are the same as before, but the products can no longer be called indigenous. Thus, in the present context it is not enough to consider articles manufactured inside the country as Swadeshi.

But Swadeshi should not merely mean goods produced in the neighborhood. The process by which they are produced and the purpose of production should also be taken into account. Goods produced by manual labor should be considered Swadeshi to a greater extent than factory-made goods, because the former help some needy person to earn his bread. By this criterion cloth produced in England from handspun yarn and woven on handlooms would really be more Swadeshi, for us, than cloth manufactured in an Indian textile mill. Similarly, goods produced for meeting the needs of oneself or one's neighbors would count as Swadeshi; but profiteering by creating artificial demand for them through advertisements and other means can never be considered Swadeshi.

Even beyond this, Swadeshi in reality involves a choice between two different lifestyles. The lifestyle in consonance with Swadeshi is that in which people engage in productive labor themselves; there is interdependence and sharing among neighbors, wants are limited, and the life led is simple. In the other, one seeks to maintain a high standard of living by exploiting the labor of others. From this point of view, Swadeshi and its opposite—Videshi, or "foreign"—are really a matter of choosing between non-possession and possessiveness, between parasitism and self-reliance through productive labor, between service to others and their exploitation, between cooperation and competition.

---

15   Common well-being.

TRUSTEESHIP

At this point it is again Gandhiji's ideas that show us a way out of the dilemma. Gandhiji emphasized that most of whatever physical strength, intellectual ability, resources, wealth, capabilities, and so on that a person possesses are either inherited from his or her predecessors, or obtained either from society or from nature. Not much of it is created by the individual without a contribution from the society and nature for what he has received from them—thus, without repaying their debt, he or she is guilty of appropriating a share or the labor of others. The Gita[16] indicts such a person as a "thief." In chapter 3, verse 12, it declares, "The gods—i.e. the elements of nature—when gratified by selfless work, give human beings the things they need. One who enjoys the gifts [of nature] without giving the gods back their due is a thief." Gandhiji therefore suggested that the simplest way of repaying one's debts to society is not to consider oneself to be the owner of one's wealth, resources, and talents, but a trustee on behalf of the society as a whole. These things are to be used for the benefit of the whole society, and especially for those weaker and less fortunate than oneself. One should use for oneself only as much as one needs for one's sustenance and efficient functioning. It is to be noted in this context that the acceptance of trusteeship has not been left by Gandhiji to the sweet will of the individual. Apart from suitable legislation, the persuasive power of Satyagraha, the concept of trusteeship, is also a unique contribution of Gandhiji to mankind.

THE JUDICIARY

There is all-around agreement on the view that the usefulness of justice lies in its being expeditious, less expensive, and easily available. We have inherited our judiciary from the British. In terms of basic principles of justice it has many welcome features, but it is also obvious that it is very expensive, greatly dependent on general procedures, and insensitive. Decisions are not handed down quickly enough. Cases remain pending for decades. Thus our existing judicial system is not useful for the poor and the rural people.

The increase in the number of disputes in society is due to the institution of private property, and to the mentality of selfishness. A restraint had been put on claims of private ownership of physical wealth in traditional Indian society by the wide acceptance of the spiritual maxims that all land and all wealth belonged to God or society. The emphasis was on the use of wealth for the good of the family or society, instead of for personal and selfish

---

16   Bhagavad Gita—one of the most important holy texts of the Hindu religion.

enjoyment. At the same time, the Panchayat system of rendering justice was evolved here, whose emphasis was on mutual understanding and giving a sense of satisfaction to the disputant of having got a fair deal, rather than on implementing provisions of the law to the letter. The system of resolving disputes by local units, as proposed for the new order, will make up to a certain extent for the shortcomings of the present judicial system. Justice will then become readily available, inexpensive, and expeditious. Except for a relatively small number of complicated or serious cases, it would be possible to dispose of most disputes at the local levels. The regional language should be used in the courts.

Experience of recent decades has shown that the role of the judiciary is not only to resolve disputes between individual citizens or groups but also to adjudicate on disputes between citizens and the government and to interpret the Constitution and the laws. Hence it is essential to keep the judiciary as independent and impartial as possible. To ensure this, the appointment of judges should be entrusted to a constitutional body insulated from political and other forms of pressure.

SAFEGUARDING DEMOCRACY

The establishment of active Gram Sabhas in villages will be the first step of people's power towards assuring its supremacy, but its consolidation for continuing the march towards full Gram Swaraj[17] and real and strong democracy makes it imperative that the people have control over their representatives at every level, from the block to the parliament. It is also necessary that they be able to prevent malpractice like intimidation, rigging, booth frauds, tampering with ballot boxes at the time of elections, and other such antisocial activities. For this it is necessary for the voters to get organized, and to take an active part in the political process. Thus, activities like organizing the voters, keeping in contact with elected representatives, the nomination of people's candidates, and so on, will be an essential part of the movement for social change.

The malpractice at election times, and evils like authoritarianism, political interference, the machinery of law and order, favoritism, rampant corruption, and other forms of criminality are serious stumbling blocks in the way to Gram Swaraj, which will be impossible to achieve without overcoming the machinations of those who want to perpetuate their hold on political and economic power.

---

17   Gram Swaraj, or village self-rule, was a central concept in Gandhi's thinking. The village (and villager) was at the centre of Gandhi's thought, insofar as India's social and political organization was concerned—at least, the type of social and political organization that he wanted to see for India.

GLOBALIZATION

Globalization began when Columbus crossed the Atlantic some 400 to 500 years ago, with his doctrine of "plunder and appropriate." Globalization is based on the same philosophy. Today's economy is based only on profit, and any economy based on profit will lead to exploitation and self-centeredness. Earlier it was different. The profit-based economy really started from the Industrial Revolution. Privatization is the culmination of what started 400 years ago. Gandhi always spoke of self-reliance. Nehru was the opposite; he actually started globalization in free India, with his dream of large-scale industrial development.

VISUALIZING THE TWENTY-FIRST CENTURY

This plundering, which has assumed that you control all the natural resources through centralization and then redistribute them to the market, was the method of exploitation. This hegemonization of resources started from British rule itself. Once you own the resources, you make the people dependent upon the market. Even a farmer who grows food has to buy his own food from the market. He is no longer self-reliant.

No, I am not pessimistic about the future; otherwise I would not be alive.

At the present time globalization is at its peak, but it will crumble under its own weight. Osama's bombing of the World Trade Center was symbolically the bombing of the economic and military power of the US. Elaborating, he said that both Christians and Muslims are fundamentalists. They have been fighting for ages. It was a clash between two peoples who want to exploit the world in their own ways. There is also a conflict of values; otherwise, how else can one explain the attitude and dedication of the followers of Osama, like the ones driving the planes who so readily gave their lives?

I do not agree that there has been no opposition and revolt against globalization. There are many agitations going on against globalization, such as the Narmada Andolan, in Rajasthan, the water Andolan,[18] which is all connected to the Gram Samaj.[19] The onslaught of globalization is very powerful. Even the media is with them. Only the *Hindu* newspaper gives weight to anti-globalization news. But globalization has its own alternative; it will crumble under its own weight within the next ten to fifteen years, and the next century will be one of alternatives. The inner contradictions

---

18   He is referring to the controversy over large dams on the river Narmada that have become a symbol of the struggle for a just, equitable society in India. The Narmada river is the largest westward flowing river in India, and empties into the Arabian Sea.
19   Village society.

of globalization will not let it sustain itself. That does not mean we become complacent or stop our fight against globalization. We have to be ready to offer an alternative as and when the situation arises.

NOT GLOBALIZATION BUT LOCALIZATION

Economic freedom is a fundamental prerequisite for the new social order. Every village would have to be self-reliant in the matter of its basic needs, and every villager ensured gainful employment. Keeping the goals of self-reliance and full employment in view, the village community should draw up its own economic plan for the fulfillment of its basic necessities on the basis of the possible resources available in the village. There is no other way for eradicating poverty and unemployment from the villages. Nowadays the government is advocating the globalization of our economy. This means that our economy should be integrated with the world economy that is today under the control of the affluent capitalist nations that have thrived initially by exploiting the poor nations. This will be disastrous for India. While there is a case for a mutually complementary role for the villages and the national economy, on the whole the economy needs to be "localized" instead of globalized.

This interview was conducted with the assistance of Ms. Chavi Sharma, a researcher from Jaipur. The original interview was conducted in Hindi, the language of northern India.

There are very few voices of hope in the era of ever-expanding globalization in India. Siddharaj Dhadda, a grand old man of the Gandhian tradition, is one such powerful voice, who not only speaks with conviction for the Gandhian alternative but also continuously works towards it. Even at his age, he moves around the country spreading the message of village reconstruction. Leading a simple life in Jaipur, he always tries to travel by train and not by air. Whenever the younger generation organizes a meeting anywhere in India with the objective of countering globalization or building some alternative, he participates and inspires them with the message of hope.

When we interviewed him he was preparing a second edition of his book, The Gandhian Alternative, *in Hindi, and asked us at great length about various grassroots movements that assert people's rights over natural resources like land, water, and forests. He also inquired about whether he could obtain the full text of some important judgments delivered by the Supreme Court of India, protecting the rights of vulnerable communities like tribal groups in recent years.*

We interviewed him in a room on the ground floor of his ancestral house, which he also uses as his office. In keeping with the Gandhian style, the room had no furniture, and he sat on a mattress on the floor with a low desk before him. All his books and papers were neatly and meticulously arranged, and whenever he wanted to show us a book or document, it was always in its assigned place. In one corner of the room stood his spinning wheel, on which he continues to spin every morning. All his clothes are made from the yarn he spins, and he makes it a point to ensure that all his objects of everyday use are handmade in nearby rural areas. His only lament was that it was becoming more and more difficult to find fully handmade footwear, and he is forced to get his shoes from a place almost 100 kilometers away from Jaipur.

MOZAMBIQUE

9

Maciane F. Zimba and Carolina J. Tamele

Traditional doctors, leaders of the Association of Traditional Doctors.

Interviewed by Maria Paula Meneses

"When [Frelimo] arrived they should have conducted a ceremony—mhamba—so that all the dead would know they had returned, that the war had ended, shouldn't they?

The person who taught me couldn't write; would he have liked to see someone writing down what he said? He would say that what he knows he has kept in his head, and until today he transmits everything he knows only through speech . . ."

Maciane F. Zimba and Carolina Tamele

By structuring the localization of bodies of knowledge, colonial policies ensured cultural fixing in undifferentiated arenas, whether in geographical or "racial" terms.[1] *The "Voices of the World" project therefore needed a new type of intervention. Through the eyes of two* tinyanga,[2] *it has proved possible both to avoid uniform and stereotypical generalization and to hear people of humble origin who have empirical knowledge—the result of their own understanding of life and the knowledge of others accumulated over the generations.*

The text begins with a personal narrative that introduces the life story, cosmic vision, and ideas about the world of Maciane F. Zimba, a Mozambican traditional doctor, now

---

1 The concept is used here in a way similar to that suggested in P. Gilroy, *Against Race: Imagining Political Culture beyond the Color Line*, Cambridge: Harvard UP, 2000. This author argues that the emergence of multiculturalism, associated with the expansion of the global economy, contributes to the partial erosion of race as a biological referent. At the same time, however, Gilroy argues that race reemerges as part of the practice of identity, as resistance against the capitalist tendency to dissolve solidarity and difference.
2 Plural of *nyàngà*—"traditional healer" in the languages of southern Mozambique (Xironga, Xichangana). I have some reservations about using terms such as "medicine man," "witch doctor," or even "traditional healer," as a translation of the term *nyàngà*. A first point has to do with the fact that Western terms contain a strong pejorative connotation in relation to this term. In fact, for a long time the terms used were close to *ganga*, *n'ganga*, or even traditional doctor. With the implantation of the colonial order from the end of the nineteenth century, two other terms came to be used, following the various studies of Westerners on this question (for example, E. Evans-Pritchard, *Witchcraft, Oracles and Magic among the Azande*, Oxford: Clarendon, 1950):

1. "Medicine man," used in opposition to the term "doctor," the last being exclusive to representatives of Western medicine;
2. "Witchdoctor." This term, of a profoundly colonial stamp, is a clear indicator of the level of disrespect and disqualification of local medical knowledge.

In many places in Africa, heavy legal restrictions, and even prohibitions, were introduced against traditional medical practices because the traditional healer is a person of extraordinary social prestige, able even to act as a mediator in conflicts (thus exceeding the capacities of biomedicine). In this paper, therefore, the preferred word is *nyàngà* (as stipulated in the statutes of AMETRAMO, where the equivalent Portuguese designation is "médico tradicional") when translating/transcribing the interviews into Portuguese. The English equivalent is "traditional doctor" or "traditional healer."

the president of AMETRAMO (Associação dos Médicos Tradicionais de Moçambique—Association of Traditional Doctors of Mozambique). Also present is the voice of Carolina Tamele, Zimba's wife, and head of the Association's Department of Culture. She interposes her own thoughts, complementing the discourse or opening new subjects for discussion.

Zimba and Tamele provided me with much enriching companionship and contact with other forms of knowledge and healing—about the importance of the body, person, and community. Given the confidence they had in me, being capable to some extent of maneuvering and transforming me into a listener-interviewer, it is important to pose a question: Was it I who selected them or was it they who selected me? This clearly implies the establishing of relations of confidence in both directions.

The joint interview that constitutes this narrative took place over a number of sessions. Far from being the result of a single meeting, this narrative consists of information collected over almost two years of interaction. The different people, localities, and questions we discovered and explored turned into a continuous context for the development of friendship. On each meeting I felt greater proximity and openness. We shared common memories, in a spirit of respect for one another's knowledges, and understanding and confidence increased.

Whenever possible, the text is constructed with the words of those interviewed, although my questions are also present. Through the historical background and context of the Association, I have attempted to understand the reasons for the present struggle for the constitution[3] and for the strengthening of the Association, and its perspectives for the future. This history in itself reflects the struggle—and far from linear course—of Mozambican history, including the desires, visions, and conflicts between modernity and the traditional, between the state and other moderating forces of social control: in other words, between apparently dissonant worlds that share numerous points of contact, whether in the colonial period or after independence.

This text, far from attempting to map a well-defined terrain, has the objective of presenting only a partial view of traditional healing in Mozambique. Although the interviews were conducted in one of the suburbs of Maputo, the interviewees had distinct and complex histories, with identities superimposed one upon the other, having multiple references of cultural integration.

As I am not fluent in Xichangana, and as those interviewed were weak in Portuguese—apart from the fact that "our healing is done in our languages," as Carolina Tamele expressed it—the interviews were often conducted in Xichangana, the language spoken in southern Mozambique. In order to achieve the richness of the interviews, I had the help of Zefanias Matsimbe, who played a crucial role in translation. The participation of this competent interpreter and translator made the construction of this work even more intensive, as little by little the words flowed and the flourishing knowledge of the people appeared.

---

3   This refers to the constitution of the association.

Maria Paula Meneses: *Mr. Zimba, tell us a little about yourself. Where were you born? Here in Maputo?*

Maciane F. Zimba: No, it was not here. I was born in Gaza, in Bilene-Macie. I am aged now—it's a long time ago I was born. Now I am sixty-something, not yet seventy, not quite, because I was born in 1934.

MPM: *Are you married?*

MFZ: Yes, but my wife died. I have two wives [*laughs*]. Now my wife is Carolina Tamele.

MPM: *How many children have you got? Some of them have houses on your land and live there, don't they?*

MFZ: I've got many children: ten of them. The eldest is already married, but is in South Africa. He has a house here. The other children are still young; they still go to school.

MPM: *Did you study? Did you go to school at all?*

MFZ: I studied a bit in Bilene. Here in Maputo I studied to the second class, thanks to the spirits.[4] I came to Maputo in those times of the Native Pass, that long ago[5] [*laughs*]. First I worked in a hotel—I don't remember the name. I washed dishes and all that, and cleaned the bedrooms. Then I went back home to Gaza. Home is there; here it's only for work, you see. After I got there, I then went to South Africa, on the mines.

MPM: *So you went to the mines?*

MFZ: Yes, South Africa. I went to the mines, I worked there two years.[6] Then they took me out [of the mines] to work on the land. The spirits attacked when I was in South Africa. That was an *nguni* spirit.[7] Its name

---

4   Reference to the support of the ancestral spirits. This relation between ancestral spirits and living members of the community is extremely important. Through the nature of the genealogical relationship, the spirits are a perpetual guest of the family and community, giving protection and benefits in exchange for periodical offerings that ensure this linkage. It is the role of the eldest (chiefs, traditional doctors, and so on) to maintain this contract of security and protection.

5   The Native Statute (which existed until 1961), as a political system imposed by the colonial state, was based on a structure of social identity that, through blood or association to a particular lineage, ensured basic rights of residence and land cultivation in a wider political community. The laws, statutes, and policies that differentiated a citizen from a native defined colonial citizens as those who could move freely within the territory, engage labor, and acquire property, as distinct from those for whom these things were not possible—the natives. To travel from one locality to another in Mozambique, a native had to possess a passbook, indicating his destination, which had to be confirmed by an employing entity.

6   Even today, it is common for young southern Mozambican men to migrate to South Africa to work. For a long time this labor was channeled particularly to the Witwatersrand gold mines.

7   The Nguni group, from the early nineteenth century, occupied extensive areas of south-central Mozambique as a result of the Mfecane migrations (a period of political disruption and population migration in Southern Africa which occurred during the 1820s and 1830s).

is Kondjani. It's the spirit I have. It's a spirit from the bush, deep in the bush, in the river. It's a spirit of the river, of the water.

And when I got back from South Africa, I was much afflicted. I returned [to Mozambique] when my head was a bit touched. The spirit came out and I felt pain, it hurt a lot; my head was not alright; and when I was there in South Africa, one day when I was sleeping, there came a spirit, a man almost, which said: "Go back home!" But I told no one—they would not understand. This was after only six days in South Africa. I still stayed some time working in South Africa, about four months, but I got worse—the spirit came out more in my body, and I got sick. I could no longer work. Then a Boer[8] saw me with his own eyes, and said "You've got a spirit. I don't know what you're going to do." And then he asked me something. I said I didn't know what is happening. But when it's a spirit, that spirit wants me to do [the spirit's] work. What to do? The Boer said: "You have to go back, back to your home." But I stayed there, worked and worked and worked, finished to the end of the contract, and came home. When I got home, got here, the spirit was coming out—again. As soon as I got to Bilene, I got there, and said to my brothers, "Here I am" and straightaway they sent me to study to be a healer. I studied a lot. I was *thwasàna*[9] two years. I began the course in 1952, and in 1954 the course finished. Two years—then I could be a traditional healer. First I had to begin learning *ndau*, *nguni*, the language of the spirits. Not the language we speak,[10] it's another. Then, [sometime in the 1960s] I came to Maputo. I have stayed here until now.

MPM: *So because you're a traditional healer, you worked a lot to create AMETRAMO?*

MFZ: Yes, I am the president of AMETRAMO, but it was a lot of work to create this association. I started in 1974, 1975[11]—even before independence;[12] but it was a lot of work. But before it was called an

---

8 Expression used to refer to white South Africans of Dutch origin. In this case the word is used as a synonym for "white chief."

9 Student of traditional medicine.

10 The maternal language of Zimba and of Carolina Tamele is Xichangana, one of the languages spoken in southern Mozambique. The Nguni languages are predominantly spoken in South Africa (KwaZulu-Natal, Transkei, and Eastern Cape); Cindau (the language of the Ndau group) is spoken in the central region of Mozambique.

11 At that time, various traditional doctors working in southern Mozambique contacted the Commission for Restructuring Health Services of the then transitional government. They wanted to create a School of Traditional Medicine and, based on this, to form an organization of traditional doctors. The request was denied, for the constitution of such an organization "would mean the institutionalization of the obscurantism of the medicine men by the Government" (B. Tomé, "Medicina Tradicional: estudar as plantas que curam," *Tempo* 460 [1979]: 13–23).

12 Mozambique celebrated its independence in June 1975.

organization, we began by working, talking with the healers—we gave help if they asked.

MPM: *You helped them. How, with money as well?*

MFZ: With money collected among the healers. There was a subscription, but it was small, very small—in those days each contributed five escudos [*laughs*].

We got independence, and father Samora[13] came when we were working on our organization. After a time they blocked us from doing our work. When the traditional doctors went to work, a member of the militia would arrive and take the money [of the doctor]. They would say: "We are working, you are not; we are going to take away these chickens." Also, on the way, on the road they would have those keeping watch on the people; they would stop the buses, make everyone get off, look at the identification [*laughs*]. At the roadblocks,[14] when they encountered a traditional doctor—then, you have to eat all you are carrying, all the medicines! They would force you to eat, right there in front of them. You only had to play the *gosha*[15] a little, and very quickly the militia would seize and burn these work instruments of the traditional doctor. We suffered a lot. There were other doctors who were sent to Lichinga, sent to Niassa.[16]

MPM: *To the re-education camps?*

MFZ: To the re-education camps, and many died there; others managed to get back. We tried to get round the problem, but at that time the Frelimo party[17] wanted to exclude us altogether; but we continued to work, to do our various activities. They took the decision because some of us complained.

MPM: *There were complaints from among you, from those who disagreed with the organization?*

MFZ: Yes, there was complaint; they wanted an organization, but some said I was taking their place and. . .

MPM: *Meaning you were at that stage already the president of the organization?*

MFZ: We were only secretaries. When we saw that our concerns were running badly, I found a way to talk with Jossefate Machel.[18] I spoke with him about the problems of the traditional doctor, that they were burning the things we use for our work, and other problems, and he replied: "I

---

13   Reference to Samora Machel, the first president of Mozambique, and then also president of Frelimo.
14   In the first years of independence there were several control points on the main roads, where identification was checked.
15   Percussion instruments made from gourds used by the *nyàngà*.
16   Province at the extreme north of Mozambique, where many "re-education camps" were located.
17   The party then in power. A multi-party system was introduced only in the 1990s.
18   Brother of Samora Machel.

cannot say anything, and neither can President Samora talk about this, the one who can talk is papá."[19] We went to talk with him in Jossefate's house, and we spoke a lot about our tradition, and he said: "I am only the father of the president, I am not an authority; but I say that even the Portuguese attempted to block the traditional doctors from working, but they did not succeed; my son will also not be able to prohibit it. But I cannot decide anything about this—only the president can decide." Then we were told that Samora was gong to Chilembene[20] to present Graça[21] to his parents, and also to visit his mother's grave. It was Moisés himself who helped us, invited us to go to Chilembene. We arrived there and papá Moisés received us and began to explain to his son[22] what we wanted; the president told us to wait. When it came to our turn, we were told to go into the house, and Samora came with his companions and wanted to know exactly what our problem was. I was with my colleague, who should have done the talking, but he couldn't speak for fear.

MPM: *Fear of the president* /laughs/?

MFZ: Fear of the president. But I managed to talk to Samora, and I said that I came to look for him because he used to say: "Even chained lions are free; and all my people are free." I said to him: "We are traditional doctors, sons of tradition, who look after traditional spirits. Who is going to liberate us if not you? Which president is going to liberate us, since we have heard that traditional medicine is not allowed?"

MPM: *And why did Frelimo not allow traditional doctors to work?*

MFZ: They said that after the whites [the Portuguese] had gone away, now it was us who were the opportunists. We were the black marketeers [*laughs*]. After I had explained everything that had happened, he asked: "Have you ever heard me say 'Down with the doctors'? Also, when we say down with something, it doesn't mean the end of it, only to diminish it. I want to tell you that traditional medicine is not going to end, but those who vaccinated the Portuguese so that they could come to Tanzania and murder Frelimo people without being seen, those are our enemies. As you have explained everything and came to see me, I am authorizing you—go and work!" He asked me if I played the *tilholo*,[23] and if I was *nyamusòro*.[24] I said I was, and then he told us to continue our

---

19   Moises Machel, father of the president.
20   His birthplace, in Gaza.
21   His future wife.
22   Samora.
23   Small divining bones used as an aid in diagnosis by the traditional doctor.
24   A traditional doctor who treats only with the benefit of the spirits. A doctor who treats only on the basis of knowledge of characteristics and qualities of plants and animals is known as *nyàngàrhume*.

work, but he recommended us not to *kotsolem*,[25] not to aid abortion, not to take soil from the footsteps of others so as to kill.

MPM: *He did not accuse you of creating confusion among families?*

MFZ: No, he only told us to work to heal people. We thanked him for this reply, and he asked if we had anything more to say. We said no—there was nothing to add; it was the only matter we mentioned. He told us to go and tell the [Frelimo] party that he authorized us to continue working. Then I said: "The party is your son, we are your sons; we don't have the power to talk to the party; it would be better if the chief himself spoke to them. If I say that the chief authorized it without you [the president] saying it, they can kill us." And Samora gave us a letter, and told us to hand it over to the party.

When we got back to Maputo, I met with some of the doctors and told them we had to give the letter to the party, but they refused. They said: "We cannot go there, we have already seen this—they will arrest us all." So I went alone to the party to hand over the letter. On the spot, when I met Sigaúque—he was the secretary of all the suburbs and districts of Maputo—when he saw the letter, he called his friends and they asked me who had given me the letter. I replied, saying that the one who had given me the letter had signed his name. They asked me if I had complained about them.[26] I said no, that we only wanted to find a way to continue to work as traditional doctors, without problems, and in freedom. They advised me to send the letter to the Ministry of Health; at the time the minister was Hélder Martins, and he worked with the secretary [general of the Ministry], Albino Maheche. The party gave me a car to take me there and leave me with Maheche, there in the Ministry. He gave the letter to the minister, Hélder Martins. The minister called to talk with me.

MPM: *On another occasion?*

MFZ: The same day. He called me via Secretary Maheche. When I arrived, the minister told me to sit down, and asked where I had got that paper [the letter]. I said "From the one who wrote his name. It has his signature there. You can see the signature." "What's this? Is he your family or what?" asked the minister. "No, he is not family, he is our president," I said [*laughs*]. "Then it's alright," he said. He got a bit angry. "So he wrote a letter directed here?" was his question; then he said that first I would have to go to the notary, make a formal application, then authenticate

---

25 According to Zimba's subsequent explanation: "To make a 'spell' so that a husband can totally control his wife without her knowing. In relation to the footsteps, what matters here is the fear of a 'spell' which may pursue people and cause them to miss the path, or be persecuted by bad spirits."

26 The party's city committee.

the signature and come back to the Ministry. Then he said he would send everything back to the one who had written the letter. He said that he would tell Samora that I should be shot [*laughs*].

MPM: *And then?*

MFZ: Then I said: "If they shoot me, that's no problem, at least I'll die working." Then the document was done, and the letter authenticated at the notary and sent to the Ministry. I did everything and made a photo-copy and brought it to the Ministry. The minister said: "So, he has come back? Where is he? Go and call him!" Secretary Maheche came to say this to me. I replied: "I am going to send this document to our president. If he decides this person has to die, so be it." I had already been in big trou-bles, and this minister was a small fish—Samora could kill me in Gaza, not this minister. The secretary said: "Don't worry, Mr. Zimba, here in the Ministry there is no traditional medicine, nor private medicine. Samora wants a space here for traditional medicine to work with us." "Then that's alright," I said. Maheche then said: "After two or three days come here with your family; tell them to come with you. If you're going to be shot, you can say good-bye." And I said alright, I would say good-bye. After three days, I went there again. When I got there, Maheche said: "Your reply has already arrived. There's no problem, I am going to arrange a room for traditional medicine; I am going to work with you." Maheche went with me to see the minister. Hélder Martins clapped on the table [*laughs*]: "Right, have you said good-bye to your family?" I said yes. Then he said: "Albino, take this letter to your office." Maheche took the document to study in his office; no one had to be shot. He told me to work in the Ministry with the doctor Leonardo Simão.[27] I studied with him about traditional medicine. Afterwards, they took us to the Agro-Economic Institute[28] to study how to collect medicinal plants.

MPM: *And were there many traditional doctors who went to work in the Ministry?*

MFZ: Yes, there were many of us, because they asked us to bring people to work there in the Ministry.[29] We were more than a hundred. But before this, when I spoke with Simão, he wanted to know where we had our meetings, and I told him we met in Mazanga, there in Avenue Acordos de Lusaka. Janet Mondlane and others, led by Leonardo Simão, came to see where, and told us to register people to study the collection of plants.

MPM: *All these people were traditional doctors?*

MFZ: Yes, it was the group of doctors. Carolina was also there.

---

27   The current minister of foreign affairs.
28   National Institute for Agro-Economic Research.
29   The GEMT (Gabinete de Estudos de Medicina Tradicional— Office for the Study of Traditional Medicine) was then formed—a unit within the Ministry of Health charged with relations with the traditional medical field.

MPM: *But who chose the people?*

MFZ: I chose them. I also went to study; they even published a photo in that magazine, *Tempo.*

MPM: *And now you are not afraid of talking about the old times, the old problems?*

MFZ: Speaking the truth doesn't kill people, but speaking liberates them, removes the guilt that many placed on us doctors, and which in the end was not correct. It's necessary to bring things out, as I am doing, how I felt. Everybody shouted, "Down with the witch doctors!" You as well.

MPM: *Mama Carolina also participated in the meetings with the people from the Health Ministry?*

Carolina J. Tamele: Yes, I was there. I became a doctor when very young, a long time ago.

MPM: *You met Mr. Zimba when you were already a doctor?*

CJT: Yes, it was through this—I was already an adult then. I got that illness of the spirit in 1973 in Chókwé. I am from there; I was born in Lionde, in Gaza. I studied there with *b'ava*[30] [Zimba] for two years. It did not take long. It takes a long time when the spirit is much delayed; when it is advanced, it doesn't take long. I will explain how the training is done.

MPM: *So you studied the plants, going to find them in the bush?*

CJT: Everything, everything you learn when you go looking for medicines in the bush and help cure people until the spirit comes out; and you are taught how to speak and to do the treatments. If you have a patient who is really ill, you sleep and the spirit will show you where to find the best plants to make the patient better. It is the spirit that shows you. You go and find the plant there. Lastly, you learn to accompany the spirit to the *ndhùmbhà*,[31] where you are going to work, when the person is fit to do some of the tasks of the doctor. There is a ceremony, when the training is finished, called *kuthwasa.*[32]

MPM: *What is "nthwasa"?*

CJT: It is the study course. First [I will] explain the *nguni* spirit, and then the *ndau* spirit. This is in the first year; in the second, you learn the medicinal plants. Then the master [*b'ava*] has to see that the person has properly learned to handle the spirits, both the strong and the weak; with the *ndau* spirit is where there are most problems. A person can get possessed of strong spirits and simply die. At first the spirits mistreated me, took hold of my whole body. At that time I was very thin [*laughs*]. The spirits made me that way, because at first I was in denial, and went almost mad.

---

30 Literally, this means father. By extension it applies to the respected elders, as being the teachers who train the future *tinyàngà*.

31 House reserved for the cults of ancestral spirits, where consultations are conducted.

32 Shangaan word referring to the long process whereby a person is cured of spirit possession and trained to work as a *nyamusòro*.

MPM· *And the spirits always run in the family, don't they?*

CJT: Yes. My grandmother was a doctor, the mother of my own father. She had two of these spirits; she died a long time ago. These are the spirits that are helping me now.

MPM: *But in what language do you talk with these spirits?*

CJT: Zimba has already explained that—we speak Manguni,[33] we speak Mandau. I didn't know, did I? I am from Gaza, but I have got that spirit and it teaches me also to understand and to speak. Do you see? I can reply when that spirit appears. Even the doctor's assistant has to be able to speak Manguni and Mandau. They have to be learned, and explained, these languages.

MPM: *What do you call the assistant? Do all the doctors have an assistant?*

CJT: Yes, they have to have an assistant—to help find plants, to dress the doctor. They are called *nyawuthi*. The *nyawuthi* tell the doctor when the spirits appear: they have to greet them, when they appear in the doctor's body, and receive their message when they speak; they have to know how to speak with them and understand their message. It's difficult; you will have to learn to be an assistant with us!

MPM: *Does the also have spirits?*

CJT: No, it's only with some people.[34] They only appear in the doctor.[35] At home in Gaza, the *valòyi*[36] may often be hidden in a tree, but the *nyàngà* has to climb the tree, and the *nyawuthi* also to help the *nyàngà* search, because the *nyàngà* might die up there. Working with spirits is very difficult.

MPM: *But now you are used to it, it's easier!*

CJT: Not really. It requires patience, because some spirits are really difficult to deal with. So there are people who take longer to train; it could take three or four years to finish the course.

MPM: *Do you think today people look on the* tinyàngà *with more respect than formerly?*

CJT: Yes, today they have more respect for us. They respect our work. Before, in Samora's time, they shouted, "Down with the *tinyàngà*!"

MPM: *How? What did they sing? Can you speak about those times?*

CJT: In those times it used to go like this [*singing in Xichangana a song from the first days of independence*]:

---

33   These languages are widely spoken in the southern part of the country, together with several others, including Portuguese.

34   Spirits run only in some families.

35   Because he does not have the power of the ancestral spirits, the *nyawuthi* can only become a *nyàngàrhume*, at best.

36   Plural of *nòyi*. The *nòyi* is a spirit with the power to do ill, and is able to cause problems far away through the intercession of the person in which it acts.

Down with the *tinyàngà* because they produce family intrigues,
Down with the *tinyàngà* because when they play the *tilholo*, they accuse
your mother of being a witch,[37]
Down with the *tinyàngà* because they make disorder [in society].
Are those who work with spirits going to live in Mozambique?
We have to be strong so as to make our country overcome all the
obstacles and advance,
Down with the *tinyàngà*, down with them!

You see? They were speaking about us.

MPM: *I did not know that there were these songs about the* tinyàngà. *Did you [traditional doctors] sing these songs?*

CJT: They sang them; we could not sing this about ourselves. But I remember it all and know that this was done—they sang those songs. I heard them sung in meetings.

MPM: *But why didn't you sing?*

CJT: Why should I sing against myself, against my own person?

MPM: *It was for this reason you prepared to form the doctors' association?*

CJT: Yes, I began a long time ago, in 1977. First I was working there in Zixaxa, near Xipamanine, near Vulcano,[38] where they had meetings. The *tinyàngà* came from Gaza and other regions, and we met in Mr. Mathe's house. He spoke many languages, even English and French. Here, Mr. Zimba was with someone else—Mazanga is his name. The meetings were in Mazanga's house, in Urbanization suburb; we were invited.

MPM: *So there were many groups meeting in Maputo city?*

CJT: There were many, but we separated because after a time Frelimo decided the *tinyàngà* should not do their work freely. It was President Samora himself. He said: "The spirit does not decide to enter children. Saying this is a child, it cannot be a *nyàngà*—the spirit will not listen. The child might be very small, but the spirit only has to wish it, and the spirit enters and the child won't be able to go to school." That was it, the government stopped meeting regularly with us. It was a long time. . .

MPM: *But did they persecute you, as the song says?*

CJT: Yes, those of the Grupo Dinamizador,[39] others from the OMM.[40] Do you see? In the time of Samora it was even difficult to sell medicines. At Xipamamnine we sell, but only under the counter, so we sold very

---

37 According to Carolina, the mother and aunt of the house are the most often accused by the *tinyàngà* of being witches.
38 Suburb of Maputo.
39 Structure formed to promote organization at the basic ward/neighborhood level.
40 Organização da Mulher Moçambicana—Mozambican Women's Organization; a structure of the Frelimo party.

little in those days. So we looked for ways to meet Samora, because
the *tinyàngà* were suffering; they could not beat the *tingoma*[41] and other
instruments used by the *tinyàngà*. No one, no one at all could work
during the day. We could only work at night, as if we were thieves.
This was here in Maputo, but the doctors out in the countryside were
alright—they could work without problem; you could take goats and
chickens for the work [as payment]. But it was difficult for us here. How
could you explain the goat or chickens as payment? But because the
nyàngà has renown, and is respected, he is offered many things. We had
many difficulties—if you traveled [from Gaza] to Maputo, the *mutundu*[42]
were confiscated at the roadblock at Bilene-Macia. They burned much
of our *mutundu*; and we in Maputo would go to help them at Macia.
They would ask if we were *tinyàngà*, said we were doing nothing—it
was obscurantism. Today, though, those Frelimo people come to ask
the *tinyàngà* whether their congress [to be held in 2002] will be successful with this multiparty system, with these conflicts, this lack of unity.
They didn't consult anyone else. We spoke of the errors that Frelimo
committed in the past.

MPM: *They admitted the mistakes?*

CJT: They did! They came to meet with us. They may not have changed,
but they heard. We told them they should bring the radio and television to broadcast the information, so that people could see what they
came to ask us; secrecy is not a good thing. Today they want to follow
tradition, but they forget that we have our heroes, *tinyàngà* who died in
prison, when they said that after the exit of the white exploiters, that
left the *tinyàngà* as exploiters, and they persecuted us. The *tinyàngà* were
eaten by lions;[43] they forgot this. I said: "First, you lost tradition. Before,
when the Portuguese were the district administrators or governors,
they respected tradition, they worked with the chiefs; for that reason
they were successful in their government. Why cannot we ourselves,
we blacks, do the same thing? When Frelimo arrived, why didn't they
call on us? Frelimo came a long time ago, didn't they? Chissano was
the first to come as prime minister in the transition, but he didn't do
anything like this. When Samora came, the *madoda*[44] called him and told
him he ought to know of the times he spent in the bush where there

---

41   Plural of *ngoma*, a large skin-covered drum used to announce the action of the
traditional doctor and aid in the calling of the spirits.

42   A typical basket in which the traditional doctor keeps instruments, etc.

43   A reference to Operation Production. Conducted in the mid-1980s, when all those
considered unproductive, without a work card (signifying attachment to an apparatus
overseen by the state), were sent out of the city to distant areas where they were to
undertake productive activities.

44   The elders—the most experienced, who form a counsel.

are cobras and lions. These animals are dangerous, but they didn't do Frelimo any harm, because these areas where Frelimo went were treated by the *tinyàngà*." I said all this. I remember that one time we spoke with one of our [Mozambican] administrators, who said he didn't know why we worked hidden away. He said we should explain what we knew, that our knowledge was very important, that it was as a result of the help of the *tinyàngà* that many people were saved during the armed struggle,[45] owing to the lions and cobras in the bush. But as Frelimo worked well with the *tinyàngà* at that time, nothing happened to them.

You know, these Frelimo people forget that the bush, where people died, where the colonial soldiers burned houses, needs to be visited in the traditional way. The government should organize this, but it doesn't happen—they only go to visit the Heroes Monument.[46] And those who don't rest there—who visits them?

In the meeting [with the Frelimo chiefs], I said: "People know there are spirits of our forefathers in every area; each zone has its chief. Where the chief is buried, there is also an *nyàngà* buried. To be a chief, ceremonies have to performed with the *nyàngà*. All those who have the power to be chief have to pass via the *nyàngà* to obtain that power. But you don't know this as you won power so long ago, and won the country! How do you explain that Chissano has had a peaceful government since he assumed power?"

MPM: *Are you a member of Frelimo?*

CJT: Me? Yes, I am, for more than ten years. I joined in Samora's time.

MPM: *Now they no longer sing "Down with the tinyàngà!"?*

CJT: It seems they have forgotten, but I still remember the music [*laughs*]. We in AMETRAMO have a Department of Culture. We sing and dance. When presidents arrive, we go to the airport to wait for them and sing.

MPM: *How did the idea of AMETRAMO come about?*

CJT: The idea came up because the revolution did want traditional doctors. Some doctors were ruined because they wanted to do away with them. We had to struggle with the government in Samora's time to build AMETRAMO. But there were always plenty of problems, do you see? There was much conflict over power.

MPM: *Mr. Zimba, what happened after you went to collect plants and work in the Ministry? That was all? You did nothing more?*

MFZ: We learned to collect and dry the plants. But some of my colleagues tried to complain about me, but they didn't succeed at all—neither in the party nor the Ministry.

---

45 Reference to the period of armed struggle for independence (1964–74).
46 The monument in Maputo where the bodies of some of the nation's heroes are interred.

MPM: *What did they accuse you of?*

MFZ: They said I subordinated them and gave unclear guidance that were different from those of the party. They went to complain to Maheche, and he told the minister that the doctors had presented a problem. These people said that they were the first to go to the meetings, that I always wanted to be in charge, and so many other things—he said this and that and so on. There was a big meeting, with Samora, with the minister. Maheche said to Samora,[47] "Don't speak in Portuguese, speak in Xichangana so everyone can understand; I will speak in Portuguese for the minister." They spoke a lot, those who had complained. When they finished, Maheche said, "Zimba, you have been accused of many things; you have to react to the problems." I stood up and said they did not complain about me but about him [Maheche], "because what they complain about is what you are telling me. I am not to blame because I transmit the guidance that I get from you and the minister." Maheche translated for the minister Hélder Martins [*laughs*]. Then the minister got very angry, and said if there were any more complaints from those doctors, he would have them all arrested.

MPM: *So the minister got angry?*

MFZ: Yes, with those who had gone to complain: "Because what we want you to do is what Zimba says. When he went to speak with the president, where were you? When he asked for the letter and when the chief gave the letter, where were you? If you want unity it is better to work in coordination with Zimba, because it won't work otherwise—we only recognize him. Let us work together in coordination." And there the meeting ended.

MPM: *They all wanted to be chiefs?*

MFZ: Yes, they wanted to be chiefs.

MPM: *And afterwards, how did AMETRAMO arise?*

MFZ: The party called us in again about traditional medicine. It was they, the party, who brought out the name; they helped give the name— AMETRAMO; it was a party idea. When the party understood the power of the doctors, they called them all in for a meeting. I was not told: my district told me nothing. It was at that meeting that Ms. Banú Idrisse was elected president of the Association.

MPM: *The organization changed its name to an association?*

MFZ: Yes. [The party] wanted to help us turn it into an association. It was around 1989 or 1990.

MPM: *It was then the Association began?*

---

47   In 1986 Samora Machel died. The new president of Mozambique, in office until 2005, was Joaquim Chissano, of the Frelimo party. Armando Emílio Guebuza succeeded him.

MFZ: Yes. Well, it became an association and was led by Banú until the First Conference.[48] Then there was a time when I myself was the secretary of Banú. Banú had friends in the party, and that group of complaining doctors supported her. They even complained that I used the money contributed by the doctors. There were many problems, and they sent me away. Many of them wanted to put me in jail. At that time I was on holiday, but they could have got my stand-ins to find me; but they didn't bother with that, just accused me. Then the party came to speak to me to resolve the problem. We went to meet the people from AMETRAMO. When we arrived there, the party was also present; the person who accompanied me spoke: "Some are complaining; they don't want Zimba as one of the leaders of the Association, they themselves want to lead." Many people spoke, and the party member said that they should not overturn the orders of the president and destroy the Association. He said I should work in AMETRAMO. They then received me and said I should be a judge of the Association, and I said didn't want to judge.

MPM: *It was to solve the doctors' problems?*

MFZ: I said that I wasn't in a position to judge the problems of the doctors; they would have to find another solution. They said they would have to hold an election between me and Zacarias Mangaze—the one who was put in my place—and so we held elections.

MPM: *Which office was it for?*

MFZ: President of the district. I got twenty-seven and he got zero [*laughs*]; he didn't get even one vote. I then worked in the district for four years, and was then transferred to the city in place of the president there. That was it—he wasn't removed; the doctors held elections in the city and district and the people [*tinyàngà*] chose me as president. But the leaders of Maputo city AMETRAMO reduced my votes in favor of Alcinda Hunguane.[49] I remained calm, and was her vice-president for almost three years; when they saw that she didn't work well, they moved her to the National Executive Commissariat, and I occupied her place in the city. I stayed to work here in the city.

MPM: *What were your tasks?*

MFZ: Mobilize the doctors to enroll in the association, pay their dues, and get the membership card. I worked in the city [for the association] from 1990 until 1996. I saw that the people [*tinyàngà*] complained because the Association was unregistered. I went to speak with President Banú and told her that the *tinyàngà* were complaining of the lack of registration, but she said she had sent the papers to the lawyers, to make statutes. These

---

48   In 2000.
49   This refers to electoral fraud.

papers were submitted in 1993, but she never followed them up. As Mama Carolina was head of culture for the city, she spoke with Chissano. There was much confusion at that time. Chissano gave orders for Baptista Cosme[50] to find out what had happened to the application. Cosme told Banú to find the number of the file and give it to him [*laughs*]. I went to tell the leaders of AMETRAMO this, but they didn't have the number, they knew nothing. The secretary general didn't have it either, and told the supervisor to go with me to Banú to get the number; Banú didn't have the number, and said it was with the Association's lawyers. I asked: "How do we look for information without the file number?" Then, one day, at the airport, Carolina was there dancing and the president[51] came in from a journey; he asked for the number of the file sent to Cosme. Baptista Cosme came and berated us a lot, saying that he had ordered that the number be given quickly—if it didn't appear, they would put him in prison.

MPM: *Who did he say this to?*

MFZ: To me. I saw that there was a big problem, that little had been agreed. I was afraid to go to the lawyers on my own to get the number, in case this came to seem treacherous; so I took a secretary with me. We went to the Commercial Registry and found out that the file was entered in 1994, and had been returned to the lawyer because some items were lacking. It was complicated—all the documents were completely out of date. The lawyer said it was necessary to start all over again. He telephoned Banú, and she said she did not recognize the people who had gone to the registry—they were infiltrators. The lawyer took fright, and beat around the bush, so I asked him: "Do you want to be taken for a good lawyer or a deceiving lawyer? Which do you prefer?" I said that it was the president who wanted the number, not Banú, and threatened to go to the president and tell him that the lawyer was refusing to give me the number. He was much afraid, and his secretary came to help us rapidly make the Statutes of the Association, so as to get the necessary file number. We did all the documents; the Statute went to Banú, and she agreed. I went there every day to see if the process was going correctly in the Registry, even in the Ministry of Justice. It took a short while, but the minister of justice signed, and then ten people had to go to the registry to sign a copy of the statute. We organized seven people with documents all ready, but Banú got to hear of it and went to remove these documents, so as to put her own people in their place. Anyway, we went to see them sign.

MPM: *And you, Mr. Zimba, who had organized it all, were left out?*

---

50   Then mayor of the city.
51   Chissano.

MFZ: Yes, I was only present; after organizing it people appeared saying I was the chief of AMETRAMO.

Then we had to have an election, to choose the president of AMETRAMO, because now there were the statutes of the Association. But that lady[52] refused, did nothing more, because she wanted to remain at the head—she just wanted to be president. She went to complain at the party, but she was put off. The people [the *tinyàngà*] demanded an assembly, but she refused, saying they couldn't—that they were slighting her, that they didn't want her as president because she was a woman. The *tinyàngà* denied this and said they only wanted an assembly so they could choose a chief. While she was head, nothing was done. She left none of the subscription money, nothing; AMETRAMO did not even have a floor mat. It had no headquarters, nothing.

At that time [1999] the *tinyàngà* rejected her continuation in power, and even arranged lawyers to organize things properly. Alice Mabota[53] helped us to put AMETRAMO correctly on paper. She said we had to have a General Assembly to choose a president. Banú didn't want this, and confused things so as to boycott our work. She chose the date of the assembly, but then she didn't want to go ahead. We had some money from contributions, and held the assembly in April [2000], and I won the election. I became national president of the General Assembly of AMETRAMO.

MPM: *How about the Provisional Assembly in Beira, in 1991?*

MFZ: There were also many there—200 to 300 people. Each one of whom paid out of their own pocket.

MPM: *In this assembly in 2000, were there problems? You mentioned no delegates from the north came.*

MFZ: It was in the flood season.[54] And then, how would they come without resources? There was only money for the Assembly, not to pay for travel. To call the presidents[55] from other places, we used the telephone, from Gaza to Cabo Delgado.

MPM: *So who was present in this Assembly? Only the doctors from Maputo?*

MFZ: Yes, and Gaza. It was impossible for others to get here; there was no money, and the roads were impassable to get to Maputo. The representative from Inhambane wanted to come, but Banú prevented it, because that's her base—she has family there.

MPM: *Did the problems with Banú stop there?*

---

52   Banú Idrisse.
53   President of the Mozambican League of Human Rights.
54   In 2000 one of the largest ever floods occurred in the south of the country, making travel between the south and the center-north impossible for some time.
55   Provincial representatives of AMETRAMO.

MFZ: No. There was a big problem with her. She accused us of saying that she took money from AMETRAMO. She reported we spoke badly of her. But she diverted a lot of subscription money. We discovered it, talked with her, but she went to lay a complaint in court. Our lawyer helped, and now in June said the case had come to an end, that Banú was in the wrong.[56]

MPM: *Does Banú have a position in the new administration?*

MFZ: We offered her a job as a counselor, but she declined. Now she doesn't much come to meetings. She only wants to be in control, as president. But there are others who have been in this struggle for AMETRAMO, and we have worked together with them for a long time.

MPM: *So now are there no problems among the AMETRAMO people?*

MFZ: They still continue. We organized a headquarters, a new membership card, money in the bank; but the statute says each year we have to have new leaders. So others want a change. A year is very little to do a lot of work. We have still not succeeded in having a meeting in all the provinces, to elect the provincial presidents. This has only happened here in Maputo and in Inhambane; only now will we advance to the center and north.

There is much argument now. People want to occupy this post, be president, but they don't do anything to warrant it. There is a woman who wants to be leader. We only began to work last year, after the election—it's not sufficient to do the many things we want to do. These people who are leaders[57] have work to do, but they don't actually do it. They want to be the big boss! The people of the leadership must work. There is no time for just sitting and giving orders. All the doctors have to work, to bring in money to AMETRAMO, pay the subscription. The leader should not be alone. Otherwise, what would I be president of? Chief of what? All alone!

MPM: *Now that you have a headquarters, all ready and functioning, what is the aim of AMETRAMO?*

MFZ: It seems good to have all traditional doctors engaged in the association. The association is what responds to the problems of the doctors.

MPM: *What problems?*

MFZ: There is the problem that if you cure one person, another might die, even in the doctor's house. If it happens in hospital, no one is arrested; but our doctor, he will be arrested. Then, another might say that the doctor cured him, that he is well, but he may well come back and speak badly to the doctor, and say: "You didn't cure me well; I want to take my money back." You see this? [*laughs*]. Another time the doctor does his work,

---

56   Banú's legal moves to interrupt the process were defeated.
57   The contesting parties are main members of AMETRAMO's leadership.

treats the person, and takes his money; then the person complains, says he is not properly cured. When the person complains to the Association, we resolve that problem.

There is a problem the doctor encounters among the people: [a person] comes to the house and says: "There is a witch," and so on, and so on; then he goes to the doctor and he will explain what the witchcraft is. Formerly some courts blamed the doctors for giving medicine or drugs that killed people. Some sent people to the doctors to resolve the problem of witchcraft.[58] Now, with the Association registered, it is easier—do you see? Now when this happens [when the doctor makes a mistake, or his work is perceived as being "wrong"], when it doesn't turn out well, the doctor is defended. That is the *nyàngà*, who didn't do well. This is why I asked all the doctors, male and female, to join the Association, because there are other causes of such misfortune; they should all belong to the Association, to AMETRAMO. Those who are members of AMETRAMO should say, if it is a doctor who did this, whether it is one who is not yet a member, who does not know the order, does not know the law.[59]

MPM: *Does AMETRAMO have links with other parties, such as Renamo?*

MFZ: No, we still have no links; we are going to make this link. Until recently, there was only one party, so we only have links with Frelimo. But AMETRAMO is not part of the Frelimo party. Renamo, Dhlakama do not want AMETRAMO, they do not want *machangane*;[60] they say a *machangane* when president should go to Gazankulu in South Africa. We deny this—we are born here. Now can he say where we should go? We were born here; we don't know Gazankulu. So where should we go? Dhlakama is very bad now.

MPM: *But is there still collaboration between the party, the courts, and AMETRAMO?*

CJT: Yes, there is. There are many, many accusations of witchcraft. A man accuses his wife of wanting to do him ill with drugs acquired from a *nyàngà*; we have to try to clear up the confusion: call the *nyàngà* who prescribed or applied the medicine, to explain what the objective was.

---

58   The patient consults the *nyàngà* to alleviate pressures and social tensions that he or she has. Apart from "physical" ailments, the *nyàngà* is capable to identify social tensions and grievances, as well as antisocial conflict, which may produce ill feeling, misfortune, and even death in the community. The identification of a witch under the influence of evil spirits means identifying the breaking point of the community's harmony. Bringing him or her to confess this "anti-community moment" is seen as the draining and annulment of blame, of the evil that the person has internalized, thus enabling the restoration of good community relations.

59   A *nyàngà* acting wrongly—or rather, perceived as having acted against the majority of the family and community—changes his status to witch doctor.

60   Ethnic group.

Then we might find another *nyanga* to cleanse the couple, so that they can continue to live in harmony.

MPM: *When this problem occurs, who resolves it in AMETRAMO? Do you all work together?*

CJT: We have departments, each with its own area. I am head of Culture, where the aim is to promote cultural activities. There is the Department of Legal Affairs for legal problems the doctors encounter in their work. There are other departments, Social Welfare, Women, also. . .

MPM: *Is there any punishment for things badly done?*

MFZ: There is punishment within AMETRAMO. It is not with the *xamboco*.[61] You have to pay a fine if things are badly done. It is in the statutes that if a doctor fails, we have to see whether it is the first, second, or third time. The fine is 50,000, 100,000 or 200,000 meticais.[62] You see, if it is a major mistake, we try to control things based on the statutes. AMETRAMO supervises.

There is the Supervisory Panel that supervises people. Now, let's see what happens with many people. For example, you go to see a doctor because you want an abortion, and it goes wrong; it is the doctor who is in trouble. The woman will say, "I went to a traditional doctor, he gave me medicine to end the pregnancy, but it went wrong." She goes to the hospital, and has to explain how it got to this stage. So the traditional doctor has to go and explain things [and is confronted with]: "Why are you doing the abortion? Don't you know it's illegal!?" Then there are problems. So the doctor has to go to explain in AMETRAMO. The affected person presents a complaint to AMETRAMO. The Supervisory Panel deals with these problems, it supervises the doctors.

MPM: *Who controls the money?*

MFZ: Ah, that is the Department of Administration and Finances; along with the treasurer, they deal with money.

MPM: *Are all the people in the assembly and the office-holders from Maputo, or do they come from the provinces?*

MFZ: There is Sabina Nhaca from Gaza—she has already been a Frelimo representative. Natália Massango is from Maputo province, from Matola. There is also a man who lives in Mozambique, but is Malawian—he lives in Maputo. We will have presidents from the other provinces; they don't have to be in Maputo, but they have to be national members.

MPM: *What does a traditional doctor have to do to become a member of AMETRAMO?*

---

61 Corporal punishment with a whip.
62 Up to a maximum of US$10—in a country where the minimum monthly wage is no more than US$40.

MFZ: Fill in a form, and then he will be a member; others are honorary members. There are some who are already registered as honorary members.

MPM: *How does the Association know that a person is a good doctor? How do you know that a person is a doctor?*

MFZ: For AMETRAMO, the person has to have two testimonials, from doctors practicing for a long time, who live in the same ward as the one who wants to be a member. It works in wards [neighborhoods]. They specify that they did the course over what period; after they are trained, they have to become members, they have to register. That's the only way to get the membership card.

MPM: *Are there many doctors living in the built-up city?*

MFZ: There are, but the majority are not Mozambican. There is one, Dr. Ébo, who appears on television. He is not Mozambican. He says he is a member of AMETRAMO, but he is not known among AMETRAMO members. But AMETRAMO does not accept the kind of publicity that he does. He has signs up in front of his house: "Licensed traditional doctor," and so on. That AMETRAMO does not accept. Even publicity in the newspaper or on the radio is not advisable, even if you are a member of AMETRAMO. Because if we all did that, the newspaper would be overflowing with doctors' announcements. He says it is because he is not Mozambican that he puts announcements in, so people will know him; but AMETRAMO does not accept that—it is not the way we do things. A traditional doctor when he moves into a house, rented or whatever, he cleanses the spirits with song and dance, so people know through this that he is a doctor.

MPM: *Perhaps these foreign doctors know how to treat other illnesses?*

MFZ: It may be, I don't know. I think we should be more united and study the worst of the present illnesses—malaria, AIDS, and others; some know how to treat them, so they should share their experience.

MPM: *So when the* tinyàngà *have doubts, they consult their colleagues? There is a* bandhla?[63]

MFZ: They may consult. It is important to exchange experiences about illnesses, so that the person can be properly cured. AMETRAMO is important. There are days for meetings to discuss illnesses, treatments. . .

CJT: We talk a lot, and work alongside other doctors. When a doctor cannot resolve a problem, he talks with a colleague. There are always several doctors in a neighborhood. There is unity among us. When it is impossible to resolve a problem, they take the sick person to *b'ava*. When we see that it is a hospital case, we send to find a doctor there. When we suspect malaria, we send to make *pica*[64] there, but we help the

---

63 A meeting, party, or feast in a village. By extension, today *bandhla* means the different associations of people with common interests, such as the *tinyàngà*, for example.
64 A blood test.

patient with our medicines. Our obligation is to help those who come to us. When the course ends, we swear an oath we have to uphold. In the course we learn to cure all illnesses, but knowledge of some diseases is gained with experience, and discussion and learning with colleagues.

MPM: *What was it like formerly? Only a man could be* b'ava, *or could women also be?*

MFZ: It was the same as now. *B'ava* is a form of respect; it can be a man or woman. That is a problem of Portuguese.

MPM: *Mama Carolina is a* b'ava?

CJT: Yes, I am *b'ava* to the students I have, men or women. Their name is *mathwasàna.*[65] *B'ava* is the teacher who has the ancestors' knowledge. The *b'ava* can be a man or woman, you see. I am a woman *b'ava*, Papa Zimba is also *b'ava*, but he no longer does training. I still have pupils. Even for the men pupils, I am *b'ava* for them. After the person finishes training, when they have done the *kuthwàsa* ceremony, they come to find me at home to consult me if they have any doubts: "*B'ava* Carolina, such and such happened, I have come to seek your opinion." I speak, give my opinion, say do this or that.

MPM: *Do you know what are the main illnesses, the medicines and the quantities used for these illnesses? Or does each doctor do it his own way?*

MFZ: In this new leadership of AMETRAMO we are trying to study illnesses—how the sick are treated. There are many diseases that are not well understood, such as AIDS. We are still studying to understand this AIDS. Formerly there were STDs; now it's changed—we have AIDS. It's not the same. When a patient with AIDS comes, he doesn't say that he has this problem, but when the *tilholo* are used, you see that it is this disease. Medicine may help even AIDS. Many come from South Africa with this disease.

MPM: *How is your relationship with traditional doctors in South Africa? I heard there was a meeting. . .*

MFZ: That's right, there was a big meeting—there were more than 150 people there. It was at the frontier near Nkomatipoort. Even Doctor Nhlavana Masseko, the international president of the Traditional Healers Organization, [attended].[66] They came, and we went too, in a group of fourteen from AMETRAMO. It cost a lot to get there. Those people in the South African embassy always object when they see the person is a traditional doctor.

But the meeting went well. There was a great feast; two cows were killed. Now they will come to Mozambique [September 2001] for a conference at our headquarters in Maputo. They want a meeting to

---

65 Students of traditional medicine.
66 An association of South African traditional doctors.

learn to cure better. Masseko said we should make an agreement with all African traditional doctors' associations. He said they had already visited many places, including Europe. *Xei*, he has a lot of money—overflowing with money. They are helping us with alterations in AMETRAMO headquarters, there in Xipamanine. We are going to become a real association, with a secretary to receive people and everything.

CJT: We need contact with these South African doctors, but they need us more. When the meeting ended, they said that Mozambicans know better how to cure, that they must be above those of all countries. In South Africa, the traditional doctors are useless! Some of their people come to be treated here, to get the power to be a good doctor there in South Africa. We know how to shake the *tilholo* to understand what a patient has. There they do not work well with spirits—they only know how to give medicine, and that with a poorly done consultation.

MFZ: We have really to talk with these South African doctors. They run out of medicines to cure people, and come here to Maputo and Gaza to find them. A Mozambican doctor who is in South Africa pays his subscription there, not in AMETRAMO; it shouldn't be like that.

MPM: *You mean there are doctors here with greater spiritual power, and who know more?*

CJT: Yes. This Mr. Masseko studied there in South Africa; he found work there as a *nyàngà*. But he was clever—he knew he had to come to Mozambique to find medicines. He learned that the *mandau* spirit requires its own remedy, so he had to come away [from South Africa] to the north [of Mozambique]. There in the north he didn't find anything. He returned another time and went to Inhambane, found nothing there, and came to Chókwè [Gaza]; there he found good spirits and knowledge. He only has the spirit from the south [*nguni*].

MPM: *Which are the most powerful spirits?*

CJT: All the spirits from the *machangane* area have the power to help the doctors. We [the *tinyàngà*] here in the south have rules. We work with two spirits, each of which has its role. The *ndau* spirit has its task, and the *nguni* spirit also. The *nguni* spirit has the task of shaking the *tilholo* to know what the illness is, know the problems of the people; we do not work like the hospital doctor, who asks where you feel pain, does blood tests to discover what the person has.[67] We use the *tilholo* to tell what the

---

67 Traditional medicine and biomedicine do not share the same sense of knowledge, and so do not follow the same criteria. While the former shapes its therapeutic efficacy to the intended result within the wider social order, the latter is bound be a model of scientific objectivity, where the etiology of symptoms and treatment must be organized as part of an autonomous, separate universe, which develops only in terms of its own internal advances and discoveries.

illness is, and if we see that the illness is caused by *nòyi*, the *ndau* spirit is used to take out this spirit. With *kufemba*,[68] it is possible to make contact with the patient's ancestors. The spirit speaks with the patient, saying what they want. Often these are matters that the ancestor did not resolve before dying; so these problems remain with a single person, and it is therefore a heavy burden.

MPM: *So there is a division between the two?*

CJT: Yes, there is a division of tasks. For this reason the majority of traditional doctors have these two spirits. The *nguni* is the one that throws the *tilholo* and looks for cures; the *ndau* spirit has the job of bringing out the evil spirits, or those of the ancestors that show anger towards you for a variety of reasons. The *ndau* spirit can enable you to speak with your ancestors so as to find a solution for your problem.

MPM: *Do you cooperate with the South Africans?*

MFZ: Yes, we are going to meet, for training on AIDS. This disease is a great problem.

MPM: *What is the attitude, the position of AMETRAMO, towards other traditional doctors in the world? There are the Chinese, the Indians. . .*

MFZ: When you're engaged with doctors from other countries it can be very good, because of the exchange of experiences. They give you the knowledge that they use for treatment, and then we add it to what we know from here, so you know better.

CJT: You know, I think the problem is because we don't know all the doctors, they are undermining our power. If you are a traditional doctor, you should come to AMETRAMO, become a member, and work. . .

MPM: *Are there many patients who come to consult you?*

MFZ: There are, but many also go now to those churches, the Zionist churches.

MPM: *But do the* mazione[69] *work like traditional doctors?*

MFZ: Yes, they say they know how, and manage to take away the spirits of the dead like us. But we do the treatment properly—the result of study; they only use water, or sometimes oil. And they charge much more than we do. And then there are these other Brazilian churches. People think they are better than us. But they don't know how to cure our diseases.

---

68   When the protective spirits of a doctor take hold of the body and detect the presence of evil spirits. When a *nòyi* is found, this is indicated by a sneeze (*wetshi*).

69   The Mazione church is a Pentecostal form of Christianity, which emphasizes spiritual renewal through the Holy Spirit. The imported religions (Christianity, Islam) have come to generate various syncretic movements in Mozambique, whose specificity rests in the fact that their religious work includes therapeutic functions. This increases the range of therapeutic resources available, showing once again the medical plurality that exists.

CJT: What we see as wrong is that increasingly the religion is accepted. There are already poor habits: there are churches where prayer is conducted with people who are naked, but these churches request a license from the government to work in the country. There are so many Brazilians, they could fill the country up. Don't they [the government] see that they come only to make money from Mozambique? It's full of people, Brazilians with their churches; everywhere they open is completely filled with people, but it is a matter of money only, nothing else: if you pay, pay well—they say they will cure anything [*laughs*]. They have a special day of the week for curing. . . .

MPM: *You are talking about the IURD?*[70]

MFZ: Yes, that church. Things are not going well. Traditional doctors are not working well: people are running away from our tradition, and going to that church. Things are not at all good. Those *mazione* churches are no different from the IURD. They are all in the same group. They don't work in the same way, but what they do, they are in the same bracket. It is true. They don't like traditional doctors. They make propaganda against doctors in their services. They use funeral ceremonies to tell people they shouldn't go to consult the traditional doctors, that the doctors are not good, and they say: "You must follow religion. The doctors kill people—they are sorcerers." They speak a lot against us. If a doctor were there, it would not go well; it would be a shame [*laughs*].

MPM: *You don't feel they are discriminating?*

CJT: Yes, they are discriminating against us. Let us try to speak with them.

MFZ: Now that our Association is registered, I am going to send for all those terrible *mazione* folk and talk with them.

MPM: *What about the Catholic Church?*

MFZ: There is no problem with the Catholics. A doctor can freely enter the church.

MPM: *They don't object when enter a Catholic church?*

CJT: There is no problem; the Catholics don't make a fuss. I am a Catholic, I go to church! I never say that I have no time because there are people waiting to consult me. I go, and attend them when I return from church.

MPM: *So what causes the difference? What do the* mazione *do to impede your work?*

MFZ: The *mazione* don't allow us to enter the church to attend the services. When a traditional doctor comes, and he really wants to be a believer, they send him to burn his *mutundu*—everything that belongs to a traditional doctor. Afterwards a prophet will appear—a doctor becomes a prophet. Even it the wife of a *zione*[71] has the spirits, the husband will not

---

70   Igreja Universal do Reino de Deus—Universal Church of the Kingdom of God.
71   Same as *mazione*.

allow her to do the doctor's course. They leave the person to carry on sick. Now I am thinking of having a meeting with them so as to arrive at an understanding. Because there are times when they use traditional medicine. Where do they learn it? They are not traditional doctors. How is it they manage to identify a root, vaccinate, give medicines, close a house for protection, do all these things? That is not their work. They can only use the word of God, oil, ashes, water—nothing else.

CJT: Also, we can never refuse to intervene. If anybody asks for help it is because we are needed, and our spirits indicate the proper answer. To deny help to a person is a great lack of respect for our spirits. Even when we are with our families, if a patient appears, we leave everything to help the person. This is our role. It has to be like this. Those who don't act like this are chastised by the spirits. And we ourselves earn our living this way. But the *zione* only attends in the church.

MPM: *These days it is often said that sons and daughters accuse their mothers of being witches so that they can acquire the house. Is this true?*

CJT: It's true, unfortunately. They often say that the offspring accuse the mother of being a witch so they can obtain her house, along with the goats, the chickens. But the ones saying these things are the *mazione*, and they throw the blame on the *nyàngà*. These are the *zione* who make up accusations against the mother. The *tinyàngà* were the first to exist, a long time before these *mazione*, and then there was no such accusation. The *mazione* work like the *tinyàngà*, but talk like a person who wants to do away with traditional medicine; they make a recipe for roots, vaccinate the person, purify with the blood of goats and chickens. But the old *mazione* did not work this way—they did not require payment; but now they demand 3 to 5 million meticais, even as *mazione*. Often, when their treatment doesn't work, we shake the *tilholo* and discover that the *zione* has done nothing to aid the family—he has only caused confusion among the family ancestors. But when the people go to complain, they don't think it's the *zione*; they always say it is the *nyàngà* who causes confusion. Then, in the Association, at the police, when asked to bring the *nyàngà* who caused the trouble, in fact they take along a *zione*.

MPM: *With the Muslims, are there any problems?*

MFZ: No, there aren't; nor with the Protestants.

MPM: *And how was it in colonial times?*

MFZ: It was more or less alright in colonial times; the traditional doctor just had to keep quiet.[72] You paid tax to the chief—fifty escudos, once

---

72 The *tinyàngà* represented a source of authority independent of the colonial administration. In those days, as today, in times of trouble these elements reinforced their political function. In the previous century, they sometimes acted against the colonial administration, attempting to widen the areas under their control; as a result, the colonial

a year. I used to pay this. The chief knew how many traditional doctors he had, and who was doing the course. If they thought you were a great doctor, you paid 100 escudos. It depended on the number of people who went to see the doctor, whether he had a wide reputation or not.

MPM: *In colonial times, did you have large meetings?*

MFZ: No, each one did as he wished; a *bandhla* was not necessary.

MPM: *Were there no instructions from the government and the chiefs to the doctors?*

MFZ: The chiefs only wanted the money from the tax; if someone made a mistake or failed, he was tried and arrested if necessary, or he might remain at liberty. If the *b'ava* had *mathwasàna*, there might be problems; but when a chief or elder came to my house, I would tell him that I had a person in training. They would tell me to go on working, and when the time for the end of the course came, I would call them to come and see, and that was that.

MPM: *Tell me something—was there a great change after independence in relation to the* tinyàngà?

CJT: What I see quite clearly is the collaboration between us. In colonial times we did not know each other, everyone worked in his own house; before, we helped each other very little in exchanging information about medicines when treatment by another doctor was not going well. Each depended on his own *b'ava*. If the *b'ava* was far away, there was no solution. But now I can communicate with another *nyàngà*, just by speaking on the telephone and requesting help to see what is wrong with the patient, and how to treat the illness.

MPM: *The cell phone solves everything* [laughs].

CJT: [*laughs*] I can also go personally to a colleague's home, and he gives me the medicine I need for my patient. Before, when I went to the house of another *nyàngà* he would say I wanted to bewitch him, and accuse me of being envious. There are still some *tinyàngà* who think like that.

MPM: *Formerly* timamba,[73] shingundu,[74] shikubo,[75] *and other things were worn. Now they're no longer used?*

CJT: Now they aren't used, because it is difficult to wear them when you travel in a *chapa*-taxi.[76] The *chapa* gets full, and these things perturb other

---

government imposed legal sanctions, including prison and exile for those who openly defied the colonial state's norms. Afterwards, whether during the war of independence or during the civil war, the *tinyàngà* acquired a newly enhanced role in the struggle for supremacy. In times of conflict the *nyàngà*, in re-establishing the exigencies and expectations of the collectivity over the individual, acquires considerable political influence; during the war of liberation, they were at times included in Frelimo's political project.

73   A type of leather support on top of which several strings of cowries are fixed—like a belt. It can also be a hat.

74   Hat or plume of feathers, used by the nyàngà when he is possessed by ndau spirits.

75   Hat made of vegetable fiber painted crimson, similar to a wig.

76   The *chapa* is the popular name for the small buses circulating in Maputo. Many of them are open trucks.

passengers. The [fare] collector may not even let you enter. Formerly, when a person finished training, he went about dressed that way to show he had finished, that he was now a *nyàngà*. These days it's too much, to have the body cluttered with those things. When I did the course, my *b'ava* was already modern—he didn't accept the use of such things just to be with the spirits. It was up to your spirit to bring clients—it was not necessary to go about dressed up to advertise yourself [*laughs*].

MPM: *Mama Carolina, why do you use a special* capulana[77] *when you do a consultation?*

MFZ: I also use one.

CJT: I always put on a *capulana*. When there's a party meeting, I put on a *capulana*; at home I always have one on. When I go shopping, in the fields, there may be times when I leave it off. But it's good when you have to go in the *chapa*-taxis. When I travel, I always take *capulanas* with me; when I go visiting the family also. But for parties here in Maputo it's not used—only when I go to dance for the president, in the airport.

MPM: *No, I mean that special—that one you used in the party that time. . .*

CJT: That's the spirits' *capulana*. It is special—it shows that the person accepts the spirits he or she has.

MPM: *And a male* nyàngà, *how does he go? Does he also put on such a* capulana?

CJT: No, a man does not go about dressed in the *capulana*. He can use it at home. He folds it up and puts it in his bag when he's going out. But when he gets to the place, when he's going to sleep he puts the *capulana* under his head. When we go to the AMETRAMO meetings, both men and women take the *capulana* in a bag, so it's the same for Zimba. When a man goes to such a meeting, he takes his *capulana* in a bag, and when he arrives he takes it out and puts it on. We have to do this, otherwise the spirits don't help us. It has to be done, it's tradition. It was always like this.

MPM: *But there are times I have seen Mama Carolina without the spirits'* capulana.

CJT: Maybe I was menstruating. When you are menstruating, you cannot touch the spirits' things. You have to wait for it to finish. You don't work in that period—you can't do *kufemba*, nothing at all. You can't involve yourself in things of the spirits in that period. Even if someone simply wants his medicine, wants further treatment, I have to chew charcoal—then I can work. Then I have to have a medicated bath, made with these leaves [*shows them*]. They are well pounded, and then I take a bath with it. You have to take away the smell of the blood.

MPM: *The men don't have such a problem?*

MFZ: We do—it's in our tradition. If you have sex with a woman, you

---

77 A piece of bright cloth normally worn around the waist, mainly by women.

have to take a bath with a special medicine before going to work treating people. Only in this way do spirits return to the doctor.

MPM: *And the women* tinyàngà *also have to take a bath after sex?*

MFZ: Yes, you have to take away the smell, and make the spirits return.

MPM: *Mr. Zimba, can you tell us why you stopped collaborating with the Office for the Study of Traditional Medicine (GEMT)?*

MFZ: I worked well with Leonardo Simão. He knows a lot from me, because I worked with him. I stopped working with the Ministry of Health a long time ago, because the minister changed, everything turned upside down—the one who was good for traditional medicine left, and now they don't talk to me. They no longer talk with the doctors; some say the doctors don't know anything, and ask what do the doctors go there for? I said no, I was already trained in traditional medicine a long time ago, I will simply stay at home and work.

The [new] people of GEMT don't accept that we know anything. They don't even call us doctors. They say we are "practitioners." What does that mean? Practitioners of what? That word is no good. We study, do an exam, know medicines, know how to help a person. When necessary, those people from GEMT come to talk with us; in fact they recognize that we know plants, know how to treat diseases, but then they call us "practitioners." Practitioners of what? A practitioner is someone who only sells medicine, but doesn't know how these medicines cure.

MPM: *Mama Carolina, tell us what you feel is the big difference between how they treat people in the hospital and the treatment done by the traditional doctors?*

CJT: Each has knowledge—they both study and know things. But there are Mozambican diseases that only we know, only we traditional doctors understand. The sickness of the spirit, only we understand and can treat. Hospital treatment cures the external disease, but doesn't get inside to make the illness come out of the person. So it doesn't go, it comes back again. When we break with tradition, misfortunes occur—a death might occur naturally, but it might come from some evil thing that was done. A woman who is widowed has to obey tradition before having relations with a man; if not the man will get ill.

When we go far away, the danger is greater. We get there, and there will be spirits that mean harm to us, which want to get what we have—they want to see if we are strong. If we begin to be half-mad, to have problems, which we cannot explain, that's how it is—it's a sign that there are going to be problems. We know that. Often the good spirits warn us of a problem, that a *nòyì* is following us.

MFZ: A person can go to the hospital, but there are things that can never be cured there—there is no medicine for it. Modern doctors only bother to give medicines. There are illnesses that require ceremonies; if not there'll be no cure. There are illnesses only the traditional doctor can cure—it is not knowledge everyone has. You have to know what it is, how to treat it, know which medicine to get from the bush to give to the person—it's not easy.

MPM: *When that lady came here because her son had a problem, he couldn't sleep because of his girlfriend—did you treat them?*

MFZ: [*laughs*] That's already done—he's all right now. First I treated him personally here, then I gave him medicaments to take at home. He got better. Mama Carolina made the medicines at home. *Xei*, it was a big problem. He wasn't sleeping, he wasn't eating. He got sick, thin, didn't work; it was bad. He had to come to the doctor; we did our work, gave him medicine to make him vomit, to take out what had entered inside. He takes the medicine, and when it finishes, he sees what was inside—it comes out and he gets better. But you have to go to a proper traditional doctor, a strong one, to fight that malady.

MPM: *At times a woman is not too good. . .*

MFZ: [*laughs*] Not just at times, it's always!

MPM: Xei, *that's not so—at times men are no good; they need medicine to get a lover. Don't they come here for that too?*

MFZ and CJT: [*laughing*] Yes, they certainly do!

MPM: *Do you make those medicaments, Papa Zimba?*

MFZ: No, I don't do that. I want people to live properly. Not to get mad—thinking only about women, you go mad. I don't want that. When he spoke with me, Samora also told me that he didn't want that.

MPM: *Tell me why, when you do your consultations, you always call on members of the patient's family?*

MFZ: Obviously, the family is necessary to know what happened. We meet the family to discuss what happened and understand the causes of the unhappiness of the person. The family comes and explains the problem, tells it all, the whole history of the problem, even before the illness was felt, to discover what happened—to see if the patient forgot to do something in relation to the forefathers, if anyone was doing mischief, or if the family forgot the ancestors, if they didn't do *mhamba*.[78] Then the doctor talks with the patient—you have to talk. The doctor calls the spirits also when we rattle the *tilholo*—you know how it's done, we already explained. We have to discover who is to blame for the illness: if it was only forgetfulness, or if they didn't want to know any more about such things.[79]

---

78 Ceremony for the ancestors; the plural is *timhamba*.

79 A further point of interest is that the cause of the misfortune—the illness that occurs—may not appear in the person who commits the act or who failed to perform a given ceremony, but in another member of the family who, not being protected by vaccines, ends up being most affected.

MPM: *When someone dies as a result of misfortune or accident, when someone is murdered, what do you do then?*

MFZ: When someone kills someone else, deliberately, the spirit of the victim returns to the family of the killer, and brings much unhappiness, even disaster. The family, trying to find out what is going on, goes to the traditional doctor. He is the only one who can try to find out what has happened, and what treatment and ceremonies need to be done to resolve the problems. It may be that a family member who is not so protected gets sick.[80] The spirit thus survives, and comes back to trouble the family of the killer. In that family, there is sure to be ill fortune, all kinds of bad luck, because the spirit will enter someone's body and do mischief, but the whole family will be affected—all of them. For this reason, they all come to consult the traditional doctor.[81]

MPM: *On the question of vaccines, is it just a matter of making incisions?*

MFZ: There is one that lasts a long time. When it is only for one thing, you make a *xitsungulu*[82] so that it is always with the person. You sew it well in the cloth; *xitsungulu* is a medicine to protect the person. It's protection for living, to protect everyone: those who don't work envy those who have employment, have money, possessions, television. It's important to avoid this.

MPM: *If I wanted to be a minister, how do I get protection to get to that position?*

MFZ: There the doctor is clever. Giving medicine to become a minister if you've only got second grade won't work. A gardener wants to be a director with only first grade: it's not possible! If you're already on the way, the doctor gives protection. Getting to be a director is not easy. You need to have in the family at the time a spirit of one who was a director, and who will help. You have to have a ceremony for that spirit to become a director or a minister. You have to say: "You have to help me, you were once a minister." Then the spirit will help you get where you want to go.

MPM: *What are the main illnesses that people come to you with in Maputo?*

MFZ: The most serious is AIDS, and tuberculosis. These diseases are very

---

80   The one who is not "vaccinated." As a prophylactic treatment, incisions for the vaccine are made in the areas most vulnerable to external attack; the vaccine (normally a paste made up of between five and twenty ingredients) is spread directly by the *nyàngà* in each cut. The components of the vaccine are of vegetable origin, dried, ground, and mixed in an oily solution (cobra fat). The vaccine is made essentially as a protection against the *valòyì*, the "infections" of witches, malevolent medicines placed near the house of the patient, nightmares, lightning, and bullets, and to bring good luck. These days, vaccines contain more than they used to, because there are now more problems and illnesses.

81   It is interesting to note the pressure exercised on the family, and the fact that this large, organic unity is the target of the spirit's anger. This indefiniteness about who will be the target of the spirit may work either in favor of or against the culprit.

82   A small bag of medicaments normally hung from the neck.

complicated, but there are those who say it's malaria, for it's a disease that almost everyone has—we call it *dzedzeze*. Or misunderstandings in the family—a man and woman don't get on, you see. . .

MPM: *But, for example, can a couple who can't have children go to the hospital and to the* nyàngà *at the same time?*

CJT: But it may not be through illness. But it's better to go to the hospital first.

MPM: *And if the hospital doesn't succeed?*

CJT: If not, they go to the *tinyàngà*. The doctors will try to find out why— there may be pains in the abdomen, they may be sterile, the man or the woman. Sterility may stem from failing to do the traditional ritual, such as communicating to the spirits the fact of the woman having left home to go to the man's house. If so, she will not get pregnant; she should have a small ceremony at her home, and then as soon as she comes back to her new home, she will become pregnant straight away, without any need for medicine. If we do a treatment, after a month we tell them to go to the hospital to do the tests. Then they come back and we do a treatment to secure the pregnancy—protect the baby in the mother's belly. It's all important, the hospital and our medicine. There's no problem with that.

MPM: *Are there many people with these problems?*

CJT: Yes, this is a very old condition.

MPM: *So why don't you cooperate more with the hospital doctors here in Maputo, to exchange experiences?*

MFZ: We are still struggling with the Ministry of Health. But the association is still young. It's only a year.[83] Each one knows his own affairs. We could work together. People have to go slowly; little by little will take us there. Now they accept our certificate to say that a person was sick and was treated by a traditional doctor.

MPM: *And there is no problem with the hospital doctors?*

MFZ: There are problems when the patient doesn't respect us—neither the traditional doctor nor the hospital doctor. It happens. They begin to feel better, and forget everything. Complications arise, and they come running back. It can't go on like that—we don't know what the person has or what he wants. That is difficult. But our obligation is to cure people.

MPM: *How do you work on AIDS? The situation is difficult, with many dying. . .*

MFZ: A sick person goes to the hospital and the doctor says: you have AIDS. Then he does nothing. When you have malaria, he does the blood test and then gives medicine, and the person gets better. So what is happening? The doctors don't know how to treat AIDS? Where does the disease come from? It's the whites who brought it. The whites see

---

83   A reference to the time Zimba has been in the leadership.

that they haven't managed to finish off the blacks, and send their AIDS. It's a struggle against Africans, against blacks. We have been living here a long time. We were all born here—there's never been a lack of medicine to treat people. Now they say there's nothing to treat AIDS. Many are dying, practically only of this. What's going to happen? It's a big war now. Many Africans are dying of AIDS—they say there is no cure, and no one helps. The AMETRAMO doctors have to do something. We may be poor, but we know something. This present minister of health has never called us. He knows we could help, but doesn't call us, doesn't talk with the traditional doctors. We know how to make medicines to help those who are told they have AIDS, and can help cure people. We are doctors. Why doesn't the Ministry call people to help in the treatment? Because they only want people to reveal the plants that are used. Only African plants can do the trick. So why don't we work together?

This Jeito[84] of theirs is also no good. It's that which brings AIDS, it's no good. When you use Jeito, there are no more children. When we die, there'll be no one to replace us—it will be empty.

MPM: *I don't know—in Europe they say that the disease first appeared in Africa!*

CJT: No, it's not so! Because the disease came with the Portuguese. The whites bring diseases from outside. When sailors came here they came with different diseases. There were no STDs in our country. Those who think dogs could have sexual relations with people are the people who brought diseases—because animal blood does not mix with that of a person; but they don't know this, and say we are the ones to blame [*laughs*]. So a Mozambican is in danger only because he is black; in Samora's time there were those who had sex with dogs just to get a few dollars—those foreigners!

MPM: *So what's wrong now?*

MFZ: If the government doesn't help us, we can't do anything; we will go on doing what we are doing, but if the government helped us, we could do much more.

MPM: *In South Africa they have a plant for treating AIDS. It looks like manioc. Do you know it? It was discovered by traditional doctors, but the pharmacies want this medicine to make money. Who is the owner of the plant?*

MFZ: There in South Africa there's much trickery, but they cure AIDS very well.

MPM: *The plant doesn't cure but it is used as treatment, it gives strength. But the traditional doctor has lost his plant; it's like Medimoc,[85] which buys all the medicines and charges for them.*

---

84   The name of the best-known condom available in Mozambique.
85   Mozambican company charged with the import and export of medicines, including those in the form of raw material.

MFZ: The traditional doctor's right—he's the one who knows He's right.

MPM: *What sort of help do you need now? Financial or. . . ?*

MFZ: The government has always to consider us its own, and let us collaborate with the Ministry of Health. Now with this AIDS disease—those people of GEMT came to talk, to ask us help again to identify the plants that cure AIDS, that I can use to help treat people. They bring people here to AMETRAMO, but nothing more happens. I don't even know who these people are. They come here, talk, ask our help, and then only say they are going to put our names in a book. They don't want to give money for the AMETRAMO headquarters, but we are the ones who know. We have always lived here—we have the old medicines, which only we know. So how is it going to be? Do they want to trick us again? We worked [in GEMT] with Leonardo Simão. Then it stopped. We want to speak with the minister of health, with the prime minister, but we can't get an audience. They go to the provinces, leave Maputo without even speaking to AMETRAMO; they go only with the people from their offices. They go to the countryside, do their meetings, call the traditional doctors, and ask a lot of questions. Sometimes they pay something, but it's not enough. We [AMETRAMO] are struggling against all this. It's not right. We are the ones who know, but the ones with the money are the ones in the Ministry offices. It's not correct. . .

MPM: *Do you normally explain how you treat diseases, and what medicines you use?*

MFZ: No—we tried this and it wasn't worthwhile. Teaching everyone is not going to cure people. They are going to know everything, our knowledge. Our work shouldn't end like that. We can teach others, but not everyone. We teach, but only those who will not affect us. Our medication is made with various plants and other things. It's not just one, as those office people have it in their book.[86] We helped them do it, and they don't recognize our work, our names. Formerly, we didn't teach anyone—only those who had spiritual illness, who were going to be *tinyàngà*. Those we teach so that they can cure others.

MPM: *Does what you learn stay only in your head, or do you write it down, Mama Carolina?*

CJT: It is only in my head.

MPM: *Then how do you explain to people all that you know?*

CJT: You can write history, but to teach others it won't work because they won't study that: they have to know how to do it only from their heads. The person who taught me couldn't write. Would he have liked to see someone writing down what he said? He would have rejected this: even

---

86 P. Jansen and O. Mendes, *Plantas medicinais: seu uso tradicional em Moçambique*, Maputo: Ministério da Saúde, 4 vols, 1983–94.

obliging the person to abandon his training. The *b'ava* might say that his house isn't a school, that it was not necessary to write all he knows. He would say that what he knows he has kept in his head, and until today he transmits everything he knows only through speech. The *b'ava* could present different types of medicinal roots and their uses one by one. Formerly he used gourds to keep his medicines; each contained its medicament, which we had to know well, without fail; the *b'ava* taught what each medicine was for and what illness it cured. The *b'ava* didn't write. Would you have the courage to write? If you tried to write, he would say: "You didn't come through the force of the spirit," and throw away the paper. But I was embarrassed a lot at first, because there was so much at the same time and place. There was the medicine that has to be boiled before being put in its place; many, many roots; others to be mixed before applying, with water, with oil. . .

MPM: *Now you can buy the medicines here, can't you?*

CJT: Yes—there is a person we know who brings it when we ask him to go and find it.

MPM: *Who is it that sells medicines at Xipamanine?*

CJT: You see? They even sell medicines at Xipamanine. When you get there, you see them selling medicines—but they don't know anything, they don't know how to cure. In an area of *nkonola*,[87] the *tinyàngà* will go to search with his hoe, dig and dig, and take out the whole root. Then he will put the soil back so that the root will grow again. That root is good for stomachache. But there are people who don't know how to do it, and remove everything, so nothing remains and the next time there's nothing: it's those mobile sellers, selling there in Xipamanine. There are many of them; they aren't traditional doctors, it's just a business. They don't know how to remove the plant. The medicine is not taken just like that—it has to be prepared, taken how the doctor says, kept in a certain place. This is a problem we have, we *nyàngà*, and we have to see if we can resolve it.

MPM: *How are you managing to fight against this?*

MFZ: I am going to succeed, I am going to fight against that business. It's for this purpose we have introduced some inspectors to bring medicines from there. One of these days there will be no more of that plant. Nearby here, the bush has gone—it's a long way away. There are those who go and search and bring to sell here, others who don't know to how to remove the plant properly. . .

MPM: *Have you thought of cultivating medicinal plants?*

MFZ: No, not yet, because these plants would turn the house into bush.

---

87 *Terminalia sericea*—a medicinal plant.

You could plant in a field, but someone would come and dig them up and steal. . .

MPM: *There is a lot of violence—many people die, there are murders. It seems that people are increasingly forgetting that it is necessary to have respect—they don't do the ceremonies.*

MFZ: That's right, because it's true Frelimo struggled until it won—but it wasn't only the warriors, it was also the dead, the ancestors. They were there to protect them. When [Frelimo] arrived, they should have conducted a ceremony—*mhamba*—so that all the dead would know they had returned, that the war had ended, shouldn't they? So there would be no more problems. But papa Samora didn't do that. This Joaquim Chissano also doesn't do it. But in other countries they do it; I have seen it on television. When he does the election campaign, when he has won the votes, Mandela calls all the traditional doctors to a ceremony [including playing the *tingoma* and summoning the spirits] so the dead will remain at peace.

MPM: *Papa Zimba said that many leaders come here to get medicines to become strong.*

MFZ: That's right—to get a vaccine in order to have strength. We traditional doctors have to vaccinate to strengthen people. Leaders use *xitsungulu* in their pockets. That Chissano also uses *xitsungulu*. If another person wants to harm him, he won't not succeed. . .

MPM: *These leaders, these people who go about in suits, none of them say they are going to a traditional doctor, to the* nyàngà; *it seems they are embarrassed. . .*

MFZ: Because they don't want everyone to know that the president, the minister goes to the traditional doctor.

MPM: *But do they actually go?*

CJT: Many do [*laughs*]. They even call for us in party meetings nowadays—I already talked about this. They are embarrassed to come to a consultation during the day, so they come and knock on the door at night!

MPM: *There are complaints by the elderly that the young don't follow tradition.*

CJT: That's very true.

MPM: *How do you see this?*

CJT: Because we no longer obey tradition.

MFZ: People today, from the way of dressing, mainly the women, do things wrong. Women are much respected because they give life; but when they go about almost undressed in the street, the country gets ruined. Men dress well, but the women go about in short clothes; they say it is modern, but it's not, it has no sense. It's highly improper to show these parts [thighs]. And women are deceived by the policy that teaches that abortion is no danger to them; that when someone dies, they can have sex with no problems, without doing a purifying treatment. So many young people die through not following tradition. This is what is ruining our land. Formerly there was none of this, because the chiefs put in by the Portuguese knew they had to do ceremonies for the land. Today this no longer happens. At times they do ceremonies in Portuguese. How are the spirits going to understand that?

CJT: It is not only a question of tradition—it's that they don't do things right for us to live properly. A black is a black. There is always something difficult to resolve. He should find someone to look well into his life and its traditional base, to hear properly what the ancestors have to say to him. Why did Samora die early? He didn't follow tradition when his mother died. Our country will fail like this. But Chissano is worse—he is selling everything, even the land, to foreigners. He is selling our country—we know but we don't want to say it. This Chissano, it seems his head is not right. The power of the chief is traditional—he is chosen by God, by the ancestors. Samora? He himself bungled by calling in the Russians; when he was a baby his body was completely rolled up by a snake when he was with his mother in the fields; no one knows how the snake disappeared—it was a complete mystery. When they called the father to see what had happened, they found no sign of the snake. It was there they did the ceremony for him, where power was given to him. There is a real snake and a snake of the spirits. His was of the spirits. Now no one defends us—they have no respect, there is no chief, since Samora died.

MPM: *Why do so many want to do harm these days?*

MFZ: It is a sign of the times. There are many people here in the city. It's not like before. It has filled up with people—some are employed, others don't work, but want to take the jobs. There are many with no work; they only do petty trade, and when they see people with money they think they will kill them and keep the money. The city is filling up. In colonial times, you can say [the colonialists] divided the people. It was a different time; only with an identity card—this one comes from Macia, that one from Gaza, this one from Maputo—could you stay. Those from the north, no—they went to São Tomé: when people did wrong here, the Portuguese put them in ships and sent them to São Tomé. But not to remain as a prisoner; it was not to stay at ease, doing nothing. No, they were distributed among people there to work. They were not in prison. They used to work there, in the fields or whatever, until they came back after two or three years. Also in those days, there was no bus to Beira, no bus to the north, to Nampula, to anywhere there—there was no bus there. You went by boat, very slowly. Nowadays, as there is the bus, you can send people away [from Maputo]; but when they get there, as they have money, they buy a ticket to come back [*laughs*]. What are you going to do? You may be sent there, you get back—In Samora's time, it was more or less alright. The bus didn't always go there, you needed travel authorization, you didn't go about so easily. Now there are many who are stealing, killing. . .

CJT: Papa Zimba was speaking of those who murdered and were sent to São Tomé. These days, thieves are not punished. When I was a child, I was very scared when I saw people taken for *xibalo*,[88] people chained at the feet. It was difficult to walk—they seemed to be jumping; they were the prisoners from the jail at Magude. But it showed there was order in society. Today, where is the law? These days people only spend a few days in prison, and then they get out. Aren't they going to murder someone else? So there is no longer deportation,[89] and they can no longer send people as a punishment to the north—they say the law doesn't allow it. The prisons themselves are covered with grass, but they don't order the prisoners to clean up because they fear they will kill the warders. In the prisons, people get out in an instant. It's like a hotel. It is dangerous for a wronged person to accuse a wrongdoer—he might even risk his life. It's the thief who is protected by Frelimo, not the victim of the theft.

MPM: *It is certainly bad—it is increasingly difficult to tell who is a good doctor, who is a false one.*

MFZ: That's right. Now we have these modern doctors, when people die suddenly, in an accident or whatever—they are very busy. It is certainly very poor what they are doing; they remove the whole of his life [from the deceased, remove the good organs to be used in transplants]. What are they doing? What is the purpose of that life? It's just to make money. When you die like that, with no illness, that's what they do, even here in Mozambique. They take things out bit by bit. There are people telling us about this. The family says he had an accident and went to hospital; he died in an accident, and the family finds him in the hospital with everything removed. They've taken the tongue, the eyes.[90] In South Africa they sell these things [*indicates the genital organs*] to make medicaments, to give strength [*laughs*].

MPM: *For men to get more potency?*

MFZ: [*laughs*] I don't know. No, it's not necessary—it's the medicament, the plants, those in the bush that make men more forceful, bring strength.

MPM: *So why do the doctors in the hospital do that?*

MFZ: I really don't know why they do it, or what is the use of the parts the doctors take, the sex parts and all. I don't know what life it is we lead with this government.

---

88   Forced labor.
89   To São Tomé.
90   In the hospital this procedure is carried out for the transplant of organs.

MPM: *You voted for the "Better Future"?*[91]

MFZ: The "Better Future" is that: cheat others. The "Better Future," because formerly it was all reed huts here.[92] The whites didn't allow free construction. Now Frelimo has entered, everything has changed—they say it is a "Better Future," but it is just the same: there is reed, but no way of using it. The confusion of bureaucracy is the same.

MPM: *If it's all the same, then one of these days we'll have* xibalo *back.*

MFZ: We already did—Operation Production was *xibalo*. It seems we voted for it. The question of the chiefs is another thing not well done. The chief knows his own cults. He is a chief, a son of the land. The chiefs worked for the colonials, it's true; but when independence came, they shouldn't have taken away the chiefs. They should have explained to them a new way of working with our new government. But they took away the chiefs, the ones who played *timhamba*[93] to cause rain, to promote well-being, so the people wouldn't worry them. They removed those chiefs only to put in the Grupo Dinamizador;[94] they brought a person from Inhambane to be head of this neighborhood without him knowing the local customs here. What is he going to know about us *machangane?* You can't. . .

MPM: *National unity is needed.*

MFZ: Yes, it's national unity, but in the meantime he doesn't know anything about the people from here. National unity is being negated [*laughs*]—there is no national unity in it. He doesn't know the deceased from here, doesn't know what is what. Ah, no, it cannot work like that. They have to go back to appointing chiefs.

MPM: *Isn't it better for the people in each village to choose who should be chief?*

MFZ: The chief is not supposed to be chosen by the people. There is the family of the chief who died: the son or nephew, it should be—if not, then they can put another. Frelimo likes "national unity," but this doesn't fulfill "national unity"—that cannot be if our rules are not fulfilled.

CJT: You know, now is the time for Frelimo to go about getting votes. But in the period it didn't respect tradition, what was the party thinking? Did it think the *nyànga* wasn't a person? Why can't a pair of *tinyànga* go to parliament to help solve some of the problems? They only choose among themselves. But if they had only one *nyànga* from Gaza, one from somewhere else, they could help overcome problems—that struggle in the parliament. There is much disagreement; I have seen it on the television. It would be good to have people to study the conflict to

---

91 The slogan of the Frelimo party in the last election.
92 The suburbs of the city, nowadays called areas of temporary construction.
93 Acts of communication and communion with the dead.
94 Dynamizing groups.

find a way out—it could reduce the confrontation; but they don't see this. If I were well set up to go to parliament, and had explained my work and had the aid of the spirits, I could discover the protagonist of the conflict, and he could be sent away. And he would also stop using harmful medicines to provoke confrontation in parliament and obstruct solutions.

MPM: *You wouldn't be included in the discussions? You would be counselors? Or even deputies?*

CJT: We couldn't be counselors; our work would be to calm confrontation between deputies. Isn't what they say that all are Mozambicans, that all are equal under the law?

MPM: *Have you already tried to speak with the leaders of the government, of the parties?*

CJT: We have no way to go and speak with them directly. We have made requests for an appointment, a meeting, but they always refuse. We *tinyàngà* only want to give advice.

To reflect on Voices *has not been easy. To speak of traditional medicine necessitates explanations of systems of knowledge that in the end are linked to profoundly human dilemmas, as well as to the emotions that these bring with them—illnesses, the loss of loved ones, social conflicts, jealousies, desperation, and frustrations. In the words of Zimba and Tamele, references to the world of the ancestors are part of the permanent dialogue about knowledges, about the reason for their being, bypassing the trap of the modern scientific world. Spirits and witchcraft are categories that refer to the existence of profound crises in the lives of each of us—and they are also a theme about the nature of our lives.*

There is no doubt that interviews not only contain the potential to present other worldviews, but that they also constitute expressions of struggle and of political memory, allowing areas to become visible that until now have been obscured by the hegemonic force of the politics of knowledge-production. In this project, where sometimes the same facts have been narrated differently in the distinct voices of Zimba and Tamele, the boundaries between the seen and the unseen, between fact and fiction, between memory and the events that are dissolved and lost—this project introduces the human into the domain of the social sciences, with the defects and desires, the jealousies and traumas of each and every one, proving that the representation of facts is itself the object of contestation as an event. The gathering and preservation of human memory narrated by the voices in this text do not in any way defend the permanence of a unique vision of the world; on the contrary, the voices are a challenge and an alternative route to the power instituted by scientific history. The opinions expressed in the interview anticipate a constant negotiation between various normative spaces, indicative of a permanent reflexivity concerning the attitudes and goals of decisionmaking, as well as revealing the great inequalities of power in the social fabric of Mozambique.

I listened to the tape recordings countless times, ending always at a crossroads in relation to the text produced from the interviews, especially with regard to the question of self-reflection. It is a matter that obliges one to engage intimately with everyone who lived through independence and the Mozambican Revolution, and which obliges us to go back in time and almost to offer a mea culpa. In the end, like so many others, I also went shouting in the street, at the rallies: "Down with obscurantism!" We were young, the transformations in our identities were vertiginous, it seemed that we bore the world within us and that everything was possible. Now I look back and ask myself how we could have been so insensitive to all those impartiality problems, I would almost say of martial law, that the spirit of militancy inculcated in many of us. It was the time of "either you're with us or against us," and, clearly, I was in favor of this. Who would not want to play a part in the first battle of the "new man"?

The rebellion arose much later, when the cultures entered into contact and conflict: other people, other revolutionary situations, all of them with problems. In the end, things no longer seemed so easy. Was it for that that we took the country? The contact with the USSR was painful, and from it arose my first great crisis of identity with the Party. Indeed, in the end, to belong to the Party was, in those days, to be Mozambican, believing it to be a national project.

But soon the disenchantments began to accumulate, and the exit routes were each time poorer. The greatest shock came when the mulatos and whites were questioned during that famous constitutional revision following the death of Samora, in which suddenly the nation seemed eternal, secured only in the roots that tied people to the blood of the land, "to my ancestors, all of whom were born here." For a few moments I thought that my place (as a mulata) was not there—another identity crisis—but was there, and so I moved again; I fled rapidly to a doctorate that diverted me from questions of power, from the cultural conflicts that were each time greater.

In the middle of all this, family matters. My links to the Revolution (and I believe that the same thing occurred to many of us) caused my family's elders to become weary with us, because we had left our traditions. Things had ceased to be how they used to be, and we truly felt ourselves to be lost. Whenever I returned to Mozambique I approached my elders; it was my link to my country, my attempt at a profound connection to the land that I loved so much and about which each time I knew and perceived less. Struggles over power, and reconciliations, everything was mixed up together while detours in the direction of capitalism helped nothing.

I confess that it was during this time that I began to frequent these healers, at the beginning as a joke, and later because they helped me to understand myself. They showed me that I was human and that, in the end, it was there, in the simplicity of unhurried conversations, that we all understood each other. Everybody had problems, but it was the profound feeling of help and support, of friendship, that was fundamental. At a time when my parents had left the country, this became crucial for me. But I made these trips, as I mentioned to Mama Carolina, clandestinely. Only now, looking at these tinyàngà *as an "object of study," do I for the first time have the courage to leave my materialism behind and confess where I used to go (always with the excuse of doing fieldwork). I found friends, strong ones, in people who showed me a total dedication that I had never thought it possible to have. They are the ones who deserve to have their voices here; I was just the one who offered a push. In the end, this is my act of redemption. My mea culpa.*

What Zimba and Carolina speak about is impossible to transcribe—especially the acts, the forms of treatment and of social inclusion. It was with them and through them that, many times, I gained new confidence in myself during difficult periods of my life. And I forgot who I was—I left behind my titles and duties, and became Paula: she who knew how to write grant applications well and who helped AMETRAMO deal with the necessary bureaucracy. Several times I became furious during various meetings with AMETRAMO—furious at a government that had become too Western, too insensitive to its "real country," to its people, its histories, its land. A government that was deaf to the anxieties of its people, treating them like raw material; treating them, like someone who possesses data, as objects of study, but not as citizen-subjects. I do not agree with all of the views expressed here, but much of what is said in the interviews I feel as well. In the end, Mama Carolina has more courage than I do in exposing what she thinks publicly. I did not set out to conduct an interview of someone totally unknown—I feel that I have almost committed an act of betrayal, and that there are areas that will always be barred from view. I am unable to write about them because I am part of that truth, that history. Another escape that I attempted was that of avoiding exoticizing these "others," of whom I am also a part. How many times did I go to the "masses," to the ceremonies? How many times did I ask that the "stones be beaten" in order to understand problems that were afflicting me? I never wanted this to be known, but I am inside of the mirror, not the one gazing into it. For this, my apologies—but I couldn't manage to reflect in any other way.

10

Maincha Pitara

Women's rights activist, founder of a pioneering community court dedicated to disputes involving women.

Interviewed by João Trindade and Maria José Arthur

"I'm not talking about other things, but about social problems, about widows, that sort of thing. I don't know what, for me, I don't know how it is—I don't know why, but I'm ready for that, I really am . . ."

Maincha Pitara

In recent decades, the sociology of law has leveled criticisms at the legal-political paradigm of liberalism, attacking in particular the notion that our lives are commanded or conditioned by a hierarchically organized and uniform normative legal system that depends exclusively upon the power of the state. Recent studies carried out in Mozambique[1] have confirmed these criticisms on a national level.

Mozambican society is characterized by an enormous wealth and complexity in matters of law and justice systems. This is exuberantly demonstrated by the existence and operation, as well as by the interpenetration and reciprocal influence, of community courts, traditional authorities, and other non-state mechanisms for conflict resolution, to which the vast majority of citizens resort for the resolution of individual and collective conflicts.

In this category we can include the Woman's Legal Office, located in Pemba, in the northern province of Cabo Delgado, an OMM initiative,[2] which receives modest financial support from an Australian NGO. It first began by providing assistance and counseling to the victims of domestic violence, but rapidly broadened its sphere of intervention until it became what it is today—a recognized and sought-after agency for the resolution of conflicts, specializing in family relations and related matters, as well as home economics.

---

1 See the research study carried out in partnership by the Centre for African Studies of the Eduardo Mondlane University and the Centre for Social Studies of the School of Economics, University of Coimbra, between 1997 and 2000, whose report was subsequently published as a book: B. de Sousa Santos and J. C. Trindade (eds), *Conflito e Transformação Social: Uma Paisagem das Justiças em Moçambique*, Porto: Afrontamento, 2 vols, 2003.

2 Organization of Mozambican Women (OMM). Set up in 1973 in Tunduru (Tanzania), during the struggle for national liberation, as part of the global structure of the Liberation Front of Mozambique (Frelimo), its main goal was to ensure the mobilization and integration of women in the collective war effort, particularly in the liberated zones. After independence, with the exception of a short period as an independent association (1990–96), it became a women's mass organization of the Frelimo Party, responsible for integrating women into the political, economic, social, and cultural life of the country.

A simple statistical comparison of the cases of this nature brought by parties to the Office and to the Law Court of the Province[3] would reveal the population's preference for the former. This preference may be explained first and foremost by a greater cultural proximity to the type of reasoning and argumentation used by the office in constructing its deliberations.[4] However, the high costs involved in bringing legal proceedings, the lack of efficient mechanisms of legal aid, and other factors conditioning the access to justice by the most disadvantaged groups of the population also play a part.

"Mama"[5] Maincha Pitara, a highly respected local figure, has been involved in the coordination of the Woman's Legal Office since it was founded. Born in Pemba in 1949 to a poor rural family, Maincha was the second of five children. Her childhood was similar to that of most girls from this social background. She did not go to school, and began working early; at the age of ten she was already a macaiaia[6] in the home of an employee of the colonial administration. She remained there until she was sixteen, when she went back to her parents' home to undergo the rites of female initiation.[7] She married for the first time at nineteen, but separated shortly afterwards, because her husband wanted to take her to his home province of Inhambane and her family did not consent to it.[8] She was the queen of tufu,[9] helped her parents to farm, and got married again shortly after the end of the colonial war. When Frelimo came to power, during the transition to independence (1974–75), she

---

3 The present judiciary organization of Mozambique, established by Law No. 10/92, of May 6th, involves three hierarchical levels of courts: first and second class district courts, provincial courts, and the Supreme Court.

4 Boaventura de Sousa Santos calls this type of reasoning and argumentation topical-rhetorical, as opposed to the apodictic reasoning/knowledge characteristic of the formal justice produced by the courts. Unlike syllogistic deduction from general normative utterances, it develops out of generally accepted opinions or points of view, based on what is reasonable within the concrete circumstantial context of the problem to be resolved. See B. de Sousa Santos, *O Discurso e o Poder: Ensaio sobre a Sociologia da Retórica Jurídica*, Porto Alegre: Sérgio António Fabris Editor, 1988, pp. 6–7.

5 This expression is very common in Mozambique to denote a woman who deserves special respect and consideration, either because of her age or because of her specific social role.

6 This was a term used in the colonial period to denote a domestic servant who looked after the colonists' children.

7 When they reach puberty, boys and girls in rural African societies generally undergo rites specific to this phase of growth. After the first menstruation (between fifteen and sixteen years of age), girls are taken into the forest, where they receive instructions and advice about how to behave in society before their elders and their future husband. See X. Andrade, *Levantamento e anotação bibliográfica sobre a construção da sexualidade entre adolescentes e jovens*, Maputo: CEA-UEM, 2002.

8 In the northern coastal region of Mozambique, where the matrilineal system of kinship is predominant, the husband is received into the wife's family. This contrasts with what happens in the patrilineal system (predominant in the south, particularly in Inhambane), in which the wife enters the husband's family.

9 A traditional dance from the coastal region of northern Mozambique, which displays a strong Islamic influence.

became a member of OMM, elected in the neighborhood where she still lives today (Bairro Eduardo Mondlane). In 1978 she became secretary of that organization in the city of Pemba, a post she held until 1986. In 1979 she attended an adult literacy course in Nampula,[10] *which lasted for six months. She has three children, born in 1980, 1985, and 1991. She was a member of the former Provincial Assembly of Cabo Delgado, is an elected (lay) magistrate of the Provincial Court, and a member of the National Coordinating Committee of the OMM. In the local elections of November 19th, 2003, she was elected representative to the Municipal Assembly of the city of Pemba, on the Frelimo party ticket.*

Because of the distance between the cities of Maputo and Pemba (around 2,500 km) and the interviewer's professional commitments, the interview had to be divided into two sessions, five months apart; they involved a total of around ten hours of conversation.[11] *The dialogue was greatly facilitated by the mutual respect and trust between interviewee and interviewer, which had already been established in previous contacts. In order to ensure maximum rigor and fidelity in the transcription of the conversation, we have sought to preserve as far as possible Maincha's way of expressing herself in Portuguese, including the formulas and expressions she used and the numerous interferences from her mother tongue, Macua. As the conversation sometimes lingered on matters that were merely circumstantial and unrelated to the central topic of the interview, some cuts have been made.*

João Carlos Trindade: *Mama Maincha, the first thing that I'd like you to talk about is your life—when and where you were born, who your parents were, your life as a child. . .*

Maincha Pitara: Talk everything about my life, right? Well, I was born right here in Pemba. My late mother, like my father, said that I was born in the hospital, right here in the capital, Pemba, on February 20th, 1949. My parents had five children. It's a pity, but my dad had a son with a different mother. My dad had six children. Then one died, so we are four. The oldest is my sis. She's in good health, even today. As for me, since I was a child, I was a *macaiaia*—from ten until I was sixteen.

JCT: *And you didn't go to school?*

MP: Ah, no, nothing like that. It was only through literacy and adult education classes.

JCT: *That was after independence?*

---

10   Capital of the province with the same name and the main city in the north of Mozambique.

11   On my second trip to Pemba, I benefited from the valuable collaboration of Maria José Arthur, a member of the project's research team, who helped me to outline and conduct the interview. The comments and suggestions offered by Teresa Cruz e Silva, coordinator of the project in Mozambique, and Paula Meneses, another team member, were also very important. I therefore extend to them all my acknowledgements and gratitude.

MP: Yes, after independence I stayed in Maputo for three months, at school, in the campsite; then, after I left, in '79, I went to school over in Nampula too for six months of training. Then, after six months, when I left, I started here in Pemba at the literacy and adult education classes at night.

JCT: *You're a Muslim, aren't you?*

MP: Yes, yes, I'm Muslim.

JCT: *Didn't you go to Madrassa school?*

MP: Madrassa school—no, no, I didn't go to that. Only when I got married, I went there with my husband who was at that school.

JCT: *So, you were saying that you worked as a macaiaia until you were sixteen. And then what happened?*

MP: Then I went back to my parents' and when I arrived—at that time I was a virgin; they did an initiation ceremony for me. And when I was nineteen I married a man from Inhambane. I had a child, a boy; but it died, I lost it. Then my husband was called back to his province, his parents called him. In those days, when he said he wanted to take me to Inhambane—in those days, you couldn't just go around like that; people were afraid to go to other provinces, it wasn't easy at that time, so I ended up not going. My parents said it wasn't worth it, for if they died, I wouldn't be around, things like that. So I listened to what my parents were saying, and I stayed. So at that time I helped my parents with the land. I was a simple peasant girl—I worked in the *machamba*[12]— and when the people started dancing that dance, *tufo*, I was the queen, I was the queen of *tufo* in this neighborhood. Then I got married again, and a child was born—a boy—but I lost that child again. Then, when Frelimo appeared, at the time of the Transitional Government,[13] before independence, I was chosen by the people of this neighborhood, Bairro Eduardo Mondlane, Wimbe, I was chosen for the OMM. Until national independence, I was head of the OMM. In '78 I was chosen to be the city secretary. I was also elected in '87 as magistrate of this province; I was also elected provincial representative of this province of Cabo Delgado. I worked as secretary of the OMM of the city of Pemba; I worked as elected magistrate in the court of the province of Cabo Delgado, and I was a provincial representative. In '78 too, I was taken to Maputo, to do the literacy course, as I said before. I stayed there three months, and when I got back, barely one month later, the nation called me,[14] so I

---

12 Agricultural property, cultivated land.

13 The Transitional Government, which developed out of the General Peace Agreement that Portugal and Frelimo celebrated in Lusaka (Zambia) on September 7th, 1974, ruled the country until the proclamation of independence on June 25th, 1975.

14 The "nation" here refers to the central power structures. It is very common in

went abroad—I went to Italy. I stayed two weeks in Italy, then I came back. When I got back from Italy, I was called again to Maputo, to do another six-month literacy and adult education course over in Nampula. In Nampula I stayed another six months away from my husband—that was in '79. Then, in '80, '81, a child was born, my daughter. In '85 another child was born—all this when I was secretary of the OMM of the city.

JCT: *What year did you stop being city secretary?*

MP: In '86.

JCT: *Why did you give it up? Were you tired of it?*

MP: No, not at all. It was because when it was said that the provincial secretary of the OMM should be. . . the city of Pemba is small, it should only have a provincial secretary, not a city secretary and a provincial one. And so they kept only the provincial secretary. So I stayed there just to assist—I didn't have a job, but always collaborated with the OMM. Then, at the First Congress, I was elected as a member of the National Coordinating Committee of the OMM, as always happens with collaborations.

JCT: *What year was that?*

MP: That was in '96. When Paulina[15] was elected, that same day I was elected.

JCT: *And are you still part of that Coordinating Committee?*

MP: Yes. Very much so. When I stopped being secretary of the OMM of the city, I kept collaborating with the OMM, and I stayed like that, as a collaborator, and it was then that some people turned up here—a lady from Australia, called Dona Ana. When she arrived, she asked for a woman advisor for the Legal Office: "We need a woman who can help other women, solve problems, social problems, I don't know what. . ." So the OMM, together with some other people and the lady too, who already knew me—she used to stay here at the beach of Wimbe with people that she knew—she went to find out and the OMM said, "She has no work; she was the secretary, but now she comes here to collaborate with us. But she doesn't have a permanent job, so she should be the advisor—she's a person we know; we know how she behaves and everything." Then the lady also said, "I know her. We play a lot on the beach—she has actually helped me with my work, giving lectures, talking to the people and things; and so, if we elect her for this job, she'll manage it all right." So that was when I was elected, the governor approved—it was Governor Simbine at the time; the court also approved, as I had also had experience in the provincial court. I was chosen to work in the Legal

---

Mozambican political jargon to say "I was called to the nation" or "We received a delegation from the nation."

15   She refers to Paulina Mateus, the present secretary-general of the OMM.

Office. That was in '92. So I did a MULEIDE[16] course, and then we started working, until now.

JCT: *We'll talk about the Legal Office in just a minute. Could you go on telling us about your family? So you have two daughters, one born in '81, and the other in '85?*

MP: I've got three. In '91 I also had a child, the last one.

JCT: *And do you have any grandchildren?*

MP: That daughter that was born in '81 has already got two children. She got married very young.

JCT: *And your husband, where does he work?*

MP: He's a carpenter for the municipal council.

JCT: *And what's his name?*

MP: Abudo Sumail.

JCT: *Don't you use his name? Pitara is your father's name, right?*

MP: Yes. He is Abudo Sumail and I am MP, my father's name.

JCT: *And when did people start to call you "Mama Maincha"?*

MP: I, since my [*laughs*]. To tell the truth, it was already used at home, by my family. I've always been respected in my family, since my childhood. So, because of this work that I do, it became the habit to call me "Mama." Everybody calls me "Mama, Mama," and Maincha is my name.

JCT: *Fine. Let's go back. I've seen that, when independence came, you were working, you were very active.*

MP: Yes, I was working, I was very active. . .

JCT: *And your husband too?*

MP: My husband is not doing this kind of work—but he supports my work a lot; he hasn't any problems with it, with the things I do all the time. My husband doesn't have a problem with that. I can work freely, as I want. I can stay away from him—he doesn't have a problem with that. Sometimes I'm away from my husband for six months, but when I get back, it's all right, he doesn't have a problem. He stays and looks after the children—my children are even more used to their father, because he is always with them. It's me who is always moving about a lot compared to my husband.

JCT: *But husbands are not like that normally. . .*

MP: No, they're not, you're right. I've been lucky to have this husband. Lucky—everybody says that. To tell the truth, I could spend my whole time out on missions without meeting up there at home, without being

---

16 Women, Law and Development—a non-governmental organization set up in 1992, whose main objectives are to improve the social status of women, to contribute to the elimination of inequality in the access to resources and power, and to promote debate about the legal situation of women in Mozambican society, petitioning the competent authorities for the repeal of laws that discriminate against women.

there, and that wouldn't be a problem. Not at all. A person might need to talk to me, maybe at night, and I'd go and talk in the sitting room with that person, and my husband doesn't. . . I have no problems at all, to tell the truth.

JCT: *Is he from right here, from this neighborhood?*

MP: Yes, he's from here, from Nhanimbe. Nearby, just a short distance away, up there. His mother has a family, a sister, a brother, I don't know what. He's a man that seems like he's not from here, but his parents and my parents are neighbors.

JCT: *Have your families known each other for a long time?*

MP: Yes, they have, and the families get along fine; there's no problem.

JCT: *Is he much older than you?*

MP: Maybe—he's fifty-seven and I'm fifty.

JCT: *So you met and got married still during the colonial period?*

MP: Yes, yes.

JCT: *And then, when independence came, were your parents still alive?*

MP: No, it hadn't come yet. That was before independence, in the colonial time.

JCT: *Both of them died before?*

MP: Yes, they did.

JCT: *But had Frelimo appeared by then?*

MP: Yes. My father, he died in an accident. A car ran him over; he was on the road. My mother died before. She was the first. She left a child that was still breastfeeding, so I raised that child.

JCT: *Were you the eldest?*

MP: Although I had an older sister, I was the one that had the patience to raise the baby, and so I ended up doing it.

JCT: *What did you father do?*

MP: My father was. . . He worked on the boats; I don't know what it's called. He was a worker that when a boat came in. . .

JCT: *Stevedore?*

MP: Yes, that's it.

JCT: *Did he ever sail?*

MP: No, he stayed at the port.

JCT: *What about your mother?*

MP: My mother was a peasant.

JCT: *You said you had five brothers and sisters, didn't you?*

MP: We were five altogether. It's a pity—one died. She also left a baby with me, my niece.

JCT: *So, you were three sisters and two brothers?*

MP: No, we were four women and one man. We lost a lady, so now we're three women and one man—the man's alive.

JCT: *And do they all live here, or have some of them gone off to other parts of the country?*

MP: No, they all live here.

JCT: *And the house where you live, was this the family house or was it built by you and your husband?*

MP: It was built by me and my husband.

JCT: *Together?*

MP: Yes, yes.

JCT: *But the land there, was that your family's?*

MP: The land over there was the family's. We settled among relatives, but we moved to another place because that was at the time of the communal village. So we moved and went to a place like this.

JCT: *Ah, you were farther away. So those streets that we can see in the neighborhood, that was the communal village, the communal village project. Does it have a school too? And a health center?*

MP: Yes, yes. We have a school, a health center.

JCT: *Then you got a drinking fountain. Is it working?*

MP: Yes, it is.

JCT: *Did you have land for farming[17] here?*

MP: There's land for *machamba* up there, near the cashew trees. There are people who have *machambas* with only beans and manioc.

JCT: *To sell, or just for the family?*

MP: To eat. Then, when someone wants to make a bigger *machamba*, he goes out to the green zone, at Mieze, some way from here. I've actually got a *machamba* there.

JCT: *Is it the family's machamba? Does it belong to the whole family?*

MP: Yes, yes.

JCT: *And do you still cultivate it?*

MP: Yes, we're still cultivating it.

JCT: *And is it enough for you all to live on? Part of your food must come from there. . . ?*

MP: Yes, we get the *chapa*[18] to go there, to Mieze.

JCT: *And does it still give manioc, beans. . . ?*

MP: It still does. Bigger manioc, even, because that's the area where it is produced.

JCT: *Do you go there too?*

MP: Yes, on weekends.

JCT: *How do you find the time?*

MP: I have a young man permanently in my *machamba*.

---

17   *Machamba.*
18   Name given throughout the country to the system of collective passenger transport managed by private entities.

JCT: *Is he a relative?*

MP: No, he's just a young man that I pay and give something to.

JCT: *Does he live there and take care of. . . ?*

MP: Yes, yes, and he has his wife there too.

JCT: *Those things that you get out of the* machamba, *are they just for you, or do you have enough to sell?*

MP: It's just to eat—we don't sell it.

JCT: *And doesn't your family do a bit of trading? Over in Maputo everyone sells something, a little bit. Is it not like that here?*

MP: No, only at the market. Here there are also ladies who sell things at the market—that have things to sell at the market. They also sell vegetables, those things that they can get out of the *machambas*; they also sell things from the *machamba*. They usually make cakes, those women, and also bread. They get their children to sell them, or the women themselves will sell cakes, bread, and anything else they can.

JCT: *But you in your family—you yourself don't have the time, do you? To increase your income?*

MP: Oh no, I haven't the time; we are like this: I manage to get a little money with this or that, but we are many. Being in a family is a serious thing. You have to help. I also have to help because there were people that helped me at the time when I wasn't working, when I had nothing, nothing, nothing. My relatives helped me a lot until the time when I could get by.

JCT: *In your house, with your family, what language do you speak?*

MP: We speak Macua.[19]

JCT: *Don't you speak Ki-mwane?*[20]

MP: No, we all know Ki-mwane, but out mother tongue is Macua.

JCT: *A while ago you said that you were the "queen of* tufo*" in your neighborhood. Could you explain what that means?*

MP: I was a dancer—I led the group of dancers.

JCT: *And does that make one famous in the neighborhood?*

MP: Yes, it does.

JCT: *And do the women that do that find it easier to marry, because they're known?*

MP: They're very well known. I was the leader of them all.

JCT: *And was that how your husband noticed you and liked you?*

MP: He noticed me, and said that he had to have that woman [*laughs*].

JCT: *And your husband's family, do they mind the fact that you work in the Legal Office and spend a lot of time away from home?*

---

19   The most widely spoken language in Mozambique, with around 5 million speakers in the provinces of Nampula, Cabo Delgado, Niassa, and Zambézia.

20   Language spoken in the coastal strip of the province of Cabo Delgado, and predominantly in Pemba and on the island of Ibo.

MP: They don't mind. I have my sisters-in-law who are good friends of mine. They think it's fine.

JCT: *It's just that in the south, for example, the husband's family often orders the wife around more than the husband himself does; and even when he doesn't mind, if the family says no. . .*

MP: Here it's different. Only your husband can tell you what to do—only him, not his family. If you want to help, you do it—you go to your mother-in-law's, you may take a barrel to carry water. . . in your own way, of your own free will. But they've got no right to make you, to tell you what you should do. No, it's very different, a bit different.

JCT: *And your family, did they also get involved in the OMM, DGs[21] and things like that?*

MP: No, no. None of my relatives were involved with the OMM or anything.

JCT: *Not even your siblings? Your brother didn't join the DG?*

MP: Oh, my brother had joined the Dynamizing Group, or something. But soon after, he didn't get to. . . Afterwards he left.

JCT: *But your family, what did they think about you being so active? Did they think it was OK or did they tell you not to waste your time?*

MP: No. At that time, relatives. . . that's why I could do so much: I didn't go around with my children in my arms. I left my children at home. My sister did everything for my children. People that knew me knew that I had a baby, but I always went around without my child.

JCT: *So family support was important?*

MP: I got a lot of support from my family, I really did. I didn't have to carry my child around with me, take it to work, never. My children always stayed with relatives at home. Until now, no child of mine has had to trail around after me—I couldn't understand that thing about the child following around, crying, calling for its mother not to leave it; with me it was not like that. When I left home, my children were fine, just said bye-bye, no problem. They got more used to their aunties.

JCT: *And in your family, after the deaths of your father and mother, who became head of the family? When there is a problem? How is it sorted out? Who makes the decisions?*

MP: To tell the truth, it was me that took charge of the family to a huge extent, even though I'm a woman. Took charge really, I can't say. . . Any conversation, whatever it is about, my relatives come to me. I am the one who decides, they sit in my house, they plan it there, when it's something

---

21 Dynamizing Groups—grassroots political organs set up by Frelimo in the period of transition to independence, with the purpose of mobilizing the masses for the three great tasks of the moment: consolidating national *unity*, increasing productivity in *work*, and *vigilance* in relation to the enemies of the revolution.

they want to do, then they come to me. I have uncles and aunts, even they don't talk about anything without me being there. That's why I even have my hut—I have my house in the Cariacó neighborhood, a neighborhood right here in the center [*indicates the direction with a gesture*]. When Dona Ana was here, I told her that my problem was always having to walk to work, so she said, "I will help you at least to buy a place, a hut where you can live, cut the distance from Wimbe to there." So she bought me a piece of land and I built my house, and I'm building another up ahead, but when I think of moving there, sometimes I feel sad. Right now, while I'm still alive, I think it's a big pity to be away from my family—that's why I'm still here.

JCT: *You mean, you sometimes stay there when you have a problem? When you finish work you sleep there, when it's late?*

MP: Yes, yes—when I see that I'm late, and I have no transport, I can sleep there in my own house.

JCT: *And your family, do they understand what's happened when you don't turn up?*

MP: Yes, they know I'm there. So I can't just leave here—a pity, really.

JCT: *Also because it was here, in your neighborhood, that you began working at the OMM. . . ?*

MP: Yes, yes.

JCT: *And those people, I imagine you know them all?*

MP: I know them, I've worked there a lot, even the people. . . I've done a lot for the people, at least giving them guidance—when they want to dig a well, for instance, and we got a health center. I was the one that got the people going to clean, build, so that we'd have a health center here, as the city is a long way away; at least those things. It's a bit of a headache, but at least we sorted it out here. I'm the sort of person that will make an effort to talk to people, to talk with the folk—I've done that a lot. Now, it's not only my relatives, but also the whole population; if I abandon them and go somewhere else, they won't like it.

JCT: *But what is the organizational structure in your neighborhood now? Do you have a secretary? Do you have someone responsible from the OMM in your neighborhood?*

MP: Yes, yes, we do. When I was secretary here, and then was transferred to the city, they elected one, but as an associate. So, when there's something—when they want to do something, or receive visitors, anything—they also ask me for help.

JCT: *You mean, the neighborhood structure still depends on you for advice?*

MP: Yes, yes, it does, yes. As I'm living right here, they still depend on me—they still ask me things, want me to collaborate when they're planning something, they call me.

JCT: *What does the OMM do now in the neighborhood? What is its role?*

MP: Now the OMM doesn't do as much work as I did. Now it's only. . . but at that time there was work: a person presented the work they were doing as OMM work—they presented it; but now it's only like that a bit.

JCT: *And the young people—your daughters, are they happy with life? I mean, do they get on all right with their husbands?*

MP: Actually, the other one isn't married yet—she's still studying. She's fifteen. She was born in '85—she's at school. She's been saying she doesn't want to get married now. I don't know—she's more involved in her studies.

JCT: *What do you want for your daughters?*

MP: I want that—I want them to study. At least study, know things—they are going to take over their mother's work. I want my daughters to study. Many of those that are interested in studying, who are not yet busy with children, and things like that, I want them to study. And the youngest too.

JCT: *How old is the youngest?*

MP: The youngest is ten.

JCT: *And the one that is studying, is she in secondary or primary school?*

MP: She's in the seventh grade.

JCT: *And your eldest daughter, did she not study? Didn't she want to study?*

MP: She wants to, yes, but she's got children. She's also away—she's in her husband's house. She's saying that if she were like me, she'd have someone to look after the children, and she'd go to school, yes.

JCT: *So she wants to study?*

MP: She wants to, but. . . I'm a busy person; even if I want to help with the children, I haven't the time. I haven't the time, but she really wants to study—she just doesn't have time. Studying is very important.

JCT: *Is she the only one that's a little way away, that doesn't live in the neighborhood?*

MP: She's away, yes.

JCT: *I'd like you to talk a bit about your work, your activism at the time of independence. Had you heard of Frelimo before? How did you get those new ideas? How did you start to work?*

MP: Yes, at that time, before independence, I began to work at Frelimo, because when Frelimo arrived, at the beginning, we couldn't just join. They said they were looking for a person to be responsible in the community—to be responsible,[22] to be a part of the OMM, to be secretary. So that meant all the people sitting down and choosing who it would be. It was then that I was elected—I was the person chosen. In the community, each family assembled in four places. They said, "You should choose the

---

22   In Mozambican political vocabulary, the term *responsible* is today generalized as a synonym for "leader," at the level of political parties or the state.

name of the person to be responsible at the OMM." So, of those four groups, one group chose another lady, and three groups chose the name of Maincha. So, as there were three groups, they said it would be me. That was when I was chosen as secretary of the neighborhood.

JCT: *So there was another candidate besides you, Mama Maincha? How did you get nominated? Who was it that suggested your names to be candidates?*

MP: At that time, the men's organizations were called. . . So, they were called to go and speak with the directors—they were given the task of coming to the community and speaking to the people about choosing a person.

JCT: *So those people suggested names—is that right?*

MP: So, when those people in charge came, they told the people, "You are going to sit in the church—these churches here—you are going to sit down, you too, to choose the name of the person you need to be responsible." So, we got together, they came to tell us that each group should see the person they needed. So that group was all my family there—from my clan to tell the truth; they chose my name, the other clans also chose my name. So, as someone has to be generally responsible here in the neighborhood, then it should be so-and-so.

JCT: *And the other candidate, the one that was chosen by one of the four groups, did she continue to work in the OMM or did she quit?*

MP: Then, at the time that I am talking about, it was before the OMM, right at the beginning. It was set up after that.

JCT: *And that men's organization, the one that was called to receive the task, what organization was that?*

MP: They still exist, those organizations, some people don't work there now—that thing of changes; I don't know, let's put that. . . Dynamizing Groups.

JCT: *Was it them that were called?*

MP: Yes, it was them. So it was at the time when people were choosing what the structures were going to be. It was those groups, when things started, before independence. It was at that time that I was chosen. So, the other things I did, working in the court, being secretary of the city, that was because I was very active. So I was chosen there by the directors, to see who works in each neighborhood, who does I don't know what. . .

JCT: *Were you ever a party member?*

MP: At that time.

JCT: *Were you a member when the Frelimo party was structured?*

MP: When I was chosen at that time, I was a member.

JCT: *Going back to your election as secretary of the neighborhood, how did the people react?*

MP: The people said, "Although. . ."—because at that time I was young—
". . . although she's young, she's a person that respects people. Maincha
knows how to respect people; she knows how to get on with adults,
including young ones like her, so we need her." And at that time people
danced here with pleasure [*laughs*]—and I was there, sitting in the middle.
But with real pleasure! I actually cried at that moment, because I didn't
know what would be in store for me—because at that time, when we
heard "You will wear trousers," things like that; "Go into the woods"—
that thing of saying "You will go into the woods" made us uncertain,
because those who had fought knew what had happened; but for us that
stayed, all that was new: "You will leave your home. . ." I don't know
what—it made me feel uncertain about what would happen ahead.

JCT: *Did people say these things to make you afraid?*

MP: Yes—but then, all right, groups from organizations came and said,
"Mama Maincha, don't you cry; we've registered your name because the
population chose you. We're not going to hurt you." I said, "All right."
So we stayed, had meetings and whatnot, and then later I got used to
that work. So, before our national independence, it was in the district
of Mueda, in a place called Diaca, that we had the first meeting of many
people like us. We stayed there ten days, and when I returned the people
said, "Let's have a party." So they had a party for me—that thing of
being happy and all that for me. So, they had a party, they cooked food,
others danced, things like that. Later, I was with the OMM, and then
they transferred me to here. They said, "Now we will transfer you to the
city—the city then, she has to do"; because any work that I was given, I
did it properly. So those groups, like this old man that was here—people
saw that I was doing work in the interests of the majority. So, when I
went to do the course in Maputo, I stayed ninety days there. At the time
it was Graça Machel, who was Minister of Education, that did the closing speech. To each person, she asked, "What did you see during the
course?" So, when I also spoke, I said that the course was something very
important—I said what I saw during the course. So, she asked my name,
made a note of it, and soon, when I arrived here I was called right away
before the week finished, to go abroad—to Italy, Rome, where I stayed.
And that's how I started to work.

JCT: *But when was the first time you understood what the OMM was all about—
the discourse against the exploitation of women, the new ideas brought by the
revolution?*

MP: Yes, at the time when people said that the woman also had the right
to speak in public [*laughs*]. Because at that time the late Samora said,
"Women also have the right to speak in public, while before women
weren't anything," and things like that: "Who doesn't support women?

I am the first person to support women." So people, the men, said, "So do I! So do I!" [*laughs*] As the president himself was saying, "I support women," the men also had to [*laughs*]—even those that didn't want to, they got up too [*laughs*].

JCT: *Sometimes, some of them got up just because they were ashamed not to.*

MP: Yes, yes, they were ashamed. I saw this when we were at a conference in '84—before [Samora Machel] died, because during that time he didn't come here again: "Who doesn't support women? Who? I support them—I am the first, I support women; I give women respect. Who else?" So all the men there at the conference got up too. [*laughs*] It was at that conference that they said that women should also work in the police, that they should work in the court, to see if it would help resolve things, see the woman question, too. Because sometimes a woman can go to court, she might be right. I don't know. But as there is no figure of a woman there too, to defend the woman's side a bit. . . That's why it's important that women should be magistrates, work in the police, also to see other things. At that conference[23] we talked about a lot of things.

JCT: *What sort of reaction did you feel from the people, the men and the women, to that speech?*

MP: Some didn't accept it well—they didn't agree that the woman also has this and that; they didn't accept those words very well. They were looking at it from a distance. Now it's different, they are beginning to accept other things—but then they were looking at things from a distance. So they argued a lot, others also argued, "Women are not to be in the front—what's that then?" But there were words, like. . . I don't know how I can say it—some didn't feel right about it, didn't like it much.

JCT: *And were women able to participate? Weren't they forbidden to go by their husbands, as happened in other places?*

MP: Here too. Most of the women here couldn't work because of that.

JCT: *In those days, the OMM held meetings at night, didn't it? Sometimes the ladies would come out of the meetings at ten, eleven at night?*

MP: Yes, yes. Some of them lost their husbands then. It meant actually losing their husbands, divorcing, yes—it meant actually divorcing. They would say, "I have a wife that is of the OMM, that goes to work and whatnot, the whole day without seeing her, she goes out in the district, I don't know what. Well really, for me it's not right." Some people lost husbands because of this.

JCT: *But they preferred not to quit the OMM?*

MP: Yes. At that time, even the. . . what's-her-name. . . when the secretary was Salomé Moiane, one day she asked here, "Husband—Maincha has a

---

23   The First Extraordinary Conference of the OMM, held in November 1984.

husband?" The people answered yes. "Because I, , , every time I come to visit Cabo Delgado, she's the person that I always see. Does she have a husband?" referring to my husband. The people said, "Yes, she has a husband."

JCT: *So, she was surprised that you still had a husband, despite your work?*

MP: Yes, going to courses, coming here—when she arrived for meetings she always see Maincha there, so she asked, "But does she have a husband?" They said yes. It was very interesting that my husband did not stop me from doing that. But other women lost husbands, or didn't marry, only worked at the OMM. It's because of this that some feel sorry. There are people who died—they were from the OMM; there are people that are still alive, those that worked at that time, that haven't got a job.

JCT: *And how did you divide the work with the DG? How did you know what was from the DG and what was from the OMM?*

MP: They divided up well, yes. What the OMM does is its work, the Dynamizing Group does. . . the party does its work. So there, where I am, I do my work, just plan it and do it. No one looks now—it doesn't depend on the party, or anything; each place only does the sort of work that it has learned. Only when there is a meeting, organization such-and-such calls us to office such-and-such; when we want to have a meeting, we have to visit the office, and that's it.

JCT: *But did you never have any problems with the DGs? I mean, did they never interfere with the work that you were doing at the OMM?*

MP: That couldn't be helped, couldn't be helped. They said, "You should know, in order to be jurists, about legal things. . . I don't know what." That couldn't be helped, but we got on with our work.

JCT: *A bit afraid of what you were going to do?*

MP: A bit afraid—a bit afraid. It's only human. [*laughs*] That exists too in the world.

JCT: *Mama Maincha, let's suppose that there was a national proposal for you to stand for secretary-general of the OMM. How would you react?*

MP: Ah, no. That's too much, that. I can't. . .

JCT: *Why not? If they told you that you were being chosen to be secretary, would you accept or not?*

MP: Not at all.

JCT: *Why not?*

MP: Not at all. It's a big confusion. [*laughs*]

JCT: If you were secretary-general, you could perhaps change a lot of things—do things that the OMM is not doing now?

MP: Not at all. I prefer working at the base. Yes, as I grew up in the OMM, I am the branch that came from the main root of the OMM. I can collaborate with the OMM, but it can't be in an intolerable position like that—nothing like that. I can't.

JCT: *And how do you see the problems that the country is facing today, after so many promises in the first years of independence that still have to be fulfilled? What do you think of the present situation?*

MP: Yes—the country is in trouble. Now, from a person's point of view, it seems like it's not worth anything. That's why some things don't go well—the country is in trouble, yes. Even the chiefs are in trouble. Now, one person alone is not enough—one person's opinion doesn't get heard.

JCT: *Let's talk now about your experience as elected magistrate at the provincial court. That was until what year?*

MP: That was in '87. I began in '87—that was when I was elected.

JCT: *Then it went on until when?*

MP: It is still going. I'm still an elected magistrate today.

JCT: *So, you work whenever the court meets?*

MP: Yes, but according to a schedule. Each year has a schedule of two months. But me—as I work near the court, sometimes when a magistrate is missing, they call me.

JCT: *And don't they interrupt your work at the office sometimes?*

MP: Sometimes they interrupt my work at the office—when they see that there's a problem that is big. They come and get me, and I go to work.

JCT: *And here in the office, how do you go about solving cases? What do you do to find the best way?*

MP: The best way to find a solution to a case—a social problem, to do with the home—first of all you have to have patience. We have to begin by asking questions with patience. But first, when people start to speak, first they raise that first point. To begin at the beginning for the person that is giving you information—we have to take that down, to listen, when it is a woman. Starting from there, we ask how and when they started to have the problem. First we ask the years of marriage—how many years of marriage. The person speaks. Then, in the early years, how did you live? Then the person starts telling everything. The conflicts related to the problem began in which year? Like that. The person also starts to explain. Then, they start explaining everything—sometimes, when we want to ask a question later, we write it down. That's what I do myself—we write it down there to ask the question later, when the person stops speaking. Then, we give the word to the others, if they have anything to ask that first person that spoke; if the others have a word, have something to ask, then they ask; if they haven't, then we start by saying, "Let's allow the man to speak too." Then we get the question that we were going to ask. Then the man too, when he begins he denies it all or he might say, "It's true what my wife is saying"—so then we also begin to understand what she said. So, like this we get what is important about the person—we get what the person says; then, with all those questions, it's when we see who is right. Because not everyone can be right. We have to say that this person, or this man is right, or this woman is right, and she is right because of this and that. Because the man asked you this, or the woman asked that, you wouldn't allow it, you refused—at another time you refused this, you wouldn't let her do whatever it is; you continued to do that. So, that's why the woman is right. Then, later, we ask if there is love or not. Then, if we see that there is love, but [he or she says] "I don't like what my partner is doing," if we try to make him or her do those things less, will the marriage continue? Then, if they say that it will continue, we have a reconciliation—we say that it's all over; the problem is finished. Then, when we see that things are like this, we want to study it together, so we ask for a break and the people go out. I sit down with my colleagues: "Let us go over what we've heard." Then we all talk it over until we find the same path. Then we call the people back for the final sentence. Like that—we don't wait for another day, we may do it on the same day. But if we see that it's a bit more complicated, we let the people have a break, go home and think it over. Then, when they've thought it over at home and all that, you come back; and when you come back we meet again, we finish the problem. Because there are people who come in angry on that day, then the next day they arrive as if they had no more problem: they had sat down with the lady before, they had agreed on something. "Let's leave this behind. . . what are we going to say to the Legal Office?" They reach an agreement or something—they arrive there, and just like that, it's over. So, first we hear the person's point, then we begin to analyze.

JCT: *So, you can even solve a problem on the same day, if the parties keep their calm?*

MP: Yes, we can. It can all be over the same day.

JCT: *Otherwise, it might take you two or three days?*

MP: Two, three days—right. On the first day the person makes the complaint; so the first day we begin resolving that case, but it might not be over on the very first day. Because the Legal Office is for reconciliation, we give lots and lots of advice to the person. First, reconciliation, we advise the person, I don't know what; then we give them some time to think: "Go away for so many days—thirty days, say, go away and think, stay together." When the day arrives, they come back to the office. Then, when they say "We're staying with our husbands," then we clap and it's all over, for the best, with the marriage and all that. There are cases when we do a reconciliation twice. But on the third day, if we see that the love doesn't stick, there's no way; so then we accept a divorce.

JCT: *When love doesn't stick anymore. So could the case last a month or so?*

MP: No, it doesn't take that long. It could take a month if there are these reconciliations—that, yes. And also, if the problem is a problem of. . . sometimes there are people that have problems while the person is pregnant. When we see that she's pregnant, then we do the reconciliation until the birth; when we see that the birth was normal—take your baby, keep going. Now let's see if there's a divorce—let's see.

JCT: *But you don't decide on a separation at the time of the pregnancy?*

MP: At the time of pregnancy we don't accept that—that's right.

JCT: *And are there people that show up and say, for example, "I hit her because tradition lets me hit her"? Are there people that show up saying that—saying that it is tradition that counts?*

MP: Yes, yes. We usually have people like that. "I hit her because I couldn't stand it anymore, she provoked me," or whatever. "I get a bit angry." I say, "You can't do that—say 'I hit her,' as if it was a game. I don't know, you could kill the person." In playing around like this, a person could die.

JCT: *And in those cases, when people say, "I'm right, because tradition says I'm right," what do you do?*

MP: Yes, when the person says "I'm right," we start to tell them again: "You're not right—what you're doing is not right because of this, this and that; you shouldn't do that, you should do this or that." So later, the one that said "I'm right" becomes a bit more subdued; then, later [he says], "Yes, Mama, I wasn't right in that thing, for sure." "So, starting from there, don't do it any more." That's it, if a person accepts they'll say...

JCT: *And they say that in front of the family?*

MP: In front of the family, the wife's companion, the man's companion. That's right.

JCT: *Has it ever happened that a man came to make a complaint against his wife?*

MP: Yes, a lot—a lot, a lot of men.

JCT: *What do they come to complain about?*

MP: They come to complain about their wives.

JCT: *But what sort of things do they usually complain about?*

MP: Adultery—the woman is committing adultery. There are also parents that say, "My daughter was raped." The men usually make the complaint. Also, there's the woman that speaks too much in front of her husband, that doesn't have respect—the men usually complain: "My lady has no respect." There are also women that violate the men's rights, such as getting pregnant by so-and-so, and this man does everything, thinking she is pregnant—"I got my lady pregnant." And later he comes to say, "She's pregnant by another person, by Luís," or whoever. So men come and make complaints. Those are the kinds of things men complain about.

JCT: *And cases of witchcraft—do you get any of those? For example, they often accuse a woman whose child has died of I don't know what.*

MP: Yes. Actually, the other day I met a woman who said, "My husband said let's kill your father, because you're my wife; I myself—I want to make sure that I have my wife, to trust you, to have our things, riches, the property at home. I will trust you more—let's kill your father." But the lady didn't agree. She didn't agree, and that's when she came to the Legal Office, to say she didn't agree. So there, by making the man feel ashamed, he didn't want to be married to her anymore; there was love, but as she shamed him, he didn't want to any more. And the lady didn't want to either.

JCT: *And how did the case end?*

MP: It ended in divorce.

JCT: *And does it not happen that you sometimes get cases where the people, out of shame, tell you that they agree but, deep down, they don't? Have you ever had anyone who tried to do something here at the office?*

MP: Do something—what do you mean?

JCT: *I don't know, use some kind of drug. . . ?*

MP: Ah, yes, yes. Once there was a man—I don't know, it was a drug that he had, I don't know what. And when I started to talk to him, he started to chew something there—it was right inside his mouth. So, as soon as I found out, I said, "It's not necessary to do those things, because this is a social problem; go slow here, calm down. Now, I don't know if that's to shut me up, to keep my mouth closed, I don't know—please, Papa, you've got something in your mouth; I can see." "Sorry," [he said], and he started taking out that thing. That was it—it was over. It happens. [*laughs*]

JCT: *Really, you've got to be attentive all the time, haven't you?*

MP: Yes. Even Dr. Pondja, the judge that signed the first agreement of our office, gave me some advice when I was starting off. He said, "Careful with the people, now—you should watch out when the people come in, because they're not all alike in the world; people have many different ways of thinking. Careful, Maincha, the work you've taken on here is a work that could make you an enemy for others; some, yes, others, no, so be careful."

JCT: *Besides that, have you ever been threatened?*

MP: Not at all. From the time I started working, only among them, they would say, "This lady, you be careful!" Among them, saying to the women right there, "Be careful with this lady". . . That happens quite a lot.

JCT: *How do you usually get home?*

MP: I usually go like this. . .

JCT: *Do you get a lift?*

MP: Nothing of the kind. When I leave in the morning for work, I don't have a problem; but the problem is getting back.

JCT: *Do you go on foot?*[24]

MP: On foot—that's right, slowly. Until I get home.

JCT: *Do you take the road, or do you take short cuts?*

MP: The road.

JCT: *Sometimes you come home when it's dark, don't you?*

MP: Yes, yes. When I go back when it's dark, it's very difficult to get a lift, because most people don't know me on that road.

JCT: *Your early reports mention that the Legal Office, at the beginning, was called "Office for Women and Development," and you began with activities related to disseminating information about women's rights—projects like crocheting, cake-making, and so on. Suddenly things changed. When did that happen, and why?*

MP: We changed, yes. That was around '94 or '95, through the work that was being developed. Even with Dona Ana,[25] we thought we should change the name to Legal Office, yes.

JCT: *But at that time, at the beginning, when it was the Office for Women and Development, the Australian organization that supports you was already helping, wasn't it?*

MP: Yes, it was helping. Because at first it was a project that they said that would be for four years, then it would stop. So they went [to the office] and saw the amount of work at the office. So they said, "Let's keep this going another three years." And they have continued until now—we don't know when it's going to finish.

JCT: *And those projects in the first years, supporting the ladies, did they go well? Did they get off the ground?*

MP: They went on for a bit, but it was the ladies themselves that killed it. They let it drop. Some used the money up—they let it drop. So Dona Ana herself said, "How can we go on trusting a work that has no peace? So let's drop it." It stopped.

JCT: *So, at first it was more about giving advice—but then the people started coming to you for help with solving their problems, didn't they?*

MP: Yes, yes. It was through those works, doing work that people liked, doing things that people needed—the same thing. So, they changed the name, the thing changed—it started to be the sort of work we're doing today.

JCT: *A little while back, you said you'd made an agreement with the court, with Dr. Pondja—is that right?*

MP: Yes, because even Dona Ana, when we started... when that office was founded, then it was Secretary Filomena Nachaque that informed the

---

24   The neighborhood where the interviewee lives is located around 10 km from the building where the Woman's Legal Office operates.

25   The representative of the Australian NGO, the International Women's Development Agency—the main sponsor of the Legal Office's activities.

governor, when it was Mr. Simbine—then he accepted it, signed it, so the national OMM also signed, that it should be this office. Then I and Dona Ana went out together to the judge's office; he also signed, then we started working.

JCT: *So it was a kind of recognition of your existence, rather than a collaboration, wasn't it?*

MP: Yes.

JCT: *Has that document with the signatures been kept? Who keeps it?*

MP: It might be Secretary Filomena. She must have a copy of it.

JCT: *And working with the police, did that come later?*

MP: Yes—with the police it was later, after we'd already started.

JCT: *And that agreement with the police says what? It's to do what?*

MP: It's to say that, when the office asks for support, then the police have to give it, I guess. . . They said yes, we're ready.

JCT: *But are there cases that are actually for the police? For example, if I go to the office with a criminal case, a case of rape, say—if you send me to the police, will they take care of it?*

MP: Yes, they do, very well. They know that when we get a case, even of violence, even that crime, we pass it on to the police, with a document, and they receive it. They too, when they get a social problem that needs the Legal Office, they also send it over with a document.

JCT: *In some places, women's organizations have problems with the police because they're all men. When a woman goes there complaining that her husband hit her, instead of taking her complaint seriously, they ask, "What did you do to your husband to make him hit you?" How do things work here?*

MP: In relation to the police here, because first we met with the police chief, the commandant himself, he told the police how to react. Also, in our opening session, when we do seminars, mini-courses, and so on, the police, the judge, and even the governor are present. So, every chief has guidance from the office—every chief knows what the Legal Office's work is.

JCT: *So you've never had problems with the way the police handle the cases that you've sent to them?*

MP: No, no. We've even had some advice: we were told that if a policeman—because policemen also marry and have problems with their wives—says that it's for you yourselves to decide a police case, and if he doesn't accept it, then we're ready, you can do the document and send it over. The police said that—yes, they actually said that. Here we don't have problems with the police; we have great support, really good support. I'm grateful for that; that's why the office of the Cabo Delgado province, here in Pemba, is really safe. Yes, it's really safe.

JCT: *That agreement with the police is quite recent, isn't it? More or less two years, right?*

MP: Yes, yes.

JCT: *And what about the community courts?[26] How have your relationships with them developed? They didn't react to the fact that the office was solving cases that fell under their jurisdiction?*

MP: At first, yes, they were jealous. But it didn't last long, because they send cases over here—they transfer cases to the Legal Office. Although they charge money, but when they see that they can't do it there, they send it to us, over here, without money; because they use up the money and can't do anything, and then send it over here. Sometimes, when a person gets here, we say, "Go back to your neighborhood and ask for it to be transferred to here"; the person gets there, but they don't want to do it, especially when they know that there is something in it for them— they don't want to, or whatever. So we notify the man and we sort it out; as an office that helps people, we don't have to say, go bring so much, I don't know what. We start the work, and that's it; and that's why the others, the women, try not to pass other places and come directly here; we also receive a person only after we see things with her; then we do the document, tell them to ask there where they've issued the document, say something, or get the initial report.

JCT: *And we have also heard that you had activists in the neighborhoods, didn't you?*

MP: Ah, yes, we did—we do. They are working, sometimes when we ask them to come over at least one day, once a month—then they work. As for the rest, we leave it—they might not come; we leave it because sometimes we haven't anything to give. Nowadays no one will do work for nothing.

JCT: *But had you thought of those activists in the neighborhoods also to resolve problems, or just to provide guidance?*

MP: To provide guidance, at least—to make people understand when they see those problems, because these are daily problems that affect people.

JCT: *So, they go and persuade the women by saying, "Go there and make your complaint." Is it for that?*

MP: "Go there..."—or even go with them. Go with them as an activist. They are there and see how the people are living; when they find something, they tell them: "You can't sit there with your arms crossed; go on—I'll go with you to the office, don't you know it? OK, let's go."

---

26   The community courts, which were set up by Law No. 4/92, of May 6th, "permit citizens to resolve small differences within the community, contribute to the harmonization of various justice practices and to the enrichment of rules, uses and customs, and lead to the creative synthesis of Mozambican law."

JCT: *But when the office began, it was just you and Cristina, wasn't it?*

MP: Yes, it was me and Cristina—the two of us. Then Cristina stayed in the Secretariat of the OMM.

JCT: *And Mapewa and the others came?*

MP: Before Cristina went to the Secretariat, then Mapewa, Madalena, and Isabel were activists too. Then, at the time when I was working with Cristina, that was when Dona Ana arrived—as she was always visiting—so I asked her. I said, "Dona Ana, here there are two of us working, but the work is not... that time when we started, now there's a lot of work. So I'm asking, as we have activists, at least one month, can an activist come to work? I don't know if we can manage at least to give maybe 150, at least, so that when that month is over, she will receive a little bit of change, go home and buy a little something, do business—something to help at home; so, let's also have another person." Dona Ana said, "Ah, yes, Maincha, your idea, you want to eat with your companions, good idea. You don't want to eat alone." I said, "Yes, the work shouldn't be done alone." She said, "Good idea." So, that was when I called Isabel and Madalena and Mapewa. Now the office is organized like this: Maincha—president; Mapewa—responsible for finances; Isabel—responsible for receiving cases and for organizing them; Madalena—clerk; Teresa—responsible for information.

JCT: *Why did you choose those women? Because they were more dynamic?*

MP: And there were more, also from here, from Maringanha, Wimbe—there were other people. Then those there, they stuck on. They were more active—and they also started to ask; Isabel said, "Mama, I may not receive anything, but we'll continue to work all the same." I said, "Ah, is that so?" She said, "Yes." Isabel, Madalena and Mapewa started working as volunteers. That went on and on, until we got to the point when we could [pay].

JCT: *Teresa only joined later?*

MP: It was later that Teresa joined, that's right.

JCT: *And when did the office start having its activists? Was it when it changed from being the "Office for Women and Development" and became the "Woman's Legal Office"?*

MP: It was later, when we'd already started with the work

JCT: *Did you choose people that you already knew from the OMM?*

MP: Ah, those activists had all passed the courses—yes, we were together.

JCT: *And how did you choose people for the courses?*

MP: It was through Maputo—they came to give lectures; they came to give courses. So they determined the number of people—so we that are here, that are from here, that know the people, we started to call people.

JCT: *Were they OMM activists, or only women you knew, that each of you knew from the neighborhood?*

MP: They were women. . . together with OMM activists, there were ladies from the companies, and others.

JCT: *Besides the structure you referred to, the work organization inside the office, I heard that you have a support house. Could you explain what that is?*

MP: It's our shelter. It's here on the beach at Wimbe, near the village. It's a house where women can rest. Sometimes there are conflicts inside the home, so a person can't stay there. Because sometimes our husbands. . . sometimes they get angry, they don't let their wife stay in that place. Then, serious problems, fights, I don't know—beating each other up; they can't stay in that place. So, when they get to the Legal Office, instead of saying "go back there," we take them to the shelter so that they can rest there a while, until the end of the trial, to resolve the problem; when it's over, then we know where the lady will go, or if she continues in her house.

JCT: *When you mentioned the cases that end up at the office, you said that many of those cases are of jealousy. Could you explain that jealousy a bit better?*

MP: Household jealousy. A woman is jealous when her husband takes another wife, and so, out of jealousy, they start to fight, fight, until later on, it can cause a divorce.

JCT: *When the man gets a second wife. . . ?*

MP: Yes, yes.

JCT: *Is there much polygamy here?*

MP: Here? Yes, there is a lot.

JCT: *And the wives don't accept a second wife well?*

MP: No—the women don't accept to be two people. Because sometimes they appear when they are living together—from the beginning, when they get property, when they get their house. . . Then later, if a person, if a man gets another wife, then later the lady starts feeling that "we suffered a lot; now that we managed to get what we got, now I'm no longer a lady—I'm not your wife; I don't know, you got yourself another person..." That's how jealousy starts, and later on it can cause divorce.

JCT: *And the man then stays with his second wife?*

MP: Then he stays with the second wife. But then, when he stays with the second wife, sometimes he doesn't take any notice of that one—the older one: he doesn't take any notice of her. A woman might even say, "I'm here since my husband got himself another wife. I've stayed six months, or even a year—he doesn't pay me any attention; he doesn't make love with me. . . " This happens a lot—a person, as a human being, feels...

JCT: *Yes, of course. A case like that is complicated. How do you resolve it?*

MP: Yes. Often, that second wife is just a kid. There's a word that we use here—we say she's a "little fourteener." These are things. . .

JCT: *Fourteen years old, you mean?*

MP: Yes. He doesn't look back any more—always ahead, always ahead. It's a pity. You even meet people, with that feeling of "Is that really my husband, that one? My husband? . . . Let's talk about it." Even when a woman says, "My husband. . ."—there, in the office, they speak; even when a woman says, "My husband, come back, come and talk to me," the man goes home and wants to sleep in the sitting room; if he sleeps in the bed, it's like he's been tied down, it's like he's being forced to sleep there—he doesn't feel that "I slept with a woman." So, sometimes we meet ladies, it seems that they're going to get anemic. I've actually met a lady who said, "It's been six years—it's not months, six years that I've not been with my husband." You see! "That I don't know my husband as a husband"; and a person starts thinking, "Is he my husband? That man that I used to talk to, with love, to arrange our things; nowadays I'm nothing." You see? Then we ask the men, and they say, "No, at that time it was like this—my lady should also begin with love, but this one here doesn't give me love. When I get home she just asks things and I can't stand that, and that's why I go out sometimes." But it's a lie—a way of trying to escape, not wanting the lady. Those are the kinds of things that appear.

JCT: *And is there a solution for those cases?*

MP: There's a solution, when we say, "Go and try—go and try to call up the love of this lady, as you're saying it's not divorce." Because sometimes they start by refusing, saying that they love them—they start by refusing, so as not to have to share their property with the lady, knowing that there really isn't any love. They try to get out of it; but knowing that they're trying to escape, we try in the beginning a bit of reconciliation; and when we see that things are getting worse, then they can come again.

JCT: *And then the decision is made?*

MP: Yes, it is. It could even go on a year, saying that things are already more or less back to normal; it can even take two years—until the time when they say, "Yes, my husband is not so bad; he's not like he used to be"—but, like that, through a reconciliation.

JCT: *So, those women, actually, don't come asking for a separation?*

MP: No.

JCT: *They come asking for advice, to see if he'll come home?*

MP: They ask us for advice, to see if he'll come back—to analyze it really, to have a consultation, to know if there is love or not. "Was he truly my husband until now or not?" Women don't go there only to get divorced.

JCT: *They come asking for help for you to call the men, so that they can talk, because they don't do it by themselves?*

MP: Yes, help to call—exactly, yes. It's exactly those things. A woman even says, "I've come to ask for your help, Mama—to see if what my husband is doing to me is real, or is he still my husband. If he's my husband, Mama, I need help." A woman even says, "I've come to ask for help; I thought of coming here to the Legal Office to ask for help."

JCT: *For example, a woman that lives twenty, twenty-five years with a man and separates, can she get herself another man?*

MP: No, very difficult—very difficult!

JCT: *They just want "fourteeners"?*

MP: Yes. It's very difficult to get a man. It's easy only for a man to get a woman when he divorces his wife—he might be an old man, but he can get one. For a man, when he's working, it's very, very easy to get a woman, but for a woman, when she divorces her husband, it's very difficult to find another husband—very difficult! She could even die like that, without a husband, but she could stay twenty years with that husband—fifteen or twenty; if she divorces him it's very difficult.

JCT: *And a boyfriend, can't she get that? Just a boyfriend?*

MP: A boyfriend, yes, she can—but find one that she can say, "I've got a husband"; no, that's difficult. If she finds a boyfriend, it's a man belonging to a lady or whatever, and later there will be problems, like falling into the river, down the well, I don't know what—things like that, with the man's wife.

JCT: *You mean to say that divorce is bad for the woman not only because of her survival, but also because the divorce will put an end to her love life?*

MP: Yes, it does. There's a case too that I had today, a marriage of twenty-five years, with four children—the man wanted to divorce that wife. We tried to do a reconciliation last year, but it didn't work: the woman came back, said [the problem] continued. We did a second reconciliation, it continued. So, today, the time has come for separation, already divorce. There's no way. So, I said, "The house—who will keep that?" He said, "The house is for my children." "How can it be for your children who are minors? How will that be? The lady, how will she be? The house was just one, just that house—you have already left, you live in the house of another woman, and you are also building another house. How can you now throw this lady out? Where will she go?" He said, "The lady can stay there, with my children, until she gets a man—then she can leave my house." "How can she leave? Where will she go? If she finds a man who is alone, it's not to get married, not to get her a house; the man that should get her a house is you, who lived many years with her! When you married her, she was young. Today, be careful about what you're going to do. To find a house, who's going to come along now and give her a house? It was you that took her youth from her." He said, "All right, she can stay—she can stay in that house."

JCT: *But will he put that in writing?*

MP: Yes, he will make a declaration to say she can stay. So the woman later said, "Yes, I see I can stay in that house—but I don't want to stay in that house because my husband got married near to that house; everything he's doing with that woman, I can see; I have children there. Yesterday my son said, 'See, my father's over there—we are hungry here, my father's there eating with that woman.' So, me too, as a mother, as a wife, I feel it; so, I want my husband at least to get a house somewhere else, so that I can stay with my children, or sell that house." So we've ended up deciding to sell that house, to move away, because it's near; we've finished like that. He's already done the declaration, and also another to provide for the children—to give something for the children every month. He's agreed, and they ended up divorcing. But the lady was really sad, you see—it's twenty-five years; she's not thinking of having another man, but she ended up getting divorced. Things happen.

JCT: *Now, how did the office grow—because now it's big, it's setting up offices in the districts, isn't it?*

MP: Yes, yes, we are. It's been like that, growing. And, as I said, the OMM, which is also following the office closely, talks to other people too, and to other organizations. Also, when people and other organizations come to visit, they want to know the Legal Office. So they come to see the work, how it's getting on—they see that it's really getting on in this office, so they talk to others, and that's why we... because, in the past, people would come here from a long way off, from other districts, such as Montepuez, Ancuabe; people were transferred to here. Because we began to promote our work in the districts. We left here, went to have meetings with the populations of those districts. So, through that, people started to like it. People also started to ask, "Why don't you set up offices here? Because Pemba is far away. Here we are out of it, most of us—we still don't know about those rights that a woman has, that she can make a complaint in a place. So we want to have an office near us too." That's why we set up offices there in the districts, so that those who want to come to the office in Pemba, but can't, can have their problems solved there. That's why we have set up those offices, at the request of the majority.

JCT: *So, was it the OMM or the populations themselves that asked for offices in the districts?*

MP: It was the populations, yes—because of the promotion we did of our work. Yes, yes—they liked it; because these are things people experience very closely.

JCT: *So, you now have offices in all the districts of the province?*

MP: All the districts of the Cabo Delgado province. And those advisors attend courses.

JCT: *Did they do the course here?*

MP: Yes, here in Pemba.

JCT: *Who was it that ran the course?*

MP: It was the people from Maputo.

JCT: *I'd like to know how many training courses there have been here in the office. The documents that we looked at mentioned a course on August 5th and 6th of '92. Have there been any more courses since then?*

MP: There have been more courses. Dona Beatriz came, as well as Dona Becas of the OMM—they gave a course too.

JCT: *What did they teach on those courses?*

MP: Courses on women's rights, that kind of thing. Women's rights, the home, domestic violence. . .

JCT: *Did you take full advantage of it? Was it good?*

MP: Yes, we did. It was good, but we also want courses that are closely connected to our work, because, when I went to Nampula, I saw a course—that one that I said I went to—to talk about the experience of the office; so the person who was giving that course is a lawyer from Nampula, and I liked the course he was giving. He even gave me other documents with guidelines, and I said I liked it. I attended [the course], but I would also like my companions—those that work in the districts as advisors, those that are also from the office—to benefit from what I saw, because it's very important, it's really connected to our work. He said that actually he was here the week before last, he visited the office. So I said, "If we get a little of this [*makes a gesture referring to money*], we will call you." And he said, "I'm ready."

JCT: *I heard that next month the provincial court is going to organize a seminar about mediation. Have you been invited?*

MP: No, we've not been invited, but I've heard that we are going to be—I've spoken to Mr. Lima.

JCT: *But do you think it's necessary to do more training? For you people here?*

MP: For me, yes; I could be there, but. . . [*laughs*] but everything that is discussed. . .

JCT: *You've experienced it?*

MP: A lot—a lot. I can say that people learn laws there, they ask me all sorts of things, and I can, even like this. . .

JCT: *Even without having studied those laws. But you use your common sense?*

MP: Without taking anything, a person can say, nothing is finished… Other things, besides those laws, I'm not talking about other matters, but about social problems, about widows, that sort of thing—not beating up, not killing people, social problems. . . I'm ready for that—I really am.

JCT: *And the other women that work for the office, do they plan to study more, to get more training?*

MP: They have—they can also study. They are also inside the issues. They are getting there. All that's needed is a bit of patience—a lot of patience.

In November 1998 and February 1999, the interviewer spent a total of six weeks in Cabo Delgado coordinating the team of researchers from the project on "The Administration of Justice in Mozambique," carried out by the Centre for African Studies of the Eduardo Mondlane University and the Centre for Social Studies of the School of Economics of the University of Coimbra (see note 1).

During the first trip, the team conducted several interviews with different members of the community courts in the neighborhoods around the city of Pemba, and mention was made repeatedly of the Woman's Legal Office, to which certain "social cases" that were difficult to solve had been transferred. None of the researchers knew or had even heard of that institution, but the respect and deference with which it was mentioned by all interviewees, as well as the praise given to its coordinator, aroused the curiosity of the team.

That was how we made contact with MP and her co-workers. Since then, we have continued to follow the office's work and popularity (although intermittently, due to the distance and to the various programs in which we are involved). Today, this alternative means of conflict-resolution has delegations in all the sixteen districts of the province of Cabo Delgado, involving a total of thirty-eight people.

PORTUGAL

11

Fátima Carvalho

Textile worker, grassroots trade unionist, leading activist in the struggle for the rights of working women.

Interviewed by Boaventura de Sousa Santos

"Sometimes, I ask myself, 'What is my role in all this? Is it worth being a unionist nowadays?' Everything takes such a long time to change . . ."

Maria de Fátima Carvalho[1]

No history has yet been written of the trade union movement in the Portuguese textile industry, undoubtedly one of the sectors suffering the sharpest decline in competitiveness over recent decades. This decline is due not only to the low salaries offered and the relatively unskilled nature of the workforce but also to the industry's failure to modernize or introduce innovation, as regards both technology and the definition of effective strategies that might enable it to assert itself as a productive sector with know-how and experience in Portugal and abroad.

Any history or narrative that may eventually be written about the Portuguese textile sector over the last thirty years cannot ignore the important role played by Fátima Carvalho. But her most important contribution has been within a more circumscribed area—the domain of those that have personally experienced the impact of the systemic processes taking place in the industry. It is here that her way of being and acting are acknowledged for being so different, and for offering an example of how to overcome the many crises that are presently shaking the sector—including, of course, the crisis of trade unionism.

Fátima Carvalho was born in 1948 into a family of modest means in the village of Casal Vieira, Batalha county, in the district of Leiria. Her childhood and adolescence were spent helping her parents work the land or look after animals in order to ensure the family's basic subsistence.

At sixteen she went to work in the textile industry, at one of the plants in Mira de Aire, and would make the daily 10 km journey between home and work on foot. Faced with the whims of the bosses and a generalized feeling of exploitation, contractual irregularities, an absence of fixed wages, and discrimination between men and women, she gradually developed a moral and civic conscience. Since then, she has been wholly committed to the struggle for equality and social justice. This commitment has led her to seek opportunities for reflection and intervention in order to stimulate debate and collective participation. Thus, in 1964, she joined the Young Catholic Workers association (Juventude Operária Católica—JOC), where she took a militant role, acting as head of the diocese, under the motto "See, Judge and Act."

1   The text has been produced with the precious help of Sílvia Ferreira.

With the "Carnation Revolution" of April 25th, 1974, Fátima Carvalho devel-
oped an irresistible urge to participate, a desire that revolutionized her life. When she
was elected trade union delegate, her personal dreams became subordinated to those
of the group. Of that moment, which proved so important for her life, she retains
the memory of a general enthusiasm, blind courage, and dynamism that led her to
confront a boss who was preventing his workers from taking part in general meetings
by threatening them at gunpoint. She also remembers the excitement generated by
their victories, both small and large, gradually made possible by the new political
conditions and the dawning awareness on the part of the workers of their own poten-
tial and right to self-respect.

In 1975, she became leader of the Wool Workers' Union of Mira de Aire. Two
years later, she took part in the merger of various textile unions from the districts
of Coimbra and Leiria, and, since then, has occupied management positions in the
organizational structure representing these unions. In 1986 she joined the National
Council of the CGTP-IN (Confederação Geral dos Trabalhadores Portugueses,
Intersindical Nacional—General Confederation of Portuguese Workers, National
Trade Union Congress), and recently (2006) joined the Executive Committee of the
National Council of that confederation.

In addition to her activities as trade union leader, Fátima Carvalho has also
held important posts on the Boards of the Federation of Textile, Wool, Clothing,
Footwear and Leather Unions of Portugal (FESETE), organizing concerted and
reciprocal union action between the various sectors.

In 1986 she joined the National Committee supporting Maria de Lourdes
Pintasilgo's presidential campaign, and still today takes part in initiatives organized
by the movement that emerged from this committee, which brought together people
of different political and social backgrounds. More recently, she has made a point of
intervening actively in civic movements, such as Pro-Urbe and the City of Coimbra
Committee. In 1994 she was on the list for Política XXI's candidature for the
European Elections, and in 2002 supported Jorge Sampaio's presidential campaign.
In 2006, having run in the local elections as an independent candidate on the Socialist
Party (PS) ticket, she became a Councilor on the Coimbra City Council.

THE NATURE OF THE CRISIS

Boaventura de Sousa Santos: *What does trade unionism mean today? How*
  do you see the present situation, particularly when you compare it to how it used
  to be? Is it in crisis? And is that a crisis of your sector, of the whole economy, of
  trade union consciousness? Or is it a crisis of organization among union bodies?
  How do you see this crisis?

Fátima Carvalho: It makes sense. In terms of industry, I don't think there
  is a generalized crisis. There are companies with serious economic and
  financial problems, because of declining markets or a lack of organization,

modernization, and management. I think the employers have not been able to adapt to today's world. And they don't work together. They don't have a relationship of cooperation; they don't share their experiences. If that is necessary, in an area dominated by a single industry, they don't take advantage of the synergies that exist—they don't join up or help each other. There is still very much the idea that "This is my patch and I can't let others into my secrets. This is my company!" So everyone works for himself. Everyone does his own thing, often badly. They don't cooperate, or organize partnerships between companies to develop joint ventures, to take advantage of resources and discover new markets, or promote their products under better conditions. There are clients out there that have a hard time getting what they need because they can't find small articles in a market that today is absolutely dominated by the big multinationals. If times change, then they have to change too.

Just a few days ago, a businessman who was trying to restructure his company was telling me that, after he had presented his project, he discovered that there was another similar one operating in another area. So he decided that it was better to keep only the commercial part, which was the most profitable, rather than try to implement the whole project. If these projects are coordinated by the Ministry for the Economy or IAPMEI,[2] then it is their job to warn businessmen about situations like this. They should tell them, "There's already another project underway that is the same as yours. What we really need is this or that..." ICEP[3] and other government structures exist, but there is no structure that coordinates it all and says, "Right, let's carry out some studies for companies that are going under, and try to find out exactly what type of support they need to make them viable. Let's provide technical support and consultancy services for companies that need it, to support those that already exist." But governments don't really care about that; nor do the technicians that analyze the projects and decide what kind of support they are going to get. They can't be bothered to educate businessmen, who often have a rather old-fashioned outlook, and think that doing business involves unrestrained exploitation, tax-dodging, and low wages. This is where the trade unions come in. We demand assistance for these failing companies so that they can be made viable again and jobs can be saved, but at the same time, we also demand respect for the rights and dignity of the workers.

As our country is mostly made up of small and medium-sized companies, we urgently need to define development strategies for each place

---

2   Institute for the Support of Small and Medium Companies, under the auspices of the Ministry for the Economy.
3   Foreign Trade Institute of Portugal.

or region. We need to set up forums for dialogue among all the bodies involved (local authorities, businessmen, trade unions, universities and other public bodies, or those that are directly or indirectly related to the companies) in order to take advantage of the know-how and skills that could generate new business initiatives and create more jobs, in all economic and social areas. And we need to study the best ways of responding to the problems and challenges that confront companies today.

BSS: *So, does this mean that entrepreneurs do not really have a capitalist vision?*

FC: I think that some have and some haven't. And we, the trade union movement, shouldn't just put them all in the same bag. We can't react in the same way to businessmen that we don't even know, or when we don't know where their companies are based; or with those that have advisors all around them telling them to run their companies in one way or another, invest in off-shores here or there; or with those businessmen who fleece their companies for their own personal profit, or who operate entirely in the parallel economy. I would like to think that this type of behavior is not typical of entrepreneurs in the textile industry, and that most of them try to stay afloat so that their company can win through!

In the past everything was a lot clearer. Today there are people around who set up all kinds of schemes to make money, and society considers them to be honest folk. They are asked to give their opinions about everything—and then they demand ten, twenty, thirty thousand contos[4] for the trouble! They've got no notion of what country they're living in! It's criminal. And most likely, the bosses they work for are the ones that pay the lowest wages to their workers.

But the boss who didn't pay the state so that he could pay his workers' wages first is seen as dishonest. It's true that he should also have paid the state what he owed. But it's the elites in our society that take three-quarters of the cake that have a very technical idea of what it's all about. And they teach the bosses to suck their companies dry and live off the parallel economy. The leftovers are for the workers, the poor, and for petty charity.

Where are they, in this country, the headquarters of those big companies? Are they actually in Portugal? Or are they helping to make others rich somewhere else? Why is it that governments, whatever their politics, never go near this subject? Could it be that they're all hoping for a cozy little position in one of those companies after they give up politics, with a nice fat salary?

In my opinion, this is the kind of economic power—a power with no values—that is running Europe and our country. It is not the governments

---

4 Unit of the old Portuguese money—the escudo (one thousand escudos = one conto).

or the politicians that are behind it—it's the people connected to the big economic groups, who often don't even pay taxes. It's the ones that say, "Why don't you take your company off to Romania, or Bulgaria, or China? You'd get loads of benefits there."

Many companies that are considered to be economically healthy and that are supported by people who really know what they're doing—even these are caving in without really knowing why. But they go bankrupt, and the people responsible don't even get their wings singed, don't even put their own assets at risk. In many cases, they are not even in this country. They're untouchable. All this is done in the name of capital and profit. Nothing is done for human beings or for the sustainable development of the country.

BSS: *But in the textile sector, don't you think that the problem is also due to the fact that they have not restructured or developed new skills? We continue to have very low salaries, and a very low skills level. Do you think that this is the way to go on? What I mean is, do you think that we should try to save particular companies just as they are, or should we instead try to upgrade them? That might involve some unemployment, but in the long run it would create new jobs in the same sector with better-qualified workers, don't you think?*

FC: Companies have never managed to restructure and reorganize. The management has got so used to having it easy, not having too many demands made on them. In the past, it was easy to just cultivate your own patch. The problem came when the market changed and modernized. Then those businessmen found themselves stuck. And the governments tried to make the odd restructuring plan here and there, such as in the wool industry. It's just that they didn't take the time to study the main problems facing each company so as to make sure it was economically sustainable. They supported all kinds of projects that, in some cases, left a lot to be desired, and all the bosses wanted was to get their hands on the funding, without bothering about whether the company was actually viable or not. So it's not really surprising that many of those projects came to nothing.

TRADE UNION PRACTICE: SAVING THE COMPANIES

BSS: *The union sometimes finds itself in the position now of having to collaborate with the management in order to get companies back onto their feet, almost helping the management to do their jobs better. How has this come about?*

FC: That's what the workers want—that we do everything possible to protect their jobs. So we have no choice, even though the trade union movement does not always understand this. It is not always easy, I can tell you, and I feel quite lost at times. If we listen to the analysts, and in the context of globalization, our industry is going to finish. Businessmen say these companies are a bad bet economically, that they can't compete in such a competitive market, where only the big companies and multinationals get by. But is that really true? Does that mean we should just give up? We can't do that! What we have to do is to change our political strategies—try out new things, row against the tide, and invest in new market niches, in quality, in creativity. Above all, we have to value the human resources that we have. Sometimes I wonder why a particular company has to close down. Some people say that a company is like a person—it has a certain lifespan, and then it dies. And I say a company might have a lifespan, but before it dies it can be transformed so as to give it another lease on life, to keep it going.

There was a time when trade unionism was more assertive, made more demands, tried to introduce changes—when there was more incentive to discuss ideas and differences. Since the 1990s, the trade union movement has been mostly concerned with protecting workers and their jobs against those ferocious attacks that are threatening to close down companies and take away the rights we have won.

BSS: *And was it this that led you to make that distinction, as you do so clearly today, between what we might call the "good" businessman, who wants his profit but at the same time also tries to keep jobs and push his company forward, and the "rogue" businessman, who just wants to take advantage of European funds or financial assistance schemes, but who has no consideration whatsoever for his workers?*

FC: Yes, it was, to a certain extent—but it was not only that. Since the 1990s, the textile sector has had serious problems. For example, Coimbra used to have 4,500 jobs in the sector, and between '91 and '92, half of those jobs disappeared—in the county of Coimbra alone.[5]

We were faced with a serious problem, and we had to react. Either we could say that it was all bad and there was nothing to be done about it, or we could do an about-turn and think, "No. This might be bad, but we have to try to find a solution. There is always a way out." So, from then on, we decided to fight. But I don't mean fight in the sense of just taking advantage—because in those desperate times, it's always easy to mobilize the workers, particularly when there are wages unpaid, when their job is at risk. In many situations, the people's struggles are used to defend other aims and ideas. But we thought that the most important aim would be to get people involved in trying to get their companies back on their feet and in protecting their jobs. That is what gets them going.

---

5   In the last ten years, in the union's area of influence, forty-five companies have closed down or have filed for bankruptcy, leading to the loss of 4,000 jobs.

The struggle for Ideal[6] is a good example. There were 500 jobs at risk, and it was the biggest experience and challenge in my life, given our determination and the workers' involvement, their tenacity and creativity, the way they all gave themselves over body and soul to defending their jobs. I think that the workers taught everybody a great lesson, showed them how important it is to be united in the struggle, and that no matter how difficult things are, it's always possible to act. The workers of that company managed to really assert themselves, and their struggle is still recognized today as a kind of turning point, the moment when they realized that they had the power to turn things around.[7]

BSS: *But you lost that struggle, didn't you?*

FC: What do you mean, we lost it? At the time, Cavaco Silva[8] was in power, and there wasn't much of a culture of dialogue, nor much sensitivity towards solving these problems. We only managed to get support and sympathy on the local level—from the civil governor and city council. As for the national level—well, the civil governor at the time, who happened to follow the same political line as the government, but who really got involved in our struggle, even went to Lisbon to meet up with Mira Amaral.[9] But he threw him out of his office, saying, "What? You've come all the way from Coimbra just to try to sort out the problems of a company? That's not what a civil governor should be doing!"

So the central government didn't want to get involved in helping to find concrete solutions for the company. That was not their strategy at that time. It was obvious that the company was very debilitated economically, but it had a lot of assets. That was when we understood that the city of Coimbra was more interested in real estate speculation than in industry. In fact, there are still a lot of people here today that think like that, who believe that the city's future lies in the service industries—although there are other cities nearby that have managed to create links between industry and the university and other services. In Coimbra, all that is still being debated, still at the virtual stage. Industries and other services are dwindling, year after year, and jobs are still being lost, without anybody doing anything about it.

---

6   Textile factory.

7   After a long process involving various tactics on the part of the workers and the union, and the support of the city, the company was declared bankrupt on December 21st, 1993. Since then, the bankruptcy proceedings have dragged out in court, and the union is still fighting for the workers to receive what is owed them in unpaid wages (worth some 600 million escudos).

8   Aníbal Cavaco Silva, prime minister between 1985 and 1995, of the center-right Social Democratic (PSD) government. Since January 2006, he has been president of the republic.

9   Minister of industry and energy in the eleventh and twelfth governments, between August 1987 and October 1995.

BSS: *Can you tell us a story where you were successful?*

FC: For example, there's COLSI in Coimbra. In 1992, this was in a situation of total crisis.[10] Anybody who looked at the company would say, "It's not economically viable. It will have to close." At the time, we fought fiercely—this was after the struggle for Ideal, but still during Cavaco Silva's government. The creditors' assembly was getting ready to file for bankruptcy, but the workers' struggle spoke louder. We managed to put those 500 women on the street, and we brought the city to a standstill. The secretary of state for social security was obliged to step in and put the company into administration—his vote was decisive, as social security was the biggest creditor.[11] He laid down a condition that was practically unheard of at the time—that the company should get rid of its previous manager, saying that he had a culture of avoiding paying the state.

The company passed into the hands of a new administrator that didn't do too well. Then, two more came in that were not doing badly. But, in October 1995, when it came out of administration, the old manager came back and took over again, to everyone's surprise. As the legislation was rather permissive, there were no safeguards against situations like that, and no one, not even the appointed administrators or the workers, could do anything to stop it—something which, in our opinion, should never have happened. He kept the company until 2000—that was five more years of not paying social security—and nothing happened. He only paid the workers. In the meantime, he set up another company inside this one, ORBIMODA, which is very common in these cases. Then he started to say that he was tired and wanted to give up the company, and so he went and got an Argentinean to run it. The Argentinean tried to take charge, using intimidation and repression to organize production, but the workers declared total war and demanded that the boss get rid of him, since it was really him and his sons that were in charge. Later, COLSI went bankrupt, and a partly state-owned company, ESTAMO, bought the premises. So ORBIMODA lost all its assets and, at the end of 2001, began to fall behind with wages. It was a critical situation.

What could the union and the workers do? No one believed in that company! But the workers said, "We're not going to let it close! We want our jobs!" And so there was only one route open to us—to fight with all our might, and knock on all doors. First, we got the minister of social security to listen to us, and he implemented the Wage Guarantee

---

10   One of Coimbra's biggest clothing companies. In 1991 it employed 700 workers, reduced to 550 in 1992. Already owing a huge social security debt, it lost one of its best customers in that year, which left it in a critical situation.

11   Social security debt, resulting from failure to pay the contributions deducted from employees' salaries, is very common among Portuguese companies.

Fund[12] so that workers who hadn't been paid for two or three months and were suffering great hardship would get something. Then we went looking for new investors, but we were disappointed by the mayor,[13] who did nothing to support industry in Coimbra. So in the end, though things had been bad with the previous mayor, now we were in the same state, or worse even.

So we started to try out new paths. The boss discovered a Canadian ex-emigrant who wanted to open a company, although he knew nothing about the clothing sector. We sent him off to SIRME/IAPMEI,[14] which undertook to help get the company on its feet.

In another company in Mira de Aire, three technicians, who were my colleagues, decided to set up a company after the revolution of April 25th, 1974. They were criticized by other businessmen, and nobody believed that they would manage to set up a new company. They began by building a small pavilion. They bought old looms from the company where they had worked and began operating them. As they earned, they invested in new machinery. Today, that is the most modern company in Mira de Aire, with the best market and the most workers—and the workers always earn a bit more than in their contract, as they are united and know how to make demands. Problems are solved through dialogue, and there are good levels of union membership, with four union leaders, and rights are respected.

Once there was a football match in which Portugal was playing, and all the men on the nightshift wanted to watch it. They asked one of the bosses if they could see the match, offering to compensate the company by working double-time afterwards. But the boss wouldn't listen, and he reacted strangely, differently from usual. "No!" he said. Conclusion: that whole section decided to watch the football match. The next morning, the older boss, who was a bit more sensible about these things, phoned the union saying, "We've got a very serious problem on our hands. You have to come over." "Why? What's happened?" And he explained the situation, saying that the sections were all stopped because there was no work to do. I was upset, because this was obviously rather complicated in legal terms. So, I said to him, "You know the law, sir." But he replied, "I want everyone to sit down and discuss this problem together. There has to be dialogue in these situations. I know I can dismiss them if I want

---

12   A social security provision designed to ensure the payment of wages owed by employers that have declared bankruptcy, insolvency, or have gone into liquidation. The maximum amount is six months' salary.

13   Carlos Encarnação, of the PSD, who became mayor of Coimbra in 2001, succeeding a Socialist Party mayor.

14   System of Incentives for the Revitalization and Modernization of Companies—a department of IAPMEI.

to, but if I didn't need them, I wouldn't have them here." That was a really sensible attitude that that businessman had, and I'd love it if others followed his example. So anyhow, we went there, fearing the worst. The twenty men started to say that they knew they'd acted illegally, but they'd done it because of the way their request had been received, and so, what they wanted was to speak to the person that had caused the situation, and they were not going to take lessons from anyone. I thought to myself, "Goodness, what on earth am I going to do here?" And I said to them, "Well, let's call them." And I told the bosses that we had come but that I was not going to be cannon-fodder. I said, "Let's all sit down around a table and listen to what both sides have to say." Everyone had their say, shouting and bawling, and then afterwards the workers suggested, "All right, sir, we'll give up a Saturday to compensate for the losses that we caused the company on that day. But next time we want to be treated with more respect, so that we can find solutions that will satisfy both parties' interests." And nothing like that ever happened again in that company.

BSS: *I'd like you to tell me more about the strategies you use in your struggle. Obviously the strategies changed in the 1990s, from a confrontational kind of unionism to one that is more interested in making companies work. Maybe strike action became less important than it used to be; but you always counted a great deal on the women to mobilize. It's a militant union with grassroots support, which operates with the support of the workers. How do you manage that? What strategy do you, as union leader, use to make sure that you don't just impose things from the top, but instead remain very connected to the people? Is it easy or difficult? How do you manage it?*

FC: I think that in these situations we need, above all, to be committed, to be prepared to make the effort to discover new ways of doing things. We also need to use a lot of common sense and to follow the heart. People have to trust us and to feel that we are completely committed, even if we don't really know what is the best thing to do. We have to make them feel that they are not alone in protecting their rights and in looking for solutions, however difficult the problem might be.

In one company, we discovered that some people had been hiding the fact that they were not eating, because their wages had not been paid, which is a common problem in our companies. I said, "Now, let's all talk about this. Why have they not had anything to eat? If there's no way of paying the wages, let's look at other alternatives. What are we going to do?"

In this case, it had been two months since the people had been paid. The easiest option would have been to go on strike. But I think that those are the worst moments to go on strike, because the whole thing could go into a coma and never recover. We didn't want to suspend contracts to get unemployment benefits. We begged them not to leave the company, because we feared that if they did, it might not open again, making it really difficult to find another course. But the people had to eat—they were earning 70 contos, it was very difficult. We're talking about the lowest wages. We don't have to go abroad to see situations like this; we have them right here on our doorstep.

We would telephone the civil governor ten times a day, if we thought it necessary, and he would say, "For God's sake!" "But Governor, these people are going hungry!" I telephoned IAPMEI and spoke to them all there, and said, "You've got to do something!" I phoned the minister of the economy and António Guterres's private advisor.[15] I phoned Dr. Paulo Pedroso,[16] saying, "I cannot have these people going hungry." And he told me to apply to PEC/IAPMEI. So we applied in the name of the workers and activated the Wage Guarantee Fund, so that the wages were immediately paid. This gave the people something to believe in and made them feel that we were with them in their problems. This inspired them to go on fighting for a solution.

That is how we work—always trying to find solutions, sometimes by looking for little gaps in the law, or by trying to get a response from institutions, pressurizing the people in power who analyze the technical files, and who say "There's no way out of this problem." I say "Are you sure? There must be. For sure there is!" And they feel so pressurized that they say, "You don't give us a break!"

THE STRUGGLE FOR FIANDEIRA AND LANIFÍCIA

FC: In Mira de Aire, where I'm from, there were two wool companies that were over sixty years old, had a lot of assets, and which underwent restructuring in the 1980s, using EC funds for the sector. These investments were made at a time when the dollar was very high, and so they started having serious problems with transactions and with the banks. Although the companies were now better equipped technologically than they had been before, they had also got themselves further into debt. And if we also count the serious problems that they had with organization, management, and commercialization, you can see how they got

---

15 António Guterres was elected prime minister in the general election of 1995, occupying the post until March 2002.
16 Secretary of state for employment and professional training in the thirteenth government (November 1997–October 1999), secretary of state for labor and solidarity, and minister for labor and solidarity in the fourteenth government (October 1999–April 2002).

into such a state. Meanwhile, the banks pulled the carpet out from under their feet and they started to default. The commercial part began to go down, interest rates increased, and the companies began to go bust. It was a great problem for almost all the wool companies that had restructured.

These companies ended up having to use Decree-Law 132,[17] and go into administration. The same thing almost happened to them as happened with Ideal. The creditors were getting ready to file for bankruptcy. There were 200 workers, which, in a small town like that, would have been a disaster. And we said, "No, these companies can't close." We held meetings with the management, who said, "There's nothing we can do. They're going to file for bankruptcy." "So we have to fight and demand support from the government and institutions responsible," I said. "We have to act right away, contacting the people responsible for getting the creditors to put the company into administration."

We went to the ministries and the situation was studied. They said, "No, FIANDEIRA and LANIFÍCIA are not viable. Technically, in the opinion of the creditors, these companies are not viable." But we replied, "These companies cannot go bankrupt!" It's a great pity that most businessmen only recognize the value and strength of the unions at moments like these. After the problems have been solved, they often go back to ignoring us again.

Given the creditors' determination to close down the companies, the idea started to develop of finding a solution through judicial foreclosure, if there were buyers interested in taking over the companies. At that time, the PS government supported this alternative, so the problem lay in finding a new investor that would take over FIANDEIRA and LANIFÍCIA. So we started the tough job of looking for other investors. We asked all the businessmen of Mira de Aire, and others, but it was no good. Then, one of the directors, who had been there since the company had been in administration and who wasn't a shareholder, offered to keep going and to try to find two or three more investors. "Ah, but the government doesn't want any of the former shareholders, and I'm not in a position to do it. I haven't any money. I've just bought a new house and I'm paying off a mortgage."

As it happened, the government, using existing legislation, had imposed the condition that none of the previous management could remain. I said, "Why can't they stay? Does the law really have to be applied in such a heavy-handed fashion?" And that's when the first war started. Because, perhaps if a chap has a name and face like a capitalist, they say, "He's a capitalist; he has the legal and financial conditions, and he's not connected

17   Decree-Law 132/93 of April 23rd, Code of Special Company Recovery and Bankruptcy Procedure.

with the past—he's good." when at times that's not true. But this was a big obstacle. A journalist once said to me, "You're not going to get anywhere that way. That didn't work in Marinha Grande or anywhere else. That route doesn't lead anywhere." So the project was rejected, not because it was not economically viable, but only because they would only take on firms that still had people from the previous board.

Everything was heading towards the project being rejected altogether, and the company going bankrupt. I spoke to Dr. Vítor Ramalho, who at the time was secretary of state for the economy, and he was very sensitive to these problems. He said to me, "Fátima, to be honest, I don't have the strength on my own to solve this problem; I need a decision from above." So we told the civil governor that, with the more recent developments, the workers had decided to go on hunger strike in front of the civil governor's headquarters in Leiria. We were so determined that, at that moment, we were ready to try almost anything.

Meanwhile, we heard that António Guterres was coming to Coimbra for a debate with the local PS politicians in the Gil Vicente Theatre, and we said to the civil governor, "Listen, we need to speak to the prime minister. He's in Coimbra, and we want to talk to him about this serious situation." It was a Saturday. The other union leader and I were waiting from nine in the morning to eight at night in front of the Gil Vicente Theatre, to see when he would receive us. He saw us at eight at night. In fact he was very understanding. Although the PS crowd and all that group of elites wanted to take him away to have dinner, he said, "No! I have all the time in the world to talk to you now." And I said, "There's a serious problem in Mira de Aire. We need your help urgently to save those companies and those jobs. So, you have to intervene so that the various ministries will make the companies viable." He said to me, "Fátima, tell me the honest truth: Do you really think that they are able to carry off the project?" For a trade unionist, that was very difficult to answer, but we wanted so much to solve the problem that we said, "Yes, we do." The most important thing was to save those jobs. So he phoned Dr. Vítor Ramalho right away and said, "Let's save those companies."

The next Monday, an IAPMEI representative phoned me and we were a whole hour talking. He said, "Although I have a great deal of admiration and consideration for your work, I have to analyze these projects technically. And technically speaking, my opinion is that FIANDEIRA and LANIFÍCIA are not viable. But listen, because of your commitment and everything you believe in, I'll give them the go-ahead. We'll approve the project, but I want to tell you that I don't believe in it." And so I said, "So let's make a deal. In a month's time, or two, or three, if the project isn't working, I'll admit I was wrong. But if it works, then you'll have to do that, OK?" Three months later he rang me. "Fátima," he said, "I was wrong. You were right all along!"

THE STRUGGLE FOR SEPORCENTRO

BSS: *One of the things that appears a lot in your practice, and which you also refer to often, is your capacity to raise the self-esteem of women. Women workers are not usually very skilled, and their bosses' attitudes don't do much to raise their self-esteem. And sometimes, in crisis situations, you have managed to get women to fight in a very advanced way. For example, in SEPORCENTRO, the women went and slept at the factory entrance for three days. How did you manage that? How did you get the idea? Because I know that sometimes these struggles are not completely planned.*

FC: In these situations, normally, when we plan things, they don't work. It's more like waking up in the morning, getting an idea, and then going and talking it over with the women. That's what happened in this case. At SEPORCENTRO, they had fallen behind with the wages.[18] We are talking about a company with advanced technology, which worked for some of the biggest brands, and which was part of a group of companies that had been set up in different parts of the country in order to take advantage of subsidies that existed there, because in Oporto, which was where the mother company was based, there were none. So they had come to areas where there was no clothing industry, but where there were a lot of women that could get support, as they'd never worked in the industry before. So they began to work, they got training, and, with so much financial assistance, it seemed like the company would have a long future. But after five years the support ended, and the company began to fall behind with salaries. So the workers decided not to work until they got paid. We held a meeting in Oporto, at the headquarters of the mother company, where they told us that they were having difficulties and that they were going to go into administration using Decree-Law 132, which actually never happened. But the workers didn't fall for it, and when the trucks came to take away the merchandise they wouldn't let them out.

From then on, the struggle was very hard; but, at the same time, those women managed to teach everyone a lesson—not just their relatives, but also the people in general. One day I phoned the mayor of Poiares and said, "You've got to help these women. We cannot let the trucks leave." He didn't think twice, and sent the council car. Things started to get complicated; no one knew how this was going to end, since positions

---

18   Factory producing sports equipment for brands like Adidas and Nike. It employed eighty women workers in 2000.

were getting more and more extreme, in an area where there was no experience of struggle. Those women had never fought before! We had a group of unionists among them, but most of them were not members. I told them that we had to extend the movement—which was not difficult; and so the struggle took on a whole different tone, which was nice. The whole town of Poiares got behind those women. The nights were cold, but they didn't lose heart, and soon wood appeared, so that they could make a fire. The baker took them warm bread; other people took food and drinks. Those women felt almost like princesses with so much support, in spite of all the sacrifices they were making.

The women began to wonder: "And so now what? We can't keep stopping these trucks without getting something." And from then on, every day, at every hour, every minute, they kept their mind on their goal, chanting, "We want our salaries." And the management told them, "It's not us that pay you. It's not the company, it's the brand Nike." "Ah, but the boss said that he didn't have it, and so we're not going to leave here until you give us the money." We got them all worried, and so they called the police, saying that it was an illegal strike—and we said to the civil governor, "If you do that, you've had it with us." He couldn't go down that route, because all the people of Poiares would have supported the workers even more.

The women did shifts. There are photographs of them with blankets there on the ground, in the middle of the road. They stayed there day and night, but when Friday arrived, we began to realize that it would be difficult to spend the whole weekend there. And, to make matters worse, there was a festival going on in the town. How could they stand it? So, that Friday, at seven in the morning, I could hear them muttering, "How are we going to last this out the whole weekend?" My colleague, Luís, was putting diesel in his car to go back to Coimbra, and suddenly I had a crazy idea. I got on the phone and called the civil governor. "We're done for!" I said. "And why is that?" he asked. "Listen, we have information that there's a group ready to burn the trucks. That's going to really cause trouble. You've got to do something right away. You'd better get on the phone to the managers and to the brand owners, tell them that if they want they can solve the problem by paying the women. One thing's for sure, though, you're not going to attack the women. It will be the end of you if you do!" The man panicked, and every half-hour he was on the phone to me: "Fátima, I'm calling an emergency meeting."

The television companies were there, broadcasting live, and the other press, sensing the worst, ended up staying with us and helped the struggle along. It's a pity that these things only work at those moments. Everyone was so nervous that someone was always asking, "So, what is going to happen?" "Ah, I don't know!" we would reply. "I don't know what's going to happen!" "You haven't planned what you're going to do?" "No, it depends." "So, you still might. . . ?" "We might. Listen, if they come to take away the trucks, we won't let them, and then there'll be blood!"

In the meantime, the civil governor managed to call the meeting. The bosses came from Oporto; also the brand representatives. There were about twenty of us in the Civil Government headquarters. I'd never seen so many reporters all around. They were all there. We had a meeting that lasted four hours, but we didn't get anywhere. I said, "You've got to solve the problem. Pay the women today, and the trucks will be allowed to leave immediately." "But all our work is there; we're running the risk of losing orders, and now you still want us to pay the workers?" "I don't know anything about that. That's your problem, and you'd better sort it out with the bosses of SEPORCENTRO. We've got nothing to do with it." There were phone calls to America, phone calls to here and there. At 3 p.m., the boss called me to say, "Fátima, we've only managed to get 50 contos." So I pretended that I'd spoken to the women, and said, "No one accepts that. We can stay here a month—we're in no hurry! We're all together on this." He replied, "Yes, even the mayor is on your side. That's what really bugs me." You see, there was also a political problem there. How could the PS be seen to be dragging their feet about this when the town's mayor, who was PSD, was on our side? Politically, they were trapped, and what was most important was that everyone ended up helping.

By then it was 5 p.m., and the brand representative phoned me: "If we give you the money, will you let us get the trucks out today?" "Of course! We don't want to keep the trucks here for any reason. All we want is money for the workers who are hungry. The workers have to fight with whatever weapons they have at hand, and this is the only one they've got." "But it's not our fault," he said. "I'm not blaming you. I'm just saying that we want the money, nothing else."

At 6 p.m. the governor called me: "Oh Fátima, there's a bit of light at the end of the tunnel, but it's still a bit gray." The man hadn't even had lunch that day! Meanwhile, they phoned me to say, "Listen, we've got a solution. You can tell the workers that they will pay you and to let the trucks out." "No, no. Only when we've got a check in our hand. We won't let the trucks go until then." "We've given our word of honor to the civil governor." "We're tired of words. We want the check." "But how do you think we're going to find a way of getting a check to you to pay you today?" This was Friday, and it was already getting dark. I replied, "Come here. You can give it to the civil governor; we don't care who receives the check. But we want the check in hand." After some hours of anguishing about it, they decided to come and give us the check. And we were all there. The press kept asking, "Do you know anything?" "I don't know anything at all," I said. But I said to the workers, "I think we're winning."

Then one of the bosses and a brand rep phoned me. Three lawyers appeared, and an Englishman from Oporto, and goodness knows how many others, and they said, "Listen, let's go to the Town Hall—the civil governor is there, and we will hand over the check there. We're not going to the plant, or else we'll have to confront all those people." And they didn't want to confront the women, because they had nothing to do with it. But we replied, "We're not going to the Town Hall. The women want you to come and hand over the check at the gate of the company." "But we don't want to be filmed." And I said: "That's your problem. Tell the press that you don't want to be filmed." So they came in their big Mercedes, and the press said to me, "You won't accept the check in secret, will you?" "You won't go away from here, will you?" And I said, "Don't worry, I'm not leaving here. I want the women to see this important act." So they came and turned their backs, and I went behind the truck and they gave me the check. It was an official letter, with a check stapled to it. They said, "You will show this just to the women. Please do not show the press, because we don't want them to know who's paid the check." After a second, I said, "Look, girls! Here's the check." And the press caught all that. Everyone clapped. It was a very moving and beautiful moment. Everyone was saying, "It was worth the effort!" "That was the most interesting moment of my life!" and "I'm never going to be the same again, now that I know that I'm able to change things!"

TRADE UNIONISM

BSS: *You are a great trade union leader, with a remarkable ability to stir up people, mobilize state institutions, and even the managers themselves. Have you always had the support of unionist women, or not? What is the membership rate among women? And what is your relationship like with women who are members and those that are not? Are they treated in the same way?*

FC: Our membership rates are reasonable, despite repression in many companies that don't allow unions. But, on the other hand, every day we lose members when companies close down. In the examples that I gave just now, the level of membership is very good, as high as 80 percent. At these times, even technicians that are not unionized are on our side, since it is our motto not to discriminate against anyone. We try to have an open shop, where everyone feels represented. When the time comes to fight for workers' rights, we are always available to help those that are members and those that are not. We just want the non-members to realize how important the unions are in society, and how they can help them sort out their problems, so that they don't just come running to the union when they need us. That's why we say to them afterwards, "Now you should also show some solidarity with the union and its members, who are the reason for our existence." But unionism is going through a bad phase. The biggest problems are lack of respect for union rights; persecution, which makes people afraid of joining; and situations when the union has to meet secretly somewhere outside the company, in a café or in the woods.

That's still quite common today. We are in companies where our members ignore us so that no one suspects that they are members, and then later they will call and say, "Sorry, I passed you just now and pretended not to know you. Don't take it the wrong way, but if they knew I was a member, I'd be done for." We still get situations like that today, where the managers see the unions as bogies! Many are women, since we usually develop much stronger empathy with women much sooner. Sometimes it can get a bit too much, and we find ourselves getting involved with the person not just as a worker, but also in other areas of their lives, such as when the person has health problems, or others of a more personal nature.

A few days ago, I was listening to the minister Bagão Félix,[19] a man with a very Catholic social vision and morality. He spoke about the change in the law designed to help companies get back on their feet, attract investors, and develop industry. There are things there that could, and should, be changed. But is that all there is to it? What about those companies where unionism is not allowed, where overtime is not paid, where workers don't have the right to organize their own lives, and have to be available at any time, including at night and on Saturdays, always ready when the big orders come in? Not to mention the rights of women, which are not always respected, such as the right to breastfeed and get family support. One woman, just because she asked the company for two hours off so that she could breastfeed her baby, had the tires on her car slashed, and other repressions. We asked to intervene two or three times and never found anything, so she had to

19   Minister of labor and social security in the fifteenth government, who proposed the introduction of important reforms in the areas of social security and labor. The reference is to the proposal for a new labor code, in negotiation with Social Concertation and involving public debate, which attracted fierce criticism from various sectors, including the unions, which accused it of eroding rights already achieved.

choose: either she could keep her job, or she could stay with the baby. So she had to resign.

These situations are still happening today—in the twenty-first century! And some of the companies that do all these things, that don't respect minimal rights, also have financial problems. So, is this just a problem of legislation? It might be in some cases, but for most companies that's not the problem, not at the heart of the matter. The bosses, in most cases, still do whatever they want with their workers. And they get away with it because the systems that are supposed to control such things don't work properly, and most businessmen have a culture of tax evasion and law evasion.

SEXUAL DISCRIMINATION IN COMPANIES

BSS: *The fact that most workers in this industry are women means that there are cases of gross violations of rights, such as, for example, the right to breastfeed. Have you had any other cases of bosses with completely chauvinistic ideas that the women complain about? What is the situation regarding sexual discrimination in companies today?*

FC: Normally in companies, and particularly in the clothing industry, most of the workers are women. In textiles, part of the intensive workforce is women, but where there is intensive capital, there are also men. The bosses are usually men, and they often strut about like roosters among so many women.

The main problem is that people don't want to talk about these things— they're afraid. For example, some women do overtime, and so someone has to take them home—and then on the road, they might try something. Once a woman reacted badly, and two months later she was fired. These are situations that people don't talk about much. Everyone knows when someone has something going with someone, but some workers think, "Maybe if I did that, they wouldn't repress me so much, I'd be treated better." These situations are not always identified, but unfortunately they do exist. But I think it was worse in the past!

BSS: *Is it difficult for you to talk about these things with the women?*

FC: Yes, it's a bit taboo. It's a problem nowadays, in our society. If it's a person's free choice, then I've got nothing against it. It's just that normally it's not. In fact, I had a problem like that myself, soon after April 25th. The bosses were very insecure. When I became union delegate, one of them—the one that maybe tried that tactic the most, and who had already had some things going about the place—started to give me a lift home every day. I lived about 5 km away, which I would usually walk every day with the other girls, and I started to get quite worried. "Oh,

Mr. Ferreira,[20] it would be better if I walked with the others, or at least, you could give them a lift as well." "No, I have to talk to you." And he started to tell me what a good girl I was, the best—how I had such a solid basis and very important principles. He offered me whatever place I wanted in the office. I could be a receptionist or go into bookkeeping; I could even get a management job, because he said I was "smart." And I once told him, "Oh, Mr. Ferreira, I've worked here for so many years, you never told me I was good at anything, and now, all of a sudden, I've become good at everything!" "No!" he replied. "We always thought that. We were just waiting for the opportunity to put it into practice." One day, on the road, we went to a place where he had a mill, and he told me that this was the best place to reflect. I realized that his reflections were heading in quite a different direction, and so I said to him, "Look, Mr. Ferreira, you be careful about what you're doing, because I'm going to tell everything in the plant. I'll tell everyone! And you know, I don't want to be a manager, I don't want to go into the office. I'll keep on just as I am, and don't think that I'm going to give up being union delegate. I want to honor my responsibilities to the workers that voted me in, and, actually, I'm liking doing it." "But you've only been delegate for a few days—how can you possibly be liking it?" "Ah, because I've realized that this is the best way of defending my rights and ideals. So don't pressure me, because I'm not going to change. If you want to get on with me, then you'll just have to accept it." After that day, he never gave me a lift again—and he didn't speak to me again either.

BSS: *As women are in the majority here, has the union had any problems in making sure that salaries are the same for people doing the same work in the plants? Is that a priority for you, or has the problem never arisen?*

FC: In contractual terms, we don't have that problem. But the companies generally give more of a push to men than to women. For example, in addition to their contractual salary, they may give perks to the men, arguing that they do heavier work and there are differences in that. We normally react, but it's not easy to combat that sort of discrimination that goes beyond what's laid down in the contract.

I don't want to suggest, though, that this happens in all companies. For example, we have a company[21] in the Coimbra area that is economically stable, and where a group of men, who have always been able to mobilize better, decided to demand a raise. And they managed it. Today, they earn more than is stipulated in their contract. One day, I called a general meeting and said, "So, girls, what are we going to do about this? There's going to be a strike to demand more money and you're not coming in with us?

---

20 Not his real name.
21 A textile company with 200 workers, and one of the few with its own brand.

You're on the contractual minimum! The men have asked for 5 contos, so let's ask for 5 contos for everyone." We managed to get the raise for everyone! But the men still say today, "If we hadn't had that joint effort, we'd be better off today."

WOMEN AND TRADE UNIONISM

BSS: *We all know that there is still a lot of chauvinism in our society, and one of the problems is the fact that women have to double as mothers and housewives at the same time as they are workers. Their husbands surely are not always very understanding about their union activity, or about activities that mobilize women. Have you got any stories of that type?*

FC: Actually, the last one. . . Nothing like that had ever happened to me in all these years as a union leader, but it happened just a short time ago. In one of the Coimbra companies, a woman worker, who was not a union member, came to join so she could get her rights, just like the other workers. She was young, and her husband too. But when the difficult period was over, he ordered her to leave the union. But she had the courage not to do that. So he came into the union headquarters saying that we were forcing people to join. He wasn't talking to me, he was talking to another leader; but I was in the same office. "Hang on a minute, what's all this about?" I had to react: I came out and asked him, "What? I've only heard your voice, I've not heard what your wife has to say. She's the worker in this sector. You're a right macho man, aren't you?" I think I lost it a bit—I was not talking normally: "You can get out of this union office right now. You've got no right to speak for your wife. She's got a mouth—she can speak for herself!"

The man had a bit of a stammer, and at that time, he couldn't manage to speak to me. But later he said, "If I catch you in the street, you won't want to know what I'll do to you!" And I said, "Go ahead, just try! It's really sad that you're trying to interfere in your wife's work. When we went to help you with your problems, you didn't mind in the least! Nor when she arrived home with the money that we managed to get for her. You're not just a macho man—you're also an opportunist!"

With women, union organization is more difficult. Only in some struggles, particularly when the heart is involved, such as when we're defending jobs and salaries—then the men don't interfere much because they've also had similar problems. But when it's about voting for delegates or leaders, then it's very hard, because the women are still the main ones in charge of bringing up the children and doing the housework. So they have very little free time. When we are able to elect leaders or delegates, in some companies, they lay down conditions: we can only carry out union activities inside the company, because they say they can't go anywhere else, to meetings outside. Because it's very difficult to get time off from the family. Normally, only those women who have had a different kind of life, who have emancipated themselves because they're not very attached to their families, or because they haven't such a structured family—it's easier to get them to participate. As well as that, I don't think the problem is helped much by the way union structures operate. The meetings are long, they don't fit in very well with family life, or with nursery timetables, and sometimes the subjects discussed go off onto other areas away from the concrete problems that they feel in their workplaces, and so they don't have an answer. Even if they're physically present, they're not always really there in spirit. They don't feel really motivated to take part.

With all these problems, despite the fact that women are in the majority in many sectors, in the unions and in middle management structures they're a minority. It's the men who usually end up in leadership roles. But, for example, one thing that I liked a lot was taking part for some years in a women's association, Frauen.[22] This was a group of independent women where I could go without representing the trade union movement or any other institution.

BSS: *How did that come about?*

FC: There was a German teacher that I met here in Coimbra, and we became friends. She had friends in that organization, and said to me, "Hey, I'll go along and talk to them, and I'll ask them to invite you to one of these meetings. You'll find it interesting, the exchange of ideas and experiences—you'll see." I didn't go to represent Portugal, I went just to represent myself. But I was the only Portuguese woman there. Most of them were intellectuals, from different countries of Europe— many were connected to the university and other kinds of work, and they had a way of thinking that was very open and very interesting.

At the first meeting, they asked me what I had thought, and I said, "I thought it was a pity that the subjects that you discussed here were not really relevant to my own life. You didn't speak about jobs, working hours, or about those things that I think restrict women the most. You spoke about women's freedom, freedom in the relationship between men and women." And it was funny, because the next meeting was all about the work economy, and later there was another about flexibility and management of working hours. After that, they got involved in all those subjects.

---

22   Frauen holds an annual international meeting to discuss the problems encountered by women in various countries (within western and Eastern Europe, Africa, Latin America, and Asia).

That exchange of ideas and experiences, without being tied down to anything, that was very useful for me—very interesting.

BSS: *Do you consider yourself a feminist?*

FC: I don't think I am much—it's that I can't really get into that very closed scheme. Sometimes feminists are very closed. That's the problem—women's rights seen through a single prism. I think that there are rights that we should defend for both women and men. I don't have the view that we have to work only for us, women. We all have to get involved, women and men. Maybe women should play a bigger role in educating men, or at least in trying to change their mentalities so that equality is not just an empty word.

BSS: *Do you think that the fact that you are a woman has determined or influenced your way of being a union leader very much? Sometimes you talk a lot about the slog, and things like that. Do you think that your way of doing things, which is extremely creative and at the same time very involved, is a personal character trait, or does it come from the fact that you are a woman? You sometimes say that, in a world of men, at least at the level of leadership, you have also known how to seize the advantage on behalf of your movement, for your organization.*

FC: I don't really know how to answer that, but I think that I've realized I am a woman, and for quite a long time, I was rather atrophied as a woman. Everything I've achieved has involved a great deal of struggle, a lot of effort. I was very blocked—I was afraid of myself, and shy. I think that it was being part of the JOC, and then participating in the revolution, that woke me up. That was when I began to think, "I can do it. I'm going to fight. I'm going to change. I don't want to be like this." And so things started to change inside me, which I'm proud of today. I like being a woman! And I think that I've learned a lot about what men are like too. Often I had that idea about the boss, that the boss was someone who was frightening, who intimidated and repressed us. Those myths started to collapse as I gradually became aware of what I was capable of standing up to. I began to understand that men also have their weaknesses. And that let me realize where their weak points were, so that I could defend myself.

It was a very difficult period. I was accused of causing all the problems in the company; everything was my fault, because they wanted me to give up, not to succeed, because I—me and my companions—we believed in what we were doing. In this chauvinistic society that we live in, if we women, who have some abilities (and there are a lot who have far more than me!), if we discover a route that we can go down, if we know how to use men's weaknesses—those men that are more chauvinistic, more macho in their outlook—then we can gain some ground. And I think that, as a union leader, I've won a few dividends out of that.

THE RELATIONSHIP WITH THE UNION MOVEMENT

BSS: *I'd like to change the subject a bit now, because there are still some other things I'd like to talk about and which I think are important—the enthusiasm that you've brought to these struggles, and which shows through when you talk about them, and the obvious successes that have made you one of the most prominent union leaders in our country. Now I'd like to talk about leadership, the "machine," as you call it. You've always had problems with that machine, particularly with the CGTP. I'd like to hear how all that developed, because it has left quite a mark on your work, hasn't it?*

FC: I think the reason for this has to do with my own particular constitution, the way I'm made. I'm just not cut out for "machines," for people all thinking alike. The root of my struggles in Mira de Aire and other places, the way I got involved in everything, was always very spontaneous and creative. That was where I learned what I know, and I felt good there.

That's why I didn't get on so well when I came to Coimbra, at the time of the merger in 1977, when four textile unions from Alcobaça and Coimbra, wool industries from Castanheira, Mira de Aire, and Coimbra, and clothing unions from Coimbra, Guarda, Castelo Branco, and Leiria all joined up together. As you know, I am from Mira de Aire, and there we always had the freedom to think for ourselves. There was always a way of working things out by discussing everything thoroughly and thinking things through, without having things imposed from outside or wherever. When I came to Coimbra, I had great trouble adapting to the way the union functioned, after the merger. It wasn't just that the union was very influenced by the Communist Party; there were ways of working that were different from what I was used to, and which I didn't adapt to very well.

I would travel 100 km to get here to the leadership meetings, but I felt very sad. I would cry a lot on the way, and spent my time hassling the chairman of the General Assembly. I would write him letters saying that I wanted to resign, because I couldn't fit in with that way of working, or with the way they thought. We would have an idea, we would start talking about it, and sooner or later, they would say, "No, we can't decide today—only in the next meeting." Sometimes they would go out to telephone, and only afterwards would they decide, after Rua da Sofia[23] had said yes or no. When I began to understand this, I thought, "What on earth am I doing here? I could stay in Mira de Aire. I work there—I could be with my coworkers and friends and do my job as union leader without being constrained all the time."

---

23   Headquarters of the Coimbra Delegation of the Communist Party.

I couldn't go to the other general meetings. I could only carry out my unionist activity in Mira de Aire, since they said that was my area, where they were not accepted. But here in Coimbra, once I went to a general meeting and they spent the whole time saying, "Shut up, shut up!" I'd hardly got going. I couldn't live like that.

In the meantime, I was appointed coordinator. I came once a week, and there were four full-time directors, so I couldn't go out to the companies. They only sent me when things got very complicated, such as once in Lousã. This was around the time of the revolution in 1974, and there was a dispute between two workers about who would get a holiday when. The two men started beating each other up inside the plant, and so the boss fired them. And I thought, then, "No! He might be able to fire them, legally, but we won't accept this dismissal." I asked for help from a lawyer friend, and he gave me some ideas. I called a general meeting of all the workers in the Paper Union. They elected a committee for the purpose, and we met up with the directors of the company and managed to get the two workers readmitted, without any punishment beyond apologizing for their behavior.

Another time, also in Lousã, there was a mistake in the contracts of the wool factories, which gave the bosses the possibility of increasing the working hours. CARVALHOS tried it, and increased the hours. This was a company that gave quite a few perks, such as bicycles, and other things; so they had their workers in the palm of their hand. However, with the support of the union, the workers decided to draw up a petition to say that they were against the increase in work hours, and the boss called them in one by one. As you can guess, they managed to persuade all the workers to sign a new petition, accepting the new timetable.

The following day, I went along to the plant and they said, "No, we're not going to talk to you. We're weaklings! First we signed your petition, and then we signed the bosses' one. We couldn't say no! We were afraid." "No, but we'll win," I told them. "How can we win, with the petition that we all signed saying that we accept the new timetable!" So I went to the bosses and I said, "Listen, if you increase the work hours, you will be the first company in the wool industry to do it, and I'll bring here all the workers from Covilhã, Gouveia, Mira de Aire, and Castanheira. So you don't know what you're letting yourself in for!" Then we called a meeting to see if we could get them to change their minds, and, instead of increasing the timetable to forty-two hours, we managed to get them to reduce it from forty to thirty-seven and a half hours, for most workers. But not all the union leaders approved of this way of working. That was back in 1979.

In 1980, there was a single list, which was common, and I warned the chairman of the General Assembly: "Listen, I'm telling you now, I don't want to be on it." "No! Stay, and we'll get a group together of independents that will have a majority in the management." "Sure! We'll get the majority, but then we won't be able to hold it together for long, and we'll give up, as has already happened." But we tried again, and, as we predicted, the independents were all demobilized, and we soon became a minority, without managing to work together as a team.

Meanwhile, the chairman of the General Assembly was in Lisbon one day—a historic day—and I went to speak to him, and I said, "Listen, I'm going to quit. I'm going to hand in my resignation, and this time you have to accept it!" And he said, "OK, let's do a deal. You'll keep on until the end, and we'll draw up an alternative list." It's true that they had a lot of support in the Coimbra district, but in the wool plants around Mira de Aire, Castanheira de Pêra, and Avelar, we were stronger.

I think the chairman of the General Assembly said that, but never thought that we would take things so far. And then, right near the date of the elections, I told him, "Hey, we've got a team." "What! You've got enough people?" "Yes, we have. All we need is you and the others from your area. We need twenty-six people." "That can't be!" he said. "But no one's going to give up!" I said. "This is going to go ahead." He replied, "Let's see. But we can still all talk, can't we?" We replied, "Only with the consent of everyone that has agreed to go on the list."

That was maybe the most difficult decision for us all, but especially for the chairman of the General Assembly, who was a member of the executive board, a historic figure, who had done a lot for the unity of our confederation. He was in a very difficult position, because, as there were two lists, he had to choose one. We had many hours of really intense talks before we managed to reach an agreement. No one wanted to give up. Everyone had their say, because it wasn't common at that time to have two lists for the same trade union center. And in the negotiation phase, we couldn't reach an agreement to do a single list.

Then, on the day when the lists were to be presented, Kalidás, the chairman of the General Assembly, was missing, as well as the people from his area, who we really wanted on our list, out of friendship and because of what they represented for the union movement and Castanheira de Pera. That was a moment of great tension; our nerves were on edge. We waited till the last minute, and then handed over the incomplete list at the last moment, as the statutes stipulated, so that the members who were missing could join the list. We didn't think we'd be able to get the list in on time. Our representative had to run up the stairs two at a time.

When we arrived, the chairman of the General Assembly said, "Right, we've got here two lists. We've got five days from now to sort out this problem. Let's talk." At that time, positions were very extreme, and there was no possibility of a consensus. And he added: "I can't see myself being on one of these lists. I don't agree with this split. You're pushing me out of the union—after I've given my whole life to the movement. Fátima, you're my friend, you're all my friends! That's why I can't understand why you're taking such extreme attitudes." And he left. It was a really bad moment. And obviously we wanted to have Kalidás on our list—it would only make sense if he was; that was the natural order of things. At that time, the right had got into the government, with Cavaco Silva, and they were saying to me, "You see, with radical attitudes and gestures like that, Cavaco has won in your region." And I replied, "So, instead of considering the fact that I'm from a really conservative part of the country where it's difficult to start a union movement at all, and fulfill the revolution's ideals, you prefer to accuse me of things like that! You know what I've been through there! Maybe Cavaco Silva has won in my area—so why have you not prevented him from winning in the whole country?" I guess I lost it a bit. They realized they'd said the wrong thing, and we went away. It was a very bad moment.

Kalidás was in a great dilemma. It was not easy to choose, what with the position he held in the union movement. The most natural thing would have been for him to have been on our list. He was a socialist, and was representing the minorities in the CGTP-IN. But if he stayed out of the union, he wouldn't be able to continue in the executive, because he wouldn't have the support of the union that he had helped to found. So he went to Castanheira de Pêra to have a think.

It was then that everyone intervened, and one day, I suddenly thought, "Right. I'm going to call Arnaut,"[24] as he had been the lawyer in the wool union. I asked him to have a word with Kalidás, who was his friend, to try to persuade him to join our list. I also phoned Lopes Cardoso.[25] Some months later, Kalidás told me: "You know, even Arnaut and Lopes Cardoso rang me to try to get me to join your list!" In those five days, he hadn't even been to the executive council, and Judas, among the other directors, phoned him and tried to get him to be on our list. Five days

---

24 António Arnaut, founder of the Socialist Party and minister of social affairs, who was responsible for setting up the national health system.
25 He was in the opposition during the period of the Estado Novo. After the Revolution of April 25th, 1974, he joined the directorate of the Socialist Party (PS), becoming minister of agriculture and fisheries in the sixth provisional government and the first constitutional government, from which he resigned. He was one of the founders of UEDS, the party that elected him to parliament, and which was dissolved in 1986 when he returned definitively to the PS.

later, a friend of mine, who was also on the executive, Mila from Oporto, rang me and said, "Don't say anything, but Kalidás is going to join your list."

We got to the last day, and he called a new meeting of the members of the two lists, and said, "Listen, I've come here today to see if we can make just one single list." "It's not worth it, mate," everyone said. And he announced that he was going to be on our list, saying that this was the one he most identified with. It was the right decision, it passed. After that, we got down to work. We got busy on the campaign, because it was very important for the autonomy of the union. We began with Ideal, as there were some 400 or so members there. I went with Kalidás—and it was not easy at that time because the other list had a lot of influence there—and tried to boycott the general meeting. But as women tend to work more from the heart (and I had won their hearts over a bit), we managed to get them to listen to us, despite all their grumbling. And, believe me, speaking to some 500 people without a megaphone is not easy! He came out and said, "So, is this how differences of opinion are respected at the grassroots level? But what sort of unity is this that we're building? It can't go on like this!" I think this made him question the whole unity of the union movement and the way that it related to people.

It was a very complicated moment, because it wasn't common for there to be two lists within the same organization. If you did it, you were called divisive. It was hard—very hard. During the electoral campaign, the whole union apparatus was behind the other list, and our list only had the support of the people on it. We had to subsidize the whole campaign ourselves, and one or two directors from other unions, that were friends, helped out with some money. But it left us with nothing!

Then election day arrived. I had the idea that we might win, but Kalidás thought we were going to lose. When they were counting the votes, we couldn't even add two and two together any more! He said, "Fátima, if we lose, I'll be the one who will have lost the most." And he was right. In political terms, he was the one with the most to lose. But I said, "But if we win, you also have a lot to gain. And I'm really pleased that that's the case. You deserve it! You will have better conditions and more authority to defend the autonomy and unity of the union movement, which are so important to you—because now the union will be on your side, defending your principles!"

When the votes came in from Mira de Aire, we were losing and the people from the other list were all radiant, never imagining that Mira de Aire would vote in mass for our list. They were the last. Kalidás, as chairman of the General Assembly, was responsible for the whole election, and so it was he who answered the phone to record the votes. I was standing next to him and helped him add it up right away, because he couldn't anymore, with that atmosphere. Then I said quietly, "We've won." There were people from the other list who took their defeat very badly, because they never believed that the votes from Mira de Aire could have ended up giving the victory to us. So they left, and we—as we had no champagne, like they had—we went out and bought a bottle of normal wine and celebrated.

Agostinho Roseta,[26] may he rest in peace, phoned and said, "Congratulations on your victory and courage," saying that attitudes like that were rare in the union movement.

BSS: *Agostinho Roseta was in the UGT at that time, wasn't he? Did he try to persuade you to join the UGT?*[27]

FC: No. Agostinho Roseta taught me a lot—he was a good friend. It didn't matter what position he was in. I don't think you should judge people by their status or position, but rather by what they are, and, without a shadow of a doubt, he was a very worthy man, always ready to defend great causes, very human and supportive. When I was elected union delegate, I didn't understand anything about it, and so I'd go to the cafés in Mira de Aire to telephone him at my own cost, to ask for help. At that time, union activity was very intense, and I was very concerned about acting properly. I was always asking him, "How should I do this?" And he was always ready to give his opinions. He was a great teacher. He sent us all the documents that he had produced to help us do our job properly, since we had so little experience. He never asked anything in return; nor did he tell us "Do this" or "Do that" in political terms. He was always available when we needed him.

BSS: *What was he doing at the time?*

FC: He was a great technician at the Southern Textile Union, at the time when Augusto Mateus was also there. Manuel Lopes,[28] who founded that union, had great masters supporting him, but after a while he went off in a different direction. Agostinho Roseta was a man of great abilities, and he also had a very wholesome way of thinking. He was sidelined because the union had started to adopt a line that was different from his.

BSS: *You have often had to confront the CGTP leadership, and its majority positions, at meetings. How did you feel in those situations? Did they try to boycott your presence or refuse to give you a voice? Did they respect you? How is that story?*

---

26 Agostinho Roseta was one of the founders of the CGTP-IN, and one of its best technicians. After leaving the CGTP-IN, he was invited by the leader of the UGT, Torres Couto, to join that union.
27 General Union of Workers, founded in 1978 with the support of the socialists and social democrats in order to oppose the hegemony of the CGTP-IN.
28 Manuel Lopes was also an official in the Southern Textile Union, and one of the founders of the CGTP-IN. He was one of the great forces in the textile sector.

FC: It's like this I think that at first especially after the split at the time of the two lists, things were not at all easy. It was a critical period, and I was seen as a divisive presence, someone to be excluded. With time, though, things began to calm down a bit. Then they heated up again when I joined the national committee, which was not peaceful at all. Although that was not something I really wanted to do, all the minorities were pressuring me to go for it, to strengthen the group. Around the same time, more or less, I was also part of the management bodies of the federation in the textile sector, but there things were a lot easier, since the various forces all got along much better, just as they do today. I would even say that it is one of the few federations[29] that have the greatest diversity of opinions, because many unions in that sector have considerable autonomy and independence. After some years, I left to give my place to another person from my union.

I have always found it very difficult to fit into mid-ranking organizations, because the debate is generally quite far removed from daily union action. And I also think that I was getting a bit disillusioned, after all the trouble when Judas left, and all the others that had broken with the party. There was no separation of the waters, and those leaders had a rough time because of the positions they had taken. Also, up until the 1990s, our struggle was more about fighting for rights generally. But when the crisis started to appear, it was necessary to switch track, to try to get companies back on their feet and protect jobs; and then I began to understand that, in this field, it's not possible just to have one common strategy, but that everyone has to act for themselves. Then, I asked myself, "So what, after all, am I doing here in these organizations?" When there is no common strategy before such difficult and complicated situations, each person is worth what they can actually do on the ground. Despite these difficulties, which go far beyond denouncing injustices and demanding rights, I still think that unity is very important, particularly when we're fighting for big causes and against the injustices caused by globalization and this faceless exploitation. Given the complexity of the problems facing us today, I feel the need to join up with people from different backgrounds—like you and other sociologists, for example, who study the complexities of the new social inequalities and try to discover new ways of dealing with them. Like that interesting debate that we had about the world of work at the turn of the century—do you remember? I think that debates like that, and other initiatives of civil society, teach us a lot and help stimulate our daily activities. They're also good for the union movement and for active citizenship.

---

29 Federation of Textile, Wool, Clothing, Footwear, and Leather Unions of Portugal.

Up until the 1980s, it was all about winning rights and consolidating what we had gained through the revolution of April 25th. Between 1980 and 1990, the struggle got more political and union-based, when there were debates at the national level, such as the one organized in Coimbra. I still have the document that you sent us for that meeting of union leaders, which we held in the Avenida Hotel. You might not remember it—when Judas and the others asked why these unionists were meeting. At that time, it was not normal practice for so-called minority groups to get together, and this was a bit scary. And then there was the desertion of the Coimbra Trade Union Federation, because of alterations that they wanted to make to the statutes, which were aimed at expelling people, like Carlos Cidade and others. And then there was a whole chain reaction of things that we had an active part in.

BSS: *After that period, did you, or do you today, think that the CGTP is the same kind of organization as the one you confronted at that time?*

FC: I think it's different today, but in essence the questions haven't changed much. The CGTP still hasn't managed to free itself from the Communist Party's hold. Today we can discuss anything and give our opinions. But when it comes to making a decision, it's always the same people that decide.

UNIONS AND POLITICAL PARTIES

BSS: *Do you think that party affiliation on the part of trade unions is very powerful in the movement?*

FC: Yes! In my opinion, it's too strong. I think it's a bad thing. Because the natural tendency is for parties to use the unions to assert themselves on the ground, and very often the roles get confused—which, in my opinion, does nothing to strengthen the unions or give them more credibility. Instead of becoming places for reflection and discussion, they are used for party struggles; and I don't mean just as a way of affirming themselves and implementing their policies on the ground. I don't want to devalue the political parties in saying this, because they are very important for democracy and for denouncing injustices. But, as we often say, "each to his own."

BSS: *But, in your own practice, have you never had any party affiliation?*

FC: No.

BSS: *But you were close to the Base-FUT.*[30]

---

30   Base Frente Unitária dos Trabalhadores (Workers' Unity Front), an organization linked to Christian movements. It organizes consciousness-raising sessions and provides training in professional skills, union matters, politics, the environment, and youth issues.

FC: My connection to Base-FUT had to do with my participation in meetings and consciousness-raising sessions that were held about trade unionism, and also because of their strong connection with some international trade union movements, which gave us the chance to share experiences and ideas. I was also connected to Política XXI[31] and the Pintasilgo Movement,[32] which I identified with strongly—that's why I supported her presidential campaign so much. She was a woman that I greatly admired. I was also close to the MES,[33] and I decided that, as an independent, I would support Ferro Rodrigues,[34] because I could see that things were getting bad and I thought that he, as social security minister, would not turn his back on all the issues that we were raising. I think that he's a very humane person, and for that reason I and other independent leaders decided to give him our support, putting down in writing our reasons for doing so.

BSS: *In those discussions, the UGT never appeared. What did you think of the UGT? Do you think it has some presence in the Portuguese trade union movement? Does it have any significance? And is that a positive or a negative presence?*

FC: I think that in some sectors—such as banking, insurance, and others, especially in the services—their unions have great organization and acceptance among the workers. In other cases, where parallel unions were set up with little grassroots influence, in my opinion, its presence has been very negative. Normally, it has served as a springboard for bosses who want to undermine workers' rights. They take advantage of the difficulties in collective negotiation, and the workers end up paying for it. They negotiated very bad contracts in our sector, removing all our capacity for negotiation. Conclusion: today, we have little or nothing left of those things that we won with such effort. There are no salary scales! The bosses do what they want—they simply send a circular around the companies saying, "We suggest these raises," but they are not binding in nature. And we, although we contest it, have no power to reverse the situation, given the lack of motivation and disillusionment that our workers feel. Although I consider myself to be open to other opinions and experiences, I could never understand the behavior of those unionists

---

31   Left-wing civic movement, set up in 1994. Fátima Carvalho was a candidate for the European Parliament, like her interviewer, Boaventura de Sousa Santos.
32   Pintasilgo Movement, connected to GRAAL.
33   Left Socialist Movement, set up in May 1974. Its origins date back to 1970, when a group of progressive Catholics and radical socialists left the MDP/CDE. In 1974, this initial group was reinforced by other dissident elements from the PS.
34   This refers to the general election of March 2002, which was held early after the resignation of the prime minister, António Guterres, in whose government Ferro Rodrigues had served, first as minister for solidarity and social security, and then as minister for social infrastructure.

who, in many cases, do not know what grassroots work is, and make decisions without consulting the workers. Those were difficult times, but we are confident that we'll get over them.

BSS: *In the UGT, in your opinion, was there the same kind of party manipulation or influence as in the CGTP?*

FC: Yes, yes—by the PS and PSD. I don't think they were trying anything different. They might in some cases be a bit more open, but in essence they were the same. You just don't notice it so much, because those parties are not so closed, and there's more freedom of opinion. Sometimes I get the feeling that someone will have to break something, because they're all asleep. The only thing that seems to bother the CGTP is the splits in the PCP.[35]

BSS: *But are those splits in the PCP reflected in the union movement? How?*

FC: In the lack of directness and transparency, the absence of debate about ideas. No one dares make much of a stand. It works mostly through conversations in the corridor. No one acts with the heart, it's all very rational—and life is not always like that. I think that this way of operating inhibits people's growth and atrophies their critical sense and capacity for debate, and it often leads to political warfare. There's still a great culture of toeing the line. Some days ago, one of the directors said, "It's better for there to be few of us, but good, rather than many who are bad." People are afraid of reacting, of rocking the boat and causing trouble, or even of getting kicked out, as happened with others not so long ago. Anyone who has different ideas is treated with indifference and distrust, as a rule.

I think that we're going through a bad patch in terms of ideas. The political situation is bad, and I think that we need to discuss new paths for the future. But we are too divided—people are not really available or open to reflection; everyone closes in on themselves.

After the general elections (that Durão Barroso won), I went to a national general meeting and decided to intervene. I wasn't going to say anything new, just this: "My friends, difficult times are ahead for us. For, although the previous government may have made a lot of mistakes, I think that it also solved many problems, because at least we had people who would speak to us. That opportunity, that culture of dialogue, that vision—we won't have it any longer. And it is crucial for the success of our activity. Just fighting—the struggle alone—won't get us anywhere! That's why we have to think seriously of how we are going to mobilize those workers from now on. Because workers today don't mobilize just

---

35 A controversy within the Portuguese Communist Party (PCP), which originated in attitudes taken by some important militants who argued for the renovation of the party against the official line. This led to the expulsion of directors Edgar Correia and Carlos Luís Figueira, and the suspension of Carlos Brito.

to fight the government. That record is worn out. The workers want to see concrete solutions to their problems. Today, it's not just a matter of blowing the whistle, like it was after April 25th, 1974."

And I said, "I think that we have not yet taken stock, since the elections, of our position—engaged in a bit of self-criticism to see where we've gone wrong or figure out how the right managed to win. We need to understand why the workers don't trust the parties of the left and voted for the right. I don't think we can keep going forward without stopping to analyze our mistakes and weaknesses—that won't help us find new paths or give confidence to the workers. Does the union movement not make mistakes too? Some people didn't see the seriousness of the political situation; others spent their lives writing to the newspapers, saying that the PS or PP or PSD were all the same thing. Anyone who thinks like that can't be too bothered now, because they'll have got what they wanted! And I'd also like to ask whether there are not people here who think that "the worse is for the better"—that culture of preferring the right to be in government to the left, because minority parties find it difficult to get into power. And I said too, "I would like to reflect here on another thing. There are a lot of unionists here who have run on number-one lists for certain political parties. Now, if we are such an influential body of unionists, why on earth was the vote so low for candidates that are so well known to the workers? Shouldn't we be asking ourselves about these things?"

The more orthodox members immediately raised their arms to speak. One unionist came up and said, ironically, "No! I think we're better off now. Because now all the PS bunch are in the opposition with us." I just said that we needed to think about it much more. With those sorts of views, I don't think it's possible to do any kind of analysis.

I came to the conclusion that the change was not going to come at general meetings, nor from the biggest organizations within the union movement. I think that changes will start from people who've got some connection to principles, to values, with the union movement, but who are not bound to any party apparatus; people who think—and you are one of those; people who have experience and can show us the way, so that the large organizations feel the pressure to become more open and respectful of others' opinions. Sometimes, I ask myself, "What is my role in all this? Is it worth being a unionist nowadays? Everything takes such a long time to change. And now we've even got a retrograde right-wing party in power. But what sort of political awareness do people have? What have I been thinking all these years? What is my role?" I wonder a lot about these things. I think that people's social conscience is still very fragile.

GIVING VISIBILITY TO SOCIAL PROBLEMS

BSS: *There's something that you often say that surprises many people—that is, "There are people going hungry." These women who are unemployed, many people today say, "Ah! But they'll find something else!" Does that really happen? Does society support them? What happens to someone after they've lost their job and have no unemployment benefits? What happens to those social groups that are less visible—the ones you are always drawing attention to?*

FC: I think this is a problem all over the world. Only a few people are cushioned from the worst, but society has got used to all these differences and social tragedies. Economic power changes people, makes them more individualistic. I'm full of praise for people who, even when they're hungry and have no job, or their salaries haven't been paid, find ways to keep on fighting, so that there's always something on the table to eat—trying to take advantage of what they have. And here, without a shadow of doubt, much of this merit is due to the women!

The problem seems to be getting worse. Some days ago I noticed this at a Local Committee for the Monitoring of the Minimum Guaranteed Income, now called the Social Insertion Income.[36] I would say that the basic problem is the lack of preventive measures to stop people from becoming unemployed and socially excluded.

As for those tragedies that so many families go through, no one agrees about the problem, but everyone talks and theorizes. Some people say that the people who live off the minimum income or unemployment benefit are scroungers, that they take advantage of those schemes and don't want to work. They're accused of all sorts of things. Others say, "They learn to get by on those schemes, and now they don't want to come off them." I would just like to ask them: Who was it who put them there in the first place? Is it not the fault of our governments, which didn't do anything to prevent these situations? I just think that, before making comments about those people, we should all look carefully at ourselves and ask what we would do if we were in their shoes. I've no doubt this situation is very difficult to solve, and we can easily lose heart, because it's getting more and more difficult to find ways out. I'm not

36 The Minimum Guaranteed Income was set up in 1996, and ensures a minimum income to Portuguese and foreign citizens that fall below this level and who agree to take part in a program of social insertion—according to which they agree, for to undertake retraining or other programs as deemed necessary by the program. Local Monitoring Committees are an important component of this, and discuss the insertion program with the beneficiary. They consist of public departments from various areas, local authority representatives, private welfare institutions, business associations, trade unions, and other nonprofit organizations. In 2002, the new government revised this measure, renaming it the Social Insertion Income.

saying that there aren't some people who might be irresponsible and take advantage of what's on offer—there always have been people like that, it's not a new thing. But most people live by struggling hard.

For example, one woman lost her job at the age of fifty. She had started working at fourteen, fifteen, or sixteen. If you yourself were to stop working now, you'd be in a kind of rhythm—you'd have a certain pace going, and you wouldn't be able to live just not doing anything, would you? You might feel tired sometimes, but stopping altogether just makes you even more tired. So, don't you think these people feel the same way? Many of them say that they are too young to retire and too old to get a new job.

One woman said to me a few days ago, "Since I've been unemployed, my life has been hell. It's like I've been jinxed. I've worked in a cafe, in a restaurant, and in a hotel. Either they go bust or I get fired. I've not had a proper job since!" Others, for example, are living off a pension of 30 or 40 contos, and others have serious health problems.

How many do you think walk into the union office saying, "And what's going to happen now, girl? What is my life going to be like? Look, I'm even starting to have health problems. How will I manage to work? I haven't had much of an education, and I've always worked in this area. And I even liked it, in spite of everything." And I say, "My God, what can I do? These people are withering up." I don't have the answers, and I think that the people who should be here dealing with these situations are the ones that have the power of decision and are well placed in society—but for them, these things just pass them by. But I have to react and give them support—that's my job. And I start: "Come on now, don't cry! You'll find something—you've got to believe in that!" Many of them answer, "No, another job, no. I couldn't do it anymore! I'm much too old." And that's when they're forty—imagine! "Yes, I'm old, too tired, too sick. . ." I think that these things have become part of people's daily lives, and we're running the risk of becoming a country of sick, unmotivated, unhappy people.

Some women do a few hours in people's houses,[37] and things like that. They do it more as a way of surviving and to keep themselves occupied, so they feel less useless. But those women stop having a social life, because they're working on their own with the broom and the pots and pans. Then they go home, and it's more of the same: more cleaning, more pots and pans. It's all routine. What I mean is, they don't have that social contact any more that they used to have with their co-workers at the plant, for better or for worse. That's one of the biggest sources of employment in Coimbra for these people today.

---

37   Domestic service.

BSS: *In your contacts with politicians and businessmen, you only seem to encounter prophets of doom and gloom! I suppose we don't know if it's only in your sector, if it's in all sectors of the economy, or if it's the whole country that is hopeless. But most of the time you seem to encounter pessimism everywhere, and you've opposed these views. What is it that spurs you on?*

FC: What spurs me on are the people. Because I think that it's through them that we'll find good solutions—if you take into account their creative power and ability to work together and in networks. But I also realize that we're a long way from there now, and all we can see are our politicians, businessmen, and other people taking a few odd measures here and there that hardly do anything to restructure or modernize our industrial fabric and get our economy going again—always bearing in mind that your greatest resource is manpower, since in a just society it is always the people that make the difference.

I think that here, as with everything else, we have to hang on to the potential that we have. We have to start investing in education, in training, in active citizenship, in everything that the people feel will give value to their ideas and their knowledge, going against traditional models of behavior. For example, I have an idea, a project, but I don't have the ability or the money to put it into practice. This is where cooperation between the university and the local authority can make a big contribution. Today, with the Internet and all those exchange schemes between different countries, we can share experiences with people connected to different organizations. And we should also be able to get better cooperation and make connections between theory and practice, in the search for new ways forward and the exchange of experiences, looking for new markets and investment. It might be a good idea to look at Brazil, where people cooperate and act in a different way. We could perhaps learn something from their experience about how to improve our own situation.

BSS: *In periods of crisis, we have seen companies in many countries that have been abandoned, or which are in the process of being abandoned, and which are taken over by the workers, who form cooperatives. Is there no experience here in the central region of the country of any process like this?*

FC: We had the experience in Coimbra at CLARCOOP, which ended up closing down. There was another in Mira de Aire, when the owner ran away to Brazil in August 1975 and the workers stayed on to manage the company, in a system of self-management. It was a very complicated period, and just when they were starting to put things right, in 1976, the boss came back. The workers, in spite of everything they had done, couldn't stop him, because legally the company was still his! Another example was at COLSI, where things were heading in a similar direction. The boss abandoned the company in December, saying, "Go and get money from the Council. I've not got enough to pay you for the month of January." And when we noticed, he was organizing the workers to come out into the street. But we arrived and asked, "What's all this about? You're going to the Council to ask for money? For 20,000 contos?" That was when they realized that he had been using the money from the business to sort out his own personal problems. So then, the workers decided to stop working. They were stopped a whole week! In the meantime, we thought, "We've got to make this fight visible," so we decided to go to the Council, to the civil governor, everywhere. We told the workers, "Listen, you make posters. You, that are here doing nothing, instead of sitting there looking at each other, think up some ideas and put them on posters or on fliers to hand around." Conclusion: the people wrote down what was in their souls—tremendous things they said. Those posters were completely different from normal, because they showed their feelings. Meanwhile, when the boss found out, he called us and said: "Girls, from today, I'm not coming back here again. I might go to prison for not paying social security, and so I've got nothing to lose!"

So the workers elected a committee to manage the company during the crisis. The leaders wanted the workers to open a bank account. We didn't agree to that, since it could put the workers in a critical situation. So we decided that the workers would manage the company, but the money would continue to go to the company's account, and the boss would authorize the workers to take out the money at the end of each month. We thought at the time of setting up a cooperative, but it was a big company, with a very heavy structure, and worked only to order. The risks were too high, and there were a lot of people, mostly women—though I don't want to suggest that women are not as able as men!

NETWORKS

BSS: *To what extent does the trade union movement need to open up more to society—to other social movements, for example? And at the same time, to what extent should other social movements understand and show perhaps a bit more openness and loyalty to the union movement? I know, for instance, that, in the many meetings that you hold, you have always pointed out that civic organizations, city movements, don't give the union movement the centrality that it deserves.*

FC: I think that would be a very important route. But our mentality is bit like "My patch is better than the other guy's." It's not just businessmen that think like that. I think everyone does, and the movements too, which often turn their back on each other. I think we need someone who can make connections and stimulate it. Perhaps there's a lack of leadership here. I'll give you an example. On the Minimum Income Committee, there are about twenty or thirty associations from the city represented. We spend a whole morning there, and in the end I ask myself: What have we been doing here? We've been spending all our time analyzing everything, and we've hardly talked about solutions. There's lack of cooperation. Sometimes I wonder: Is there really a will to change things? And I say this as a kind of little provocation to myself: Isn't it good that there are all these people around with all these problems, just to justify the existence of all these institutions? Is the aim really to make people grow? To find answers? That's one doubt I have, among others.

BSS: *So you don't think that the trade union movement could get more involved in social insertion,*[38] *for example? That's not the job of a trade union?*

FC: I think it is—of course I do! I think that unions have a very important role to play in schemes like that—they've got the experience, the know-how about working on the ground, and their values. Right now, the legislation allows the unions to participate in some organizations. In my opinion, that's not enough. We have to go further and define our role, the part we are going to play in those institutions, which should go further than just being represented on the management bodies.

BSS: *But even in the matters that are more central to trade unionism, one of the criticisms that is often made is that the unions protect jobs, but when workers become unemployed, they are left to their own devices. Unemployed people do not pay union fees—they are not there in the world of work, and the union loses sight of them. Is that true?*

FC: I don't think that has been our practice, because a certain proportion of our time and services are absorbed in giving support to those people. In most cases, when we are talking about the closure of companies, we hold periodic meetings all the time while the cases are waiting to go to court, keeping people updated on their progress. Also, even after three, four, five and even six, seven, and more years, they still come to the union offices often, or they phone, particularly when they're having problems with social security, pensions, workers' rights, and so on. I could tell you loads of cases where this has happened. The people continue to come to the union for a shoulder to cry on—someone they can trust; and they normally speak to us before taking any decision, in many cases after they've already consulted state institutions. Our motto is that we don't close the door on anybody.

As regards the bigger organization, there we have big problems! First, the people go off to their homes and they're scattered around the place,

---

38   See note 36.

which makes their union very complicated. It's a little like, "Out of sight, out of mind!" And the people also get used to that. I don't mean that they break off the relationship, but they can't really see a reason why they should meet—they stop believing in it. Each person looks after himself, and the links that join them get eroded away.

In recent years, we have also invested in vocational training for unemployed women, and the experiments have been very interesting. But, at the same time, it is very challenging to try to insert those people into the job market, or to create self-employment, which is one of the aims of the training.

BSS: *The success of training courses tends to be measured by the rate of integration into the job market. What is the rate after your courses?*

FC: For example, in Castanheira de Pêra, after most of the companies closed down, we organized short training schemes to try to help those women—first to believe in themselves, and second to improve their skills. We did the same thing in Coimbra and in other areas. It has been a very interesting learning curve as regards their integration, which is one of our great concerns, both in the job market and in the creation of self-employment. Around 50 percent, and in other cases 20 to 40 percent, have managed to get a job somewhere. We've also managed to get ten of the trainees to create their own jobs.

One example I could give, among others, is of three women from Penacova, who did our training scheme and then decided to set up their own business, with our support. We helped them draw up their projects, which were supported by the Employment Center, and we made them believe that they could do it. They went ahead, knowing that it wasn't going to be easy. But this was in Penacova, which is a very small town, and not very developed. After a month or so, they turned up in tears: "We have no work. What can we do now? No one asks us to do anything. We're desperate!" What they needed was to get known. So I said, "How can we help these women to get out of this situation? Wait, I've had an idea!" It was one of those things that appear out of the blue—not thought out at all. We got hold of the telephone directory and began looking for companies that needed work. They didn't want to call because they were shy, so I began to call up the companies, "Do you have work for these ladies?" There was one company that needed men's jackets, but the women didn't know how to do that. So they went away. They didn't phone me again; and I thought, "They've closed down." But I plucked up the courage to ring them, and I asked, "So, how are things going?" "Oh, sorry we've not rung, but we've been very busy. We followed up your idea and we began calling around, and we found a gentleman who gives us a lot of work making overalls for hospitals. And now we're making the overalls for the ophthalmological clinic on the road into Coimbra. We've even bought another machine—we're really pleased!" And they went around saying that it was the union that helped them set up their own little business and changed their lives! So, it's the accumulation of all these experiments that we've held in other areas that makes us want to keep going. Listen, don't you think that it would be important to set up a "House of Knowledge" in Coimbra? That's a great dream of mine! We think there's a lot to be done, and the government, through the IEFP,[39] needs to monitor these initiatives a bit more, offer more incentives. It's not just a matter of handing out the money and then leaving people to their own devices! Shouldn't the institutions, local councils, and other organizations have a say about this matter?

BSS: *The textile sector today is completely internationalized. Your union and the companies here are competing with companies both inside and outside Europe. Has this ever given you the idea of contacting other unionists in other countries? Do you think that could be useful, or are you in competition with each other, each one defending your own country?*

FC: No—that is a great limitation, and we don't know how to go about it. In the struggle for Ideal, we felt the need to share experiences, given the complexities of the situation. But we still haven't managed to. Don't forget, we're a small union with few resources. Normally, connections with union structures are made either by committees of multinational companies, which is a structure existing in the EWC,[40] or at least by union centers and federations—that is, at the top. As we are independent, things are more difficult!

THE EXPERIENCE OF APRIL 25, 1974

BSS: *You are today quite well known as a union leader in our country. But everything had to start somewhere. For many of us, there was a historic moment in our society that was very important (and I'd like to end our interview with this)—I'm talking about the revolution of April 25th, 1974. I know that this completely transformed your family and personal life—your life in the union, as a worker, and as a woman. I'd like you to tell me a bit about that. We'll end at the beginning. What I mean is, how was this woman, with all the qualities that you have today, how was she changed by the experience of April 25th?*

---

39   Institute for Employment and Vocational Training. This is a public body under the auspices of the Ministry of Social Security and Labor that is responsible for carrying out employment and vocational training policies, defined and approved by the government.
40   The European Works Councils are organizations providing information and consultation services for workers in European companies, and are regulated by Directive 94/45/CE. This is applicable to all companies within the European economic space with at least 1,000 workers, and which employ a minimum of 150 workers in at least two different countries.

FC: I'm from a family of modest means. My parents worked on the land. It was very hard! My sister started working in the plant at twelve, and had to walk 5 km on foot each way to get there, every day.

Then, around 1959 or '60, there was a strike that lasted over a month in the tapestry section, and my sister took part. There were over a hundred women working there, and the looms were all manual. Meanwhile, the bosses began to introduce mechanical looms, which meant that the workers had to work on a piecemeal basis, earning for what they produced. They refused, and stopped work. The bosses told them that they didn't know what they were letting themselves in for, and if they didn't all come back to work immediately, they'd be arrested. They stayed out on strike. Then, the PIDE[41] appeared, trying to find out who was behind it all, who the leaders were. They searched the houses of some of them, and around fourteen women ended up getting fired. The PIDE didn't arrest them only because they hadn't discovered any organization behind them—and, as they were women, they were considered ignorant.

When I joined the same company and was doing the same work as my sister, I had great trouble adapting, because we were working under great pressure. Each loom had three, four, or five people working on it. It was joint work—when one finished her part she had to wait for the rest. The loom overseer would shout her head off: "Get moving you lazy good-for-nothings!" When someone fell behind, they would keep going nevertheless, and then they'd get their fingers stuck. We were responsible for ourselves, and that would cause arguments between us. The bosses never cared much about us. All they cared about was our mistakes, because it was all done in such a hurry. Then, the boss was always yelling at us. People started peeing at the loom, because they couldn't waste time going to the toilet, and they would say, "You're already behind, and you still want to go to the toilet! You can wait till lunchtime." The relationships between the people were marked by pressure and fear. At lunch, for example, we had an hour to eat, but we never used it all because we had to weave a few more rows.

In the meantime, I had joined the group JOC in Mira de Aire. That was a great learning experience. Our motto was, "See, Judge, and Act." That is, look at the problems, assess them, and then act. But we had great trouble acting. There were so many injustices in our workplace; the place was ruled by fear, and there was constant pressure on us. Often, we made use of people outside the company—we'd go and talk to the priest or to other influential people, asking them to help us fight the injustices in the

---

41   The International and State Defense Police, or PIDE (Polícia Internacional e de Defesa do Estado), was the main tool of repression used by the authoritarian regime of Salazar in Portugal, which lasted for over forty years.

companies. And we were often able to do it without the boss ever finding out who was behind it.

In 1970, I and some colleagues, who are nurses, doctors, and social workers today, were invited to take aptitude tests and go to study in Coimbra. That was my dream. When I told my parents, they started to cry: "But, daughter, who will keep us? Who will pay for your studies?" It was me who was supporting the whole household at the time. My sister had got married, and had gone with her husband to live in Angola.

In 1973, a group of workers from various factories decided to start studying. We asked two teachers from the town to give us evening classes, privately. My idea was to keep studying to be a nurse or social worker. But then April 25th happened. I was studying at the time, but I was so overjoyed that I couldn't keep it up any longer. What I wanted was to really experience that moment, which was so important for my life. So I ended up just finishing the second grade, as it was called then.

At the JOC, I had heard many of the songs that were played on the morning of 25 April! When I arrived at the company, I said to the other girls, "Don't be scared. I think freedom is on its way." Someone took a very small radio into the plant, and we sneaked into the toilets every hour to listen, to find out what was going on. Some of them were afraid that there was going to be a war; others thought it was good, that it meant freedom. "Maybe not," the others said. "But can't you see how worried the boss is? We've got freedom at the door!" We were overjoyed. Soon after that, I was elected union delegate, and that's when the problems started. So, we started to think, "What shall we demand right now?" The idea was to demand something. In our section, it was only the person in charge of each loom who received the legal wages—it was two thousand escudos. The others earned 25 escudos less, and we all started to say, "We should get the same. Equality is coming, and the law has to be applied to everyone."

I was already in charge of a loom, and so I said to the others, "Listen, girls, I think that you should be the ones to ask for the raise. I'll support you, but it's you that have to go and talk to the boss." So they went, and then he called me in. "You're putting ideas into their heads, aren't you? Do you really think they're capable of doing the same work as the people in charge?" "I don't know! Ask them," I replied. "I don't think so. This is going to cause a riot! So they're going to earn as much as you and the other overseers? You just wait—you'll see what'll happen!" I started to think, and I told him, "Listen, I've had an idea. I don't want the others to earn the 2,000 escudos if you're then going to come along and tell me that they're not responsible. I'll ask them who thinks they're able to take responsibility. And those that say yes, then you'll have to agree! But let them decide." So I went back to them, and I said, "Listen girls, I've got something very important to say. The boss agrees, but now you've got to decide." They took it very seriously. That was at two o'clock in the afternoon. By four o'clock, still no one had said anything. You see, they were all afraid that they wouldn't be up to it. Some didn't want to do it, but among them there were two that he said were capable. I went to him and said, "You see! You thought they were irresponsible, but they've taught you a lesson!"

Another example: one day two of the looms were making tapestries with pictures of Indians on. I was doing the women and on the other loom, they were doing the men. Then we noticed that the ones working on the other loom had made a mistake, and I said, "Oh girls, you've made your Indians blind!" We all started laughing: "Listen. This is serious, and it's me who'll get the blame for this mistake." They didn't believe it, and I said, "He'll take advantage of this to have a go at me!" And that was just what happened. The boss, when he lost his temper, would say anything. So we decided to organize ourselves. After he would leave, we would do some more Indians so that he wouldn't notice what had happened. The whole section agreed, even the section leader. But he noticed that the Indians were blind, and he kept on top of us. So we weren't able to make more Indians. This was Friday. On Monday morning, he grabbed hold of one of the tapestries and came straight to me. When he arrived, he said, "Is this why you're a delegate, so you can tell them to do stuff like this? You see— you do want to destroy the factory, it's true!" He accused me of all sorts of things, but I just kept quiet. The man was beside himself. And the other girls at the front said, "It was us that did it wrong, and it should be us that have to pay for the mistake!" It all happened very spontaneously. Everyone stopped and came slowly to stand near me. He began to look around, and saw that he was surrounded by women. And he said, "So what're you after? Get back to work!" And they reacted, "Don't do that to Fátima. She doesn't deserve it! It's not fair. Fátima never told us to do it badly!" And I said, "Do you really think that I'd tell the others to do it wrong? If so, why would I get them to do it wrong and then do it right myself?" "Because you're sly! You'd get them to do it wrong so you wouldn't get the blame." He looked around and then started to come to his senses. "Girls," he said, "she's the only one that doesn't need a helping hand!" He went away. A bit later on, he came back and said to me, "Sorry, I was beside myself. I haven't slept a wink this weekend. But you've got to agree they made a big mistake." "No one's denying that," I said, "but you wanted to take advantage of that mistake to get at me, because I'm the elected delegate. The other girls stood by me, and I shall never forget it!" From then on, our union action in the company was more respected.

April 25th was, for me and the others, the dream of freedom and hope—the end of oppression, and the right to think and express our opinions in freedom. It was about having standards of living that we had never had. It's enough to say that when they got a raise of 1,000 escudos, they were able to improve their living standards immensely. I was able to buy a fridge for my parents, a television, a cooker. In a few months, it was possible to afford all those things. It was a time when people made great investments, getting the main things they needed to live.

BSS: *Was the union set up before April 25th?*

FC: Yes. Just that it had connections with the regime. At first, we would make the journey from our village to the factory on foot. But in the 1970s buses started to appear, and they would sometimes come five or ten minutes late, and we would be late to work. And the boss would appear right away: "Discount an hour!" It was very unfair. We would have to work an extra hour without receiving any more for it. One day we decided: "Let's all go together to the union and find out about our rights." But when we got back to the factory, we were told off! Because the boss already knew where we'd been: "If you go back there again. . ." he warned. That was when we realized that the union was on the side of the bosses and we had no one to defend our rights, although we were obliged to be members of the union.

In 1975 we got involved in a wool workers' strike to demand 1,000 escudos. We earned 2,000 escudos. We were on strike for two weeks—it was a special experience! It wasn't easy spending all those days at the workplace, because we didn't know what to do with ourselves. But everyone participated in that struggle! Our determination and the justice of the cause was so great that we managed to get 3,000 escudos—and then, soon, the minimum salary went up to 3,300 escudos.

In preparation for that strike, we held a general meeting in the union delegation, and the leader, Manuel Lopes, took part. There were around a thousand of us—it was crazy! The only workers who were not there were those from one particular company, because many of them were not from Mira de Aire and were terrified of their boss. Some people started to say, "You see, some of us are here trying to fight, and others goofing off!" So I got up onto a bench, as I'm so tiny, and I said, "Let's not criticize the poor girls. Let's go tomorrow and invite them to join the strike." Everyone agreed, and so we went to their company the next day at around six o'clock, when they were all leaving. There we got another 1,500 people to join—and in a town of that size, that was masses: just about everyone! But we didn't really know what we were going to do. And the leaders, the delegates—maybe more rational than me—started to say, "Why are we going there? He'll destroy us!" "Listen, I'm not going there, You go on your own. I'm not going with you. You've no idea what we're in for with that boss. He's been threatening us with a shotgun, and you still want us to go there!" There was only one leader that wanted to go with me.

So we set off down the road, chanting: "Boss, you're a gangster, we're gonna hang yer!" He arrived, and we were all shouting. The whole place was surrounded with people, and he shut the women up inside the factory. We yelled, "Let us talk to the women; we won't leave until you do." Then he came to the door and said he wanted to speak to two of the leaders. So I went, along with another. I thought, "He won't win me round. I'll just say no!" But he knew my family, this man, and started off by saying that I was from a good family, that I was going astray, that I'd be sorry one day. He knew my cousins, as they'd also worked there at the factory. He grabbed hold of my arm, and I said, "Let go of my arm!" I just said no, over and over again, because I was afraid of saying anything that could harm our cause. "I don't want to talk to you!" "So who do you want to talk to?" he asked. "I want to talk to the workers. I came here just to ask the workers to join us. I don't want anything from you. Let me talk to the workers." But he wouldn't, and said, "Listen, I'm losing my patience." When we went down to talk to them, I really thought I was going to die, because he had his shotgun in his hand!

But we went to talk to the workers, and he told them, "Don't listen to anything they say!" However, we talked for a bit with the women, and we managed to persuade them to join the other workers. As we were leaving, I said to them, "You're going to tell all the workers now that you are with them, and that you just haven't come out because you were afraid to." And one of them said, "You say it. I don't even know how to!" So I spoke in their name, and everyone clapped and shouted, "We've done it! Victory! It was all worthwhile!"

In the hot summer of 1975[42] the bosses were all scared to bits, and started to organize themselves with the support of the bosses from Rio Maior and Minde, to start to destroy people and intimidate them— because that was a very conservative area. In Minde, there was a lot of crazy repression. There were women who were raped, people beaten up, and the union was born and died the same moment. Even today, there isn't really much of one. Minde is 3 km from Mira de Aire. In Mira de Aire, our group was not really associated with any political party, because there were people who were very dynamic, some of them from

---

42 In July 1975, there was a series of violent actions against the headquarters of left-wing political parties and organizations all over the country (though it was more intense in the north and center). This wave of violence, associated with the conservative forces, became known as the Hot Summer.

the JOC, who were very well organized in that town. We discussed everything, spent a lot of time together, and we were a very interesting team. But we had some serious problems, because the bosses published a communiqué called "Get Going." That was an appeal to the good people of Mira, saying that the moment of truth had arrived. They wanted to destroy everything. They called everyone from Rio Maior and Minde, and joined together and decided to attack. We were on strike in '75 because of the national wool workers' contract, but the struggle for the contract in Mira de Aire turned into a struggle for freedom and for the values of April 25th. Because April 25th was not put into practice immediately on that day—and there are some places where it still hasn't been implemented!

So the people started to get organized, and we had no experience of anything. One of the doctors from the town offered his services, and we started to get support from some people. But as we'd seen what had happened in Minde and other places, we expected the worst. On the day of the strike, we all went to the factories, saying, "Listen, the bosses want to destroy us." And so, we, me and the others, were the center of attention. The union office was on the second floor in the center of Mira de Aire. We got some Molotov cocktails—the boys were making those things—and we kept them for more than a month in the union office. We slept there for fifteen days, so that no one would destroy our headquarters. We had people scattered around all the factories who would inform us when they gave the signal "Get Going," because we knew that it would all start in those factories. We had decided that, as soon as anyone knew something was coming, they would go straight to the union office to let us know. In the meantime, the Drivers Union of Leiria offered to surround all the routes out of Mira de Aire, in case the folk from Rio Maior came along too. Anything could have happened, couldn't it? The doctor had let us use his house so that we would be better protected. But we said, "No. If we're going to die, then we'll die in the union office!"

BSS: *What month was that?*

FC: It was around May 1975. Each of us went to our own factory, and I was at the gate of the plant where I worked, near the clock-in machine. I said to the workers, "Today is strike day." And some of the company bosses, who were keeping their eye on the clock-in machine, said, "Today is a working day." Everyone was very nervous. Anyway, everyone stayed out there on the forecourt, and I was among them, with the bosses all around, watching the meeting. And I said, "Listen, if you don't come out on strike today, you'll be killing freedom, putting an end to April 25th, and our union. The national strike is to defend our contract, but this strike today in Mira de Aire is also for freedom. Anyone who wants freedom should go on strike. If you don't want freedom, then don't bother. They want to destroy our organization. That's your decision." "But they're going to come and attack us," they said. "Then fight back." "But we have no weapons!" "Fight back!" They started to think, "Let's go and get the scissors, or the shuttles from the looms."

The other girls told me to stay with them, but I said, "No! Those guys want to attack me but they've got to go to the union office to do that, because that's my place. I'm not afraid." But a group of men wouldn't let me go alone. They all came with me, accompanying me like bodyguards. And everyone kept to the strike. There was between 90 and 95 percent participation—the biggest in the whole country. Only the little companies didn't really take part.

So we came to the union office—it was around nine o'clock—and nothing happened. Then ten o'clock. "So, no one has given the call 'Get Going'?" Then eleven o'clock. Then the boss from LANIFÍCIA went and set off the factory siren—because they'd all planned to give the signal at the same time. It was the "Get Going" signal. One woman jumped him from behind and said, "Let go of that right away!" And he turned to her husband, who was a union delegate, "Oh Joaquim,[43] look what your wife's doing!" "Here, she's not my wife, she's a worker. So I've got nothing to do with it." Then a group of men went up onto the roof and turned off the signal. In my company, one of the bosses also went up to set off the signal, but a worker saw it and grabbed an iron bar and said, "If you do that, you're done for! I might go to prison, but you'll lose your hand!" So he stopped and there was no "Get Going" signal. After that, we spent fifteen days guarding the union office. Nothing happened. But there were a lot of threats. Our struggle and organization was exemplary, and they started treating us with more respect. So the workers of Mira de Aire can say that April 25th was a milestone—and anyone who has lived those ideals never forgets them. It was the day when hopes were built, and the end of many days of oppression.

Then there was another attempt, but that was with the UDP,[44] which decided to go to Mira de Aire to hold a rally without arranging anything with the people from the town. It was all highly organized from inside

---

43   Not his real name.
44   Set up in December 1974, the Popular Democratic Union was a Maoist communist front that became a political organization with a Marxist-Leninist tendency. In the elections of 1975, 1979, and 1980, it elected a deputy to parliament from its lists. After that, and until 1991, the UDP ran for elections on the Communist Party (PCP) list. Acácio Barreiros, a famous militant from the student movement, was elected deputy of the UDP, and was then the most well-known voice of the extreme left in parliament. In 1983 the PS elected him deputy.

and out—really annoying. That was one of the worst things in Mira de Aire. Acácio Barreiros[45] had to run through the streets of Mira de Aire, saying he was sorry. And the bosses took him to Entroncamento. They burned everything belonging to the UDP—flags and other documents. There were people who had come from Marinha Grande and Alqueidão da Serra and other places for the UDP rally. Many people had to flee, and they were wandering about in the mountains lost for two or three days, without being able to get back to their towns. Others were driven out. And there were women beaten and even raped. It was really horrible.

BSS: *But did they attack the people that fled to the mountains?*

FC: Yes. We were indignant, because that almost destroyed us. Because, at one point, you started hearing voices saying, "Now let's attack the townsfolk." The target they wanted to get at was the union office. I was going to the rally on my own. I didn't imagine there would be such a row. I saw a worker from my factory in a tavern, and he came up to me and grabbed my arm, and said, "You're not going." "Yes I am! You can't order me about!" I think he was a bit drunk. "Sorry, pal, but you're not going to stop me from going to the rally!" But he didn't explain why. He just grabbed me and took me to the union by force. Afterwards he said, "There's going to be trouble. They were looking for you. You are one of the people they're most after." I was hiding in the union office, me and some other people; and later on, as I didn't have any clean clothes for the next day, I sneaked off home in the early morning, on a motorbike, with no lights, so that no one would recognize me.

BSS: *Your family didn't take too kindly to your activities, did they? You also went through a bad patch with them, before they realized the value of what you were doing, didn't you?*

FC: It was very hard. That was the most difficult part for me. Neither my family nor the church, which I was very attached to, could understand my commitment. I was involved in the Sunday school, and organized the classes for the whole parish, which had 6,000 people. The priest at that time was a bit more open to new ideas, and we Sunday school teachers had started to suggest that homilies could be prepared in group—and he accepted, suggesting to other laymen that they could do it with him. I was also part of that group. At the time, this was quite an advanced idea! Meanwhile, April 25th happened, and I continued to teach Sunday school. I had a wonderful relationship with those children. But one day, I started talking and they wouldn't listen to me. I asked them why, and they said, "Because our parents don't want you to teach us. They say you're teaching us communism." They wanted to complain to the bishop

---

45   Portuguese politician.

to get me expelled; but I decided to stop teaching, because I couldn't keep up a good relationship with those kids anymore. Those moments affected me a lot—made me feel that I was being rejected by the people from my own village.

In the meantime, my sister had been forced to come back from Angola with nothing—with two small children. She had been living in Malange, and had a café that got stoned. She went through some bad times, too. She lost everything she'd fought for with so much sacrifice. She didn't bring anything with her—just the clothes she stood up in. It was a very serious situation. And my family blamed me. My mother suffered a lot, because she had a very human perspective on things, and was very influenced by other people. I would go to the factory, and people would gather around the house and pressure my mother to make me give up! They told her that she would go to hell if she didn't stop me doing these things. My mother cried every day—she had visions and everything! I stayed at meetings in Mira de Aire and came home late, and they told my mother that those people were my lovers. And one night, I said that I wasn't going to be provoked any more. "I'm leaving," I said, "and I'm not coming back. I love you all very much, but I'm going to get somewhere to live in Mira de Aire." I was getting ready to leave, still in my nightie, but my parents came to get me. We were all crying!

Then, one day, my mother burned herself, and I had to take time off work to look after her. Those two weeks I stayed at home were very interesting, because my mother gradually realized who was at her side. And I asked her, "So, where are those ladies now, the ones who come and say all those things about me? Which of them is here now? Who is your friend? Is it not me, mother?" Then she started to understand, and when people went up to her to complain about me, she would say, "Tell my daughter yourself! I've got nothing to do with it. She's good to me, and I want to go on being her friend."

From then on, everyone, including people from the family that criticized me in front of her, got a response: "Her life is her own business"—and she wouldn't listen to them saying bad things about me again, or about what I was doing. With that attitude, my mother showed what a great woman she was, a great mother, and a great friend. Though she was illiterate, she could still teach a lesson or two to those around, and after that the whole relationship changed with my family and the other people in the village. Everything went back to normal—I might even have been more respected afterwards.

But at the first elections, the only reason why the local people didn't beat me up was because I was with my parents and my sister. I just heard them shouting, "Don't let her vote! She'll vote communist!" What I'm trying to say is that perhaps April 25th could have gone in a different direction if only the people hadn't fled from the villages. Because people that had different ideas avoided getting into confrontations in the villages, because it was easier to get their ideas across in the cities. It was a good moment, but in the villages it was very complicated. Today, I think that it was a very good thing that I stayed on there, because I managed to sort out my own problems. I did it—I managed to get the people to accept me again.

Afterwards, I got very involved in the problems of social security. I went to the offices of the wool industry in Lisbon to sort out problems to do with sick pay, pensions, things like that. I loved doing that work, and in the village there were a lot of people that wanted a pension but couldn't get it. At that time we were going through a period when people could discount time,[46] and there were people there who had the right, had worked in various companies, and couldn't get it. As the people in charge of the Wool Industry Pension Scheme wanted to help me, I went there and went to the board of directors, and managed to sort out their problems. That didn't happen with the people connected to the bosses. That was how I showed that I was still the same person: nothing had changed, because I was still fighting for the ideals of April! And it was really good to feel how proud my parents were when the people realized that I only wanted what was best for them, and that, despite everything, I was still prepared to help people, even those that had criticized me. It was a great lesson for life—something that has made me very proud.

A union leader since 1975, FC has had a career that has not been typical of institutionalized union practices. Her personal life history is mixed up with the history of the union and the struggles of the workers she supports. Their struggles have become her struggles, and she never considers a cause lost, even when victory seems far away.

Although she describes herself as a woman of the left, it is nevertheless difficult to identify her with any particular political party. She doesn't mind where policies come from so long as they provide responses that she thinks will help the workers and promote a fairer, more caring society. For this reason, she will often take a critical stance, when necessary, in relation to the official line of the party with which she identifies in theory, as an exercise of constant reflection and self-monitoring. The fact that this is so unusual helps explain why so many of the current political parties are so circumscribed in their outlook, unable to see beyond the limited horizons of what they have always been used to.

The awareness that change has to be implemented holistically, that it should involve everyone, has led FC not to restrict her intervention to the world of the

---

46   Meaning that time worked, regardless of where, counted in the calculation of their retirement pension.

unions. She has also participated actively in civic movements and associations, in *progressive Catholic organizations, in spaces for political representation, and in other areas where there is a need to fight for justice and human dignity, and to change the world.*

Moving as she does in many different spheres, she is sometimes confronted with "specialist" discourses, and with the complexity that presently surrounds the processes of representative and participatory democracy. Her example shows that civic responsibility is not just a privilege for the political elites. Through a process of constant translation, she reminds us that workers are people whose lives go on after those moments of crisis—people for whom unemployment and downgrading cannot be discussed in the same breath as "modernization processes" and "economic inevitability." The presence that emerges most sharply from her narratives is that of someone who needs to be with people—above all, with those who are most deprived in terms of power and rights. This is why she views the victories achieved by women worldwide within the framework of emancipatory processes generated by the collective struggle— access to the public sphere, the respect and trust of men, and, above all, empowerment with regard to their own lives and futures—as part of the learning process about what it means to be citizens with rights.

FC's struggle is, therefore, also a struggle for the humanization of causes. She fights against the kind of depersonalization and standardization that turns people into "cases" or mere statistics. Each struggle involves people and families, relationships and interactions, feelings and emotions—of the worker, the minister, the businessman, the local politician, the director of services, and the social worker. Her profound knowledge of people and processes, and the credibility that she enjoys, allow her to move among them, promoting processes of mutual respect and dialogue that are essential for problem solving.

Emancipation, seen through FC's eyes, must be a source of constant rethinking, and of the free reinvention of the notions of utopianism and citizenship.

12

Joaquim Gonçalves

Self-employed, leader of the ecological movement against co-incineration.

Interviewed by João Arriscado Nunes and Marisa Matias

"But ordinary citizens, well, it's just not allowed. We present technical evidence, we present scientific evidence, and it's like beating your head against a brick wall, because they won't let us [speak]. And then, what's worse is that, as well as not allowing us a voice, the control they have over the media is so great that they manage to misrepresent the way the message is put across . . ."

Joaquim Gonçalves

In December 1998, the Portuguese government announced the names of the two cement factories that were to be fitted with co-incinerators for harmful industrial waste as part of its strategy to resolve the problem of treating this type of waste in Portugal. One of these factories was Cimpor, which had been operating in Souselas, near Coimbra, since 1974. It is one of the largest in the country, and is considered to be one of the best equipped in technical terms.

"Used to" living ever since with the environmental problems caused by the factory's operations, the local population opposed this decision and formed a protest movement that succeeded in delaying the implementation of the government's plans and in promoting the reduction of the incineration of the type of hazardous waste that could be treated through other techniques. Accused from the outset of being parochial, this campaign managed to establish channels of dialogue and raise questions hitherto unasked in Portugal. Moreover, by positioning itself clearly against the so-called toxic culture, the struggle against co-incineration asserted itself as being at the forefront of environmental struggles in a worldwide context.

The debate surrounding the installation of the co-incinerator took hold in Portugal in an unprecedented manner. It set the political agenda for several years, and led to controversy within the national scientific community and public opinion. In addition to individual citizens, several local and national associations and entities played an important role in the movement. Among these, we should highlight the Souselas Association for the Defense of the Environment (ADAS—Associação de Defesa do Ambiente de Souselas), which, since the middle of 1997, had been monitoring the activities of the company and calling attention to their environmental consequences. With the appearance of the movement against co-incineration in Souselas, ADAS therefore emerged as the structure best prepared to argue the case and establish links with the local population.

The successive protests led to the creation in mid-1999 of an Independent Scientific Commission (CCI—Comissão Científica Independente), in order to give an expert opinion on the treatment of harmful industrial waste. One year later, because the issues relating to public health had not been dealt with, the Medical Working Group (Grupo de Trabalho Médico) was formed, which, like the CCI, claimed that the co-incineration process would generate no risks to public health, although this decision was not unanimous. Over the following years, ADAS, together with other organizations, devoted itself to studying and rebutting these reports, and acted as a "channel" of information to the people of Souselas.

Joaquim Gonçalves was at the forefront of ADAS from its beginnings until recently. As a result, he became one of the most visible faces of the protest movement. For over twenty-five years, his life was inextricably linked to his actions as the leader of this movement.

Joaquim Manuel Correia Gonçalves was born on August 30th, 1958 in Souselas, where he also married and still lives and works today. The fact that he had always lived there meant that, early on, he became interested in publicly engaging in the problems of the area, and he is one of the best-known figures in this small community. Gonçalves took an advanced course in accounting and administration, which enabled him to work as an administrative employee at Cimpor, the company that owns the cement factory, from 1984 to 1994. He left the company for personal reasons, and since then has been a self-employed insurance agent. This work, which is based heavily on personal contacts and on working "door to door," has also contributed to his extensive knowledge of the Souselas population, as well as to his deep understanding of the main expectations and concerns of his fellow inhabitants.

Among these, environmental problems have occupied a prominent position for a long time now—particularly those arising from the presence of the cement factory in the area. This situation explains his entry into the movement via environmentalism. He approached the Anti-Pollution Commission, which had existed in the area since 1976, and played an active role in transforming it into ADAS, of which he finally became president.

From 1998—when co-incineration was announced for the Souselas cement factory—ADAS became one of the main forces of opposition to the process, not only because, out of all the associations and entities involved, it is the one that is closest to the local population, but also because it is the one that best understands the environmental problems of Souselas. Having worked at Cimpor, Gonçalves is deeply acquainted with the workings of the company—an advantage that has proved important in understanding and explaining some of the more technical issues.

As events unfolded, it became clear that it was not only Souselas that was involved in the struggle, but that it was a much wider problem, related to issues of the environment, public health, and quality of life associated with toxic waste—a problem that knows no frontiers. Gonçalves understood this and helped to broaden the debate.

Due to Gonçalves's heavy schedule, this interview took place in two parts, the first at the Centre for Social Studies, and the second in his office. As a result of several previous meetings and the atmosphere of trust that prevailed between Gonçalves and the interviewers, the conversation ran smoothly, and at various points the interviewee extended his comments, going far beyond what had been asked of him, and even anticipating some of the questions that we were planning to ask him. Thus, there *are many typical discourse markers in the transcript of the recording, including pauses and resumptions of the argument, repetitions, and corrections of statements. In order to make the reading of the document clearer, we have therefore chosen to abandon the traditional "question-answer" format, and have instead organized the contents thematically from a set of main topics suggested by the interviewee's own discourse. Nevertheless, we have naturally kept the speech in the first person, thus preserving the Gonçalves's "voice" of intact.*

CIMPOR IN SOUSELAS

The environmental problem in Souselas isn't the cement factory; unfortunately, it's a much wider problem. But the struggle of the local population in Souselas began almost as soon as the factory was built, in 1972. It was a factory that started out all wrong; for example, when the Municipal Assembly discussed the authorization to site the factory in Souselas, there was a huge row about it, even then. The factory was only installed there because the president placed his casting vote in favor—the relevant minutes of the Municipal Assembly are quite explicit on all this. A cement factory is a technologically advanced factory, but it is still a factory that produces a lot of pollution, as well as cement—you only have to think of the tons, the thousands of tons, of rock that are needed. Still, it's a factory, and if you don't take care to keep to all the necessary standards involved in the production process, it's almost always compelled to cause pollution. And then, linked to this question, for me, there was a kind of megalomania involved in its construction, meaning that everything was geared towards making the maximum profit, to the detriment of the environment.

Notice that Souselas is three factories in one: there are the two twin lines, line one and line two; and then, two years later, they built line three, which produces twice as much as lines one and two combined. Because of the production processes involved, particularly the method for cooling down the kiln, lines one and two were relatively easy to manage through centralized command, and with the professional experience of those who worked there. Many of them came from our former colonies, where there was already a tradition of the cement industry, particularly in Matola[1]—some of the engineers came from there. However, when line three started operating two years after lines one and two, there were complex facts that led to an exponential increase in pollution. Why was that? Because line three produces twice the amount, and uses a completely different kind of technology. Suffice to say that—it's not the case now because they are all going to be the same—the cooling was done by water-based satellites and

---

1 Joaquim is referring to the Matola cement factory in Mozambique.

mill number three which is the one that grinds the rock into powder before it is baked, is a vertical mill, while the other two are horizontal. A vertical mill is very difficult to operate because it responds to differences in temperature and differences in pressure inside the mill itself, and "controlling the gases," as we say, is extremely complicated. And so one small oscillation can create massive discharges into the atmosphere. The records relate basically to line three—it's basically this line, because it has double the capacity and it is difficult to contain, if you can call it that, its operations. The extraordinary discharges into the atmosphere also came from there—the ones which turned Souselas the color they did, that wouldn't come off the cars that were out in the street the day before, even after they were washed; because the cement comes out hot, it falls on top of the cars at about 200 degrees. So these were terrible things—it really was an attack on the population. In addition, there were certain types of jobs that people were doing in the factory without ever being made properly aware of the environmental problems—for example, the way the quarries were laid out. In my opinion, they didn't take enough care to ensure that the blasting was done properly; they didn't study the geology of the quarry itself properly. So what happened? One of the worst events for Souselas: it was maybe in 1976—I don't remember the exact date—when they began to mine the south face of the quarry. That was when it started: they started blasting in one part of the quarry and the rocks, maybe due to human error on the part of the people in charge, were sent flying up into the air and came down on people's heads. That was the time when very serious problems began, when they closed down the primary school in Souselas (Cimpor built a new school later, to the north of the factory), and there were rocks falling down on people. Even houses and cars were damaged at that time because of the falling rocks.

CIMPOR AND SOUSELAS

I believe that industries, and the cement factory, have to exist: we need cement. We don't want the factory to move away—although now the question is raised in different terms, because the development of the world, the development in the way the factory operates, industrial development and environmental development, mean that what was true yesterday may not be true tomorrow. What we are contesting is the way the factory operates, the way it is wrecking the environment. Let's say that the factory has been operating in its own universe, separate from ours, and that it pollutes because it has to pollute, because it can't make cement any other way, but it doesn't have the slightest awareness, or there hasn't been any awareness on the part of the people in charge of the factory, that on the other side there are human beings, plants, animals, and all the things that belong to these people, which at the very least ought to be discussed. It's funny that in this struggle there are a lot of people saying that we'll accept co-incineration if we get compensation. This means just looking at the problem of pollution from the financial point of view—in other words, saying "We're being polluted, they're destroying our environment—but if they pay us some money, if they build us a lot of things, we'll end up better off, because things won't be as bad." But my question is: We are all born equal, aren't we? We all come into this world naked, we are all born from our mothers—at present, although I'm not so sure we will be in the future—and we all die the same way. We can be buried differently, but we all die the same way. And what's the difference between dying rich and dying poor? Just the funeral, that's all, because the body disappears just the same: it either gets put under the ground, in a huge coffin or a huge urn, or it's turned to ashes, if it's burned, if it's incinerated. It disappears in the same way, so, after death, we're all the same. What's the difference, then, between dying rich and dying poor? Well, let's see, people want to live as long as they can, so let's avoid dying. Now, what price compensation? Obviously Cimpor, the cement company, could have done a lot more for the place, some very concrete things; for example, the houses are completely ruined—just go and take a look: the houses have cracks all over. Where is the compensation for these people's property? And the gutters in the streets of Souselas are filthy. So, a factory that makes cement, shouldn't it, without saying a word to anyone, just come along and say, "My friends, we'll pave over the gutters, we'll take care of everything." I mean, they didn't have to be doing nothing. The real facts are there—they were the ones who destroyed it, their trucks ruined the streets on their way to the factory, wrecked the paving, wrecked everything. What would it cost? You could say that it would just be a way of cleaning up their image, getting rid of the bad image and replacing it with a good one. But there is no need to play games behind the scenes for this to happen; it's not a case of compensation.

THE FIRST LOCAL PROTESTS

The blasting from the quarry, the massive doses of pollution—all this created an almost spooky atmosphere for people living in Souselas. From that point on, people began to mobilize because these things couldn't continue. I mentioned '76—that was the time when the first records appeared of a self-elected anti-pollution commission. And who was in it? People from Souselas, unknown people, who got together without joining a proper association of any kind, but who got together, who wrote texts and raised objections (there are records dating back to '76 of this type of protest) in various places: the City Council, the Municipal Assembly, the president of the republic, the ombudsman. A whole series of things were done, and the results were practically always small—I mean, people held a demonstration, and then what did the powers that be say? That it was half a dozen people that had demonstrated, half a dozen crazies who were involved because they felt bad, and so on. Because they were just people, they weren't a group, they had no visibility. Well, things carried on a bit longer. Then another pollution issue emerged, much more complex, at least in terms of the visibility of the problem. Until around 1990 the factory ran on fuel—that is, heavy oils; then from 1990 up to now, it changed the type of fuel it burned in the kilns to coal. This, in my opinion, brought two added problems. There was the problem of the visible way in which the coal began causing problems for the local people—we live in an area where we often, very often, suffer from a prevailing southerly wind, a warm wind, especially in the summer, which is the worst time for this wind, which originates in the deserts of north Africa. In Souselas we live in a valley. The wind enters from the north, comes down here and whirls around; it's a very changeable wind, and can come from lots of different directions. Now, the coal was kept outside in the open air—thousands of tons of it in big piles. So, what happened? There would be a south wind (normally at night, when we were sleeping) and the next day you would be cleaning away cartloads of dust—from people, from houses, from all our belongings. It was like sand in the desert: it got in everywhere, you had no chance against it, you couldn't stop it—and so we were prisoners in our own houses. And this came on top of the blasting in the quarry, the stress of the four o'clock blasting, the stress for the women, especially—the Souselas housewives who had to spend hour after hour cleaning it away. It was terrible. Now they have managed to store some of it, though not all; but at least they have remedied things a bit.

ANTECEDENTS OF ADAS

So the struggle of the Souselas people has been going on for some time. Some snide remarks, from people saying that we are only fighting against the environmental problem (and there have been some insinuations to that effect), that we were only protesting against the environmental situation and against co-incineration so that we could, let's say, get some kind of financial or personal reward out of it, don't correspond to reality. Let's see now, when was it that Souselas got the most, financially speaking, out of the fact that the factory was built there? It was in the beginning, in the first phase of the factory's operations. Why? Well, it wasn't just a factory—to build one of those factories you need lots of other companies; loads of people went there, and obviously businesses, the small businesses, which are all we have—their people certainly experienced, shall we say, an influx of cash at the time. But even at that time, with all that money coming in, there were people who, independently of all this, were disputing the way it was being carried out. So the one thing bore no relation to the other.

THE EMERGENCE OF ADAS

Why did ADAS emerge? Things continued, people were getting together more and more, and the protests were getting a little louder. And what did this mean? In May 1997, we managed to, let's say, crack the secret of the deal that was being made between the government and the cement companies, which later led to the creation of Scoreco.[2] Then we started putting two and two together [and realized] what was going to happen with this agreement between the government and the cement companies concerning the elimination of certain types of waste—namely toxic or harmful industrial waste—within the cement plants. Well, as we thought, the deal went through. We knew at the time that, if it concerned anything relating to a cement factory, Souselas, because it was the largest in Portugal, would probably be involved. And with the whole history we already had of it being difficult to get the message across and to campaign systematically, consecutively, from everything that had happened in the anti-pollution commission from '76 to '97, we had the idea. There was already a much larger group of people, and we said, "Come on now, we've got to make some progress, we can't go on like this. This struggle is going to get a lot more complex. What is going to happen is going to be, in principle, much more complex. We have to set up a formal campaign." What was the idea behind formalizing our campaign? To create a legal body so that it could play an equal part in debates and could legally contest what eventually might happen. I was invited to sign the deeds of the association—its constitution dates from April 16th, 1998—therefore already after '97 and after several local protests by the Souselas people. It was established on April 16th, 1998, by public deed at the Penacova Notary Office. Our statutes were approved, and the Souselas Association for the Defense of the Environment was formed.

THE ESTABLISHMENT OF ADAS IN SOUSELAS

I can say that in this period of time—that is, from April '98 onwards—several things happened in this struggle that also affected our level of acceptance.

---

2   Scoreco is a consortium of cement factories created in 1996 in order to ensure the implementation of the co-incineration process. It is composed of Cimpor and Secil—the factories that exist in Portugal as a duopoly—in association with a French company. The creation of this consortium therefore signified a decisive step towards a decision in favor of co-incineration.

Why did we have difficulties in getting started? The sociologists can answer that one. Now, Souselas is a village with strong left-wing traditions. Why? Because, although it was an agricultural village until the 1940s, it became heavily industrialized from the '40s onwards. It began with Sesol, which used to be Mármores Batanete—that's to say, first it was a sawmill, but later it became a marble-cutting yard, Sesol, after the '40s; then, in the '60s, there was what is now Somit,[3] but was SIAF at that time; then, in the '70s, Cimpor. The industries that polluted and spoiled the environment the most were all directed towards that place without any kind of planning or any means at all of protecting the habitat, the people, the things, the animals, the flora and fauna, that existed in the place. Now, I actually engaged in that political struggle through a party to the right of local traditions. And in the beginning, because we had a local council that was, and still is, totally to the left, loyal to the CDU,[4] and because I had come from that political set-up, there were those who tried to make people believe that what we were doing was entirely a political idea—a political struggle against the status quo, against the government of the day, and so they tried to take the discussion over to the political side. One victory that ADAS won—and perhaps I played a positive part in this—was that politics and the environment were never to be mixed within ADAS. We took great care to check all the statements—although it was very difficult for me because I was, and still am, a member of the Parish Council, so I am involved in politics; but I managed never to mix the two things. Indeed, this was always fundamental: there are lots of people in ADAS who have absolutely no party connections, and I've never asked which party people were in—I couldn't care less. I never ask because that isn't the issue; I've never asked what they believe in, if they are this or that. And we've managed to make an alliance of ideas; we've managed to join forces and put politics aside. We left it completely alone, and created a campaign based entirely on environmental issues.

During the first year, during 1998 and up until mid-1999, there were some difficulties, there were some complex issues. I remember two meetings, particularly one at the Souselas Social Center, when the bad side of this kind of alliance got the upper hand (it reminds me of what is going on now in Sweden), and there was a meeting with lots of people where we had, to put it crudely, two or three people indoctrinated with the idea that they were there to be destructive, not constructive, and who tried to denigrate and ruin everything that was being built up. I think that, luckily for the Souselas struggle, for the Coimbra struggle, and for the environmental

---

3   Somit nowadays deals with the processing of wood.
4   The Coligação Democrática Unitária (United Democratic Coalition) is a coalition composed of the Partido Comunista Português (Portuguese Communist Party) and the Ecological Party (Partido Ecologista "Os Verdes").

struggle, this didn't actually happen: there was enough clear-sightedness and presence of mind for us not to let them ruin the work that was being done; there were no really violent showdowns that would have reflected badly on the credibility of the association. We overcame these difficulties; I think now they have been completely overcome.

It's now clear that our struggle concerns the environment; it has nothing to do with who governs us—if it's Party A, or Party B, or Party C—because at the moment I would say that it doesn't matter whether it's the Socialist Party or the Social Democratic Party or any other party that's in power: our situation would be the same. Because what is at stake is Souselas, and—I've said this before and I'll keep saying it—it's very difficult for people outside Souselas to understand how much we feel we have to fight against co-incineration, because we've been traumatized for thirty years by the activities of the cement factory.

Our problem is a problem that only we understand—those of us who live there, who have had our property damaged, who have had our belongings spoiled, and who know from experience how things are; even today these situations recur, although things are much better nowadays. We are the ones who know exactly what it would mean to have one more source of pollution on top of what we have already had all these years. And, as I said, Souselas is not only Cimpor; Souselas has other environmental problems at the moment as well, particularly the problem I've already mentioned of Somit. They want to open a huge sawmill to process used timber, and we don't know where it's coming from, what it was used for, what it contains—a whole series of issues that we have already put to the minister for economic affairs, in the form of some very concrete questions; but we haven't had an answer yet. But I would like to say that the Souselas struggle, in environmental terms, is almost like a laboratory: there are such different types of pollution, which, when you add them together, cause so much harm, so much damage to people's way of life, so much environmental loss, that it is a laboratory—you've got everything there. You can choose, for example, the pollution caused by cutting marble—the effluents—which is very complicated. The marble has to be cut using water—huge amounts of water that goes to waste afterwards. Before now it was done haphazardly. Now it's a little bit better—it's a ceramics factory, and everyone knows how ceramics factories work in this country, or used to work; now it's a bit better.

PRESIDENCY OF THE ASSOCIATION

Then we had the questions: What is to be done? How are we going to do it? How are we not going to do it? Who will be the president? Who won't be? I was invited, or almost forced, into becoming president. And then there was another question. Four years ago I came under heavy pressure, I was beseeched to head the list in Souselas of a party that was running for the Souselas Parish Council. I had never been very involved in the political side; I was an independent at the time, but people were pressuring me, believing that I was strong enough to head the struggle—and also because of the fact that I was already self-employed at the time in Souselas, working as an insurance intermediary, which means working door-to-door, meeting people and talking to them, and they thought that I should choose that path. I think that the work that was done, independently of political parties, [which] wasn't an issue—the discussions that took place, the positive way in which it developed—led people to think, "No, you're the right man for us—you have to be the president, you have to represent us." And I said, "OK, very well, if you think that I'm capable of handling this, I won't turn my back on the struggle. It's Souselas that matters, and it's our future that's at stake, so let's get on with it!"

PERSONAL TRAUMAS

And then [there are] some traumas that never leave you. Personally speaking, my father died of silicosis, my mother died of silicosis, and my grandfather died of silicosis—that is to say, there are some personal traumatic experiences that will always make us, at the very least, unable to trust. We are fighting to make our environment better so that the distrust lessens rather than increases, so that this lack of trust will gradually subside. So there are some things that we cannot give up on: we can't give up on spending our lives in Souselas, having our property in Souselas—we were born there, we live there, we can't just simply be thrown on the rubbish heap; we have the right to fight for the best possible quality of life.

THE CAMPAIGN AGAINST CO-INCINERATION

At the moment, ADAS is fully mobilized; it has always sought to promote and formalize the struggle on technical and scientific terms; we have never said no without reasons. Obviously, in the midst of all this, when we needed to go out into the streets, we did, but we've always tried to keep our discussions and our struggle open. And I can't help emphasizing how badly the government has failed to do anything about, for example, the problem of co-incineration. To go back a bit to the Study on Environmental Impact, to the time when all the controversy started, the study was done at the request of Scoreco, but it was never discussed. When they were in Souselas to discuss it, there was never any open information session—it was just a meeting to clean up the bad image of the past. I still say, and I have said this publicly: co-incineration is a war, and a war is won battle by battle. And we have in fact won some of the battles. I think that the Independent Scientific Commission[5] is a battle that, relatively speaking, we won. Why? Because if there hadn't been any Independent Scientific Commission we wouldn't have been able to discuss the problem in, let's say, scientific terms. If the problem had just been a political power game, co-incineration would have just been a political decision, and we wouldn't have had a chance of contesting it. At the moment we are opposing the report of the Independent Scientific Commission because, in scientific terms, it contains anomalies, and we have managed to look into these and pick out, as it were, the negative parts. We are managing to participate in scientific terms and debate in scientific terms what the Independent Scientific Commission itself has presented us with.

The problem of the Medical Group[6] still continues, in my opinion. For example, if there hadn't been a Medical Group there wouldn't have been an epidemiological study. The report of the Independent Scientific Commission says in point 5.4 that there should be active epidemiological monitoring for our population. Then, the discussions around the final vote, how the results of the Medical Group were presented, for us are symptomatic of the fact that things are not going well, and that it is possible to campaign in this area. If Professor Massano Cardoso[7] hadn't had the courage to say no, we would have great difficulties now in opposing what

---

5   The creation of the Independent Scientific Commission was the result of a proposal made by the Social Democratic Party in parliament in February 1999, arising out of the various views expressed by the entities involved in opposing co-incineration. With the establishment of this Commission (Law no. 20/99 of April 15th), the procedures for co-incineration were suspended until the group of experts had assessed whether or not it was the best method for dealing with harmful industrial waste. The Independent Scientific Commission was composed of the following members: José Cavalheiro (professor at the School of Engineering, University of Porto, and researcher at the Porto Biomedical Engineering Institute), Casimiro Pio (professor in the Environment Department at the University of Aveiro), Henrique Barros (professor of Epidemiology at the School of Medicine, University of Porto), and Formosinho Simões Sanches (professor in the Chemistry Department at the University of Coimbra).

6   The Medical Working Group was created after the CCI published the results of its study, indicating that co-incineration should proceed. Its aim was to investigate the consequences of co-incineration for public health. It was also created as a result of pressure being brought to bear on the government—this time in the form of a proposal by the Ecological Party. The creation of this group responded to one of the main demands of the protest movement since its beginning: the need to analyze the potential public health problems inherent in co-incineration.

7   Massano Cardoso is a professor at the School of Medicine, University of Coimbra, and also Director of the Institute of Hygiene and Social Medicine at the same university. He was the only one of the six members of the Medical Working Group to vote against co-incineration, stating that it brought risks to the health of the populations affected by it.

is being done in terms of the epidemiological study. For example, at the press conference we are giving tomorrow [June 26th, 2001] we are protesting and presenting facts about what is not being done in medical terms, in scientific terms. Obviously, we've got strong enough support behind us to be able to say, "My friends, we are making these statements, we are calling the Independent Scientific Commission inept and incompetent"—because we are calling them that directly—"and if necessary we have people here who can explain why."

So, we have managed to raise the level of debate, and I think that these are victories. I don't mean to say that the war has been won—not at all, because wars take a long time. You know, there was a war a few centuries ago that lasted 100 years; I don't mean that this one will last as long, but it's been going on for at least four years now, and at least we've managed to suspend or delay co-incineration for four years. It is a struggle that has advanced and retreated over these four years. At the moment, as we were saying a few minutes ago, in my opinion, the ball is in the opponent's court. There has been a political decision, and we're not out tilting at windmills here—we're fighting concrete facts, and there are politicians and scientists we can already call on, and eventually I think we will also have to take that path, calling things into question and considering the debate in legal terms. There are already people who are accountable for this, and we have to wait and see whether they have (and they will have to have) the courage to come forward, because they are well-known names. Let's wait and see how it works out.

So, we've got something to fight against. I look at it this way: there was a political decision made (by a particular government—it doesn't matter from which party: it was the government, a government decision) to install co-incineration. Let's suppose that we get co-incineration; then there is one of those accidents that everyone now says can't happen, and it happens, and there are people, or a group of people, or even one person, whose health is irreversibly damaged. Someone will have to be made responsible—someone will have to pay for what has happened, because now we have names, someone who said yes, someone who agreed to it in writing. Future governments will have to answer for what happens as a result of past actions, and until they eventually annul the decision they have to answer for what they were bold enough to do. So, there are names, and I think that from now on the struggle is going to get harder, but much more exciting, because the tougher it gets the more exciting it becomes.

Many people have asked me, "How do you still have the patience to go on with this, to be ruining your private life and getting attacked just because you represent the movement?" and I just say, "Wait and see. . ." I wouldn't say that I am ADAS, but I am its public face and, however much

I might want to, I cannot abandon those people who believed in me and still continue to do so. There may be one, there may be two, there may be three—it doesn't matter how many there are; what matters is that there are people who believe that I am right, that I represent their opinions and ideas, and that I am the public face of these ideas and this dispute. I can't say to them "I'm off now, the problem's over—it's nothing to do with me any more. Go and get someone else." I just can't, because I'm here, and that's a fact, I'm involved in this situation and I have to see it through to the end, to the very end, until it's all sorted out. And I do think that the problem will be resolved, because this is a political problem, it's an economic problem, and I think that when the country eventually changes the structure of government, this will bring matters to a head. There have been some very strong political stances taken, so that if this political change takes place, matters will at least have to be reassessed, because we have reached the conclusion that they aren't right—that, at the least, they have to be reconsidered, and then we shall see what will happen to us. So we can't lose heart. It's a public health problem; it's a human problem, above all, and we're here to deal with it.

The first protests began, let's say, when João Pardal[8] raised questions, around February '97. From then onwards, the first groups of people began getting together, and the protests began at the factory gates, already before ADAS was created. The people who were involved, most of them, were the ones who later joined ADAS, but the protests had started long before this, and they weren't specifically against co-incineration, but against the way the factory was operating. The first documents I have date from 1976.

For example, I think that the key point in the way in which the campaign was carried out was, in fact, the Medical Group. When one scientist had the courage to oppose other scientists in black and white, I think that that was when the CCI started to lose. We won and the CCI [started] to lose.

THE COMMITTEE FOR THE FIGHT AGAINST CO-INCINERATION

I should also stress two factors that were extraordinarily important for our struggle, both positively and negatively, and still are now. On the positive side, there was the Committee for the Fight against Co-incineration, which was made up of various bodies from the most disparate political quarters, from very different areas, as is the case of one particular newspaper which is above suspicion in this matter, the *Diário de Coimbra*, and also ACIC,[9] the Teachers Union, ADAS, the Coimbra Civic Association "Pro Urbe," and

---

8 A biologist and a member of the Social Democrat opposition in the Coimbra City Council.
9 The Coimbra Commercial and Industrial Association.

other institutions, such as the Ecology Group of the Coimbra University Students' Union. So, there was an enormous range of positions and people united in a common cause. It was a common cause because it was understood that what was at stake was a problem of public health, which affected the prestige of the university itself and the city of Coimbra.

THE COIMBRA CITY COUNCIL

On the negative side, I would have to point out the conduct of the Coimbra City Council, in particular the Socialist Party, which has the power to affect the fate of the city, and, fundamentally, of two people on the Council—the mayor and the councilor for the environment. I stress the negative aspects of these two individuals because they were never able to maintain a proper, focused attitude, and had no malleability whatsoever during the process–that is to say, when fingers were pointed out to them and they were directly held responsible for what was going to happen in terms of co-incineration, that was when people went to the Council, and afterwards also to the Municipal Assembly. At the time there was huge pressure from local people, and huge pressure from their own political party, the local Socialist Party, which later led to talks with the prime minister. We thought at the time that the ideas of the Council would be unshakeable, would be much stronger, much more sensible, much more dynamic. But after that I think that what prevailed was the political will of the Socialist Party, and not the will that should have guided a mayor who had been elected by the local people to preside over their destinies. The mayor followed a course that for me was so tortuous that it's not possible—at least not yet—to tell whether he really was against co-incineration. Actually, I think he is neither in favor nor against; he just defends the Socialist Party's position.

I would also point out the negative aspects of the actions of the councilor for the environment. I think that if a councilor for the environment, in any city council, hasn't got the technical background, the scientific background, to take a stance on environmental issues, he or she can only do one of two things: either resign, because they aren't able to hold the office to which they were appointed, or plead ignorance of these matters, and choose people who can speak on their behalf, analyze things for them, and just act as their spokesperson. I think that the councilor did neither of these things—he didn't admit that he didn't know and, by not admitting his ignorance, adopted an autistic stance, just like the mayor; and these autistic stances then have political backup. In other words, he states that the campaign in Souselas is a campaign by all the other parties against the Socialist Party. It's got nothing to do with that—it's a matter of public health; and usually the blame is attached to the Socialist Party because, if this is in fact a political decision from the central government, the truth is that the political representatives on the Council didn't side with the local population, and didn't oppose the politics of the central government. Now, automatically, they are in no position to say that we have no case. Finally, I would point out here, too, the position taken by the mayor in relation to the powers conferred on him by Decree-Law 120/99 concerning the final and official constitution of the Independent Scientific Commission. This states that the Commission is made up of three members appointed by the Board of Rectors [of Portuguese Universities] (or at the suggestion of the Board of Rectors, because after that the appointment is political), while the fourth member is appointed directly by the environment minister and the fifth and sixth by the respective Councils of the places where co-incineration is planned. That is to say, the fifth member has to be appointed by the Coimbra City Council and the sixth by the Setúbal City Council.[10] We know that, at this moment, no member has been nominated yet by the Setúbal City Council, or at least not officially, and that the nomination of the Coimbra City Council was for Professor Massano Cardoso, at the express invitation of the mayor, which Professor Massano Cardoso has accepted. And here's one more tortuous move, and it goes even beyond that—it's obvious political hypocrisy, in light of what we came to know afterwards. While accepting the mayor's invitation, Dr. Massano Cardoso made it clear that he would be on the Scientific Commission purely to act as a spokesman for the protests of the people of Souselas, and that he wanted clarity, transparency, and communication—that is, an openness about what the Scientific Commission thought of the entire process. He said he would be the "eyes and ears" of the Souselas people. What we have discovered, in the meantime, after a lot of pressure at the factory gates by the local people, is that while Dr.Massano is being invited, the Scientific Commission has already started tests behind the backs of the mayor, the civil governor, and apparently even the president of Scoreco himself (at least, this was the news that was published, and it hasn't been discredited). So, at the very least, what is asked of the mayor of Coimbra is that he should come to Souselas, not to defend the local people—because he has never done that—but to defend the person he himself nominated to defend the local population. Now, by not appearing, and by saying that the demonstrations of the Souselas people are just a display of folklore—and I might say that folklore, in my opinion,

---

10   The other cement factory chosen to implement co-incineration is located in the district of Setúbal, in Outão. Unlike Souselas, this factory (which belongs to Secil) was only included in the process after the publication of the findings of the CCI report, in which the decision was made to replace a previous choice of factory. It should be noted that the original factory was located in the Arrábida Natural Park, and this gave rise to innumerable protests by environmental associations.

is the purest demonstration of the desires and will of the people; folklore and ethnography are the will to revive the purest traditions people have—when he says that the protests and the demonstrations of the local people are just some kind of folk performance, that is just stupidity. I have to call the mayor himself stupid because if someone, if local people, use folk traditions in their demonstrations, it's because they are revealing what is in their hearts and souls. For me, his not coming to Souselas last Friday shows that he is taking an exclusively political stance, and is not willing to support the people who have elected him. So, once again, he has dug or irreversibly widened the great divide which separates the Souselas and the Coimbra populations. So I think that the people of Souselas and Coimbra will have to give a political response to the political position taken by the mayor of Coimbra.

THE CIVIL GOVERNOR OF COIMBRA

I cannot but mention also the stance taken by the civil governor of the District of Coimbra. As well as displaying complete openness in his dialogue with the population, he has taken up a public stance that shows a complete disapproval of and a complete disagreement with the position of the Independent Scientific Commission and, by analogy, with the government itself—and particularly the environment minister. I would like to stress the positive conduct of the current civil governor of the District of Coimbra, because throughout the entire process he has shown great openness—an awareness that the struggle in Souselas is correct, and that the population only makes demonstrations when, in effect, the Independent Scientific Commission and, by implication, the Coimbra City Council don't follow the rules of honesty, transparency, and rigor.

THE CONTEMPT OF THE POLITICAL POWERS

It is depressing, or it becomes depressing for local citizens—for example, in the specific case of the *Diário de Coimbra* petition [against co-incineration], which nearly 60,000 people signed.[11] Really, it's depressing. The attitudes of the Souselas Parish Assembly are depressing (I'm talking in political terms here). The attitude of the Coimbra Municipal Assembly is also depressing— I'm not even talking about the Executive, but on the part of the Municipal Assembly, it's depressing. That's why I say that Portugal is too politicized in a negative sense, in terms of the citizens we all are; it's very negative for all of us when we demonstrate in the only ways we can, like signing petitions.

---

11   Joaquim is referring to a petition organized by a local newspaper, the *Diário de Coimbra*. It was signed by around 60,000 citizens, but practically ignored by the government.

For me it was essential to have such a large number, such a mass of people expressing their opinion against this situation—50 percent of the people in the *concelho*[12] of Coimbra, if you look at it, and then the central government comes and says that it has no significance. In other words, the arbitrary nature of government (and I'm not saying that it's only this government)— in the end it just becomes a way of humiliating those who elected them to be our worthy representatives. I don't want to make a political campaign out of this, but if we bear it in mind, and what happened recently in Ireland, where more than 50 percent of the population were against the Treaty of Nice—and all the political leaders of all the other countries in the European Community, including the president of their own country, acted as if it didn't mean a thing! So I ask: How can citizens show what they think of the way they are being governed? A little while ago, I was wondering if we didn't suffer from some kind of complex about not being able to get our message across. The struggle is abysmal. Logistically, financially, in terms of access to the media, you can only praise anyone who has the courage to be involved in a struggle like this one, where everything is abysmally disproportionate. But, as I said, it's not just happening in our country, it's happening in Europe too, perhaps in the rest of the world, even in Europe, and the example I gave of the referendum on the Treaty of Nice in Ireland is symptomatic.

Besides, one of the questions I have raised, as a citizen and as someone sitting on a Parish Council,[13] is: What are we doing here? What is the purpose of a Parish Assembly?[14] What is the purpose of a Municipal Assembly? If the power lies solely in the hands of the Mayor, what are people doing in a Municipal Assembly?

LACK OF DIALOGUE WITH LOCAL PEOPLE

If the factory had known how to live alongside the local people, if one of its higher goals had been to create links between itself and the local environment, there would have been no need for the local population to say that it could have done things differently. Why is it that, for example, that factory and all the other factories don't have a press office, a public relations office where they can hold meetings with local people from time to time? If they don't want to do this informally, they could hold an open

---

12 An administrative subdivision of a district.
13 Local authority.
14 The Parish Assembly its the decision-making body of the Parish Council, which is elected by a universal, direct and secret ballot of the citizens who are registered to vote in the area of the local authority in question, in accordance with the proportional representation system

parish assembly—like: "My friends, we've come here to find out what the problem is, how we are doing, if things have gotten better or not, what your complaints are." Why don't they do this? It's a way of linking the factory—not just this one, all of them—to the local people they live with. But no, they shut themselves off, they shut themselves away in their own little world and don't give a damn about the local population, and there you have it. That's what happened, and is still happening, with co-incineration. What we see is that they want to turn what has been found out about co-incineration, about what it produces or doesn't produce, it's basic harmful effects—they want to turn this into a state secret.

But you have to discuss things—you have to have an open discussion. Because it was only through discussion that, for example, we reached the conclusion that there are already alternatives to the oils, there are already alternatives to the solvents, and, in principle, there might even be alternatives to the slurry.[15] That's discussion. But it seems that when we go and discuss things with the Independent Scientific Commission, we are talking to gentlemen who have been placed on a pedestal. And they shouldn't be; we are the ones who understand the reality of it—we know what our reality is. For example, I'm against this situation of going to Aveiro or going to Lisbon or to Porto to discuss matters with the CCI or with the government itself. Aren't we from Souselas? Aren't we human beings? Shouldn't we be treated like human beings, like people who produce the goods that provide the taxes to pay for everything that exists in this country, that sustains the government? Don't they know who we are? They know they can send me a letter from Lisbon telling me to pay x taxes by y date. So why don't they understand the reverse? I think that is why we need dialogue. Dialogue means right here, face to face, looking people in the eye. It doesn't cost anything. But it's what we need to do. We have to be treated as first-class citizens—we are all equal. And so when they want to impose a process on us that the scientists themselves say they can't control, that they don't have any national experience of, that all they have on it is vague or doesn't point to any bad situation, and therefore must be good; when they present all this as accomplished facts, and we experience a completely different reality, it's logical that they will never be able to win the minds of the Souselas people or make us believe that it's a good thing, because it was completely wrong at the beginning, and it continues to be completely wrong now.

One of the duties of the CCI was to promote public discussion of the situation—discussion between institutions, in order to clarify the positions

---

15   From among all harmful industrial waste, the three types declared suitable for burning in cement factories may be generically classified as used oils, organic solvents, and organic slurry. As their name indicates, these types of waste are the result of industrial processes and are highly combustible, and can thus be used to reclaim energy.

it had taken; in other words, to create a developmental, informative process out of what it intends to do. But no, the CCI shut itself off from the public. Has anyone ever heard of the CCI coming to this area to discuss anything? Never. And why won't they come? They don't need us to ask them—they should just say, "On such-and-such a day at such-and-such a time we'll be in Souselas." About this epidemiological study, tomorrow we are going to hold a press conference in which we are going to attack them, and we're going to attack them because they haven't done what they said they would do. Why isn't the epidemiological study being done? Because no one supports it. Why does it have no supporters? Because ADAS said: "We, who are here, have done a study that they haven't. We have already identified the realities that we face—they are identified and written down. It was us who went out there in the evenings to every house in the area."[16] Out of a thousand people, there were only three who wouldn't reply to the enquiry—so you can see the support that was given. And after we reached our conclusions, the CCI said it would do tests. Look, if they are going to do tests, the person they are going to do them on has to know what they are going to do to him, in a proper manner, concretely and concisely, in black and white.

So why didn't the CCI have the courage to do the same work we did? If they have funds—and I can tell you they are almost unlimited, and they are not controlled by the Court of Auditors as the Decree-Law says—let them come here. If they don't have the courage, let them ask ADAS or some other institution, and we'll go with them. That's what would bring some credibility to the process—so why is it that they won't come to us? Why do they keep themselves apart? Don't the guinea pigs have any say in the matter? What is the Helsinki Treaty for anyway? In general terms, isn't it there to say that when people serve as guinea pigs, they have to give their express agreement to be treated as such? So, what's going on? Now, we're saying that what they put down on paper is very nice—we've even read point 5.4 of the CCI [report]; we've even read what they've got now on the internet, about what they are going to do, what exactly they want to know. And yet we've got this previous history of them not even allowing us any credibility—they haven't even got a believable past history. And if they don't have this history, how am I going to believe them? It's a problem of lack of credibility. So, if it means that ADAS really does have to go there,

---

16 The implementation of an epidemiological study in Souselas was one of the main demands of the local population. The fact that this was completely ignored by the government led ADAS, with the support of the Institute of Hygiene and Social Medicine at the University of Coimbra, to take the initiative of conducting a local survey, on a door-to-door basis, with the aim of determining the state of health of the local population, in a process that resembled "popular epidemiology."

then, yes, I'll go round to people's houses if necessary. But I want to have
someone there who can tell me what is being done; I want to be absolutely
sure about what they say they are doing—because afterwards there will be
things to discuss. But it's early days yet, and I want to be absolutely sure
about things.

MEDIA INEQUALITY

No one cares about those who are against and say why: they might even be
right, but if they're not aligned with those in power, it's extremely hard for
them to get their message across. And so this is the political side of things—
shall we say, in political terms, there are still certain places where you can go
within the political structure. A president of a Parish Council, let's say, can
pretend he is crazy and go to the Municipal Assembly and disrupt it, or even
disrupt the parliament. But ordinary citizens—well, it's just not allowed.
We present technical evidence, we present scientific evidence, and it's like
beating your head against a brick wall, because they won't let us [speak].

And then, what's worse is that, as well as not allowing us a voice, the
control they have over the media is so great that they manage to misrepresent the way the message is put across. For example, except for the rare
occasions when I have been on TV news programs, and once or twice on
RTP1,[17] on TeleRegiões, the first thing they tell someone who is going to
speak is: "You've got one minute, you've got two, you've got three, now,
choose . . ." Or the journalist, let's say, channels the interview so that the
person being interviewed almost has to say what they want him to say. And
there's one thing that I'm still trying to work out in all of this—and that's,
for example, why there hasn't ever been a media discussion in Portugal,
an open discussion dealing with the whys and wherefores of both sides.
We've been at this for four years, and there hasn't been any opportunity yet
for people to sit down around a table and say, "Come on then, let's talk,"
and then let each side defend its position and bring in people from various
areas to help in their defense, like the CCI did. We would certainly have
on our side epidemiologists, people from chemistry, physics, mechanical
engineering—Professor Delgado Domingos,[18] for example, who has been
systematically branded a madman, but who is the only person in this country who understands the construction of cement kilns. But they don't give

---

17   A television channel.
18   Delgado Domingos is a professor at the Higher Institute of Technology in Lisbon,
and lectures on mechanical engineering and the environment. In addition to writing
several newspaper articles, he has also taken part in some of the initiatives of the protest
movement, arguing against the suitability of the co-incineration process for cement
factories.

us a chance to discuss things, to sit down together and "put the cards on the table." They don't even let us do this, and that's why it's difficult to get the message across, isn't it?

GETTING THE MESSAGE ACROSS

I think this is the number one problem—in other words, the difference in resources, the logistical difference. Up until the political decision, in that phase of the struggle, it was extremely complicated to get our message across, to explain our reasons. The popular protest, which, as I've often said, is what reaches the TV screens, is motivated by a desire to display anger, which sometimes acts against the voice of reason. In other words, anger is a spontaneous feeling, and sometimes shows itself in ways that are not entirely reasonable, that overstep certain limits, even the limits of decent civic behavior. In the most heated moments of the campaign, the television tried to convey the image that we were a band of people who loved appearing on TV, who wanted primetime—that this was a political struggle. At the same time, the Independent Scientific Commission were putting forward their recommendations by trying to convey to the public that they were the owners of the absolute truth—or, in other words, that we had no reason to protest because they knew the absolute truth, that what they said was indisputable, and so we had actually nothing to argue against, because science had said that everything was completely in order. So it was a very difficult time. I don't think there was a softening in attitude so much as a slowing down of the popular mass protest, because some things gradually became clear to us. First, it is always difficult to keep people active in a particular struggle in the same numbers and with the same level of commitment over a long period of time—it's difficult because people start to slacken off. Actually, the president of the Independent Scientific Commission said that the protests would end because people would eventually give in to tiredness. And we could see that.

STRENGTHENING THE SCIENTIFIC DEBATE

From then onwards [since the medical report], our protest has focused very much more on the scientific side, on the technical side. It has been more that kind of campaign—perhaps even a lot stronger, but not so visible. How has the problem of oils been dealt with, or the problem of solvents? With the great help of Quercus[19]—namely Quercus-Coimbra, which the public

19   Although we cannot speak of a strong environmentalist movement in Portugal, Quercus—the Association for the Conservation of Nature—is the most prominent environmental association in the country, in terms of both membership and initiatives, which

haven't heard so much about, but which has been winning us several battles within the Commission itself. As for public opinion, I think that anyway (at this moment there aren't any opinion surveys on this subject), as for public opinion, we're already condemned.

I've often said that now is the time when things are going to heat up, because it's now that things are starting to get a bit more complicated. And this is actually what is happening. Which is one reason why we have to be a lot more careful now: our protest has to be based on concrete facts; we can't convey the image that we're just protesting for the sake of protest, because they've already taken advantage of that before. That's why I, for example, haven't appeared at some of the press conferences that have been held, particularly in Coimbra, because there are some people who just want to take the struggle into areas that are not very creditable. You know, protesting if members of the Commission get 500,000 or 600,000 escudos—I don't think that's the way to do things. In global terms it's important, but in specific terms, raising these issues—I don't think that's the way to move forward.

What we have to try to do now, and what is going to happen tomorrow, is to concentrate the campaign on the scientific side of things. The big difference of opinion within the scientific community could, in my opinion, prevent this situation from advancing. Because what are we seeing? Within specialized areas—not in the medical field but in specifically technical fields, namely in chemistry, physics, and so on—we are seeing developments in the United States, developments arising from documents that the EPA[20] has been presenting, which prove us right—and the truth is that many people who at the time said that perhaps it was the solution now say that perhaps it isn't a good solution.

GAINING CREDIBILITY FOR THE STRUGGLE

But, to tell the truth, as I said a while back, it was very difficult in the beginning when they wanted to impose a completely political struggle on us, but we managed to gain credibility for the struggle. I think that nowadays ADAS is visible on a national, even an international, level. Many people phone me from outside Portugal to say, "Keep it up! Keep it up!"—because it's also true that the campaign has been directed towards discrediting the Independent Scientific Commission, and this is also happening on

---

have gained it increasing credibility with the public as well as with political powers.

20   The Environmental Protection Agency—an American state organization that, over the last thirty years, has produced countless research studies and reports relating to the protection of the environment and public health. Most of the existing documents on the co-incineration of harmful industrial waste, the emissions that result from it, and the associated risks, have been produced by this organization.

an international level. In other countries—I don't know whether it's due to ineptitude, or maybe to lack of discussion—co-incineration has been installed and still exists—although it is less widely used in some cases—because at the time there was no strong discussion. I think there was no discussion—I don't know whether it was because people just accepted it or what. It's not because the Portuguese are more intelligent or because the people of Souselas are more threatened than anyone else in all this; but the truth is that, if the doubts are rising rather than diminishing within the scientific community, I think that this will involve a debate on a European level, or even a worldwide level—I don't know.

And there is another factor that points to this: environmental problems have never been as much the order of the day as now. Until now, the development of the United States itself, in economic terms, was based on the successive and systematic running down of the environment. The statement of the current president[21] himself, saying that he will not sign the Kyoto Protocol, and the reasons he gave for not signing, have, I think, created a feeling of revolt among Europeans; I don't know whether this is for environmental reasons or not, but it could be. People are beginning to understand that, in the end, those who are in control and have the power also have the guts to trample on the lives of everybody else, because they want a better life for themselves. But this is our world we're talking about—I mean, we can't leave, we have to live here. I think that the struggle that Souselas started, the credibility that Souselas gave to the struggle, the fact that it separated itself off from the political side of things. . . because I think that this country is too politicized, I think that politics is put over and above everything else; or, in other words, when someone has the courage to confront whatever it is, it has to be political—I mean, we can't do anything without it being political. If we say that this river is polluted, "Well, mate, you're against the president of the Council because the president of the Council is the one who should have done something about it and he didn't, because he's on the other [political] side." Which means that whatever you do, there's politics behind it. And we managed, in my opinion, to get rid of that side of things, and I think that the credibility it gave us and the credibility it is giving us and will continue to give us will help us get our image across, and our message will get through.

ALLIANCES

I have to say that this struggle has been, fundamentally, a very rich human experience for me. Here's a funny story for you: the other day I was a long way from home, in Castelo Branco, and two elderly men passed me and

---

21   At the time of the interview, George W. Bush.

[said], "Look who it is! It's that man from the television who's protesting about all that rubbish and stuff." I mean, people know me; it's strange. I think that we have made contact—let's say, people are beginning to see that we can't be quite the lunatics they want us to appear to be. And about what Marisa was saying just now, we have actually created a network: we have strong links with people from Maceira, people from Estarreja, people from Porto, people from Leiria, people from Alhandra, people from Barreiro, people from Setúbal, which is really good and really useful. Actually, this applies to ADAS as well as Pro Urbe—we mustn't forget that Pro Urbe has played an extraordinary part in this process. Why? We were saying that on a national level there are difficulties in reaching particular places. And you don't have to go too far to see that; it seems that Souselas isn't Coimbra, and Coimbra isn't Souselas.

I often say that Coimbra has one very good thing and one very bad thing: the university. The very good aspect is the prestige it has as the oldest university in Portugal, if not one of the oldest in Europe, and [from] the fact that the scientists, the specialists, or the doctors who come out of there have a lot of credibility on a national and even an international level. But I also think that this same university works within its own little world, and isn't open enough, and doesn't create the necessary synergies between the population that surrounds it and the university itself. I think that this is a terrible drawback, and it's a drawback that can only be overcome by a change in mentality. In this specific case—co-incineration or incineration in Souselas—what happened was that the only schools that did anything were the School of Economics (including Sociology) and the Medical School. The School of Science and Technology, in particular, could have played a much more active role than it did, because it had all the technical resources, the human resources, the scientific resources to actually contest the process of co-incineration or incineration at the Souselas factory. So I think that it's a very good but also a very bad thing. The University of Coimbra has to open itself up to the local population; its scientists have to offer more, so that their knowledge can be much more fully "imbibed" by the population that surrounds them. Because it's not right, in my opinion, that Coimbra gives everything to the students: it gives them accommodation, it gives them knowledge, it gives them the university, it gives them everything— and then these students, when they've finished their degrees, go off and leave nothing for Coimbra. I think it's high time for some kind of repay- ment, for a much stronger interconnection between the university and the local population, between the people who are educated there and the local population of Coimbra.

PARTICIPATION OF WOMEN AND ELDERLY
PEOPLE IN THE MOVEMENT

There are concrete answers for these facts. First, there are women, because they are the ones who suffer most from the environmental aggression of the factory. Who cleans the house? Who clears up, almost daily, the rubbish that is produced by the factory? Who, for example, takes the children down to the village doctor? It's usually the women. It's very rare to see a father taking his children down to the health center on a regular basis. He might go with his wife, but it's always the wife who takes care of the children's health. And it's the wives who get up at night to look after the children when they're suffering from allergies, from bronchitis—they have a whole series of things to deal with. It's the women who really suffer from what Cimpor does.

The fact that elderly people are also involved is because these people, in my opinion, are much more sensitive to things. When we are young, we aren't worried about death. When we are young, we just care about living from day-to-day as fast, as urgently, and as freely as possible. As we get older, we are more haunted by the idea of dying. Why? Because people realize that their health isn't as good as it used to be, that it's deteriorating, that they have to go to the doctor more often, and they almost demand to have their health back, because they see that it's deteriorating. This struggle, if nothing else, has made people more aware of the fact that a large part of the illnesses that appear are the result of the way in which industries in general, and Cimpor in particular, have been operating over these past years. People are now more aware, since ADAS has managed to provide scientific explanations from various doctors from the University of Coimbra—many of whom are world-famous specialists, who have come to Souselas to explain why certain pathologies have occurred, what their origins and causes are. People are beginning to understand the situation: "So, I've got bronchitis, I feel ill, I've got a series of allergies, so actually it's the result of all this." And this awareness, together with the fact that they are approaching the end of their lives, means that elderly people have more of a feeling for public health than for ecology itself. But these facts have been presented effectively, because now awareness of public health is much more common in elderly people, and also in women; besides, women in the villages have more time than the men.

PUBLIC HEALTH

Public health, I think, is maybe the weightiest issue, because what is at stake here is a public health problem. We have, in fact, two great allies:

individually, Professor Massano Cardoso and, collectively, the Scientific Council of the School of Medicine of the University of Coimbra. I think that the union of the Coimbra scientific community, or at least that part of it which is linked to medicine, might, in terms of this conflict between one office and another, one science against another, lead us to win the struggle.

"MY LIFE DOESN'T HAVE A PRICE"

I can't accept what the Independent Scientific Commission said they wouldn't do. They said at the beginning that they wouldn't do dioxin tests because they were very expensive and they didn't have the money—it would cost too much. I can't accept what the CCI says at the moment about environmental monitoring, continuous monitoring—that it's not being done because they don't know how to, and they don't have the money. I won't accept this: my life doesn't have a price, and they're telling me how much my life is worth. If it's a financial problem, let them tell me how much my life is worth. Now, multiply that by one thousand inhabitants—and I'm only talking about Souselas here, about that one kilometer area—multiply it by one thousand, and how much does it cost? How much am I worth? Only I know how much I am worth. Can anyone except me add up how much I am worth? I don't know what kind of future I will have. I am now forty-three years old. What about the little kids who are being born now? What price are they going to put on their future? What are they going to make of themselves? How much do they cost? What kind of investment is it? You could say that it's unlimited. So, are we limiting the lives of these people according to economic criteria? It's all wrong. So, if they want to create this situation, if they don't want to run this risk, if they don't have the money, only two things can happen in the end: either we leave or the factory does. In the end it's a kind of extreme solution that I don't want to see us reach, but if we reduce things to financial terms, then I have to say, "Friends, I don't know what a child that's just been born, that's a few months old, is going to be in the future; it might even become prime minister of this country or another one, or even president of the United States." Who is to say that they couldn't? We're just working with suppositions—no one can deny us our ambition, our human ambition. Don't they say that human ambition is limitless? So, let's see, then: if they want to create this situation and they have no solution for us, let them take the factory away. So, after all these questions, Souselas and I myself will never accept co-incineration. I can't accept it, because the failures in the whole process are so great that only the negative side stands out. My life is at issue here—I'm not even talking about the tangible side, money or material things, but my life itself; and nobody can tell me how much that is worth—they cannot, and I won't accept it. And the CCI wants to work out how much the lives of the Souselas people are worth!

"THE STRUGGLE GOES ON"

Everything that is happening—this final part of the struggle that we are involved in, as there has already been a decision; this latest situation; the successive errors that we have found in the report; the increasingly complex questions that are being raised, that are making the Independent Scientific Commission itself lose credibility over the points it presents in its report—if it hadn't been for this struggle, what would have happened by now? We would have co-incineration there [in Souselas], without baghouse[22] filters, without a treatment unit, without anything. They'd come along, light up the fires, and just burn away. That's what has happened in other places. So there's nothing else we can do: the struggle goes on.

Conducting an interview like this one is a learning experience, and also an exercise in confronting the "other side" of the issues at stake. Joaquim articulates in an exemplary manner the different types of knowledge he has gained—through his personal experience, as an employee at Cimpor, and as an inhabitant of Souselas, as well as through his involvement in this particular protest movement. One of the most significant factors we were able to detect throughout the interview was the centrality of the problem of co-incineration in the life of the interviewee. This is exemplified by the enthusiasm, the strength, and the dedication evident in each of his replies.

In addition, we were also able to detect the opposition that exists between the traditional political struggle and the environmental struggle. The latter, as the Souselas case shows, is in fact an alternative way of carrying out a political struggle, different from the type that is channeled through political parties and traditional institutions. It is a form of political action that seeks to organize and to give a voice and visibility to emerging collective identities, which arise from problems that are experienced first of all on a local level, and then gradually link up with struggles and movements of a broader nature, focusing on the protection of the environment, environmental justice, and the right of citizens to participate in decisions that affect their life, their health, and the environment.

Throughout the interview, as in all previous contacts with the interviewee and the movement against co-incineration in Souselas, we entered into a process of learning about the articulations that make up this new form of political struggle. Citizens called for the right to participate, and even though they were not listened to, they refused to bow their heads but held their ground, and became increasingly more informed and more critical in relation to the whole process.

---

22   The baghouse is a generic name for Air Pollution Control Equipment (APC) that is designed around the use of engineered fabric filter tubes, envelopes or cartridges in the dust capturing, separation or filtering process.

13

Manuel Graça

Footwear worker, member of the army that started the April 25th Revolution, grassroots trade unionist, activist in the struggle for trade union democracy.

Interviewed by Elísio Estanque

"And then they said to us: 'Calm down, man. We've got the Eastern countries, we'll get there one day!' But we knew what was happening to their political struggle through dissident groups—we knew all about the movements in Czechoslovakia and Solidarity in Poland. We knew what was going on from the start through political circuits and other autonomous organizations on the left . . ."

Manuel Graça

I met Manuel Graça in 1989, when I was beginning my research into the industrial footwear sector in S. João da Madeira. His availability and the interest he showed in my work from the outset, combined with certain experiences we had in common (such as political involvement in the revolutionary period of 1974/75, and solidarity with workers' struggles), led to the establishment of a relationship of understanding and openness that has lasted until today. The interview presented here clearly illustrates the rapport that exists between interviewer and interviewee. Despite our different social positions—and the fact that there are always misconstructions in any kind of interaction or communication—the mutual understanding that exists between us undoubtedly contributed to the success of the interview. Indeed, it was the personal affinity between us that allowed me to obtain the biographical details of the interviewee that I will now present.

Manuel Graça was born in 1953. His parents both worked in the glass industry in Oliveira de Azeméis, in one of the largest companies in the area (the Centro Vidreiro). Given the family's economic needs and his father's loss of employment, Manuel, one of eight children, followed the example of his elder brothers and began his working life early, as soon as he completed the fourth grade of primary school at the age of ten. This was during the early years of the colonial war, and one of his elder brothers was sent to Angola in 1964. Prior to this, his father had been dismissed from the company where he worked, supposedly for having supported a strike and fraternized with people considered to be the opposition. The colonial question was then one of the hottest issues on the political agenda in the country, and, despite the harsh repression and censorship, it was one of the main subjects of café conversation, especially among those sectors of the youth population that were socially aware. Manuel first worked in the footwear factory, Praça, also based at Oliveira de Azeméis. The bosses of the company were known to have Nazi sympathies and business connections with Germany, and they even had a picture of Hitler in their factory. Manuel remembers that working conditions were terrible. They began at 8 a.m. and finished at 7 p.m. (and frequently later than this), every day of the week including Saturdays. The wage was 7.50 escudos per week. This first phase of his working life lasted for around six years, during which he experienced the hardships of those who had no other alternatives. From the age of fifteen or sixteen, he began to frequent the café more regularly, and there met up with old friends—former schoolmates who had, unlike him, continued with their studies and were about to go to college (as they were mostly the children of educated, middle-class parents). This meeting was important for him, because it put him in contact with critical opinions about the colonial war and the Salazar regime in general. This café was near a local association, ARCA,[1] to which some of his friends belonged in this period (the mid-1960s), and the atmosphere of debate that he found there, as well as the various recreational activities, greatly enriched the daily routine of this young man who was to become a trade union leader.

It was in this environment that Manuel began to gain an awareness of the conditions of exploitation in his company, where he earned less than 10 escudos per week. His more educated friends questioned his work situation, and gradually he, in turn, began to question it too. As he was, by now, able to operate in different aspects of production at the factory (preparation, cutting, assembling, finishing, and so on), he felt that he was being treated unjustly. He considered his alternatives. He moved to another shoe factory, Fémina, where he was able to earn per day what he had previously earned in a week. However, his problems continued, while, simultaneously, his awareness grew of the injustices in the workplace and in society. He sought information about his rights from the trade union of the sector (trade unions were part of the authoritarian structures of the regime), but the result was that his employer was warned about his potentially "subversive" attitudes by informers at the union (who collaborated with the political police).

At the age of seventeen, Manuel was already participating actively in the cultural activities of ARCA, particularly the film and poetry section. In the second half of the 1960s, he was already familiar with the new rock music trends then emerging in Europe and North America, associated with the hippy movement, pacifist ideas, and youth rebellion.[2] As we know, the social movements at the end of the 1960s, as well as bringing new cultural values and practices, were marked by irreverence and a critical stance towards politics. The works of writers and poets known to oppose the regime, including books that had been censored, such as those by African authors like Amílcar Cabral, circulated clandestinely among the members of ARCA. These influences profoundly affected Manuel's youth.

In addition, an event such as the robbery of a bank in Figueira da Foz, led by Palma Inácio, was also a topic for discussion among Manuel's friends, particularly as one of the participants in the robbery (Camilo Mortágua) was from that area. Although with a still somewhat undefined political consciousness, Manuel considered

---

1   Associação Recreativa e Cultural de Azeméis—Azeméis Recreational and Cultural Association.
2   The Doors, the Rolling Stones, Steppenwolf, Janis Joplin, Creedence Clearwater Revival, Frank Zappa, The Who, Deep Purple, and so on—as well as free jazz and Portuguese music by Zeca Afonso, Adriano Oliveira, José Mário Branco, and Sérgio Godinho—are a few of the hundreds of LPs that Manuel still keeps in his office.

himself an anti-fascist and critic of the regime, and therefore that event attracted his sympathy. Among his contacts were activists in the Portuguese Communist Party (Partido Comunista Português—PCP) and in more radical groups, such as founding members of the Internationalist Communist League (Liga Comunista Internacionalista—LCI).[3] *He even participated in educational initiatives promoted by that group, where authors such as Marx, Lenin, Trotsky, Mao Zedong, Ernest Mandel, and others were discussed. They even debated what stance to adopt on the subject of military conscription, raising the possibility of evasion—although the dominant position was that one should join the army and then undertake consciousness-raising activities within it.*

With this experience behind him, Manuel began his military service in January 1974, shortly before the revolution of April 25th. His anti-militaristic and anti–colonial war stance, together with the extension of his contacts to other opposition associations, made him new friends during his stay at the Viseu military barracks. There he was involved in clandestine propaganda activities against the war in the former colonies. After his training was finished, and with the military coup of April 25th imminent, Manuel was sent to Queluz,[4] *since he had meanwhile been mobilized for Guinea, though he never actually got there. His contacts with party organizations gave him access to information about the Movement of the Armed Forces (Movimento das Forças Armadas—MFA), and so he was aware of the movements connected to the attempted coup of March 16th,*[5] *as well as that of April 25th itself.*

On the night of April 24th, he waited anxiously with his ears glued to the radio to hear the José Afonso song "Grândola Vila Morena," which was the secret signal that set in motion the military operations. His comrades in the barracks doubted what he had told them confidentially about the coup, but the following day they were able to join the Portuguese people at large in celebrating the downfall of the old regime and the achievement of freedom.

Manuel left at around 6 a.m., in a jeep with a group of other soldiers, for the streets of Lisbon. He was in the area of Estrela, and later took part in the occupation of the studios of the former National Broadcasting Building on S. Marçal Street. The soldiers mingled with the people, who insisted on coming out into the street despite constant appeals to remain indoors. In Manuel's opinion, it was this stubbornness of the popular movement that ensured the success of the democratic forces. In the Queluz barracks, they wanted to dismiss the commandant, who was a supporter of the deposed regime, take control of the barracks, and elect a new commandant. Over

---

3   A small political party of Trotskyite inspiration that stood in various elections in the post–April 25th period, but never won many votes. Later it joined up with the Revolutionary Socialist Party.
4   A town near Lisbon.
5   A first attempt at a military uprising against the regime, which miscarried, as only a single column of soldiers from the military base at Caldas da Rainha tried to march upon the capital. It was intercepted by forces loyal to the regime, and its officers were arrested.

the next few days, the commandant demonstrated support for the movement, but many found his posture unconvincing, and he ended up being replaced. The struggle for democracy in the barracks immediately became an integral part of the intense political and social activity that had been unleashed on April 25th. At Queluz, as in many other military compounds, the uncontrollable desire to participate led to the breakdown of distinct areas of the mess and common rooms for soldiers, sergeants, and officers, and the same spaces began to be shared by all. At this time, when collective decisions were taken by voting with raised hands, Manuel was already carrying out the functions of leader of the "Soldiers' Committee" of the barracks. Everywhere—in companies, schools, residential neighborhoods, public offices, and so on—people and workers began to organize.

The desire to participate and the revolutionary dynamic quickly led to forms of "popular justice," sometimes arising spontaneously, and at other times as the result of manipulation by political groups and parties. This gave rise to all types of excesses, typical of the revolutionary climate of the period. Political clean-ups followed, and forms of manipulation and political opportunism multiplied. In the months after April 25th, the units of the Armed Forces, and later the COPCON,[6] began to intervene in many areas in order to arbitrate conflicts, since the institutional power had lost all legitimacy and was now paralyzed. Revolutionary legitimacy was, however, reinforced when it was supported by the MFA. Manuel was in fact involved in military groups called upon to regulate some of these conflicts, particularly in firms. His ideological training, although Marxist in inclination, allowed him to maintain a certain distance from the dogmatism of the period, especially as conveyed by the PCP. In a company in Queluz, the workers called a general meeting and, with a majority vote, decided that the boss should continue to front the company. They were opposed by a minority (PCP representatives), who wanted him to be expelled. "There I was, with a militia man and two other companions, representing the COPCON [. . .] At the meeting, I said, 'Listen, if you have all discussed it and decided the matter by vote, then that decision is valid—anything else is fraud.' I am in favor of discussion and democratic voting. After that, you can't keep insisting. That's why I said, 'If we're going off in that direction, tomorrow we won't have any legitimacy whatsoever'." Even at that time, when a significant number of Portuguese began to entertain the idea of constructing a socialist-style society in Portugal, Manuel had serious doubts. As he explained to me, his ideological background led him to recognize the need for a connection between participatory and representative democracy.

---

6   The Continental Operational Command—COPCON—was the organization that directed the Armed Forces Movement in that period. Its most influential member was the then army major Otelo Saraiva de Carvalho, a charismatic figure and operational commander of the military coup of April 25th, 1974. He stood in the presidential elections of 1976, but was defeated by Ramalho Eanes, the first elected president in the post–April 25th period. In the 1980s, Otelo Saraiva de Carvalho became involved in a legal trial, accused of being the moral author of several bombings led by the organization known as FP-25 (Popular Forces of April 25th), and he spent a long time in prison.

At that time, despite being still in the army, Manuel participated as a citizen in political activity, and had a role in different popular movements in the area of Lisbon. He was also a member of SUV (Soldados Unidos Vencerão—United Soldiers Will Win),[7] and took part in various actions and demonstrations, such as the creation of neighborhood committees and the movement for the occupation of vacant houses in Lisbon. He believed that it made no sense for houses to be unoccupied while there were people who slept in the street or in shacks, without even the most basic amenities. The populations of the poorest neighborhoods of Lisbon had been swollen by an influx of thousands of retornados—people returning from the ex-colonies, some of whom had no means of support—and these segments were also supported by committees in which Manuel was involved in that period. In August 1975 he was dismissed from the Queluz military base, together with other companions considered to be undesirable elements, by the commandant, and the dismissal note was signed by Otelo Saraiva de Carvalho. He remained at the military headquarters in Lisbon until November 25th.[8] When the subsequent presidential elections were held, he supported Otelo Saraiva de Carvalho, whom he felt represented the concerns of the popular and social movements and of the soldiers.[9]

Elísio Estanque: *So, after that period you came back here to this area?*

Manuel Graça: Yes, I came here, in the post–November 25th period. I came for the work, and went back to my job at FÉMINA. There was a series of strikes here that had begun at the time of April 25th, and which I followed. In 1975 and 1976, a collective labor contract was established, so there had been strikes in many firms. At that time, there was more participation and better organization—people were more available for the struggle. It was then, when I finished my military service, that I came back to the company and stayed there for a few years, even after I'd been elected trade union delegate and leader. Anyhow, I was there, I was elected delegate, and as I was very active and took part in assemblies and general meetings of the union delegates, I was invited to take part in that

---

7   Political organization of soldiers that developed secretly within the armed forces. It followed some radical ideological currents (Trotskyite), but was generally considered to be a creation of the PCP.

8   November 25th, 1975, is the date that symbolizes the beginning of the normalization of the democratic regime. It was when the moderate military sectors, under the leadership of the so-called Group of Nine (which favored a model of representative democracy and integration into the European Community), in the wake of a series of military operations under the command of Ramalho Eanes, neutralized the influence of the Communist Party and the revolutionary left within the armed forces.

9   The interview was conducted at the headquarters of the Footwear Workers Union in São João da Madeira. It was recorded and later transcribed. This was particularly difficult given the poor sound conditions and the language and tone of voice of the interviewee. For this reason, some of the grammatical formulations have been altered slightly, after the interviewee had read the interview and also made some corrections.

group. I participated in many activities supporting the union leadership. We created more extensive structures to support the leadership. After two years, I stood as a candidate myself. Some time later I left, and then stood again. After I joined the leadership the first time, I think I had two short interruptions and came back again in 1987, and have been here since.

EE: *Who did you find here when you got back? What I mean is, since you had at the time such a strong political and ideological consciousness, what were the ideological influences prevailing in the union leadership at that time?*

MG: Most of them were close to the MES, the UDP, and the BASE-FUT.[10]

EE: *So there was no one from the PCP? Didn't they make any alliances with you? Or was it you who didn't want to?*

MG: There were, but they were not part of the leadership, because at the time what happened was this: there was a big conflict with them because they were a very sectarian group. For example, there was a series of strikes that they boycotted. And there were assemblies with thousands of people, and they always voted against strikes. There was a time when there was a two-week strike—a very powerful action that had been decided in assembly at the pavilion—and they tried to boycott it. In the assemblies, they usually voted against strikes.

EE: *This was at the beginning of the eighties?*

MG: Yes, it was in eighty-something. They always had that policy: anyone who was not with them was against them, was their enemy. Whenever the Party was not in control, they were always against.

EE: *But though the PCP did not have a great deal of electoral support in this region, nevertheless, compared to the smaller parties, they were important, much more important than. . . ?*

MG: No! The MES and UDP had more militants.

EE: *They might have had more militants, but not electoral strength—their electoral strength was not comparable to the PCP, was it? Were they stronger than the PCP in electoral terms?*

---

10   The Movement of the Socialist Left (Movimento de Esquerda Socialista) was a small party on the radical left, with little electoral support. Nevertheless, it managed to win considerable influence among the intellectual circles of Lisbon, and also in workers' committees, trade unions, and neighborhood committees. The Popular Democratic Front (União Democrática Popular—UDP), still in existence, resulted from the merger of different groups of Marxist-Leninist inclination, inspired by the Albanian model. The UDP managed to obtain some electoral expression, and had an elected representative in the Constituent Assembly (April 1975). It also had significant influence in the industrial centers and trade union movement. The United Workers' Front (Frente Unida dos Trabalhadores—BASE-FUT) was, as the name implies, organized by the trade union movement, and was devoted exclusively to union intervention. It sought to train and organize workers and form revolutionary cadres acting within existing unions. It was a minority current that appealed for revolutionary action from the bases.

MG: At the time of Otelo Saraiva de Carvalho's campaign, I was union delegate. I had been elected for the local confederation of unions, and they invited me to take part in Otelo's support committee. The PCP supported Octávio Pato. There was also a series of LCI groups that weren't so strong, but which debated a lot, much more. The MES and UDP were the strongest groups, with the most support, after BASE-FUT. At that time those parties had more support here than the PCP.

EE: *With those more radical forces leading the union, how would you compare the union structure and the parties in terms of importance? Do you think people gave more importance to party structures or to union leadership?*

MG: I thought that they should have been combined. I think that the party should take part in social organizations, like the ecology movement, or residents' and workers' movements. I think that people, militants, should intervene there, essentially.

EE: *But, that is to say, you as a militant in a certain group, who discusses problems, strategies, visions of social change, and the union role—does that mean that when you got on to the leadership, you were going to try to put through as many of these proposals as possible?*

MG: Sure. I tried to push my own points of view! But, obviously, I was often defeated in the leadership. In maybe four different leaderships, only two or three of my proposals were passed. But I thought that was normal. Why? Because I didn't have. . . well, the aim of a proposal is to debate! And sometimes, the proposals I made, I thought they were right, but in the end they weren't. Other times they were. There were many decisions taken, and if my proposal was accepted, I would try to get some kind of balance in that way.

EE: *And what about the other forces in the leadership—did they have the same attitude? This attitude was common to everyone, wasn't it?*

MG: No, no! There were guys who had had really sectarian backgrounds in those political groups. As I already knew some groups, left-wing union groups, in France, Spain, Italy, and England, I knew that their tradition was completely different. In those countries, there was more respect for differences of opinion, for proposals. Here, in the period after April 25th, they were all much more sectarianized. This was a very interesting period from the political and social point of view, but there was always a very sectarian way of thinking in relation to other organizations on the left.

EE: *If you were to assess this period critically and self-critically in relation to naiveté, beliefs, convictions, and so on, what would you say? In the end, taking into account your role and your interest in contributing to social emancipation and to greater social justice, more dignity for the working classes, more purchasing power, and so on, if you could go back to the 1970s, let us say, would you do the same all over again?*

MG: Although history can never be repeated, I would take the same posi
tions on the basic issues, because I think that what I did was based upon
my own analysis and conviction. What happens in a discussion when
we present proposals? If there is a discussion, if we can see that there is
participation, even if I lose, I don't have to give up my positions. And I
never gave up, because I had those principles about democracy and the
Marxist dialectic. Even the other guys that had a more sectarian attitude,
after a week, at the following meeting, there was nothing left—t had
diluted completely. So yes, I think, I would do the same thing over again.

EE: *I had an experience very similar to yours in relation to that atmosphere, particularly in the area of Lisbon. I know that there was great enthusiasm, an attitude of
radicalism, participation, radical change in society. And you, you were from here,
you had worked here, and have your roots here, but after having experienced that
atmosphere of the Lisbon context, when you came back here, did you not feel a
lack of fit between the idealist discourse of socialist beliefs (about whether we should
or should not proceed towards a socialist society) that you experienced in Lisbon,
for example, and the characteristics of the working class here in this area—in the
footwear sector, particularly?*

MG: I felt it and acted accordingly—that's all! So, when I made a proposal,
and I intervened a lot, I had that situation in mind. That's to say, for
someone who has experienced that type of thing, like the development
of the workers' movement, there were many cases like that, and I felt
it. But I always had the idea that we had to try to start things from the
bottom, although there was a lot of resistance in some cases.

EE: *But in spite of all that, do you recognize that, in that period, considering that
the working class from the Lisbon industrial belt mobilized incredibly easily, you
felt a great discrepancy in relation to the reality here, in the footwear sector, when
you got back?*

MG: Of course! Because here the workers' movement was much weaker,
much more recent, and obviously those positions were and are minority
ones. Of course it was more accentuated.

EE: *Just to say it in another way: At that time, when you began to take part in the
union leadership, were there, let us say, different points of views from your own
that had been discussed, or were in competition with each other?*

MG: Sure. There were always different perspectives, particularly in relation to trade union democracy guaranteed by the right to hold different
political opinions—different perspectives on trade union unity, on the
organization of strikes, and so on. So this was reflected in the strategy
concerning the presentation of proposals. At the time of the two-week
strike, there was picketing—the PCP opposed the strike, but other
groups supported it with pickets; then there were some who wanted
the strike to go on for an indeterminate period, and others who wanted

a fixed period. At the time I was against the strike continuing for an indeterminate time—I thought that it was exhausting, and that we were also dependent upon the position of other unions that didn't support the strikes. But that was not discussed in the assemblies, only among the leadership. And, as we were very dependent on other unions, the strike could go on much longer, and we wouldn't be able to get a good settlement with the employers. But on that occasion the employers' association, even with a strike for an indeterminate time, at the end of two weeks immediately accepted our proposals—something that I had never expected.

EE: *But was that your first negotiation process?*

MG: Well, I was in that group. There was a negotiation group that belonged to the leadership, but it contained only some of the members. And at the time, the opinion I had was that they had booked a strike for an indeterminate period, and our union, which was isolated, would weaken even more. And we could have been defeated. But in fact, I went in and went onto the picket lines, and the strike had an amazing level of support.

EE: *At that time, in terms of union membership, there was great support of the union, wasn't there?*

MG: Yes, there was. But there was a period of large-scale de-unionization because of manipulation on the question of trade union unity. The CGTP-IN[11] wanted unity, and everyone from the minority groups was in favor of it, except, I think, BASE-FUT and LCI. I was against it, because it was not a democratic decision made by the workers, but rather a bureaucratic decision, and I thought that they were replacing the workers. True unity is built with concrete steps and actions. But at that time there was great repression in the companies, and the union movement was already starting to lose strength everywhere. There were many activists who were fired—and that in spite of the high level of participation in that strike, which lasted two weeks. That's why a lot of people were fired afterwards. It was the period of the greatest repression, and many people were fired—mostly the activists that had been on the picket lines. At that time, in the companies there was a very brutal repression, very direct. Now it's subtler, isn't it? It was a "clean-up" that lasted some four years; a period of great regression.

---

11   The General Confederation of Portuguese Workers, Intersyndical (Confederação Geral dos Trabalhadores Portugueses, Intersindical—CGTP-IN), is a majority federate organization operating on a national level, ideologically associated with the Portuguese Communist Party. Its main rival is the General Union of Workers (União Geral dos Trabalhadores—UGT), which is closer to the Socialist Party. The Trade Union Unity Law, approved in 1975 (during the communist-influenced governments) but revoked shortly afterwards, made a single trade union confederation compulsory at the national level.

EE: *At that time, did you, in the leadership, discuss politics too? Did you talk about changing society?*

MG: The interventions at the time always went that way. Almost everyone spoke of the need to change society, to make a more just and fraternal society, without frontiers, with equality, and so on. There were times when there were a lot of general meetings here in the union. When there were strikes, there were stronger assemblies, and of course the discussion always ended up on those points of view and more politicized proposals.

But there was a group of leaders, myself included, who were more pragmatic. Because the problem is this: if you start to talk about things too much, you end up pushing people away. If you get too demagogic about it, it won't work. So, people, the leaders, have to consider the level of the workers. They have to understand that the workers of a footwear center like this one are not on the same level as an activist or union leader—they've got a very low level, and I understand that. Often it is hard for me to make that type of speech. I prefer more concrete discussions. I always have this principle, of trying to make a society that is more just. But to talk about that systematically and deeply—no, because then I think it becomes demagogic.

EE: *If you were to assess the period from then until now—since you then had that discourse that was more advanced, and which was difficult to transmit to the workers. Do you think that that has improved, or has it become worse?*

MG: Well, the situation now is very different, totally different. At that time, there were a lot of workers who had the Eastern European countries as a reference, even socialists and independents that had nothing to do with the PCP—they saw in those countries a model for development. I didn't have that reference, but I was not systematically hostile to it either.

EE: *The union delegates that appeared at that time, did you notice if they were influenced by that ideological perspective?*

MG: Sure. Lots of people had that point of view. There were those who were union delegates or activists for political and ideological reasons, but also in order to influence the company as a whole.

EE: *In the assemblies at the time, was there much debate about this? Were there divisions about it?*

MG: Yes, yes. When there was a debate, some wanted just to strengthen their own positions and not listen to others—"Now that we are on the move, come to our side!" And that limited the debate. Obviously, we were not here on our own, because we also participated in the union movement and in the companies, and the workers were called to that discussion.

EE: *But the union leadership distanced itself from that model, didn't it? Wasn't it more concerned with transmitting to the workers the idea that they were not, say, communists?*

MG: The leadership distanced itself from those references because we knew that sooner or later that situation would change, and there was growing internal opposition. The PCP, on the other hand, conveyed the idea of the ideal model of the eastern countries to the whole union movement. But the unionists that were here—from BASE-FUT, MES, UDP, and LCI/ PSR—didn't have that reference, and that was an obstacle, not only in relations with activists but also from the political point of view. The militants from the PCP were reformists, and that was a caricature of socialism. But that did not prevent us from joining all together, united with the PCP crowd when there were struggles. But everyone thought that it was an obstacle to the development of politics and of the struggle for a socialist society—for a society based upon justice and solidarity.

EE: *I'm asking this because, at that time, in '75, here in S. João da Madeira there was a lot of resistance to the PCP hegemony in Portuguese society. Buildings were burned, and there were attacks on the PCP headquarters, weren't there?*

MG: Yes. But that was also done to the PRP[12] and MES headquarters. And they tried to attack several headquarters here in the region—even the union headquarters.

EE: *These were spontaneous actions?*

MG: No—they were organized by the right, by the ELP,[13] the most backward right that there was. Some bosses, others who were involved in other businesses, the military right, the right wing of the church, they were also involved. There were the employees of small companies, some workers who'd been manipulated, but not the workers as a whole. We had assemblies with a lot of people—thousands of people—and those people never carried out attacks. So it was done by small, organized groups that went around from place to place.

EE: *But the union had the reputation of being a communist union—radical?*

MG: Yes, yes—that's true, yes! But it was enough for anyone to claim to be of the left to be branded as a communist. There were a lot of people, even people connected to the Catholic movements—the Catholic League of Workers (Liga Operária Católica—LOC), Christians with a unionist perspective about grassroots work—who worked with us and were labeled communists, because they were union members. On almost all the leaderships of the union, we had people from the LOC.

---

12 The Revolutionary Party of the Proletariat (Partido Revolucionário do Proletariado—PRP) was also a small group, of Trotskyite persuasion, led by Carlos Antunes and Isabel do Carmo. This group was one of the promoters of the FP-25 group, whose leaders later spent some time in prison as a result of charges in the same legal case as that of Otelo Saraiva de Carvalho.

13 The self-designated Portuguese Liberation Army (Exército de Libertação Português) was a group of the extreme right, set up in 1975. It resorted to bombings against the forces and parties of the left, and was led by figures connected to the Salazar regime.

EE: *How has the union managed to reconcile the need to negotiate with employers and their associations with the need for the collective mobilization of workers? I have the idea that many workers in this area, even those belonging to the union, have never showed much interest in participating on a large scale.*

MG: We are talking about a recent proletariat, one that is not very politicized and has little experience at the level of politics, unions, or companies. So it is not very demanding. People don't identify with the collective, with collective interests, at first. They always see the individual—they always see things in terms of their personal point of view. But ten years ago, we also had a problem, which was this: How could we manage to make the connection, without this discussion, on the level of negotiation? When we were negotiating the contract, we had unions connected to the PCP with a completely sectarian posture, and we were often in open conflict with them. Why? Because they always defended the interests of the Party.

EE: *Didn't the same thing happen with the small parties?*

MG: No—it was completely different. We knew that the CGTP was mobilizing for a particular action, not in order to improve the conditions for workers but to mobilize the workers for a cause, which at times was noble, but which also served to cover the interests of the bureaucrats in the PCP apparatus.

EE: *And what about the positions of the union in the CGTP structures? Were they heard? Were they taken into account? Was there any kind of consensus?*

MG: There were times when they were heard; but at other times there was great destabilization in relation to our proposals. Because often the proposals clashed with the CGTP strategies, which are mostly connected to the PCP. They had their strategy directed towards a particular struggle, but it was never in order to improve the lot of the workers. So they often used the union movement to make those kinds of strategies, and that sometimes held up the negotiating process. It was their tactic to do that—it was a tactic of the worse it is, the better. That's to say, their tactic was: the worse things are, the better it is! That didn't work, because the result for the union movement is what we're seeing today in Portugal and in Europe—we're in a great, deep hole! And I don't share that position. I think we have to accept majority decisions from the workers. There were sectors of workers that thought that too, but they were manipulated.

And then they said to us, "Calm down, man. We've got the eastern countries, we'll get there one day!" But we knew what was happening to their political struggle through dissident groups—we knew all about the movements in Czechoslovakia and Solidarity in Poland. We knew what was going on from the start through political circuits and other autonomous organizations on the left. Of course, we knew very well what was going on—indeed, I was part of a committee supporting the struggle of the Solidarity workers in Poland—we held debates, showed films, news bulletins, and so on.

EE: *What about your experiences negotiating with employers' associations? What was your position at that stage?*

MG: Well, at that stage, as I've said, we were in a minority on the negotiating committee, so it was the PCP that always imposed its line. We never stood a chance—our proposals never got accepted in Oporto, at the headquarters of the federation and the employers' association. They would call a strike as easily as call off a strike. Those strikes only happened when there was a breakdown at the negotiating table. Because when there was that two-week strike, and other important strikes here in S. João da Madeira, we got into conflict with the union committee that was connected to the PCP.

EE: *And did those strikes get much support, despite that?*

MG: They were a success. There was great support, because they did more groundwork. But the other union—the footwear union for the Oporto/Felgueiras area—also had a lot of support, but less groundwork. Here in our union there was always the tradition of doing work in the companies, of holding meetings in the companies, of seeing the union not only here in its headquarters but also in the companies. And in those unions that didn't happen. That's to say, they have a more bureaucratic idea of union work.

EE: *But, as for that groundwork in the companies, with union delegates or more conscious workers, over the years, did you notice that there was, let us say, significant success? For example, on the question of instrumentalization that you were talking about just now, I recall that that made the workers suspicious about union initiatives, but I also have the idea that they started to get even more suspicious of the union's initiatives and proposals when they began to see that some leaders or ex-leaders had given up union activity and set up their own businesses, or had been promoted to important positions in the companies where they worked. Now, isn't it that kind of attitude, which some workers still talk about today, that leads to desertion of the union—that leads them to think, "What they want is a slice of the cake"?*

MG: Yes, that happened a lot, but not only in the footwear sector. There was a period when a lot of workers set up companies, others became foremen, and then they turned into the worst tyrants for the workers. So, the idea was created that people just want a slice of the cake, that they want a position in management, they want more money—because the aim is to earn money. But we have to be careful here, because this is something that society has created. It's the people with power that stimulate those ideas—not only in the footwear sector, but everywhere. It's a policy of division and destruction of the union movement. Here in the footwear sector, we have had phases, maybe four important phases. Until 1978 we had one cycle. The guys that were here from April 25th to November 25th—they were all fired. Then we had a period when it was like we were crossing a desert. There was a period of recession of five years—four or five years. Then there was a period of progression, and it is in the periods of progression that the activists and union leaders are trained. In the periods of recession, we often don't appear, because we have to organize to be able to resist—it's the work of a mole. In this system, there is no other way to build up a great workforce.

EE: *But despite all that, isn't it a bit frustrating, for someone who believes in system-atic and continuous intervention in order to raise the consciousness of workers, to find, after a number of years, that there are still few signs of that consciousness? What are the challenges and problems today?*

MG: For me it's not frustrating! I'll explain why. First, it's a question of conception that I have to develop unionism, the struggle of social move-ments—ultimately, political struggle. When there are decisions about certain struggles, to go on or to give up, many times there is the decision to organize a protest, and then it doesn't even go ahead. That might be for different reasons, or because the company acted and gave more money to one group and less to another—divide and rule. I understand this critically, so that this message passes to other people. Because companies have their strategies regarding bonuses, promotions of managers, brutal repression, creation of small companies to benefit everybody—people let themselves be won over by this. So, it's normal. And as for us, we are in a phase of political recession, but at the same time we are starting a new cycle of debates and projects for the labor movement.

These are world problems, and not just of a region or a union. We don't live in an oasis—we're suffering the consequences of that new cycle. Now, how are we going to resist? This discussion is significant for those that took part in the post–April 25th period, when there was a great accumulation of new forces, a great popular participation, with important social achievements. This wounded the lion, but it didn't kill it, did it? Now, this crowd that was around at that time and had that experience has to resist, it has to try to resist all that, hasn't it? There is repression; people are fired; employers and those in power try to win people over to their side. These are times when we have to discuss new schemes to resist and reorganize.

EE: *Don't you feel a bit isolated? I mean, if you look around, I don't know how many members the leadership has right now, but I ask you: In addition to your-self, a person marked by the 1970s and the post–April 25th period, are there any others, of your companions that were union leaders at the time here in the footwear industry, who are still active union militants?*

MG: There are some from that time—but they are a minority.

EE: *Are you on friendly terms with some of those people who were with you in the leadership during that period, but who left later?*

MG: Yes, with most of them. There are some I don't keep in touch with. They did a bit, but then they put on their slippers and stopped working altogether. This period of twenty or twenty-five years completely destroyed everything: the memory, the experiences of the union and workers' movement, of the left in general, and of the Catholic sectors—all that was completely destroyed. It wasn't just the most combative leaders, but the whole crowd connected to the LOC that were completely banished, as well as those from BASE-FUT.

EE: *Does BASE-FUT still exist?*

MG: Yes, it does. It holds some meetings, debates. But that crowd also suffered repression. And why? Everything that relates to the workers' memory, to causes—well, those in power try to destroy it completely by firing people or offering incentives. That's why a lot of people gave up. Now, I don't feel alone, of course not. I think that it is going to take many years—my generation and more—before we gain the upper hand again and things change in a way that benefits the workers. I don't think that it will be in my generation, nor in my children's (if I had children)—not even in a hundred years' time. It's not possible to speak of socialism as an emancipatory cause, is it? There are people who say, "Listen, are you not tired of all this? Haven't you given up?" Because I never set rigid goals. Socialism is not made to measure. A more just society, a more fraternal society—that is something that will certainly not be built in my lifetime! I don't know—it's very difficult.

EE: *But do you have the feeling at the same time of having managed to create, let us say, significant sectors of workers in the footwear industry who are sympathetic to the union, and who identify you with the union? That is, do you feel that you have support, or potential support, behind you, or not?*

MG: I don't think like that. My intervention and my thoughts don't go in that direction. Of course, as I am a union leader I'm better known—I'm one of the most active leaders, and the people recognize that, both in a negative and in a positive way. The bosses know who I am.

EE: *Do they know your political position?*

MG: Yes, they do. I don't hide my position, and I don't make distinctions. For me, one boss is just like any other, whether he respects our rights or not. If there are some that respect our rights, then that's great. But for me, they are all part of the same system. In this case, individual people don't mean much to me. I'm not hostile, and I don't foster hatreds against anybody, but my struggle is not against this boss or that one. Now, when we get down to concrete matters, then it's clear that there are differences.

EE: *But for example, in a company where there are, let us say, atrocities, illegalities—I don't know what—and you manage to turn things around and to mobilize workers, and you get the boss to change his position, to look at things in a different way, to give more benefits to the workers, to be more mindful of pregnant women's work, and so on—would you see this as emancipatory, or not? From the point of view of workers' interests?*

MG: For the workers it is an experience. It's quite an experience! I've no doubt about that. How does a system create such injustice? Because its aim is to accumulate profit! Of course people eat each other up, devour each other—small and medium bosses, all of them, don't they?

EE: *Yes, but at the same time there are so many people, as we were saying earlier, a lot of workers who are obsessed above all with making money, in having more money, more bonuses. . .*

MG: They earn such a low wage! With the miserable wage that they get in this sector, of course they have a period to balance things out—to be able to buy a house or a car, on the one hand, and to try to survive, on the other, because the money doesn't allow them to do more than that. They try to get by, day by day. And people are bombarded every day by political messages that tell them they have to compete, they have to do better, get more bonuses—and the others, that don't do that, don't have anything. In truth, we can't all be at the same level. Because the system doesn't allow everyone to compete on the same level. It has schemes to divide us up, schemes that create selfishness, individual conflicts, an idea of consumerism. They go and buy, and then they have to pay.

EE: *So it's the hegemonic logic of the system in general that. . . ?*

MG: . . . that creates those schemes. But many bosses, for example, now say this: "What kind of worker is this that never visited EXPO '98?!" From the boss's point of view, he would be an ignorant and backward person . . . And he is a serious, educated man. Why? Because they are caught up in the rationale of the system—this system.

EE: *So, what is your vision, shall we say, in the long term, regarding alternatives to the system? What encourages you to believe that it is worthwhile continuing to work, to struggle, to have patience, as you say? What alternative do you see to the system, and how does your role and union activity relate to this alternative—this alternative strategy to the social system?*

MG: Well, it wouldn't be our first experience of revolution. Nothing gets done without the constant work of discussion, organization, and action, on both the local and the global levels, to try to "put a spanner in the works"—to try to change things. I'm not only talking on the level of the union, but also about politics; about NGOs connected to ecology—to the rights of women, minorities, poor people, the homeless, the landless. There has to be some kind of connection between all of those movements, which does not exist right now. Because those movements are all breaking up, they are all disconnected, not only in Portugal but all over the world. What I mean is, nothing will happen if we don't work hard to mobilize and organize people, to reflect, so that we can all together "put a spanner in the works" and try to create stronger, more powerful movements in Portugal, in Europe, and worldwide. There are millions of people in the world who are acting now. They are acting, like that peasant leader in France[14] who invaded McDonald's. That was not a crime—it was an act against the system of normalization, of globalization, that bars everyone, fires everyone, leaves everyone unemployed, and that benefits large economic groups, and the brutal accumulation of huge fortunes. That action got a lot of sympathy from millions of people, and now what we need is to join forces in all areas.

EE: *But do you believe that it's possible for a worldwide anti-capitalist movement to emerge out of actions like this? Is that it?*

MG: Of course! We have to create alternatives to this system. If we take ecological measures to the extreme, the movement would have to be anti-capitalist, in the strict sense of capitalism, whose only goal is accumulation, since it does not aim to serve human beings. Because today humans have such knowledge of technology, as you know, that there is really no reason for such poverty. But the system is made to create this poverty and this wealth.

EE: *But I presume that you don't think that the system has been made, shall we say, by a Machiavellian conspiracy?*

MG: It has! It has!

EE: *But do you think that there is an intentional action on the part of the capitalists and politicians?*

MG: It is made by people who want to perpetuate the capitalist system. They have millions of people thinking for them. They've been thinking about capitalism for many years—for a thousand years, if not more! So, if we think of socialism, of a transitory phase for a society where it will be possible to overcome capitalism. . .

EE: *But hang on a minute! Let me just get this clear. For example, state policies of social intervention, along the lines of the welfare state, which regulate and combat employers' illegalities—that, for you, has nothing to do with socialism? Or does it?*

MG: No. That is not socialism, but those are measures that can help. I support social security and health benefits, and everyone making their contribution to social security so that the wealth can be distributed, preventing slavery, and so on. But what happens is that the workers pay

---

14   José Bové.

all the taxes and the capitalists don't pay anything! This is, in a way, what's happening with neoliberalism, isn't it? So I'm in favor of state intervention, of social policies—it seems contradictory, but it isn't! I cannot say, "OK! Wait here while I go and find the way to socialism. . ." I don't think like that. I'm saying this because I'm convinced that, if we fight, if we build and discuss, that is what socialism is. The eastern countries are not the example of socialism.

EE: *OK. But what way do you think is possible today? I'm not asking you this question in the context of 1975!*

MG: No, no! 1975 has got nothing to do with the situation today. . .

EE: *Of course it doesn't. But what is the path that you think could lead to an alternative society?*

MG: All these paths! In all areas! It is not contradictory to demand that all states put an end to misery, to unemployment—that they provide education that serves people. There are many important tools for the survival and the well-being of people. It's not contradictory. For me, capitalism is the most perfect society that has appeared until today.

EE: *Perfect?*

MG: Perfect—that is to say, compared to slavery! What was the most perfect society that existed until now? This society, despite its barbarities. I acknowledge that.

EE: *But the question is: What is the model of socialism? Is there an alternative model?*

MG: Ah! I don't have a model; that's to say, I'm just talking in terms of ideas.

EE: *But do you believe that change, when it comes, should be a gradual change, following from those global and local protest movements, or total revolution?*

MG: It wouldn't have to be total revolution. I'm not in favor of a revolution that would be led by weapons. That is not revolution. That is not the sense of transformation. When I speak of revolution, I mean with the participation of millions and millions of people, the extension of direct democracy, the participation of all the social and political movements, and not just the workers' and union movements, to help transform society. Obviously, in the countries of the east, for example, there was a complete fraud—that, for me, is not socialism. Now, I don't have the recipe for socialism. When I speak of emancipation on the level of women, on the level of rights to religious freedom, the secular state; when I defend ecology, employment, education. . .

EE: *In your opinion, is emancipation viable within the system we have at present?*

MG: I think that it's possible to have reforms in many areas—because, look, when conflicts intensify, there has to be a breakup. For that, you have to construct a large movement. It is constructing movements that will lead to the emancipation of people.

EE: *Do you agree with the idea that the working class is the engine of history? Or do you think that the "proletariat" was nothing more than an invention of Marxism?*

MG: I'm not dogmatic about Marxism or Leninism, or Trotsky. None of that. For me, Marx serves as a working method, and no more. I agree with the method, with the definition he gives of the proletariat. At that time, most workers were factory hands; today they're not. Today, there are millions of people doing other types of work—intellectual work, repetitive work, housework, and so on. But society continues to be organized as a capitalist system, doesn't it? And I think that we have to find a different system—I think that people should be given an opportunity to organize themselves. Now, Stalinism was an aberration; but Marx was right when he said that the emancipation of the workers had to come from the workers themselves. But in the case of the Soviets, when there began to be repression, when they took away freedom, that couldn't lead to socialism. I'm in favor of other parties—and I think that the organizations, the parties, have to ensure the maximum of internal democracy and respect for all shades of opinion. So, I don't argue for a state-based socialism. People have to have individual rights to emancipate themselves—more and more individual rights. But this has to happen on a global scale, on most of the planet, and not just in one country or another—because that couldn't last. There is no other possibility. I argue for self-organization, but I also believe that there should be as much negotiation as possible, wherever that is possible.

EE: *But, for example, has the union ever taken the initiative to promote cooperatives, so that the workers can produce footwear themselves?*

MG: In the 1970s there were many cooperatives, but afterwards they, and the self-managed businesses, came under attack. Right now it's very difficult. Rising unemployment in Portugal and in the other countries of Europe may lead people to organize themselves into cooperatives. But with the present political predominance of neoliberalism, they don't really have conditions for survival, in whatever area it is. But we need to resist.

EE: *And in your opinion, what should be the role of the state? Do you believe in the potential of the welfare state?*

MG: I think it can be useful, and that we have to defend it—but I don't think it is the solution. That has been proved. There are countries like Germany, where the workers have good training—they're educated, know their rights, and so on; but the problem is that the global system creates all these differences. I argue that there should be those reforms, but at the same time there should be immediate measures to help countries of the Third World. Because, if not, then things might improve in some countries, but in others they could go back to near slavery. Everything is interconnected.

EE: *But—sorry—in Portugal, and in the footwear industry in particular, there is a low level of education, a resistance to reading, a deficit in training, and poor technical know-how. I don't know if you agree with me, but my idea is this: the worker has more chances of making his demands, of being active, of participating in an organized way, and thus contesting the system, if he has better technical training and better education.*

MG: I've no doubt about that. I argue that, too; but I think that all the citizens in the world are people, and if I see a person who is oppressed, I have to defend his or her rights. Although I agree that there should be essential measures applied by the welfare state, I'm convinced that this is not the solution to everything. There has to be a growing awareness and participation—I believe those things cannot be separated.

EE: *OK. But suppose that the state, with the sensitization of employers and union participation, attempted to develop a program of change and restructuring in the footwear sector, by supporting and giving benefits to the more modern companies, based on high technology and with a highly qualified workforce, with the intensive training of workers, who could use part of their working hours to attend courses, and so on. Would your union support this kind of initiative?*

MG: Of course! Those are exactly the things we want!

EE: *And do you think that this is viable?*

MG: Yes, it is. Now, there are many companies where the workers resist this. And why do they resist? Because they don't want change. There are many workers who are opposed to training, but that is part of our demands. Now, of course, it's up to the state to do this. Indeed, the state has in fact been making investments in several sectors, including the footwear industry, and we support that. It's a pity that it's just a small cluster of companies. To let the company control its own training and restructuring on its own is not good—we don't support that. What I want is for the workers themselves to control the application of public and company money, in order to provide training and carry out restructuring in all companies.

Here there are very specific work niches, with people who've had a college education fronting businesses, which doesn't mean that there are no social conflicts in those companies. In Eco Lett,[15] for example, they have a different system of personnel management that works better. It's influenced by the Danish model, and is based on semi-autonomous teams, with productivity bonuses for the group. This brings more benefits for the worker and for the company.

---

15   Shoe factory.

EE: *So, does the union support this type of initiative?*

MG: Of course. We support anything that will reduce alienation and improve working conditions, even if it's only by a millimeter!

Now, when there are restructuring processes, we have argued that a company with 400 workers that wants to keep only 150—what we argue is this: restructuring, yes, but we have to control the process and see which people are being made redundant. How will it be done? Who are the people? And what conditions will they get for unemployment? Sometimes employers say, "These workers are not prepared for restructuring—they've been in the company many years." That's just bullshit, because we know that if a worker is given training, he can learn to work with a computerized machine. Basílius, which is owned by the former president of the employers' association, was the first in the sector to do a conversion. And they fired almost no one. At first, there were a lot of workers that came here to speak to us, very anxious about losing their jobs. The company said no, that the worker's wouldn't be made redundant, but they thought they would be, because they would not be able to do that. And we intervened, demanding that they train those workers, who were between forty-five and sixty years old. They did the conversion, introduced new technology, and there were only one or two that left—and that was out of personal choice. And with this, the company became more productive, and the workers also had better conditions. Now, we've also seen other cases in which employers decided to fire anyone who was unable to carry out a particular task, and we got involved, because these are companies that impose an authoritarian regime. They don't allow the union delegates to intervene, and they don't allow any general meetings. Some time ago, the bosses of a company closed up the union leaders inside. Their motto is "We don't want contracts; we don't want rights; they have to obey us! We pay them to obey orders!"

At Rhode, which is also a large company, with advanced technology, there is still an authoritarian system. The workers are completely alienated. They don't respect their rights—they won't stop to discuss procedures. They are concerned only with the commercial side, and with keeping up a high level of production, which leads to a crazy amount of stress. The level of absenteeism at Rhode is enormous, and there are serious psychological problems. That is what happens in many companies.

EE: *A while ago you said that, for you, a boss is always a boss. But don't you think a distinction should be made between a boss that promotes that kind of innovation, respecting social rights, and a boss that implements an arbitrary and authoritarian system, as in those cases?*

MG: In that aspect, yes. In what concerns staff policies, yes. But there are not good or bad. . .

EE: *But do you admit that there are some aspects in which the interests of the workers and the employers may coincide?*

MG: There may be cases in which greater productivity means more rights, higher wages. But for that, people have to be trained, capable of doing the work, with skills; and there has to be investment. In most cases, that is not what happens. So, in principle, I think that it's not a matter of good or bad bosses—it's a matter of policies. The problem is structural, and we are inside the system.

At the outset I mentioned that the relationship of understanding and friendship that I had established over the years with the interviewee was fundamental in ensuring that the interview took place in an atmosphere of great informality and mutual trust. As a matter of fact, this relationship has had such profound implications that it has undoubtedly impinged upon the domain of sociological research itself. Proof of this is the fact that, several times, before and after the interview, I found myself involved in situations in which the roles of researcher and participant overlapped. In addition to the many times I accompanied union leaders and delegates in action on the ground—particularly in distributing information and contacting workers near the entrances to the companies—I was able to intervene in a workers' general meeting, upon the request of MG, as a sociologist studying the sector. The fact that my studies on the footwear industry have always focused on working conditions and on the lifestyle of the working class (instead of giving priority to entrepreneurial and management problems) implies a perspective that is in line with union concerns. However, it is known that not all union leaders are sufficiently open to heterodox understandings of their activities—nor do they like being questioned about the commonplaces that they usually use to support their rhetoric. In this particular case, the differences in analysis and perspective have never divided us, and have even contributed to consolidating a relationship that is over ten years old. My occasional participation in union initiatives—such as in a debate in the union auditorium where the preliminary results of a participant observation were presented (undertaken by myself in a footwear company)—actually provoked reactions from employers (namely, the boss of the company where this research study was carried out). They accused me of working "on behalf of the union," and this, voluntarily or otherwise, represented a clear political positioning before such antagonistic social actors.

When research is carried out in such a way as to lead the researcher into profound involvement with the social actors in question, when his practice rejects the arrogant posture of top-down imposition of scientific knowledge upon other knowledges, and when the research attempts to empower alternative knowledges and collective action, it is natural that the traditional subject-object relationship will be questioned, as happened in this case. These situations are thus part of a process of reciprocal exchange. The very fact that Manuel was invited to take part in this project, and to attend the international conference held in Coimbra in November 2000, illustrates the importance of our relationship.

As I have explained, the specific situation of the interview cannot be disconnected from the general context of the relationship between interviewer and interviewee, and so I can say that the testimony presented here and, above all, the relationship that I forged with this union leader, are part of a common heritage, in the sense that the leader's experiences and discourse have penetrated the interpretation codes and theoretical frameworks of analysis that I have developed around the workforce of the footwear sector of this region. I am convinced that the reverse has also happened. The public comments that Manuel has made about my works (previously published) and his various invitations to participate in union initiatives show that, directly or indirectly, my research on this subject has had some practical application in the field of Portuguese trade unionism.

SOUTH AFRICA

14

Lydia Kompe-Ngwenya

Worker, community organizer against apartheid, campaigner for women's rights, trade unionist, member of parliament.

Interviewed by Shamim Meer

"I think I gained a lot of experience. I was really capacitated. I was really empowered. I could resist anything. I even said to myself, if I was empowered like this before my marriage I would not have divorced, because I would also empower my husband somehow or other . . ."

Lydia Kompe-Ngwenya

Mam Lydia Kompe-Ngwenya's life and person embody almost the full range of experiences and struggles of African South Africans. Born in a rural village, Matlala, in the Northern Transvaal in 1935, Lydia experienced at age fifteen the brunt of apartheid's betterment policies, which curbed agriculture among African people and forced many into wage labor. As a direct result, Lydia was unable to complete her schooling because her family was reduced to near starvation. As an African South African, and in particular as an African woman, she was denied freedom of movement into the cities of so-called white South Africa as a result of the apartheid government's influx control policies. As an African factory worker in the 1970s, Lydia was denied by that same state the right to belong to a trade union. As a child and later a young married rural woman, Lydia experienced firsthand how the traditional system of chiefs relegated women to a subordinate position. And as a worker, a trade unionist, and an organizer of the Rural Women's Movement, Lydia also experienced firsthand how employers, fellow unionists, and the state, each in their unique ways, relegated women to subordinate status as well.

Lydia has lived her life fighting these injustices. She continues in the present to look for ways to work for a more just society. Since the inception of the post-apartheid government under Nelson Mandela, Lydia has been a member of parliament. Now serving her second term as a parliamentarian, Lydia tries to link grassroots work with her parliamentary responsibilities.

Lydia resisted the onslaught of the state on her life and person by whatever means possible. In the early 1970s, when separated from her husband and having to care for three young children in Johannesburg on her own, Lydia was determined to find a job despite the influx control laws, which dictated that, as an African woman born in a Bantustan, she had no right to an urban job or residence. She presented herself at government offices as a coloured, fabricating the name Kompe, and applied for an identity document on these terms. While this allowed her to stay in the city and to look for a job (since coloured South Africans were not affected by influx control), this was not without its personal costs. In an interview in 1997, Lydia spoke of how the influx control law attacked her very selfhood—"I had to do away with my own factory culture, with my own self, and call myself a different thing so that I could come and work."[1] She had to live with the discomfort of going into restrooms and canteens reserved for coloreds at work at a time when apartheid dictated separate amenities for each race group (African, colored, Indian, and white).

Lydia completed school up to standard seven (two years of high school), after which she worked as a nurse's aid and, later on, at an electrical factory, Heinemann Electric. In 1975, while working at Heinemann Electric, a firm employing 606 mainly female workers, Lydia became involved in organizing workers into the Metal and Allied Workers Union (MAWU). This was a time when African workers were not legally allowed to be union members, and when the state and employers were bent on crushing any attempts by African workers to unionize. But it was also the time of emerging militant unions, such as MAWU, which culminated in strong industrial unions that a decade later linked with community, youth, and women's struggles to battle against capital and the apartheid state.

In early 1976, Lydia was elected shop steward at Heinemann, and was elected to the National Executive of MAWU. Lydia was at the forefront of the battle to win union recognition at Heinemann at a time when there was only one company in the entire country that had recognized a union of African workers. MAWU targeted Heinemann because they felt the company's profile would embarrass it into being more amenable to the union. Heinemann was owned by a high-profile South African company, Barlow Rand, in partnership with a US company, and the company's industrial relations director was an executive member of the South African Institute of Race Relations. Despite this profile, however, the company was intent on union bashing, and brought in the police to do just that. A demonstration of striking workers demanding union recognition in 1976 was met by what has been referred to as "the decade's most violent assault on unionised factory workers"[2] in which "Police hit everybody and everything before them. Several people were bitten by dogs. A woman about seven months pregnant was one of the victims. A policeman armed with a stick resembling a pick axe hit her all over her body. She lay still."[3]

Police brutality, which had taken many forms in the preceding decades of resistance, was to intensify in a near civil war. In May of that year a number of trade unionists were detained by the police. In June 1976 protesting schoolchildren were massacred by police and the army, and a new climate of resistance spiraled nationwide. In November 1976 a number of unionists, including the MAWU organizer and branch secretary, were banned, effectively preventing them from carrying out any union or political activity for five years.

---

1   See B. Goldblatt and S. Meintjies, "Gender and the Truth and Reconciliation Commission—A Submission to the Truth and Reconciliation Commission," Johannesburg, South Africa, 1996.

2   S. Friedman, *Building Tomorrow Today: African Workers in Trade Unions 1970–1984*, Johannesburg: Ravan Press, 1987.

3   Clive Emdon of the *Rand Daily Mail*, quoted in Friedman 1987: 116.

Lydia and other trade unionists lost their jobs after the strike. Like many others who fought in the trenches during those times, she was not deterred or intimidated by these events. Thus, when she was approached in early 1977 by MAWU to work as an organizer in order to fill the gap created by the bannings, she readily agreed. Lydia worked as a MAWU organizer for two years, and was then asked to set up the Transvaal branch of the Transport and General Workers Union, of which she was to become branch secretary.

Lydia was involved in the setting up of the Federation of South African Trade Unions (FOSATU), which brought together a number of militant trade unions in April 1979. She also was involved in the formation of the Congress of South African Trade Unions (COSATU), which included FOSATU and a number of independent trade unions in a super-federation, in 1985. In addition to taking on employers and the state in the battle against racial domination and class exploitation, she was keenly aware of battles to be waged against patriarchy in all its guises.

In a 1983 discussion on women workers in FOSATU, Lydia spoke of the problems she personally encountered as a union organizer who was a woman: "I wish I was not married, because the marriage stood right in my way. My feeling is that, of all the problems women encounter, marriage is the biggest problem that prevents their involvement in union activity."[4] Meetings after work, demanded by the pace of union organizing, upset her husband; he expected her to be home by 6 p.m. But at times she slept at the homes of friends, because there was no transport to take her the distance between work and home at night. Her husband was unhappy, and life was miserable at home. He could not see why she was involved in the union. He was scared of politics, and worried she would end up in jail. He complained that she did not have time for him. However, Lydia seems to have broken him in, and in an interview in 1982 she said that he was now getting old and used to her way of life.[5]

In addition to her personal plight, Lydia was acutely aware of the problems experienced at home by the women she organized—the women cleaners. These women left their homes in Soweto at 5 p.m. to clean offices in Johannesburg until 3 a.m. every night. They spent hours cleaning their own homes before and after work, and came home at six in the morning to homes waiting to be cleaned, having been left in a mess by husbands who had already left for work. In a 1982 interview, Lydia said: "If a man comes home earlier he hasn't the ability to go and fetch the child and look after it while she [the wife] is still working. He expects the woman to go and fetch the baby, put it behind her back, get to the stove and cook for him. And he is busy reading the paper. And we do it happily because we grew up that way, because we saw our parents do it and we think it's the African law).[6]

---

4   S. Meer, *Women Speak: Reflection On Our Struggles 1982–1997*, Cape Town: Kwela Books, 1998.
5   J. Barrett, A. Dawber, B. Klugman, I. Obery, J. Shindler, and J. Yawitch, *Vukani Makhosikazi: South African Women Speak*, London: CIIR, 1985.
6   Ibid., 106.

At work the women cleaners had to deal with supervisors who demanded sex, and who could cause a woman who refused to lose her job. Women did not get promoted to be supervisors, a job reserved for men, causing Lydia to observe that "even the capitalists think men are superior."[7]

Lydia found herself facing discrimination at work from her fellow trade unionist comrades. As the only woman organizer among men, she found she was expected to buy lunch, "with the excuse that I could choose better because I am a woman. It became a habit that every lunchtime I ran around buying lunch, making tea for them, after that washing the dishes. My job would fall behind because I'd have to finish all the jobs they left from lunchtime." Lydia fought this, insisting: "I am not the tea girl."[8]

The male-dominated unions did little to remedy women's subordinate status, despite the pioneering work of Lydia and other women trade unionists in the mid-1980s. Today, women unionists continue to wage battle within unions that espouse principles of democracy and worker control, yet which remain male bastions. Speaking of the early 1980s, Lydia said in a 1982 interview, "FOSATU tried to have a women's group. But male members felt threatened" when women pushed to be equal.[9] FOSATU was at the time trying to get more women shop stewards. Today, in the year 2001, there are still very few women shop stewards in unions, and an entrenched gender division of labor dictates that men are employed as union organizers and women as union administrators in most COSATU unions. In 1982, Lydia hoped it would take just a few years for women to get into union leadership.

Lydia appealed for women's rights to be recognized. "A woman is a human being. She needs the assistance of her husband, her family, as a human being. And we appeal for equal rights for God's sake. We don't want to be inferior."[10] Lydia asserted that women must have the same rights, that she "would like my grandchildren to actually feel free in organizations, at home, everywhere."[11]

Not battle-weary after her years of work in the trade union movement, Lydia moved on to new battles—in 1986 against state removals of African people into the impoverished bantustans, which thereby stripped them of their land and citizenship. In 1983, Lydia joined the Transvaal Rural Action Committee (TRAC), set up by the Black Sash (an organization established by white middle-class women and working closely with organizations fighting apartheid), to work with communities resisting land removals. Lydia joined TRAC because she wanted to get back to her roots to work with rural women. At the time there were a number of forced removals by the apartheid state, aimed at consolidating the Kwa Ngane and Lebowa bantustans in Northern Transvaal, and in removing African communities from urban areas throughout the country.

---

7   Ibid., 108.
8   Ibid., 104.
9   Ibid., 109.
10 Meer, *Women Speak*: 69.
11 Barrett et al., *Vukani Makhosikazi*: 109.

In addition to supporting communities in their battles against the state, Lydia worked with rural women and founded the Rural Women's Movement. The organization took up women's specific concerns, such as women's exclusion from tribal decision-making forums. Drawing on her experience of union organizing, Lydia led and supported rural women's protests and campaigns against lack of water and other services in the rural areas. The Rural Women's Movement was to make history when the organization linked with other organizations to intervene in the drafting of the country's Constitution to ensure that the rights of traditional leaders were subject to the gender equality clause of the Constitution.

Lydia battled in the trenches of trade unionism and rural community struggles throughout the two states of emergency—the first, from July 1985, affecting only parts of South Africa, and the second, a nationwide state of emergency, running from June 1986 to February 1988. She worked closely with the United Democratic Front organizations and, after the unbanning of the ANC, was active in facilitating the launching of local ANC branches. When the ANC drew up its list for parliament, Lydia found that she was on the list. She speaks in the interview here of her surprise and initial reluctance to go into parliament, as she saw herself as first and foremost a grassroots organizer.

It has not been possible for Lydia in her role as parliamentarian to advance the interests she took up so strongly in her work with trade unions and rural communities. In the following interview, Lydia laments the huge gap between the government's policies and their implementation in order to meet the need for land, jobs, and basic services for the majority of South Africans who continue to live lives of poverty. In her own home in Tsimanyane, a rural village in what used to be Northern Transvaal and is today part of the Northern Province, the tap in her yard is serviced with water only once a week, so that containers have to be filled with a supply of water to last a week. Children in neighboring villages carry or wheel drums of water at dusk, traversing the main thoroughfare, forever in danger of being hit by passing motorists. Seven years into the new South Africa, the rural constituency that Lydia serves as an ANC member of parliament lives in poverty, with little hope of jobs or infrastructure development. She speaks in the interview of criticism she faces from those who sent her to parliament and whose expectations have not been met. Lydia copes by finding glimmers of hope in the work she does in the portfolio committees of parliament and the organizing work in her constituency.

Her own strong criticism of the present government is directed at the lack of support from the government for NGOs. She notes that NGOs played a crucial role in the democratization of South Africa, and could be playing a crucial role in its development today. She is almost bitter when she speaks of her pleas for support for NGOs falling on deaf ears. What Lydia is really speaking of is the demise of the strong social movements of the past, and the state's marginalization of such movements. This is something that resonates strongly with me, an activist who has worked with community and trade union organizations in battles against racial oppression and class exploitation, and for women's rights.

It strikes me that it is unlikely that future South African parliaments will have MPs of the ilk of Lydia—since South Africa has fast moved to an era in which formal technical qualifications are seen as a more fitting match for positions that are increasingly defined as technical, and having less to do with the grassroots.

Shamim Meer: *Mam Lydia, it is such a pleasure to talk to you. For me, as for many South Africans, you represent a number of struggles, all of which are embodied in you. You have fought for the rights of workers and rural women, and in 1994 you went into parliament, taking some of these hopes and struggles with you. It is really good to have this opportunity to review some of the past as well as the present. Can you start by telling us some of your most vivid memories of your involvement in the trade unions.*

Lydia Kompe-Ngwenya: The most crucial one was when I found myself employed in the factory [Heinemann Electrical] for the first time, after being a housewife for many years, and after working in a hospital. I enjoyed it because it was a completely different experience for me from being a nurse. I found it very enjoyable, particularly when we started joining the trade union. Even though it was very difficult at that time. Our trade unions were not recognized, let alone registered.[12] So we were using all those old structures—the liaison committees, the works committees—which were not really representing the majority of workers. These were dummy structures which represented the bosses. And when the trade union organizers Sipho Kubheka and Gavin Anderson[13] came selling the Metal and Allied Workers Union to us in Heinemann, we quickly joined the union. We were many women workers there, and we joined with enthusiasm. But our boss was very, very critical of the unions. He tried to introduce works committees instead of the union committee.[14] When he realized there was a lot of pressure from us, he said, "I will bring another committee instead of the union committee." We rejected this until we went on strike, and we were all dismissed because we were involved in the strike. A lot of our people were injured, and we lost the strike because it was an illegal strike—though at the end we won our civil case, where a lot of our people were compensated for being bitten by police dogs, injured by batons, and so forth. It was really,

---

12   Many of the battles between workers and employers in South Africa in the 1970s and early 1980s were over recognition of trade unions. At the time of the Heinemann strike, only one company in the country had recognized an African workers' union, and by 1979 only four companies had recognized unions.
13   Sipho Kubheka was MAWU's Transvaal Secretary, and Gavin Anderson was a MAWU organizer.
14   Liaison and works committees were dominated by employers, and used as a means of controlling workers.

really critical.[15] We now couldn't get a job anywhere, because every time we applied for a job they would say, "Oh, you are from Heinemann." I just stopped saying I'm from Heinemann—I said I'm from the hospital, and went to get testimonials from the hospital, and then I got employed at other places, like Checkers and John Orrs.[16]

When I was at John Orrs in 1977, Bernie Fanaroff from the Metal and Allied Workers Union came to me to say, "We need you to come and assist us at the office because both of our organizers are banned"—that was Sipho and Gavin—"so we felt you were one of those who were quite strong in Heinemann, so would you mind to come and assist us as an organizer?" And they also wanted a woman organizer, because they were seven men in MAWU. So I agreed and I went to work for MAWU.

It was very difficult, you know, when I first came there, because I was the only woman among all these men, and there were a lot of things I was obliged to do like making tea, going to buy lunch—because we were eating in a group—and washing dishes afterwards, and then cleaning up. And in the meantime I was an organizer equal [to] them, so my job will delay and they will carry on. And I was also cashing all the subscription monies the organizers brought in every Friday—after collection, I was on the cash machine counting all the money, seeing that it balances. So I had a lot of work also on my shoulders.

I remember one day Jeremy Baskin[17] came to interview me in the office—that's when he came with the heading that "I am a trade unionist not a tea girl." So I started to get more empowered, and I drew a roster, and I pasted it behind the door so that everyone should have a turn to go and shop, and I said we have to go in turns to do all these jobs because we are all equal here—we are all organizers here, there is no tea girl here. And that strengthened me. I started to resist all these seven men's power.

At the same time we were going to the factories. I was the only woman organizing in mass male plants where there were very few women. I remember there were only two women shop stewards in MAWU. So I also faced problems: sometimes the others would say, because I was a bit young at that time, if you do not agree to my proposals [of sex] then I'm not going to let these people join MAWU. And you know it was such a

---

15   The Heinemann strike was a landmark strike in South African union history. Despite a seemingly liberal company—owned jointly by high-profile Barlow Rand and a US company, and with an industrial relations director who was an executive member of the liberal South African Institute of Race Relations—the firm was determined to crush the union. The company brought in the police, who brutally assaulted the striking workers using dogs and batons.

16   Checkers is a supermarket chain, and John Orrs is a department store.

17   For an interview by Jeremy Baskin with Lydia Kompe, see *South African Labour Bulletin* 18: 6 (6 June 1993).

tricky kind of thing. If they allocate me a plant, I would have to organize that factory—and they would drop us at the gates of every factory to organize for thirty minutes only. At lunchtime. And within that thirty minutes you must have said something very, very special to encourage people to come to the office in Benoni.[18] But you know, I survived. I had a lot of members, and without getting between sheets I managed! I had a lot of members. I survived, and I actually got a lot of respect from the very same men. They realized I can put my foot down and I mean what I say—that they will need to empower workers.

SM: *At that time people did not talk about sexual harassment?*

LKN: No, it was not something that was really said, because in fact we also did not address it so much in our union offices. So I was just dealing with this thing as an individual. In the offices it was just Chris Bonner and myself—Chris was an administrator then; we were very few women in the offices, and we didn't see it as a major issue. We were just dealing with it ourselves—until the time other women came to join us, and I was educating them that this is what happens and you must just put your foot down and don't take any nonsense. But we were not saying it very loudly, not as a big group, until such time as we formed FOSATU[19] and we started to organize more women from Sweet Food and Allied, from Paper Wood and Allied, and from my union Transport and General [Workers Union]. The MAWU executive chose me to get the Transport and General Workers Union off the ground, because it was only in Durban. So I started the Transport and General Workers union on the ground in the Transvaal.

Then we employed others, like Andrew Shabangu, and then when he left Jane Barrett[20] came—we were two women; there were two of us, and we could balance, and it was very nice. Then we started getting women cleaners—the office cleaners from AMPROS and other places. Then more women came, and we started a women's forum in FOSATU, and that's when the issues of sexual harassment started to emerge from the workplace and within our union. We did not make a lot of noise within our offices because we just said, we can deal with it. We were a small group, so we could say, "Hey, stop your nonsense—hey stop your nonsense!" But as a big forum we came and started to address these issues. We came with good maternity leave agreements, and all those issues.

---

18   East of Johannesburg.

19   The Federation of South African Trade Unions (FOSATU) was formed in April 1979 as the first federation of the militant unions that re-emerged in the 1970s, and which included MAWU and the Transport and General Workers Union.

20   Union employees.

Between FOSATU and the formation of COSATU[21] in 1985, there were long discussions on unity talks, bringing all the progressive unions together. Our FOSATU unions were called workerists, and even within ourselves in FOSATU there were kind of different ideologies. Others saw it as a clear working-class struggle. Some of us saw it as mixed—that you could not divorce the politics and the union. So we differed ideologically, but we survived. I just thought, I'm not going to leave this FOSATU after I worked so hard to get people together just because of the different ideologies; I am going to stay. And I had backing from other progressive unions outside that: "Mam Lydia, we are with you—stay there." Then I stayed there until we formed COSATU. After we formed COSATU, I just felt, "Oh, my dream came true," and I left the unions. We had strong women's groups—forums—in FOSATU and COSATU. Then all the women in FOSATU became COSATU, and we had other unions that joined us like the Mine Workers Union, which was the major one, and we had Emma Mashinini[22] joining us, and all smaller unions.

SM: *What did workers gain from joining trade unions? What were some of the major issues?*

LKN: I think we eliminated a lot of unfair dismissals. Because we had house agreements where we discussed disciplinary procedures, and how the workers had to be disciplined, and how the workers had to be finally dismissed, and the intervention of the shop stewards and the officials had to be made. There was no longer a situation like any worker being just kicked out. And we also controlled the way of strikes. Remember, before, when workers wanted to strike, the police would jump in quickly and let them get bitten by dogs like at Heinemann. Those kinds of things actually came to a stop. We had agreements that actually stipulated lawful strikes, and you've got to be discussing while workers are demonstrating outside. So we did not see it as a strike, but as a demonstration while discussions were held. It also helped the bosses as well, because there was

---

21   The Congress of South African Trade Unions (COSATU), a trade union federation acting as an umbrella body for its affiliated trade unions, was formed in 1985 by a merger between FOSATU and a number of independent trade unions. COSATU constituted a major pillar of the democratic anti-apartheid movement in South Africa.

22   Founder and president of the Commercial, Catering and Allied Workers' Union of South Africa (CCAWUSA). She was arrested in November 1981, and spent the next six months in solitary confinement at Pretoria Central Prison. After her release from prison in 1982, she defied advice to live abroad and instead resumed her post at CCAWUSA for another four years. In 1985, Mashinini was involved in the formation of the Congress of South African Trade Unions (COSATU), a body that united trade unions across the country. She resigned from her position as president of CCAVMSA in 1986. In the same year, she was appointed director of the Anglican Church's Department of Justice and Reconciliation. In the early 1990s, she became the president of the Mediation and Conciliation Centre in Johannesburg, and was appointed commissioner for the restitution of land rights in 1995.

this interaction. We slowly started signing all these agreements whereby, in the end, workers started to take a bit of control over their workplaces. And we also managed to have full-time shop stewards who had their own offices in the factory, like Chris Dlamini at Kellogs. These were the first full-time shop stewards who were responsible for the interests of the workers inside the plant.

So it really reduced a lot of strikes, a lot of dismissals—and they received increases in wages in a lot of the factories. And, particularly, what really made me very pleased was the agreement that we signed between big bosses like AMPROS (Anglo American Property Services) and their employees, who were like lifetime women night workers—which was to me heartbreaking, because these women never really saw their children. Because they didn't even have a night off. They did not have any place to rest for an hour, and in our agreement all those things were dealt with. I had found them sitting on cardboard on the concrete: cold and hot weather, it was the same; and we started by tackling one by one all of the issues until all these things were improved, and we signed the agreement. They now had chairs. They could relax. They had changing rooms, they had showers, after we had signed the agreement.

Transport and General benefited from all those ordinary cleaners' stop orders, because we were actually struggling. Transport is a very difficult union to organize—because workers are split, you can't find them easily, they are always on the road. But we tried—we sacrificed, to go and organize them at night, during their breaks; and we managed because we had access to them. And we met also very early in the morning, when they knocked off—they came to our offices. We also managed to get time off when we had meetings with the bosses, and that night the shop stewards were not going to work. Those were the things—I mean they look very petty, but they were so important to workers who came from that kind of background. Those were things we really won—the maternity leave, they increased some of the UIF,[23] and that UIF would pay so much and the bosses would also pay so much for so many weeks. Those were some of the things [from which] the workers benefited—and leave was also increased from two weeks to a month when you finished a year, and so forth. And the security guards as well—their conditions were improved tremendously. So every security guard applied to work at AMPROS, because their working conditions were completely different from other security guard workplaces. So I think that's why, when we launched COSATU, I just felt, "Oh my dreams came true. I am going to leave this union with the younger people, because now they don't

---

23   Unemployment Insurance Fund.

have to run around. Stop orders are now legalized. Unions are registered. It's just a matter of strengthening the whole thing. The young ones can go around to the workshops—there's no more going to the gates pleading that people should join. People just come because they can see the benefits of trade unions." Then I went to join Black Sash.[24]

SM: *Mam Lydia, before we move off from trade unions, can you tell us what some of the things were that you personally gained from being involved in the trade union movement?*

LKN: I think I gained a lot of experience. I was really capacitated. I was really empowered. I could resist anything. I even said to myself, if I was empowered like this before my marriage I would not have divorced, because I would also empower my husband somehow or other. Because I started to understand why people fight sometimes. Even in the family. I realized, if you are both not employed, if there is not enough food and care in the home, there's always tension. Somebody is tense because you have not got enough money to supply the home—particularly men who feel they are responsible for bringing in money. You resort to violence. I started to realize these things later when it was too late. But I learnt a lot of things.

   And I learnt to live with all races. Because I want to say, before I was very, very bitter with white people because of the laws that affected my life so much—particularly influx control.[25] I never thought I would ever be friends with whites. When I saw white people, I just saw enemies. Every time when I see the police harassing us, I just pray to God that Mandela gets released and we win the struggle and we get into power— then I'm going to join the police force and get revenge. And I'll be the first one to arrest all these white people and give them their medicine to taste—the way I was bitter inside. But the trade unions changed me, and other organizations I joined like UDF.[26] I started mixing with whites, and I realized, no, I was wrong. I was so behind times. I did not know there

24   The Black Sash was set up by white liberal women, initially to protest racist laws. The organization later set up advice offices, and in 1983, in response to requests from communities for assistance in resisting forced removals, the Black Sash set up the Transvaal Rural Action Committee (TRAC).

25   Apartheid laws controlled the movement of African women and men into towns through passes in order to control the growth of "surplus" labor in towns, and to redirect labor to farms. The influx control laws denied African people permanent rights of residence and citizenship, viewing them as temporary residents whose homes were in the bantustans. Millions of African South Africans were prosecuted under these laws, and were either endorsed out of town or sent to farms as wage labor.

26   The United Democratic Front (UDF) was formed in 1983 to mobilize resistance against the apartheid state, to build organization, and to conduct campaigns. The UDF promoted the ANC, nurtured a political culture, and emphasized democratic rights and people's power.

were such progressive people who are white. I just thought all whites
were bad.

Because I was coming from the rural areas, I identified all whites as
bad—coming from that background where the whites took our land in
1949, 1950 betterment schemes.[27] My parents were peasants. We did not
suffer. We were eating very well. The big boss came and took our cattle,
took our land, brought other people to our mission, and we just got
packed there, and I could see our family getting poorer and poorer, and
my mother had to leave the family and go and work for us as a domestic
worker. And we stayed with my father. Because my father couldn't find
work. He was too old to work in the mines. So my mother said, "Let me
go and work and you stay with the children." So that's how we grew. I
was about fifteen. It really made me so bitter—bitter. Knowing that we
never used to suffer—but now those white guys came to impoverish us
so much for nothing. And, you know, I was still very young, but I did
not know the reason why. Why do they do this to us? And I just became
so bitter being a young girl, and I grew with this thing. I couldn't even
complete high school—because my parents couldn't afford it anymore.
They were so poor. And I grew with this bitterness—that I could have
been so far with my life. Because I aimed to be so far with my education. And I knew I was going to go so far because my father was a very
hard worker. He was plowing, planting sweet potatoes, exchanging with
cows—he would sell a cow and pay school fees for us. That made me
more bitter.

SM: *Is this what made you go back to working with rural women?*

LKN: Exactly. After I got so empowered, I felt I owed the women that I
was struggling with at home some kind of knowledge that I had gained
as a rural woman and an uneducated person. I was empowered. I could
stand for myself. So why can't I go and work with rural women? I joined
Black Sash because they had a project that worked with rural people—
Transvaal Rural Action Committee, concentrating on restoration of land.

Aninka [Claasens] had left the trade union for Black Sash, and when
she started this project, it grew up and she needed more people. Then
she recruited me. She said, "Come and work with me—this is what we
are doing." It was really a coincidence, because I left at the right time
when we launched COSATU. It was not like I dumped them. No—
we launched it properly, and I worked for three months. I gave them
three months to organize themselves. I really loved my trade union. I

---

27   Apartheid government measures to control people and land usage in the bantustans. Betterment resulted in the removal of people into rural villages and in limiting the
livestock they could keep, and forced many into wage labor. There was widespread and
often violent resistance to betterment in the 1950s.

had a very nice party. But it was so bitter when I left—the women were screaming, crying, particularly the women cleaners. When I joined Black Sash they used to come and fill up my office. Those women would come in the morning and cry to me, "You told us you were going home, but now here you are in Black Sash. Why do you do this to us?" And I said, "I did not know how to say—you know, I couldn't say I got another job so easily. I thought I was going to tell you as time goes on." But I really felt guilty that these women felt I had dumped them; but I also had a lot of work to do elsewhere, you know—where people don't concentrate. And I feel I want to go back to my roots and go and help the rural women. I mean, I did a lot from 1974 until now. It's a long time. I trained Susan Shabangu.[28] I trained Jethro from AMPROS to carry on. Susan was a secretary, but when I left she was an organizer, because I just said, "Now work with these people." So she carried on working. So it was not like I dumped everybody. No. So I now went into TRAC[29] and worked with them.

SM: *While you were at TRAC you founded the Rural Women's Movement. Can you tell us about that? What made you set up this organization?*

LKN: I worked a lot in the Western Transvaal and Eastern Transvaal, because that's where major forced removals took place—in the Driefontein, Daggakraal, Piet Retief, and Amsterdam areas. Those were where the forced removals of Kwa Ngema[30] took place a lot. While moving around these areas, I experienced the same thing I saw when I was growing up, and where women were just excluded. I never saw my mother go to the Kgotla,[31] you know, during those times. I experienced this also when I stayed in the rural areas with my husband—we women were not going to the Kgotla. I saw the same now. I realized these things, and I said, somehow this will have to stop. Because a lot of men are in town and a lot of homes here are looked after by women. And if a few men go to the Kgotla under the tree and take decisions, who is representing us? We also want a part of the whole set-up here in the village, and if we are excluded because our husbands are not here, who is going to tell us what decisions are made? Sometimes we just hear that the Kgotla has decided that every household has to collect 5 rand to do something for the chief. When are we going to have a say? With the forced removals, when men were taking decisions on how they should resist, the women were not part of

---

28   Susan Shabangu is currently the South African deputy minister of minerals and energy.
29   The Transvaal Rural Action Committee was set up by Black Sash in 1983 to work with communities resisting apartheid government land removals.
30   One of the bantustans.
31   Traditional council of elders.

these decisions. And yet they were the ones who were left behind with the children. These men will make their decisions and leave for work on Sunday, and these poor women don't even know what was decided. And I felt, no, this was very wrong.

I first spoke to men themselves, and said, "I think this is wrong, what you are doing. You make decisions yourselves, and you don't convey this to women, and you don't plan with women, and they are the ones who are actually holding the knife at the sharp end. At the end of the day you are gone. So I think you must also invite them even if it is just to listen." Then they said yeah yeah yeah, just to listen—yeah yeah yeah. Then I started working with the women now—I talked to the mothers what we can plan what we can do as women. We planned that the women must go to the Kgotals and talk to those men, that the women must stand up and speak.

That's how we started. And we decided to join with other groups of women. TRAC gave us money, and when we had a meeting with the Magkopa group we called the neighboring ones like Mathopestad, the others nearby, and we held a joint meeting. So sometimes we even had a big one. The first one was in 1986, when we met at Mathopestad. Kgosi Patrick[32] was tough, but not a very difficult chief. So he agreed we could meet because [his] wife was very involved with us also. We had a big feast there. We brought together nine groups of women from different places where forced removals were taking place. We had a cow slaughtered. We had a big feast and our Black Sash people came to celebrate with us there. That was the beginning of consolidating the Rural Women's Movement. At that time it was just a Rural Women's Forum. You remember, 1986 was during the state of emergency,[33] so everything we were doing was behind closed doors. So that's why we chose Mathopestad, because it was so isolated. It was right outside. So the police wouldn't really come there, and if they came the chief was fine. If they came, he [would] say, "No—this a prayer meeting." He was on our side. So nothing happened, really. We went to the grave-yard to honor the ancestors, because the priest came and gave us holy communion. It was a mixture of everything. And I realized this is the first good step forward.

---

32   Leader of the Mathopestad Group.
33   During the mid-1980s the UDF and COSATU launched nationwide protests and work stay-aways. In townships across the country, youth organizations, women's organizations, and civic associations spearheaded protests. The state retaliated with a state of emergency in parts of the country from July 1985 to mid 1986. From June 1986 to February 1988 the state of emergency was extended throughout the country. Unprecedented numbers of UDF and union members were detained, and many were forced underground. Severe restrictions were imposed on the media.

And the next time we had a big launch we had mobilized more people now from Braklagte, Driefontein, everywhere in the northwest—we had organized a lot of groups of women. Then, in 1991, we launched it and gave it a name, the Rural Women's Movement, and we even invited FEDTRAW,[34] because we were actually aligned with the broader movement. We were not working in isolation. I was a strong member of FEDTRAW, so whenever I did things I invited Ma Sisulu[35] and them. And she had delegated people to come and talk about the FEDTRAW constitution. And I remember Mrs. Motsoaledi, the wife of the late Elias Motsoaledi, came to our launch, and June Mlangeni—they came to our launch. We wanted to concentrate on mobilizing and empowering these rural women, and also involving projects so that they can feel they are doing something—not just fighting against forced removals, and not just doing something to empower themselves; that they can work toward being independent. Even when their husbands left them they could still survive. Life would still go on, because one thing that rural women lack is that self-confidence. They just feel that the husband is the last resort: if [my] husband dies, then my life is finished. And we wanted to change that. Yes, my husband is a very valuable asset at home; that we respect, it's our culture. But it's not the end of the road. People's lives continue even without the husband, like life continues without a wife at home. So those are the things we wanted to encourage women to do—as you can only do that with the means of empowering women through projects, giving them some sort of talent so that they could do things out of nothing, where they could make plastic mats and other things.

SM: *You also took up problems like lack of water?*

LKN: The women were at the forefront. They became really at the forefront of the struggle. Moutse was the area that I was allocated to work with. I spent a lot of my time during the crisis and the struggle against Moutse's incorporation into the homeland Kwa Ndebele. That was very hot. Moutse refused to be part of any homeland structures. They said, "We are just fitting in the central government until such time when we get our liberation." Because we had hopes that one day this country will be free. We don't know when—but one day. We were always putting pressure. So we [are] not moving to any devil structure now; we are just staying here. And the government said, you stay there with nothing, no

---

34   The Federation of Transvaal Women (FEDTRAW) was affiliated with the United Democratic Front, a key anti-apartheid front set up in the 1980s that led much of the internal resistance to apartheid.

35   Albertina Sisulu is the wife of Walter Sisulu, one of the defendants of the Rivonia trial. She was elected as one three UDF presidents at its inception. Caroline Motsoaledi and June Mlangeni were married to Rivonia trialists Elias Motsoaledi and Andrew Mlangeni, respectively, and were themselves political activists in their own right.

resources. Central government said, you are not part of us, because you refuse to go to Kwa Ndebele, you refuse to go to Lebowa.[36]

So we just started to push them, because they still had offices that operated, and we said let's take up this water thing, because people cannot survive without water. And we really went to publicize and make our voices heard, and the only way we could make our voices heard is when we make a big, big march. We planned that at one of our workshops. I said, "Why don't we take something up and make ourselves heard as women? What do we think we can take?" And people said, "What about water—because we don't have water. What can we do?" Then the women started to come up with ideas—"Let's march; let's march to Mosate."[37] I said no, not to our Mosate. Mosate is not the one that refuses water to us. We march to those very offices where the magistrate is. We are going to ask permission to use the stadium, that little stadium. Then we started sharing tasks; everybody was still hot and enthusiastic. Then some women said, "We will go to Mosate and ask Mosate to talk to the magistrate for us." We said the chief must go to talk to the magistrate. Who is going to go to the chief? Then we wrote down: Who is going to go to ask for the permit? So and so will go. Who is going to do this? Who is going to do this? I am going to go to TRAC to ask for a little bit of funds to transport our people from point A to point B. The next week, we went again to find out how things are being coordinated. We found out everybody has agreed. We went to the civic[38] and to all these structures. We touched everybody, and everybody was supportive.

We went to the youth; they were 100 percent supportive. We said, "Youth, you are going to be our marshals, but you are not going to take any control of anything. You just give us the space. All you have to do is protect your mothers today—that's all. But not to take the lead." But, you know how they are: they said, "No no—when you deliver the memorandum we want to be part of it." I said to the women, "Look, let's not be arrogant with these kids. Let's leave them. But we are going to hide one thing. Our march is going to be a different march. We are not just going to give the memorandum, and talk and talk and talk, and leave. That's not what I want. I hate that. I want something that will be fruitful. We can't organize such a big march, walking such a long distance, being older women, for nothing: we want immediate negotiations." That's what the unions had motivated me about—to get fruit, not just to talk and *toyi toyi*,[39] and not come up with something. So I said, "Let them go

---

36   Kwa Ndebele and Lebowa were two bantustans.
37   The chief and his officials.
38   Community-based organizations set up to address community concerns.
39   *Toyi toyi* refers to a military chant and dance that became a symbol in the war of liberation.

and hand in the memorandum, and we keep the secret—you don't move out of the office before they give you the date of the meeting: never. Let the youth come out, and you just stay there. That's the secret." We said to the women, "Don't tell these boys what we are going to do. Let them go with us." And the youth were in the foreground when we got to the office. They grabbed the memorandum, jumping *toyi toyi toyi toyi*, and I just said to the women, "Let's stand and hold our flag." We stood with our flag, which says "Women hold the knife on the sharp end." We stood there with all our groups, and four women went in—Martha Matlala was one of them, and Mita, and two others. They went in. We stayed outside. And after they got the memorandum, the officials were surprised to see these women not moving out. Then the women pulled up chairs, and they sat down and said, "Could you please sit down—we want to talk to you. We want you to set up a date. Those women want to go out with a date for a meeting when we will sit down and discuss water problems. We are not just making a joke here. This is the beginning of making our voices heard. But we want the fruit—we want to see water delivery. And we do not want a long time. Could we suggest a date?" And the women suggested a date of the 31st—three or four days after the march. And they agreed with the date. And we came back, and we said to the boys, "You watch out. You will strike a rock." And on the 31st we came back and said, "Here we are, the women-led delegation—we want water now. By whatever means, but now." We had thought of tankers, and we said the role of the youth would be to move around as volunteers with the tanker trucks, to make sure that they get clean water. That's the job we gave the young boys. Since then, Moutse has been drinking clean water, and some are still drinking tanker water from that time.

So that's how, really, we managed to do things. We were tackling a lot of issues like the trauma women experienced during the incorporation time, and I think that itself has really strengthened the Moutse women. Today, you can see they are progressing—their projects are really successful. In 1992 the Rural Women's Movement started this community radio. We had to decide where to start the community radio—in which of the three strong regions. Then, unanimously, the conference said, "Lets go to Moutse," because they realized Moutse women were much more strong. I spent a lot of my time there. And we started the radio. It is still there—a creation of the women.

SM: *Soon after that, you found yourself on the ANC list to parliament, and by 1994 you were in parliament as an MP. You are now serving your second term. Can we go back to the time when you learned you were on the ANC list: What did that feel like?*

LKN: I rejected it completely. Last time I was at Luthuli House[40] it was like

---

40 ANC offices in Johannesburg.

a joke. Some women were saying, "Hey Mam Lydia, do you remember how you gave us tough times when we told you you were on the list and we asked you to come and sign the papers, because the branch in Yeoville brought your name up, the branches in the North-West brought your name up, and you just refused?" When I was told I was on the list I said, "What about my job? What about TRAC?" I said no. I did not understand why I should be on the list. Because really I thought, seriously, people like myself should not even dream of being in parliament, because I assumed only well-known, educated people should go there—and not me. Who am I, really? And what about my women, hey?

And I was told, no, women are the ones who want you to go there. Because the women I was working with were the UDF women—now they were the ANC women. They were on the branches, and these women were the ones who said I must be there. I said, "No, man!" I know the rural women are hiding behind all these little structures to survive from apartheid, but I didn't think its time yet now for me to leave them, because I didn't think they are that well empowered. They said no, they will survive. "You are not actually going to stay in parliament; you will be coming to the rural areas"—because I did not understand how parliament works. I did not even know we are going to have our constituencies and office, where we can still link with our people, because I never had anything to do with all those little apartheid structures, like homelands. I never wanted to go near them—I hated them. So I did not even know what went on in those little parliaments of theirs. Really, to be honest—I didn't know what was happening. You know how these things can work to an uneducated rural woman. I tell you, sometimes I am so sorry I do not have the required skills, you know. People persuaded me, and the women started phoning me. At that time I still had a bad back, and I had an operation. And they said, "No Mam Lydia—you will be fine." I also had such a lot of pressure, even from my colleagues that I worked with. They said, "Mam Lydia, you must go." I then went to sign. I am sure I was one of the last ones to sign.

I was very, very active in organizing for the ANC at that time. We even had a choir in Yeoville—you know, to launch other branches. Yeoville was one of the first branches to launch, and I was on the executive; and we started a choir. Then we launched Berea and Hillbrow. We launched other groups with this choir. But I still didn't see that I am expected to go to parliament. I just wanted to be on the ground—to work on the ground. We were just starting to feel this liberation, starting to feel the warmth of it. You could sit in the park, you could do what you want, you could apply anywhere, have a meeting anywhere—things we had never dreamt of. Particularly myself, I was not even allowed to be in the proclaimed area of Johannesburg when I first came to the city many years ago. Now I just felt I could display myself—that here I am now, a South African. So, to go to parliament—this will isolate me from what I really want to do, to show that I really won the struggle I fought for. But I went there.

SM: *So what was it like when you got there?*

LKN: Ah, we were all dom[41] you know. Nobody was more clever—everybody was starting to learn. We were juggling about with the whole set-up in parliament. I expected that those who are more educated would get it quickly. But it wasn't like that—they were getting lost like me in parliament. What really annoyed me every morning was when I entered parliament. I look at my right; I see that boys choir[42]—including Verwoed and Vorster and the whole group over there, you know. That was the most revolting thing to me to watch every morning. And even if you try to ignore them, your eye will always go there and, ah, it stayed with us for many years. I don't know why. I kept on saying, "When are we going to change these people?" Everywhere there were these photographs. Only one picture of a woman—Suzman, in the front entrance when you get to the new wing. In the old assembly there's this bunch of men—all those vicious ones, no smiles even. That contributed a lot of bitterness inside me. But because I could see people changing, I had nobody to share this with. I hate watching these people. I really hate it. It opens wounds. As if we were adorers, or we really put a stamp on them that they are heroes. Why couldn't we just for the first day get them out? But it's just because I am a very strong activist, who believes in getting things done now regardless of what the procedures and protocols are. We did not even know about those things—procedures and protocols.

SM: *And you had also set up your own organizations—the trade unions where workers had control, the Rural Women's Movement, where rural women run things. And now you were sitting in these halls set up by the apartheid government.*

LKN: Exactly—the bureaucracy that takes its own pace and time to do things, its own way. Yet with us we just said, we will do this, and we carry on, and it worked. And that's where it took us to—this liberated era. You know, even now we do not have our heroes on the wall of parliament. I will leave my second term without seeing our heroes—Mandela, Tambo, people who liberated us—on the walls of parliament. I have no control over it. Maybe I am just one of those people who wanted things to work my own way because of ignorance.

Yes, for three years, 1994, '95, '96 I had it hard. Particularly in the chamber itself. I was sometimes filled up with anger when I heard the

---

41   Stupid.
42   Portraits of apartheid-era presidents and MPs adorning parliament.

opposition parties criticizing us for this thing and that thing, for not speeding up things. You know, in two, three years they expected us to have done miracles. That actually made me so angry. If I wasn't inter- acting, making noise that I irritate people, I would have collapsed with anger. Because I really get so filled up with anger inside me to say, "Who are they to tell us?"—you know. Because from day one they were just starting to criticize: the ANC is not doing this, the ANC is not doing this—not even having changed their critical damn laws. They had caused the whole trauma: now they want us to change within a wink of an eye. How can we? For so many years, forty-eight years of apartheid imple- mentation on us, and expecting us to change everything in a few years. Honestly, I think they were so unrealistic.

The only thing that I enjoyed, and that kept me surviving at the end of the day, were the portfolio committees and the study groups. Because at least with those smaller groups I could contribute, I could partici- pate—particularly on land affairs, because it was like my previous work. It just came to me, you know. And the first law that we passed was the Restitution Act—that we could take people back to the land, that our people would be settled. That made me so excited, and I enjoyed it. But the implementation became so dragging and so dragging that slowly I just became discouraged. Because I thought, "Ah, this Act is going to make us heroes," you know. Because we were just going to get people the land back, develop them, and negotiate to get them alternative land in some cases, like the Act says. I thought it was just going to be like that. Particularly with the R15,000 grant,[43] and all this. Oh, I thought it would work easier. Because I though they will involve the NGOs to help those people they are working with already, to implement all the laws that we have passed. Because they are excellent laws. All we lack is implementation—that's all. But, you know, the whole term went by. I thought, should I go back or stay out? People said "No, go back again and try again." Then I went back the second term.

Before the end of 1999 I started to cope a little bit with the bills, and I could understand the bills now. Because before I couldn't—I was struggling. I was just reading these bills for a whole two hours, not under- standing anything. I served on committees on land affairs, agriculture, water affairs, and sanitation, which was combined, and women, and on the Reconstruction and Development Programme. I had a lot of meet- ings, and I was also on the private membership committee. It was just too much. But my priority was land, agriculture, and water affairs. So

43   In terms of the post-apartheid government's land redistribution program, a market- led land reform program, approximately US$1,875 is granted to a family earning less than R3,000 per month (approximately US$375) in order to purchase land.

I concentrated there a lot. Particularly now that the RDP has started improving our water system here in my constituency, that has actually given me courage that at least we are doing something—even though we were struggling to really have physical implementation. But I think we are just lacking resources, power, and capacity from our third-tier government—the local government. But otherwise I am starting to cope. I reduced most of the committees. I am left with water affairs and forestry and women, and I just thought: this is what I can handle now, at the age of sixty-five. It's enough on my plate.

SM: *And you have your work in your constituency. Can you tell us about this?*

LKN: Yeah, for five years I was working here in the area where my home is. I strengthened the projects we had before I went to government—the rural women's groups, you know, which we were organizing while I was still at TRAC. It gave me a good chance, because now we have some resources with us in my office. We had our administration—we had two administrators. One was a fieldworker working on land issues here at home. We sent him to go out and talk to some groups while I was in Cape Town. So it was very much easier. Then we have the administrator in the office. The fieldworker could also help with the women here, when they had visitors. He could help them take notes, because our women are still very unskilled—they need some training. Something I learnt from TRAC was fundraising. I learnt to fundraise, and it really assisted me because now I can manage to make a small business plan and send it to funders such as ESKOM.[44] ESKOM is our best partner here in this area. They supply us with a lot of resources, and they give our women workshops of empowerment and capacity-building. I always have somebody from my office to supervise, to see how they are doing, how they are getting on—because ESKOM does not have follow-ups, because they have a lot on their plates also. So when we have somebody from our ranks, he can follow up and see that things are done properly, and assist here and there. I also involve the councilors, but when I am away they can assist the women to see to it that the projects are nice, and that they are also accountable to the funders. So that's one thing that I really enjoy so far. But we have very little time for our constituency; constituency work only happens during parliamentary recess—one week or so. During weekends we just rush, come home, have a small workshop, some briefings here and there. We don't really have continuous, constant follow-ups with women. You know, they need time—the rural women need time. They don't need rush; when you rush them you confuse them more.

SM: *You also have almost a day's travel to get here from Cape Town.*

---

44   South Africa's Electricity Supply Commission, a para-statal organization.

LKN: When I get here I am tired already, but the following day I must go out to the groups. I contribute very little—sometimes I am tired. But I survive.

SM: *You seem to be trying to continue grassroots organizing with being in parliament. What about those links? Do you feel you are able to link what's happening at the grassroots with your work in the portfolio committees and the assembly?*

LKN: That's the little time that we have. In my opinion I think we should restructure parliament. Now that lots of laws have been passed, we are not dealing with a lot of bills like on our first term. Maybe this would be a nice time to restructure, so that those who are activists should be given the chance to be home for some time and do work, physical work. So we can meet the demand of our president that our focus should be on eliminating poverty, particularly in the rural areas. We cannot do that if we are not physically there for some time to assist. Because our local councilors are also new, they need some kind of boost and assistance from us at the top there. Sometimes we should come down and work with them—not to step on their feet, but to work as a team and assist wherever we can with the experience we have—and particularly when we find that the councilors are mainly men, you see. And it does not really match very well with the women's groups we have, particularly in my area. I think we have very few women councilors. If some of us are back home at certain intervals, and come and interact with them and let the big brains up there do some work, then we can link our work. I mean, we are not academics: we are good at other things, and they are not good at the grassroots. So all these things link together, you know.

SM: *You spoke earlier of the NGOs—for example, with land reform—that things would have worked better had they been brought in to assist with implementation. What can you say about NGOs and the social movements of the 1980s—about what role they are playing at the moment?*

LKN: You know, it is a big disappointment to me. Because I have raised this from day one of the establishment of the RDP with our minister, because I was sitting on the RDP. I suggested that, let's not shy away from the fact that we have good NGOs, progressive NGOs—that some of us come from that background, that those people are there, and now the ANC has won the struggle, we are in power—we are not going to be funded like before, when we were struggling. So those NGOs are going to suffer. And we are going to lose a lot of good people. They are going to vanish. So why don't we task them and assist them to continue the work they have been doing? They know the people on the ground. They are the ones who have been empowering those people. I mean, I was within those people. So why should we lose such cream? Why don't we use them to interact with our people on the ground? Had we done that, we should not be having these houses that are halfway built for a year in my area. I'm telling you, if we had an organization that is accountable, that reports back to the Ministry of Housing or ministry of whoever, I'm telling you, all these unfinished things would be completed. I agree that we have some NGOs which were not progressive, but 95 percent of them were really good. And now, because of funding, they closed down, which to me it's a real big pity—really, a big pity. Because the government from up there, even from the province, are not going to manage to deal with the bread and butter issues on the ground while they are dealing with legislation. It's not going to be very easy.

That's why I always think that maybe the other alternative, since government does not want to use NGOs, is that some of us should come down and come and assist. We are still not going to be as accurate as an organization that would take responsibility, which would see it as their job and be accountable to a department. I'm telling you, things would have gone very, very smooth. Because a lot of money has been spent from the welfare department—the money is supposed to go to the poorest of the poor, to help them uplift their lives. Who is actually in charge of that money, to see to it that it reaches its goal? Who is in charge? Because we need somebody who is very appropriate, really committed, who has these very people in her heart. So I really don't know how to deal with that issue. But I still think my dreams are not yet met towards uplifting the poor, and actually meeting the goals of the president that we need to stick our heels into uplifting the lives of the poor. My question is: How? How are we going to do that? Because money has been allocated. How is the money going to be utilized? Next time, it is rollover or disappearance, because there is no one who takes the real responsibility that we can say, "What did you do with the allocation?"

SM: *You said that your hopes and dreams have not been realized. We still have poverty. And I want to ask, from the point of women who wanted you in parliament, women in the ANC branches and the Rural Women's Movement, and other organizations, in terms of their hopes, in terms of what they felt you'd be able to achieve in parliament—do you have a sense, any feedback from them, as to how they feel you have been doing in parliament?*

LKN: All I get sometimes from those groups you have mentioned is just criticism, constructive criticism—that "Mam Lydia, we didn't expect you people to do us down like you do. We know you can't change the system in a short space of time, but we need to see progress; we need to feel your presence; we need to see things happening. We want to do things with you people." I'm sure there are some other members who really don't go to their constituency. And even us, who go to our constituency sometimes, we go empty handed, you know.

SM: *It is very hard. Some areas, like your own, do not have water. In your own home here you get water once a week. Those old issues that we hoped liberation would change are still there—lack of water, lack of jobs maybe is our biggest problem. . . ?*

LKN: Yes, and lack of sanitation. I'm telling you, I don't know—the health, the roads; you can see how they are. But I want to say, until the local government is totally empowered and takes control we are not going to manage to do things properly. Because I think those are the people who should actually do that. All those developments you have just mentioned have to be under their control. We can't expect to run our cars on those kinds of roads—we can't run an ambulance on the road that passes the hospital in my area. A drip won't even stay on those roads; instead it will injure a patient. You can't expect a hospital to be on a dirt road, where it concerns people's lives. Those are the things that should be prioritized. And I really don't know how we should do it. We also try and put pressure as parliamentarians for our constituency. To say, "Hey, you— MEC![45] Come and have a roadshow and see how things work here." He will come and see, and he won't come back again. I have not given up with my government. It is just the will that needs to be turned a bit to positive kind of ways, where people will say, yes, this is what we are expecting. And give these people some jobs—say, here is the money; we don't have enough money to employ and to pay, but we have money to get this road going, for your gain and your betterment. People will do it, I am telling you. Even without pay, people will do it. This taxi man will go out of his way to fix the road, because it will be for his own benefit. If they have enough money to put tar and concrete but not enough to pay labor—people will come and do it. If you have enough money to put a bridge but not enough money to pay, people will put it up. Because they know at the end of the day they are the ones who will benefit—it will save tires, save lives. Every time I am here at home, I see ambulances with their front wheels up being towed to garages. What's the use of repairing it and then putting it again on that kind of road? Isn't it like working at a loss? To me, you've got to really heal the wound, not just the surface.

SM: *Where do you see hope in the future?*

LKN: I think, if we can be allowed to sit down and plan and share ideas, particularly with the people who are directly involved in these things— who have not run to the suburbs yet. We are still here, we experience things. If my people don't have water, then I don't have water as well. It's an experience that happens to me as well. I'm not saying these things in a sympathetic way—like, shame, these poor people are not having water.

---

45   Member of the Executive Committee within the provincial legislatures. They are in effect the provincial equivalent of national cabinet ministers.

I'm saying we don't have water, actually meaning including myself and my family; and I think we are the ones, like the MPs in Gauteng,[46] those who still stay with the masses in the township. I respect them. Because when they talk about violence, when they talk about improvement of their area, they talk about themselves as well. They are not saying, every morning I drive from Houghton and I go to Soweto to where I am deployed; they are saying, we are here, we experience these things. We listen to the guns every day, we see the crime with our own naked eyes. We are still staying in Hillbrow. We see all these things happening. We have not run away. These are the people who people should listen to—and sit with them, and plan with them how best to do things. That's my idea.

SM: *Is there a final comment you would like to make?*

LKN: I'm still recommending and praising our government for the good things they have done—passing good laws. I'm still optimistic that, if we can get together and people change their mind-sets and just make sure we fulfill what we have said, our priority this time is to improve the lives of the poor, especially the poorest of the poor in these rural areas. And people should learn to come down to the rural areas and just come and see how people survive, and bring some investments here. No investor would come and invest here when we are in such a devastated situation—no one wants to break his car, no one wants to come and dump his things where there are no resources. We have some resources, like you have seen. In my village we have electricity—we have, once a week, water in my yard. We were forced to buy more drums to fill up water for a week. It's not a very healthy situation, but it is better than pushing wheelbarrows. When you go out from my village, as you saw, children pushing wheelbarrows on the main road at night—you can't even see them, and they are in danger of being run over by cars. It breaks my heart. We really need to do something. And I sometimes feel pity for these poor councilors who really don't even know what to do when the situation is like this. Maybe slowly, slowly. But people are getting impatient. Because what I've learnt, if people don't get water, if people don't get better health. . . And water is one of the preventions from bad health. So prevention is better than cure. So, if we start by improving our lives it will improve the state of health.

It has not been possible for Lydia in her role as parliamentarian to advance the interests she took up so strongly in her work with trade unions and rural communities.

---

46   Gauteng is the province that includes Johannesburg and Pretoria. With increasing class mobility for a small black elite, many black elites are moving out of the formerly black areas to the formerly white suburbs.

In this interview Lydia laments the huge gap between the government's policies and implementation in meeting the need for land, jobs, and basic services for the majority of South Africans who continue to live lives of poverty. In her own home in Tsimanyane, a rural village in what used to be Northern Transvaal and is today part of the Northern Province, the tap in her yard is serviced with water only once a week, so that containers have to be filled with a supply of water to last a week. Children in neighboring villages carry or wheel drums of water at dusk traversing the main through road, forever in danger of being hit by passing motorists. Seven years into the new South Africa, the rural constituency Lydia serves as an ANC MP lives in poverty, with little hope of jobs or developed infrastructure. She speaks in the interview of criticism she faces from those who sent her to parliament, whose expectations have not been met. Lydia copes by finding glimmers of hope in the work she does in the portfolio committees of parliament, and the organizing work in her constituency.

Her own strong criticism of the present government is directed at the lack of support from government for NGOs. She notes that NGOs played a crucial role in the democratization of South Africa, and could be playing a crucial role in development today. She is almost bitter when she speaks of her pleas for support for NGOs falling on deaf ears. What Lydia is really speaking of is the demise of the strong social movements of the past, and the state's marginalizing of such movements. This is something that resonates strongly with me, as an activist who has worked with community and trade union organizations in battles against racial oppression and class exploitation, and for women's rights.

It strikes me that it is unlikely that future South African parliaments will have MPs of the ilk of Lydia—since South Africa has fast moved to an era in which formal technical qualifications are seen as a more fitting match for positions that are increasingly defined as technical, and less to do with the grassroots.

Index